Horace and Seneca

Beiträge zur Altertumskunde

Herausgegeben von Susanne Daub, Michael Erler,
Dorothee Gall, Ludwig Koenen und Clemens Zintzen

Band 365

Horace and Seneca

Interactions, Intertexts, Interpretations

Herausgegeben von
Martin Stöckinger, Kathrin Winter
und Andreas T. Zanker

DE GRUYTER

ISBN 978-3-11-068525-1
e-ISBN (PDF) 978-3-11-052889-3
e-ISBN (EPUB) 978-3-11-052861-9
ISSN 1616-0452

Library of Congress Cataloging-in-Publication Data
A CIP catalog record for this book has been applied for at the Library of Congress.

Bibliografische Information der Deutschen Nationalbibliothek
Die Deutsche Nationalbibliothek verzeichnet diese Publikation in der Deutschen Nationalbibliografie; detaillierte bibliografische Daten sind im Internet über http://dnb.dnb.de abrufbar.

© 2019 Walter de Gruyter GmbH, Berlin/Boston
This volume is text- and page-identical with the hardback published in 2017.
Druck und Bindung: Hubert & Co. GmbH & Co. KG, Göttingen
♾ Gedruckt auf säurefreiem Papier
Printed in Germany

www.degruyter.com

Foreword

This volume is based on a conference held in the Seminar für Klassische Philologie at the University of Heidelberg in July of 2015. In its production we would like to register our sincerest thanks to the Alexander von Humboldt Stiftung and Amherst College, as well as to the Mommsen Gesellschaft, for their generous funding. We would also like to thank Jürgen Paul Schwindt and Gerrit Kloss for their support of the project, as well as the administrators and student helpers who made the conference itself run so smoothly. The typescript was edited with aplomb by Eugenia Lao.

We would like to dedicate the volume in the name of all of its contributors to the memory of our keynote speaker, John Moles, who, with his customary generosity and enthusiasm, contributed greatly to the original gathering. Only two months after we met in Heidelberg we were deeply saddened to hear that he had passed away. The three editors of the present volume still remember, and always will, our walk with John across Heidelberg's Alte Brücke over the Neckar on the late-summer afternoon before the conference began.

Notes concerning the texts and translations employed are provided in the individual contributions. Abbreviations of names and titles follow the conventions of the LSJ and OLD. Latin titles, when cited in full, are generally printed in the original, save for Horace's *Odes*, *Epodes*, *Satires*, and *Epistles*, whose frequency in the scholarship, we feel, overrides our aspirations to uniformity (this also allows Seneca's *Epistulae Morales* to be more clearly differentiated from Horace's *Epistles*).

Martin Stöckinger, Kathrin Winter, Andreas T. Zanker

Table of Contents

Introduction —— 1

I Philosophy in Literature – Literature in Philosophy

Barbara Del Giovane
Dressing Philosophy with *sal niger*. Horace's Role in Seneca's Approach to the Diatribic Tradition —— 27

Francesca Romana Berno
Nurses' Prayers, Philosophical *otium*, and Fat Pigs: Seneca Ep. 60 versus Horace Ep. 1.4 —— 53

Catharine Edwards
Saturnalian Exchanges: Seneca, Horace, and Satiric Advice —— 73

II Horatian Verse in Senecan Tragedy

Richard Tarrant
***Custode rerum Caesare*: Horatian Civic Engagement and the Senecan Tragic Chorus** —— 93

Christopher Trinacty
Horatian Contexts in Senecan Tragedy —— 113

Tobias Allendorf
Sounds and Space. Seneca's Horatian Lyrics —— 137

Jonathan Geiger
Strictness, Freedom, and Experimentation in Horatian and Senecan Metrics —— 159

III Themes and Concepts

Gregor Vogt-Spira
Time in Horace and Seneca —— 185

Barak Blum
***Studiorum instrumenta*: Loaded Libraries in Seneca and Horace —— 211**

Elena Giusti
The Metapoetics of Liber-ty. Horace's Bacchic Ship in Seneca's *De Tranquillitate Animi* —— 239

Alexander Kirichenko
Constructing Oneself in Horace and Seneca —— 265

IV Modes of Quotation and Issues of Reception

Ute Tischer
***Nostra faciamus.* Quoting in Horace and Seneca —— 289**

Nina Mindt
Horace, Seneca, and Martial: 'Sententious Style' across Genres —— 315

Victoria Moul
Seneca, Horace, and the Anglo-Latin 'Moralising Lyric' in Early Modern England —— 345

Table of Correspondences —— 371

Works cited —— 401

Contributors and Editors —— 431

General Index —— 433

Introduction

The pairing of two authors may appear both old-fashioned and arbitrary in twenty-first century classical studies: the comparison of Homer and Virgil, Pindar and Horace, Sallust and Tacitus, and Virgil and Lucan has provided topics for numerous books, articles, and chapters over the decades. The abundance of such studies has in part been balanced by the changing scholarly modes of dealing with the literary relationships involved – terms such as *imitatio* and *aemulatio*, 'influence,' 'anxiety of influence,' 'allusion,' 'reference,' 'intertextuality,' 'tradition,' 'dynamics of genre,' and 'reception,' to give but a few examples, each come with their own emphases and framings of the connections between texts and authors. But why add another pairing to this vast body of scholarship? And why the particular pairing of Horace and Seneca?[1] A preliminary, and somewhat blunt, answer is that to the best of our knowledge no one has undertaken it before, at least not with due consideration to the entire oeuvres of both authors.

Several studies from the nineteenth and early twentieth century address or touch on Horace and Seneca in tandem, often as part of an investigation of an author-specific topic such as 'Seneca's technique of imitation' or 'tropes in Senecan tragedy': by way of example we might note Zingerle (1873), Gaheis (1895), Kapnukajas (1930), and Keseling (1941). Two scholars of this period focused exclusively on the relationship between Seneca's tragedies and Horace's *Odes* – Gerber (1883), who explored Seneca's use of Horatian metre, and Spika (1890), who listed verbal parallels and imagery common to both Horace's *Odes* and the choral odes of Seneca. Although these studies still offer much useful material, their methodology is of course dated. In more recent decades, we find two brief overviews by Mazzoli (1974 and 1998) and an influential essay by Berthet (1979), in addition to a number of articles devoted to specific problems and topics by other scholars.[2] Important observations concerning the relationship of Horace and Seneca have been made by Tarrant in his commentaries on the *Agamemnon* (1976) and the *Thyestes* (1985), as well as in a series of articles, such as those on Seneca (2006) and the reception of Horace (2007). What is still required,

---

[1] One might compare the recent volume of Berlincourt / Galli Mitić / Nelis 2016, whose title, *Lucan and Claudian*, reveals the same traits as *Horace and Seneca*. In their introduction, the editors note that the similarity to traditional studies of the aforementioned variety is intended, yet clearly state their aim not to neglect more recent theoretical points and methodologies. Cf. Berlincourt / Galli Mitić / Nelis 2016, 2–4.
[2] E.g. Dionigi 1980; Degl'Innocenti Pierini 1992 and 2013; Blänsdorf 1998; Stevens 1999; Schöpsdau 2015; Littlewood 2016.

however, is a comprehensive study of the relationship of the Horatian corpus to Seneca's philosophical *and* poetic works, one that takes into account modern critical theory and methodologies. First steps in this direction have recently been taken by Trinacty (2014), with a focus on Horace's Roman Odes, and by Rimell (2015a, 82–147), whose study of the concept of enclosed space includes an analysis of the Horatian *angulus* and its reception in Seneca's prose.

But beyond this need to fill a gap in the scholarship, the study of the interplay between these two authors is attractive for a variety of other reasons. Horace and Seneca reveal, for example, in many respects striking similarities, but are at the same time paradoxically dissimilar precisely at these points of contact. Both authors write philosophy in a literary framework and thereby engage continually with the same themes and questions – for example the idea of the good life, the proper use of time, the formation of the self, the *desideratum* of moderation – yet do so from different philosophical angles (namely quasi-Epicureanism and Roman Stoicism). Both have been criticised for their proximity to political power, yet this proximity takes a different form in each case – Horace slowly approaching the centre of power from great distance, Seneca swiftly distancing himself from his position of great intimacy with Nero's court. Both work in a variety of different genres in the course of their long careers, which, although the precise genres diverge greatly, constitute analogous forms: philosophical letters (whether in poetic *sermo* or in prose), dialogue (as can already be noted in the authors' use of the terms *sermo* and *dialogus* as descriptors for individual works), the influence of diatribe and satire (housed in completely different genres), and of course lyric – and here Seneca's choral songs would be unthinkable without Horace's *Odes*, even if they exist in a different context and serve a different end. Finally, we might mention the similarities when it comes to the authors' ironic style, together with the formal correspondences – even down to the *minora* – which make the case for a deep underlying connection between the two authors all the more compelling. None of these items is precisely replicated, and yet the similarity is too clear to be denied.

Even from a superficial *syncrisis* such as that just outlined one recognises the fundamental and perhaps unique character of the relationship between Horace and Seneca: it consists in similarity rather than uniformity. The corpora are of course extremely different, yet when set next to each other they reveal themselves to be interlaced with non-systematic parallels and congruencies in their composition, their workmanship, and in numerous details (although never in their entirety). The relationship has the appearance of being both intimate and distanced. It is precisely in this that the fascination of the theme 'Horace and Seneca' lies, as well as its great difficulty: sweeping attempts to describe the relationship exhaustively or to provide an underlying axiom for its analysis generally lack persuasive force, and mapping out the connections demands of the critic both subtlety and a willingness to deal more frequently with twilight potentialities than with clear moments of open interaction. We believe that the very obstacles to the study of Horace and Seneca in tandem in fact present an opportunity: they not only open up the possibility of examining an interesting relationship between two eminent authors of the Roman literary canon, but also force us to touch on a number of fundamental issues of literary criticism, and as such to reassess the tools and terminology that we are accustomed to apply in such investigations. In what follows we shall give a few examples to show precisely why we think it is worth exploring this particular relationship and note some of the aforementioned obstacles, before describing the rationale and contents of the volume itself.

1 Intertextuality between Horace and Seneca: Problems and Prospects

At this point, one would normally turn to a concrete example of a point of contact between the two corpora, yet this is precisely where things become interesting in the case of Horace and Seneca: it is a simple fact that Seneca quotes Horace only four times in his entire corpus verbatim (if we admit an example from the disputed *Apocolocyntosis*).[3] This is remarkable, since Seneca uses quotations frequently in his prose works, especially from the writing of Virgil and Ovid, the two other principal Augustan poets.[4] None of Seneca's few citations of Horace differs significantly from his citations of other authors, nor do these sparse moments of direct reference offer any real insight into the way in which Seneca viewed Horace in general, apart from as a source of moralistic descriptions. To

---

[3] The references are as follows: Sen. Ep. 86.13 (Hor. S. 1.2.27), 119.13–14 (Hor. S. 1.2.114–116), 120.20–21 (Hor. S. 1.3.11–17), Apoc. 13.3 (Hor. Carm. 2.13.34). Cf. Berthet 1979, 941–942. Mazzoli 1974, 234, calls the number 'irrisorio.' Note the distribution of these citations towards the end of the collection of Seneca's *Epistulae Morales*, and that three of them are taken from a single book of Horace.

[4] Cf. Mazzoli 1974, 215–232, 238–247, and Mazzoli 1998. Interestingly Seneca's father, Seneca the Elder, does not cite Horace at all in his *Controversiae* and *Suasoriae* (according to the indices of Winterbottom's Loeb and Håkanson's Teubner), even though Virgil and Ovid are both referenced numerous times.

give one of the briefest of the four quotations as an example, Seneca employs Horace as a component in an attack on the growth of luxury in Ep. 86:[5]

> Descripturus infamem et nimiis notabilem deliciis Horatius Flaccus quid ait?
> Pastillos Buccillus olet.
> Dares nunc Buccillum; proinde esset ac si hircum oleret, Gargonii loco esset, quem idem Horatius Buccillo opposuit.
>
> What says Horatius Flaccus, when he wishes to describe a scoundrel, one who is notorious for his extreme luxury? He says: 'Buccillus smells of perfume.' Show me a Buccillus in these days; his smell would be the veritable goat-smell – he would take the place of the Gargonius with whom Horace in the same passage contrasted him.
> (Ep. 86.13)

There is clearly not much to go on here. Given how few actual quotations of Horace there are in Seneca, tracing the relationship between the two corpora becomes a complex affair that involves marking not only clear allusions and commonalities of content but also subtle links such as the usage of imagery, topoi, and aspects of style.[6] It should go without saying that these are not explicitly marked, and at times Seneca seems even to obscure the link with the source text (as we shall see below).[7] In approaching this particular pairing of authors, we are simultaneously required to be more open to the possibility of a connection than we might normally wish to be[8] and to apply a correspondingly higher degree of philological care in the evaluation of the posited connection: greater philological openness requires a more careful eye for the specific contextual details.

The study of this type of connection has become somewhat easier of late. The paradigmatic early applications of intertextual theory to Latin literature generally revolved around poetic texts (where intertextual links are often easier to spot and verify).[9] More recently, however, scholars have begun to investigate the relationships between prose texts, as well as the connections between

---

[5] The text of Seneca's *Epistulae Morales* and *Dialogi* is taken from Reynolds's OCT; the translation of the letters is from Gummere's Loeb (with minor changes); the translation of the *Dialogi* is from the Loeb of Basore.
[6] On topoi in general see below, section 2.
[7] Cf. Mazzoli 1974, 235.
[8] This kind of openness is formulated by Gibson 2002, 232–233, in his discussion of the term 'parallel.'
[9] Cf. Conte 1986, Fowler 2000, Hinds 1998, Thomas 1999.

prose and poetry (and the modes whereby such links were forged).¹⁰ Yet the question of genre does indeed force us to face up to certain realities: since we cannot rely on shared epic or elegiac conventions, metrical *sedes*, or poetological catchwords (such as *lepidus* in neoteric poetry), we are required to employ other strategies to reveal or argue for an intertextual connection. One such strategy might consist in the identification of common narratological structures rather than lexical parallels – for example, by tracing structural patterns of the *katabasis* found in the *Odyssey* throughout later texts (the descent into Trimalchio's mansion in the *Cena Trimalchionis* springs to mind).¹¹ Yet it should be noted, of course, that this particular technique is of necessity imprecise and less helpful when it comes to the links between philosophical works, given the individualised argumentation of philosophical discourse. It is therefore necessary to adopt a variety of different approaches in evaluating the relationship between Horace and Seneca – one single technique is insufficient.

Senecan texts can reveal quite different degrees of proximity to their Horatian precursors: some links are close and easily spotted, while others offer greater 'resistance.' We hope to demonstrate this by means of three examples – two of which involve possible instances of Horace's poetry being embedded in Seneca's philosophical writings, one in his choral lyric. Our first example is frequently cited as an example of Seneca's muted indebtedness to Horace; the following is taken from the beginning of Ep. 28 on travel:¹²

> Hoc tibi soli putare accidisse et admiraris quasi rem novam quod peregrinatione tam longa et tot locorum varietatibus non discussisti tristitiam gravitatemque mentis? <u>Animum debes mutare, non caelum</u>. Licet vastum traieceris mare, licet, ut ait Vergilius noster, 'terraeque urbesque recedant,' sequentur te quocumque perveneris vitia.
>
> Do you suppose that you alone have had this experience? Are you surprised, as if it were a novelty, that after such long travel and so many changes of scene you have not been able to shake off the gloom and heaviness of your mind? You need <u>a change of soul rather than a change of climate</u>. Though you may cross vast spaces of sea, and though, as our Virgil remarks, 'Lands and cities are left astern,' your faults will follow you whithersoever you travel.
>
> (Sen. Ep. 28.1)

---

10 Cf. e.g. Woodman 1998 for historiography (and Woodman 2012 for general reflections); Morgan / Harrison 2008 for the novel; Whitton 2013a, 32–34, and Schenk 2016 on intertextuality in Pliny; Van den Berg 2014, 208–293, on intertextuality in Tacitus's *Dialogus De Oratoribus*; on the widening of the scope in intertextual studies see Baraz / Van den Berg 2013. Hutchinson 2013 discusses the intertextual relationship between Greek and Latin literature as a whole.
11 Cf. Morgan / Harrison 2008, 228–230; for further examples see Paschalis 2011, 73–98.
12 The parallel is also pointed out by Mazzoli 1974, 236, and Berthet 1979, 944. See also Mindt, 338, in this volume.

The phrase *animum... mutare, non caelum* is found almost verbatim at Hor. Ep. 1.11, where the traveller is told that he will not alleviate his sorrows by changing the sky above him but only by exercising *ratio* and *prudentia*:[13]

> ...nam si ratio et prudentia curas
> non locus effusi, late maris arbiter, aufert,
> <u>caelum, non animum, mutant</u> qui trans mare currunt.
>
> For if 'tis reason and wisdom that take away cares, and not a site commanding a wide expanse of sea, <u>they change their clime, not their mind</u>, who rush across the sea.
> (Hor. Ep. 1.11.25–27)

It is of course entirely possible that the expression in question is proverbial,[14] but on closer inspection we find a connection between the two texts that suggests that Seneca had Horace in mind. Ep. 28 starts at the point where the Horatian letter ends: Seneca's addressee, Lucilius, has undertaken a *mutatio caeli* and yet experienced no *mutatio animi*. In an analysis of both letters, Schöpsdau has shown that Seneca renders the first section of his letter 'Horatian' by opening with the unmarked quotation of Horace, working through the implications of the themes *mutatio caeli* / *mutatio animi* (Ep. 28.1–5) in what follows, and then applying a formulation (5 *bene vivere*) that plays once again on Horace's Ep. 1.11.[15] Yet even though Seneca's letter has reached a fitting conclusion at this very point, its author continues on: the sections that follow the Horatian opening, which involve Seneca's advice on the theme of *mutare animum* (Ep. 28.6–9), clearly deviate from the points that Seneca had made in connection with Hor. Ep. 1.11.[16] Seneca moves beyond his apparent Horatian model to elaborate further on the topic of *mutatio animi*. This movement is in fact reflected right at the beginning of Seneca's letter, where the syntax of the phrases is reversed because the Horatian line, which contains a description (<u>caelum, non animum</u> mutant, qui... currunt), is transformed into a statement of advice (<u>animum</u> debes mutare, <u>non caelum</u>).

---

[13] The text is Shackleton Bailey's Teubner; the translation of the *Epistles* is taken from Fairclough's Loeb, that of the *Odes* from Rudd's Loeb.
[14] Cf. Schöpsdau 2015, 451–452.
[15] Sen. Ep. 28.5 *cum illud quod quaeris, <u>bene vivere</u>, omni loco positum sit*, '...although that which you seek, – to <u>live well [i.e. happily]</u>, – is found everywhere'; cf. Hor. Ep. 1.11.29–30: *petimus <u>bene vivere</u>. quod petis hic est, | est Ulubris*, 'we seek <u>to make life happy</u>. What you are seeking is here; it is at Ulubrae.' Schöpsdau 2015, 457–461.
[16] The details of the argumentation and the differences from Hor. Ep. 1.11 are given by Schöpsdau 2015, 465–469, esp. 466–467.

This example demonstrates one particular difficulty in determining Seneca's employment of Horace's text: the engagement involves alteration, reworking, and a movement beyond the original thought. Nearly all such moments where Seneca seems to be borrowing from Horace involve a transfiguration of some kind, whose degree varies in ways that are generally not the result of the mere insertion of Horatian material into a new context. How, then, do we gain certainty about Seneca's relationship to Horace given the fundamental dissimilarity lodged within the very similarities?

To move on to a second example, it seems that on occasion Seneca deliberately hides a quotation of Horace by means of another citation. The *carpe diem* from Horace's Carm. 1.11 should need no introduction:

> ...sapias, vina liques et spatio brevi
> spem longam reseces. dum loquimur, fugerit invida
> aetas. carpe diem, quam minimum credula postero.
>
> ...strain the wine and cut back far-reaching hopes to within a small space. As we talk, grudging time will have run on. Pluck the day, trusting as little as possible in tomorrow. (Carm. 1.11.6 – 8)

Seneca's *De Brevitate Vitae* contains an expression that looks very similar to Horace's famous one:

> Quo spectas? quo te extendis? Omnia quae ventura sunt, in incerto iacent: protinus vive. Clamat ecce maximus vates et velut divino ore instinctus salutare carmen canit:
>   optima quaeque dies miseris mortalibus aevi
>   prima fugit.
> 'Quid cunctaris?' inquit 'quid cessas? nisi occupas, fugit.' Et cum occupaveris, tamen fugiet; itaque cum celeritate temporis utendi velocitate certandum est et velut ex torrenti rapido nec semper ituro cito hauriendum. Hoc quoque pulcherrime ad exprobrandam infinitam cunctationem, quod non optimam quamque 'aetatem' sed 'diem' dicit. Quid securus et in tanta temporum fuga lentus menses tibi et annos in longam seriem, utcumque aviditati tuae visum est, exporrigis?
>
> Whither do you look? At what goal do you aim? All things that are still to come lie in uncertainty; live straightway! See how the greatest of bards cries out, and, as if inspired with divine utterance, sings the saving strain:
>   The fairest day in hapless mortals' life
>   Is ever first to flee.
> 'Why do you delay,' says he, 'Why are you idle? Unless you seize the day, it flees.' Even though you seize it, it still will flee; therefore you must vie with time's swiftness in the speed of using it, and, as from a torrent that rushes by and will not always flow, you must drink quickly. And, too, the utterance of the bard is most admirably worded to cast censure upon infinite delay, in that he says, not 'the fairest age,' but 'the fairest day.' Why, to whatever length your greed inclines, do you stretch before yourself months and

years in long array, unconcerned and slow though time flies so fast?
(Dial. 10.9.1–3)

The general topic of both texts is the nature of time and its correct usage, and there is a fundamental tension in each between two aspects of time in particular: on the one hand its continuous progression, on the other the fact that only a single point is accessible to human experience at any given time. For this reason, although scholars have been struck by the similarity between the phrases *carpe diem* and *protinus vive*,[17] they have generally argued that the underlying idea is different. Whereas Horace implies that one can seize the moment and thus remove oneself from time's irresistible flow, Seneca considers this move to be impossible (hence the subsequent expression, *et cum occupaveris, tamen fugiet*);[18] according to the philosopher, human beings can nevertheless gain control over time by imposing discipline on their lives through paying attention to their employment of the present moment, even if this will not affect the progression of time itself.[19] This subtle difference is reflected in the similes and metaphors that Horace and Seneca employ: while Horace makes use of garden and agricultural imagery with the terms *resecare* and *carpere*, which imply a certain degree of peace and leisure for the carrying out of these activities, Seneca's flowing torrent conveys the sense of headlong haste, in that the possibility to drink its water will not always exist. Does this, however, entail that the phrases *carpe diem* and *protinus vive* have nothing to do with each other? It is difficult to determine: on the one hand, the expressions share no words in common, but it is nevertheless hard to deny the strong syntactic and thematic similarities between them – for example, the presence of an imperative in each, the brevity of the individual words, the slogan-like concision of the statements as wholes. The two phrases are conspicuously similar yet ostentatiously different.

We might be tempted to leave things here, were it not for further consideration of the two phrases in their respective contexts. Immediately after the phrase *protinus vive*, with its Horatian nuances, Seneca swiftly alludes to a statement made by that *maximus vates* from his *velut divino ore*: he is of course not referring to Horace but to Virgil (the quotation is from the *Georgics*).[20] It does seem,

---

17 E.g. Williams 2003, 21–22.
18 Cf. Vogt-Spira 2001, who argues that Horace ascribes a different quality to the seized moment, which is why it is removed from the continuous flow of time. See also Vogt-Spira in this volume.
19 Williams 2003, 21–22.
20 Mazzoli 1974, 216, notes that Seneca praises Virgil by the use of various eponyms, as well as epithets such as *noster*, thus revealing him to be his favourite poet. Compare his staid 'Horatius

however, that Seneca has Carm. 1.11 at least in the back of his mind: in praising Virgil's poetry Seneca points out how fitting the choice of the word *dies* is in comparison with *aetas* – the distinction concerns the fundamental tension between the continuous progress of time (an attribute of *aetas*) and the correct use of the moment (encapsulated by the word *dies*) – yet the same juxtaposition of opposites and stress on their different status is already found in Horace's poem (Carm. 1.11.7–8: *fugerit invida | aetas. carpe diem*). Seneca did not get this contrast from Virgil. If Seneca were indeed modelling his *protinus vive* on *carpe diem*, Horace's name would seem to have been quite wilfully suppressed throughout. Similarly, in the case described above (Sen. Ep. 28.1), Seneca's potential unmarked quotation from Horace, *mutare caelum*, is directly followed – smothered, as it were – by a direct and marked quotation from *Vergilius noster* ('our Virgil').[21]

But this particular excerpt from the *De Brevitate Vitae* yields even more reason to suspect a submerged link. In explaining the fleeting nature of time Seneca employs two phrases that appear to be reminiscences of Horace: the expressions *temporum fuga* and *annos... seriem* (Dial. 10.9.3) find correlates in the *annorum series* and *fuga temporum* of Horace's famous Carm. 3.30, a further meditation on time:

> Exegi monumentum aere perennius
> regalique situ pyramidum altius,
> quod non imber edax, non Aquilo impotens
> possit diruere aut immemorabilis
> <u>annorum series</u> et <u>fuga temporum</u>.
>
> I have finished a monument more lasting than bronze, more lofty than the regal structure of the pyramids, one which neither corroding rain nor the ungovernable North Wind can ever destroy, nor the countless <u>series of the years</u>, nor the <u>flight of time</u>.
> (Carm. 3.30.1–5)

The theme of this ode does not seem immediately germane to the context encountered in the *De Brevitate Vitae* – it reflects on the immortal and imperishable fame of the poet and his poetry rather than on the correct usage of time. We must therefore ask ourselves – can a secure connection between these lexical commonalities be established or are they merely a coincidence? In support of

---

Flaccus' in introducing the marked quotation from Horace above (but cf. *egregie Horatius negat* at Ep. 119.14).
21 This strategy, i.e. hiding a correspondence under another quotation, is found elsewhere in Seneca; an example (a quotation from Sallust) is analysed and discussed by Berno in this volume.

the former, we might note that the collocation of *temporum* and *fuga* occurs only twice in Latin literature (i.e. in these same passages). It is of course possible that the Senecan phrase is simply a loose reformulation of the more famous Virgilian *tempus fugit* (Georg. 3.284), which was imitated several times in the first century AD,[22] yet the combination of *anni* and *series* is not particularly frequent either,[23] and its placement right after *temporum fuga* in the Senecan excerpt mirrors the pattern found in Horace. The question nevertheless remains – how are we to interpret this?

A bold critic may even wish to see a more sophisticated strategy in play here. The correspondence between *carpe diem* and *protinus vive* at the beginning of the passage from the *De Brevitate Vitae* is uncertain – and probably deliberately left so. Given this, the phrases *temporum fuga* and *annos in seriem* may be intended not as an allusion to a specific Horatian ode but rather as an oblique hint to the poet Horace himself: the second, fleeting gesture towards the Augustan poet discussed in the previous paragraph, then, would reinforce the first, recalling Horace without explicitly mentioning him. In this regard, it is interesting to note that the lines of Carm. 3.30 that immediately follow the one just discussed (i.e. *annorum series et fuga temporum*) concern the immortality of the author via a metonymical identification with his poetry:

> Non omnis moriar multaque pars mei
> vitabit Libitinam.
>
> I shall not wholly die, and a large part of me will elude the goddess of death.
> (Carm. 3.30.6–7)

Horace would seem to be obliterated from memory, broken up into *disiecta membra* and reincorporated into Seneca's prose right at the point where he declares his poetic immortality. On this reading, Seneca would seem to be wryly suggesting the futility of poetic aspirations towards immortality by means of the curtness and vagueness of the link with his Horatian pre-text.

We have seen that the argument for allusions and references to Horace in Seneca's prose works often takes the form of a *sorites* paradox: how much similarity and correspondence is required in order to posit a connection convincingly? How bold must the critic be in order to argue for an intentional strategy of name-avoidance on the part of Seneca? One weak correspondence between the two authors may not persuade, but when it is found together with further

---

[22] E.g. Ov. Met. 15.183; Ov. Fast. 6.771–772; Sen. Ep. 108.24; Sil. 11.385.
[23] Aside from Hor. Carm. 3.30.5 and Sen. Dial. 10.9.3, the collocation can be found at Ov. Pont. 4.12.21; Col. 3.10.6 and 4.19.1; Apul. Mun. 22.

(potentially similarly weak) instances, the critic may start to question even his own scepticism. We may feel that we are on surer ground when it comes to the relationship between Horace's *Odes* and Seneca's choral odes – in part because the question of genre is not in question, in part because Horace's influence on Senecan choral metrics is undeniable.[24] This does not mean, however, that the connections between individual excerpts are any easier to pinpoint and categorise. Seneca's usage of Horace's *Odes* in his tragic choruses is not reflected in verbatim quotations as such, nor do his references appear to rework specific Horatian source texts in systematic ways; at times, Seneca uses a motif or image similar to one found in Horace's lyric without any specific lexical quotations.

Echoes and reverberations, however, are once again difficult things to isolate and pin down; a prime example of this issue can be found in delicate interplay between the opening stanzas of Horace's Carm. 3.3 and the third choral ode of Seneca's *Agamemnon*. Our discussion of these passages will be somewhat more expansive. To take the Horatian passage first:

> Iustum et tenacem propositi virum
> non civium ardor prava iubentium,
>   non vultus instantis tyranni
>   mente quatit solida neque Auster,
>
> dux inquieti turbidus Hadriae,   5
> nec fulminantis magna manus Iovis:
>   si fractus illabitur orbis,
>   impavidum ferient ruinae.

The man of integrity who holds fast to his purpose is not shaken from his firm resolve by hot-headed citizens urging him to do wrong, or by the frown of an oppressive despot, or by the South Wind, that unruly lord of the restless Adriatic, or by the mighty hand of thundering Jove. If the firmament were to split and crash down upon him, he will still be unafraid when hit by the wreckage.
(Carm. 3.3.1–8)

The image evoked here – we might call it a vignette – is that of an individual who remains unmoved and impassive in the midst of a world being plunged into chaos; political disturbance, the elements, and natural disaster cannot faze him. The vignette invokes an internal peace that contrasts with the external turmoil, a fixed

---

[24] Cf. Gerber 1883 and Geiger in this volume. On Horace's influence on Senecan tragedy in general see Billerbeck 1988, 15, and Blänsdorf 1998.

focal point from which all threats can be observed rationally and faced calmly.²⁵ The syntactic structure of the two stanzas reinforces this contrast: the man, who is mentioned prominently in the first (*iustum virum*) and final (*impavidum*) lines of the two stanzas, remains the accusative object throughout. Between these two points we find a range of grammatical subjects (*ardor, vultus, Auster, dux, fulminantis manus Iovis*) that denote the danger and destructive forces that rage around him like a storm and appear to affect the entire world (*fractus orbis*).

The parallels with the third choral ode of Seneca's *Agamemnon*, where the Trojan women lament their fate, have been discussed by Tarrant and more recently by Trinacty.²⁶ The similarity, of course, lies not only in the theme of the fall of Troy (which emerges shortly after the quoted excerpt of Hor. Carm. 3.3) but also in the lexical and syntactic parallels in the opening of each:²⁷

> Heu quam dulce malum mortalibus additum
> vitae dirus amor, cum pateat malis   590
> effugium et miseros libera mors vocet,
> portus aeterna placidus quiete.
> nullus hunc terror nec impotentis
> procella Fortunae movet aut iniqui
>   flamma Tonantis.   595
> pax alta nullos civium coetus
> timet aut minaces victoris iras,
> non maria aspersis insana Coris,
> non acies feras pulvereamve nubem
> motam barbaricis equitum catervis,   600
> non urbe cum tota populos cadentis
> hostica muros populante flamma
>   indomitumque bellum.

> Oh, the sweet evil implanted in mortals,
> this fearsome love for life, though escape from troubles
> lies open, and death's freedom beckons the wretched—
> a tranquil harbour of eternal calm,
> untouched by any terror, by any storm
> of raging Fortune, by any fire
> from the hostile Thunderer.

---

25 The vignette is used quite frequently by Seneca, e.g. in Tro. 15–26 or in the second choral ode of the *Thyestes*, (Thy 348–368), where it is used to reflect on the attitudes of a ruler (piquantly, of course, with regard to the Tantalids); cf. Tarrant 1985, 146–147.
26 It is already mentioned by Spika 1890, 37: 'Imitatio vero illius carminis est apertissima.' Tarrant 1976, 288–290. Tarrant 2007, 283–284. Trinacty 2014, 146–150. See also Tarrant, 105–107, in this volume.
27 The text of Seneca's tragedies is Zwierlein's OCT, translations are taken from Fitch's Loeb.

> That deep peace fears no <u>throngs</u>
> <u>of citizens</u>, no <u>conqueror's angry menace</u>,
> no <u>seas maddened by wild norwesters</u>,
> no ferocious battle lines or clouds of dust
> raised by barbarians in horseback squadrons,
> no downfall of peoples and whole cities
> as enemy fires ravage the walls,
> no untameable war.
> (Ag. 589–603)

If we move past the first three lines, which lament the 'fearsome love for life' (*dirus amor vitae*) in the face of the 'tranquil harbour' (*portus placidus*) of death, we find the same vignette as the one presented in Carm. 3.3.1–8: the idea of a fixed and immutable centre around which chaos unfolds – be it in the form of fortune, Jupiter's thunderbolt, agitated crowds, threatening rulers, sea-storms, battle, or a world in general turmoil and devastated by war. When it comes to drawing a comparison with Horace, however, the aspect that strikes one is that the topic is not an individual (*iustus vir*) but rather a place, the harbour (*portus*), and subsequently a mere pronoun (*hunc*) whose referent is left conspicuously vague: it either refers back to the harbour or takes as its antecedent an unspecified individual who experiences the storm of dangers (mentioned later in line 605).[28]

We may further note that the syntax of Ag. 593–595 resembles that of the opening of the Horatian ode in clear ways (and this is a recurrent feature of Seneca's engagement with Horace's Odes in his choral lyric): Seneca's polysyndeton *nullus... nec... movet* imitates the *non... non... quatit... nec* found in Horace's Carm. 3.3.2–6, and the accusative *hunc* (whether it refers to the harbour or to an individual) is followed by the sentence's grammatical subjects (*terror, procella*, and *flamma Tonantis*), as had been the case in Horace (*iustum... virum*). From line 596 (*pax alta nullos...*) onwards, however, the distribution of subject and accusative object is reversed: the grammatical subject *pax alta*, the internal state of calm, introduces a new line and is followed by a list of the threatening and destructive forces that it does not fear (*non timet...*). Just as was the case with Seneca's <u>animum</u> debes <u>mutare, non caelum</u>, we find the Horatian parallel disguised by an alteration in syntax.

---

28 The shift is so unexpected that it has given rise to the suspicion of a lacuna: Tarrant 1976, 287. Cf. Tarrant in this volume, 107 n. 21.

It is in lines Ag. 596–598 that we come across the closest lexical correspondences with Carm. 3.3, as listed by Spika and Tarrant.[29] In addition, from line 596 onwards the metre also appears to take a 'Horatian' turn:[30] although the *canticum* employs rhythmic patterning quite freely – it opens with asclepiadic and sapphic metres (589–594),[31] which already add a strong Horatian nuance – the metre of lines 596–600 makes use of the alcaics of 'Seneca's immediate model,'[32] thus underscoring the link. From line 599, the choral ode deviates from its model by expanding the short phrase *fractus orbis* in Carm. 3.3.7 into a fuller description of war, and the metre once again adopts greater variety at this precise point.

The final part of the vignette, as it is presented in the following lines of Seneca's choral ode (Ag. 604–610), employs the same technique of amplification as before. The fearless man, the Horatian *vir iustus*, is the focus here and is once again unequivocally set in the midst of the chaos:

> Solus servitium perrumpet omne
> contemptor levium deorum,   605
> qui vultus Acherontis atri,
> qui Styga tristem non tristis videt
> audetque vitae ponere finem:
> par ille regi, par superis erit.
> o quam miserum est nescire mori!   610

> Who can fully break out of bondage?
> Only one who scorns the fickle gods,
> who looks without gloom at gloomy Styx,
> looks upon dark Acheron's face,
> and has courage to set an end to life:
> such a one is a match for kings, for gods.
> How wretched to be unschooled in dying!
> (Ag. 604–610)

The *contemptor levium deorum* recalls the fearlessness (*impavidum*) of the Horatian intertext, but also ensures a seamless transition from the preceding section, aligned as it is with the expression *pax alta non timet* – just like the deep peace of death itself, the *contemptor* has nothing to fear. It is for this reason that the

---

29 Spika 1890, 37–38; Tarrant 1976, 288: *civium ardor – civium coetus; vultus instantis tyranni – minaces victoris iras; Auster, dux inquieti turbidus Hadriae – maria aspersis insana Coris; fulminantis magna manus Iovis – iniqui flamma Tonantis.* Cf. also Trinacty 2014, 148.
30 Cf. Allendorf in this volume, 148–149.
31 See the *descriptio canticorum metrorum* in Zwierlein's OCT, 468.
32 Tarrant 1976, 288.

syntactic structure of the Horatian ode found in lines 593–595 has been altered from line 596 onwards: it prepares the ground for the last section of the vignette. By means of this move, Seneca's *contemptor* appears far more active than the Horatian *vir iustus*; although the focus is more on what he could or will do than on what he really does, his active role is clear: he will break every form of bondage (*servitium perrumpet omne*). Whereas the Horatian *vir impavidus* for all his stability remains passive, the Senecan *contemptor* will take action.

Seneca's reworking of the Horatian vignette can also be noted in more subtle ways. For example, we have already seen that both scenes rely on the contrast between an internal state of mind and the chaos of the external environment, and that this is relayed by means of antithetical adjectives: in Horace's ode, words such as *turbidus* and *inquietus* describe the surroundings, while the *mens* of the *iustus vir* is characterized by the adjective *solida*. In Seneca, however, the opposition is reinforced by the polyptoton *qui Styga tristem non tristis videt* – the Styx itself may be *tristis*, but cannot make the onlooker so. The technique of contrasting inside and outside is the same in both texts, but Seneca condenses and expands what is merely suggestive in Horace. The conclusion of the vignette in the choral ode is also both similar to and different from that of Carm. 3.3: the individual who remains unmoved when looking at imminent destruction and dares to end his own life is the gods' equal (*par ille regi, par superis erit*). In Seneca's ode, the attitude is similarly exceptional, but serves simply to free the individual from all kinds of domination and pressure.[33]

The complexity of the interplay between the beginnings of Carm. 3.3 and the third chorus of Seneca's *Agamemnon* should be clear from this discussion. Seneca does not follow his Horatian model in all respects but moves beyond it to create something fresh – one might compare Horace's own reworkings of Greek lyric at the beginning of individual odes (the mottoes), whereby the initial allusion to the model is swiftly superceded in what follows. But the key difference is that Seneca does not abandon Horace completely – while he uses overt verbal borrowings only rarely, he nevertheless employs Horatian vignettes that underlie quite extended passages of text. The question is what one does with this material – how does the scholar write about it in a responsible and engaging way? With what shorthand do we allude to such allusions? We are a far cry from the classic poetic intertexts found in Stephen Hinds's *Allusion and Intertext*, or in the ago-

---

[33] Cf. Carm. 3.3.9–15, where the individual's fearlessness at the sight of turmoil and death is said to be a skill (*ars*) that led to the apotheosis of Bacchus, Hercules, and Romulus (and eventually Augustus). In Seneca, the same connection between the mental quality and divine power is established, albeit in a very different way.

nistic references discussed by Richard Thomas.[34] Such questions bring us to a second crucial point to consider when discussing the link between Horace and Seneca.

2 Topos or Multi-layered Intertextuality?

The heterogeneous and uneasy relationship between the two corpora is not the only problem: the works of Horace and Seneca do not emerge from a void and consequently cannot be compared as if independent of other influences, and it is important to account for the broader literary and sociocultural contexts in which they are embedded. The fact that a text can be influenced by multiple sources in different ways is reflected in the correspondingly broad contemporary critical vocabulary for describing the processes involved – for example, 'topos,' 'multiple reference,' 'imitative series and clustering,' 'window reference,' 'chains of reference' ('Transformationsketten'), and 'palimpsest.' In what follows, we shall describe the problems introduced by this 'multi-layered' intertextuality via an example that involves a third author; for reasons of space, our choice of focus will be specifically on a moment when (a) this influence is situated between Horace and Seneca (i.e. the third entity serves as an intermediary for Seneca's reception of Horace). Elsewhere in this volume other situations will be discussed, for example those in which (b) the third author precedes Horace and Seneca in terms of chronology, with the result that Horace serves the intermediary or point of comparison for Seneca's reception of another work,[35] or (c) the possibility that the third author follows (sometimes at a great distance) Horace and Seneca, whereby the question becomes in which order and with which emphases Horace and Seneca were read by posterity.[36]

In the *De Consolatione ad Polybium* (Dial. 11.18.2),[37] Seneca advises Polybius to take care of, and indeed prolong, his brother's memory in his literary works: *fratris quoque tui produc memoriam aliquo scriptorum monimento tuorum* ('And, too, prolong the remembrance of your brother by some memorial of your writing'). The word *monimentum*, which can mean 'memorial' as well as 'building,' triggers the following comparison of Polybius's writings to a monument:

---

[34] Thomas 1999, esp. 12–67.
[35] Such a procedure is discussed by Berno in this volume.
[36] For examples, see Mindt and Moul in this volume.
[37] The following interpretation owes much to a seminar paper by An de Vos (2014); we are grateful for her permission to quote her unpublished material.

hoc enim unum est e rebus humanis opus, <u>cui nulla tempestas noceat quod nulla consumat vetustas</u>. cetera quae per constructionem lapidum et marmoreas moles aut terrenos tumulos in magnam eductos altitudinem constant, non propagant longam diem, quippe et ipsa intereunt; immortalis est ingenii memoria.

For among human achievements this is the only work <u>that no storm can harm, nor length of time destroy</u>. All others, those that are formed by piling up stones and masses of marble, or rearing on high huge mounds of earth, do not secure a long remembrance, for they themselves will also perish; but the fame of genius is immortal.
(Dial. 11.18.2)

The comparison of literature to buildings in terms of longevity is well known and goes back at least to Pindar (Pyth. 6.7–18). It was made prominent in Roman literature by a series of authors in the Augustan and early imperial age,[38] and is picked up in two epigrams ascribed to Seneca himself (Anth. Lat. 417 and 418).[39] The evidence suggests that we are here dealing with a literary topos (i.e. commonplace), a rhetorical category that Hinds, in his seminal discussion of Roman intertextuality, describes as follows: 'rather than demanding interpretation in relation to a specific model or models… the *topos* invokes its intertextual tradition as a collectivity, to which the individual contexts and connotations of individual prior instances are firmly subordinate.'[40] That is, the topos is traditionally, at least, classed as an inert conglomeration of comparanda rather than an active phenomenon.

It is indisputable that Seneca is walking a well-trodden path in the quoted excerpt from the *De Consolatione ad Polybium*. The theme of achieving fame by means of literary production serves as a leitmotif throughout the entire consolation, and the passage provided above should be read in connection with Dial. 11.2, where the literary achievements of Polybius's brother rather than Polybius himself are described: his writings grant him eternal fame – a fame supplemented by those of Polybius's own. Nevertheless, there are reasons to believe that there is a special link between this passage and Horace's Carm. 3.30: unlike, for example, Prop. 3.2.15–26, where the speaker promises eternal fame to his mistress, both Seneca's and Horace's texts are concerned with literary fame – in the case of Seneca with the fame of Polybius's brother, in the case of Carm. 3.30 with the fame of the author himself (as already noted). The underlined

---

38 Verg. Georg. 3.1–48; Hor. Carm. 3.30; Prop. 3.2.15–26; Stat. Silv. 5.1.
39 Kurth 1994, 220–221.
40 Hinds 1998, 34; Hinds of course then proceeds to put life back into the notion of topoi. Cf. Curtius, 1993, 89: 'Im antiken Lehrgebäude der Rhetorik ist die Topik das Vorratsmagazin. Man fand dort Gedanken der allgemeinsten Art: solche, die bei allen Reden und Schriften überhaupt verwendet werden konnten.'

phrase recalls the relative clause at the opening of the Horatian poem (the referent of *quod* is the *monumentum aere perennius* of the opening line):

> ...quod non imber edax, non Aquilo impotens
> possit diruere aut innumerabilis
> annorum series et fuga temporum.
>
> ...one which neither corroding rain nor the ungovernable North Wind can ever destroy, nor the countless series of the years, nor the flight of time.
> (Hor. Carm. 3.30.3–5)

The link between Seneca's work and Carm. 3.30 is further enhanced by his encouragement to Polybius to become the *primus inventor* of Latin fable in the style of Aesop (Dial. 11.8), just as Horace had boasted of being the first Roman to write in aeolic metre (Carm. 3.30.13–14). Even the motif of an ascension from a humble position (Carm. 3.30.12 *ex humili potens*, 'rising from a lowly state to a position of power') finds a response in the description of Polybius's promotion at the hands of the Emperor (Dial. 11.6.2).

Yet there is of course a third text in play – the epilogue of Ovid's *Metamorphoses* (15.871–879), whose first lines run as follows:[41]

> Iamque opus exegi, quod nec Iovis ira nec ignis
> nec poterit ferrum nec edax abolere vetustas...
>
> And now my work is done, which neither the wrath of Jove, nor fire, nor sword, nor the gnawing tooth of time shall ever be able to undo.
> (Ov. Met. 15.871–872)

This text was both heavily indebted to Horace's *Exegi monumentum aere perennius...* (Carm. 3.30.1) and well known to Seneca, who had exploited the Ovidian phrase *parte meliore* (Met. 15.875) earlier in the De Consolatione ad Polybium itself (2.6).[42] Moreover, the link with Ovid in particular is strengthened by the parallelism within the metaphor of consumption, which is applied to *vetustas* in both Ovid and Seneca (compare *opus... quod nulla consumat vetustas* in the excerpt above with Ovid's *edax vetustas* at Met. 15.872) – in Horace's Carm. 3.30.3, it is instead applied to the corrosive rain (*imber edax*). The correspondences between the three texts suggest that something more than a topos is at work here: the question is, however, precisely how they interact.

---

41 The text is from Tarrant's OCT; the translation is from F. J. Miller's Loeb.
42 Ovid's influence on Seneca is well known, cf. Jakobi 1988; Tarrant 2002.

Three possibilities emerge: (a) the first involves the two source texts (those of Horace and Ovid) being blended into a third (that of Seneca). If this is so, a further question follows: are the source texts balanced within the *De Consolatione ad Polybium*, or is there a hierarchy in terms of their respective influence? While Seneca's use of the metaphor of consumption in connection with aging is indeed very similar to Ovid's phrasing, the general structure of the argumentation, together with the ordering of the images evoked, is closer to what we find in Horace. We encounter *nulla tempestas noceat, nulla consumat vetustas* in Seneca, and in Horace we observe a similar pattern: first we hear of a storm (Carm. 3.30.3 *imber edax* and *Aquilo impotens*), and immediately afterwards of old age (5 *annorum series et fuga temporum*). In contrast, Ovid begins his succession of antagonistic powers with Jupiter's anger and fire (Met. 15.871), which one could of course see as a parallel to the storms in Seneca and Horace, yet then adds in the following verse a reference to iron (Met. 15.872 *ferrum*: probably a metonym for martial violence), and only then speaks of the effects of old age. Seneca's formulation, which had at first appeared highly Ovidian, thus displays a clear similarity to that of Horace in terms of the order of thought.

A second possibility (b) is to regard the relationship as a history of reception, with Ovid 'rewriting' Horace, and Seneca 'rewriting' Horace through Ovid. Again, the terminology used to describe the phenomenon is of importance: the established term, 'window reference,'[43] would seem to suggest that Seneca activates aspects of Horace's ode within the Ovidian framework; the respective source texts (for Ovid, Horace's ode; for Seneca, both Ovid and Horace) are viewed, validated, and then treated as inert matter given its form by the final author in the chain. On the other hand, a greater dynamism between the texts would suggest a 'chain of transformation,' a categorisation that implies a reciprocal procedure, one in which it is not merely the case that a receiving text is influenced by a received text but in which the influence occurs in both directions.[44]

If we were to apply this last conception of the relationship to the situation at hand, one might argue that there is a political valence to Seneca's allusions: Seneca wrote the *De Consolatione ad Polybium* while in relegation on Corsica – a fact that he mentions in the text (Dial. 11.13). His abject flattery of the emperor Claudius (Dial. 11.7, 12–14, 16) makes it quite clear that he is as concerned for the mitigation of his own misery (and particularly its cause, i.e. relegation) as he is for the apparent goal of the text, the alleviation of Polybius's misery. Is it possible to see a similar subtext in Horace and Ovid? Scholars have noted in both

---

43 For this concept, see Thomas 1999, 130–132.
44 Böhme 2011, 11; see Mindt in this volume.

cases that – in different ways – political motivations, and in particular Augustus, loom in the background.⁴⁵ Seneca's overtly political text, so it might be argued, supports such interpretations of the texts to which he refers. A nuance that was perhaps still embryonic in the earlier texts is foregrounded via the link with the receiving text, in which the theme of politics is central. Yet, to follow this form of argumentation, the support is mutual and has an influence on the receiving text: if one, encouraged by the political dimension of the Senecan *consolatio*, reads the *Iovis ira* of Ovid (Met. 15.871) as the anger of Augustus (as Jupiter), it is possible to make the inference that Seneca judged the actual enemy of memory to be neither erosion nor old age, but rather the *Erinnerungspolitik* of the emperor.⁴⁶

Finally, one might simply (c) step back and view the relationship between the three texts as participation in a shared topos: given the subtle differences between the texts and the variation they disclose, scholars might still be inclined to infer that Seneca is merely drawing on a communal repository of motifs, metaphors, and terms, i.e. the discourse of literary output as a physical structure, rather than on a specific model. This does not of course mean that interpretation of Seneca's application of the topos must cease, a point well made by Hinds his general discussion of topoi in *Allusion and Intertext*: as he notes, the question as to what role the individual pre-texts played for an author remains justified, even if the reconstruction of an 'ideal reader,' who accords the individual texts precisely the same importance as the receiving author (i.e. Seneca), is impossible.⁴⁷ According to Hinds, the problems that confront the scholar in dealing with topoi are symptomatic of all sophisticated forms of the study of intertextuality.⁴⁸

---

45 Concerning Horace's Carm. 3.30, Koster 1983, 39, and Simpson 2002, 90, suggest a planned memorial for Augustus as a possible contemporary point of reference. The *pontifex* of line 9 may have had something to do with the demands made in the twenties (Res Gestae 10) for Augustus to fill the office of Pontifex Maximus even before the death of its incumbent, Marcus Aemilius Lepidus. Cf. De Vos 2014, 6 n. 36; Simpson 2002, 92–93; Nisbet / Rudd 2004, 373. The word *princeps* (line 13) has been the cause of much speculation; cf. De Vos 2014, 6 n. 39; Till 1968, 100; Koster 1983, 38; Simpson 2002, 94; Sutherland 2002, 232. For possible political connotations in the epilogue to Ovid's *Metamorphoses*, cf. Schmitzer 1990, 296–297 (in reference to the formulation *Caesaris ira* in Tr. 3.11.72) and Hardie 2013, 621 and 624.
46 This possibility, incidentally, provides a further example that interpretations involving intertextuality are not necessarily purely formalistic but may also draw on political and historical discourses. On this phenomenon see Fowler 2000, 127–131.
47 Hinds 1998, 46: 'The ideal reader, who sees exactly the same cues within the *topos* as the author, and constructs them in the same order and in the same way, will always in the final analysis be unattainable.'
48 Hinds 1998, 47: 'With *topoi*, and indeed with allusive discourse at large, one can never step into the same river twice. No two readers will ever reconstruct a set of cues in quite the same way.'

Besides this methodological added value, the study of topoi can also lead to further sociological considerations: in the previous example, it is noteworthy that Seneca appears to be the first to make use of the relevant topos in prose. From this, one could pose the question as to whether Seneca, by means of employing this particular topos, creates and reinforces certain advantageous group-identities: on the one hand between himself, his educated addressee Polybius, and his broader readership (consisting of the emperor and other members of the political elite), to whom the poetic texts in which the topos arises would have been well known and for whom there would have been sense of recognition or *déjà vu* in reading the Senecan passage; on the other, between himself as an author of prose and the famous, already canonised poets who employed the topos. The creation and reinforcement of such group-identities is particularly relevant in Seneca's situation in exile, far away from the political and literary circles of Rome: it constitutes a means of projecting to others, and engendering within himself, a sense of self-assurance, i.e. of 'belonging to the club.'

3 The Volume

We have discussed but a few of the difficulties that confront us in trying to draw out the links between these two eminent authors, and would like to stress that we have only presented the tip of the iceberg here. Further issues will be discussed throughout the present volume, which we have divided into four parts.[49] The first ('Philosophy in Literature – Literature in Philosophy') focuses on the interaction between literature and philosophy: Barbara Del Giovane ('Dressing Philosophy with *sal niger*. Horace's Role in Seneca's Approach to the Diatribic Tradition') describes the way in which Horace serves as a filter for Seneca's reception of the Bionic tradition of Cynic philosophy, focusing on specific points in this long-standing debate and providing an in-depth consideration of Horace's Carm. 3.16, while Francesca Romana Berno ('Nurse's Prayers, Philosophical *otium*, and Fat Pigs: Seneca Ep. 60 versus Horace Ep. 1.4') considers the interface between Epicureanism and Stoicism in Horace's Ep. 1.4 and Seneca's Ep. 60: Seneca employs Sallust's preface to the *Bellum Catilinae* in order to criticise Horace's *pinguem... Epicuri de grege porcum* (Hor. Ep. 1.4.15– 16). Catharine Edwards ('Saturnalian Exchanges: Seneca, Horace, and Satiric Advice') then discusses the role of the Roman Saturnalia against the Horatian back-

---

[49] For a summary of the conference on which the volume is based, including information about the keynote address of John Moles, see Soldo 2015.

drop, arguing that Horace's S. 2.3 and S. 2.7 serve as an important point of contact with Seneca's Ep. 18.

Part two, 'Horatian Verse in Senecan Tragedy,' mainly concerns links between the lyric portions of the two corpora, Richard Tarrant ('*Custode rerum Caesare*: Horatian Civic Engagement and the Senecan Tragic Chorus') arguing that the role of the chorus of Senecan drama is meaningful in the context of Neronian Rome: the secretive and cloistered features of Nero's court are captured in the behaviour of the chorus, whose ignorance concerning the actions of the protagonists is mirrored by the position of the Roman people at the end of the Julio-Claudian dynasty. This stands in contrast to the benevolence of Augustus in Horatian lyric. Christopher Trinacty ('Horatian Contexts in Senecan Tragedy') then discusses specific intertexts in Seneca and Horace, touching on many of the issues that we have made in the preceding pages but also going beyond them: where does an intertext stop? How much of the surrounding Horatian context does Seneca hope to activate via his allusions? There follow two paired contributions: Tobias Allendorf ('Sounds and Space. Seneca's Horatian Lyrics') considers the role of sound in the poetry of the two authors, long considered an important feature of discussions of Horace but a point of common concern for both, while Jonathan Geiger ('Strictness, Freedom, and Experimentation in Horatian and Senecan Metrics') closes part two with a discussion of the details of the relationship between Horatian and Senecan metrics: how did these authors work to standardise the Greek lyric metres, and what types of latitude did they allow themselves? And how did Horace help determine Seneca's usage of these forms?

Part three, 'Themes and Concepts,' is predictably wide-ranging: Gregor Vogt-Spira ('Time in Horace and Seneca') considers the all-important issue of time – both authors are fascinated by the question of how best to allocate this precious resource, but their answers are decidedly different. Barak Blum ('*Studiorum instrumenta*: Loaded Libraries in Seneca and Horace') discusses the idea of the library in each author, emphasising the ethical aspects of maintaining collections of books and the possibly negative motivations for doing so. Elena Giusti ('The Metapoetics of Liber-ty. Horace's Bacchic Ship in Seneca's *De Tranquillitate Animi*') then discusses the role of Bacchic ecstasy in Seneca's *De Tranquillitate* and Horace's early poetry, while Alexander Kirichenko ('Constructing Oneself in Horace and Seneca') looks at the complex ways in which Horace and Seneca deviate from each other in terms of their creation of their unique personae, considering the fracturing of the self in Seneca's tragic choruses.

Techniques of citation, both within and of the works of the authors at hand, are broached in part four, 'Modes of Quotation and Issues of Reception.' Ute Tischer ('*Nostra faciamus*. Quoting in Horace and Seneca') throws under the spotlight the very techniques by which Horace and Seneca incorporated 'foreign' texts into their own works. Nina Mindt ('Horace, Seneca, and Martial: "Sententious Style" across Genres') discusses the role of point and epigram in the writing of the two authors, and particularly how they were received by Martial: how did Martial construct his 'hidden canon'? Finally, Victoria Moul ('Seneca, Horace, and the Anglo-Latin "Moralising Lyric" in Early Modern England') takes us all the way down to the Early Modern period, where we find Horace and Seneca read in very much the same ways: the writing of each served as an ethical lodestar – to the point that they barely resisted being amalgamated.

Although the contributors to the volume have not confined themselves to intertextual issues in a narrow sense (i.e. lexical parallels), we have decided to close the volume with an index of parallels between the two authors. The idea is borrowed from the indices in the studies of Knauer (Virgil / Homer) and Nelis (Virgil / Apollonius);[50] while they have certainly encountered criticism, these indices have been of lasting importance for scholars working on these poets, and we hope to offer a similar tool for the study of Horace and Seneca. The list is not computer-generated: we have sorted through the difficult listings of Spika and Zingerle, as well as the material provided by Kapnukajas, Berthet, and Mazzoli, checking and adjusting their parallels and adding entries offered by our own contributors. We are particularly grateful to Elena Giusti, Richard Tarrant, and Christopher Trinacty on this score. The index of course deals with cross-generic relationships, and we have modified the system of abbreviations of Knauer and Nelis accordingly (they are explained in the index itself). In order to be as clear as possible, we would like to stress (1) that we do not necessarily assume authorial intent in the compilation of these points of resemblance, and (2) that by ending our volume with them we do not want to suggest that they represent anything like the 'final word': provisional and incomplete as it remains, this list is simply meant as a possible starting point for further research into the relationship between Horace and Seneca.

---

50 Knauer 1964 and Nelis 2001.

I Philosophy in Literature – Literature in Philosophy

Barbara Del Giovane
Dressing Philosophy with *sal niger*. Horace's Role in Seneca's Approach to the Diatribic Tradition

This contribution aims to offer new perspectives on Seneca's approach to the diatribic tradition and to show how Horace's poetry works to mediate Seneca's use of diatribic style and topoi.[1] The analysis provided will on the one hand reopen a controversial chapter in the history of classical literature and philosophy, and shed light on the relationship between Seneca and Horace on the other.

The 'controversial chapter' is, of course, the debate over the so-called genre of Cynic-Stoic diatribe.[2] The qualification 'so-called' is indicative of the difficulty in dealing with this literary and philosophical genre – a genre that never actually existed. While I agree with the consensus view of modern scholars, who refuse to consider diatribe a specific genre,[3] I nevertheless want to argue for the value of using terms like 'diatribe' and 'diatribic' – once these terms are properly understood and qualified.[4]

The literary genre that was allegedly invented by Bion of Borysthenes is a construction of modern scholarship that appears to have originated with Usener.[5] Usener associated the Greek term *diatribai* with the work of Bion,[6] which

---

I would like to thank the Fondation Hardt in Vandoeuvres (Genève), where, between April and May 2015, I found the perfect environment in which to develop this paper.

[1] On the relationship between Seneca and diatribe (with up-to-date bibliography), see Del Giovane 2015b.
[2] The only monograph on diatribe so far published is Oltramare 1926; Fuentes González 1997, a critical edition with commentary on Teles's fragments, is the most recent work that focuses on the debate on the legitimacy of diatribe as a genre: cf. in particular the chapter *La question de la 'diatribe'*, 44–78; for the definition of diatribe, see also Kindstrand 1976, 21–25; Stowers 1988, 71–83.
[3] On the notion of genre and generic theory, see especially Harrison 2011, 1–18 with bibliography.
[4] For a review of authors who agree on the usefulness of employing the term 'diatribe,' cf. Fuentes González 1997, 73 n. 5.
[5] The essential work on Bion of Borysthenes is the commentary by Kindstrand 1976: the general introduction is at 21–55. Further texts are Weber 1895, 6–33; Hense 1909, C–CVIII; Pennacini 1982, 55–61; 1989, 451–456; 2007, 59–78.
[6] Usener 1887, LXIX: 'Bio Borysthenita sermonibus suis (διατριβαί nomen erat) genus cynicum severitate risuque mixtum perfecit.'

had previously been termed *sermo* in the scholarship: the link with the title of Horace's *Sermones* is not accidental. Diogenes Laertius, in reporting an apophthegm quoted by Aristippus, was the first to connect the word *diatribai* with the work of Bion and 'of the people associated with him.'[7] The primary meaning of *diatribē* is linked with the concept of 'wearing away,' especially in terms of time; but it can also mean 'pastime,' 'occupation,' 'discourse,' 'ethical treatise.' By extension, the term can signify 'philosophical school' and, more generically, 'a place for teachings.' It follows, as Halbauer[8] first pointed out, that the term *diatribē* implies nothing about style that could justify its construal as primarily a literary genre. Nevertheless, Jocelyn's vehement polemic goes too far:[9] he not only rejects the use of the word *diatribē* to indicate a genre but also the interpretation that it denotes 'speech' or 'conversation' in relation to Bion and his pupils. For Jocelyn, a proper 'conversation' should involve at least a second interlocutor. Thus, Bion's monologues cannot be characterised as dialogue. However, I believe that the word *diatribē* might have been used by Diogenes Laertius to mean a sort of transcription of a speech by a teacher that could involve, in its original oral form, an additional student-interlocutor.[10] The *adversarius fictus*, a stylistic feature of the fragmentary texts by Bion and Teles[11] and one also employed by Seneca and Horace to give voice to a dissenting opinion, may be interpreted as a rhetorical device derived from an original dialectical stage. While on the one hand the word *diatribē* might well have indicated a philosoph-

---

[7] D.L. 2.77 'ὥς φασιν οἱ περὶ τὸν Βίωνα ἐν ταῖς Διατριβαῖς, 'ἀπόχεε,' ἔφη (scil. ὁ Ἀρίστιππος), 'τὸ πλέον καὶ ὅσον δύνασαι βάσταζε,' 'Like the people in Bion's circle say in their speeches, Aristippus declared: "Pour away the greater part and carry no more than you can manage"'; the text of Diogenes Laertius is that of Dorandi; translations are taken or adapted from Hicks's Loeb.
[8] Halbauer 1911, 3.
[9] In three different articles Jocelyn rejected 'the notion that in some registers of ancient Greek the word *diatribē* could denote a type of philosophical discourse or writing with definable characteristics': Jocelyn 1979, 145–147; 1982, 3–7 (quote at p. 3); 1983, 89–91.
[10] In D.L. 4.77 the composition of *apophthegmata* and *hypomnemata* is also ascribed to Bion. The term *hypomnema* has many meanings, but I am especially concerned with the definition 'notes, commentaries,' which I interpret as written notes transcribed by the preacher Bion after a preliminary oral lesson.
[11] The *vox ficta*, together with the rhetorical device of addressing a second interlocutor with questions or with simple 'mechanised interrogative formulae' (Zangrado 1998, 91), is present in Bion's fragments, although, as Kindstrand 1976, 30 states, it is a stylistic feature that 'has been too strongly stressed by earlier scholars as the cases in the preserved fragments are comparatively few and of a completely rhetorical character.' However, these features are employed in Teles and will recur in Epictetus's preaching, whose speeches, in Arrianus's transcription, are defined with the term *diatribai*.

ical speech in Diogenes Laertius's text, there is no evidence that Bion himself used it to refer to the general nature of his work or employed it as its title.

As there is no evidence of a literary genre called 'diatribe,' we may well ask what justifies our use of the term. In my view, we are warranted by a tradition whose most significant traces are to be found in Horace and Seneca, and which, in Mazzoli's words, 'adunava sotto i comuni colori del cinismo stoicheggiante, dell'εἶδος σπουδαιογέλοιον, della mordace contestazione e della retoricità una materia etica priva di precise σφραγίδες scolastiche.'[12] This tradition can be observed in a cluster of topoi but also in many stylistic features: according to Grimal, the 'style diatribique' is marked by a taste for metaphors and a passionate eloquence.[13]

In other words, we cannot neglect the fact that there existed a corpus of texts, prominently represented by Bion but in general incomplete and fragmentary, from which Cicero[14] and Seneca specifically quoted, to which Horace alluded,[15] and which probably circulated in an anthologised form from Cicero's time onwards. However, essays such as Oltramare's well-known contribution tend to interpret classical moralistic literature in a 'pandiatribic'[16] way, and analyse the influences of diatribe on authors like Horace and Seneca merely in order to produce a sterile numbered list of topoi or specific features of the 'genre.'[17] In my view, it is important to consider the individual rhetorical and expressive contexts in which the diatribic influence is recognisable without renouncing analysis of their background and forms of mediation.

I will begin my inquiry by demonstrating Horace's involvement with the Bionic tradition; I shall then explore Seneca's engagement with diatribe in order to show Horace's fundamental influence on Seneca's *modus operandi*.

---

12 Mazzoli 1970, 237.
13 Grimal 1978, 262.
14 Cic. Tusc. 3.62 (= fr. 69 Kindstrand).
15 Hor. Ep. 2.2.60 *Bioneis sermonibus et sale nigro* (= t. 14 Kindstrand), 'Bion's discourses, with their black salt'; the text of Horace is that of Klingner's Teubner; translations are taken or adapted from Fairclough's Loeb for the *Satires* and *Epistles* (unless otherwise indicated), and Rudd's Loeb for the *Odes*.
16 On Oltramare's flaw of 'pandiatribism,' see Citroni Marchetti 1991, 82 n. 1; Lana 1992, 110.
17 Oltramare 1926 provides first a catalogue of *pensées diatribiques*, then a list of the same topoi identified in Seneca's works; one might also mention works like Weber 1895, which first presents a list of diatribic stylistic features, and then analyses these same features in Seneca and Horace. The value of this essay lies in its demonstrating the many affinities between Seneca and Horace against a common diatribic background.

1 Horace's Bionic Paternity

According to a fascinating hypothesis advanced by Heinze and reprised by Moles,[18] the word *sermo* in Horace's expression *Bioneis sermonibus et sale nigro*[19] functions as a translation of *diatribē*, the word used to define Bion's works. Along the same lines, Gowers interprets the verb *delasso*, employed by Horace in S. 1.24 to indicate the action of 'wearing out' through the many examples of *mempsimoiria* ('discontent with one's lot in life'), as a translation-gloss of the Greek verb *diatribein*.[20] These scholars proceed from the assumption that Horace was aware of the title *Diatribai*. Nevertheless, although the name 'Bion' provides clear proof of Horace's intention to connect his own poetry to the Bionic tradition, we do not have sufficient evidence to establish conclusively whether the word *sermo* was deliberately used by the poet and whether it attests to his knowledge that Bion's works were called *Diatribai*.

However, the Horatian expression *sal niger*, used by the poet at Ep. 2.2.60, has also been read as an allusion to the text of Bion. As we know from Diogenes Laertius, Bion told the king Antigonus Gonatas that his father was a freedman 'who wiped his nose on his sleeve,'[21] an action that indicates the father's occupation as a dealer in salt fish; this anecdote seems to be recalled by the Horatian *sal niger*. Besides this, Moles has provided a list of seventeen points to show how Horace in S. 1.6 sketches an autobiography modelled on the biography of Bion as a means of claiming the philosopher as a literary model.[22] In what follows I will add one point to this impressive list in order to further illustrate the bond between Horace and Bion, arguing for Horace's knowledge of Bion's works.

In the autobiographical fragment by Bion mentioned above (1a Kindstrand), the king Antigonus addresses the philosopher to gather information about him, quoting the Homeric verse τίς, πόθεν εἰς ἀνδρῶν; πόθι τοι πόλις ἠδὲ τοκῆες, 'who are you and where do you come from? What city is yours, who are your pa-

---

[18] Heinze 1889, 6–7; Moles 2012, 446–447; 2007, 165–166.
[19] Ep. 2.2.60 = t. 14 Kindstrand: Horace uses this expression to represent his satiric work.
[20] Hor. S. 1.1.13–14 *Cetera de genere hoc – adeo sunt multa – loquacem | delassare valent Fabium*, 'The other instances of this kind – so many are they – could tire out the chatterbox Fabius'; cf. Gowers 2005, 54 n. 41; 2012, 66.
[21] Fr. 1a Kindstrand (= D.L. 4.46) 'Ἐμοῦ ὁ πατὴρ μὲν ἦν ἀπελεύθερος, τῷ ἀγκῶνι ἀπομυσσόμενος (διεδήλου δὲ τὸν ταριχέμπορον) γένος Βορυσθενίτης,' '"My father was a freedman, who wiped his nose on his sleeve" – meaning that he was a dealer in salt fish "a native from Borysthenes"'; fr. 1b (= Suda α 249 Adler); 1c (= Suda σ 1377 Adler); 2 Kindstrand (= Stob. 4.29.13).
[22] Moles 2007, 166–167.

rents?', which occurs seven times in the *Odyssey* and once in the *Iliad*.²³ After explaining his family circumstances, Bion himself quotes a verse from Il. 6.211: ταύτης τοι γενεῆς τε καὶ αἵματος εὔχομαι εἶναι, 'This is the stock and this the blood from which I boast to have sprung.' The addition of the Homeric quotation to the description of his humble background is to be interpreted, according to Bonandini,²⁴ as a programmatic declaration of his distance from the world of *epos* and its ideals. The same Homeric apostrophe employed by Antigonus is used by Zeus to address the philosopher Menippus, the main character of Lucian's dialogue *Icaromenippus*.²⁵ Even more relevant to our argument is the fact that in Seneca's *Apocolocyntosis* Hercules employs the verse τίς πόθεν εἰς...,²⁶ with one small variation,²⁷ to address the emperor Claudius, who has just arrived at Olympus. Claudius, like Bion, replies with a Homeric quotation that is in this case linked to the phrase just employed by Hercules.²⁸ The use of the Homeric apostrophe might well be a topos of a diatribic as well as Menippean tradition: my assumption in what follows is that Horace's S. 1.6 must be read in light of this Bionic tradition.

The example of Tillius, candidate for the position of tribune of the plebs, in S. 1.6.24 stirs up a reflection on the envy that afflicts men involved in politics (24–26 *Quo tibi, Tilli, | sumere depositum clavom fierique tribuno? | invidia adcre-*

---

23 Cf. Od. 1.170, 5.264, 10.325, 14.187, 15.264, 19.105, 24.298; Il. 21.150; at 7.238, the verse presents a variation in its second hemistich. The first hemistich is also quoted by Xenophanes (VS 21 B 22.4).
24 Bonandini 2010, 67.
25 Luc. Icar. 23 Ὁ δὲ Ζεὺς μάλα φοβερῶς, δριμύ τε καὶ τιτανῶδες εἰς ἐμὲ ἀπιδών, φησί 'Τίς πόθεν εἰς ἀνδρῶν, πόθι τοι πόλις ἠδὲ τοκῆες;', 'Zeus, however, looked at me with a fierce, Titanic stare and said in a very terrible voice: "What is your name, sir, whence do you come, and where is your city and hearth-stone?".' The text and translation of Lucian's *Icaromenippus* are taken from Harmon's Loeb; cf. Camerotto 2009, 130; see also 130–131 for passages by Aristophanes where, even without using the Homeric verse, characters ask for information about other figures' origins.
26 Sen. Apoc. 5 Accessit (scil. *Hercules*) itaque et quod facillimum fuit Graeculo, ait: τίς πόθεν εἰς ἀνδρῶν, ποίη πόλις ἠδὲ τοκῆες;, 'So Hercules went up to him and, as was extremely easy for a Greekling, said "Who are you, and from where? What kind are your city and parents?"'; the text and translation from the *Apocolocyntosis* are both taken from Eden's edition (Cambridge Greek and Latin Classics); 'Homeric verses, and this one in particular (cf. esp. D.L. 4.46–47) had a long history of parody and humorous misapplication,' Eden 1984, 85; cf. Weinreich 1923, 68–71 and O'Gorman 2005, 96–98, who interestingly focuses on the '"knowing your Homer" competition' between Hercules and Claudius.
27 Cf. Eden 1984, 85 for the ποίη instead of the πόθι τοι.
28 A passage by Epictetus (3.21.92) also presents Alexander addressing Diogenes the Cynic and quoting a Homeric verse. The Cynic replies with the line following that quoted by Alexander.

vit, privato quae minor esset, 'What good was it to you, Tillius, to assume the stripe once doffed and become a tribune? Envy fastened on you afresh, but would be less, were you in a private station'). Horace then focuses on the condition of men who decide to hold a senatorial position, represented by the broad stripe and black sandals, and thus expose themselves to inquiries about the origins of their ancestors (27–29 *nam ut quisque insanus nigris medium impediit crus | pellibus et latum demisit pectore clavom | audit continuo 'quis homo hic est? quo patre natus?'*, 'For as soon as any man is so crazy as to bind the black thongs halfway up his leg, and to drop the broad stripe down his breast, at once he hears: "What fellow is this? What was his father?"'). In the questions *quis homo hic est? quo patre natus?* one may hear a clear echo of the Homeric verse πόθεν εἰς ἀνδρῶν; πόθι τοι πόλις ἠδὲ τοκῆες employed by Antigonus in the quotation from Bion but also found in the Menippean texts by Lucian and Seneca. This detail seems to confirm the hypothesis that there was a tradition in which Homeric quotations were the customary way of asking after a character's family origin, which probably found in Bion a significant, if not the very first, exponent. Horace seems to be aware of this tradition: in S. 1.6, the questions *quis homo hic est? quo patre natus?* are not pronounced by an authorial figure to address an interlocutor, as in the cases mentioned above, but occur as utterances of a *vox ficta* to exemplify the common tendency to inquire about the origins of senators (27 *ut quisque*; 29 *audit continuo*). Horace seems to go further than the tradition, by not only translating the formulaic Homeric verse but also manipulating it and turning the questions into an index of the excessive concern for family descent commonly shown by the Roman public. The specifically Roman context, together with the typically moral aim of Horace's *Satires*, leads Horace to formulate the two questions in universal terms, addressed to all who aspire to power. Horace cannot put Antigonus's probing questions into Maecenas's mouth, just as he cannot afford to identify himself with the man desirous of obtaining political power: the satirical sketch is thus exhausted by the reference of paradigmatic questions to an unspecified human 'type.'

After the comparison with the pretty-boy Barrus, who causes girls to examine each and every part of his body (S. 1.6.30–33), Horace reaffirms that whoever aspires to take care of the Roman state 'compels all mortals to be anxious to find out from what father he's born, whether he's disgraced by having an unknown as his mother' (36–37 *quo patre sit natus, num ignota matre inhonestus, | omnis mortalis curare et quaerere cogit*). Here, it is also the mention of an *ignota mater* as a cause of shame that seems to evoke Bion's family situation. As he himself writes, Bion had a mother 'such as a man like my father would marry, from a brothel' (fr. 1a.7 Kindstrand). Horace not only alludes to Bion, as if he were claiming his satirical legacy, but also turns Bion's reference to his family into a paradigmatic example of publicly declaring one's own humble origins, a situation that concerns, as specified at verse 37, 'all mortal people' (*omnes mortales*).

2 'The God Who Offers the Chance to Change One's Life.' A Bionic Tradition?

I have attempted to show how Horace not only knew Bion's texts, but also considered Bion's work paradigmatic of a tradition characterised by a brilliant mordacity – a mordacity that Horace transferred to his own satirical work. Seneca reveals himself to have read Bion as well, since he quotes Bion three times.[29] However, according to many scholars,[30] it appears that Seneca did not read Bion directly,[31] but through the mediation of a different author or a collection of apophthegms (*gnōmologia*) that consisted of practical maxims (*gnōmai* or *chreiai*).[32] The correspondences between Seneca and Teles[33] are also to be interpreted in terms of a mediation through a *gnōmologia*.[34] My aim here is to show that Horace's poetry plays the role of a 'filtro prezioso,' as Mazzoli has pointed out,[35] for Seneca's approaches to diatribic topoi: in other words, Horace represents for Seneca the most refined interpretation of the diatribic model and thus prepares the ground for Seneca's own version of it. I will first give as an example a topos that is strongly foregrounded in Horace's *Satires* and point out that Seneca employs it as well, even though he is not listed among the authors who engaged with it. Moreover, I will also show how it is precisely Seneca's use of this topos that corroborates the hypothesis of its diatribic background.

The theme I refer to is that of the god who makes an offer to human beings. Following the examples on the theme of *mempsimoiria* in S. 1.1, Horace imagines

---

29 Sen. Dial. 9.8.3, 15.4; Ben. 7.7.1.
30 Cf. Setaioli 1988, 166 for a review of the different scholarly interpretations: Hirzel 1895, II, 29 n. 2, supposes the mediation of a *gnōmologia* for Seneca's quotations of Bion; Heinze 1890 and Oltramare 1926, 261–262 think of Aristhon as an intermediate author; Hense 1893, 38 of Athenodorus.
31 Weber 1895, 5 and Kindstrand 1976, 86–87 believe that Seneca read the text of Bion directly.
32 For an explanation of the differences between a *chreia*, an *apophthegma*, and a *gnōmē*, cf. Kindstrand 1986.
33 Cf. Hense 1909 passim, who appends a great number of parallel passages by Seneca to Teles's texts.
34 See on this point Setaioli 1988, 166.
35 Mazzoli 1998, 63.

a god who offers to humans the chance to change their roles in life, a proposal that is, however, rejected by the unhappy mortals:

> ...si quis deus 'en ego' dicat
> 'iam faciam quod voltis: eris tu, qui modo miles,
> mercator; tu, consultus modo, rusticus: hinc vos,
> vos hinc mutatis discedite partibus. eia,
> quid statis?' nolint. atqui licet esse beatis.
>
> If some god were to say 'Here I am! I will grant your prayers forthwith. You, who were but now a soldier, shall be a trader; you, but now a lawyer, shall be a farmer. Change parts; away with you—and with you! Well! Why standing still?' They would refuse.
> (Hor. S. 1.1.15–19)

Both vocabulary and imagery are drawn from the field of theatre, and, as scholars have noted, theatrical metaphors, despite being a widespread 'literary topos'[36] when related to *mempsimoiria*, seem to be consistently employed in the diatribic tradition.[37] Another Horatian passage features a god who shows up and fulfils a wish (S. 2.7.24);[38] in this case, it is Davus who proposes to Horace the idea of a god who provides the opportunity to live in olden times, whose way of life is praised by the poet. Here the 'hypocrisy of H.'s own *mempsimoiria* is attacked'[39] since Horace, as Davus promptly suggests, would certainly reject the god's offer (24 *usque recuses*).

In considering the origins of the topos of the 'god who gives something,' scholars have invoked popular philosophy,[40] the Menippean tradition, and mime,[41] and have focused particularly on Menander's *Theophoroumene*, where

---

[36] Fuentes González 1997, 150–151.
[37] See Teles fr. 2, 16.4–17 Hense (= fr. 16a Kindstrand).
[38] Hor. S. 2.7.24–27 *Siquis ad illa deus subito te agat, usque recuses, | aut quia non sentis, quod clamas, rectius esse, | aut quia non firmus rectum defendis et haeres | nequiquam caeno cupiens evellere plantam*, 'And yet, if on a sudden some god were for taking you back to those days, you would refuse every time; either because you don't really think that what you are ranting is sounder, or because you are wobbly in defending the right and, though vainly longing to pull your foot from the filth, yet stick fast in it.'
[39] Cf. Gowers 2012, 67.
[40] 'The figure of the god who shows up to solve human wishes was recurring in popular philosophy: cf. Bion *ap*. Tel. Pp. 3–4 Hense,' Minarini 1977, 52.
[41] Oltramare 1926, 67; Gowers 2012, 67; even though he does not mention the topos of *mempsimoiria*, compare Socrates's address to Alcibiades in the *First Alcibiades* 105a, ascribed to Plato: 'Suppose that at this moment some god came to you and said: "Alcibiades, Will you live as you are, or die in an instant if you are forbidden to make any further acquisition?".' Moreover, as a confirmation of the Socratic tradition about the god and the hypothesis of 'living or dying,' in

Craton speculates that a god appears (1 εἴ τις προσελθών μοι θεῶν) offering human beings the chance to be born again in the form of another creature. Craton begs not to be transformed into a human being, since humans are unlucky and depressed, unhappy in their destiny – a prefiguration of the diatribic topic of *mempsimoiria*. An oration by Maximus of Tyre[42] outlines a thought experiment in which a god treats humans like actors, offering them new lives but nevertheless failing to reduce their unhappiness thereby.[43] A passage by Teles featuring Bion's metaphor of life as a play (fr. 16a Kindstrand)[44] in which men are dissatisfied by their role has led scholars to suppose that the passages in both Maximus and Horace have a diatribic background. In particular it is notable that the Horatian passage features not only a role reversal offered by a god, but theatrical language as well (S. 1.1.18 *mutatis... partibus*). After noting Bion's theatrical metaphor, moreover, Teles quotes another speech by Bion (fr. 17 Kindstrand), in which a personified Poverty addresses men. Heinze[45] connects the Horatian *si quis deus* with the Bionic εἰ λάβοι... φωνὴν τὰ πράγματα..., which had introduced the metaphor in Bion's text.

I believe that Seneca's Ep. 96 may reinforce this interpretation. At the end of the letter, Seneca prays that the gods not allow Fortune to keep Lucilius in a state of luxury: Ep. 96.4 *neque di neque deae faciant ut te fortuna in deliciis habeat*,

---

Memorabilia 1.2.16 Xenophon imagines a situation in which a god proposes to Critias and Alcibiades, portrayed as an evil for the state, the choice 'between the life they saw Socrates leading and death.' Thus the god concludes that 'they would have chosen rather to die.'
42 Max. Tyr. 15.1 Hobein 'If one of the gods were to strip each of these men of his present life and aspect and reclothe him in those of his neighbour, like actors in a play, then once again these same people will be found longing for their previous lives and bemoaning the present.' Translation by Trapp (OUP).
43 A passage by Lucian from *The Ship, or the Wishes* is also worth mentioning. In chapter 13, Adeimantus imagines what would happen if a god had granted him ownership of the grain ship that he and his friend had seen.
44 Fr. 16a Kindstrand (= Teles fr. 2, 5.3–6.1 Hense) Δεῖ ὥσπερ τὸν ἀγαθὸν ὑποκριτὴν ὅ τι ἂν ὁ ποιητὴς περιθῇ πρόσωπον τοῦτο ἀγωνίζεσθαι καλῶς, οὕτω καὶ τὸν ἀγαθὸν ἄνδρα ὅ τι ἂν περιθῇ ἡ τύχη. καὶ γὰρ αὕτη, φησὶν ὁ Βίων, ὥσπερ ποιήτρια, ὁτὲ μὲν πρωτολόγου, ὁτὲ δὲ δευτερολόγου περιτίθησι πρόσωπον, καὶ ὁτὲ μὲν βασιλέως, ὁτὲ δὲ ἀλήτου. μὴ οὖν βούλου δευτερολόγος ὢν τὸ πρωτολόγου πρόσωπον· εἰ δὲ μή, ἀνάρμοστόν τι ποιήσεις, 'Just as a good actor must perform properly whatever role the poet assigns him, so too must a good man perform whatever Dame Fortune assigns. For she, says Bion, like a poetess, sometime assigns the role of a firstspeaker, sometimes that of second-speaker; and sometimes that of king, sometimes that of vagabond. Do not, therefore, want the role of first-speaker when you are a second speaker. Otherwise you will commit some discordant act.' Translation by O'Neill (Scholars' Press).
45 Heinze 1889, 17.

'May neither gods nor goddesses keep you in the lap of luxury.'⁴⁶ Here we may first note the theme of Fortune deciding the roles in the play of life, which we saw in the Bionic fragment (16a Kindstrand). Right after this, Seneca presents Lucilius with the idea of a god who lets him decide whether to live in a market or in a military camp, using the same formulaic expression as Horace: *si quis deus*⁴⁷ (5 *Ipse te interroga, si quis potestatem tibi deus faciat, utrum velis vivere in macello an in castris?*, 'Ask yourself: if some god gave you the choice, would you rather live in the food market or in the military camp?'). The passage also features the metaphor of life as a battle, a standard theme in diatribe,⁴⁸ summarised by the phrase: 'life, Lucilius, is a campaign,' *atqui vivere, Lucili, militare est*. Unlike in the Horatian passage, the choice proposed by the god does not here involve *mempsimoiria*: this rhetorical device is exploited by the 'philosopher' Seneca to admonish the would-be wise man Lucilius on the necessity of choosing a Stoic life.

Seneca also elaborates on the topos of the 'god giving a gift' at Ben. 7.8.3, a passage hitherto unnoticed in this context, where he imagines a situation in which the god offers possessions to the Cynic Demetrius, who, according to Seneca, would have surely refused: *Demetrio si res nostras aliquis deorum possidendas velit tradere sub lege certa, ne liceat donare, adfirmaverim repudiaturum dicturumque*, 'If some god wanted to give our wealth to Demetrius to keep, on the condition that he not be allowed to give any of it as a gift, I venture to claim that he would reject the offer, saying as follows.' It is interesting to note how the topos serves here as a prompt for Demetrius's speech: the Cynic, after rejecting the god's offer, addresses the divinity with a long reply. As in Ep. 96, the refusal of the god's offer is not meant to merely reprise a theme in the tradition of *mempsimoiria*. In fact, Seneca goes well beyond this tradition, and, by employing a metacritical approach, makes use of the thought experiment as a means of introducing the Cynic-Stoic idea of *autarkeia*: what motivates the rejection of the

---

46 The text of Seneca's *Epistulae Morales* is from Reynolds's OCT; translations are by (or adapted from those of) Graver and Long (University of Chicago Press).
47 Cicero (Cato 83) also refers to the image by employing expressions similar to those used by Horace (*si quis deus... valde recusem*) in a similar context; the proposal is to change one's age: the god offers to the aged Cato the possibility of going back to his youth – a possibility that Cato, however, refuses: *Et si qui deus mihi largiatur ut ex hac aetate repuerascam et in cunis vagiam, valde recusem*; the text of Cicero's *Cato Maior de Senectute* is from Powell's OCT; Juv. 5.132–133 (see Santorelli 2013, 163 ad loc.) and Mart. 1.103.1–3 depict a god who offers money to a man.
48 On the use of military metaphors in Cynic-diatribic tradition, cf. Fuentes González 1998, 481–483; Oltramare 1926, 28; military metaphors are naturally not exclusive to diatribe and are common in Roman literature. Cicero and Lucretius, for example, employ this repertoire of images: on this cf. Fitzgerald 1978, 85 and n. 35; Mastrorosa 2000, 277–310.

god's offer is a belief in the self-sufficiency that entails the refusal of external goods. In comparison to Seneca, Horace in S. 1.1 apparently shows a more conventional approach to the topos: nevertheless, as we have noted, in S. 2.7 Davus's mention of Horace's certain rejection of the god's proposal reveals a metacritical consciousness that makes the philosophical commonplace less predictable.

3 Quotations of Horace in Seneca. The Case of Ep. 119

In this section I shall continue to focus on direct quotations from Horace in Seneca's works. These quotations, placed in contexts in which Seneca manipulates diatribic topoi while developing what looks like a properly satiric style, represent a moral *sphragis* on the subject matter. Horatian quotations, with the exception of that from Carm. 2.13.34,[49] are indeed all drawn from the *Satires* and included in the final letters of the collection,[50] which suggests that Seneca reread Horace's *Satires* in his old age.[51] When it comes to explaining the small number of quotations (only three), I agree with Mazzoli and his idea of a self-censorship carried out by Seneca:[52] Horace as a poet deserves the same treatment as the *lyrici* who, according to the philosopher, 'are frivolous by design';[53] his poems, therefore, lack the moral gravity suitable to a Stoic. As may be seen elsewhere in this volume, the deliberate nature of Seneca's silence about Horace's *Odes* in terms of explicit reminiscences is demonstrated by his very works, which show an impressive closeness to Horace's poems and reveal Seneca's deep engagement with the

---

49 I refer to Apocol. 13.3 *Itaque quamvis podagricus esset, momento temporis pervenit ad ianuam Ditis, vel, ut ait Horatius, 'belua centiceps,'* 'So, although he was gouty, he came in an instant to the gateway of Dis where lay Cerberus or, as Horace says, "the hundred-headed beast".' This case, as Mazzoli 1970, 234 suggests, can be interpreted as more of a 'reminiscence' than a proper quotation: the rarity of the word *centiceps*, 'one hundred-headed,' and the uniqueness of Horace's description, which conveys a different tradition from the one of three-headed Cerberus, seem to suit the context of the *Apocolocyntosis*, which is marked by hyperbolic tones; cf. Trinacty 2012a, who investigates 'Seneca's rationale for quoting a half line of Horace.'
50 Hor. S. 1.2.27 (and 1.4.92) in Sen. Ep. 86.13; Hor. S. 1.2.114 in Sen. Ep. 119.13–14; Hor. S. 1.3.11–17 in Sen. Ep. 120.20–21.
51 Mazzoli 1998, 63 talks about a greater openness on the part of the Stoic apostle towards Horace's indulgence.
52 Mazzoli 1970, 235–236.
53 Sen. Ep. 49.5 *Illi* (scil. *lyrici*) *ex professo lasciviunt*.

poet.⁵⁴ Horatian quotations from the *Satires*, I hold, function as an authority, a sort of moral stamp that individuates and certifies human vices.⁵⁵ The Bionic nature of the *Satires* allows Seneca to recall and to express the salty persona that Horace explicitly claims for himself.

Ep. 119 is an excellent specimen of a diatribic substrate articulated by means of Horatian echoes. The quotation from S. 1.2.114–116 concludes a discussion of 'true wealth,' which Seneca identifies with the ability to recognise the natural limits of desire; it is, moreover, inserted into a context marked by stylistic imitation of the same satire. The quotation appears at section 13 of the letter, following an allusion to one of Bion's maxims:⁵⁶ fr. 36 Kindstrand (= D.L. 4.50) 'Referring to a wealthy miser he said, "He has not acquired a fortune; the fortune has acquired him"' (πρὸς πλούσιον μικρολόγον, 'οὐχ οὗτος,' ἔφη, 'τὴν οὐσίαν κέκτηται, ἀλλ' ἡ οὐσία τοῦτον'). Seneca compares those who are surrounded by wealth but are paradoxically devoted to a 'bustling poverty' (*occupata paupertas*) to people afflicted by fever:

> Nam quod ad illos pertinet apud quos falso divitiarum nomen invasit occupata paupertas, sic divitias habent quomodo habere dicimur febrem, cum illa nos habeat. E contrario dicere solemus 'febris illum tenet': eodem modo dicendum est 'divitiae illum tenent.'
>
> As for those in whose minds an overworked poverty masquerades as wealth, they have wealth in the same way that we are said to have fever, when actually it has us. We often put it the other way round, saying, 'The fever has hold of him': in the same way, we should say, 'Wealth has hold of him.'
> (Ep. 119.12)

In the case of sick men we should not say that they have fever, but that fever has them: the same might be said about people who possess wealth, Seneca says, echoing Bion's maxim (*divitiae illum tenent*, 'Wealth has hold of him'). Furthermore, through the prescription 'and in the same way we should say' (*eodem modo dicendum est*), Seneca claims the efficacy of the diatribic topos. My view is that Horace's Ep. 1.2 works as an interpretative filter for Bion's maxim. This poem seems to be invoked already at paragraph 6: 'The one who has enough has attained the one thing the rich can never get: a stopping point' (*qui satis habet consecutus est quod numquam diviti contigit, finem*). The goal of obtaining what is *satis* – a term which represents a proper existential measure – seems to

---

54 It is worth acknowledging the 'thematic concordance' between the choruses of Senecan tragedies and Horace's *Odes*, in both moral content and style: cf. Degl'Innocenti Pierini 1992.
55 Cf. Berthet 1979, 943: 'Les verse du poète constituent donc des *exempla*, technique de citation chère aux Romains.'
56 As first noted by Ménage 1692, 181.

rephrase an ideal naturally aligned with the Horatian sentiment. In Ep. 1.2.46, the *satis* coincides with the idea of satisfaction as constituting fulfilment: *quod satis est cui contingit, nil amplius optet*, 'the man who has enough, should not desire more'; its fortuitous quality, marked by the present *contingit*, seems to be echoed by Seneca's *contigit*. In the same letter, at line 56, after describing the avaricious individual as affected by an eternal lack (*semper avarus eget*, 'the avaricious is ever in want'), Horace exhorts us to find a limit to our desires ('aim at a fixed limit for your desires,' *certum voto pete finem*); the force of the warning is here emphasised by the imperative *pete* combined with the term *finis*. In S. 1.1.92 too, Horace advises us to set a limit, a *finis* (*denique sit finis quaerendi*), via a lexical echo of Lucilius (1331 Marx): *virtus quaerendae finem re scire modumque*, 'virtue is knowing the limit and the end of seeking a thing.'[57]

Returning to Horace's possible influence on Bion's maxim as quoted by Seneca, I would like to focus on Horace's Ep. 1.2.47–49: Horace reflects here on how wealth is not useful in removing sickness and distress; on the contrary, it is useless if he who possesses it has ill-health. Property, here exemplified by the house, the land, and the pile of gold and silver, is not enough to heal people afflicted by fever nor to rescue people from their troubles: 47–49 *non domus et fundus, non aeris acervus et auri | aegroto domini deduxit corpore febris | non animo curas*, 'No house or land, no pile of bronze or gold, has ever freed the owner's sick body of fevers, or his sick mind of cares.' In the original maxim by Bion the miser is represented as possessed by wealth; in Seneca, the phrase about wealth possessing men is introduced after the description of how fever possesses those affected. Horace's association of the pile of riches, which are devoid of any therapeutic properties, with fever afflicting the sick body, might have stimulated Seneca's elaboration of Bion's maxim.

As for the Horatian quotation in Ep. 119: Seneca has just reaffirmed the need to identify the measure of natural desires (12 *nihil ergo monuisse te malim quam hoc, quod nemo monetur satis, ut omnia naturalibus desideriis metiaris, quibus aut gratis satis fiat aut parvo*, 'There is no advice I would rather give you than this, which no one can hear too often: you should measure everything by your natural desires, which can be satisfied either at no cost or only a little'). This claim seems to be linked conceptually to the lines in the Horatian poem that precede those quoted by Seneca, where Horace argues for the establishment of a natural limit for the purpose of regulating one's passions: S. 1.2.111–113 *nonne, cupidinibus statuat natura modum quem, | quid latura sibi, quid sit dolitura negatum, | quaerere plus prodest et inane abscindere soldo?*, 'Wouldn't it be more profitable

---

[57] Cf. Gowers 2012, 79; translations of Lucilius's text are taken from Warmington's Loeb.

to enquire what limit nature sets for the desires, what she can do without and what will cause pain if denied her, and to sunder what's empty from what's solid?'.

From a lexical point of view, the adjective *parvus* in the Senecan excerpt immediately evokes the rhetoric of frugality – the *parvo vivere* – first articulated by Ofellus in Horace.[58] Besides this, the Senecan exhortation to not confuse vices with desires (12 *tantum miscere vitia desideriis noli*, 'Just don't mingle those desires with vices') seems to echo lines 75–76 of the same satire (S. 1.2). Horace contrasts listening to Nature with the action of 'confounding what is to be avoided with what is to be desired,' expressed by the verb *inmiscere*, which is echoed by the Senecan *miscere*.[59] In an attempt to mimic the modes of S. 1.2, Seneca starts asking questions with the verb *quaeris*, revisiting the hemistich of the Horatian quotation (Ep. 119.13 *Quaeris quali mensa, quali argento, quam paribus ministeriis et levibus adferatur cibus?*, 'Are you asking about the quality of the table your food is being laid on, the quality of the silver, the matched pairs of waiters with their smooth skin?' cf. S. 1.2.114–115 *num... quaeris | pocula?*) and also adducing traditional examples of luxury. After the actual quotation,[60] Seneca avers the moral truth of Horace's poetry, recognising Horace's role as a guarantor in the detection of vices:[61] 14 *Egregie itaque Horatius negat ad sitim pertinere quo poculo [aquae] aut quam eleganti manu ministretur*, 'That's why Horace gets it just right when he says that thirst cares neither for the cup nor for the elegance of the server.' With regard to the actual quotation, we may observe that it is in fact cut in half: Seneca omits the verses about the sexual stimulus (116–118 *tument tibi cum inguina, num, si | ancilla aut verna est praesto puer, impetus in quem | continuo fiat*, 'When your organ is stiff, and a servant girl or a young boy from the household is near at hand and you know you can make an imme-

---

[58] It is Ofellus who shows *quae virtus et quanta, boni, sit vivere parvo*, 'What and how great, my friends, is the virtue of frugal living' (S. 2.2.1).
[59] Hor. S. 1.2.73–76 *At quanto meliora monet pugnantiaque istis | dives opis natura suae, tu si modo recte | dispensare velis ac non fugienda petendis | inmiscere*, 'But how much better and opposed to those ideas is the advice of nature, who is rich in the resources at her disposal, if only you were ready to manage them properly and not to confuse what you should avoid with what you should seek.'
[60] Sen. Ep. 119.13 *Num, tibi cum fauces urit sitis, aurea quaeris | pocula? num esuriens fastidis omnia praeter | pavonem rhombumque?* (Hor. S. 1.2.115–117), 'Your throat is parched with thirst: do you demand a golden cup?'.
[61] This will be also highlighted in Ep. 120.21, in which Horace is quoted again: *Homines multi tales sunt qualem hunc describit Horatius Flaccus...*, 'There are many people like the one Horatius Flaccus describes...'

diate assault'),⁶² and it seems to me that this deliberate omission is a proof of how the philosopher disapproved of the excessive freedom that marks Horatian *sermo*.

But if censoring Horace's overly provocative Muse seems a simple matter, Ep. 119 offers evidence of how Horace's text is so deeply rooted in Seneca's memory that it emerges almost unconsciously during the composition of Seneca's work. In commenting on his quotation of Horace (14 *egregie itaque Horatius...*), Seneca affirms that it makes no difference what goblet we drink from or how elegant the hand that serves the water is (*elegans manus*). In the Horatian quotation there is no mention of how the cup is actually served. But if we look at the piece of Horace's text that Seneca leaves out, we find a claim about the irrelevance of having a maidservant or a household slave-boy (S. 1.2.116–117 *num, si | ancilla aut verna est praesto puer*) at the highest moment of excitement. 'The elegant hand' could be indeed a reminiscence of that *ancilla* or that *verna* depicted by Horace; although not directly mentioned, they seem to naturally emerge from Seneca's poetic memory by a type of metonymy. This interpretation finds further support in the declaration that follows, in which Seneca reaffirms that, given a natural stimulus such as thirst, we should not care about the hairstyle of the slave or the gleam of the goblet (*nam si pertinere ad te iudicas quam crinitus puer et quam perlucidum tibi poculum porrigat, non sitis*, 'If you think it matters to you whether the slave boy has curly hair and the cup is of some translucent material, you are not thirsty'); here, moreover, the *crinitus puer* seems to be a clear recollection of the *puer* featured in Horace's censored verses.

The conclusion of Ep. 119 provides the first mention of the things that, thanks to laws given by the divinity, are 'already acquired and ready to hand.'⁶³ The opposition between the *euporista* and the *dysporista*, the things easily found and those hard to find, especially concerning food and drink, is a topos broadly endorsed by Epicurean philosophy as well as by the diatribic tradition.⁶⁴ This topos finds its full development in Seneca, with the oppositions

---

62 The translation is taken from Rudd's Penguin.
63 Sen. Ep. 119.15 *Id actum est ab illo mundi conditore, qui nobis vivendi iura discripsit, ut salvi essemus, non ut delicati: ad salutem omnia parata sunt et in promptu, delicis omnia misere ac sollicite comparantur*, 'The world's creator, the author of our laws of life, established the conditions for us to be well cared for without being pampered. Everything we need for our welfare is ready and available, but luxuries come only at the cost of misery and trouble.'
64 Epic. *ad* Menoec. 130.9; fr. 469 Usener; Teles fr. 2, 7.4 Hense, where we find the same thematic affinity, but without the terminology *euporiston / dysporiston*; Muson. fr. 18a–b *On Food* 94.9–15, 104.12–15, 105.1–3 Hense; on this topic, see Oltramare 1926, 57, themes 53 and 53a; Berti 2004,

here being drawn between the things *parata... et in promptu* and the *deliciae* which cause trouble and torment. *Paratus*, just like Horace's *parabilis*, translates the Greek *euporiston* and, after the aforementioned lines on sexual stimulus, Horace declares his preference for a love which is *parabilis* and *facilis* (119).

To conclude our discussion of Ep. 119 and its elaborate engagement with Horace's poetry, it is worth adding that the juridical detail about the laws created by God (*vivendi iura*),[65] which guarantees Seneca's compliance to Stoic orthodoxy, may also recall the verb *statuo*, employed by Horace at S. 1.2.111 in order to indicate nature's action in giving its laws (*nonne, cupidinibus statuat natura modum quem*, 'Wouldn't it be more profitable to enquire what limit nature sets for the desires...?').

4 A Poetic Model for Diatribic Language: Horace, Carm. 3.16

As previously suggested, the *Odes* influenced Seneca more than the philosopher wanted to admit. In this section, I shall suggest that there is one particular poem by Horace that has never aroused much attention in this regard but that represents a key model for Seneca in terms of both language and content: Carm. 3.16.[66] Fraenkel did not appreciate this poem, as it represents, in his view, a 'frigid allegory' that has 'no wings,' oddly developing a 'moral diatribe' closer to a *sermo* than a *carmen*.[67] The 'moral diatribe' concerns Horace's rejection of the wealth offered by Maecenas for a choice of life marked by *autarkeia*.[68] Nisbet / Rudd's words are particularly enlightening: they state that within the poem 'great estates are rejected with the hyperboles of diatribe and the paradoxes of Stoicism,'[69] thus confirming that Carm. 3.16 creates a language in which diatribic

---

124–125. On the vocabulary of diatribic texts which marks food as 'at hand' or hard to get (e.g. *difficilis / parabilis*; the Greek *polytelēs / euitelēs* etc.), cf. Van Geytenbeek 1963, 99.

65 Ep. 119.15 *Id actum est ab illo mundi conditore, qui nobis vivendi iura discripsit, ut salvi essemus, non ut delicati*, 'The world's creator, the author of our laws of life, established the conditions for us to be well cared for without being pampered.'

66 On Carm. 3.16, cf. Frank 1925, 27–28; Schork 1971, 515–539; Santirocco 1984, 248–250; Nisbet / Rudd 2004, 199–211; Citti 2000, 79.

67 Fraenkel 1957, 229.

68 The choice is similar to that of Carm. 3.1, where the poet claims he would not exchange the Sabine valley for more impressive wealth: 47–48 *cur valle permutem Sabina | divitias operosiores?*

69 Nisbet / Rudd 2004, 200.

morals are interpreted through the stylistic form of the paradox. Moretti's definition of paradox is particularly appropriate here: 'a rhetorical arm for ethical radicalism.'[70] I consider the language of this poem close to that employed by Seneca when modelling imagery and topoi that embody an ethics characterised by the same radicalism.

> Inclusam Danaen turris aenea
> robustaeque fores et vigilum canum
> tristes excubiae munierant satis
>   nocturnis ab adulteris,
> si non Acrisium, virginis abditae   5
> custodem pavidum, Iuppiter et Venus
> risissent: fore enim tutum iter et patens
>   converso in pretium deo.
> Aurum per medios ire satellites
> et perrumpere amat saxa potentius   10
> ictu fulmineo; concidit auguris
>   Argivi domus ob lucrum
> demersa exitio; diffidit urbium
> portas vir Macedo et subruit aemulos
> reges muneribus; munera navium   15
>   saevos inlaqueant duces.
> Crescentem sequitur cura pecuniam
> maiorumque fames. Iure perhorrui
> late conspicuum tollere verticem,
>   Maecenas, equitum decus.   20
> Quanto quisque sibi plura negaverit,
> ab dis plura feret; nil cupientium
> nudus castra peto et transfuga divitum
>   partis linquere gestio,
> contemptae dominus splendidior rei,   25
> quam si quicquid arat inpiger Apulus
> occultare meis dicerer horreis,
>   magnas inter opes inops.
> Purae rivus aquae silvaque iugerum
> paucorum et segetis certa fides meae   30
> fulgentem imperio fertilis Africae
>   fallit sorte beatior.
> Quamquam nec Calabrae mella ferunt apes
> nec Laestrygonia Bacchus in amphora
> languescit mihi nec pinguia Gallicis   35
>   crescunt vellera pascuis,
> inportuna tamen pauperies abest,

---

[70] Moretti 1995, 160.

nec, si plura velim, tu dare deneges.
Contracto melius parva cupidine
    vectigalia porrigam   40
quam si Mygdoniis regnum Alyattei
campis continuem. Multa petentibus
desunt multa; bene est cui deus obtulit
    parca quod satis est manu.

When Danae was locked up in a tower of bronze, doors of stout oak, and fierce patrols of watchdogs would have protected her well enough from lovers-by-night, had not Jupiter and Venus laughed at Acrisius, the nervous jailer of the girl whom he had hidden away. For they knew that the god would have open and undetected access once he had turned into a bribe.

Gold has a way of passing through the middle of body-guards, and breaking through rocks more effectively than a stroke of lighting. The house of the Argive seer collapsed, plunged into ruin by the love of money. The man of Macedon split open city gates and undermined rival kings by making presents; presents ensnare savage admirals.

As money grows, it is attended by worry and a craving for more. I have had a horror, quite rightly, of raising my head to an eminence that could be seen from far and wide, Maecenas, glory of the Knights. The more a person denies himself, the more he will receive from the gods. Destitute myself, I want to join the camp of those who desire nothing; a deserter, I am eager to abandon the side of the rich, and thus acquire more credit for being master of the wealth I reject than were I said to hide away in my barns everything that the tireless Apulian reaps, a pauper surrounded by great riches.

A stream of clear water, a few acres of woodland, a harvest that never lets me down – this is a more fortunate lot, though the glittering lord of fertile Africa is not aware of it. Although Calabrian bees do not bring me honey, and Bacchus does not mellow for me in a Laestrygonian jar, and I do not have thick fleeces growing in the pastures of Gaul, nevertheless, I am free from nagging poverty, and if I wanted more you would not refuse to give it. By reducing my desires I shall enlarge my small income better than if I joined Alyattes's kingdom to the plains of Mygdon. Those who seek a lot lack a lot. All is well for the man to whom God with a frugal hand has given enough.

Horace first makes use of the mythical exemplar of Danae and Jupiter, who penetrated the bronze tower after turning into gold (1–8). This is followed by the example of Amphiaraus (9–13), whose house, literally submerged by avarice (*ob lucrum demersa*), was ruined by gold. We should remember here how Amphiaraus was an emblematic example of greed in diatribe, as revealed in the phrase 'The earth swallowed Amphiaraus, but you have swallowed your land,' with which Bion addresses a man who has wasted all his goods (fr. 45 Kindstrand = D.L. 4.48). The power that arises from the possession of riches is, moreover, represented by Philip II of Macedon (13–15), who was able to 'burst the gates of the cities' (*diffidere urbium portas*) by means of bribes. After alluding to the freedman Menas / Menodorus (15–16), Horace shifts the perspective from the efficacy of wealth to his own behaviour, marked by a refusal of and detachment from the goods Maecenas has offered to him. The gnomic statement 'anxiety, and the hunger for more, pursues growing wealth' (17–18 *crescentem sequitur cura pecuniam | maiorumque fames*), which works as a connecting passage to the second part of the poem, sums up the reason for Horace's refusal. Wealth that provokes an escalation of needs and desires is a topos in the language of *sermo*. Suffice it to quote here the metaphor of dropsy, which occurs in Ep. 2.2.146–148 (*si tibi nulla sitim finiret copia lymphae, | narrares medicis; quod, quanto plura parasti, | tanto plura cupis, nulline faterier audes?*),[71] but also in Carm. 2.2.13[72] and Ep. 1.2.56, where the miser is condemned to be forever in want: *semper avarus eget*. The comparison between avarice and inextinguishable thirst is a topos that probably derives from Aristippus[73] and subsequently made its way into Cynic anecdotes.[74] The Socrates depicted by Xenophon, for instance, tells us how already Antisthenes used to compare misers to people who eat but are never satisfied.[75] An apophthegm by Diogenes testifies to the connection between the *philargyros* and the *hydrōpikos*,[76] and a maxim by Bion (quoted by Teles) also highlights the presence of the simile in diatribic preaching.[77] Bion's maxim is particularly interesting since the metaphor is preceded by the paradoxical observation that 'if anyone wants either to have himself free from want and scarcity or to free someone else, let him not seek money from him.'

---

[71] Hor. Ep. 2.2.146–148 'If no amount of water could quench your thirst, you would tell your story to the doctor: seeing that the more you get, the more you want, do you not dare to make confession to any man?'.
[72] Hor. Carm. 2.2.13–14 *Crescit indulgens sibi dirus hydrops | nec sitim pellit*, 'Dreaded dropsy grows by indulging itself and you cannot drive away the thirst.'
[73] Cf. fr. 4a 73 Giannantoni (= Plut. De cup. 524a–b).
[74] On this topos, a collection of passages can be found in Nisbet / Hubbard 1978, 44–45; Brink 1982, 362–363; Fuentes González 1998, 397–398; Kindstrand 1976, 241.
[75] Xen. Smp. 4.37 ὅμοια γάρ μοι δοκοῦσι πάσχειν ὥσπερ εἴ τις πολλὰ ἔχοι καὶ πολλὰ ἐσθίων μηδέποτε ἐμπίμπλαιτο, 'For in my eyes their malady resembles that of a person who possessed abundance but though continually eating could never be satisfied'; the text of Xenophon's *Symposium* is from Marchant's OCT; translations are taken from Todd's Loeb.
[76] Stob. 3.10.45 Διογένης ὡμοίου τοὺς φιλαργύρους τοῖς ὑδρωπικοῖς, ἐκείνους μὲν γὰρ πλήρεις ὄντας ὑγροῦ ἐπιθυμεῖν ποτοῦ τούς τε φιλαργύρους πλήρεις ὄντας ἀργυρίου ἐπιθυμεῖν πλείονος, 'Diogenes compared the avaricious with the men who suffer by dropsy: those people, despite being filled up with water, still desire running water; the avaricious, being full of money, still desire money'; Stobaeus's text is from Wachsmuth / Hense's Weidmann; translation is my own.
[77] Fr. 34 Kindstrand (= Teles fr. 4a, p. 39.1–4 Hense) 'And if anyone wants either to have himself free from want and scarcity or to free someone else, let him not seek money for him. For it is, says Bion, as if someone, who wants to relieve the thirst of a man suffering from dropsy, would not treat the dropsy but would supply him with springs and river'; cf. Brink 1982, 363, where the Horatian *nulla… copia lymphae* is considered 'actually closer to Bion's κρήνας δὲ καὶ ποταμοὺς, while the visit to a doctor recalls Aristippus.'

A line by Lucilius confirms that the topos is familiar to the satiric tradition[78] (fr. 764 Marx), and both Epictetus[79] and Seneca,[80] the latter comparing the sickness that provokes thirst to the 'insatiable soul' (*inexplebilis animus*), further support the popularity of the image.[81]

The final stanza of Carm. 3.16 also asserts the necessity of limiting one's *cupido* in order to maximise one's resources: lines 39–40 ('I can eke out my income more effectively by constraining what I desire,' *contracto melius parva cupidine | vectigalia porrigam*) show a paradoxical perspective that not accidentally recalls a passage from Cicero's *Paradoxa Stoicorum*.[82] Moreover, it shows an affinity in both formal and thematic terms with an Epicurean lesson translated by Seneca in Ep. 21.7.[83] The theme of desire as that which proves our poverty recurs in the diatribic tradition[84] and is especially developed by Seneca. The paradoxical identification of the poor individual with the man whose greed is greater than the goods he possesses is found in the Cynic Demetrius in Ben. 7.10.6: *quidquid habet, ei, quod cupit, conparet: pauper est*, 'then let him compare what he

---

[78] Lucil. 764 Marx *Aquam te in animo habere intercutem*, 'That you have dropsy-water on the brain.'

[79] Epict. 4.9.4 'Do you not know what kind of thing the thirst of a man in fever is?'; translation is taken from Oldfather's Loeb.

[80] Sen. Dial. 12.11.3 *Ista congerantur licet, numquam explebunt inexplebilem animum, non magis quam ullus sufficiet umor ad satiandum eum cuius desiderium non ex inopia sed ex aestu ardentium viscerum oritur; non enim sitis illa sed morbus est*, 'Though all these things are amassed, they'll never satisfy his insatiable soul, just as no amount of fluid will be enough to satisfy the man whose craving arises not from a lack of water but from the heat that scorches his insides; for that isn't thirst but disease'; the text of Seneca's *Dialogi* is from Reynolds's OCT; translation of Seneca's *Consolatio ad Helviam Matrem* is taken from Williams (University of Chicago Press).

[81] It is worth drawing attention to Tantalus's portrait in Seneca's *Thyestes* (152–175). Tantalus is affected by both eternal hunger and inextinguishable thirst. It is precisely his unquenchable greed (cf. Thy. 158 *quamvis avidus*) that makes him the most relevant Senecan character embodying a characteristic disagreeing with the *satis*.

[82] Cic. Parad. 51 *Non esse cupidum pecunia est, non esse emacem vectigal est; contentum vero suis rebus esse maximae sunt certissimaeque divitiae*, 'Not to be avaricious is money, not to be spendthrift is income: in fact, to be content with your own money is the greatest and most certain wealth'; the text of Cicero's *Paradoxa Stoicorum* is from Mueller's Teubner; the translation is by Webb (Texas Tech University).

[83] Sen. Ep. 21.7 *'Si vis' inquit 'Pythoclea divitem facere, non pecuniae adiciendum sed cupiditati detrahendum est,*' 'He says, if you want to make Pythocles rich, what you must do is not add his money but subtract from his desires' (cf. fr. 135 Usener).

[84] Cf. Teles fr. 4a, 42.2 Hense.

has with what he desires – he is still a poor man.'⁸⁵ The same topos and vocabulary feature in the already quoted Ep. 119, where the statement 'He who has much desires more – a proof that he has not yet acquired enough' (6 *qui multum habet plus cupit, quod est argumentum nondum illum satis habere*) introduces the negative example embodied by Alexander. The Macedonian's cupidity is represented by the action of shattering the very bolts of the universe (*ut dicam mundi claustra perrumpit*), which seems to amplify the action of 'bursting the gates of the cities' (*diffidere urbium portas*) that Horace attributes to Philip in Carm. 3.16. The digression on Alexander in Seneca's Ep. 119 is sealed first by a further paradoxical phrase (*neminem pecunia divitem fecit*, 'Money never made a man rich') and then by another gnomic reflection, which emphasises how money increases both avidity and desires (*pecunia contra nulli non maiorem sui cupidinem incussit*, 'On the contrary, money always smites men with a greater craving for itself'), while in Carm. 3.16.17–18 money causes 'anxiety, and the hunger for more' (*cura pecuniam maiorumque fames*).

Moving on in Carm. 3.16, at lines 21–22 Horace proposes another paradox and asserts the importance of denying as much as possible to ourselves in order to secure more important favours from the gods: *Quanto quisque sibi plura negaverit, | ab dis plura ferret*, 'The more that a man denies himself, then the more will flow from the gods.' Horace describes himself as naked – that is, 'disarmed' according to the military meaning of the word *nudus*⁸⁶ – and belonging to the camp of people who desire nothing. At the same time, the poet reflects on deserting the party of the wealthy through the use of the word *pars*, which, taken in its military usage,⁸⁷ indicates one of two opposing groups fighting each other.⁸⁸ Through the military metaphor of the opposing camps, Horace seems here to infuse his meditation with tones that I would be tempted to define as 'rather Cynic,' as it were, and which find their clearest expression in his adherence to the party of people who 'do not desire anything.' The expression *nihil cupere* is employed by Seneca in the *Thyestes* in the paradoxical representation of the *rex sapiens* (388 *rex est qui cupiet nihil*, 'a king is

---

85 The text of Seneca's *De Beneficiis* is from Hosius's Teubner; translations are by Griffin / Inwood (University of Chicago Press).
86 Cf. OLD, s.v. *nudus*, 4 having no armour or weapons, unarmed.
87 OLD, s.v. *pars*, (meton., sg. or pl.) one of two opposite groups or individuals, a party, side; 16 a (in war, esp. civil war).
88 The terms *transfuga* and *castra* are both employed by Seneca in Ep. 2.5, albeit in another context: *Hodiernum hoc est quod apud Epicurum nanctus sum – soleo enim et in aliena castra transire, non tamquam transfuga, sed tamquam explorator*, 'Today it is this, which I found in Epicurus – for it is my custom to cross even into the other camp, not as a deserter but as a spy.'

he who shall naught desire') and also in two passages of *De Beneficiis* (7.3.2 and 7.2.4). The passages from *De Beneficiis* are even more meaningful since they are both placed after the two speeches by the Cynic Demetrius, and describe the behaviour that suits the *sapiens*. After the premise that 'the sage is the only one who possesses everything and can retain it without difficulty,'[89] Seneca concludes that the wise man desires nothing since there is nothing beyond everything: *nihil cupiat, quia nihil est extra omnia*.

As for the passage at Ben. 7.2.4, a Horatian theme is echoed in the exhortation to not depend on the future, but to enjoy the things that one possesses at present: *Hic praesentibus gaudet, ex futuro non pendet; nihil enim firmi habet, qui in incerta propensus est*, 'This is the person who rejoices in the present and is not dependent on the future – for anyone who relies on uncertainties has no solid ground.' Compare Carm. 2.16, in which lines 25–26 (*laetus in praesens animus quod ultra est | oderit curare*, 'the mind that is happy for the present should refuse to worry about what is further ahead'), while not focusing specifically on present goods, still stress the value of the present as the best temporal dimension. First Cynicism[90] and then diatribe focused on the importance of present goods, as fragment 4a of Teles – *A Comparison of Poverty and Wealth* –[91] shows: to be satisfied with present goods coincides with the capacity to adapt to circumstances. The philosopher Crates explains how we have to be ready to open our bag in order to donate its contents: an indifference to the bag's contents is engendered by a satisfaction with present things, especially when we do not possess anything and consequently desire nothing. This particular moral message finds an echo in Carm. 3.16 and is encapsulated by phrases such as *nihil cupere* – οὐκ ἐπιποθήσεις.

To return to the passage in Ben. 7.2.4, the expression *nihil cupit* describes the wise man as someone free from worries, hopes, and desires; he is removed from danger and content with himself.[92] Just after that, in reference to the wise man,

---

[89] Sen. Ben. 7.3.2 *Unus est sapiens, cuius omnia sunt nec ex difficili tuenda*, 'The sage is the only one who possesses everything and can retain it without difficulty.'

[90] Especially with anecdotes about Antisthenes and Diogenes, cf. Xen. Smp. 4.38; Phil. 18.122.

[91] Teles fr. 4a, 38.4–39 Hense 'And therefore Crates replied to the man who asked, "What will be in it for me after I have become a philosopher?" "You will be able," he said "to open your wallet easily... Rather, if the wallet is full, that is how you will view it; and if you see that it is empty, you will not be distressed. And once you have elected to use the money, you will easily be able to do so; and if you have none, you will not yearn for it, but you will live satisfied with what you have, not desiring what you do not have nor displeased with whatever comes your way".'

[92] Sen. Ben. 7.2.4 *Magnis itaque curis exemptus et distorquentibus mentem nihil sperat aut cupit nec se mittit in dubium suo contentus*, 'Therefore, being free of major worries that torment his

Seneca exhorts his reader not to believe that being content with oneself means being content with little: *Et ne illum existimes parvo esse contentum*, 'And you should not think that in doing so he is content with little.' I believe Seneca wants to stress here his surpassing of the moral imperative of self-sufficiency upheld by Ofellus, as demonstrated by the Horatian line *qui contentus parvo metuensque futuri* (S. 2.2.110 'He who, satisfied with little and fearful of the future'). The wise man described here by Seneca is not only unafraid of the future, having dispensed of all illusion of hope: by bringing an end to desire, he takes paradoxical possession of everything: *omnia illius sunt*, 'Everything belongs to him.' The example of Alexander, whose lust for conquest is a symptom of poverty, goes back to the topos of avidity as a characteristic that neutralises the value of material possessions. The sentence 'whatever he desires is something he lacks' (*tantum illi deest, quantum cupit*), seems to reprise once more the concluding message of Carm. 3.16, *multa petentibus | desunt multa* (43–44), confirming that the greatness of the lack is determined by one's desires.

Finally, I want to draw attention to *De Tranquillate Animi* 8. Here Seneca quotes Bion and presents Diogenes the Cynic[93] through Teles's anecdote of the slave Manes.[94] I shall focus on the adjective *nudus*, 'naked, unarmed,' metaphorically employed by Horace in Carm. 3.16 to refer to the condition of not desiring anything. At *De Tranquillitate Animi* 8.5 Diogenes is associated with the immortal gods by virtue of his autarchic way of life: *si quis de felicitate Diogenis dubitat, potest idem dubitare et de deorum immortalium statu...?*, 'If anybody doubts Diogenes's happiness, can he also have the same doubt about the condition of the immortal gods...?'.[95] Right after that, the gods are described as naked, captured in the action of giving everything even though they possess nothing: *nudos videbis deos, omnia dantes, nihil habentes*. The similarity between Diogenes, 'who stripped himself of all the gifts of Fortune,' and the gods is later reaffirmed (Dial. 9.8.5 *hunc tu pauperem putas an diis immortalibus similem, qui se fortuitis omnibus exuit?*, 'Do you think a man who has shed all his gifts of fortune is a pauper, or like the immortal gods?'). The same connotation of nudity as what marks god's condition is put forward in Ep. 31.10, where it is associated with

---

mind, he hopes for nothing and desires nothing; not committing himself to what is unreliable, he is content with himself.'
93 Sen. Dial. 9.8.3, 9.8.7.
94 Teles fr. 4a, 41.13–15 Hense; the anecdote is also present in Stob. 4.19.47, D.L. 6.55, and Ael. VH 13.28.
95 Translations of Seneca's *De Tranquillitate Animi* are taken from Fantham (University of Chicago Press).

the lack of property: *Deus nihil habet. Praetexta non faciet: deus nudus est*, 'God owns nothing. A tunic bordered with purple will not do it; God is naked.'

I would like to stress here the affinity between Horace's nudity and Seneca's depiction of Diogenes as close to the gods because of his self-liberation from his possessions. Although Horace does not formulate an identification with the god, he too emphasises the god's benevolence, which depends on the human capacity to deny oneself as much as possible: Carm. 3.16.21–22 *quanto quisque sibi plura negaverit, | ab dis plura ferret*. The action of *sibi negare* is recalled in *De Tranquillitate Animi* 8.8 when Seneca describes Diogenes as *felicior* because of his self-sufficiency: *quanto ille felicior, quo nihil ulli debet nisi cui facillime negat, sibi!*, 'How much more happy the man who owes nothing to anyone except himself, whom he can so easily refuse!'. At Ben. 5.4.3[96] Diogenes is additionally depicted as a naked man[97] who walked through the Macedonian treasures, treading on the royal wealth. The paradoxical image of Alexander beaten by Diogenes in power and wealth, because what the philosopher does not accept is greater than what Alexander could give him, may well be seen as a parallel to the image of Horace who rejects Maecenas's offers.

To return to Carm. 3.16 once again, Horace's self-description as *contemptae dominus splendidior rei* (25) seems to recall the paradoxical concept expressed by Demetrius in Seneca's Ep. 62.3,[98] where the shortcut to wealth is demonstrated as the contempt of richness (*contemptum divitiarum*). In line 28, Horace additionally formulates a paradox in which he describes himself in the hypothetical condition of being wealthy, defining himself *magnas inter opes inops*, 'poor in the midst of riches' – or rather, what the crowd interprets as 'riches.' This particular

---

[96] Sen. Ben. 5.4.3 *Necesse est a Socrate beneficiis vincar, necesse est a Diogene, qui per medias Macedonum gazas nudus incessit calcatis regiis opibus; 4... multo potentior, multo locupletior fuit omnia tunc possidente Alexandro; plus enim erat, quod hic nollet accipere, quam quod ille posset dare*, 'Of necessity I shall be outdone in benefits by Socrates, of necessity by Diogenes who passed through the Macedonian treasures naked, trampling on the king's wealth; ...Far more powerful, far richer was he than Alexander, who then had all things in his power; for what Diogenes would not accept was greater than what Alexander could give.'
[97] 'Cynics were not really naked but wore a cloak of coarse material without underwear (D.L. 6.22); yet in the Roman period there is a statue of Diogenes nude, the nudity representing freedom from want and contempt for the body,' Griffin 2013, 26; Juv. 14.308–309 will name Diogenes *nudus... Cynicus*; for the image of the 'naked' Diogenes: cf. Zanker 1995, 176–179.
[98] Sen. Ep. 62.3 *Contemnere aliquis omnia potest, omnia habere nemo potest: brevissima ad divitias per contemptum divitiarum via est*, 'No one can have everything, but there is someone who can despise everything. The quickest way to wealth is to despise wealth.'

paradox, whose origin seems to lie in the Cynic tradition,[99] is reformulated by Seneca in Ep. 74, where rich people are described as *in divitiis inopes*,[100] and in the *Consolatio ad Helviam*,[101] where poverty *in summis opibus* coincides with the exceeding of natural limits. Seneca endorses the same paradoxical concept also in Ep. 119.9 and Ben. 7.8.6,[102] where he ascribes great 'wealth' to the poor man. However, in Carm. 3.16 the rejection of Maecenas's gifts does not involve the sort of poverty that Horace defines as *inportuna*, 'grinding.' This specification, put forward after the material I previously defined as 'Cynic,' appears to once again align the ode with the theme of the *aurea mediocritas*, which is invoked in the poem's conclusion: 43–44 'he's happy to whom the god grants just enough, from a careful hand,' *bene est cui deus obtulit | parca quod satis est manu*.

La Penna, in a memorable paragraph of his essay *Orazio e la morale mondana europea*, entitled *Satira e diatriba: l'instabilità della morale oraziana*,[103] sheds light onto Horace's position with respect to Cynic-diatribic *autarkeia* and the concept of *metriotēs*. In Horace's oscillation between the golden mean and interior freedom, La Penna envisages a precarious balance, a sort of ambiguity. This hesitation derives, in La Penna's view, from the tendency to make *autarkeia* a more socially integrated virtue; this version of self-sufficiency, unlike the one embraced by the Cynics, aimed at abandoning its transcendental aspect in order to be accepted into high society. Nevertheless, a degree of turmoil is unavoidable here, since social integration is possible only at the cost of sacrificing

---

99 Cf. the words by Antisthenes in Xenophon's *Symposium*: 4.35 ὁρῶ γὰρ πολλοὺς μὲν ἰδιώτας, οἳ πάνυ πολλὰ ἔχοντες χρήματα οὕτω πένεσθαι ἡγοῦνται ὥστε πάντα μὲν πόνον, πάντα δὲ κίνδυνον ὑποδύονται, ἐφ' ᾧ πλείω κτήσονται, 'For I see many persons, not in office, who thought possessors of large resources, yet look upon themselves as so poor that they bend their backs to any toil, any risk, if only they may increase their holdings.'

100 Sen. Ep. 74.4 *Occurrent, quod genus egestatis gravissimum est, in divitis inopes*, 'Others who endure the worst form of poverty, for they are bankrupt in the midst of wealth.'

101 Sen. Dial. 12.11.4 *Qui continebit itaque se intra naturalem modum, paupertatem non sentiet; qui naturalem modum excedet, eum in summis quoque opibus paupertas sequetur*, 'So the person who keeps himself within the bounds set by nature will not feel poverty, while the man who goes beyond those bounds will be pursued by poverty even amid the greatest wealth.'

102 Ep. 119.9 *Adferat censum et quidquid habet et quidquid sperat simul conputet: iste, si mihi credis, pauper est, si tibi, potest esse*, 'Let him state his total wealth, counting whatever he has in hand and all that he is hoping for. In my view, if you will accept it, the man is poor; even in your view, he could become poor'; Ben. 7.10.6 *Cum bene ista, per quae divitias suas disposuit ac fudit, circumspexerit superbumque se fecerit, quidquid habet, ei, quod cupit, conparet: pauper est*, 'When he has surveyed the ways his wealth is invested, and spent and made himself feel proud about it, then let him compare what he has with what he desires – he is still a poor man.'

103 La Penna 1993, 54–62.

one's inner liberty. While La Penna interprets S. 2.2 as the best example of this 'unconscious compromise,' I suggest that Carm. 3.16 might also be read in light of this turmoil, which clearly appears in the oscillation between material nakedness, freedom from desire, and the golden mean that rejects 'grinding poverty' (*inportuna paupertas*). Seneca too, in the 'radical' passage of Ben. 7.2.4, claims a neat self-sufficiency that is distinct from the moral of *parvo vivere*, elsewhere repeatedly praised by Seneca. I believe we can find many traces of the same oscillation in Seneca, in his attempt to adhere to a strict Stoicism on the one hand and his human awareness that he cannot do so on the other. Through the lens of this interpretation one might focus on the end of section 9 of *De Tranquillitate Animi*. Here Seneca seems indeed to soften the tones of his exhortation after the 'Cynic-diatribic parenthesis,' ended by the quotation of Bion and the example of Diogenes. He professes that the ideal amount of money 'is one that neither sinks into poverty nor departs far from it,' *optimus pecuniae modus est, qui nec in paupertatem cadit lice procul a paupertate discedit*, an amount that Horace would have surely approved of.

5 Conclusion

The sophisticated relationships between Seneca, Horace, and the diatribic tradition can be articulated on different levels. What I find most relevant is the way Seneca, by means of Horatian language, gives a new interpretative force to a topical tradition that could have presented itself to him as inert.[104] As Gianotti notes,[105] Seneca has the merit of having reformulated and given new meaning to literary material that was conventional but also susceptible to being used in an endless variety of ways, and of doing so also by problematising, from a theoretical point of view, the very topoi of the diatribe. Horace's poetry, which also engages with diatribic material, constitutes a starting point and an inspiration for Seneca's treatment, which is a testimony to the Stoic's skill in blending sources from the worlds of rhetoric, philosophy, and literature: to quote Traina's words, 'infine, Seneca è un artista... La tradizione è diatribica, ma l'arte è di Seneca. Frammenti di mimi danno alla sua pagina il sapore della vita.'[106]

---

104 Hinds 1998, 34–47 and 94–95 skillfully illustrates how a topos should not be interpreted as inert, but as something fluid and mobile, reflecting a deep literary background and the complexity of the multiple sources: 'with *topoi* and indeed with allusive discourse at large, one can never step into the same river twice,' at 47.
105 Gianotti 1979, 101–143.
106 Traina 2009, 29.

Francesca Romana Berno
Nurses' Prayers, Philosophical *otium*, and Fat Pigs: Seneca Ep. 60 versus Horace Ep. 1.4

The covert nature of the complex relationship between Seneca and Horace means that Horace shows up in Seneca more often in an indirect way than through explicit quotation.[1] It is my intention to focus on what I consider an example of this relationship by dealing with two epistles, one by each author. After a short discussion of Horace's and Seneca's epistles from the perspective of literary genre, I will go through the texts and propose my interpretation of them: namely, that Seneca in Ep. 60 intends to reply to his troublesome predecessor by means of a rhetorical device similar to the so-called technique of 'multiple reference.'[2] In other words, Seneca alludes to Horace in order to revise the Augustan poet's philosophical positions, which he does by citing another author. Thus, there will be a third figure at play in this essay: Sallust.

1 Introduction

When we approach Seneca's *Epistulae Morales* from the perspective of literary genre,[3] we find that the contemporary scholarship mentions Epicurus, Cicero, and sometimes Plato as sources, but gives little attention to Horace. Horace's *Epistles* should nevertheless be considered a model for Seneca's: even if the former writes in poetry and the latter in prose, we must admit that these works (in particular when it comes to the first book of Horace's *Epistles*) share many features: an addressee in whom the author combines a historical character with a more general 'reader,' an exhortative tone, a light and sometimes colloquial dic-

---

I would like to thank Victoria Rimell and the editors for proofreading my English.

1 See the Introduction, 3–16. Seneca's tragedies have been widely analysed for their connections with Horace; on citations and allusions in Seneca's prose works there is less bibliography: see Berthet 1979; Dionigi 1980; Negri 1988; Bruno 1993; Minarini 1997; Di Virgilio 1998; Mazzoli 1998; Montiglio 2006; Berno 2014.
2 Thomas 1999, 135–140.
3 See e.g. Cugusi 1983, 195–206; Muñoz Martín 1995, 87–93; Mazzoli 1989, 1856–1860; Op Het Veld 2000, 19–23.

tion, ironic hints, and an epistolary status half-way between the authentic and the fictional. Moreover, both texts are among their respective authors' final works: in a way, this is their last message to their readers, which Horace for his part presents as a conversion from poetry to philosophy. And this is the main point at issue: Horace's *Epistles* are often explicitly philosophical in both tone and content; the recent analysis by Moles is significant in this regard.[4] On the Senecan side, the title itself – *Epistulae Morales* – already highlights the importance of the issue of moral philosophy. In my opinion, a systematic analysis of the first book of Horace's *Epistles* on the one hand and Seneca's collection of letters on the other would produce interesting results; but let us make a start by investigating just two letters, Horace's Ep. 1.4 and Seneca's Ep. 60.

Horace's Ep. 1.4 is well known: this is the letter in which he defines himself as 'a fat and glistening pig from the flock of Epicurus.' There is a vast bibliography on this short text: I will focus on individual themes and questions strictly related to the subject of my research, that is, the philosophical issues at play. Seneca's Ep. 60, by contrast, is not well known: its brevity and position (after two long and theoretical letters that deal with Platonic questions), have caused it to escape most scholars' attention. Because of this, these texts have never been compared to each other: only in the commentaries to Horace's Ep. 1.4 does one find Seneca's Ep. 60 cited (alongside other texts) as a parallel to Horace's charge against the prayers made by nurses. In my opinion, however, these two epistles share far more than one single commonplace: in Horace one can find praise of Epicurean *otium* and mild denigration of its Stoic equivalent; Seneca reverses this position, and in doing so he uses motifs (such as nurses' prayers, the distinction between apparent and actual goods, and references to a pig-like existence) that were already in Horace's poem.

2 Horace, Ep. 1.4:[5] A Handsome, Sad Friend and a Fat Pig

Albi, nostrorum sermonum candide iudex,
quid nunc te dicam facere in regione Pedana?
Scribere quod Cassi Parmensis opuscula vincat,

---

[4] Moles 2002. On philosophical issues in the *Epistles* see also McGann 1969; Grilli 1983; Gagliardi 1988; Ferri 1993, 59–143 (111 on Ep. 1.4); Kilpatrick 1996, 304; Laurenti 1997, 579–580; Johnson 2010; Cucchiarelli 2015, 30–33.
[5] To the classic commentaries by Kiessling / Heinze 1914, 45–47, and Mayer 1994, 133–136, we can add Fedeli 1997, 1055–1063 (with accurate bibliography), Maurach 2001, 314–315, and most

>   an tacitum silvas inter reptare salubris
>   curantem quidquid dignum sapiente bonoque est?   5
>   Non tu corpus eras sine pectore. Di tibi formam,
>   di tibi divitias dederunt artemque fruendi.
>   Quid voveat dulci nutricula maius alumno,
>   qui sapere et fari possit quae sentiat et cui
>   gratia fama valetudo contingat abunde,   10
>   et mundus victus non deficiente crumina?
>   Inter spem curamque, timores inter et iras,
>   Omnem crede diem tibi diluxisse supremum.
>   Grata superveniet quae non sperabitur hora.
>   Me pinguem et nitidum bene curata cute vises,   15
>   cum ridere voles, Epicuri de grege porcum.

Albius, impartial critic of my chats, what shall I say you now are doing in your country at Pedum? Writing something to outshine the pieces of Cassius of Parma? Or strolling peacefully [see *infra*] amid the healthful woods, and musing on all that is worthy of one wise and good? Never were you a body without soul. The gods gave you beauty, the gods gave you wealth, and the art of enjoyment. For what more would a fond nurse pray for her sweet ward, if he could think aright and utter his thoughts – if favour, fame, and health fall to him richly, with a seemly living and a never falling purse? Amid hopes and cares, and fears and passions, believe that every day that has dawned is your last. Welcome will come to you another hour unhoped for. As for me, when you want a laugh, you will find me in fine fettle, fat and sleek, a hog from Epicurus' herd.
(Hor. Ep. 1.4)

The letter is addressed, as scholars generally agree, to the poet Albius Tibullus,[6] just like Horace's Carm. 1.33, with which it shares a similar opening: in both cases the personal name stands in the vocative – *Albi... memor* (Carm. 1.33.1), *Albi... iudex* (Ep. 1.4.1) – and in both poems we find an opposition between a *you* (Albius) and a *me* (Horace). There is a clear connection between (1) *Albi*, the aristocratic name of the addressee with which the poem opens and which derives, according to an ancient etymology, from the adjective *albus*, and (2) the adjective *candide*, which defines the *iudex* Albius at the end of the same line. The function of the name within the poem has been variously interpreted by scholars.[7] As is well known, *albus* and *candidus* are used to denote the colour 'white' (with greater or lesser brightness) both on a concrete and metaphorical

---

recently Cucchiarelli 2015, 124–126. Other essays and commentaries will be cited below. Horace's text is that of Klingner's Teubner; I use the translation of Fairclough's Loeb for Horace's *Satires* and *Epistles*.
6 Fedeli 1996, 608–609; Cucchiarelli 2010, 297.
7 Only a hint in Mayer 1994, 133 ad loc.; cf. Fedeli 1997, 1057. For the debate on *candidus* see Formicola 1995, 251–252.

level. Horace clearly intends here to establish a correspondence between the name 'Albius' (a *nomen gentilicium* supposedly originally based on physical complexion) and its bearer's moral virtue (the purity of his soul and judgement), a correspondence that he will again underline in line 6: *non tu corpus eras sine pectore*.[8] Yet Horace, I shall argue, presents a sad and dissatisfied Tibullus wandering alone in the woods (lines 1–5): he should not indulge this mental state, since the gods have given him everything a nurse could wish for her ward: health, wealth, beauty (lines 6–11). Nevertheless, he is still distressed. Tibullus should appreciate all aspects of life, and take his cue from Horace, who lives a joyful Epicurean existence (lines 12–16).

The two characters of the poem are set in opposition to each other not only in terms of their roles as speaker and addressee, but also in their philosophical attitudes, for the description of Tibullus has a distinctly Stoic flavour. At line 4 we find the verb *reptare* to describe Tibullus walking amid the woods.[9] This verb is commonly interpreted as describing a slow walk.[10] It seems to me, however, that the expression does not have an entirely positive connotation – it means something more than a simple stroll. Indeed *repto* – an *unicum* in Horace and extremely rare in Augustan poetry – is not commonly used for walking. It normally refers to the slithering of reptiles (OLD 1.b),[11] or to the uncertain wandering or crawling of small children or the blind (OLD 1.a and 3.c). When used of human beings, it connotes slowness, frequent pausing, or fatigue;[12] these connotations arise from its being the frequentative form of *repo*, a nuance that can be noted in the following verse from Plautus: *maior pars populi aridi reptant fame*

---

[8] Préaux 1968, 70 *ad* line 1.
[9] On the commonplace of the opposition between town and woodland / countryside in Horace in general, see Harrison 2007b, 121–131; Danielewicz 1997. Horace himself owned a little *silva* (Carm. 3.16.29–30; S. 2.6.3), and also presents himself as walking in a *silva* in Carm. 1.22.9–16: in this poem, a wolf runs away from him without even touching him while he sings of his love, Lalage; evidently he is presenting himself as a newborn Arion or Orpheus. This *silva* was not far from Tibullus's, in that it was located in the Sabine country to the south of Rome, while the *regio Pedana* was to the east of the city (near Tivoli). But Horace is happily singing about love in Carm. 1.22, while Tibullus is described as wandering alone and depressed in Ep. 1.4.
[10] Wilkins 1926, 116 ad loc., Kiessling / Heinze 1914, 45 and Mayer 1994, 134 ad loc. Contra De Pretis 2004, who goes too far (Horace 'is a reptile,' 157), following Putnam 1972, 87; see also McCarter 2015, 95–96. My interpretation follows a hint in La Penna 1993, 189: 'Tibullo... cammina lento e silenzioso (*reptare* è di una finezza intraducibile).'
[11] The verb *repo* in Horace could be used of animals (S. 1.3.99: *prorepo*), such as a fox (Ep. 1.7.30).
[12] Cf. Hor. S. 1.5.25: *milia tum pransi tria repimus...*, 'then we breakfast, and crawling on three miles...'; Plin. Ep. 1.24.4.

('the greatest part of the inhabitants, shrunk up with hunger, crawl along the streets' Boeot. Fr. 1.9 = Gell. 3.3.5).[13] Horace himself in the famous opening of S. 1.9, in a scenario similar to that of Ep. 1.4, uses the verb *eo* in the sense 'to stroll': *Ibam forte via Sacra, sicut meus est mos, | nescio quid meditans nugarum* ('I was strolling by chance along the Sacred way, musing after my fashion on some trifle or other').[14] It is therefore possible that in Ep. 1.4 the verb *repto* denotes not the serene walking of the meditating sage, but the uncertain pacing of a distressed man.[15] The verb itself could hint at Tibullus's internal anguish, paradoxically as he searches for tranquillity; on this reading, Tibullus's state of mind is somewhat akin to the condition of a Stoic *proficiens* who tries to follow the right path but sometimes loses his way. The most striking parallel for this sense seems to me a passage from Seneca's *De Vita Beata* (Dial. 7.18.2):[16]

> Nec malignitas me ista… deterrebit ab optimis; ne virus quidem istud… me inpediet quominus perseverem laudare vitam non quam ago, sed quam agendam scio, quominus <u>virtutem adorem et ex intervallo ingenti reptabundus sequar</u>.
>
> And your spitefulness… shall not deter me from what is best, nor shall even this poison… hinder me from continuing to vaunt the life, not that I lead, but that I know ought to be led; from <u>worshipping virtue and from following her, albeit a long way behind and with very halting pace</u>.
> (Dial. 7.18.2)

I would further argue that *reptare*, if read with line 5 of the Horatian epistle (*curantem quidquid dignum sapiente bonoque*), has a philosophical charge. A number of elements can be quoted to support this argument. Rather than writing poetry (line 4), Tibullus is seeking to become *sapiens* and *bonus* (line 5), that is to reach perfection from both a cognitive and an ethical point of view (this corresponds to line 6, *non tu corpus eras sine pectore*: i.e. *kalokagathos*, both physically and spiritually excellent). Moreover, the gifts of the gods are wisely used

---

13 The edition is that of Leo (Berlin); the translation has been taken from Rolfe's Loeb to Gellius (1).
14 Cf. S. 1.6.75; 1.5.94–95: *longum | carpentes iter*, 'covering a long stage'; 2.6.43: *iter faciens*.
15 Putnam 1972, 97, and McCarter 2015, 96, quote in this regard Cic. Att. 12.15: *in hac solitudine careo omnium colloquio, cumque mane me in silvam abstrusi densam et asperam, non exeo inde ante vesperum. Secundum te nihil est mihi amicius solitudine*, 'in this lonely place I do not talk to a soul. Early in the day I hide myself in a thick, thorny wood, and don't emerge till evening. Next to yourself solitude is my best friend.' Text and translation are from Shackleton Bailey's edition (Cambridge University Press).
16 The text of Seneca is that of Reynolds (OCT); the translation is from Basore's Loeb. Cf. Sen. Nat. 5.15.4.

by Tibullus (line 7 *artemque fruendi*), and among the nurse's prayers we find a peculiar one: *sapere et fari possit quae sentiat* (line 9). *Sapere* in Horace's *Epistles* always alludes to philosophical knowledge (Ep. 1.2.40, 1.15.45, 1.18.27), and the expression as a whole, even if we do not want to read into it a reference to the philosophical exhortation *par excellence*, *nosce te ipsum*, implies a perfect coherence between action and thought, which was one of the characteristics of the Stoic sage most praised by Seneca (Ep. 9.22, 120.22).

Thus Tibullus, in Horace's epistle at least, can be understood as interested in philosophy. In my opinion, this interest can be more precisely characterised as a Stoic one.[17] In fact, Horace insists on describing Tibullus as a fortunate man, with a list of wonderful gifts received from the gods, especially beauty and wealth (*forma*, *divitiae*, lines 6–7). These correspond to the nurse's highest aspirations for her charge (*gratia*, *fama*, *valetudo*, line 10), qualities that the poet Tibullus himself admits possessing in his poems;[18] yet he evidently does not care about them, otherwise he would be happy and not wandering distressed through the wood.[19] This disregard for his own apparent blessings represents a Stoic ideal: the Stoics maintained that the so-called external goods, that is material goods and physical qualities, do not belong to the soul, so they cannot be real goods. They belong to the category of *adiaphora* (*indifferentia*), indifferents, and thus are of secondary importance (SVF I.191–196, III.117–168).[20] The general theme of despising material goods is not the only Stoic element here: the specific polemic against nurses is also well attested in Stoic thought. As is well known, Stoics strongly criticised permissive education, stressing that deprivation and punishment would make the child's character stronger. In contrast, Epicureans maintained the importance of a pleasant and permissive education.[21] Commentators regularly illustrate the Stoic attitude with a passage from Persius in which

---

17 A doubtful and generic consideration about this can be found in Formicola 1995, 258 and 264. Terranova 1969, 196–197 sees in line 5 an explicit reference to Stoic philosophy. The mocking of Stoicism is often explicit, e. g. in S. 1.3.120–142, Ep. 1.2.1–4 (McGann 1969, 37).
18 Tib. 1.1.41–42; cf. Martin 1960, 601.
19 Cf. also Tib. 1.1.77: *ego composito securus acervo | despiciam dites despiciamque fames*, 'secure in my laid-up heap, I shall look down on wealth, look down on hunger too' (Kiessling / Heinze 1914, 46 *ad* line 6). The text and translation of Tibullus are as given by Putnam (University of California Press).
20 See e. g. SVF III.119 = D.L. 7.104, where among the *adiaphora* the author notes πλοῦτος, δόξα, ὑγίεια, ἰσχύς καὶ τὰ ὅμοια, 'wealth, reputation, health, strength, and the like' (from the Loeb of Hicks).
21 Cf. Vegetti 1983, Brunschwig 1986.

the poet deprecates nurses' prayers:[22] as we will see below, Seneca's Ep. 60 is even more relevant in this regard.[23]

Another Stoic element can be found in the passions against which Tibullus is fighting: hope, anguish, fear, and anger (Ep. 1.4.12: *inter spem curamque,*[24] *timores inter et iras*).[25] Scholars have not stressed that these are the logical consequences of nurses' prayers: nurses' prayers are themselves inextricably bound with hope, and are thus necessarily linked to anguish and fear: we always fear that something we wish for might not happen, or (and this is Tibullus's situation) that something we have could suddenly end or be taken away. If this happens to the benefit of someone else, then we feel angry.

These, then, are the passions to which nurses' wishes are subject – but they also belong to the main passions classified by the Stoics. This school classified passions into four categories, two applying to the present (pain and pleasure) and two depending on the future (fear and desire).[26] The emotions mentioned in line 12 clearly belong to this latter duo: hope (*spes*), that is a desire projected into the future; two kinds of fear (*cura* and *timor*); and anger (*ira*), which is the

---

22 Persius 2.31–40: *ecce avia aut metuens divum matertera cunis | exemit puerum... tunc manibus quatit et spem macram supplice voto | nunc Licini in campos, nunc Crassi mittit in aedis: | 'hunc optet generum rex et regina, puellae | hunc rapiant; quidquid calcaverit hic, rosa fiat.' | ast ego nutrici non mando vota. Negato, | Iuppiter, haec illi...,* 'Look – a grandma or superstitious aunt has lifted the boy from his cradle... Then she rocks him in her arms and in earnest prayer launches the scrawny prospect now towards Licinius' estate, now towards Crassus' palace: "May some king and queen pick him for their son-in-law, may girls tussle over him. Wherever he treads, may there be roses." But I entrust no prayers to a nurse. Say no to her wishes, God...' (from the Loeb of Morton Braund). The passage was already quoted by Kiessling / Heinze 1914, 46 *ad* 12. The motif comes from Plato Alc. 2.143a. See also Hor. Ep. 1.16.59–62, where a man asks Janus and Apollo to help him cheat his clients (something similar in Sen. Ep. 95.47–50). Cf. Harvey 1981, 67 *ad* 2.39–40; Hooley 1997, 190–192.
23 Cf. Cucchiarelli 2015, 125 ad loc.
24 On the emphasis on *cura* (line 5) see Terranova 1969.
25 Kilpatrick 1986, 60, notes that all these passions are present in Tibullus's elegies as a consequence of love (2.6.27: *spes*; 1.5.37 and 2.6.51: *curae*; 1.2.15; 1.6.59–60: *timor*; 1.6.57–58; 1.10.57–58 and 63–64: *ira*).
26 SVF III.378, 385, 386; Citti 2012, 30–35. Cf. Cic. Tusc. 4.80: *si spes est expectatio boni, mali expectationem esse necesse est metum. Ut igitur metus, sic reliquae perturbationes sunt in malo,* 'and if hope is expectation of good, fear must be expectation of evil. Just then as it is with fear, so with the remaining disorders; their element is evil' (translation from the Loeb of King); 4.57: *libidinosum igitur et iracundum et anxium et timidum censemus esse sapientem?* 'do we therefore suppose that the wise man is lustful and irascible and anxious and fearful?'.

desire to take revenge following an offence.²⁷ We find these same passions in other epistles by Horace, especially in connection with people who are dissatisfied with their lives: *qui cupit aut metuit* ('the one with fears or cravings,' 1.2.51); *qui non moderabitur irae* ('he who curbs not his anger,' 1.2.59); *gaudet an doleat, cupiat metuatne* ('whether a man feel joy or grief, desire or fear,' 1.6.12).

Fantham describes Tibullus as 'a victim of his emotions.'²⁸ We might put it in a more positive way and say that he is trying to defeat them: ignoring external goods is the first step to getting rid of the passions linked to them. Yet despite his struggle towards Stoicism in the Horatian epistle, Tibullus is still searching for something. In spite of ignoring the 'indifferent' qualities with which he has been endowed, like a good Stoic, he hesitates and is distressed, and has evidently not profited from his adherence to the Stoic regimen: Horace therefore exhorts him to retreat from his Stoic ambitions and to get the best from every moment, as Horace himself does as a fat Epicurean pig.

Let us concentrate on this image, found in the final two verses of the poem. Just as the end of the first epistle contradicts all of the philosophical issues previously discussed with an ironic *aprosdoketon* (the sage will always be happy – unless he develops a cough), so too this letter, addressed to a friend who meditates too much, ends with the image of the author as a pig.

Latin words for 'pig' (for example, *maialis*, *sus*, or *porcus*) were indeed a quite common insult, and implied a combination of dullness, lust, gluttony, and dirtiness in various contexts and literary genres.²⁹ In his speech against Piso, for example, Cicero mocks his adversary in terms that Horace seems to recall: *Epicure noster ex hara producte non ex schola* ('my worthy Epicurus, though product of the sty rather than the school,' Pis. 37);³⁰ one might also consider the insult *maialis* in the same speech, with which Cicero alludes to Piso's dullness (Pis. 19).³¹ We find the pig used already in Plato as a symbol of ignorance

---

27 This is the traditional definition of this passion, which Seneca repeats many times in his *De Ira* (Dial. 3.1.1, 3.3.2: *diximus [iram] cupiditatem esse poenae exigendae*, 'I spoke of [anger as] the desire to exact punishment').
28 Fantham 2013, 416.
29 See also Hor. Ep. 1.2.26 with Moles 2002, 150–151; Opelt 1965, 25 (Atellan farce: awfulness); 66 (comedy: hunger); 139–140 (satire: political fighting; political speeches: immorality); 229; 233–35 (scientific-philosophical debate: ignorance); Dubrueil 2013, 72. On the traditional link between pigs and Epicureans, Di Marco 1981, 59–91, who finds the first witness of this mockery in Timon of Phlius (fr. 55 W. = 51 D.); Cucchiarelli 2015, 126 ad loc.; Finzi 2014, esp. 37–44 and 85–91; *infra* 65–69.
30 Translation taken from the Loeb of Watts.
31 This passage is often quoted by the commentators of Horace's Ep. 1.4. Cf. Bonsangue 2004, 214.

(Rep. 7.535e: 'and he doesn't get irritated when his ignorance is revealed as a flaw, indeed he revels placidly in his ignorance like a pig').³² The pig was commonly used, in physiognomic studies, as a metaphor for sexual excitement (Ps.-Arist. Physiogn. 808b35–37),³³ dullness (812b26–28), but also of violence (Physiogn. 14),³⁴ of someone *immundus, stultus, insatiabilis* (Physiogn. 18), *immundus, vorax, stultus* (Physiogn. 48; cf. 17: *indocilis inquinatus vorax*).³⁵ Generally, round and corpulent faces were seen as symbolic of laziness: *Omnis vultus cum est plenus et crassus, ignavum significat et voluptatibus deditum* ('when the entire face is swollen and fat, it signifies a lazy individual given to pleasures,' Physiogn. 50).

Horace evidently wants to avoid the association of dirtiness by means of his reference to neat skin (*nitidus*, Ep. 1.4.15),³⁶ but he ironically attributes to himself the other associations, interpreting them as representing true enjoyment of life: ignorance, laziness, and love of physical hedonism – in other words, the refusal to think too much about individual questions, retirement from public life, and the enjoyment of whatever time is allotted to one.³⁷ Such a view fits well with the stereotypical image of the Epicurean as depicted on a famous silver cup from Boscoreale (now in the Louvre), where a skeleton named *Epikouros Athenaios*, with a little pig at his side, takes food from a plate while saying τὸ τέλος ἡδονή ('my aim is pleasure'); nearby a Stoic skeleton, named Zeno, is lost in his words and does not touch the food.³⁸ It is no coincidence that the fifth-century bishop Sidonius Apollinaris describes pictures he has observed with *Zenon fronte contracta, Epicurus cute distenta* ('Zenon with knitted brow, Epicurus with unwrinkled skin,' Ep. 9.9.14).³⁹

---

32 Translation taken from the Loeb of Shorey.
33 The edition is the Loeb of Hett.
34 The edition is that of J. André (Paris).
35 Dullness and violence: see also Physiogn. 53. Dullness: Ps.-Arist. Physiogn. 811a30–31; 811b29–30. Dirtiness: Physiogn. 51.
36 *Nitidus* is clearly linked to the *candidus* at the beginning of the poem, and usually refers to someone who cares too much for his physical appearance (Fedeli 1997, 1062–1063 *ad* 15–16; cf. Carm. 3.19.25, 3.24.20; S. 2.1.62–65). Moreover, the neat skin itself makes him look similar to Proci and Phaeacians, Ep. 1.2.29: *in cute curanda plus aequo operata iuventus*, 'young courtiers... unduly busy in keeping their skins sleek'; in Persius 4.18 we find a similar description of bearded men with depilated limbs: *adsiduo curate cuticola sole*, 'pamper your skin with continual sun.' See Dilke 1966, 86 *ad loc.*; Mayer 1994, 135 *ad loc.*; Préaux 1968, 72–73 *ad loc.*; Formicola 1995, 264; Fedeli 1997, 1062 *ad loc.*; Cucchiarelli 2015, 298; McCarter 2015, 97; for the origin of this image, Di Marco 1981, 82–87.
37 On Epicurean *otium* in Horace see Roskam 2007, 166–178 (166–167 on Ep. 1.4).
38 Cf. Baratte 1986, 65–67; Dunbabin 1986, 226–228; Guzzo 2006, 186.
39 The text and translation are from Anderson's Loeb. Cf. Kiessling / Heinze 1914, 47 *ad* line 12; Formicola 1995, 263–264; Fedeli 1997, 1062 *ad loc.*, who adds Hier. Adv. Jovin. 2.36: *favent tibi*

The mildly comical representation of the characters within the poem as a Stoic and an Epicurean, building on ancient stereotypes, fits well with the structure of the poem itself, which contrasts a *you* with a *me*.[40] This parallel is also found in Carm. 1.33, where Horace enters the poem at the end to console his friend Tibullus by claiming to have felt the *same* condition of eagerness as the elegiac poet (*ipsum me...* line 13); in Ep. 1.4 he likewise enters at the poem's end, but defines himself explicitly as Tibullus's opposite.[41] Tibullus is rich, handsome, famous, and distressed. If my reasoning makes sense, then the you / me opposition is enriched by a philosophical subtext: handsome / sad / Stoic versus fat / happy / Epicurean.[42] In this we can see a reframing of the opposition explicitly depicted in the first epistle, finely analysed by Moles,[43] between the Stoics and Aristippus (lines 16–19);[44] elsewhere (e. g. in Ep. 1.2) we find a similar opposition between Stoics and Epicureans. In other words, Ep. 1.4 interacts with the theme found in the first, programmatic letter, in that it proposes two different kinds of philosophical life.

I have argued that the Horatian letter establishes an opposition between a Stoic way of life (despising external goods, fighting against passions) and an Epicurean one (enjoying life for the moment without excessive reflection). Horace clearly inclines to the latter attitude. Seneca would obviously prefer the first, as he demonstrates in Ep. 60.

3 Seneca, Ep. 60: Fighting against Nurses and Pigs with Sallust's Assistance

Horace's Ep. 1.4, as we have seen, is quite short; it begins with two direct questions and has a lightly censorious tone. Since it presents typical Stoic passions (fear, hope, anger, distress) in opposition to Epicurean tranquillity, I have infer-

---

[*Epicuro*] *crassi, nitidi, dealbati*; McGann 1969, 44–45. On the literary and iconographic representations of Epicurus, see Zanker 2009, 136–145; [B.] Fischer 2007 and 2014; Beretta 2014 (with reference to Lucretius).
40 An opposition noted by all scholars, e. g. Mayer 1994, 134 *ad* 15; Fedeli 1997, 1062 *ad* 15–16.
41 Something similar occurs in Ep. 1.3 to Julius Florus (Pantzerhielm Thomas 1936, 46; Martin 1960, 608–609).
42 Moreover, the expression *Epicuri de grege...* seems to recall the *Chrysippi... grex* of S. 2.3.44: Kiessling / Heinze 1914, 47 *ad* 15; Mayer 1994, 136 *ad* Ep. 1.4.16.
43 Moles 2009.
44 On Aristippus and the distinction between him and Epicurus, see Traina 1991.

red that Horace is implicitly comparing these two ways of life. Now I will turn to what I consider Seneca's reply to this poem: Ep. 60.[45]

1. Queror, litigo, irascor. Etiamnunc optas quod tibi optavit nutrix tua aut paedagogus aut mater? Nondum intellegis quantum mali optaverint? O quam inimica nobis sunt vota nostrorum! Eo quidem inimiciora quo cessere felicius. Iam non admiror si omnia nos a prima pueritia mala sequuntur: inter execrationes parentum crevimus. Exaudiant di quandoque nostram pro nobis vocem gratuitam. 2. Quousque poscemus aliquid deos? Ita nondum ipsi alere nos possumus? Quamdiu sationibus implebimus magnarum urbium campos? Quamdiu nobis populus metet? Quamdiu unius mensae instrumentum multa navigia et quidem non ex uno mari subvehent? Taurus paucissimorum iugerum pascuo impletur; una silva elephantis pluribus sufficit; homo et terra et mari pascitur. 3. Quid ergo? Tam insatiabilem nobis natura alvum dedit, cum tam modica corpora dedisset, ut vastissimorum edacissimorumque animalium aviditatem vinceremus? Minime: quantulum est enim quod naturae datur! Parvo illa dimittitur: non fames nobis ventris nostri magno constat sed ambitio. 4. Hos itaque, ut ait Sallustius, 'ventri oboedientes' animalium loco numeremus, non hominum, quosdam vero ne animalium quidem, sed mortuorum. Vivit is qui multis usui est, vivit is qui se utitur; qui vero latitant et torpent sic in domo sunt quomodo in conditivo. Horum licet in limine ipso nomen marmori inscribas: mortem suam antecesserunt.

1. I file a complaint, I enter a suit, I am angry. Do you still desire what your nurse, your guardian, or your mother, have prayed for you in your behalf? Do you not yet understand what evil they pray for? Alas, how hostile to us are the wishes of our own folk! And they are all the more hostile in proportion as they are more completely fulfilled. It is no surprise to me, at my age, that nothing but evil attends us from early youth; for we have grown up amid the curses invoked by our parents. And may the gods give ear to our cry also, uttered in our own behalf – one which asks no favors! 2. How long shall we go on making demands upon the gods, as if we were still unable to support ourselves? How long shall we continue to fill with grain the market-places of great cities? How long must the people gather in it for us? How long shall many ships convey the requisites for a single meal, bringing them from no single sea? The bull is filled when he feeds over a few acres; and one forest is large enough for a herd of elephants. Man, however, draws sustenance both from the earth and from the sea. 3. What, then? Did nature give us bellies so insatiable, when she gave us these puny bodies, that we should outdo the hugest and most voracious animals in greed? Not at all. How small is the amount which will satisfy nature? A very little will send away contented. It is not the natural hunger of our bellies that costs us dear, but our solicitous cravings. 4. Therefore those who, as Sallust puts it, 'hearken to their bellies,' should be numbered not even among the animals, but among the dead. He really lives who is made use of by many; he really lives who makes use of himself. Those men however, who creep into a hole and grow torpid, are no better off in their homes than if they were in their tombs. Right there on the marble lintel of the house of such a man you may inscribe his name; for he has died before he is dead.

---

45 The translation of the *Epistulae Morales* follows Gummere's Loeb; the text is that of Reynolds (OCT).

Seneca's Ep. 60 is one of the shortest in the corpus: it starts with harsh criticism of Lucilius[46] and a direct question that concerns nurses' prayers (60.1). These prayers are not only misapplied, but positively damaging, especially those regarding wealth (60.2–3). People who live in useless retirement are to be considered spiritually dead (60.4).

In this letter there are no quotations or *iuncturae* that hint directly at Horace. There are, however, similarities in form (the opening) and tone (critical), and a significant overlap in content: nurses' prayers, wealth, and retirement. Seneca criticises these items with the violent and passionate tone of the Stoic moralist; Horace praises these same things in a light and ironical way. The philosopher focuses on wealth, which finds little space in Horace; but then, after a quotation from Sallust, he turns to the subject of retirement, which is described as a trivial version of Epicurean *otium*, and considers it a waste of one's life. The first section seems to reply to Horace's statements about nurses; the final section introduces a contrast to Horace's fat pig. We might say that Seneca is trying to answer Horace by taking the side of Tibullus's character in Hor. Ep. 1.4. In the middle there is Sallust, who in my opinion constitutes a sort of intermediary between the two.

The criticism of nurses' prayers, and on a higher level of prayers that ask for material goods in general (cf. Ep. 31.2–5 and 10.5),[47] is a predictable move for a Stoic, in that nurses (as well as mothers) wish for things that do not give authentic happiness – false goods linked to appearance, which, as we have seen, were classed by the Stoics as *adiaphora*: health, wealth, and beauty.[48] On the contrary, as Seneca often points out, external goods should paradoxically be considered negative because they easily lead human beings into vice, while poverty and suffering offer virtue the opportunity to reveal itself: *Optaverunt itaque tibi alia parentes tui; sed ego contra omnium tibi eorum contemptum opto quorum illi copiam* ('your parents, to be sure, asked other blessings for you; but I myself pray rather that you may despise all those things which your parents wished for you in abundance,' Ep. 32.4). Ep. 60 offers us a detailed example of this attitude: in the first section of the letter, nurses' prayers are defined as something bad (*quantum*

---

[46] This criticism is interpreted by Motto / Clark 1993b as a rhetorical device to lead the reader to follow Seneca's precepts.
[47] Seneca himself wrote a *De Superstitione* (Vottero 1998, 45–57; F 64–F 75); Nat. 3.praef.14; Petr. 88.8. Not only parents and nurses, but also poets invite us to consider wealth and glory as the most desirable things (Sen. Ep. 115.11–12). On this motif cf. Scarpat 1977, 41–56; Guglielmo 1997, 65–69; *supra*, n. 22. As for Tibullus, see 2.1.83–84; for Horace and Seneca, McGann 1969, 28–29.
[48] *Supra*, 58–59.

mali), and are compared to an evil enemy (*inimica nobis*): both ideas are foregrounded, as they are expressed twice in a chiastic pattern (first, *quantum mali, inimica nobis*; then again, *inimiciora, mala*). We then have the paradoxical definition of nurses' prayers as curses (*execrationes*). All this is the opposite of what Horace says in lines 8–11 of his verse epistle.

Seneca then turns to the prayers by which we ask the gods for external goods (Ep. 60.2), another theme found also in Horace's poem (lines 6–7). There, Horace mentions several external goods: Seneca concentrates on the vice of greed (*ambitio*, Ep. 60.3) in its worst manifestation, as a vice which reduces a person to his unappeasable stomach,[49] an organ far more ravenous, despite the relatively small size of the human body, than those of huge animals such as bulls (*taurus*) or elephants (*elephanti*). This hunger is a struggle that reverses the natural hierarchy in which (according to Stoic theory) human beings are at the top and every lower animal exists in order to guarantee human well-being.[50] When they pursue this vice, men are reduced not only to the status of animals, and are hence irrational and focused on material needs, but to something even worse – to a blind organ, and indeed the most primitive and trivial one: the stomach. It is not coincidental that the stomach is the subject of many of the verbs in this passage. At the end of the letter, Seneca unsurprisingly considers such people, as he does elsewhere, to be dead inside.[51] They are not only slaves to their stomach: they also are also identified with it.

We do not find such motifs in Horace's Ep. 1.4,[52] but I think that the Sallustian expression *ventri oboedientes*,[53] with which Seneca contemptuously defines men who live in retirement (Ep. 60.4), is intended to pick up on Horace's *pinguem... Epicuri de grege porcum* (Hor. Ep. 1.4.15–16), which Horace had used to describe an attitude of enjoying life that encompasses all physical pleasures. Seneca does not mention pigs but generic animals (*animalium loco numeremus*): Sallust on the other hand makes a general reference to *pecora*. But it is the pig,

---

[49] Cf. Citroni Marchetti 1991, 135–139 (99–100 on Sallust; 100–104 on Horace); Citroni Marchetti 1997, 563–564.
[50] Cf. *SVF* II.1152–1167; Cic. Leg. 1.8.25 = *SVF* II.1162: *itaque ad hominum commoditates et usus tantam rerum ubertatem natura largita est, ut ea quae gignuntur donata consulto nobis, non fortuito nata videantur*, 'for this reason, Nature has lavishly yielded such a use that what she produces seems intended as a gift to us and not brought forth by chance.' The translation follows the Loeb of Keyes.
[51] Cf. Ep. 55.4.
[52] For a similar attack on avidity see Hor. Ep. 1.6.56–64.
[53] A further quotation from Sallust can be found at Ben. 4.1.1, and a famous analysis of Sallust's style at Ep. 114.17–19.

as we have seen, that functions as the literary symbol of insatiability (cf. *insatiabilem... alvum*, Ep. 60.3) and the Epicurean way of life.

A more detailed reading of Sallust will support my point. The citation comes from the very start of Sallust's *Coniuratio Catilinae*, but the whole proem of this monograph, which deals with the opposition between body and soul (and their goods), has much in common with Seneca's Ep. 60.[54] After the definition *ventri oboedientes*, the historian affirms that the pursuit of *divitiarum et formae gloria* (1.4) is vain and short-lived. There follows a brief history of the world, from its peaceful start to the beginning of *lubido dominandi* (2.2–5), when laziness (*desidia*) took the place of hard work (2.5). Sallust claims that the life of those *dediti ventri atque somno* is similar to death (*eorum ego vitam mortemque iuxta aestumo*, 2.8). In the end he turns to the noble art of writing history, which leads to authentic *gloria* (3.2), and to a description of his youth, tormented by the vices of that time, and most of all *ambitio* (3.3–4), described as an *honoris cupido* (3.5–4.2).

A consideration of the context of the Sallustian citation shows us the extent to which Seneca must have had Sallust's text in mind: the image of men in po-

---

[54] Sal. Cat. 1.1: *Omnis homines, qui sese student praestare ceteris animalibus, summa ope niti decet, ne vitam silentio transeant veluti pecora, quae natura prona atque ventri oboedientia finxit. 2. Sed nostra omnis vis in animo et corpore sita est: animi imperio, corporis servitio magis utimur; alterum nobis cum dis, alterum cum beluis commune est... 4. Nam divitiarum et formae gloria fluxa atque fragilis est, virtus clara aeternaque habetur... 2.5. Verum ubi pro labore desidia, pro continentia et aequitate lubido atque superbia invasere, fortuna simul cum moribus inmutatur... 7. Quae homines arant navigant aedificant, virtuti omnia parent. 8. Sed multi mortales, dediti ventri atque somno, indocti incultique vitam sicuti peregrinantes transiere; quibus profecto contra naturam corpus voluptati, anima oneri fuit. Eorum ego vitam mortemque iuxta aestumo, quoniam de utraque siletur. Verum enim vero is demum mihi vivere atque frui anima videtur, qui aliquo negotio intentus praeclari facinoris aut artis bonae famam quaerit.* 'All humans who are keen to surpass other animals had best strive with all their might not to pass through life without notice, like cattle, which nature had fashioned bent over and subservient to their stomach. 2. All our power, however, is situated in mind and body; we employ the mind to rule, the body rather to serve; the one we have in common with the gods, the other with beasts... 4. For the renown of riches or beauty is fleeting and fragile; excellence is a shining and lasting possession... 2.5 But when hard work is replaced by laziness, self-restraint and evenhandedness by willfulness and insolence, there is a change in fortune accompanying the change in character... 7. Success in agriculture, navigation, and building structures depends entirely upon prowess. 8. Yet many mortals, being given over on their stomachs and sleep, have passed through life untaught and unrefined, like mere wayfarers; to such men indeed, contrary to nature's intent, this body has been a source of pleasure, their intellect a burden. The life and death of such men I place on a par since there is no report of either. But to be sure, only that man appears to me to be alive and make the most of life who by devoting himself to some enterprise, seek fame for a glorious deed or good practice.' The translation is from the Loeb of Rolfe.

litical retirement as 'dead men walking' had already been used by Sallust (*eorum ego vitam mortemque iuxta aestumo*, 2.8: cf. *mortem suam antecesserunt*, Sen. Ep. 60.4). Seneca took this image to the extreme by focusing on the stomach itself, thus reframing the image of *ventri oboedientes* in a way that was more precise and effective than Sallust's.

Scholars see in this expression an allusion to the widespread commonplace that contrasts animals bent down towards the earth (and so, men enslaved to vices) with men who look at the sky (that is, who are focused on their rational lives);[55] they agree that the tone of Sallust's preface is anti-Epicurean,[56] in that it clearly alludes to Epicurean expressions such as 409 Us. 227 Arr. ἀρχὴ καὶ ῥίζα παντὸς ἀγαθοῦ ἡ τῆς γαστρὸς ἡδονή: 'the pleasure of the stomach is the principle and root of every good.'[57] We can infer that Seneca is alluding to this same polemic.

Thus, setting aside the different contexts, Sallust offers an opposition between an Epicurean way of life (*ventri oboedientes*) and another that is active, associated with writing history, and seems to be compatible with the Stoic ideal;[58] as we have seen, in Horace and Seneca we find something similar, with special reference to the contrast between Epicureans and Stoics. This opposition is described in similar ways by all three authors. To the considerations made above in this regard, we can add that the *divitiarum et formae gloria* in Sallust corresponds to the divine gifts and the nurse's prayers that Horace finds realised in Tibullus (Hor. Ep. 1.4.6–7: *formam... divitias*; 10: *gratia, fama, valetudo*),[59] and that the opposition between body and soul in Sallust's preface (1.2: *omnis vis in animo et corpore sita est*; 2.8: *corpus voluptati, anima oneri fuit*) is the one which Horace finds resolved in Tibullus (Ep. 1.4.5: *non tu corpus eras sine pectore*).

It is possible, then, that this is an example, albeit a peculiar one, of multiple reference:[60] a well-studied process in poetic texts, which might well be expected to exist in prose as well. Indeed, we can find something similar in certain Senecan passages where, while commenting on a Virgilian quotation, the philoso-

---

[55] A commonplace that derives from Plato Rep. 9, 586a–b; Tim. 90a–b: cf. Husner 1924, 103–109; Vretska 1976, 32–33 ad loc.; Pellegrino 1982. Cf. Ov. Met. 1.84–86.
[56] Vretska 1976, 31 *ad* 1.1; Mariotti 2007, 122 *ad* 1.1.
[57] Quoted by Ath. 12.546f = 7.280a. Usener also quotes Cic. Pis. 66: *abdominis voluptates*, 'the pleasures of the belly'; Plut. Contr. Epic. Beat. 1098d = Metrod. *ad* Tim. fr. 13 p. 51 Duen.
[58] Vretska 1976, 28 lists Posidonius among the sources of Sallust's proem.
[59] Pantzerhielm Thomas 1936, 43.
[60] For the definition of this technique see Thomas 1999, 135–140.

pher alludes to passages from Horace (e. g. Ben. 5.17.5–7 and Ep. 12.9).[61] I think the case that we have been considering, however, could be an even clearer instance of this rhetorical device. Seneca cites Sallust with reference to the wider context of his letter, that is the polemic against Epicureanism as a way of life which makes men resemble animals; in this way, Seneca enlists Sallust as an ally against Horace, to whom he alludes by criticising the nurses' prayers: the Sallustian expression *ventri oboedientes* perfectly fits the aim of castigating the fat, sleek Epicurean pig in the terms of the stereotype noted above.

We may follow this line of reasoning further. *Ventri oboedientes* in Seneca's Ep. 60 operates as a sort of hinge between two themes, that of insatiability (*aviditas, ambitio*) and that of wasting one's life, to which Seneca refers by means of the verbs *latito* and *torpeo* (Ep. 60.4).[62] Insatiability is a key concept in Sallust; wasting one's life in lazy *otium* is symbolised by Horace's pig. The verbs chosen by Seneca to define a life coinciding with spiritual death are highly significant: in particular, *latito* hints at the Epicurean exhortation λάθε βιώσας ('live unnoticed').[63]

This characterisation also recalls another recurrent motif in Seneca's works, the correspondence between fattened animals and men who waste their life in physical pleasures. We find a good example of this in the *De Beneficiis* (4.13.1), where Seneca criticises the Epicurean way of life:[64]

> Vobis [sc. Epicureis] voluptas est <u>inertis otii</u> facere corpusculum et securitatem sopitis simillimam adpetere et <u>sub densa umbra latitare</u> tenerrimisque cogitationibus, quas tranquillitatem vocatis, <u>animi marcentis</u> oblectare torporem et cibis potionibusque intra hortorum latebram <u>corpora ignavia pallentia saginare</u>...

> Your idea of pleasure is to give your contemptible body over <u>to idle sloth</u>, to seek a freedom from care tantamount to sleep, <u>to hide out in thick shade</u>, to divert the torpor of <u>a lethargic mind</u> with the softest thoughts, which you call 'tranquillity,' and <u>to stuff bodies pallid from idleness</u> with food and drink in the privacy of your garden...

The same verb found in Ep. 60, *latito*, refers here to Epicurean *otium* as a human equivalent to the process of fattening animals. It is noteworthy that the combination of *nitidus* and *pinguis* used by Horace corresponds with *saginatus*, a connection that we find also in Seneca.[65]

---

61 Cf. Berno 2014, 130–136.
62 *Torpeo*: cf. Dial. 10.2.1; Ben. 5.25.6, 7.2.2.
63 For similar evaluations of *otium*, cf. Ep. 82.2–3 (*iaceo, torpor*), 55.4–5 (*lateo*).
64 The translation is that of Griffin / Inwood (University of Chicago Press).
65 Ep. 110.13: *alia [animalia delectant te] si diu pasta et coacta* <u>pinguescere</u> *fluunt ac vix* <u>saginam</u> *continent suam: delectat te* <u>nitor</u> *horum arte quaesitus*, 'other [animals are more pleasing] if after

We can, in addition, note other letters in which this equivalence leads to its logical consequence (that is, the consideration of the Epicurean / self-indulgent way of life as a spiritual death). For example, Ep. 88 delineates the same idea via an abrupt metaphor (88.19: *quid enim, oro te, liberale habent isti ieiuni vomitores, quorum corpora in sagina, animi in macie et veterno sunt?* 'For what "liberal" element is there in these ravenous takers of emetics, whose bodies are fed to fatness while their minds are thin and dull?').[66] In a number of other passages, we find the so-called *pingue otium*, the opposite of the Stoic model of activity, compared to the practice of fattening animals and thus corresponding to spiritual death.[67] This condition is compared to the Epicurean way of life as understood

---

long feeding and forced fattening they almost melt and can hardly retain their own grease. You like the subtly devised flavour | gleam [Gummere translates *nidor*, found in some mss.; I print Reynolds's *nitor*] of these dishes.' *Saginatus* is used, also in poetry, for pigs fattened for sacrifice (e.g. Prop. 4.1a.23; Plin. Nat. 13.49). The habit of fattening animals was attacked by moralists, and was forbidden by a law supported by Cato the Censor (the *lex Fannia*, 161 BCE; Plin. Nat. 10.139–140): Bottiglieri 2002, 138–150.

[66] One might compare the more detailed comparison at Ep. 122.4–5: *Aves quae conviviis comparantur, ut inmotae facile pinguescant, in obscuro continentur; ita sine ulla exercitatione iacentibus tumor pigrum corpus invadit et... iners sagina subcrescit. 5. At istorum corpora qui se tenebris dicaverunt foeda visuntur... et in vivis caro morticina est. Hoc tamen minimum in illis malorum dixerim: quanto plus tenebrarum in animo est!* 'Birds that are being prepared for the banquet, that they may be easily fattened through lack of exercise, are kept in darkness; and similarly, if men vegetate without physical activity, their idle bodies are overwhelmed with flesh and... the fat of indolence grows upon them... they are lackadaisical and flabby with dropsy; though still alive, they are already carrion. But this, to my thinking, would be the last of their evils. How much more darkness there is in their souls!'. We can add that in a fragment from a satire by Varro (435 Cèbe), those who live *in tenebris* are considered the equivalent of pigs: see Cèbe 1996, 1791–1792 ad loc.; Krenkel 2002, 798–802. Cicero alludes to something similar in referring both to Epicurus and Aristippus in Ac. 2.139.

[67] Dial. 2.3.4: *illum fortem virum dicam quem bella non subigunt... non cui pingue otium est inter desides populos*, 'the brave man, I should say, is he whom war cannot subdue... not he who battens at ease among the idle populace'; Dial. 1.2.6: *languent per inertiam saginata nec labore tantum sed motu et ipso sui onere deficiunt*, 'Bodies grown fat through sloth are weak, and not only labour, even movement and their very weight cause them to break down'; cf. Ep. 51.10. Particularly interesting is a passage about fish that live under the earth and poison those who eat them: Nat. 3.19.2: *perierunt quicumque illos ederant pisces... Nec id mirum: erant enim pinguia et differta, ut ex longo otio, corpora, ceterum inexercitata et tenebris saginata et lucis expertia*, 'everyone who ate them died. This is not surprising, for their bodies were plump and bloated, as a result of long indolence; they have had no exercise, and had been fattened by the darkness and deprived of light'; translation from Hine (University of Chicago Press). Something similar to Horace can be found in Apul. Met. 9.11: *illa otii saginaeque beatitudo*, 'that happiness of leisure and fattening.' There is only one passage in Seneca (Ep. 73.10) where the expression *pingue otium* has a positive meaning.

in its trivial sense – a life of lazy retirement, devoted to physical pleasure. This is the implication of the conclusion of Ep. 60.

In my opinion, then, this letter begins with an anti-Horatian polemic (against nurses' prayers), continues with Sallustian themes and argumentation, and then uses Sallust to turn once more against Horace's Epicurean pig. I suggest that the Sallustian quotation, with its anti-Epicurean implications and its comparison of men and vile animals, provides Seneca with an argument against Horace, and also leads the philosopher from a Sallustian subject (the vice of *ambitio*) to an (anti-) Horatian one: the vice of lazy retirement.

Moreover, by linking 'fat' *otium* with death, Seneca implicitly declares Horace's exhortation to live each single day as if it were our last (Ep. 1.4.13: *omnem crede diem tibi diluxisse supremum*) to be impossible. Seneca enthusiastically shares this view, but he does not think that the Horatian way is the right one to achieve it. This attitude becomes clearer if we read the subsequent letter (Ep. 61),[68] which starts by stating the need to reject boyish desires, i.e. desires for external goods, which naturally closely resemble nurses' prayers. In Ep. 60 Seneca rebukes Lucilius for paying attention to these things, while in Ep. 61 he proudly affirms that he himself has managed to ignore them: *Desinamus quod voluimus velle. Ego certe id ago <ne> senex eadem velim quae puer volui* (Ep. 61.1). And, just like in Ep. 60, Seneca explicitly defines these wishes as *mali: in hoc unum eunt dies... inponere veteribus malis finem* (Ep. 61.1). The link with the preceding letter is evident.

After these statements, but still in the first section of the letter, Seneca refuses the '*carpe diem*' way of life (*nec mehercules tamquam ultimum rapio*),[69] and gives a paraphrase of the Horatian line *omnem crede tibi diem diluxisse supremum* (Ep. 1.4.13) with the following phrase: *id ago ut mihi instar totius vitae dies*

---

68 Ep. 61.1: *Desinamus quod voluimus velle. Ego certe id ago <u>ne senex eadem velim quae puer volui</u>. In hoc unum eunt dies... inponere <u>veteribus malis</u> finem. Id ago <u>ut mihi instar totius vitae dies sit</u>; nec mehercules tamquam ultimum rapio, sed sic illum aspicio <u>tamquam esse vel ultimus possit</u>...* [cf. Hor. Ep. 1.4.13: <u>*omnem crede diem tibi diluxisse supremum*</u>.]... 4. *Vixi, Lucili carissime, <u>quantum satis erat: mortem plenus exspecto</u>.* '1. Let us cease to desire that which we have been desiring. I, at least, am doing this: <u>in my old age I have ceased to desire what I desired when I was a boy</u>. To this single end my days are passed... <u>to put an end to my chronic ills</u>. I am endeavouring <u>to live every day as if it were a complete life</u>. I do not indeed snatch it up as if it were my last: I do regard it, however, <u>as if it might even be my last</u>... 4. I have lived, my dear friend, <u>long enough. I have had my fill: I await death</u>.'

69 Cf. Hor. Epod. 13.3–4: *rapiamus, amici, | occasionem de die*, 'let's seize the opportunity offered by the day' (Rudd). On the motif of the proper use of time in Horace and Seneca, see the paper by Vogt-Spira in this volume.

sit... sic illum aspicio tamquam esse vel ultimus possit (Sen. Ep. 61.1);[70] finally, he turns to another Epicurean commonplace used by Horace, that of comparing life to a banquet (61.4: *Vixi, Lucili carissime, quantum satis erat: mortem plenus exspecto*). This passage clearly evokes not only some famous verses by Lucretius (3.935–939), but also Horace's first satire:[71]

> Inde fit ut raro qui se vixisse beatum
> dicat, et exacto contentus tempore vita
> cedat uti conviva satur, reperire queamus.

> Thus it comes that seldom can we find one who says he has had a happy life, and who, when his time is sped, will quit life in contentment, like a guest who has had his fill. (Hor. S. 1.1.117–119)

It seems that Seneca is saying that the right way of interpreting the Horatian statement about living every day as if it were the last is the following: as an invocation not to adopt the laziness of a pig, but rather the serious attitude of an old man; to follow not the path of Horace's Ep. 1.4, but that of S. 1.1. If Ep. 60 is the *pars destruens*, Ep. 61 represents a *pars construens* of the argumentation, which seems to correct Horace by allusion to Horace. Letters 60 and 61 can be read as a counterpoint to Horace's Ep. 1.4: here, Horace the Epicurean blames a Tibullus who is remarkably Stoic in his philosophical outlook, and presents himself as an example of tranquillity; there, Seneca the Stoic blames Lucilius for an Epicurean attitude (Ep. 60), and presents himself as an example of tranquillity (Ep. 61).

I am aware that many of the quoted motifs are in fact philosophical commonplaces shared both by Horace and Seneca. But I believe I have shown that the elements in common in this particular context are particularly numerous and significant, to the extent that we can consider this case not only in terms of the revisitation of topoi but as an example of intentional allusion.[72]

---

[70] Cf. Ep. 12.9 with Berno 2014, 131–134; Hor. Carm. 1.9.14–15, 1.11.8, 2.16.25–26. The sentence, in its formulation by Hor. Ep. 1.4.13, became proverbial in medieval times: Fedeli 1997, 1061; Tosi 2003, 292–293 n. 613.
[71] Berno 2008, 557.
[72] Cf. the case of Ep. 86, on which cf. Del Giovane 2012, 157–158; Rimell 2013, esp. 7–12.

Catharine Edwards
Saturnalian Exchanges: Seneca, Horace, and Satiric Advice

In the *Apocolocyntosis*, his satiric account of the apotheosis of the emperor Claudius, almost certainly composed shortly after Nero's accession, Seneca uses the idea of a perpetual Saturnalia to characterise the reign of Nero's predecessor, referring to: *Saturno... cuius mensem toto anno celebravit Saturnalicius princeps*, 'Saturn, whose month the Saturnalian emperor celebrated all year long' (Apoc. 8).[1] The festival of the Saturnalia, traditionally celebrated over a number of days in December, was associated with feasting, drinking, jokes, gift-giving, distinctive dress (in particular, abandonment of the toga for the Greek-style *synthesis* and wearing the *pileus*, a cap associated with newly freed slaves), and the removal of normal restrictions on behaviour (dice-playing and gambling, for instance, were thus permitted).[2] The festival was also characterised by a particular licence for slaves, who might, perhaps, make jokes at the expense of their masters without fear of punishment. As Macrobius, writing in the early fifth century, comments: 'On the Saturnalia, slaves are allowed all licence' (*Saturnalibus tota servis licentia permittitur*, Macrob. 1.7.26).[3] Given that Claudius was notorious for being subservient to his own freedmen, the perpetual Saturnalia was an especially fitting figure for Seneca's critique of this emperor.[4]

The *Apocolocyntosis* itself is often seen in the tradition of Menippean satire (whose premier exponent, Varro, also included philosophical elements in his satires, according to Cicero).[5] A different satiric tradition, that of Horace, is, I shall

---

With particular thanks to the organisers of and participants in the Horace and Seneca conference at Heidelberg (July 2015). I am especially grateful to Francesca Romana Berno and Barbara Del Giovane for generously sharing their work with me, to Janja Soldo for ongoing conversations about the letters and to the editors for suggesting numerous improvements to my text.

1 Translations are my own except where otherwise indicated, while texts are taken from the OCT edition. Most scholars agree in attributing this work to Seneca. For the debate around authorship, see Freudenburg 2015, 93–95. Some have suggested that the work was first performed at the Saturnalia in 54 CE (a year before the events at the festival described in Tac. Ann. 13.15, discussed below). See Whitton 2013b, 153; Nauta 1987.
2 On the customs associated with the Saturnalia, see Versnel 1993.
3 Text and translation are taken from Kaster's Loeb edition.
4 Dickison 1977.
5 O'Gorman 2005; Relihan 1993, 75–90. On Varro's satire, Cicero comments, Cic. Ac. 1.8: *multa admixta ex intima philosophia*, 'much was added from the very heart of philosophy.' A later sat-

argue, a significant but usually underappreciated point of reference for Seneca's later work, the *Epistulae Morales*, composed after Seneca had fallen from favour and withdrawn from Nero's court. In the letters, too, however, as indeed in Horace's satires, the Saturnalia serves as a telling figure. Bakhtin famously underlined the association of Saturnalia with satire as a literary genre.[6] Indeed the festival of the Saturnalia may be seen as constituting, in Freudenburg's words, 'the quintessential satiric moment.'[7] Horace chooses to set two of the eight poems of his second book of *Satires / Sermones* (2.3 and 2.7) during the season of the Saturnalia, while a third (2.4), in expounding a complex set of philosophically-informed rules relating to food, implicitly plays on Saturnalian customs.

My essay, exploring Seneca's engagement in his letters with Horatian satire, will focus particularly on Ep. 18. Opening with the Saturnalia, this letter at once alerts Seneca's reader to satire as a point of reference, but there are, I would like to suggest, some more particular points of engagement with Horace; in exploiting the Saturnalia as an occasion for a specifically Stoic critique of excess, Seneca echoes Horace S. 2.3, where Damasippus's Stoic rant takes place during the festival. Prescriptions for how to manage one's diet echo S. 2.4.[8] Also significant is S. 2.7, in which the slave Davus offers pointedly Saturnalian advice (again ostensibly derived from a Stoic source) to his master. The implications of these satiric resonances are complex and, we might even conclude, potentially destabilising for Seneca's Stoic project.

First, however, let us consider some more general parallels between Horatian satire and the *Epistulae Morales*. Horace's father, he claims in his first satire, offered moral guidance to his son in what might be seen as a characteristically Roman manner: *ut fugerem exemplis vitiorum quaeque notando*, 'to enable me to steer clear of follies, he would brand them, one by one, by reference to examples' (S. 1.4.106).[9] This practice Horace himself follows, to a degree at least, in writing his satires. Indeed, the three passages from Horace's *Satires* cited explicitly in Seneca's letters offer instances of such examples, such as (exemplifying those who, to avoid offending in one way, adopt an equally offensive remedy) *pastillos*

---

ire, which explicitly positions itself as Menippean, is that of the emperor Julian, the *Caesars*, set during the Saturnalia.

6 In *Rabelais and his World* (1968), esp. 6–8, 26–27. Bakhtin's approach and its usefulness in relation to Roman texts is well discussed by P. A. Miller 2012.
7 Freudenburg 2001, 114. Cf. Freudenburg 1993, 211–235; Gowers 1993, 133–136, 159–160; [P. A.] Miller 2012.
8 On the Saturnalian associations of Hor. S. 2.4, whose elaborate and richly detailed prescriptions on how to eat well also satirise didactic philosophy, see Gowers 1993a, 135.
9 On the use of examples within Roman moralising tradition, see Roller 2004.

Buccillus olet, 'Bucillus stinks of breath-mints' (quoted at Ep. 86.13).[10] Yet Horace's *Satires* offer an idiosyncratic take on exemplarity, engaging with a range of philosophical doctrines and problematising traditional Roman moralising practice; Horace himself often features as a key *exemplum* of the failings that appear to be under attack.[11]

Seneca in his letters also makes much of the importance of using examples to highlight vices. *Exempla,* he asserts, are superior to *praecepta* as a vehicle for moral instruction (Ep. 6.5). The letters are full of vividly realised portraits of moral failings, such as those of the decadent aristocrat Pacuvius in Ep. 12 or the wealthy freedman Calvisius in Ep. 27.[12] While in these respects, Seneca's writing, like that of Horace, draws on traditional Roman moralising, the self-reflexivity of both these texts is marked; just as Horace in his *Satires* often addresses admonitions to himself (or puts words of criticism in the mouths of others), Seneca also frequently serves as his own addressee: *haec mecum loquor, sed tecum quoque me locutum puta,* 'I say this to myself but imagine me saying it to you, too' (Ep. 26.7). More often than not, indeed, it is Seneca himself who is made to exemplify a flaw that needs remedying.[13]

Seneca's letters deploy a wide range of registers, at different times intimate, hectoring, poignant, humorous, and, especially later in the series (124 letters survive), rigorously philosophical. Yet conversational advice is perhaps their dominant mode.[14] Seneca often imagines, or indeed claims to quote, the words of his correspondent Lucilius. Indeed he comments in Ep. 75.1: 'I prefer that my letters should be just what my conversation would be if you and I were sitting together,' *qualis sermo meus esset, si una desideremus... tales esse epistulas meas volo.* The analogy with conversation is often invoked by ancient critics analysing letters as

---

10 The phrase adapts the first part of Hor. S. 1.2.27 *pastillos Rufillus olet, Gargonius hircum,* a line which Horace himself repeats at 1.4.92, summing up his own practice; it thus, in Henderson's words, 'stands as a one-line essence of Horatian satire.' The name 'Rufillus' is changed by Seneca to 'Buccillus,' evoking the *bucca,* loud-mouth or puffed cheek, associated with satire (Hor. S. 1.1.20–21, Henderson 2004, 117). Seneca also quotes Hor. S. 1.2.114–116 in Ep. 119.13–14 (discussed below) and Hor. S. 1.3.11–17 in Ep. 120.20–21.
11 Their complexity is well emphasised in Gowers's 2012 edition of Book 1.
12 Whose satiric qualities are noted by M. Wilson 2001, 175–176.
13 Notable examples include 56.15, 63.14–16, 87.1–7. As Jones argues (focusing particularly on Ep. 87), scholars' preoccupation with Seneca's hypocrisy (still evident e. g. in E. Wilson 2014) can be seen as a misconstrual of the performance of moral weakness which is necessarily entailed by the project of personal letters composed by a would-be Stoic (2014).
14 Recent introductions to the letters include M. Wilson 2001; Ker 2009a, 147–176; Berno 2011a; Edwards 2015.

a literary form.¹⁵ Horace, we might note, underlining the varied, polyphonous, colloquial nature of his satires, refers to them also as *sermones* (Ep. 2.1.250). Though Seneca rarely quotes Horace in the *Epistulae*, the extent of his implicit engagement with Horace's work, notably the *Odes*, has been underlined by Berthet and, more recently, (particularly in relation to Ep. 12) by Berno.¹⁶ Aspects of the relationship between Seneca's *Epistulae Morales* and Horace's *Satires* in the context of the diatribe tradition and Cynicism are suggestively explored by Del Giovane.¹⁷ It is striking that the three direct quotations from Horace in the *Epistulae Morales* all come from the *Satires*.¹⁸ Horace the moralist seems to come to the fore here; yet the complexity of Horace's *Satires* may mean that Horace turns out to be a rather ambiguous precedent for Seneca.

Seneca's Ep. 18 starts with a reference to the time of year, *December est mensis*, 'the month is December,' a deceptively simple opening. Such a comment on the season is rare in the *Letters*, and not to be taken literally – or at least, we should be aware that any reference of this kind always has a moral point, as Seneca himself underlines (Ep. 23.1).¹⁹ The season, more specifically, is that of the Saturnalia: *ius luxuriae publice datum est*, 'licence is explicitly given to self-indulgence' (Ep. 18.1). This festival, Seneca protests, once restricted to a few days, has now taken over the whole month.²⁰ Indeed, in his view, the whole year has become one long frenzy of Saturnalian excess (*olim mensem... nunc annum*). This comment surely recalls his own characterisation of the reign of the emperor Claudius in the *Apocolocyntosis* (8), quoted above.²¹ Despite the winter season, the whole city, it seems, is in a sweat: *cum maxime civitas sudat* (Ep. 18.1).

Seneca's Ep. 18 opens, then, in tones of satiric indignation, in keeping with its Saturnalian setting. Yet if, in some respects, the Saturnalia seems to rule all

---

15 E. g. Lib. *De forma epistolari* 2: 'a letter is a kind of written conversation'; cf. Ps.-Demetr. *De elocutione* 223.
16 Berthet 1979, Berno 2014. See also Mazzoli 1970, 233–238. For an acute analysis of Seneca's engagement with Horace in Ep. 86, see Henderson 2004, 117–118.
17 Del Giovane 2015b. Cf. also Del Giovane's essay in this volume.
18 See note 10 above.
19 Cf. Ep. 67.1. At Ep. 23.1, Seneca dismisses references to the weather as *ineptiae* except where they are used as a point of departure for philosophical argument (Griffin 1992, 3–4).
20 Augustus had responded to complaints about the increasing number of days devoted to the Saturnalia by limiting the festivities to three days, a restriction that was short-lived (Macrob. 1.10.23–24). Claudius extended the limit to five days (Dio 60.25.8), again failing to contain the celebrations.
21 For the idea of perpetual Saturnalia to convey unconstrained indulgence, see also Petr. 44.4.

year round, the festival itself offers particular challenges to the would-be philosopher. Thus Seneca says to his correspondent Lucilius:

> Si te hic haberem, libenter tecum conferrem quid existimares esse faciendum, utrum nihil ex cotidiana consuetudine movendum an, ne dissidere videremur cum publicis moribus, et hilarius cenandum et exuendam togam.
>
> If I had you with me, I should be glad to consult you and find out what you think should be done – whether we ought to keep our daily routine the same, or whether, in order not to be out of sympathy with the ways of the people, we should dine in jollier fashion and leave off the toga.
> (Ep. 18.2)

Seneca proposes here two possible options for the would-be wise man during the festival. Lucilius, his correspondent, is imagined advocating the latter possibility ('If I know you well, *you* would advise that we should neither resemble the crowd in all things nor mark ourselves out as different in every respect...' cf. Ep. 18.3). This course of action is praised as indicative of *temperantia*, 'moderation,' a term of central importance in Academic, as well as Stoic, philosophy; such an approach, indeed, might seem wholly consonant with that of Horace's *Satires*.[22] More generally, the earlier letters in Seneca's collection acknowledge that extreme withdrawal from the norm can have dangers; Ep. 5.1, advocating *temperantia*, notes that to mark oneself out conspicuously from the crowd may provoke hostility.[23] In Ep. 18, Seneca himself, while observing that *hoc multo fortius est, ebrio ac vomitante populo siccum et sobrium esse*, 'It shows much more courage to remain dry and sober when the mob is drunk and vomiting' (Ep. 18.4), concedes that greater *temperantia* is shown when one does as the crowd does but in a different way. 'One may keep holiday without extravagance,' *licet enim sine luxuria agere festum diem* (Ep. 18.4).

Seneca goes on to suggest, however, a further possibility, that Lucilius should adopt a new practice, one very far removed from Saturnalian excess:

---

[22] E.g. S. 1.1.92–94 (moderation in the use of wealth), 1.2.24–28 (sexual moderation), 2.2.65–66 (moderation in diet); cf. Carm. 2.16.37–40. For the Academic association, see Cic. Tusc. 3.16.3.
[23] Ep. 5.2 *asperum cultum et intonsum caput et neglegentiorem barbam et indictum argento odium et cubile humi positum, et quicquid aliud ambitionem perversa via sequitur evita*. 'A rough appearance, a shaggy head, an unkempt beard and a marked aversion to silver and a bed placed on the ground and whatever else pursues self-display by perverse means, avoid.' Cf. Ep. 14.14 *non conturbabit sapiens publicos mores nec populum in se vitae novitate convertet*, 'the wise man will not upset common custom, nor will he attract popular attention through the novelty of his way of life.'

> Interponas aliquot dies quibus contentus minimo ac vilissimo cibo, dura atque horrida veste dicas tibi 'hoc est quod timebatur?'
>
> Set aside a certain number of days, during which you shall be content with the most meagre and cheap food, with coarse and rough clothing, and say to yourself: 'Is this the condition that I was afraid of?'
> (Ep. 18.5)

This will be a strenuous and demanding project, more taxing than simply remaining *siccus et sobrius*. To overcome one's fear of poverty by accustoming oneself to the basic minimum is to win *securitas*, a key goal for the would-be wise man.[24] Developing the ability to be satisfied with coarse bread Seneca presents, in a later letter (Ep. 123.1–3), as emblematic of such *securitas*.[25] Wealth and its trappings are matters of indifference for the Stoic; happiness depends on virtue alone. Seneca underlines that this exercise is not meant to be conspicuous; it is not playing at poverty, Marie-Antoinette style. Thus it is to be distinguished from the Timonesque picnics practised by those who want a diversion from the monotony of wealth (Ep. 18.7)[26] – or indeed by those who like to parade their philosophical pretensions. This is not a game (*lusus*), but an exercise or trial (*experimentum*).[27]

In Ep. 18, the impression one makes on others is no longer a concern (in contrast to the preoccupations of Ep. 5). Whether Seneca intends that this period of abstinence should coincide with the festival of the Saturnalia is not altogether clear (though this does seem to be the implication of his insistence in Ep. 18.3 that it is a particular mark of *firmitas* to abstain from pleasure 'on these days above all,' *his maxime diebus*). We might note, however, that while the festival often involved the laying down of elaborate rules for extended feasts, it was also associated with the transgression of normal practice with regard to eating (such as joke food, particularly).[28] Given that the Saturnalia is often character-

---

[24] The letters which comprise Book 2 (13–21) return repeatedly to the fear of poverty and how it is to be overcome. Ep. 17 stressed at length the ways in which property might distract the would-be wise man from philosophy, while poverty by contrast is *expedita* and *secura* (Ep. 17.3). The would-be wise man should be either *pauper* or *pauperi similis* (Ep. 17.5), practising a *frugalitas* which is *paupertas voluntaria*. At Ep. 20.12, Seneca asserts that the rehearsal of poverty can make the real thing *iucundum*. On this kind of spiritual exercise, see Newman 1989. For the influence of the Cynic tradition, see Del Giovane 2016, 247–248.
[25] See Inwood ad loc. On restricting one's diet see also Ep. 108.15–16, 110.18.
[26] Cf. Ep. 100.6 and Martial 3.48, Gowers 1993a, 18.
[27] The military associations of such repeated exercises are developed at Ep. 18.8. On Seneca's use of military imagery, see Lavery 1980, Galimberti 2001, Sommer 2001.
[28] See Gowers 1993a, 17, 71–72, 133–136.

ised by reversals, this embracing of extreme abstinence could itself be read as a Saturnalian move.

In taking as an example Epicurus's experiments with basic diet, as Seneca goes on to do (Ep. 18.9–10), the letter returns us to the question of pleasure, *voluptas*, so often a focus of the early books in the series. In strong contrast to those seeking gross pleasure in the messy excesses of Saturnalian revelry alluded to earlier in Ep. 18, Epicurus is described extracting finely calibrated pleasure from the minimal satisfaction of bodily needs, boasting that he can manage on half an *as* worth of food a day, in contrast to his less advanced associate Metrodorus, who requires a full *as*. Seneca here fully endorses the pursuit of this kind of minimalist pleasure.[29] To convey the experience of pared down contentment which is the goal of his ascetic exercise, Seneca uses the terms *satur* (Ep. 18.7) and *saturitas* (Ep. 18.10), paradoxically evoking the excess of satire and indeed Saturnalia.[30] A quotation from Virgil *Aeneid* 8 (the words of Evander, inviting Aeneas into his simple home, 8.364–365) lends authoritative epic endorsement to frugal living and marks another shift of register.[31] Yet satiric concerns also remain in play. The moderation of appetite – and the provision of humble hospitality – themselves frequently figure in Horatian satire (examples will be discussed below).

The conclusion of Ep. 18 changes focus to address the dangers of anger and the importance of mental *sanitas*.[32] We have moved from the sweaty bustle of the Saturnalia via the competitive asceticism of Epicurus to the torrid heat of the passions. Temporal patterns are significant in this letter; the monthly practice of the inverse Saturnalia advocated for the *proficiens* is a mirror image in miniature of the annual celebration of the traditional festival, which itself is translated from an overblown month of celebration into a metaphor for licentious living

---

[29] For Epicurus's comments on the pleasure of satisfying one's appetite with the barest minimum, see Ep. Men. 130–131. On Seneca's engagement with Epicurus, particularly in the earlier books of the letters, see Schiesaro 2015. Later letters, e.g. Ep. 90.35, are much more critical of the central role of *voluptas* in Epicurean philosophy.

[30] Isid. Orig. 20.1.8 observes: *saturitas... a satura nomen accepit, quod est vario alimentorum adparatur compositum*. Seneca uses the term to convey the excess of the gourmand at Ep. 119.14 (quoted below). For Horace's use of the term *satur* see note 36 below.

[31] It is perhaps relevant, as Martin Stöckinger points out to me, that Evander concludes his previous speech by showing Aeneas the Arx Saturnia (Verg. A. 8.357–358: '... *hanc Ianus pater, hanc Saturnus condidit arcem | Ianiculum huic, illi fuerat Saturnia nomen*,' 'This fort father Janus founded, that one Saturn; this one was named Janiculum, that one Saturnia').

[32] A return to the concern with the health of the *animus* which dominates the opening of Ep.15; cf. Ep. 17.7.

all year round. Yet just as the Saturnalia may become a permanent state, so too, as the letters often remind us, may extreme poverty.[33]

But let us consider further the relation of this letter to the concerns of Horatian satire. There are some significant contrasts, of course. The second satire in Horace's Book 2 also explores the advantages of accustoming oneself to a simple diet, with strenuous exercise serving as stimulus to the appetite. But in Seneca's Ep. 18 the diet itself has become the exercise. Horace's farmer Ofellus, the dominant voice in S. 2.2, praises the economical and health-giving properties of simple, home-grown food (as opposed to imported luxury).[34] He notes, however, that the practice of restraint may be enlivened by occasional indulgence when holidays come:

> ...ad melius poterit transcurrere quondam,
> sive diem festum rediens advexerit annus
>
> ...Yet at times he will be able to turn to better fare, when the revolving year has brought some holiday.
> (S. 2.2.84–85)

There is no anxiety here about celebrating the Saturnalia. And Horace's rustic philosopher has criticism, also, for those who live too meanly: *sordidus a tenui victu distabit*, 'a mean style of living will differ from a simple one' (S. 2.2.53); his *sapiens* will be *in neutram partem cultus miser*, 'in his mode of living unhappy in neither direction' (S. 2.2.66). Extremes, here as elsewhere in Horace, are to be avoided. Importantly, wealth is a positive good, which may be spent well (or badly) or saved to serve as security for the future. For the Stoics, by contrast, wealth was simply a matter of indifference, the bleakest poverty no obstacle to living a virtuous and therefore good life. In Seneca's Ep. 18, although a middle way is mooted, in the end a more strenuous path is preferred, one by means of which the fear of poverty may be wholly extirpated.

A particular preoccupation of Horace's *Satires* is the perennial dissatisfaction dogging humankind. Seneca's *Epistulae Morales*, too, return repeatedly to this major source of unhappiness and how it can be tackled.[35] In his program-

---

[33] See e.g. Ep. 47.10.
[34] See also the idealised simple supper of beans and bacon offered at Horace's Sabine farm in S. 2.6.
[35] See e.g. Ep. 15.9; 17.5 *tolle itaque istas excusationes: 'nondum habeo quantum sat est...,'* 'So do away with those excuses: "I haven't yet got enough"'; 19.7; 70.17 *quemadmodum suus finis veniet in mentem omnia sine fine concupiscentibus?*, 'How should they conceive of their own ends when their desires for all things are unlimited?'; 73.2; 74.11 *nec implere nos ulla felicitas potest*, 'No

matic first satire, which begins by posing the question: 'How is it that no one living is content with the lot that either his choice has given him or that fortune has thrown his way?', Horace likens the wise man, one who knows how to be content with life, to a satisfied dinner guest, *conviva satur* (S. 1.1.119).[36] This analogy has strong Epicurean connotations.[37] Lucretius's personified Nature chides one who cannot bear the prospect of death: *cur non ut plenus vitae conviva recedis | aequo animoque capis securam, stulte, quietam?*, 'why not, like a banqueter fed full of life, withdraw with contentment and rest in unworried peace, you fool?' (Lucr. 3.938–939).[38] The sensations of satiety and well-being which follow an evening of food, wine, and conversation serve as a positive model for the concluding phase of a life well-lived.

In Seneca's *Epistulae Morales*, gastronomic imagery is almost always deployed to negative ends; the repellent eating habits of the luxurious feature frequently, in vividly realised detail.[39] Certainly, Seneca's attacks on the corrosive consequences of the pursuit of excess draw on satiric tradition, as we have already seen. In Ep. 119, Seneca quotes (with slight alteration) Horace's S. 1.2:

> Num, tibi cum fauces urit sitis, aurea quaeris
> Pocula? Num esuriens fastidis omnia praeter
> Pavonem rhombumque?
>
> When your jaws are parched by thirst, do you ask for cups of gold? Or when you're starving, do you turn up your nose at everything bar peacock and turbot?
> (S. 1.2.114–116)

---

good fortune can make us feel satisfied'; Armisen-Marchetti 1989, 143–144; Berno 2008, 562–564.

36 *Qui fit, Maecenas, ut nemo, quam tibi sortem | seu ratio dederit, seu fors obiecerit, illa | contentus vivat...?* Hor. S. 1.1.1–3. Gowers ad loc. comments, '*conviva satur* also covertly labels the genre H. is writing in.'

37 As Cicero makes clear, Tusc. 5.118. The sentiment is also associated with Bion of Borysthenes, a contemporary of Epicurus, known for his rousing diatribes (Kindstrand 1976, 281–282). A similar comment is also attributed to the Stoic Chrysippus; see SVF III 768, ἔοικε γάρ, φησιν, ὁ βίος μακρῷ συμποσίῳ.

38 *Satur* in Horace's line (as Gowers notes ad loc.) also evokes Lucretius 3.959–960, *ante | quam satur et plenus possis discedere rerum?*, 'before you can withdraw glutted and having taken your fill of things?' These passages are suggestively analysed, in relation particularly to Sen. Ep. 61.4 (*mortem plenus expecto*), by Berno (2008).

39 E.g. Ep. 47.2, 78.23–24, 83.24, 95.23–29, 122.3–4. Consumption and digestion occasionally have more positive associations, as in the analogy of the bees in Ep. 84.3–4, though their behaviour is far removed from that of insatiable humans.

Seneca then comments:

> Infelicis luxuriae ista tormenta sunt: quaerit quemadmodum post saturitatem quoque esuriat, quemadmodum non impleat ventrem sed farciat, quemadmodum sitim prima potione sedatam revocat.
>
> These are the torments of unhappy luxury; it seeks the means by which, though satisfied, it may still be hungry, the means by which it may stuff the stomach rather than fill it, the means by which thirst, assuaged with the first gulp, may be revived.
> (Ep. 119.14)

The luxurious, compelled to pursue excess, are repeatedly nauseated by surfeit. A vicious circle of deluded desires and frenzied attempts to satisfy those desires generates only wretchedness. Here, too, the gastronomic model has purchase in other spheres, notably those of material wealth and political ambition. It is part of the perverse human condition always to want more, a condition that cries out to be remedied by philosophy.

Only the *sapiens*, for Seneca, is wholly satisfied with life. A passage from his *De Beneficiis* (5.17.5–7), advising that satisfaction may be gained from being grateful for the pleasures one has experienced (*gratum adversus perceptas voluptates*), has a somewhat Epicurean flavour.[40] Yet, as Berno underlines, while Seneca exploits the idea of *satietas* in characterising the proper approach to living and dying, he does so without invoking the more specific associations of eating.[41] Lucretius's phrase *plenus vitae*, detached from even a metaphorical *convivium*, is now applied to the perfect life of the Stoic sage, from which nothing is lacking; at Ep. 98.15, Seneca observes, *ipse vitae plenus est*, 'he himself has lived a complete life.'[42] Certainly Ep. 18 celebrates the minimalist approach to satisfying bodily appetite exemplified by Epicurus, while later letters parade Seneca's developing ability to be happy with the coarsest bread. Nevertheless, for Seneca, the pleasures of the table ultimately offer not a satisfying analogy

---

[40] Discussed by Berno 2014, 130–131.
[41] Berno 2008, 556. One possible exception to this is Ep. 77.8, where a Stoic philosopher advises the elderly Marcellinus on the proper approach to death; he should persuade his slaves to help him die by giving them gifts, to make clear he recognizes his life had come to an end: ...*non esse inhumanum, quemadmodum cena peracta reliquiae circumstantibus dividantur, sic peracta vita aliquid porrigi iis qui totius vitae ministri fuissent*, 'it was not unnatural, just as when, after a dinner party is over, the remains are divided among the attendants, so when a life is complete, to offer something to those who had given service throughout that life.' Marcellinus's gentle end is then described as *non sine quadam voluptate*, 'not without a certain pleasure' (Ep. 77.9).
[42] Cf. 72.8. This is a kind of materialisation of *sapientia*, as Berno notes (2008, 565).

for, but an insidious threat to, the would-be philosopher's mental tranquillity.[43] The perfect Stoic's state does not truly resemble that of one who has spent an enjoyable evening eating, drinking, and conversing; the refined and pleasurable moderation of Horace's table holds no real attraction for this Stoic.

Yet if Seneca bridles at the Saturnalian feast, the frenzy of play, his engagement with the political dynamics of the festival (particularly as they operate in Horatian satire) is more complex. The more specifically Saturnalian elements in Horace's *Satires* themselves require further probing here. Horace's second book of *Satires* (with the exception of S. 2.6) generally lets others do the talking. Indeed, Book 2 particularly showcases the satirist's willingness to expose himself to Saturnalian abuse.[44] In S. 2.3, the satirist has withdrawn to his Sabine farm to escape the excesses of Saturnalia in the city (*Saturnalibus huc fugisti*, 2.3.5). The poem takes the form of a conversation between the satirist and the assertive voice of Damasippus, a former art-dealer, fallen on hard times, who is a new convert to Stoicism. His presence at Horace's Sabine farm is rather mysterious. Miller suggests he might be seen as Horace's client, and thus, as a member of the household, taking advantage of holiday licence to abuse his betters.[45] Damasippus reproves the satirist, taking him to task for drinking and sleeping too much (*vini somnique benignus*, 2.3.3) – and for failing to write poetry worth talking about (*nil dignum sermone canas*, 2.3.4). All is perhaps not lost, however: 'You have made your escape to this spot and kept yourself sober in the middle of the Saturnalia. So say something worthy of the promises that you made!' (*at ipsis | Saturnalibus huc fugisti sobrius. ergo | dic aliquid dignum promissis*, 2.3.4–6).[46] Yet the satirist is allowed little space to express himself, as Damasippus rushes to offer what he claims is a Stoic critique of vice, quoting at length the Stoic teacher Stertinius (literally 'the Snorer'), who castigates in turn the avaricious, the ambitious, the self-indulgent, and the superstitious.[47]

---

43 As Berno (2008) observes in relation to Seneca's *Thyestes*, the mental satiety Thyestes claims to desire (at *Thy*. 393 *me dulcis saturet quies*, 'sweet quiet satisfies me') is expressed in terms which might evoke more corporeal pleasure – but this serves to anticipate the all too corporeal, viscerally nauseating satiety with which the play will culminate, when Thyestes is tricked by his brother into eating the flesh of his own sons.
44 Gowers 1993a, 159.
45 [P. A.] Miller 2012, 319.
46 [P. A.] Miller 2012, 319, sees the satirist's escape from the Saturnalia as itself a Saturnalian inversion. Normal hierarchies of the simple satiric diatribe are inverted (Freudenburg 2001, 112–114).
47 Damasippus's words dominate the poem: S. 2.3.1–15, 18–26, 27, 30, 31–299, 303–304, 307–323, 323–324, 325.

The satirist himself is then reproved (S. 2.3.307–323) for aping the ways of his superior Maecenas, for writing poetry – and for his bad temper.

While Damasippus takes the role of Stoic moralist here, he emerges as a distinctly flawed character.[48] A bankrupt speculator and art-dealer, he was himself, he claims, only rescued from despair by the philosopher Stertinius. Damasippus's account of Stoic teaching is by no means compelling. This is the longest of Horace's *Satires*; there is a striking contradiction between the temperance Damasippus advocates in relation to food and drink and his profligacy in relation to words, as Gowers has observed.[49] We might perhaps detect an unsettling parallel with Seneca himself, who frequently insists on the importance of limiting one's diet and avoiding wine (most notably at Ep. 108.15–16), but who might himself seem vulnerable to the charge of repetition and writing to excess. In Horace's poem, moreover, it is the satirist who, despite licensing Damasippus's critique, gets the last word, dismissing the soi-disant philosopher Damasippus as himself the more deranged (S. 2.3.325). This is a distinctly unflattering precedent, we might think, for Stoic advice in the context of the Saturnalia.

The role of the slave in the Saturnalian texts of Seneca and Horace also repays attention. For Seneca in Ep. 18, the basic circumstances of the slave's life offer a model the would-be wise man can embrace as a philosophical exercise. He has just proposed as a monthly undertaking a three or four-day period of limited food, a simple pallet to sleep on and a rough cloak to wear:

> Non est tamen quare tu multum tibi facere videaris (facies enim quod multa milia servorum multa milia pauperum faciunt).
>
> There is no reason, however, why you should think you are doing anything major (for you will merely be doing what many thousands of slaves and many thousands of poor men do every day).
> (Ep. 18.8)

Frequently in the letters Seneca presents the material conditions of the slave, but also the slave's total lack of social and political capital, as a bracing image of pared down human possibility.[50] If a slave may attain virtue – and therefore happiness – there is no barrier to anyone else doing the same.

---

48 Probably to be linked to the Damasippus, a dealer in ancient statues mentioned in Cicero's *Letters* (Fam. 7.23 = SB 209, Att. 12.29, 33 = SB 268, 269). On the construction of personae in Horace and Seneca see also the paper by Kirichenko in this volume.
49 Gowers 1993a, 134.
50 See esp. Ep. 80.10, Edwards 2009.

But this is not the only respect in which slavery has a role; the slave is supremely good to think with. The pursuit of bodily *voluptas* associated with the Saturnalia can itself be seen as a manifestation of mental slavishness (in this respect the low pleasures which slaves in particular were licensed to pursue during the festival provided reassuring confirmation to their masters that they were truly suited to their servile status). It was a notorious Stoic paradox that only the wise man is free; all others are slaves.[51] Earlier in the series, Ep. 14 presents the relation between mind and body as properly that of master and slave, thus emphasising how wrong it is to be enslaved to one's bodily appetites: *multis enim serviet, qui corpori servit*, 'he will have many masters who makes his body his master' (Ep. 14.1–2).[52] This is an issue Horace explores at length in S. 2.7.[53] Here the slave Davus is permitted by his master to take advantage of Saturnalian licence to speak freely ('with December liberty,' *libertate Decembri*). Davus uses arguments he attributes to a Stoic philosopher, Crispinus, in order to criticise his master's enslavement to pleasure: *manum stomachumque teneto, | dum quae Crispini docuit me ianitor edo*, 'hold back your hand and temper, while I set forth the lessons taught me by the porter of Crispinus' (S. 2.7.44–45). Crispinus himself, we might note, has already been lampooned earlier in Horace's *Satires* for his uncontrolled and excessive writing. Horace concludes his first satire with the words:

> Iam satis est. ne me Crispini scrinia lippi
> Compilasse putes, verbum non amplius addam.
>
> Well, that's enough. I won't add another word, or you'll think I've been rifling the rolls of bleary-eyed Crispinus.
> (S. 1.1.120–121)

Crispinus's reputation is significant. In S. 1.3, Crispinus exemplifies a variety of failings. He is criticised as an inept stylist, as well as for his advocacy of severe Stoic views (indeed all of Horace's first three satires conclude with a dig at verbose or foolish Stoics).[54] At S. 1.4.13–14, he challenges the satirist to a writing contest but for Crispinus only quantity matters. His own rambling writings are

---

[51] See Cic. Parad. 5.33 *dictum est igitur ab eruditissimis viris nisi sapientem liberum esse neminem*.
[52] Cf. Ep. 90.19, 92.33.
[53] Fitzgerald 2000, 18–24; Oliensis 1998, 52–55; Freudenburg 1993, 223–227. The wisdom of slave advice is also touched on at Hor. S. 2.3.265: *servus non paulo sapientior* – though this mainly serves to highlight the folly of the master, mad in love.
[54] As Gowers (2012, 58) observes.

howling bombast, the antithesis of Horatian elegance and moderation (S. 1.4.19).⁵⁵

Emboldened by Crispinus's teachings, then, Davus chides his master, 'You are the slave of another man's wife' (*te coniunx aliena capit*, S. 2.7.46). Living in fear of being caught by his mistress's husband, the satirist is, Davus insists: 'many times a slave!' (*totiens servus!* S. 2.7.70). At the same time, Davus's master is a slave to his friend and patron Maecenas (S. 2.7.81), ready to drop everything the moment Maecenas summons him.⁵⁶ The only man who is truly free, Davus claims, is the *sapiens*, who fears neither poverty nor death, who is not subservient to his passions, nor to ambition. Such sentiments are entirely in line with Seneca's own advice in the *Epistulae Morales*.⁵⁷ The satirist, however, has no desire to hear these wise words and sharply reminds his slave of the limits to Saturnalian free speech. If Davus doesn't leave him alone, he'll be sent away from Rome to become a labourer on Horace's Sabine farm.

In S. 2.3 and 2.7, the figure of the satirist himself becomes an object of criticism on the occasion of the Saturnalia. In both cases the critique is articulated in Stoic terms but the authority of the critic is also significantly undermined. While the Saturnalian setting of Seneca's Ep. 18 might evoke generally satiric resonances, the Stoic content in Horace S. 2.3 and 2.7 invites us to trace a more particular set of allusions. In evoking these Horatian precedents, Seneca could be seen as highlighting, through contrast, the greater moral seriousness of his own Stoic epistolary project. Yet there are at least some moments when the slippery nature of satiric advice, particularly on the occasion of the Saturnalia, can also appear a destabilising analogue. In Seneca's apparently personal letters, as in Horace's satires, the figure of the author claims authority but also exposes himself to criticism.⁵⁸ The *Epistulae*, like the *Satires*, if not to quite the same extent, open up space for a variety of voices, the supportive friend, the querulous invalid, the old-fashioned moralist, the self-aggrandising litterateur – and the mordant satirist, as well as the aspirant Stoic.⁵⁹ The Stoic voices in Horace offer moral guidance, which bears a notable similarity to that conveyed by Seneca himself, but these speakers are also explicitly mocked for their excessive seriousness, for their own moral flaws – and for their prolixity. Might we detect some element of self-mockery in Seneca's Saturnalian allusion? Was he perhaps even teased in the literary circles of Neronian Rome for his resemblance to Horace's Dama-

---

55 Freudenburg 1993, 112–113.
56 On this aspect of S. 2.7, see Fitzgerald 2000, 18–24.
57 Most obviously Ep. 47. See Edwards 2009.
58 Above note 13.
59 Edwards 1997.

sippus or Crispinus?⁶⁰ Even at his most seriously philosophical Stoic Seneca, perhaps, cannot altogether escape the railing of satirist Seneca. If this is another facet of Seneca's performance of his own failings – the self as an example – it is one particularly fraught with risk.

And what of the slave status of Davus, who self-deprecatingly channels Stoic sentiment in Horace S. 2.7? The slave, given rare licence to speak freely during the Saturnalia, might seem a far cry from the senator, now devoted in his retirement to philosophy in the serviced comfort of his own villa. As I have been arguing, however, the satirical elements in the letters are conspicuous and, as Freudenburg suggestively comments: 'To play the part of the satirist is to play the part of slave, parasite, lowlife.'⁶¹ In contrast to the words of Horace's Davus, Seneca's advice in Ep. 18 is mostly *in propria persona* (though with comments putatively attributed to his correspondent Lucilius and a quotation from Epicurus). Slavery, often deployed as an analogy for relations between Rome and her conquered subjects, as well as for relations between emperors and the senate, serves many purposes in Roman texts of the early principate.⁶² In Stoic thought, all of humanity, with the exception of the Stoic sage, could be characterised as fools – and as slaves, as was noted above. Seneca, often disposed to slip between the figural and the literal, engages, at least occasionally, with the perspective of actual slaves.⁶³ Seneca's Ep. 47 reflects at length on master | slave relations, inviting the reader to sympathise with the slave's position. In this letter, the Saturnalia, at least as it is imagined to have been in the distant past with masters and slaves at table together, is held up as a positive model (Ep. 47.14). Reprehensible masters, by contrast, (a type more characteristic of Seneca's own time, it seems), immersed in the pleasures of the flesh – and wholly insensitive to the humanity of their attendant slaves, forbidding them even to speak (Ep. 47.3–4) – are described as enslaved to their passions (Ep. 47.17). First person plural verbs implicate Seneca and his readers here (Ep. 47.5, *tamquam iumentis abutimur... cum ad cenandum discubuimus*, 'we abuse them as if they were animals... when we have taken our places for a dinner'). Instead Seneca ad-

---

60 Tacitus (Ann. 14.52) comments on the resentment generated by Seneca's literary influence at Nero's court. Sullivan (1985a, 174–175) interprets elements of Petronius's *Satyricon* as a response to the 'philosophical posturing' and 'stylistic exuberance' of Seneca, seeing Ep. 47 (on which see below) as a particular target in section 70.10. There are also echoes of Sen. Ep. 86.4 at Petr. 73.2.
61 Freudenburg 1993, 214. As Fitzgerald (2000, 18) points out, comments made by Davus in S. 2.7 echo Horace's observations *in propria persona* in S. 1.2. Oliensis (1998, 51–63) explores more generally how the satirists of Book 2 satirise the satirist of Book 1.
62 Fitzgerald 2000, Lavan 2011.
63 Edwards 2009.

vocates conversation with one's slaves – at least, if they are of good character (Ep. 47.15–16).[64]

In advocating humane treatment of slaves, Seneca warns that masters often behave toward them as kings do toward their subjects, raging at them quite unnecessarily; slaves (like subjects...?) are, after all, powerless (Ep. 47.19–20). Some scholars have suggested that Nero himself should be seen as the primary addressee of Seneca's *Epistulae Morales*.[65] The letters are surely aimed at readers more readily disposed to pursue a course of philosophical self-improvement than Nero seems to have been. Yet there are many moments when the nightmarish atmosphere of Nero's court, for so many years the central focus of Seneca's life, seems to inflect (if only implicitly, for Nero is never mentioned) a train of thought or an image.[66]

Despite the optimism of the *Apocolocyntosis*, the unpredictable autocrat Nero (whom Seneca served for many years as tutor and then advisor) could also, like his adoptive father Claudius, be viewed as a *Saturnalicius princeps* – and not only because of his improper relations with his freedmen (a feature of the latter part of his reign). Tacitus (*Annals* 13.15) describes how, in the course of a Saturnalian party soon after his accession in 54 CE, the lot fell to Nero to be master of the revels; he exploited the opportunity to humiliate Britannicus (Claudius's son, whom Nero had displaced as heir). This was an awkward coincidence of the supposedly temporary *regnum* of the Saturnalian lord of misrule with the all too permanent autocratic power of the emperor. The attempt backfired as Britannicus, the underdog, deployed Saturnalian licence to criticise Nero. Yet ultimately this was to have fatal consequences for Britannicus himself. For the subaltern, at least, Saturnalian licence was strictly limited.

Nero's reign was, it seems, a riot of licentious pleasure-seeking; game-playing, disguise, and status inversion are recurrent motifs in later accounts.[67] In pursuit of his own uninhibited pleasure, Nero is said to have roamed the streets in disguise, sporting a *pilleus*, the freedman's cap particularly associated with the suspension of normal constraints on behaviour during the Saturnalia.[68] Like Claudius, Nero was seen as too close to his own freedmen; rumours circulated

---

[64] As Bradley underlines (1994, 135–145) Stoic discussions of slavery, including Seneca's comments here, are primarily concerned with the moral health of slave owners. Nevertheless such Stoic advice may have brought incidental benefits to actual slaves.
[65] Too 1994.
[66] Edwards 2017 (forthcoming).
[67] On the historiography of Nero's reign, see Elsner / Masters 1994, Bartsch / Freudenburg / Littlewood 2017 (forthcoming).
[68] Suet. Nero 26.

that Nero had celebrated a marriage ceremony with one of them, himself playing the role of the bride – inverting every conceivable norm of gender and status.[69] This licence – figuratively but not temporally Saturnalian – was not extended to Nero's critics, as Britannicus's fate had already made clear. It was on Nero's death the Roman people would later celebrate their own Saturnalian freedom, wearing the *pilleus* (according to Suetonius, Nero 57) to symbolise their liberation from servitude.[70] The author of the *Apocolocyntosis* was all too soon well aware of his own subservient status at the court of this new *Saturnalicius princeps*. As Nero's subject, Seneca may well have regarded his own freedom of speech as no less constrained than that of Horace's Davus, whose master mocks his Stoic advice and threatens to banish him to the fields. As the author of the *Epistulae Morales*, however, he, like the Horatian satirist, can still have the last word.

---

69 Suet. Nero 29 gives his name as Doryphorus, while Tacitus (Ann. 15.38), dating the event to 64 CE, refers to him as Pythagoras. Champlin 2003, discussing this particular episode at pp. 160–171, uses the Saturnalia as his lens in Chapter 6 of his suggestive analysis of Nero's reign.
70 Though Suetonius also reports that others mourned him (Nero 57). Tacitus suggests it was the lower and more pleasure-seeking sort (the *plebs sordida*), who remembered him fondly (Hist. 1.4).

II Horatian Verse in Senecan Tragedy

Richard Tarrant
Custode rerum Caesare: Horatian Civic Engagement and the Senecan Tragic Chorus

This paper falls into two main sections, which proceed in inverse order to my subtitle. The first section focuses on the Senecan tragic chorus and its curious relationship to the action of the play. Here I argue that the disjunction that is sometimes visible between the perspective of the protagonists (who often represent ruler figures) and that of the chorus (who often represent their subjects) is a deliberate choice by Seneca, and that it reflects the position of the Roman people in an imperial environment. In the second section, I contrast Seneca's dramatic portrayal of the relationship between ruler (actor) and ruled (chorus) with that presented by Horace in the *Odes*, which rests on trust in a ruler whose actions are both knowable and reliably benevolent. In a brief closing section, I suggest that in depicting the place of the individual in his tragic world Seneca looks back to and rejects the Horatian model of *aurea mediocritas*.

Seneca's choruses perform many of the same functions as the chorus of Greek tragedy. They both deliver scene-dividing lyric compositions and engage with the actors in the dialogue portions of the play. That fact is in itself significant, since it would appear that Seneca had a range of available options for the role of the chorus. There was the chorus of Greek New Comedy, which was restricted to performing interludes between the acts, or the chorus of Roman Republican tragedy, which seems to have done the opposite, taking part in the action but not providing choral songs between the acts.[1] The meager fragments of Augustan tragedy, which I have argued was probably the strongest influence on the form of Senecan tragedy,[2] do not give us a clear picture of the role of the chorus, but two fragments of Varius are in anapaestic metre, which suggests a choral song.[3] Finally, if the *Phoenissae* is complete as it stands—which seems to me at least possible—Seneca could conceive of a tragedy with no chorus. If, therefore,

---

1 Manuwald 2011, 74: 'Many tragedies and some praetextae... had choruses. These choruses did not provide choral interludes, but were rather integrated into the action.' A more detailed study of the chorus in Republican tragedy is forthcoming from Tobias Allendorf, who argues for a closer connection between Republican tragedy and Seneca in this regard than has often been posited.
2 Tarrant 1978, 258–263.
3 Ribbeck *inc. fab. fr.* 1 and 2.

DOI 10.1515/9783110528893-005

Seneca normally gave the chorus a role at least outwardly similar to that of its Greek counterpart, he did so as a matter of choice rather than of generic compulsion.

But while the chorus of Senecan tragedy may seem to resemble its Greek predecessor, its relationship to the tragic action is significantly different. The Greek chorus typically provides the audience with a larger context in which to interpret the action of the play, while the Senecan chorus often demonstrates the inadequacy or absence of such an interpretative framework. What is more, the Senecan chorus is often unable to interpret the surrounding action because it lacks knowledge of what is really happening.

Let me be clear that I do not regard this difference as in any way implying decline or inferiority on Seneca's part. Instead I am suggesting that the ignorance of the chorus in Seneca is an essential aspect of its role and is itself a powerful component of the plays' overall impact.[4]

In Greek tragedy, once the chorus has entered the orchestra it remains there for the duration of the play; if the presence of the chorus would impede the stage action, the dramatist must give some reason for the chorus to withdraw and then return, as Sophocles does in the *Ajax*. Senecan practice is quite different. Characters often engage in discussions that would have to provoke a response from the chorus if it were present, but no response is forthcoming and no explanation is provided for the chorus's failure to react. A notable example is the second choral song of the *Thyestes*, which opens as follows (336–338):

> Tandem regia nobilis,
> antiqui genus Inachi,
> fratrum composuit minas.
>
> At last this famed royal house,
> issue of ancient Inachus,
> has settled the brothers' threats.[5]

After a long scene in which Atreus plots in considerable detail with a subordinate the revenge he will take on his brother, the ode that immediately follows is predicated on the false belief that Atreus intends to be reconciled with Thyestes. In this case the chorus is not simply ignorant of the truth, but has somehow been given a false account of the situation. Another example comes

---

[4] Kirichenko 2013, 253–255 sees the chorus's fluctuating relationship to the action and its occasional misapprehension as contributing to the plays' character as 'instructive deceptions' (lehrreiche Trugbilder).
[5] Translations of passages of Senecan tragedy are from Fitch 2002, 2004.

in the *Medea*, following the extended necromancy scene. While Medea has not yet hit upon the idea of killing her children to get revenge on Jason, she has elaborately prepared to send a poisoned garment to Jason's new wife. And yet the chorus wonders what crime she may be plotting (849–852):

> Quonam cruenta maenas
> praeceps amore saevo
> rapitur? quod impotenti
> facinus parat furore?
>
> Where is the bloodstained maenad
> being driven impetuously
> by savage love? What crime
> is she planning in uncurbed fury?

It is true that the Greek tragic chorus often fails fully to comprehend the action of which it is a part. A notable example is the brief ode (1086–1109) sung by the chorus of Sophocles's *Oedipus Tyrannus* immediately before the entrance of the shepherd who will reveal that Oedipus is the son of Laius. The chorus's optimistic speculations about Oedipus's origins are painfully misguided—as both Jocasta and the audience know—but their ignorance is shared by Oedipus himself. The ignorance displayed by the Senecan chorus in the cases I have noted is of a more fundamental character.

One might be tempted to explain the limited awareness shown by the Senecan chorus by supposing that the chorus left the stage after each of its songs and was therefore not present during the iambic portions. But matters are more complicated, since the same chorus can be closely involved in the action at one point and completely dissociated from it at another. In the *Troades*, for example, the chorus's first song (67–163) is a *kommos*-like exchange with Hecuba, but its next lyric (371–408), following the Messenger's report of Achilles's ghost and the debate between Agamemnon and Pyrrhus, shows no knowledge of those events: the chorus denies the existence of an afterlife even though the appearance of Achilles's shade would suggest otherwise, and it does not react to the news that both Polyxena and Astyanax are to be killed to allow the Greeks to sail home. There is also the fact that in every Senecan tragedy (except, of course, *Phoenissae*) the chorus participates as a speaker in at least some of the iambic portions of the play.

In using language such as 'leave the stage' I do not mean to take a position on the much discussed (and perhaps now rather tired) question of the performance or non-performance of Senecan tragedy.[6] While the movements of a chorus would certainly be more evident in a staged production than in a recitation, and conversely the shifting relationship of the chorus to the action would be easier to accept in a recitation than on stage, the frequent disjunction between the chorus's knowledge and the actual events of a play would be evident no matter in what form the play was presented.

I turn now to another detail of Seneca's handling of the chorus that marks a clear difference from regular Greek practice: while almost all the extant tragedies of Sophocles and Euripides end with a choral statement, no genuine tragedy of Seneca has a choral conclusion. That fact has often been noted, but to my knowledge its potential significance has not been explored.

First a word about the Greek examples. In Sophocles and Euripides they are short and gnomic. As examples I cite the end of Sophocles's *Ajax* and the lines found in the same form at the end of four Euripidean tragedies.

Sophocles, *Ajax* 1418–1420:

ἦ πολλὰ βροτοῖς ἔστιν ἰδοῦσιν
γνῶναι· πρὶν ἰδεῖν δ' οὐδεὶς μάντις
τῶν μελλόντων ὅ τι πράξει.

Mortals may know many things
when they have seen them; but before seeing,
no-one is prophet of how he will fare in future.

Final lines of Euripides's *Alcestis, Andromache, Helen,* and *Bacchae:*

πολλαὶ μορφαὶ τῶν δαιμονίων,
πολλὰ δ' ἀέλπτως κραίνουσι θεοί·
καὶ τὰ δοκηθέντ' οὐκ ἐτελέσθη,
τῶν δ' ἀδοκήτων πόρον ηὗρε θεός.
τοιόνδ' ἀπέβη τόδε πρᾶγμα.

---

6 G. W. M. Harrison 2000 is a useful collection of essays representing all viewpoints, and Harrison and Liapis 2013 provides a clear and fair-minded summary. The most recent contribution, Kohn 2013, is firmly on the side of stage performance, and includes a complete set of stage directions for each tragedy. My own views on this issue have not remained fixed. The same year I began to work on Seneca's *Agamemnon* as a graduate student (1966) saw the publication of the fullest case yet made against stage production and in favour of recitation, Otto Zwierlein's *Die Rezitationsdramen Senecas*. At the time I found Zwierlein's arguments compelling and still feel that they have considerable weight, but in recent years I have become less dogmatic on the matter and now tend to a position of agnosticism: we cannot know how Seneca's plays were originally presented, and nothing rules out the possibility that some or all of them were given a stage performance of some kind.

> Many are the shapes of what the gods send,
> the gods accomplish many things contrary to our hopes;
> that which is looked for is not fulfilled,
> but god finds a way for the unexpected.
> Such was the outcome of this matter.

Now no-one would claim that these are profound or original sentiments, and accordingly the choral conclusions are often written off as perfunctory tags; in some cases even their authenticity has been questioned. But Deborah Roberts convincingly argues that the choral endings of Greek tragedy perform an important closural function, in marking the boundary that separates the world of the play from the world of ongoing life. In itself that would make them analogous to seeing the words THE END come onto the screen at the conclusion of a film, but as Roberts also notes, these endings also situate the action of the play within a larger context and hint (albeit in a rudimentary way) at a means of understanding that action.[7]

Against that background the absence of any choral endings in the genuine Senecan tragedies assumes potential significance: one might infer that Seneca did not want to provide a sense of closure to the tragic action and that he did not choose to suggest a broader framework for interpreting that action.

That line of argument receives some support from the fact that the two plays that have been attributed to Seneca but that are probably or definitely not his work, the *Hercules Oetaeus* and the *Octavia*, both end with a choral statement. For the sake of brevity I will assume that the *Hercules Oetaeus* is not the work of Seneca. The point is still disputed, but to my mind the numerous examples of borrowings from the genuine plays that do not fit their new surroundings are sufficient proof of non-Senecan authorship.[8] Furthermore, most scholars who believe that Seneca did have a hand in the *Hercules Oetaeus* restrict his involvement to roughly the first third of the play (lines 1–705); there is general agreement that the end of the play, the part relevant for my argument, is not by Seneca.

In the *Hercules Oetaeus* the chorus have a short concluding song, hailing the apotheosis of Hercules and praying for his continuing protection against new sources of fear. These are the opening lines (1983–1988):

---

7 Roberts 1987.
8 The cases adduced by Axelson 1967 are not all equally persuasive, but many do seem to withstand scrutiny. Two particularly telling examples are Her. O. 867–869 (modeled on Oed. 1036–1039) and Her. O. 991–994 (an inept reworking of Ag. 972–975). For discussion see Axelson 1967, 92–94.

> CHO. Numquam Stygias fertur ad umbras
> inclita virtus: vivite fortes
> nec Lethaeos saeva per antros
> vos fata trahent,
> sed cum summas exiget horas
> consumpta dies,
> iter ad superos gloria pandet.
>
> Never does glorious valour pass
> to the Stygian shades.
> Live, all, with courage
> and the cruel fates will then not haul you
> over Lethe River.
> No: when the final hour is imposed
> at the end of your days,
> glory will open a path to heaven.

The *Octavia* ends with an extended lyric exchange between the chorus and Octavia, in which the chorus joins Octavia in lamenting her exile. The chorus has the final word (978–982):

> CHO. Urbe est nostra mitior Aulis
> et Taurorum barbara tellus:
> hospitis illic caede litatur
> numen superum;
> civis gaudet Roma cruore.
>
> Compared with our city, Aulis is kinder
> and the barbaric land of the Tauri:
> there they appease the gods of heaven
> by slaying strangers;
> Rome revels in her citizens' blood.

Bearing in mind the fact that the author of the *Hercules Oetaeus* and the author of the *Octavia* are undoubtedly different people, it emerges that of the three dramatists of the first century CE whose work survives, two adopt a choral conclusion and one, Seneca, does not.[9] Senecan practice on this point may have been distinctive rather than simply the norm.

If we pursue the matter and ask why Seneca resisted offering his audience a feeling of closure and interpretability, two answers suggest themselves. One is

---

[9] Zwierlein 1986, 320–328 and Ferri 2003, 50–54 arrive at opposite conclusions regarding the relative chronology of *Hercules Oetaeus* and *Octavia*, but both take it for granted that the authors of the respective works are different.

that the actions of his characters are so extreme in their nature and their consequences as to render any attempt at containing or explaining them futile.

The ending of *Medea* provides the most explicit example of that phenomenon. After Jason's last words (1026–1027), any statement from the chorus would be both dramatically and intellectually feeble.

> IA. Per alta vade spatia sublime aetheris,
> testare nullos esse, qua veheris, deos.
>
> Travel on high through the lofty spaces of heaven,
> and bear witness where you ride that there are no gods.[10]

The second explanation relates to the chorus's function as representatives of the community: in Senecan tragedy the community appears to lack the ability to judge or interpret the actions of the protagonists.

To conclude the first section of this paper, I would propose linking the contrasting roles of the chorus in Greek and Senecan tragedy to the respective circumstances of their composition, in a democratic Athenian polis vs. an empire ruled by a single person. (The precise chronology of Seneca's plays in relation to the Julio-Claudian dynasty is not at issue here; while I think there are good reasons to date some of the tragedies to the reign of Nero, the suggestion I am offering would apply equally to the time of Tiberius, Gaius, or Claudius.)

That contrast in political context gives added meaning to the chorus's ability or inability to interpret the tragic action. The presence of the Greek chorus asserts the role of the community in containing and understanding the action of the drama. Even though the chorus members of Greek tragedy do not usually represent Athenians, they typically model the reactions that Athenian citizens might have to the events presented on stage. Similarly, we might interpret the helplessness that the Senecan chorus often displays with regard to the plot as mirroring the inability of Romans to control the direction of a state subject to the will or whim of a near-absolute ruler. In this respect it matters little whether we believe the Senecan chorus represents a communal utterance or – as it often seems –an individual voice, since neither singly nor collectively did Romans represent a force sufficient to counter the power of the emperor. It is useful here to glance again at the *Octavia*, where the chorus of Romans does, remarkably, assert itself and rise up in protest against Nero's treatment of Octavia. That depic-

---

10 Seneca's word order in 1027 suggests a different and even more pointed sense: 'bear witness that, where you go, there are no gods.'

tion would itself be sufficient proof that the play was composed after Nero was safely dead and his memory disgraced.

The changed political context also helps to account for the difference I noted earlier between the Greek chorus, which is assumed to be present unless it is explicitly sent off, and the Senecan chorus, which often shows no knowledge of what is happening on stage. The action of Greek tragedy takes place in the open, in full view of a community that observes it and evaluates it. In Seneca, when characters – especially rulers – plot in secret, they are able to do so while escaping the notice of their subjects.

The ignorance often displayed by the Senecan chorus is the perfect dramatic analogy for the situation so vividly portrayed by Tacitus in the *Annales*, in which the secrets of rule (the *arcana imperii*) are jealously guarded and public proclamations are typically false and misleading. One thinks, for example, of the circumstances surrounding the death of Augustus, when Livia issued optimistic statements about his health until Tiberius's accession had been secured.[11] A *tragoedia praetexta* on the subject could have featured a choral ode rejoicing at Augustus's recovery, much as the chorus of *Thyestes* rejoices at the false report of the brothers' reconciliation.

In its often futile efforts to comprehend events that are baffling and deceptive, the Senecan tragic chorus is an all too faithful reflection of the Romans of Seneca's time. It is not a coincidence that the *Thyestes* presents the most striking examples of choral ignorance, since it is the play that focuses most closely on the abuse of tyrannical power, and also the play with the strongest Roman resonances.[12]

The political explanation I have offered for the peculiar relationship of the Senecan tragic chorus to the action of the plays presupposes a specific conception of the roles played by ruler and ruled. In the second half of my paper I would like to explore that issue in more detail, with Horace as the point of comparison.

Whether consciously or not, Seneca systematically subverts the paradigm of the ruler-ruled relationship as presented by Horace in the *Odes*. A central feature of that relationship is the sense of safety and security that the ruler provides.[13]

---

[11] Ann. 1.5.4 *acribus namque custodiis domum et vias saepserat Livia, laetique interdum nuntii vulgabantur, donec provisis quae tempus monebat simul excessisse Augustum et rerum potiri Neronem fama eadem tulit* ('For a strict cordon was placed around the house and its approaches by Livia and happy news was occasionally broadcast. Once provision was made for the 9 occasion's demands, word went out simultaneously that Augustus was gone and Tiberius in control.' Translation from Damon 2012).
[12] On Roman elements in *Thyestes* see Tarrant 1985, 48.
[13] Lowrie 2015, 329–335 discusses the Horatian passages under the heading 'security and the body of the leader' and places them in conjunction with Virgil's description of the bee king in

We can see this idea developing in the course of Horace's lyric corpus. A first key text is Carm. 3.14, which begins as a celebration in honour of Augustus's return from Spain and then, as so often in a Horatian ode's central stanza, expands the meaning of the event (lines 13–16):

> Hic dies vere mihi festus atras
> exiget curas; ego nec tumultum
> nec mori per vim metuam tenente
>   Caesare terras.
>
> This holy day will truly drive away
> all my black cares; I shall have no fear
> of war or violent death while Caesar
>   is master of the world.[14]

Here Augustus's power is described in quite direct terms (*tenente Caesare terras*). In the two odes of Book 4 that are addressed to Augustus, a different conception is introduced, that of the ruler as *custos*. We see it in the opening address of Carm. 4.5: *optime Romulae | custos gentis*, 'best guardian of the race of Romulus'; the poem goes on (lines 25–28) to proclaim freedom from anxiety in terms similar to, but more specific than, 3.14:

> Quis Parthum paveat, quis gelidum Scythen,
> quis Germania quos horrida parturit
> fetus, incolumi Caesare, quis ferae
>   bellum curet Hispaniae?
>
> Who could tremble at the Parthian? At the chilly Scythian?
> At the shaggy brood that Germany produces,
> while Caesar is safe? Who could think of war
>   with the savages of Spain?

The final poem of *Odes* 4 returns to the theme, this time with the emphasis on civic order and tranquillity (lines 17–20):

> Custode rerum Caesare non furor
> civilis aut vis exiget otium,
>   non ira, quae procudit ensis
>   et miseras inimicat urbis.

Georgics 4, especially 212 *rege incolumi mens omnibus una* est ('when the king is safe, all hold to the same purpose').
14 Translations of passages of Horace's *Odes* are from West 1997.

> While Caesar is guardian of the state, neither civil war
> nor civil madness will drive away our peace,
> > nor will anger beat out its swords
> > > and set city against unhappy city.

In all three passages Caesar's name appears in an ablative absolute; in each case the construction specifies a condition that is necessary for the truth of the principal statements. In the lines from Carm. 4.15 the ablative absolute has moved to the forefront of the stanza, and the word *custos* now occupies the first place: a rendering that brings out its connotations might be 'as long as the state remains in Caesar's safekeeping.'

In Horace's conception, the benevolent rule of Augustus does not circumscribe the freedom of the citizens, but actually guarantees it. That point is made in a striking way in the closing stanzas of Carm. 3.14, where Horace celebrates Augustus's return by ordering up a private symposium to be graced by the presence of the prostitute Neaera. The conclusion of Carm. 4.15 (lines 25–32) imagines a more decorous occasion, but one that in its own way takes advantage of the security provided by Augustus:

> Nosque et profestis lucibus et sacris   25
> inter iocosi munera Liberi
> > cum prole matronisque nostris
> > > rite deos prius apprecati
>
> virtute functos more patrum duces
> Lydis remixto carmine tibiis   30
> > Troiamque et Anchisen et almae
> > > progeniem Veneris canemus.

> And on ordinary days as on holy days,
> among the gifts of cheerful Bacchus, having first
> > with our children and our wives
> > > offered due prayers to the gods,
>
> we will sing a song to the Lydian pipe in praise
> of leaders who have shown the virtues
> > of their fathers, in praise of Troy, Anchises,
> > > and the offspring of life-giving Venus.[15]

---

[15] I have altered West's translation ('let us first... offer due prayers to the gods | and sing') in order to retain the crucial future tense of *canemus*.

These lines have become something of a battleground in Horatian criticism, with some writers applauding Horace's blending of the personal and the public while others lament the apparent extinction of Horace's individual voice,[16] but for my argument what is important is that the subject of this future song is not Augustus himself (except to the limited extent that he is included in the *progenies Veneris*), but rather the Roman past. The ideal ruler does not demand to be the subject of the people's adulation.

I do not need to say much to show how the picture given by Seneca represents a complete inversion of this Horatian model. We have only to consider Atreus, Seneca's most fully developed ruler figure and the one who offers the most explicit statement of his approach to rule. Even at the best of times in the *Thyestes* – which is to say, even when he is not plotting murderous revenge on his brother – Atreus derives a sadistic pleasure from imposing his will on his subjects: *quod nolunt velint* (212 'they must want what they do not want'). He rejoices in the false praise his position allows him to extort. *Maximum hoc regni bonum est, | quod facta domini cogitur populus sui | tam ferre quam laudare* (205–207 'This is the greatest value of kingship: that the people are compelled to praise as well as to endure their master's actions').

Atreus's oppressive regime finds its topographical expression in his palace, looming high above the city and keeping the rebellious citizens in check (641–645):

> In arce summa Pelopiae pars est domus
> conversa ad Austros, cuius extremum latus
> aequale monti crescit atque urbem premit
> et contumacem regibus populum suis
> habet sub ictu.
>
> On the summit of the citadel is a section
> of the House of Pelops that faces south. Its outer flank
> rises up like a mountain, hemming in the city
> and holding in its range a populace defiant
> to its kings.

To return to Horace, another aspect of the ruler's portrayal is a close relationship with the gods. At times this closeness seems to verge on identification, as at the end of Carm. 1.2, where Caesar takes on the appearance of Mercury; at others Augustus is associated with the gods, as in Carm. 4.5.31–35, where he is venerated with prayers and wine-offerings and his *numen* joins the Lares; in another place

---

[16] Thomas 2011, 260 cites some representative statements.

(the opening of Carm. 3.5) his status as a *praesens divus* is predicated on his subjugating the Persians and Britons. One note that is struck in several odes articulates a hierarchical relationship in which the ruler willingly subordinates his control to that of the gods. Thus the closing stanzas of Carm. 1.12 (51–52, 57–58):

>   Tu [Jupiter] secundo
> Caesare regnes
>
> te minor laetum reget [Caesar] aequus orbem;
> tu gravi curru quaties Olympum.
>
>   May you reign
> with Caesar second to you;[17]
>
> as your subordinate he will rule a joyful world in equity;
> you will shake Olympus with the weight of your chariot.

A similar idea provides a kind of frame for the Roman Odes. After the personal opening of Carm. 3.1, Horace continues (lines 5–6):

> Regum timendorum in proprios greges,
> reges in ipsos imperium est Iovis.
>
> Dread kings hold sway over their flocks;
> over kings rules Jupiter.

Conversely, in the final poem of the series, failure to respect the gods' superior position leads to disaster for Rome (Carm. 3.6.5–8):

> Dis te minorem [cf. 1.12.57] quod geris, imperas;
> hinc omne principium, huc refer exitum.
>   di multa neglecti dederunt
>   Hesperiae mala luctuosae.
>
> You rule because you hold yourself inferior to the gods.
> Make this the beginning and the end of all things.
>   Neglect of the gods has brought many ills
>   to the sorrowing land of Hesperia.

Here too Atreus offers the strongest possible contrast. At the moment of his triumph over his brother, when he feels himself fully a ruler, he first dismisses the

---

17 The meaning of *secundo* ('in second place' rather than 'favourable') is clarified by *te minor* in line 57.

gods and shortly afterwards wishes that he could drag them against their will to witness Thyestes's cannibal feast (885–895):

> Aequalis astris gradior et cunctos super
> altum superbo vertice attingens polum.
> nunc decora regni teneo, nunc solium patris.
> dimitto superos: summa votorum attigi...
> utinam quidem tenere fugientes deos
> possem, et coactos trahere, ut ultricem dapem
> omnes viderent.

> Peer of the stars I stride, out-topping all,
> my proud head reaching to the lofty sky.
> *Now* I hold the kingdom's glories, *now* my father's throne.
> I discharge the gods: I have reached the pinnacle of my prayers...
> Indeed I wish I could stop the gods fleeing,
> round them up and drag them all to see
> this feast of vengeance.

Atreus wishes that he could impose the same coercion on the gods that he employs with his subjects.

This passage also contains a clear Horatian intertext, *altum superbo vertice attingens polum* ('my proud head reaching to the lofty sky') recalling the end of Horace's first ode (Carm. 1.1.36) *sublimi feriam sidera vertice* ('my soaring head will touch the stars'), describing the elation he would feel if Maecenas judged him worthy to join the ranks of the canonical lyric poets. Given the delight Atreus takes in planning and executing his revenge, it seems likely that he is appropriating Horace's phrase to show that he has attained his own form of artistic supremacy.[18]

In Senecan tragedy it is not only rulers who have an antagonistic relationship with the gods. A passage from the *Agamemnon* shows this antagonism in ordinary human beings, and here reworking of Horace plays a central role. These are the first words of the play's second chorus, a group of Trojan captives led by Cassandra (589–610):

> Heu quam dulce malum mortalibus additum
> vitae dirus amor, cum pateat malis   590
> effugium et miseros libera mors vocet,
> portus aeterna placidus quiete.
> nullus hunc terror nec impotentis

---

18 Cf. Schiesaro 2003, 59: 'Atreus sees his actions as artistic achievements comparable to those of famous poets.'

```
          procella Fortunae movet aut iniqui
              flamma Tonantis.                                595
          pax alta nullos civium coetus
          timet aut minaces victoris iras,
          non maria asperis insana Coris,
          non acies feras pulvereamve nubem
          motam barbaricis equitum catervis,                  600
          non urbe cum tota populos cadentis
          hostica muros populante flamma
              indomitumve bellum.
          perrumpet omne servitium
          contemptor levium deorum:                           605
          qui vultus Acherontis atri,
          qui Styga tristem non tristis videt
          audetque vitae ponere finem,
          par ille regi, par superis erit.
```

Oh, the sweet evil implanted in mortals,
this desperate love for life, though escape from troubles
lies open, and death's freedom beckons the wretched—
a tranquil harbour of eternal calm,
untouched by any terror, by any storm
of raging Fortune, by any fire
    from the hostile Thunderer.
That deep peace fears no throngs
of citizens, no conqueror's angry menace,
no seas maddened by wild norwesters,
no ferocious battle lines or clouds of dust
raised by barbarians in horseback squadrons,
no downfall of peoples and whole cities
as enemy fires ravage the walls,
    no untameable war.
He will break out of all bondage
who scorns the fickle gods;[19]
he who looks without gloom at gloomy Styx,
looks upon dark Acheron's face,
and has courage to set an end to life,
such a one is a match for kings, for gods.

It has long been recognised that this passage is a reworking of the opening two stanzas of Horace's third Roman Ode (Carm. 3.3.1–8):

---

[19] I have altered Fitch's translation at this point. Fitch's text of 604 reads *solus servitium perrumpet omne*, Zwierlein's combination of the manuscript readings *perrumpet omne servitium* (E, adopted here) and *perrumpet omne solus* (A).

Iustum et tenacem propositi virum
non civium ardor prava iubentium,
    non vultus instantis tyranni
        mente quatit solida neque Auster,

dux inquieti turbidus Hadriae,   5
nec fulminantis magna manus Iovis:
    si fracta illabatur orbis,
        impavidum ferient ruinae.

The just man who holds fast to his resolve
is not shaken in firmness of mind by the passion
    of citizens demanding what is wrong,
        or the menace of the tyrant's frown, or the wind

of the south, rebellious king of the unquiet Adriatic,
or by the mighty hand of Jupiter who wields the lightning.
    If the round world were to break and fall about him,
        its ruins would strike him unafraid.[20]

In my *Agamemnon* commentary I emphasised Seneca's closeness to the Horatian source-text; here I would like to note some divergences that lend the Senecan passage a darker colouring. Horace is describing an upright man of firm purpose. In Seneca the antecedent of *hunc* in 593 is not explicit (a fact that caused some editors to rearrange the lines or to posit a lacuna), but both the preceding lines and the conclusion of the passage strongly suggest that it is the man who willingly ends his life.[21] Another difference concerns the characterisation of Jupiter. In both texts he is the Thunderer, but Horace associates him with other forces of nature while Seneca couples him with 'uncontrolled Fortune' and adds the hostile adjective *iniquus*. When Seneca carries on beyond Horace, he does so in de-

---

20 Kathrin Winter points out that the *Agamemnon* passage also resembles the stanzas of Carm. 3.14 and 4.15 cited earlier, in describing absence of fear in negative terms. What is missing is the guardianship of a benevolent ruler as the source of security.

21 The transmitted order of lines makes it natural to understand *portus* as the antecedent of *hunc*, which is unproblematic given the storm imagery of 593–595 but which becomes difficult as the passage continues with phrases that must apply to a person. My note on 593 ff. canvasses various proposed alterations but concludes aporetically 'in the absence of a wholly satisfying solution I have left the transmitted text unaltered, but the possibility of a lacuna... should be considered.' In the discussion following my paper Jürgen Paul Schwindt observed that *hunc* in this case seems to point forward rather than back. Martin Stöckinger ingeniously suggested that *hunc* might refer to Horace's *vir iustus et tenax*; Horace's figure certainly looms large in the background, but I would hesitate to attribute to him that degree of textual presence.

cidedly non-Horatian terms, praising the man who scorns the fickle gods (*contemptor levium deorum*). The term is elsewhere applied to impious characters such as Virgil's Mezentius (*contemptor divum*, A. 7.648) and Ovid's Pentheus (*contemptor superum*, Met. 3.514), and there carries a strongly pejorative force. Here the tone is the opposite, and the blame rests with the gods, whose behaviour makes them suitable objects of scorn. I suggest that we can see here a counterpart to the breakdown in harmonious relations between human authority figures and those over whom they have power.

A counterpart, but perhaps also a consequence. In the logic of ruler-cult, if rulers are seen as godlike, gods can be seen to take on the qualities of rulers; the more negatively rulers are portrayed, the more negative will be the image of their divine avatars. This process can already be seen at work in Ovid's *Metamorphoses*, where Jupiter is both associated with Augustus and depicted as a rapist and deceiver.[22]

What can the individual do or hope for in such a world?

Two Senecan choruses directly address that question, and each does so by reinterpreting the same ode of Horace, Carm. 2.10.

Seneca, *Oedipus* 882–891

CHO. Fata si liceat mihi
fingere arbitrio meo,
temperem Zephyri levi
vela, ne pressae gravi   885
spiritu antemnae tremant:
lenis et modice fluens
aura nec vergens latus
ducat intrepidam ratem;
tuta me media vehat   890
vita decurrens via.

If I were allowed to fashion
fate to my own desire,
I would trim my sails to the light
westerly wind, lest the sailyards
shake in a heavy gale.
A gentle, moderate breeze
that does not heel the side

---

[22] Jupiter and Augustus, cf. Met. 1.200–205, 15.858–860; Jupiter as rapist, cf. (e.g.) 1.588–600 (Io), and note 605–606 (Juno) *suus coniunx ubi sit circumspicit, ut quae | deprensi totiens iam nosset furta mariti* ('she looked around to see where her husband was, since she was by now familiar with his often-detected affairs').

would guide my untroubled boat.
Running a middle course,
my life would carry me safe.

Oedipus 980–982, 987–990

CHO. Fatis agimur: cedite fatis;　　　　　　　　　　980
    non sollicitae possunt curae
    mutare rati stamine fusi...
    omnia certo tramite vadunt
    primusque dies dedit extremum;
    non illa deo vertisse licet,
    quae nexa suis currunt causis.　　　　　　　　　990

We are driven by fate, and must yield to fate.
No anxious fretting can alter
the threads from that commanding spindle...
Everything travels on a path cut for it,
and the first day decides the last.
Not even a god can change events
which run in a woven series of causes.

These choral sections of the *Oedipus* (lines 882–910 and 980–993) have generated much discussion because they are structurally anomalous: if each of them is regarded as dividing one act from another, the result is a six-act play, which would be unique in Seneca.[23] In addition, they are conspicuously short: even their combined length of 43 lines is far less than the average for a Senecan choral ode, and contrasts sharply with the first two odes of the play, which fill 92 and 106 lines respectively. It may be best to understand these two brief choral utterances as articulating a final act in two scenes that correspond to the twofold actions that conclude the play, Oedipus's self-blinding and Jocasta's suicide. Certainly these two choral passages are conceived as a pair, each beginning with a form of the noun *fatum* (the overarching *Leitmotiv* of the play) and stating opposed attitudes toward that concept: in the first, the chorus contemplates the possibility of shaping its own destiny: *fata si liceat mihi | fingere arbitrio meo* ('if I were allowed to fashion fate to my own desire') and opts for the safety of a middle course: *tuta me media vehat | vita decurrens via* ('Running a middle course, my life would carry me safe'); the second renounces any attempt to chart a course in life, stating bluntly *fatis agimur: cedite fatis* ('we are driven by fate and must yield to fate') and offering no hope for an escape from complete

---

[23] That is the solution adopted by the most recent commentator on the play; cf. Boyle 2011, 335.

determinism: *omnia secto tramite vadunt, | primusque dies dedit extremum* ('Everything travels on a path cut for it, and the first day decides the last').

The *media via* that the first of these two choral statements longs to follow is the equivalent of the *aurea mediocritas* that Horace recommends in the ode to Licinius (2.10.5–8).

> Auream quisquis mediocritatem
> diligit, tutus caret obsoleti
> sordibus tecti, caret invidenda
>   sobrius aula.

> Whoever loves the Golden Mean
> is safe (no squalor for him in a filthy garret),
> and temperate (for him no mansion
>   that men will envy).

Incidentally, I am not sure if it has been observed that this passage in praise of 'being in the middle' occurs in a poem that stands at the midway point in the middle book of *Odes* 1–3.

Even as the Senecan chorus aspires to this condition, its language strongly implies that its wish may not be fulfilled. *Fata si liceat mihi... fingere* expresses a hypothetical possibility, not a reality, while the choice of *liceat* suggests that the chorus sees the ability to shape its own destiny as contingent on some form of permission. By contrast, the way of life advocated by Horace is a free choice that is open to every individual.

The first chorus of the *Agamemnon* displays a similar progression of thought in miniature (102–107):

> Modicis rebus longius aevum est;
> felix mediae quisquis turbae
>   sorte quietus
> aura stringit litora tuta   105
> timidusque mari credere cumbam
> remo terras propiore legit.

> Modest estate is longer-lived.
> Lucky the man content with the lot
>   of average folk,
> who hugs the shore where the breeze is safe,
> fears to trust his boat to the sea,
> and rows a course close in to land.

The first three lines evoke a condition similar to that commended by Horace (*quisquis* might even be a nod to the Horatian passage), but the succeeding lines describe the path of extreme caution explicitly disavowed by Horace (lines 1–4):

> Rectius vives, Licini, neque altum
> semper urgendo neque, dum procellas
> cautus horrescis, nimium premendo
>   litus iniquum.
>
> You will take a better course, Licinius,
> if you do not always thrust over the deep sea,
> or hug the dangerous coast too close,
>   shivering at the prospect of squalls.

This passage of Seneca may contain another Horatian intertext, if Seneca's *aura... tuta* points to the end of Carm. 3.29 (lines 62–64):

> Tunc me biremis praesidio scaphae
>   tutum per Aegaeos tumultus
>   aura ferat geminusque Pollux.
>
> When that time comes, the breeze and Pollux
>   and his twin shall carry me safe in my two-oared dinghy
>   through the Aegean storms.

The shared nautical imagery perhaps encourages the connection. Horace asserts that his self-sufficiency and independence give him the ability to survive metaphorical shipwreck, while the Senecan chorus seeks safety by clinging to the shoreline.

It may be significant that these rereadings of Horace come from the *Oedipus* and the *Agamemnon*, the two plays in which Seneca experimented with lyric forms based on Horatian cola but combined in ways foreign to Horace.[24] One might see those metrical refashionings as analogous to the way Seneca reinterprets and in some cases inverts Horatian themes and ideas.

The material I have presented constitutes only a tiny subdivision of the larger Neronian engagement with Augustan literature, but in the area on which I have focused Horace occupies a special place.[25] Horace presented the most fully elaborated Augustan view of the ideal relationship of ruler, state, and citi-

---

[24] On the polymetric odes in *Agamemnon* see Tarrant 1976, 372–381; for the *Oedipus* odes see Töchterle 1994, 132–134.
[25] On Seneca's reception of the main Augustan poets see now Trinacty 2014.

zens – and therefore offered a particularly ripe target for Senecan reinterpretation.[26]

---

[26] I am grateful to the organisers and participants for helpful comments. Special thanks to Tom Zanker for the care and patience with which he guided this paper to its published form.

Christopher Trinacty
Horatian Contexts in Senecan Tragedy

'Be influenced by as many great artists as you can, but have the decency either to acknowledge the debt outright, or to try to conceal it.' – Ezra Pound

'Therefore give up the hope that you can fully understand the genius of great authors by piecemeal summaries; the whole must be studied by you, the whole must be considered.' (*quare depone istam spem, posse te summatim degustare ingenia maximorum virorum; tota tibi inspicienda sunt, tota tractanda.*) – Sen. Ep. 33.5

Senecan tragedy flaunts its intertextual nature. Open any of the recent commentaries by Boyle and you will see how pervasively the language of the Augustan poets influences Seneca's imagery, characterisation, and poetic fabric.[1] Intertextual connections with Latin poets supplement and complicate Seneca's poetic language, and Seneca explores how the words of Virgilian epic or Ovidian elegy can be resurrected and reframed in his tragic worlds. But how much of the larger context of the source text does Seneca have in mind when he recalls the works of Virgil, Ovid, and Horace? Does an intertextual connection suggest simply that line or stanza of a Horatian poem, or does it conjure up the poem as a whole?[2] This paper investigates moments in which Seneca evokes the works of Horace in his tragedies with an eye to the complete ode, epistle, or epode. Seneca has a clear understanding of the particulars of each poem and uses these intertexts to call to mind the complete poem and provide his interpretation of it.[3] Only by reading the intertext with its larger Horatian context in mind will the reader understand how Seneca is referencing the poem as a whole in his

---

[1] Cf. Boyle 2011 and 2014. For ramifications of such intertextual play, cf. Schiesaro 2003, Littlewood 2004, and Trinacty 2014 and 2016. I have been influenced primarily by Conte 1986, Fowler 2000, and Hinds 1998 in my intertextual readings and am especially taken by Hinds's idea that 'there is no discursive element in a Roman poem, no matter how unremarkable in itself, and no matter how frequently repeated in the tradition, that cannot in some imaginable circumstance mobilize a specific allusion' (Hinds 1998, 26).
[2] In the examples that follow I focus primarily on moments in which one can find shared language between examples, although I also believe that situations or themes can be intertextually linked (e.g. the 'golden mean' ode of Sen. Oed. 882–910 may not share much language with Hor. Carm. 2.10, but could still evoke a connection in the reader's mind).
[3] One can see a comic application of this practice at Apoc. 5.4 where a line of Homer is capped by the following line. In the Horatian intertexts that follow it is clear that Seneca knows the rest of the poem and wishes to place the entire poem in dialogue with his play.

DOI 10.1515/9783110528893-006

tragedy.⁴ Seneca the literary critic and Seneca the poet unite at these moments, which reveal how Seneca understands the larger significance of Horace's striking language and how he adapts its meaning to his tragic material. Seneca's intention in alluding to his distinguished precursor is either to further emphasise important tragic themes or to provide his own dramatic spin on the Horatian material. These readings of the Horatian source provide insight into Seneca's own reading and (re)writing of Horace's poetry.

1 Horatian *Medea*

Horace's Ep. 1.2 ruminates on the importance of reading Homer for gathering philosophical insight and claims that the *Iliad* and the *Odyssey* can teach 'what is beautiful, ugly, useful and not' better than the philosophers Chrysippus and Crantor (Ep. 1.2.3–4). Halfway through this epistle, where he becomes more interested in ethics per se than simply describing how to read Homer, Horace writes:

> nam cur
> quae laedunt oculum festinas demere, si quid
> est animum, differs curandi tempus in annum?
> dimidium facti, qui coepit, habet: sapere aude:
> incipe.
>
> Why do you rush to remove things hurtful to your eye, but if
> Something harms your soul, you postpone taking care of it for a year?
> He who has begun is halfway done: dare to be a *sapiens*, begin!⁵
> (Ep. 1.2.37–41)

Seneca has these lines in mind when he has his Medea urge herself on to crime after Jason's departure:

> Discessit. itane est? vadis oblitus mei
> et tot meorum facinorum? excidimus tibi?
> numquam excidemus. hoc age, omnis advoca
> vires et artes. fructus est scelerum tibi
> nullum scelus putare. vix fraudi est locus:

---

4 For an additional example of this practice in his tragedies, cf. Trinacty 2014, 21–23. For a discussion of the idea of evoking the context in a quotation and further examples (also from philosophical texts), see the chapter by Tischer in this volume.
5 In this paper I use Shackleton Bailey 2001 for Horace, Zwierlein 1986 for Seneca's tragedies, and Eden 1984 for Seneca's *Apocolocyntosis*. All translations are my own.

> timemur. hac aggredere, qua nemo potest
> quicquam timere. perge, nunc <u>aude, incipe</u>
> quidquid potest Medea, quidquid non potest.

> He has left. Is that it? You wander off disregarding me
> and all of my deeds? Do you forget me?
> I will never be forgotten. Come on, summon all your
> strength and skills. The reward of your crimes is that
> nothing is considered a crime. The opportunity for criminality
> is slim: I am feared. Attack where nobody could ever fear.
> Continue, now dare, begin whatever Medea can do, whatever she cannot.
> (Med. 560–567)

Horace's call to philosophical action (*sapere aude | incipe*) has been appropriated by Seneca's Medea to enact her own characteristic (literary) qualities.[6] If Horace's epistle attempts to show a route to gaining wisdom (*sapere*), Seneca is primarily interested in fleshing out the limits of Medea's daring (*quidquid potest Medea, quidquid non potest*).[7] Horace's directives to live a philosophical life are to be obeyed at once because time is of the essence, but Seneca's Medea needs to act quickly because of the mere hours she has remaining in Corinth.[8] Although Horace is acting as a sort of moral teacher as well as Lollius's teacher on how to read poetry in this epistle, Seneca bifurcates Medea's personae into both teacher and addressee,[9] as she speaks to herself and urges herself to ac-

---

6 This is the only instance of the adjacent imperative forms of these words in Latin literature, according to the *Packard Humanities Institute* website (http://latin.packhum.org/search?q=aude +incipe, seen 22.5.2016). Hinds 2011 remarks on how this Ovidian intertextual play between Ov. Ep. 12.69–71 and Med. 560–562 can act like an Alexandrian footnote, and he puts in the mouth of Medea the following speech: 'Can you *still* not remember (as a husband, as a reader…) all that I am to you, how the *topoi* of our story are shaped? Well then, let me repeat the lesson, and perhaps this time it will stick' (28). If one thinks back to Jason's words to Medea *sana meditari* <u>incipe</u> *| et placida fare*, 'begin to think sanely and speak calmly' (Med. 537–538), one can see how that didactic advice is trumped by Medea's use of *aude incipe*.
7 As shown in the differing language surrounding the use of *aude, incipe* found in each work. For the *Epistles* as a work that unites philosophy and poetry, cf. Moles 2002 and 2007. Medea's later uses of *audere* indicate how her daring is measured by the scope of her vengeance and her ability to transcend the 'normal' limits of revenge, cf. Med. 908–909 (*quid manus poterant rudes | <u>audere</u> magnum, quid puellaris furor?*, 'what great evil could unskilled hands dare, what could the madness of a girl?') and Med. 918–919 (*decrevit animus intus et nondum sibi | <u>audet</u> fateri*, 'my spirit has decreed it yet does not dare to admit it to itself').
8 An issue that will return at the end of the play when Jason urges her to get on with her 'inchoate crime' (*<u>coeptum</u> facinus*, Med. 1014).
9 On the construction of personae in Horace and Seneca, see the chapter by Kirichenko in this volume.

tion.¹⁰ It is telling that Medea moves from second to third person at the conclusion of this outburst, which reveals how she takes on the traditional role of 'Medea' at this moment (in the following lines she indicates to the Nurse her explicit plans for revenge).¹¹ Medea's literary self-consciousness is an aspect of her character that has been remarked upon at least since Wilamowitz's famous 'This Medea has read Euripides,'¹² but whereas her self-awareness of her own mythological tradition is one thing, here we may conclude that 'This Medea has read Horace.' As we shall see, Seneca incorporates this moment from Horace's *Epistles* to show how the literary tradition about Medea, like that surrounding the characters of the *Iliad* and the *Odyssey*, can be activated to question and to define her 'proper' actions.

If one recalls the entire epistle, especially the second half, one can see that certain themes from Horace's poem reappear in Seneca's tragedy. For instance, Horace formulates pithy, almost Senecan *sententiae* about the need to moderate one's anger, which, after all, is a brief madness (*ira furor brevis est. animum rege*, Ep. 1.2.62).¹³ Seneca writes about anger in a similar way at Dial. 3.1.2: *quidam itaque e sapientibus viris iram dixerunt brevem insaniam* ('Certain wise men have said that anger is a brief madness'), and the play between *ira, dolor, furor*, and even *amor* forms the passionate foundation to the actions of Seneca's tragedy. Horace turns to the topic of anger here to parallel his initial reading of the *Iliad* and the play between love and anger found therein:

---

10 Star 2012, 76–82 points out how Medea uses her self-directed commands in two opposed ways: both to maintain the vigour of her passion, but also to tamp down her passions and 'act better.' The eventual elevation of her revenger persona shows how the Horatian 'advice' that could be drawn from this story may be trumped by the literary overdetermination of Medea, even other Horatian iterations of Medea, see below.
11 Boyle 2014 ad loc. remarks 'the switch to the third person here is overtly self-dramatizing and metadramatic.'
12 Wilamowitz-Moellendorff 1919, 162.
13 Ep. 1.2.55–63 features much short philosophical instruction and a quick glance at Mayer 1994 ad loc. shows many Senecan parallels in thought, language, and effect. Note how Horace's *animum rege* (Ep. 1.2.62) is mirrored in Jason's advice to Medea *fervidam ut mentem regas*, 'rule your blazing mind' (Med. 558) before he hurries offstage. By placing Seneca and Horace in dialogue with one another, the reader may muse upon the way Seneca could 'influence' Horace: see the special issue of *Classical Receptions Journal* 5.2 (June 2013) devoted to Martindale's *Redeeming the Text* (1993) for more on how this two-way dynamic of reception functions.

> Nestor componere litis
> inter Peliden festinat et inter Atriden;
> hunc amor, ira[14] quidem communiter urit utrumque.
>
> Nestor hurries to settle the quarrel
> Between the son of Peleus and the son of Atreus:
> Love burns the first, and anger burns both together in common.
> (Ep. 1.2.11–13)

Medea unites both love and anger and shows the destructive quality of both of these emotions, claiming early in the play that she must gird herself with anger and prepare to kill in full fury (*accingere ira teque in exitium para | furore toto*, Med. 51–52), but also that she had committed no crime out of anger up to this point ('I performed no crime out of anger. Unhappy love raged...,' *nullum scelus | irata feci. saevit infelix amor*, Med. 135–136). Seneca even pairs these identical Latin terms when his chorus wonders about Medea's next move:

> Frenare[15] nescit iras
> Medea, non amores.
> nunc ira amorque[16] causam
> iunxere. quid sequetur?
>
> Medea does not know how to rein in
> Her anger, or her love.
> Now anger and love have united in this cause,
> What will follow?
> (Med. 866–869)

Medea provides a mythological example of the very subject matter that Horace analysed in Ep. 1.2, but, if we are meant to view Seneca as responding to the larger ideas of Horace's epistle, he would seem to be indicating that his *Medea* is a

---

14 Also note *ira* at Ep. 1.2.15; of course, the repetition of this word would remind the reader of the first word of the *Iliad*.

15 Note how Horace himself uses this same metaphor with anger at Ep. 1.2.63: *hunc frenis, hunc tu compesce catena*, 'subdue this with reins, with chains,' which Seneca also alludes to at Med. 174–175 (*compesce verba*). Seneca's previous chorus encapsulates many of these aspects in its description of a scorned wife: *caecus est ignis stimulatus ira | nec regi curat patiturve frenos | aut timet mortem* ('Blind is the fire aroused by anger. It does not want to be ruled or endure the reins or fear death,' Med. 591–593).

16 The nominatives *amor ira* and *ira amor* are never placed next to each other in Latin poetry except in these respective poems.

better example of the literature to be read and reread and mused upon.¹⁷ Through these intertexts, Seneca makes the reader reflect upon the *exempla* and themes of Ep. 1.2 as a whole. Horace's own encouragement to read and re-read Homer for moral ends is trumped by Seneca's use of Medea. But to what ends? It is important to note that Horace himself is pursuing his advice through the very medium of poetry, and points out the importance of interpreting Homer's epics as verse.¹⁸ As Keane clarifies:

> The case of Circe [in Horace's poem] constitutes an example of how summary and moral interpretation can obscure the narrative complexity of a literary work… Horace's summaries of the epics have a misleading structure and orientation, but they promote a deeper message by being embedded in a book that encourages and rewards careful and individualized reading.¹⁹

Seneca is making a similar claim about the possible interpretations of his tragedy. The position of Euripides's *Medea* as a seminal text in the teaching of philosophy (even by Chrysippus)²⁰ would seem to indicate that Seneca knows such a moralising Stoic reading is *a* possible hermeneutic strategy of his *Medea*. But, of course, it is not the *only* possible approach. In fact, the way Horace reads Homer in Ep. 1.2 challenges summary reductive readings of poetry and encourages individual readers to 'identify the problems with certain reading methods.'²¹ Seneca, then, recalls Horace to make a similar point. The poetry of his *Medea* can be used for moral and ethical advice, but it is also poetry and encourages a variety of individual interpretations.²² A philosophical reading may ultimately be a

---

17 Keane 2001 believes that Ep. 1.2 represents the way 'Horace engages his own reader in an interpretive exercise that underscores Homer's multifaceted didactic value and showcases Horace's own ingenious teaching strategies' (427). Medea herself embodies the passions that Horace chooses to focus on in Ep. 1.2. His own reading of Odysseus's character, not discussed above, can be seen at Med. 161: *numquam potest non esse virtuti locus* ('there is always a place for virtue') which recalls Horace's *quid virtus et quid sapientia possit* ('what virtue and wisdom are able to do,' Ep. 1.2.17).
18 Cf. Skalitzky 1968, 449 on Ep. 1.2: 'For Horace true poetry always has to some extent a philosophic content.'
19 Keane 2001, 447. Seneca's own 'careful and individualized' reading of Horace leads to his conception of Medea as a figure of philosophical reflection vis à vis Horace's strictures.
20 Cf. Müller 2014, 64–66, and Gill 1983 for Chrysippus's understanding of *Medea*. See Hine 2000, 27–28 for an overview of the way *Medea* was read by Epictetus.
21 Keane 2001, 432.
22 One can see Seneca himself practising various reading methods in Ep. 108.29–37. The question of how Stoic Seneca's tragedies are and the connections between Seneca *philosophus* and Seneca *tragicus* continues to rouse debate, see Hine 2004, Wiener 2014, Fischer 2014, and Star 2016.

reductive reading of Medea's character, her decisions, and her makeup, not to mention Seneca's expansive and challenging poetics.

It is well known that this is not the only poem of Horace alluded to in the *Medea*. In fact, the Horatian influences on this play are particularly pronounced, especially in the Argonautic odes.²³ An additional reference that calls to mind another Horatian poem *in toto* occurs early in the play when Medea prays to the Furies, 'Now, now be present, goddesses who avenge crime,' *nunc, nunc adeste sceleris ultrices deae* (Med. 13). Here Seneca alludes to the prayer of Horace's witch Canidia:

> o rebus meis
> non infidelis arbitra,
> Nox, et Diana, quae silentium regis,
> arcana cum fiunt sacra,
> *nunc, nunc adeste*, nunc in hostilis domos
> iram atque numen vertite!

O faithful helper of my affairs,
Night, and Diana, who rules over the silent dead,
When my secret rites are held,
Now, now be present, now turn your anger
And your power against my enemies' homes.
(Epod. 5.49–55)

Seneca's play opens with Medea's long prayer to the gods, both those that oversaw her wedding and those more nefarious forces to whom 'it is more fitting for Medea to pray' (*quosque Medeae magis | fas est precari*, Med. 8–9). Medea's invocation at this point has moved beyond Canidia's Nox and Diana, embodied in *Hecate triformis* (Med. 7), and is focused on the Furies and the punishment that should be doled out to the Corinthian royal family.²⁴ The hostile homes (*hostilis domos*) of Horace's poem fits the current moment of Seneca's tragedy as Medea contemplates destroying Creon and Creusa ('Shall I not attack my enemies?', *non ibo in hostes?*, 27), but she will also define Jason as an enemy (*hostis meus*, 920), who, like Canidia's Varus, is 'hostile' because of his desire for another woman.²⁵ The larger dramatic situation of Horace's poem, however, should be taken into

---

23 Cf. Spika 1890, 14–20; Biondi, 1984; Trinacty 2014, 154–164; Boyle 2014 passim; Littlewood 2016, 373–377.
24 In Seneca's description of Hecate *tacitisque praebens conscium sacris iubar* ('offering light for secret rituals,' Med. 6), one may also see an echo of Epod. 5.51–52: *quae silentium regis, | arcana cum fiunt sacra* ('you who rule the silent hours | when sacred rites occur').
25 Cf. Degl'Innocenti Pierini 2013 for more on this representation of Medea. The messenger of the play announces 'the whole house has fallen' (*domus tota occidit*, Med. 886).

consideration, since Canidia is casting a spell and preparing to murder a child in order to win back the object of her affection, actions of course reminiscent of Medea's own. Canidia also fashions herself as a Medea-like figure and mentions the ointment by which Medea destroyed the *paelex* who tried to steal Jason.[26] An understanding of the Horatian context will complicate Medea's words in Seneca's play: is she already planning to destroy her own children?[27]

One might first be tempted to suppose that this is what is happening, with Seneca, if you will, showing Horace how such prayers and magic are to be done, and with the real Medea, not some counterfeit Medea. But the intertext, especially if it evokes the entire epode, should cause the reader to recall Medea's previous murder of her young brother Absyrtus.[28] After all, the way the boy curses Canidia and threatens to become an avenging *umbra* (5.93, cf. *Med.* 963: *umbra*) parallels what happens at the shocking conclusion of Seneca's play.[29] Because of the surprising addition of the ghost of Absyrtus and the way he haunts Medea and causes her to kill her first child (958–971), this initial intertext must foreshadow his ghostly presence at the play's climax.[30] In order to call attention to this, Seneca repeats the language of the opening prayer (and the line that echoes Horace) when Medea sees the Furies (*ultrices deas*, 967 – *ultrices deae*, 13), and asks the ghost of her brother to send them away. Boyle remarks on the irony in Medea's original summoning of the Furies: 'since one of their original functions was the punishment of bloodshed within the family.'[31] Thus the resulting appearance of the Furies and the ghost of Absyrtus parallels the avenging

---

[26] Canidia mentions Medea by name ('why are the foul poisons of barbarian Medea not working?', *cur dira barbarae minus | venena Medeae valent*, *Epod.* 5.61–62) and her retelling of the plot of Medea's time in Corinth features language that Seneca utilises (*paelex, venena, nupta*). Note how Seneca references *Epod.* 5.65–66 at *Med.* 838–839, and *Epod.* 5.63–64 at *Med.* 641–642, but there to tell the story of Hercules's death.

[27] This speech will go on to offer numerous hints of infanticide, cf. Trinacty 2014, 97–101. Prince 2013, 620 points out how Horace links Canidia's magic to Medea's to associate 'this lust-driven hag with Medea as a deadly witch, but failed practitioner of love magic, and as an anti-mother figure, one sacrificing an innocent child because of unrequited love.'

[28] That Absyrtus is to be imagined as a young boy is confirmed by his description as a 'little companion mutilated by the sword' (*parvus comes | divisus ense*, *Med.* 131–132).

[29] The inclusion of direct speech from both the young boy and Canidia in iambic metre may also have encouraged Seneca to incorporate *Epod.* 5 in an iambic section of his tragedy.

[30] One may also look back to *Epod.* 5 as a predecessor for the long incantation scene in Act 4 of Seneca's *Medea*. There is no precedent in Euripides or Ovid for the ghost of Absyrtus to have such an active role in the destruction of Medea's children, and it speaks to Seneca's quest for novelty as well as a way to further entangle Medea's infanticide within the reciprocal retribution the Furies demand.

[31] Boyle 2014 ad loc.

spirit that the boy in Horace Epod. 5 will become after his death.[32] Medea's killing of her first son must appease the Furies in their traditional guise as avengers of bloodshed in the family, and the ghost of Absyrtus guarantees this infanticide (and Medea's own suffering).[33] The identification of Canidia with Medea moves beyond the mere idea that both are witches who are about to kill a child, but that Medea both has done this in the past (her brother), and presently will have to kill both of her own sons ('I have enough for my brother and father, I have given birth to two,' *fratri patrique quod sat est, peperi duos*, Med. 957). Absyrtus threatens Medea and the dying boy states that he will take vengeance on Canidia.[34] The literary 'ghosts' of Horace can thus be seen to prowl in this play from its very beginning, only to explode onto the scene at the conclusion and force Medea's hand, perhaps in a manner that the character of Medea did not imagine.[35]

In both of these examples (Ep. 1.2 and Epod. 5) one can see how Seneca has his Medea echo Horatian language to cause the reader to question her actions – what does it mean to act like the literary tradition behind Medea or Canidia?[36] Obviously, this is a major concern of the play as a whole (e.g. 'Now I am Medea,' *Medea nunc sum*, Med. 910), but the larger Horatian context behind these references causes the reader to reconsider her motivation, actions, and rationale for vengeance. The intertext with Epod. 5 shows how the actions of Horace's most famous witch can help to clarify the shocking way that the ghost of Absyrtus prompts Medea's revolutionary onstage murder of her sons.[37] The larger philosophical concerns of Horace's *Epistle* such as the force of anger and moralistic readings of Homer are now critiqued in his poetic vision of Medea. Seneca

---

[32] Medea claims: 'I placate your spirit by this sacrifice' (*victima* manes tuos | placamus ista, Med. 970–971, when she kills her son), and the boy curses Canidia: 'My foul curse will be expiated by no sacrifice' (*dira detestatio | nulla expiatur victima*, Epod. 5.89–90).
[33] 'As in the cases of Procne and Althaea in Books 6 and 8 of Ovid's *Metamorphoses*, infanticide paradoxically becomes the means of atonement for wrongs done to siblings... This motive for Medea's infanticide, like the (actual or imagined) appearance of the Furies and Absyrtus, is not in Euripides' (Boyle 2014 ad 958–971).
[34] Watson 2003, 188 states, 'Instead of having his services appropriated by the witches, he will return Fury-like to persecute them, driving them to sleeplessness and terror. These threats help to underscore Canidia's fecklessness and ineptitude.'
[35] Here one may think of Littlewood's discussion of 'deviant intertextuality' in Senecan tragedy (2004, 263–269).
[36] For the importance of Canidia for Horace's poetry, cf. Oliensis 1998, 64–101. Seneca's appropriation of this epode could even suggest that he recognises her importance to Horace's iambic project and how Canidia, as singer of magical songs (epōdai), complicates Horace's conception of his 'epodes.'
[37] An action that conflicts with Horace's dictum in the *Ars Poetica*: 'Medea should not kill her children onstage' (*ne pueros coram populo Medea trucidet*, Ars 185).

thus comments on his conception of the tragic genre – it is made to be a forum for concerns ranging from the limits of vengeance to philosophical selfhood, and these interests are mediated through his poetic language. This language itself is revitalised through intertextual echoes of Horace that reveal Seneca's reading of the entire Horatian poem. Seneca thus reshapes the anxieties of Horace's poetry in the tragic frame of the *Medea* to indicate how Horace's works can be self-consciously evaluated, adapted, and expanded in the tragic genre.

2 Odes and Choral Odes

As a knowledge of Ep. 1.2 or Epod. 5 informs Medea's 'literariness' and the larger philosophical concerns of the *Medea*, so Seneca's recollection of Horace's Carm. 1.19 and 4.1 can be seen to influence the depiction of desire in his *Phaedra*. The play investigates, in part, the effects of excessive passion: whether it is the desire of Phaedra, the misogynistic fury of Hippolytus, or Theseus's quick trigger finger in his vengeance against the 'guilty' Hippolytus. Marked references to these two Horatian odes appear in Seneca's play and point to their position as particularly influential formulations of love's fire, the tropes of erotic poetry, and the sacrifices such passion engenders.[38] In both odes, Horace is representing the trope of falling-in-love-again reluctantly, which likewise forms the background for Phaedra's own unwilling desire for Hippolytus.[39] These references accumulate and reverberate in the course of Seneca's play (appearing in multiple acts and choral songs), which illustrates how Seneca creates an ongoing dialogue with these Horatian odes to focus and refocus their implications for Phaedra, Hippolytus, and the Chorus.

The second choral song of Seneca's *Phaedra* is a meditation on the power of Venus in all spheres of the universe (human, animal, divine). The opening lines address Venus in language similar to the opening lines of Horace Carm. 1.19:

> Diva non miti generata ponto,
> quam vocat matrem geminus Cupido:
> impotens flammis simul et sagittis

---

[38] In all of his tragedies, Seneca only names Venus in *Phaedra* and *Agamemnon*; e.g. Phaed. 124, 211, 447, 467; Ag. 183, 927.
[39] Horace himself may have been influenced by Euripides's *Hippolytus* with the description of Aphrodite who, 'if she streams upon us in full flood, cannot be withstood' (Hipp. 443, where the Nurse is addressing Phaedra) and his 'Venus attacks me with all her power' (*in me tota ruens Venus*, Carm. 1.19.9) – cf. Nisbet and Hubbard 1970, 238–239 and *ad* 1.19.9.

iste lascivus puer et renidens
tela quam certo moderatur arcu!

The goddess born from a savage sea,
Whom the twin Cupids call mother,
Wild both with fire and arrows,
How that lusty child, smiling, aims his bolts
With sure bow!
(Phaed. 274–278)

Mater saeva Cupidinum
Thebanaeque iubet me Semelae puer
et lasciva Licentia
finitis animum reddere amoribus

The savage mother of the Cupids,
The child of Theban Semele
And lusty Licence order me to give my soul back
To finished passion.
(Carm. 1.19.1–4)

Wine, *Licentia*, and Venus attack Horace, resulting in the rekindling (*finitis... amoribus*) of his passion for Glycera.[40] Seneca's Venus is likewise savage (*non miti generata ponto*), and identified in her role as the mother of Cupids (note repetitions of forms of *mater* and *Cupido*). Seneca transfers the *puer* from Horace's description of Bacchus to Cupid himself, who likewise takes on the adjective *lascivus* from Licentia. In this way, Seneca combines the qualities of Bacchus and the personified Licentia into facets of the power of love and Cupid in particular, who becomes a more universal force in this chorus, even overwhelming Jupiter (Phaed. 300–307).[41] The opening position of the reference (first words of the

---

[40] Note Nisbet and Hubbard's characterisation of Carm. 1.19: 'it is not about a girl, but about literature and Horace... When the goddess of Cyprus descends on Horace he dreads her onslaught; yet being less obstinate than Hippolytus, he decides on a policy of appeasement' (Nisbet and Hubbard 1970, 238–239; my emphasis). Seneca recognises how Horace has adapted Euripides in Carm. 1.19 and rewrites this situation in his own tragedy about Hippolytus to return it to its 'true' context and genre, cf. Kiessling / Heinze 1930, 94 for more on Horace's connection to Euripides.

[41] If these forces 'order' (*iubet*) Horace to fall in love again, in Seneca's ode the power of desire 'orders the gods' (*iubet... superos*, Phaed. 294) and can cause all hatred to end 'when love has ordered' (*cum iussit amor*, Phaed. 354). This same tendency to transfer and recontextualise language can be found in the following section about Bacchus *infra* and at Phaed. 348–350 (with

chorus, first lines of the poem) makes the identification of the intertext more persuasive and sets up the Senecan reader for a description of desire that will broadly follow the seductive and insistent emphases of the Horatian poem.[42]

'But wait,' one may interject, 'Horace utilises the same line, *mater saeva Cupidinum*, at Carm. 4.1.5; so how do we know that Seneca wishes the reader to think about Carm. 1.19 at this moment and not Carm. 4.1?'. While the additional verbal connections would probably lead one to identify Carm. 1.19 as the source, it is important to note that, of course, Horace himself is linking the two poems and wishes the reader to think back to Carm. 1.19 when reading this line in Carm. 4.1.[43] Note that Horace further describes the 'loves' as 'sweet' *dulcium*... *Cupidinum* (Carm. 4.1.5), and the Greek translation of Glycera's name is 'sweet.' Horace employs this bilingual intratextual connection to increase the bond between these two poems.[44] By repeating the line in two poems about love, Horace here is enacting the very subject matter of these odes; his language and metre repeat themselves, thus pointing out that he is in love again (and writing love poetry again), in spite of his professed resistance. Seneca highlights Horace's own internal intratextual link, and he stresses the similarities between the Horatian poems in this tragedy's intertexts to both. Essentially, Seneca reads the two poems as one master Horatian text about love and love poetry, the frustration of unrequited desire, and the emotional turmoil such passion causes.[45] Through this intertext, Seneca makes his Phaedra the next in the line of figures who unwillingly fall in love, and his tragedy places the tropes of Horace's erotic poetry under the microscope.[46] There are additional intertexts to both of these odes in

---

its source in Verg. Ecl. 5.27–28) where the mourning of pastoral animals at the death of Daphnis is now caused by the force of love and, by extension, foreshadows the death of Hippolytus.
42 One may find parallels in the opening of Virgil's *Eclogue* 3 and its recollection of the opening of Theocritus's fourth *Idyll*.
43 Putnam 1986, 42 writes, 'Horace also makes a careful and, for him, unusually conspicuous bow to his own creative past by incorporating, as line 5, the whole opening verse of *c.* 1.19... This literary self-consciousness, as the poet places himself in the line of his lyric inheritance and in relation to his own past, will prove of equal importance in the two poems that follow...'
44 Thomas 2011 ad loc. notes the connection with Carm. 1.19, but stresses Greek antecedents to the phrase, not the intratextual indicator.
45 Horace's prayer that Venus go away 'where the pleasing prayers of young men call you back' (*quo blandae iuvenum te revocant preces*, Carm. 4.1.8) may be recalled by Seneca's description of Cupid who 'stirs up the fierce fires of youths and revives again the extinguished passions of tired elders' (*iuvenum feroces | concitat flammas senibusque fessis | rursus extinctos revocat calores*, Phaed. 291–293), and note *rursus* at Carm. 4.1.2.
46 Trinacty 2014, 67–93 points out how Ovid's elegiac tropes act as background for Phaedra's self-conception.

Seneca's play, which keeps these poems in the reader's mind and helps to position Phaedra as a stand-in for Horace's older lover.[47]

For instance, both Glycera and Ligurinus are recalled in the third choral ode when we read of Hippolytus's beauty. The concrete details of Hippolytus's physique mimic those of Horace's beloveds, not the Ligurinus of Carm. 4.1, who is like a dream image (more on this below), but the Ligurinus of Carm. 4.10, who will soon lose his beauty:

> et quae nunc umeris involitant deciderint comae,
> nunc et qui color est puniceae flore prior rosae,
> mutatus, Ligurine, in faciem verterit hispidam,
> dices 'heu,' quotiens te in speculo videris alterum,
> 'quae mens est hodie, cur eadem non puero fuit,[48]
> vel cur his animis incolumes non redeunt genae?'
>
> And when your hair has been cut, which now flies over your shoulders,
> And when your complexion, now like that of the first flowering of a red
> rose, has changed, Ligurinus, into a bristling beard,
> you will say 'alas' as often as you see your reflection in the mirror,
> 'Why when I was a boy, did I not have today's wits,
> or why don't my perfect cheeks return with this wisdom?'
> (Carm. 4.10.3–8)

When Seneca's chorus remarks on beauty as a fragile gift of fortune and the inevitable dissipation of Hippolytus's own beauty, they draw upon language and imagery from this Horatian poem:

---

[47] A later echo of Carm. 4.1 shows a similar methodology at work. In the course of this poem Horace argues that he is not of the appropriate age for an affair and has no suitable partner (Carm. 4.1.29–32). If Horace, protesting perhaps a bit too much, claims he has no 'gullible hope' (spes animi credula mutui, 4.1.30) of finding a shared soul, Phaedra recognises this as part of love's allure. After Hippolytus states that he will 'fulfill the role of your husband,' Phaedra remarks in an aside, 'O the gullible hopes of lovers, O deceptive Love! Haven't I said enough?' (O spes amantum credula, o fallax Amor! | satisne dixi?, Phaed. 634–635). In addition, the Nurse hopes to teach Hippolytus to learn to love and 'to bear mutual flames' (mutuos ignes ferat, Phaed. 415).

[48] It is possible that Seneca himself is picking up on another intratextual repetition of Horatian language. Cf. Ep. 1.1.4: non eadem est aetas, non mens ('My age is not the same, nor my mind'); and note Fraenkel's comment, 'In this connection we should also notice that in the poem it is Horace who utters the words which he knows Ligurinus will utter in years to come. This device suggests to the reader that what is put in the mouth of Ligurinus comes in fact from an experience through which the poet has gone himself' (1957, 415).

> languescunt folio lilia pallido
> et gratae capiti deficiunt rosae,
> ut fulgor teneris qui radiat genis
> momento rapitur nullaque non dies
> formosi spolium corporis abstulit.
>
> Lilies falter with their pale petals
> And roses, fit for garlands, wither,
> More quickly the flash which young cheeks emit
> Is snatched in a moment and no day
> Has not taken away something from the body's beauty.
> (Phaed. 768–772)

Horace ultimately hopes to convince Ligurinus that his beauty is transitory and that he should not be so arrogant, which Seneca's chorus likewise wishes to stress: 'beauty is a fleeting thing: use it while you can' (*res est forma fugax...* | *dum licet, utere,* Phaed. 773–774).[49] While Hippolytus's beauty is stressed throughout the play, it is notable that he does not look like the standard *eromenos* of erotic poetry, but is rather a hardened, hirsute, and rugged individual (e. g. Phaed. 453–462, 657–660, 803–808). Additionally, there is a clear intertext with Carm. 1.19 as the choral ode continues:

> Vexent hanc faciem frigora parcius,
> haec solem facies rarius appetat:
> lucebit Pario marmore clarius.
> quam grata est facies torva viriliter
> et pondus veteris triste supercili!
> Phoebo colla licet splendida compares...
>
> Let the cold buffet this face more sparingly,
> And the heat burn this face more rarely:
> It will shine brighter than Parian marble.
> How pleasing is his manly, glowering complexion
> And the heavy weight of his bristly brow.
> Although you may compare his shining neck to Phoebus...
> (Phaed. 795–800)

---

49 Thomas 2011, 210–215 stresses that Carm. 4.10 must be viewed within the tradition of Hellenistic epigram, which 'deals with boys whose pederastically appealing bloom is contrasted with the mature, unappealing state in which they will soon find themselves' (211).

>   urit me Glycerae nitor
> splendentis Pario marmore purius:
>   urit grata protervitas
> et vultus nimium lubricus aspici.
>
> The glow of Glycera sets me aflame
> She who shines more clearly than Parian marble:
> Her pleasing wantonness burns me
> And her face too dangerous to look upon.
> (Carm. 1.19.5–8)

Here we see another expansion from the larger Horatian poem with terms such as *grata* now used to highlight Hippolytus's virile form, while his neck's splendour (*splendida*) is seen to rival Glycera's intertextually.[50] Hippolytus, however, is more like the mature Ligurinus (bristly beard, muscular, etc.) and could only become as bright as Glycera if he succumbs to a life of indoor luxury, which is anathema to his character. The distance between the real Hippolytus and the idealised object of desire is thus brought into productive dissonance by these choral ruminations, even as Phaedra herself realises all too well her attraction for him (Phaed. 646–660). When Hippolytus spurns her, Phaedra formulates her desire again in a manner consistent with Horace, now Carm. 4.1, when she says, 'I will follow you through fire, through the mad sea, cliffs, and rivers which the flood seizes with its wave' (*te vel per ignes, per mare insanum sequar | rupesque et amnes, unda quos torrens rapit,* Phaed. 700–701), a sentiment that she repeats before her death: 'I will madly follow you through the waves and lakes of Tartarus, through the Styx, through fiery rivers' (*et te per undas perque Tartareos lacus, | per Styga, per amnes igneos amens sequar,* Phaed. 1179–1180).[51] These lines are reminiscent of the end of Carm. 4.1 where, in his dreams, Horace chases after Ligurinus:

>   nocturnis ego somniis
> iam captum teneo, iam volucrem sequor
>   te per gramina Martii
> Campi, te per aquas, dure, volubiles.

---

[50] Note Seneca's use of a comparative form of *clarus* found earlier in the chorus at 744 and of *clarus* at 1111 and 1144. Trinacty 2015, 40 argues, 'The eroticism of the Horatian ode will prove problematic in *Phaedra* as forms of *clarus* soon describe the contrast between the living and dead Hippolytus (1111) and culminate in the "shrill laments" (*claris... lamentis*, 1276) that conclude the play.' Seneca often manipulates the language of intertexts throughout his dramas, showing how he understands the original and transforms its meaning in the course of his play.
[51] Although Zwierlein believes these lines should be deleted, I think their repetition is warranted and purposeful, cf. Coffey and Mayer 1990 ad loc. for a defence of these lines.

> In my dreams I hold you in my arms at one moment,
> But then I follow you as you rush through
>   the grass of the Campus Martius,
> I follow you through rolling rivers, hardhearted one.
> (Carm. 4.1.37–40)

Phaedra will chase the shade of Hippolytus in the same way that Horace's speaker chases the dream-image of Ligurinus, and thus we may think of the Horatian poem as offering a quasi-script for Seneca's character. The repetition of this 'I will follow' trope in Seneca's play attains further significance when it is seen as an intertextual signpost to the Horatian lines – in general Seneca's repetitions often act as signposts for intertextual or thematic expansion.[52] Whereas Richard Thomas mentions the evocative way in which Horace's dream imitates the Virgilian dream of Dido (A. 4.465–468) and the dream simile evoked by Turnus (A. 12.908–912),[53] Seneca conjures up this poignancy in Phaedra's initial comment to Hippolytus (Phaed. 700–701), but then alters its meaning in her mad *post mortem* pursuit of Hippolytus's shade over fiery Underworld waters (Phaed. 1179–1180). The idealised objects of one's desire, like dreams and ghosts, are fleeting simulacra; Seneca's intertext to Carm. 4.1 highlights this similarity and, befitting his tragedy, he stresses the deadly ramification of such desire: Horace's dream becomes a nightmare. Seneca's final death tableaux featuring both Hippolytus and Phaedra double down on the claim in the final line of Carm. 1.19 that perhaps Venus 'will come more kindly when a sacrifice has been made' (*mactata veniet lenior hostia*, Carm. 1.19.16). In fact, both Hippolytus and Phaedra will be sacrificed in the course of the play, revealing Seneca's tragic interpretation of these Horatian poems as well as creating much of the dramatic irony lurking behind the sequence of events. His play becomes another iteration, recasting the prototypical version of this account (Euripides's *Hippolytus*) through intertexts with Horace's lyric language, but stressing the grave results of such obsessive desires. Seneca has read these Horatian poems in tandem, taking their shared line (*Mater saeva Cupidinum*) as an indication of shared intent, and found ways to apply the tropes, imagery, and especially the complete text of these poems in his *Phaedra*.

---

52 Cf. Gunderson 2015, 124–125 for repetition in the *Phaedra*, and Hinds 1998, 1–10 for the idea of signposts or 'Alexandrian footnotes' in Roman literature.
53 Thomas 2011 ad loc.

3 Nothing to Do with Bacchus?

A final example of the strong intertextual relationship between Horace and Seneca and the manner in which Seneca incorporates an analysis of an entire Horatian poem by means of a single cue can be found in the dithyramb to Bacchus in his *Oedipus*.[54] The opening of this *populare carmen* (Oed. 402) evokes the beginning of Horace's *Carmen Saeculare*:

> Effusam redimite comam nutante corymbo,
> mollia Nysaeis armatus bracchia thyrsis,
> > lucidum caeli decus, huc ades...
>
> Your long hair bound by nodding ivy,
> Your soft arms wielding Nysa's thyrsus,
> Bright honour of heaven, come here...
> (Oed. 403–405)

> Phoebe silvarumque potens Diana,
> lucidum caeli decus, o colendi
> semper et culti, date quae precamur
> > tempore sacro...
>
> Phoebus and Diana, mistress of the woods,
> Bright honour of heaven, O you ever worshipped and
> Always to be worshipped, grant what we pray
> At this sacred time...
> (Saec. 1–4)

Seneca's chorus usurps the language of Horace's chorus.[55] Commentators such as Boyle and Töchterle have noted the parallel, but the ramifications of this opening nod to the *Carmen Saeculare* have not yet been fully explained. First, we can see the way in which the identification *lucidum caeli decus* has been moved from Phoebus and Diana to Bacchus, who is not mentioned in the *Carmen Saeculare* but is the only god whom the Theban chorus addresses.[56] Seneca often

---

[54] Cf. Stevens 1999 for another interpretation of this ode in tandem with Carm. 2.19.
[55] Lowrie 2009, 130: 'The *Carmen saeculare*'s preoccupation with the relation of performance to writing responds to the dialectic it explores between social groundedness and aesthetic freedom.' A similar strand of criticism can be seen in the question of the performance of Seneca's tragedies, cf. Kirichenko 2013, 249–279.
[56] Bacchus takes over the powers of both Diana and Apollo, in a sense, and Seneca notably stresses his androgynous appearance to indicate the way this shape-shifting god can embody both Diana and Apollo (*virgineum caput*, Oed. 408; Oed. 419–420 passim)

finds ways to incorporate the language of important intertexts throughout a play, and this phrase is no exception.⁵⁷ Earlier, Oedipus himself prays to Phoebus as the 'greatest honour of the universe,' *maximum mundi decus* (Oed. 250), which is recalled here in a way that, in the words of Boyle, 'suggests to the audience an analogy, even identity, of Bacchus and Apollo.'⁵⁸ Additionally, Creon tells Oedipus that only avenging Laius's death will cause 'bright day to run in the heavens' (*caelo lucidus curret dies*, Oed. 219).⁵⁹ This will be further elaborated in the course of the choral ode, but it is important to note how Oedipus puts his trust in Phoebus and follows his oracular pronouncements, while the chorus looks to Bacchus as its saviour 'as long as the bright stars of aged heaven run' (*lucida dum current annosi sidera mundi*, Oed. 503).⁶⁰ The only remaining moment in which *decus* is mentioned in the play is near the conclusion, when Jocasta addresses herself and says that the 'whole honour of human law, having been muddled up, dies through you, incestuous woman' (*omne confusum perit, | incesta, per te iuris humani decus*, Oed. 1025–1026). Thus Seneca deploys the language of the tag *lucidum caeli decus* at important moments of the play to indicate the relationship the characters have with the gods.⁶¹ In essence, this is also his reading of the *Carmen Saeculare*.

Horace's lyric choral song is refashioned in Seneca's tragic choral song, which is particularly concerned with defining itself as emblematic of tragedy. Aspects of this ode reflect on its own theatricality, as Bacchus is described as playing a role (*imitatus*, 419; *simulata*, 420), and is dressed in a long robe (*syrma*, 423)

---

57 Cf. Trinacty 2014, 193–197 and passim for examples of this.
58 Boyle 2011 ad loc. Although there has been much ink spilled on whether Horace's line refers to Diana alone or Apollo and Diana, for Seneca we see variations of the line used of Apollo here, Diana at Phaed. 410: *clarumque caeli sidus et noctis decus* ('Brilliant star of heaven and honour of the night') and the sun at Her. F. 592: *O lucis almae rector et caeli decus* ('O ruler of nourishing light and honour of the sky'). Seneca's application of the term to Bacchus shows how he is willing to extend the characteristics to a god who usually does not share these traits, hinting at his vital importance to the play.
59 These earlier formulations may prime the reader for the eventual clear intertext to Horace.
60 Also recalling the *mitia sidera* of Phoebus's oracle at 233.
61 *Caelum* is a very common word in Senecan tragedy and appears seventeen times in *Oedipus*. Note how Oedipus believes his presence has polluted the heaven (*fecimus caelum nocens*, 'I have made the sky polluted,' Oed. 36), which can become salubrious again after his exile at the play's conclusion (*mitior caeli status | posterga sequitur*, 'A more gentle sky follows in my wake,' Oed. 1054–1055). Jocasta's admission of incest and legal language contrasts with the focus on childbirth and marriage laws in the *Carmen Saeculare*.

that is traditionally considered part of the theatrical costume.[62] Bacchus himself is the god of drama, and Seneca's use of the dithyrambic form may recall Aristotle's idea that tragedies developed from dithyrambs in honour of Dionysus,[63] or Livy's description of drama's introduction to Rome as a response to a plague, much like the dramatic situation of this play.[64] The reference to Pentheus's death in Seneca's song (Oed. 439–444) reminds one of Dionysus's role of writer / director / producer in the *Bacchae*, as well as the lengthy description of Pentheus's death that concludes Ovid's *Metamorphoses* 3.[65] The Horatian gods that were important for Rome (Apollo, Diana, Jupiter, Ilithyia) now play second fiddle to Bacchus, and the world domination present in Horace's song (Saec. 53–56) is reflected in Bacchus's own conquests (Oed. 424–428, 478–483). Seneca's metrical mélange incorporates Horace's sapphics, but only in one section of the choral ode (Oed. 416–428); otherwise, Seneca prefers to show his metrical sophistication by including polymetric sections and organising the song with hexameter section breaks.[66] Seneca is clearly trying to rewrite elements of the *Carmen Saeculare* as a *tragic* chorus and to emphasise his transformation of it in this choral song. The chorus prays to Bacchus to alleviate the plague, stresses his powers of transformation and fertility, and metadramatically underscores the efficacy of the tragic genre.[67] The ideological heft of the *Carmen Saeculare* and the hopeful poetic 'magic' of that *carmen* is manipulated in Seneca's chorus where the *lucidum caeli decus* is to be embodied by Bacchus as both dramatic god and

---

[62] Cf. Curley 1986, 119–120. The yellow (*lutea*, 421) belt 'is also the colour of the tragic dress... traditionally worn by an actor playing Bacchus / Dionysus' (Boyle 2011 ad loc). *Syrma* stands for tragedy at Mart. 12.94.4–5 and cf. OLD s.v. *syrma*, b.

[63] Cf. Nisbet and Hubbard 1978, 316 for more on Bacchus as patron of the theatre and Schiesaro 2016 for Bacchus in Roman drama.

[64] Liv. 7.1.7–7.2.13. Note how Horace's account of the development of Latin drama (Ep. 2.1.139–155) is preceded by his description of the chorus who seeks the aid of the gods to 'avert disease' and 'expel fearful dangers' (*avertit morbos, metuenda pericula pellit*, Ep. 2.1.136).

[65] Agave will be mentioned again in the play (Oed. 616, 933 by name, and as an *exemplum* for Jocasta's behavior at 1004–1007), as is Pentheus (Oed. 617–618). If the *Aeneid* was the primary intertext for Horace's *Carmen Saeculare*, Ovid's *Metamorphoses* fulfils that role in Seneca's ode and stresses the importance of transformation as a theme to the *Oedipus*. Note how the stories of the 'dolphinification' of the pirates (Met. 3.577–700) and Ino (Met. 4.416–542) are capped in Seneca's ode.

[66] The hexameters could recall those of the Sibylline oracle.

[67] Boyle 2011 ad loc. rehearses these points and concludes, 'the ode has a metapoetic and metatragic function, indexing the transformative powers of tragic drama' (208).

patron god of Thebes.⁶⁸ The intertext with the *Carmen Saeculare* also suggests a strong connection between Thebes and Rome, which has also been seen in the Theban tales of Ovid's *Metamorphoses*.⁶⁹ Both choral songs are ultimately optimistic expressions, although Seneca's is contextualised within the grim events of his tragedy, and thus can only be an assertion of a tentative hope for the future amidst the present plague-ridden devastation of Thebes.⁷⁰ This contrast in locale is crucial for our understanding of Seneca's reception of the *Carmen Saeculare* in his *Oedipus*.

Of all of Horace's poems (perhaps, all ancient Latin poems) the *Carmen Saeculare* is to our eyes the most emphatically tied to a time (3 June 17 BCE), place (the song was performed on the Palatine and Capitoline hills), and event (the *Ludi Saeculares*). The *Ludi Saeculares*, 'by which the new regime chose to celebrate its own definitive establishment, sealing the past and looking forward to a new, brighter future,'⁷¹ were religious, political, and, most importantly, Roman.⁷² The intertext and the knowledge of the full poem and its performance would conjure the larger social, religious, and political framework of Augustus's *Ludi Saeculares*. Seneca's reference to the *Carmen Saeculare* thus takes on a political dimension, especially if one remembers that Claudius himself had cele-

---

68 For more on the magical nature of *carmina*, cf. Putnam 2000, 130–150 passim. At *Oed.* 561, Tiresias employs a 'magical song' (*carmen magicum*) to summon the dead and learn how to combat the plague.
69 Hardie 1990. Hinds 2011 applies Hardie's findings to Seneca's *Oedipus* and *Phoenissae*.
70 There are other intertexts to the *Carmen Saeculare* in Senecan drama, but most do not evoke the song as a whole. As an example, Saec. 28 *iungite fata* is given a sinister turn at Phaed. 1183–1184: *non licuit animos iungere, at certe licet | iunxisse fata* ('It was not permitted for us to join our spirits, but it is permitted to join our deaths'). In the *Carmen Saeculare* it is a call to the fates to join 'good fates' (*bona… fata*, Saec. 27–28) to those already past (*peractis*, 27), whereas Seneca exploits an additional definition of *fata* ('deaths'), and the yoking imagery is a strong motif throughout the play. Seneca once again twists the hopefulness of Horace's language into something forlorn in the context of his play, but without suggesting the complete *Carmen Saeculare*.
71 Günther 2013, 431.
72 The question of Horace's partisanship is vexed, but in a more moderate sense many of his poems, including the *Carmen Saeculare*, are political, cf. Putnam 2000, 144, 'But Horace is creating a world for politics, not serving as a henchman to the mighty or as an aesthetic today. He is exerting a poet's power not only to imagine what the Roman polis should be but to bring that vision into being by means of his originality, whether in the poem's grand sweep or in the emphases of bright detail.' The religious feeling of the *Carmen Saeculare* would also be strongly felt in the *Oedipus* because of the various prophetic activities that are staged or reported, including visits to the Delphic Oracle, *extispicium*, and necromancy, cf. Ahl 2008, 121–123.

brated the *Ludi Saeculares* in 47 CE.[73] While we do not have much information about these *ludi*, we can assume that choral songs, sacrifices, and spectacles (including theatrical shows) were integral to the celebration.[74] Seneca had no love for Claudius, and the identification of Thebes as a surrogate for Rome casts ominous overtones to this iteration of the *Carmen Saeculare*.

Through this intertext Seneca questions whether the Rome of his day has truly lived up to the new, brighter future that Horace had ushered in and pronounced in his *Carmen Saeculare*. The character Oedipus exhibits features that would evoke Claudius (his limp, incest, his interest in *haruspicina*) and even the patron god, Bacchus, may evoke Claudius through Mark Antony's identification with Bacchus.[75] It must be remembered that Antony was Claudius's grandfather (a point that Seneca himself makes at Dial. 11.16.1). Whereas Horace celebrated Augustus's cultural revolution in the *Carmen Saeculare*, Seneca lambasts Claudius's disastrous rule in the *Oedipus*. The intertext with the *Carmen Saeculare* and the dramatic irony involved in its position in this hymn makes this contrast clear. In the *Apocolocyntosis* Claudius is said to be worse than a monster ('Then Hercules at first glance was really disturbed, as one who had feared monsters, but not yet all of them,' *tum Hercules primo aspectu sane perturbatus est, ut qui etiam non omnia monstra timuerit*, Apoc. 5.3) – and Oedipus's monstrous nature is stressed throughout the play ('a monster more confounding than his own Sphinx,' *magisque monstrum Sphinge perplexum sua*, Oed. 641).[76] While Horace's chorus praises Diana and Apollo (*doctus et Phoebi chorus et Dianae | dicere laudes*, Saec. 75–76) to ensure the fecundity of Augustus's Rome, the praises for Bacchus (*laudibus*, Oed. 402) sharply contrast with the bleak reality of Thebes and, by implication, Claudius's Rome. This intertext is a clue that Seneca wishes the reader to remember recent *Ludi Saeculares* and thus lead to an identification of Oedipus with Claudius.[77] Nothing beneficial will come to the city of Thebes until Oedipus leaves, which may be paralleled by the picture Seneca paints in

---

73 Fitch 1981 dates the *Oedipus* in a group of 'early plays' at some point before 54 CE. Boyle 2011, xviii, lxxx–lxxxi believes that it could be Claudian in date, especially 'the post-Messalina Claudian court.' I concur with Boyle and would date the play to the early 50s. Claudius figured his games from the traditional founding date of Rome, 753 BCE.
74 Cf. Suet. Claud. 21.2, Tac. Ann. 11.11; Pighi 1965, 76–78, 131–136 provides the evidence for Claudius's *Ludi*. See Schnegg-Köhler 2002 for more on the Augustan games.
75 See Stevens 1999, 285–287 for more on Antony and Bacchus, and his entire article for a similar allegorical interpretation. Hardie 2016, 16–17 for current bibliography and discussion of this identification in Augustan literature.
76 See Staley 2010, 96–120 for the central position of 'monsters' in Senecan tragedy.
77 Tac. Dial. 3.3 indicates how mythological tragedies can contain hidden criticisms of contemporary politics.

the *Apocolocyntosis* of Rome at the death of Claudius and the new golden age ushered in with Nero. An intertextual reading of the *Carmen Saeculare* accentuates how the larger historical and political circumstances of the Horatian original is evoked in the *Oedipus* with an eye to political critique as well as literary emulation and adaptation.

4 Conclusion: Recontextualisation is Interpretation

Seneca's intertextual technique goes beyond simple 'borrowings.' He utilises intertextuality for a variety of functions, and this paper has shown how he can sophisticatedly evoke the complete poem from where the intertext is drawn. This is not always the case (see n. 70 *supra*), but the recontextualisation of certain Horatian sources in Seneca's tragic genre serves as a Senecan reading of those Horatian poems.[78] This recontextualisation happens when one recognises Horatian language, but now in the mouth of Phaedra or Medea, or resounding in a tragic choral ode. Seneca will often continue to evoke the Horatian poem in the course of his tragedy to reiterate its importance or hint at the way he is interpreting Horace's original in the tragedy. The intertextual dynamic in these encounters creates further consequences, whether literary critical, philosophical, political, or metapoetic. Other examples spring to mind, such as the civil war narrative of *Epod*. 7 and the way Seneca deploys it to comment on the fratricidal *furor* of the *Thyestes*, or the strife between Eteocles and Polyneices in the *Phoenissae*.[79]

---

[78] The fact that he draws upon various genres of Horace's poetry from iambic epodes to hexameter epistles reveals how Seneca conceives of the tragic genre as an amalgamation of various genres of poetry, cf. Trinacty 2014, 6–9, 18–21.

[79] The opening speech of Furia (Thy. 23–67) features two intertexts to Horace Epod. 7, which Seneca reads as a graphic statement of civil war violence and social upheaval. Seneca echoes Epod. 7.1: *quo quo scelesti ruitis?* ('Where where do you criminals rush?') at the end of the speech: *siste, quo praeceps ruis?*, 'Stop, where do you rush headlong,' Thy. 67), and both feature the phrase *furor caecus* (Thy. 27, Epod. 7.13). Also cf. *effusus omnis irriget terras cruor* ('the gush of blood waters all the lands,' Thy. 44 – and its context) and the end of Horace's *Epode*, *immerentis fluxit in terram Remi | sacer nepotibus cruor* ('the blood of innocent Remus | flowed into the land, a curse to his descendants,' Epod. 7.19–20). Because Epod. 7 deals with civil war, one can see the way in which Seneca is figuring the interaction between Atreus and Thyestes as a civil conflict, and Roman touches can even be seen in his use of *penates* (Thy. 24, 52). Also visible is the way in which this *furor* is later evoked in a passage about civil war (Thy. 339–341). An echo of *sacer cruor* (Epod. 7.20) at Phoen. 277–278 indicates how Oedipus's incest will result in the mutual slaughter of the brothers, Eteocles and Polyneices. Watson's description of Epod. 7 is appo-

This paper has investigated three case studies of such intertextual play and recontextualisation in Seneca's *Medea*, *Phaedra*, and *Oedipus*. Seneca's evocation of Ep. 1.2 in his *Medea* shows how the ethical *exempla* derived from literature can actually spur on Medea's evil plans ('begin whatever Medea can do, whatever she cannot'), while the echo of Epod. 5 highlights Medea's previous killing of Absyrtus and the way such literary antecedents can influence the action of the play. In both cases the larger generic context of the Horatian source influences the manner in which Seneca handles the material – the philosophical *Epistles* a have a different resonance than the hostility underlying the *Epodes* and Seneca draws upon each in a distinctive manner. Encouraged by the identical line in Carm. 1.19 and Carm. 4.1, Seneca reads these Horatian lyrics together as a master text of reluctant desire that helps to flesh out his characterisation of Phaedra, foreshadow her actions, and indicate how this emotional repetition is also grounded in *literary* repetition.[80] A similar impulse can be found in Latin love elegy, as Kennedy elucidates: 'within the lover's discourse, the achievement of "real" love is always deferred... object "choice" may be developed, determined and prosecuted within strategies of *unattainability*, with even the ostensibly "attainable" being projected as "beyond reach" within the lover's discourse.'[81] While Seneca's choral odes oscillate between figuring such desire as universal or uniquely applicable to Hippolytus, Phaedra applies the Horatian trope to her own longing with grave results that the source material only intimates. The *Oedipus*'s choral song references the most important choral song of the Augustan regime in order to reflect upon itself as a tragic chorus. It stresses Bacchus's ability to subsume characteristics of other gods and the tragic genre's ability to integrate literary material from a variety of sources. Additionally, it appraises the recent political situation in Rome through the evocation of the larger ideological, religious, and social background of Horace's *Carmen Saeculare*. By pointing to these larger contexts, whether literary or cultural, one can under-

---

site for the worlds of the *Thyestes* and the *Phoenissae* as well: 'the Romans are locked into a never-ending cycle of internal *stasis*' (2003, 269).
80 Here I think of Nick Hornby's 1995 novel *High Fidelity* and his musings about pop music: 'What came first – the music or the misery? Did I listen to the music because I was miserable? Or was I miserable because I listened to the music? Do all those records turn you into a melancholy person?' (24–25).
81 Kennedy 1993, 70–71.

stand more clearly how Seneca interprets and manipulates the complete Horatian work through his reception of it in his tragic settings.[82]

---

[82] I want to thank the editors, Kathrin Winter, Martin Stöckinger, and Tom Zanker, as well as the participants at the *Horace and Seneca: Interactions, Intertexts, Interpretations* conference for their comments and questions.

Tobias Allendorf
Sounds and Space. Seneca's Horatian Lyrics

'And from high hills the streamlet lightly leaps with sounding footfall,'[1] ...*montibus altis | levis crepante lympha desilit pede*, writes Horace in *Epode* 16.[2] This dark poem, whose interpretation is famously contentious,[3] announces to the Romans that the continued civil wars will destroy the state. The best course of action would be, the poem sets out, to abandon their homeland and make for the Happy Isles. In the lines cited, however, we are in the middle of an imagined idyllic landscape, with an abundance of water. Note how Horace uses the sound of his poetry to mimic the sound of water: in the repetition of liquids (*altis | levis... lympha desilit*), the accumulation of front (so-called 'bright') vowels (*altis | levis crepante lympha desilit pede*), and the rhythm and speed of the line (Porphyrio writes, *sonus versus imitatur et velocitatem et strepitum aquae currentis*, 'the sound of the line imitates both the speed and the sound of the flowing water').[4] The sonic mimesis is put into relief by the poet's self-conscious use of *pes*, 'foot,' of course referencing the anthropomorphic water as much as the metrical form of the line ('metrical feet').[5] What is more, the Horatian line also fuses the description of sound – the sonic effects of the line, which include its metre as

---

Research for this article was facilitated by an AHRC Doctoral Award. Attendance at the Heidelberg conference was made possible by a Craven Award from the Faculty of Classics, Oxford. I would like to thank the editors of the present volume for inviting me to speak at the conference, and for their suggestions on my contribution. I am also grateful to the other speakers for useful discussions, and to Kalina Allendorf, Stephen Harrison, Tobias Reinhardt, and Richard Tarrant for their constructive feedback on my paper.

1 Unless noted otherwise, I follow Zwierlein's OCT for Seneca's tragedies and Shackleton Bailey's Teubner text for Horace. English translations of Horace (*Epodes* and *Odes*) are taken (sometimes adapted) from West (Oxford University Press); for translations of Seneca, I have used Fitch's Loeb. All other translations are my own.
2 Hor. Epod. 16.47–48 (I owe thanks to Martin Stöckinger for suggesting to me that I do something with these striking Horatian lines).
3 The bibliography provided by Setaioli 1981, 1744–1762 gives an idea about the scope of scholarship on the poem.
4 See Porphyrio (Holder 1894) ad loc.
5 Such self-conscious use of *pes* is common, and goes back to the very beginning of Latin poetry: cf. e.g. the hexameter with which Ennius most likely opened his *Annals*, *Musae quae pedibus magnum pulsatis Olympum* (Ann. fr. 1 Skutsch).

DOI 10.1515/9783110528893-007

well as its content, the sound of swift streams – with the description of a place, the idyllic space of hills whence water flows. In the present paper, I will show in a series of case studies that 'sound' and 'space' are important components of both Horace's and Seneca's lyrical compositions. I shall suggest that Seneca's fusion of sonic effects with the mapping of space and descriptions of places has close precedent in Horace's lyrics. Many of Seneca's Horatian allusions, furthermore, are marked either by sonic or spatial elements pointing to Horace.

Sound and space have been important for the study of Horace's poetry, especially with regard to the *Odes*. What would Horace's lyric undertaking be without its sound and rhythm, without his classicising standardisation in Latin of the lyric metres of his predecessors, especially the alcaics and sapphics?[6] There are further dimensions of Horace's mastery of sound: from Lee and Wilkinson, for instance, one learns about Horace's 'verbal music' (including devices such as alliteration and onomatopoeia).[7] The importance of space, topography, and landscapes has also been acknowledged for Horace's poetry: the dimensions of the Horatian aesthetic of space, as well as the Augustan mapping of the geography of the Roman empire, have rightly received detailed scholarly attention.[8]

The sounds of Seneca's lyrics cannot but echo their Horatian precedent: one of the key features of Senecan sound on the formal level is of course metre – his metrical practice is essentially based on Horace's. Without the Horatian precedent, Seneca's lyrics would probably have looked very different (perhaps more like the lyrics of Republican drama).[9] Like Horace, Seneca is a poet well aware of the possibilities of poetic spatiality. The geography of his plays, though dealing with recognisably Greek subjects, is distinctly Roman. A case in point is the *Thyestes*, where, as Tarrant has pointed out, 'Roman realities are so thoroughly fused with Greek as to create a strange hybrid world, a Mycenae populated by Quirites, a royal palace protected (however ineffectively) by Lares and Penates, and a kingdom whose borders are threatened by Parthians and Alans.'[10] In this respect, Seneca shares the landscape of the Augustan poets, with the

---

[6] See esp. Heinze's foundational study of Horace's use of metre (Heinze 1960), and Nisbet / Hubbard 1970, xxxviii–xlvi.
[7] Wilkinson 1963, Lee 1969.
[8] On Horace's landscapes see Harrison 2007b, who focuses on a central Horatian opposition, town vs. country (cf. the material collected in Troxler-Keller 1964). See also Schmidt 2002, 117–153, and Schwindt 2005, where the representation of space in Augustan poetry is closely linked to conceptions of time; on Horace, see esp. 15–18.
[9] Of which unfortunately only about eighty lines survive.
[10] Tarrant 1995, 226.

phantasma of the Parthians always lurking on the margins (as they are depicted in Horace, Virgil, and Propertius).

The mapping of poetic landscapes alongside the creation of a tragic space, moreover, is at the heart of the poetics of Senecan drama.[11] Schmidt has recently pointed to some of the ways in which Seneca's management of physical space can be conceptualised (in close connection with the management of dramatic time).[12] While this approach may have advanced our understanding of the theatricality of Seneca's plays, this will not be the domain of my paper. Instead, I will be concerned with the aesthetic dimensions of 'space' in Seneca's tragedies.

Many spatial moments in Senecan tragedy are, I suggest, accompanied by an emphasis on sounds. These sounds are of two different types: sounds that are described, produced, or heard by the characters in the plays (including the Chorus), and sounds that are created in the poetic form of Seneca's lines. The latter include the devices studied by Wilkinson and Lee in Augustan 'golden' poetry: 'verbal music,' rhythm, and metre. On both levels, Senecan engagement with Horace is important for a full understanding of the intertextual and allusive dynamics.[13]

---

[11] Seneca's use of space has long been noted as a striking feature: esp. his extended topographical *ecphraseis* have been analysed as a feature that points to Senecan drama's mere 'rhetorical' character (Leo's *tragoedia rhetorica*) and unstageability (Zwierlein). Recently, scholars have attempted more positive approaches to these descriptions, examining them as crucial building blocks of Senecan tragic architecture: see esp. Aygon 2004, Winter 2014, esp. 158–159, and Allendorf 2013, 132–134, where I place the Senecan spatial descriptions within his 'poetics of uncertainty.'

[12] See Schmidt 2014.

[13] I distinguish between 'allusion' and (Kristevan) 'intertext' (see Kristeva 1967): while I agree with Hinds about his reservations concerning 'philological fundamentalism' (Hinds 1998, esp. 17–51), I believe that there is no surplus in a critical environment in which studies in intertextuality and allusion routinely talk about 'intertexts' even if the scholars in question believe in conscious involvement of the authors. For an excellent overview of the differences between 'allusion' (authors consciously involved) and 'intertext' (a relationship between [in the system of] texts) that I rely on in this paper, see Fowler 2000.

1 Metre and Meaning in Latin Poetry and in Seneca

Seneca's tragic use of lyric metres is at the centre of his engagement with the Roman lyric tradition,[14] and most notably with Horace.[15] Metre is as much a semiotic unit to be taken seriously in literary studies as are words, images, and figures of thought.[16] The Romans were certainly aware of this. In studies of intertextual allusion we probably need to give closer attention to the sounds of poetry, which may be obscured by our contemporary readerly practice, with its overwhelming focus on the visual experience. Unlike us, ancient readers would read aloud, even when on their own.[17] Moreover, for ancient readers metre and sound were among the most obvious forms of allusive practice in poetry. The fact that ancient audiences were able to appreciate metrical subtleties becomes clear from a number of examples. Horace, Ars 263 (*Non quivis videt immodulata poemata iudex*, 'Not every judge discerns unrhythmical verses') is a

---

14 See Leo 1878, the groundbreaking study for the description of Seneca's colometry in general and for the way in which Senecan metre derives from Horace in particular (the polymetric odes are discussed at 110–134). Leo, however, underestimated the value of the A tradition. See also Tarrant 1976, 372 (with further references). Apart from the anapaests and the polymetric odes, Seneca's tragedies have choral odes in the first asclepiad, in glyconics, in sapphics, and one in catalectic iambic dimeters with three *clausulae*. There are also lines in dactylic hexameters, and some lyric metres used outside the choral odes. See Zwierlein's OCT *conspectus* (1993, 464–469).
15 Seneca also looks back to Catullus. The first choral song of *Oedipus* provides perhaps the most prominent instance of Seneca's use of Catullus: cf. Boyle 2011, 145, who describes Seneca's 'overt use' of Catullus 11 (and Catullus 51: see Boyle 2011, 157).
16 Fussell 1979 provides three ways in which metre 'means': (1) as the 'primary convention of artifice in poetry,' distinguishing it from ordinary language; (2) as a commentary on its own form, meaningfully 'varying from itself'; (3) by association 'with certain kinds of statements and feelings.' See the discussion by Morgan 2010, 4–7, who is predominantly concerned with the third way of meaning in his study. For Seneca's choral odes, it will be most profitable to view Seneca's practice with Fussell's second and third categories in mind, though these categories are in no way mutually exclusive.
17 Reading in antiquity often constituted a type of 'private recitation': see again Kenney 1982, 12. The evidence for *silent* reading in antiquity is discussed by Knox 1968. Silent reading seems to have been the exception rather than the rule; even the use of *lectores* was much more widespread (see Starr 1991). Burnyeat 1997 shows that some ancients were used to reading silently in his discussion of passages from Ptolemy and Plotinus that equate reading silently and concentrating hard. For an overview of the question in scholarship, see Johnson 2010, 4–9, who then goes on to discuss further ramifications in his book, moving the focus to the broader question of 'reading culture.' See also Busch 2002, and, on the Greek practice, Vatri 2012.

case in point: Horace clearly meant recipients to pick up the metrical joke in a line that, containing no middle caesura, is as *immodulatus* as can be.[18] Ancient rhetoricians and grammarians were aware of the semiotic possibilities of metre. One of Seneca's contemporaries, Caesius Bassus, who, according to Quintilian, was the only Roman lyric poet worth reading besides Horace, is particularly relevant as a source for contemporary readers' abilities to appreciate and analyse metrical subtleties.[19] Quintilian, moreover, who cites examples from tragedy, comments on the use of short and long syllables, saying that shorts produce *celeritas*, longs add to *gravitas* (Quint. Inst. 9.4.139–141).[20]

Seneca's mastery of rhythm, not least in the anapaests (as Fitch has shown),[21] makes clear that he is a poet well aware of the expressive effects of metre. Consider, for instance, the following examples that Fitch provides. In these Senecan lines, the conglomeration of longs – which create a spondaic rhythm out of the anapaests (spondees underlined below) – serves to express slowness (as at Thy. 873: see 1 below), the motionlessness of cold winter (Phaed. 966–967: 2 below), and heaviness (Phaed. 973–974: 3 below):[22]

(1) custosque sui tardus plaustri   – – ᴗ ᴗ – – – –
    and the slow guard of the *Wain*
    (Thy. 873)
(2) ut nunc canae frigora brumae   – – – – – ᴗ ᴗ – –
         nudent silvas,   – – – –

---

[18] See e.g. Wilamowitz-Moellendorff 1921, 9. Another case in point is the satirists' practice from Lucilius to Juvenal, who deliberately break metrical conventions when also transgressing on the level of content, or achieve effects by the dichotomy of the base language and the highly formalised metrical form (see Morgan 2010, 4 and 310–345). In prose, too, writers as late as Tacitus would have expected their readers to comprehend metrical allusions such as at the very beginning of the *Annals* (*Urbem Romam a principio reges habuere*), where the archaising hexameter clearly points to Ennius's great foundational epic poem of the same title as Tacitus's annalistic undertaking (against Goodyear 1972 ad loc.). The flaws of the hexameter, which seems to Goodyear 'so faulty indeed that it may not have been felt to be a hexameter at all,' are in fact noted features of the Ennian hexameter: a four-syllabic word at the end of a line, and the *hephthemimeres* as the only caesura. On the significance of metre and rhythm in Tacitus see e.g. Kloss 2009, a case study of Tacitus's sophisticated practice in Ann. 3.55.

[19] See Quint. Inst. 10.1.96. Caesius Bassus is also the addressee of Persius, Sat. 6, and one of the most significant ancient theorists to argue that all metres derive from a selection of prototypical basic metres (see Leo 1889, with the modifications of Leonhardt 1989). What he describes as a theorist of metre, Seneca, it can be argued, achieved as a practitioner in his plays, especially in the experimental arrangement of cola in the polymetric odes.

[20] See Hutchinson 2013, 157.
[21] Fitch 1987, esp. 77–85.
[22] The examples are selected from Fitch 1987, 77–78.

>   so that now the chill of frosty winter denudes the forests
>   (Phaed. 966–967)
> (3) sub quo vasti pondera mundi   – – – – – ᴗ ᴗ – –
>   librata suos ducunt orbes.   – – ᴗ ᴗ – – – – –
>   under whom the masses of the mighty heavens trace in balance their proper orbits
>   (Phaed. 973–974)

Conversely, Seneca's use of short syllables – especially his use of multiple anapaests in anapaestic lines – can express the lightness of a nightingale's song, as at Ag. 672 (containing no spondees: see excerpt 4 below). Often, they can create a sense of speed, as at Oed. 755–758 (see 5 below), where one should note how the anapaests in the lines correspond with the speed of Actaeon's anxious flight, whereas woods, mountains, and valleys are spondaic in their bulk (*silvas*; *montes*; *saltus*):[23]

> (4) Ityn in varios modulata sonos   ᴗ ᴗ – ᴗ ᴗ – ᴗ ᴗ – ᴗ ᴗ –
>   inflecting 'Itys' in varied notes
>   (Ag. 672)
> (5) praeceps silvas montesque fugit   – – – – – ᴗ ᴗ –
>   citus Actaeon agilique magis   ᴗ ᴗ – – – ᴗ ᴗ – ᴗ ᴗ –
>   pede per saltus ac saxa vagus   ᴗ ᴗ – – – – – ᴗ ᴗ –
>   metuit motas zephyris plumas   ᴗ ᴗ – – – ᴗ ᴗ – – –
>   Swift Actaeon fled headlong amidst forests and hills; through brush, over rocks, he wandered on more agile feet,[24] fearing the feathers moving in the breeze
>   (Oed. 755–758)

2 Reception Contexts

The semiotics of metre, of what metre can mean, also raises questions about the pragmatics of reception, of how metrical compositions are received and made sense of by audiences, listeners, or readers.[25] At Rome, some might say not with-

---

[23] These and more examples are given in Fitch 1987, 81–82 (I follow Zwierlein's colometry).
[24] On 'feet' cf. above, n. 5.
[25] In my critical approach, it will not make a difference whether Seneca's plays were *originally* intended for staging, recitation, or reading. While the Horatian elements in Seneca's choral lyrics could point towards similar reception contexts, i.e. recitation, the question is probably underdetermined by evidence. Scholars will have to make up their minds based mainly on internal evidence: a doxographical overview on the staging question is provided e.g. by Kugelmeier 2007, 14–23. In the end, he corroborates Zwierlein's findings, who argues for recitation (1966). Staged theatre is imagined as the primary Senecan performance context by Boyle (see his Introduction to his commentaries), and see also the volume [G. W. M.] Harrison 2000.

out reason, poetry was written for recitation.²⁶ It was, however, also written for reading. While we know of many significant forms of recitation,²⁷ the Latin poets themselves demonstrate that they acquired their knowledge of previous Greek and Roman poetry predominantly through reading.²⁸ When it comes to Horace's and Seneca's lyrics, a comment by Cicero is worthy of note: according to him, 'one can derive more pleasure from reading lyric poetry than from hearing it.'²⁹ At the time of Pliny the Younger, 'the reading of these [i.e. lyric poems] is customary.'³⁰ What might be – and has been – posed as a dichotomy involving two mutually exclusive options can be resolved by drawing a clear distinction: while recitation is the answer to the question of the first reception, reading is the answer to the question of the subsequent circulation and influence of poetry.³¹ Poets who have themselves encountered earlier poets in reading are unlikely to write only with recitation in mind. My analysis in the following will mainly trace those points of contact between Seneca's and Horace's lyrics that would be most easily noticeable to readers. I should reiterate here that, in ancient reading practices, sound effects would come out strongly, since Roman readers favoured reading aloud even when in private.³² My insistence on the reading and re-reading of Senecan drama also coincides with Lowrie's attractive view on the reception contexts of Horace's *Odes*: as she argues (and exemplifies in detailed

---

26 Cf. Kenney 1982, 3: 'nearly all the books discussed in this history [i.e. the *Cambridge History of Classical Literature*] were written to be listened to.' On the important practice of *recitatio* in small circles see, in addition to Kenney 1982, esp. 11–12, the material collected by Funaioli 1914. The practice of Roman (semi-)public recitation was probably started by Asinius Pollio (see Sen. Con. 4 praef. 2).
27 Including readings arranged by professionals, readings to rather private audiences, and readings by the authors themselves (see also above, n. 26). Perhaps most famously, we have testimony of Virgil having read the *Georgics* and some books of the *Aeneid* to the imperial family: see e.g. Serv. A. 4.323 and 6.861.
28 Important examples include Horace reading the scripts of Old Comedy (see Hor. S. 1.10.18), Horace reading Lucilius (Hor. S. 1.10.56), and Catullus needing a library to compose poetry (see Catul. 68.33). Examples adduced by Parker 2009, 212.
29 Cic. Tusc. 5.116: *multo maiorem percipi posse legendis iis* [sc. *cantibus*] *quam audiendis voluptatem*.
30 Plin. Ep. 7.17.1–3, esp. 3: *At horum* [sc. *lyricorum*] *recitatio usu iam recepta est*.
31 Cf. now Wiseman 2015 for the wider Roman context.
32 Cf. Cic. Tusc. 5.116 (see above, n. 29) on the superiority of reading lyric poetry over listening to it. According to Fantham 1982, 34–49, esp. 48–49, moreover, Seneca does not differ from the forms of publication of, say, Ovid or Virgil.

case studies), the *Odes* invoke the idea of repeated 'performance' as a symbol for repeated reading.³³

3 Sonic allusion in Seneca's practice

In both Horace and Seneca, sounds are crucial for creating a setting. In fact, sound effects of the kind studied by Wilkinson under the rubric of 'verbal music' are key for how Seneca sets himself within the intertextual dynamics of literary history. Apart from metrical form itself, devices such as alliteration, anaphora, and onomatopoeia can acquire semiotic force, especially when they occur in clusters. They also function as strong markers of allusion in Seneca. This is the case not only with regard to his relationship to Horace's lyrics.

In order to make Seneca's creation of sonic intertextual – and allusive – spaces more broadly plausible, I have chosen an example taken from Rome's earliest tragedian, Livius Andronicus. In addition to demonstrating Seneca's technique of sonic allusivity, this passage may go some way towards showing just how far back the models of Senecan drama reach.³⁴ The following three lines must have been included in a backstory account of how the Greeks returned from Troy. The fragment is taken from Livius's play *Aegisthus* (with my highlighting of verbal parallels with the Senecan passage below):³⁵

>   Nam ut Pergama
> <u>accensa</u> et <u>praeda</u> per participes aequiter
> <u>partita</u> est.
>
> For, once Pergamum had been burnt out and the spoils shared fairly among the men taking part in it...
> (Andr. trag. 2–4 Warmington = 9 Schauer)

---

33 See Lowrie 2009, 63–97, with a discussion of the implications of the term 'performance' at 64–71.
34 The interaction between Republican literature (including drama) and Senecan drama may have been underestimated; I am currently reviewing the evidence and literary dynamics in a chapter of my DPhil thesis on the Senecan Chorus.
35 The fragment is preserved at Nonius 512.31. The link to Sen. Ag. 421–422 is already noted by Ribbeck 1875, 28–30, but often not given due attention by later (Senecan) scholars. But cf. the brief acknowledgements of the parallel passages at Warmington 1936, 2–6 ad loc., Waszink 1972, 892, Tarrant 1976, 13–14, and Schauer 2012, 41 ad loc.

Seneca's messenger's account about the same Trojan backstory in the *Agamemnon* begins like this:

> Ut Pergamum omne Dorica cecidit face,
> divisa praeda est, maria properantes petunt.
> Once all of Pergamum fell to Dorian fire, they shared out the spoils and made in haste for the sea.
> (Sen. Ag. 421–422)

One may harbour some initial scepticism as to the likelihood of conscious allusion here. In talking about a common subject, the fall of Troy – a mythopoetic building block *par excellence* – the two poets' creativity may have simply coincided in producing similar lines. I would argue, however, that the careful shaping of sound effects in Seneca's rendition makes conscious allusion likely. Within the intertextual space of the description of Troy, the text's relationship to the Republican tragic script is carefully arranged by Seneca's conscious use of sonic effects. While the verbal affinities may or may not be due to poetic contingency, the plosive alliteration in Eurybates's utterance in Seneca clearly picks up and develops the prominent plosive alliteration in Livius: praeda per participes aequiter partita est and Seneca's praeda est, maria properantes petunt. This is all the more relevant since the Republican poets' predilection for alliteration is unmistakable, and would have been known to Seneca, who expresses his views on archaic features of Latin vocally in his prose writings (see e.g. Ep. 58).

If Livius, moreover, had included the lines towards the beginning of the play, as our conventional ordering of the extant fragments from the *Aegisthus* would have it, Seneca would be quoting lines that must have been rather memorable. Beginnings of poems and plays are prominent spaces for signalling intertextual debts, allusion, and emulation, and conversely, the alluding poet often chooses to engage with lines from the very beginning of the relevant pre-texts. In Seneca's practice, this is also true of his metrical appropriations and allusions: in his metrical engagement with Horace's lyrics, his choice of metre can have proemic force.[36]

---

[36] In the *Medea* and the *Thyestes*, for instance, the Horatian inheritance trumps the Greek tradition: metrical allusion to Horace's 'proemic' metre (that of Carm. 1.1) has replaced the established Greek practice of the Chorus's anapaestic entry. Cf. Boyle 2014, 136.

4 Sonic Spaces of War: Metrical Allusions to Horace in the *Agamemnon*, *Oedipus*, and *Thyestes*

Seneca's interest in the poetic possibilities of metre, rhythm, and verbal sounds can be illuminated by comparing his practice with Horace's. The third choral song in the *Agamemnon* (Ag. 589–658) is one striking instance of a Senecan polymetric ode where the reworking of Horatian poetics pertains to content and spatial imagery as much as to the rearrangement of metrical cola taken from Horace. The chorus reminisces about the disasters of Troy and engages in an elaborate discussion of the question of how to face death.[37] The Horatian poem that is most important for understanding Seneca's arrangement at Ag. 589–658 is Carm. 3.3. The Horatian cycle of the so-called 'Roman Odes,' a group of alcaic poems that has been considered an organic formal and thematic whole from very early on in the history of its reception,[38] is one of Seneca's favourites in the tragedies. The range of topics explored in the markedly post-civil-war Roman Odes is clearly relevant to concerns of Senecan drama.[39] While the vicious downward spiral of the *comparativus Horatianus* at the end of the Roman Odes may not yet be teleologically fixed, the poetic cycle of decay initiated in Horace receives its dark closure in Seneca's texts.

In the third choral song in the *Agamemnon*, the overt thematic link to Horace coincides with a conspicuous metrical announcement of poetic inheritance. The ode begins thus:

---

[37] Thus setting itself up from the beginning as a conspicuously Epicurean meditation, one that is reminiscent of Horace's own noted Epicureanism: on Horace's Epicurean view of death, see Fish 1998.

[38] There is some uncertainty whether the Roman Odes, certainly forming a distinct group (Heinze 1960, 190–204 discusses important questions concerning the unity), were in fact meant to be divided as they are now in most editions. They are in the same metre (change of metre being 'the principle by which Horatian odes should be divided,' Heyworth 1995, 144) and can be read as one coherent poem without much force. Pomponius Porphyrio, the earliest and most important ancient commentator on Horace that we have (probably from the third century: see Nisbet / Hubbard 1970, xlvii–xlix; text: Holder 1894), read Carm. 3.1–6 as one poem. See Heyworth 1995, 140–144, who makes the argument for the unity of Carm. 3.1–6. Cf. Nisbet / Rudd 2004, xx–xxi and Syndikus 2001, 3–6 for the opposite view and some discussion (with further references).

[39] A detailed narrative and analysis of the Roman Odes is provided by Lowrie 1997, 224–265.

> Heu quam dulce malum mortalibus additum
> vitae dirus amor, cum pateat malis
> effugium et miseros libera mors vocet,
> portus aeterna placidus quiete.
> nullus hunc terror nec impotentis
> procella Fortunae movet aut iniqui
>   flamma Tonantis.

> Oh, the sweet evil implanted in mortals, this desperate love for life, though escape from troubles lies open, and death's freedom beckons the wretched – a tranquil harbour of eternal calm, untouched by any terror, by any storm of raging Fortune, by any fire from the hostile Thunderer.
> (Ag. 589–595)

While alcaics, the metre of Horace's Roman Odes, only enter later, the ode nevertheless begins with an asclepiadic line reminiscent of Horace – one that has, however, been meaningfully varied. The addition of a long syllable gives the line a dactylic rhythm (– – – ∪∪ – – – ∪∪ – ∪ –), thus setting the scene for the ode's curious combination of epic material and lyric frame by means of the metre itself. Generically, Seneca goes beyond Horace in his use of the earlier poet's technique of 'generic enrichment':[40] not only does Seneca infuse tragic and epic material into a lyric form (as does Horace, especially in Carm. 3.3), but also, in an experimental arrangement that combines metrical units from different sub-genres of lyric, pushes against the boundaries of a clear-cut conception of lyric. Trinacty has recently provided material for an analysis of the ode's genre in his discussion of Ag. 589–658 as a 'commentary' on Carm. 3.3, also bringing in the noted parallel passages from *Aeneid* 2 – another intertext found within the Senecan choral song.[41] The focus of my analysis will be on the way Seneca uses metre to convey meaning.[42]

After the asclepiadic beginning, invested with a dactylic rhythm, Seneca's ode continues in a clearly Horatian vein in the use of the asclepiads. This is the stichic metre that opens the Horatian collection of *Odes* and thus functions as a strong marker of Horatian presence when it is used at the very beginning of

---

40 For this concept, see Harrison 2011, especially 1–33 on the theoretical justification, and 168–206 on (mostly) epic and tragic material 'enriching' Horace's lyrics.
41 Trinacty 2014, 150. For the noted allusions, see Tarrant 1976, 291 and 293–294 ad loc.
42 Boyle 2014, cxlviii calls this 'the semiotics of Seneca's lyric metres.' W. Marx 1932 was the first to study the relation between metrical form and function of Seneca's choral metres. Although not all of the generalisations in his synoptic article are persuasive, Bishop 1968 remains useful.

a Senecan ode.⁴³ While the second line is a pure (and perfectly Horatian) asclepiad (*vitae dirus amor, cum pateat malis*, Ag. 590), the divergences from Horatian practice in the lines draw attention to themselves. As Leo has shown, Horatian cola are to be expected as the usual baseline in Seneca's practice.⁴⁴ This basic finding is vital for interpretation: wherever Seneca's lines divert from the 'ideal' Horatian line or colon, they stand out metrically and should be given close attention in our reading. One might note, then, that the metrical form of 591 gestures towards its own content, with the double shorts substituting the conventionally long second element (*effugium et miseros libera mors vocet*). *Effugium*, 'flight,' is swift: in the line, it is accelerated by the double shorts that stand out in a position where one would expect the long element. After depicting the desperation that *vitae dirus amor* produces in humans and the swift escape from troubles offered by *libera mors*, line 592 continues the Chorus's train of thought: once one has rushed into death, fleeing all the evils of this world, there is 'a tranquil harbour of eternal calm' (*portus aeterna placidus quiete*).⁴⁵

At this point in the ode, the change in metre accompanies the change in topic and tone: the sense of calm is disturbed in the following lines (Ag. 593–595) by being set against the backdrop of imagined threats and terrors. At the same time, the pure sapphic line is disturbed: it is turned, by *detractio*, into – ∪ – – – ∪ – ∪ – – (*nullus hunc terror nec impotentis*) in 593, and, by *adiectio*, into ∪ – ∪ – – – ∪∪ – ∪ – – (*procella Fortunae movet aut iniqui*) in 594. The adonius (595) lends its closural force to the rather unsettling *flamma Tonantis*.⁴⁶ The following line (Ag. 596) contains the first clear verbal echo (and one of the very few) of Carm. 3.3, the poem that provides an allusive backdrop against which Seneca's ode can be read. After the display of Horatian cola in the metrical experiment of Ag. 589–595, the metre of the alcaic Carm. 3.3 makes a conspicuous appearance in 596, which is made up of the first half of an alcaic (*pax alta nullos*: – – ∪ – –) and the first half of a sapphic line (*civium coetus*: – ∪ – – –). The alcaic beginning of the line can be read as Seneca's signpost to the metre of Horace's

---

43 Also note the first line of the next choral song in the *Agamemnon* (the other polymetric ode in the play), which also starts with a (pure) asclepiadic verse.
44 See Bußfeld 1935, 6: Seneca's intention was not primarily to produce pure Horatian lines, but to produce new ones based on the Horatian cola.
45 This is probably the most Epicurean moment in the ode. Seneca here exceeds Horace's Epicureanism in Carm. 3.3, where limiting one's desires is, as noted above, linked with a concept of *virtus*, which can be identified as a rather Stoic position. On some philosophical implications of the imagery cf. Vogt-Spira in this volume, 198–199.
46 The colometry of E is clearly right: see Bußfeld 1935, 27.

Roman Odes.⁴⁷ Given the thematic and structural similarity of the preceding lines to the first two stanzas of Carm. 3.3, the alcaic colon in the first half of the Senecan line clearly points to Horace, and prepares us to hear his *civium* (Carm. 3.3.2) reverberate in Seneca's use of the same word in the second half of Ag. 596: *pax alta nullos civium coetus*.

Another example occurs in the *Oedipus*. In the third choral song, the Chorus describes the evils gathering for civil war (*civile nefas*, 748). After mention of the first *monstrum*, a hissing 'serpent having risen from the deepest valleys' (*anguis imis vallibus editus*, 726), the next evil is portrayed in a Horatian manner:

> aut feta tellus impio partu
> effudit arma:
> sonuit reflexo classicum cornu
> lituusque adunco stridulos cantus
> elisit aere
>
> Or else the earth, in unnatural parturition, poured forth weapons; the battle call sounded from the winding horn, and the trumpet blared out strident notes from its curved brass (Oed. 731–734)

The weapons and their sounds cannot belie their Horatian pedigree – they seem to have come immediately from Horace, Carm. 2.1:⁴⁸

> iam nunc minaci murmure cornuum
> perstringis auris, iam litui strepunt,
> iam fulgor armorum fugacis
> terret equos equitumque vultus.
>
> But now you assault our ears with the menacing thunder of horns, now the clarions blare, now the dazzle of armour puts fear into fleeing horses and the faces of horsemen. (Carm. 2.1.17–20)

Seneca's use of alcaic cola (– – ᴗ – –: *aut feta tellus*, 730; *effudit arma*, 731b; *elisit aere*, 734) again points to the metre of the Horatian model, Carm. 2.1: while the alcaic cola here do not coincide with verbal allusion, they nevertheless function as signposts to Seneca's literary inheritance,⁴⁹ especially in a passage where

---

47 On this idea, see also the Introduction to the present volume, 14.
48 See e.g. Spika 1890, 30 and Canter 1925, 54. Jakobi 1988, 118 does not consider this instance an Horatian reminiscence, since the topic is too common; I argue that the Senecan passage also points to Horace by means of the alcaic cola and the reworked focus on sounds: conscious engagement with Horace at Oed. 731–734 is not unlikely.
49 As demonstrated above, Seneca uses the same practice at Ag. 596.

metre and sound are crucially important. Particularly striking is the emphasis on war sounds in Seneca's lines.⁵⁰ Seneca's masterly command of metre is especially significant in a passage with a pronounced focus on the effects of rhythm and sound. At the exact points where the Senecan Chorus sings about a 'winding' horn and 'curved' brass trumpet, the poet has also inverted the cola of the sapphic line. What usually constitutes the first half of the sapphic line is exchanged with the second half in 732 and 733: might this be read as mimicking, on the level of form, the sound that issues from the inverted and curved instruments? The original Horatian synaesthetic arrangement at Carm. 2.1.17–20 must have appealed to Seneca. This will have been encouraged by the context of tragedy that is evoked in the original Horatian arrangement: crucially, Carm. 2.1 functions as a commentary on the poem's famous dedicatee's literary output – most relevantly, Pollio's tragedies.⁵¹ In a sustained mode of temporal deixis engaging all senses in the *enargeia* of war, the Horatian lines are restored to the context of tragedy in Seneca's play and adapted to the Theban pre-war situation. The Chorus picks up on the most prominent sense to which Horace appeals in his synaesthetic description – hearing – in order to explore the sounds of war.⁵² At the same time, the earthy note in Horace's account, where we see

---

50 This deviates from the cognate accounts in Apollonius Rhodius and Ovid's *Metamorphoses*: see Jakobi 1988, 118. Boyle 2011, 283 ad loc. also notes that the 'focus on the noise of battle is absent from the Ovidian narrative' [i.e. from the one at Met. 3.3–130]. While sound effects are absent on the content level in this Ovidian passage, note nevertheless how Ovid characteristically relies on sound effects for the recipients: note e.g. the effect of the alliteration at Met. 3.111, merged with the visual emphasis on the content level (*surgere signa solent primum ostendere vultus*). Sounds are also remarkably present through their very absence, in the *mutua vulnera* (Met. 3.123 and 7.141).
51 On Horace's lyric re-presentation of Pollio's 'tragical history' and on lyric 'here getting into the mindset of tragedy,' see Henderson 1998, esp. 121–122. Sallmann 1987 examines the way in which the tension between different genres constitutes the poem; according to him, 'die Exkursion in die gefährdende Welt der Geschichte [wird] durch die Gegenwart der lyrischen Muse glücklich überstanden' (84). The way in which Carm. 2.1 combines allusions to historiography, most notably Pollio's own *Histories*, and echoes of Greek tragedies is discussed by Harrison 2017 (forthcoming). The tragic echoes include the reference to the Muse of tragedy at 2.1.9 and the metaphor of dicing at 2.1.6, 'several times used in Greek tragedy for the aleatory operations of fate and the gods in the context of war' (Harrison 2017 (forthcoming) ad loc., with comparable passages). The mention of the 'Attic buskin' at Carm. 2.1.11–12 in turn echoes the 'Sophoclean buskin' in Virgil's praise of Pollio at Ecl. 8.10. On the role of synaesthesia in Sophoclean tragedy, see Segal 1977.
52 As Spika 1890, 44 and Tarrant 1985, 172–173 ad loc. note, Carm. 2.1.17–20 is also clearly echoed at Thy. 573–575. See below for further analysis of this.

(or, rather, hear)⁵³ the generals 'dirty with no inglorious dust' (*duces | non indecoro pulvere sordidos*, 2.1.21–22), may have acquired significance in Seneca's Chorus, and turned into the autochthonous origin of war, 'pour[ing] forth weapons' (731b).⁵⁴ In the pessimistic view of Seneca's Theban Chorus, nothing, not even earth and dust, can be without involvement in the present disaster: even they are made to collaborate in the evil of civil war, infected, and, as *feta… impio partu* (731), cast as the source of the monsters of civil war. In a rather different context, but one that expresses the possibility of madness, Horace also links synaesthesia and spatial description: *auditis? an me ludit amabilis | insania? audire et videor pios | errare per lucos*, 'Do you hear? Or does some seductive madness mock me? I seem to hear you and to be wandering through sacred groves' (Carm. 3.4.5–7). Synaesthesia, both Horatian and Senecan, turns out to be a privileged mode in which mental and moral madness, most notably in war situations, can be depicted poetically.

The sensory attraction Carm. 2.1 had for Seneca can be corroborated by his use of the same section of that poem in the third choral ode of the *Thyestes*:

Iam minae saevi cecidere ferri,
iam silet murmur grave classicorum,
iam tacet stridor litui strepentis:
alta pax urbi revocata laetae est.

Now the menace of savage steel is fallen, now hushed the trumpets' blaring din, now quiet the strident clarion's scream; deep peace is restored to the joyful city.
(Thy. 573–576)

---

53 I remain unconvinced by Bentley's famous conjecture *videre*, adopted by Shackleton Bailey 2001 and Nisbet / Hubbard 1978 instead of the MSS reading *audire* at Carm. 2.1.17: *audire magnos iam videor duces*. Changing to *videre* not only introduces a slight metrical licence (Horace does not normally have an opening short syllable in his alcaics), but also underestimates the synaesthetic thrust of the whole passage, which effectively creates *enargeia*, as noted already by Porphyrio: *Iam, inquit, videor videre et audire ea quae historia refert: per quod significat, vi eloquentiae Pollionem certamen speciosum in relatione pugnarum inducere* (Porphyrio ad 17, text: Holder 1894). With e.g. Kiessling / Heinze 1930, Lowrie 1997, 182–183, esp. n. 71, and Harrison 2017 (forthcoming) ad loc., I would retain the apt *audire*, and point to Horace's own synaesthesia at Carm. 3.10.5–8 ('hearing' the process of water | snow turning to ice) and Verg. A. 2.705–706 (the brightness of the flames is 'heard'). On synaesthesia in Latin literature more generally, see Catrein 2003. For the combination *audire… videor*, see Pl. Aul. 811: *vocem hic loquentis modo mi audire visus sum*, and cf. the close link between 'seeming' and 'hearing' at the (syntactically slightly different) Carm. 3.4.5–7 (cited above).
54 Descriptions very similar to (and most likely influenced by) the Senecan passage are found at Luc. 1.237–238 and 7.475.

The third Chorus in the *Thyestes* occurs after the apparent reconciliation of Atreus and Thyestes, and just before the Messenger's report. Several verbal allusions to Carm. 2.1 are unmistakable: the triple *iam* (Carm. 2.1.17, 18, 19; Thy. 573, 574, 575); *murmur* (Carm. 2.1.17; Thy. 574); genitive plural of 'war-trumpets' (*cornuum* at Carm. 2.1.17; *classicorum* at Thy. 574); 'strident clarions' (*litui strepunt* at Carm. 2.1.18; *stridor litui strepentis* at Thy. 575).[55] While the ode begins with a sense of surprised relief at the reconciliation of the royal brothers, the most striking aspect of this ode throughout is probably the loss of excitement and an accompanying sense of resignation, which unfolds through the unbroken monotony of the sapphic hendecasyllables. But the Chorus's resignation, not trusting their own initial excitement, comes through not only in the choice of metre; perhaps most significantly, as Tarrant notes, words 'denoting "fear" and "dread" recur with almost obsessive regularity throughout, suggesting that anxiety has been suppressed rather than allayed.'[56]

Given this resignation, then, it may seem initially striking that the Horatian lyrics at 573–576 occur with such sonic prominence. The anaphora of *iam* gives the passage its sense of immediacy, creating a sense of lyric 'nowness' about the event. The lines, describing the sounds of war, also stand out in an ode that otherwise tries hard to give an impression of being calm and controlled. What, then, to make of it? Is Seneca's audience to share in the lines' excitement at this point, rejoicing that peace has returned to the city? Not quite. Seneca's *enargeia* is mimesis of a second – or rather, third, or even higher – degree: in addition to the verbal allusions, Seneca's lines are mimicking Horace's textual sounds, which in turn mimic Asinius Pollio's, and so on. But this re-presentation of Horace's lines is crucial here. While civil war breaks into the poem in Horace, who makes no attempt at containing it and its sounds before the last stanza, the Senecan Chorus attempts to silence the sounds: *iam silet murmur grave classicorum, | iam tacet stridor litui strepentis* (574–575). The Chorus's attempt, however, is a failure, and with the Horatian allusion, they bring back the sounds of civil war – sounds that demand expression. The point here is that, paradoxically, the sounds that the Chorus is trying to silence are in fact only given their power through the Chorus's very song.[57] The Senecan Chorus's sounds, despite their attempt at silencing, even exceed the Horatian precedent in onomatopoeia: the alliterative Senecan *stridor litui strepentis* has replaced the (mere) *litui strepunt* of the Horatian poem.

---

55 See Tarrant 1985, 172–173 ad loc.
56 Tarrant 1985, 169.
57 I owe the idea in the preceding section of this paragraph to the combined suggestions of Kathrin Winter and Richard Tarrant.

The allusion to Horace, I suggest, collaborates in the irony of this ode, which is sung by a Chorus that, as we have seen, does not quite express what it feels and desires to express. With these lines, the Chorus not only 'recalls' 'deep peace' but, through the Horatian echoes of Carm. 2.1, rather disturbing textual traces. Carm. 2.1, we should remember, is a poem in which the Horatian poetic texture seems to go back before the peace announcements of such poems as Carm. 1.2. Instead, Carm. 2.1 returns, in the meditation on and re-presentation of Pollio's work, to the civil wars – in a notably tragic manner.[58] It is only consistent, then, that in the Senecan ode in the *Thyestes* the closing adonius should lend its closural force to the unsettling *turbine versat* – and not to a reassuring *te duce, Caesar* (as in the sapphic Carm. 1.2).[59]

5 Sonic Set-Up: Sound Effects in Seneca's Spatial Descriptions

We have now lingered for quite a while over the significance of sounds, especially metre, in order to determine how Senecan drama negotiates its place in the dynamics of literary history. These metrical and verbal allusions and intertextualities may or may not coincide with the creation of poetic spaces and landscapes. There is a general background of a war setting common to all the examples I have chosen – and this may indeed be significant for Seneca's own canon of Horatian lyric – but a closer link between Seneca's use of sounds and spatial descriptions is needed. We can then once again compare this with Horace's practice.

The third choral song in the *Troades* is built on an erratic poetics of space,[60] guided by little else, it seems, than the sounds and poetry of names. Already Jasper Heywood, Seneca's Elizabethan translator, knew that this is at the core of the Senecan ode, as Davis points out in his analysis.[61] The sixteenth-century reader, very much aware of the sound effects of Seneca's Latin, accompanies his decision not to translate the ode with the comment, 'For as much as nothing is therein but a heaped number of farre and straunge Countries, considerynge with my selfe, that the names of so many unknowen Countreyes, Mountaaynes, Desertes,

---

[58] See above, n. 51. I plan to discuss 'Horace's tragic mode' in this poem in a separate article.
[59] Cf. also Tarrant in this volume, esp. 101–104.
[60] Davis 1993, 246.
[61] Davis's reading of this ode has informed my analysis, and I am indebted to him also for his reference to a 'poetics of names.' See Davis 1993, 243–248.

and Woodes shoulde have no grace in the Englishe tongue, but bee a straunge and unpleasant thing to the Readers.'[62] The landscape of the Elizabethan translator and his audience will, however, not have been that of Seneca's audience: to them, Seneca, in painting the Trojan landscapes, would probably have mixed obscure place names, which create a sense of otherness and exoticism, with easily identifiable places with strong associations and Homeric pedigree.[63] This creates an effect opposite to that of the Homeric catalogue of ships, a noted source of the Senecan ode, where the sounds of places aid the memory of the bard as much as they do the recognition of his audiences. In Seneca, by contrast, the oscillation, the alternation between what is clearly known to be real and what is obscure, creates effective confusion. This Senecan construction poses a riddle to any audience, who, in turn, will be caught up in a confusion not dissimilar to that of the Chorus of Trojan women: they are lost and are left to speculate about where their enforced journey will take them.

Some of Horace's geographical poems display a similar interest in sounds and the poetry of names. Horace's Carm. 1.22 and 2.6, both in sapphics just like the Senecan ode in the *Troades*, are worth comparing briefly. First of all, the use of sapphics in geographical poems (as found in Seneca, the two Horatian poems, and Catullus 11) may not be coincidental:[64] as West has noted, sapphics carry Near-Eastern connotations of exoticism already in the Greek poets.[65] A similar connection of exoticism with the sapphic metre is found in the conspicuously post-Horatian and post-Catullan sapphic ode in the *Medea* (579–669), the only properly stanzaic ode in Senecan drama. In Carm. 1.22, such a geographical interest is coupled with the poetic possibilities of names, most notably in Horace's beloved's 'speaking' name Lalage: the name's sonority, its echoing of its own syllables, is a commentary on its meaning (it is etymologically connected with Greek *lalagein*, 'to chatter').[66]

Another of Seneca's spatial moments occurs in the hunter's song at the beginning of *Phaedra*. Here, the geographical vista, expressed in what one could

---

[62] Newton 1927, 4 (with Davis 1993, 242).
[63] See Fantham 1982, 325–326, who points out that 'until the final section we have... an apparently random sequence of names from Homer's catalogue of ships (only Tempe, ?Mothone?, Peparethus, Eleusis, and Pisae do not occur). ...his [i.e. Seneca's] epithets may be Homeric in sense, or Ovidian in form, but they are redistributed, and his descriptive phrases blend poetic precedent with his own interest in mythology and geography.'
[64] Cf. Morgan 2010, 211–212.
[65] See West 1982, 29–34 on likely Indo-European origins of the sapphic stanza. Morgan 2010, 181–283 traces the sapphic 'ethos' in Roman poetry.
[66] See Nisbet / Hubbard 1970, 268 ad Carm. 1.22.10.

call a kinetic poetics, full of deixis and motion, is far-reaching and global. It is very much 'Roman,' as Tarrant put it.[67] I would add that the global perspective at the beginning of the anapaestic song is eventually narrowed down to the very small space of a single item, the 'curving knife,' *curvus... culter* (52–53).[68] This spatial concentration, starting from a full, sometimes global or cosmic, view, boiling down to the obsession of one small detail, is very Horatian. Probably most famously, we come across this feature in Horace Carm. 1.9, which is, in a sense, not only the 'Soracte Ode' – it is also the 'small finger' ode: Edmunds and Schwindt have made much of the poem's movement from big to small, outside to inside, its narrowing down of space, moving from the mountain from the beginning to the finger at its close.[69]

6 Seneca's Horace's Sonic Spaces: Horatian Allusions in the *Hercules Furens*

In the second choral ode of Seneca's *Hercules Furens*, sound effects also signal allusive engagement. The whole ode, a song about Hercules's labours, delights in the effects of sound. Not only is the poem a major achievement of Seneca's *melopoeia* on a formal level, but we can also see – or hear – how sounds, as well as the conspicuous absence of sounds, accompany spatial descriptions.

The asclepiadic metre, especially after its use as Horace's 'programmatic' metre (that of Carm. 1.1),[70] seems to work as a means of domesticating Euripidean material to the Roman world of Senecan tragedy.[71] Following the first Cho-

---

[67] See Tarrant 1995 and Goldberg 2014.
[68] This technique is typically Senecan: cf. also Thy. 180–191 and 640–664 (on the latter, see Rimell 2015a, 133–135) for two other examples. Rimell has also detected a similar technique of narrowing down space and a concentration on 'corners' and 'circles' in Seneca's *Letters*: Rimell 2015a, 113–147.
[69] On this spatial movement in Carm. 1.9, see Schwindt 2005, 15–16, with Edmunds 1992, 18. See also Rimell 2015, 86–87 and 90–92.
[70] See above, with n. 43.
[71] The second ode of Her. F. is very Euripidean (cf. the second Chorus of the *Heracles*): see Fitch 1987, 256–257. The Euripidean (and Ovidian) pedigree of this choral song is well documented in Kapnukajas 1930, 29–30, and his comments ad loc. Note that Seneca's Chorus differs from the Euripidean account in at least two significant aspects: in Seneca, the apostrophised *Fortuna... non aequa* (524–525) is the driving force, not Zeus; whereas the Euripidean Chorus doubts that Heracles will ever return from the underworld, the Senecan Chorus, positive about Hercules's successes in all the most difficult labours that are singled out from the myth in this ode,

rus, arguably the Senecan ode whose Horatian inheritance is most obviously recognisable,⁷² the Horatian verbal presences in the second ode are scarce: they are, however, all significantly linked to spatial moments. Thus, Her. F. 533 (*intravit Scythiae multivagas domos*, 'He came among Scythia's nomad homes') engages with Horace Carm. 3.24.9–11 (*campestres melius Scythae, | quorum plaustra vagas rite tradunt domos | vivunt*, 'The Scythian plainsmen, whose wagons carry their roaming houses in their accustomed way, live better lives').⁷³ The Senecan creative neologism *multivagus* occurs at a significant point, placing emphasis on the dangerous instability of exotic countries. In the Senecan realm, it is not important to distinguish between the time and place in which the wavering occurs: unlike Lucretius and Virgil's *montivagus* and *noctivagus*, Seneca just has *multivagus*. The Senecan neologism points to the ubiquity of wavering in this tragedy.⁷⁴ The allusion to the *vagae domus* of Carm. 3.24, which would be subtly continued in *illic* at the starts of Her. F. 537 and 550 (echoing the same deictic gesture at Carm. 3.24.17) could evoke Horace's Roman vision of exoticism in the Senecan Chorus's ecphrasis of the Amazons' country. Asclepiadic metre and local allusion to Horace would be collaborating in the domestication of the Other in the Roman poetic imagination. For Said, the Other (in the following phrasing, specifically the 'Orient' in its nineteenth-century French representation) can be 'an exotic yet especially attractive reality.'⁷⁵ In the Senecan lines in the *Hercules Furens*, the exoticism of the mythic material is Romanised through the Horatian presences and the asclepiadic metre. What for Horace was still an essentially Greek metre is made fully Roman through Seneca's reception: at Seneca's stage in literary history, his fusion of metrical and verbal recall of Horace can rely on Horace's previous intervention. But it is only through the later poet's use and reception that the asclepiad can carry weight as a truly Roman metre. At the same time, these gestures of poetic domestication may adumbrate a political and moral statement that is not unlike the one we encoun-

---

strongly believes in the success of his chthonic transgression as well, which is of course appropriate for announcing Hercules's subsequent entry on stage.

72 See Spika 1890, 1–2. Apart from verbal presences, note especially the use of the priamel structure (*alium – alius – me*) at Her. F. 192–198, reminiscent of Carm. 1.1.
73 English translation of this Horatian passage taken from Rudd's Loeb. The parallel between the Horace and Seneca is noted by Kapnukajas 1930, 35, and Fitch 1987, 259 ad loc.
74 *Vagare, vagus*, and other expressions of wavering or erring movement are favourites of Seneca's, and constitute the appropriate physical reaction of the characters (and inanimate objects) to a poetic world in which everything is disjointed: see Tarrant 1985, 47, esp. n. 161.
75 Said 1995, 170. For a brief account of Roman Republican responses to ethnic others, see Syed 2005, esp. 362–366 for attitudes towards the Greeks (on which see in detail Petrochilos 1974).

tered in the use of the Roman Odes in the third choral ode of the *Agamemnon*:[76] again, Seneca revisits and comments upon a Horatian poem concerned with the aftermath of civil war, one that highlights the depravity and extravagance of post-civil-war Rome, even at the cost of praising as morally superior such peoples as the Scythians and the Getae. In the Senecan ode, nothing is to be found any more even in Horace's promised lands: the Scythian lands lack waves – and sounds (cf. 536–537: *et mutis tacitum litoribus mare.* | *illic dura carent aequora fluctibus*, 'and [hushed] waters with silent shores. There the hard surface is void of waves'). There is a conspicuous absence of sound in this typically Senecan depiction of a desperate place. In the realms of Senecan drama, the Horatian positive fantasy of a *Gegenwelt* far away has been turned into a wasteland.

7 Conclusion

There are many other interesting instances of Horatian presences in Seneca's choral odes. But what are we contributing by studying them? Is such scholarly and critical endeavour merely adding one more thread of intertexts, one more level of allusions, echoes that are considerably rarer than the all-pervasive Ovid and Virgil? Quite the reverse: I would argue that recognising and interpreting the Horatian presences in Seneca's choruses will make a difference of category, not of degree. Many scholars have recognised that Seneca's choruses can be very aware of their own literariness;[77] this sense can be strikingly heightened or ironically undercut by recognising the Horatian echoes, affinities that often go beyond mere verbal parallels. Rather than studying Seneca's odes negatively – for their non-integration into the dramatic action, their non-stageability, and their non-Greekness – an analysis of Seneca's Horatian lyrics can lead the way towards an acknowledgement of Seneca's choral odes as what they really are: the poetic core of the tragedies. While this paper has merely focused on some spatial and sonic moments, it has highlighted one way in which Seneca's choral odes are firmly inserted into the textualised, but not necessarily soundless, canon of Roman lyric poetry.

---

[76] Indeed, Carm. 3.24 'has much in common with the so-called Roman Odes': see Nisbet / Rudd 2004, 271–273.
[77] Most recently, Kirichenko 2013, 249–279, but esp. 260–264.

Jonathan Geiger
Strictness, Freedom, and Experimentation in Horatian and Senecan Metrics

The extent to which metrical questions in Horace's *Odes* and Seneca's tragedies are comparable is not self-evident, especially given the differences in genre, metre, and era. Nevertheless, it is a worthwhile enterprise to identify differences in the authors' attitudes to the metrical foundations of their art. The project is especially attractive when a small but significant area of overlap is taken into consideration: Seneca adopts Horace's Aeolic metres in his choral odes.

In the following chapter I will show how the two authors adopt metrical structures from their predecessors, as well as consider the constraints they impose upon themselves and the licences they allow. Although both Horace and Seneca display a typically Roman tendency to standardise their metres, they differ as to the areas in which they apply greater strictness. This difference in practice showcases their different approaches to the technique of versification and their distinct attitudes towards metrical experimentation.

For Horace, I will first focus on the metres that are most common among his odes, going over their characteristics in detail. I will then investigate a specific trait in depth: Horace's tendency to repeat technical features of his versification. I will then move on to outline Seneca's use of metre in his tragedies. After one or two short notes on the trimeter and hexameter, I will examine Seneca's adoption of Horatian metres, considering the positioning of the relevant metres within the plays and the stricter technique Seneca displays with the metre he uses. I will also present a number of examples that can be classified as metrical experiments on Seneca's part.

1 The Characteristics of Horace's Lyric Metres

1.1 Stricter Technique

In some respects Horace's versification technique in the *Odes* is much stricter than those of his predecessors, Alcaeus, Sappho, and Catullus. I will focus my

---

I want to take this chance to thank the organisers for giving me an opportunity to delve into a topic I was not overly familiar with, for reviewing my chapter, and for providing useful criticism; I am also thankful to the other participants for the discussion of my talk.

examination on the lesser asclepiad, as well as the alcaic and the sapphic stanza.[1]

1.1.1 Quantities

One feature of Aeolic verse is that the number of syllables is fixed, but not their quantities. The fourth syllable of the sapphic hendecasyllable (– ⏑ – × – ⏑ ⏑ – ⏑ – –), the first and fifth syllable of the alcaic hendeca- and enneasyllable (× – ⏑ – × – ⏑ ⏑ – ⏑ – and × – ⏑ – × – ⏑ – –), and the quite free usage of the Aeolic base in the asclepiadean are all variable elements in both Sappho and Alcaeus. These features – the preference for the spondaic realisation of the Aeolic base (already visible in Catullus, although he uses phalaecian hendecasyllables) and the clear preference for the long fourth syllable in sapphic hendecasyllables – Horace elevates to the level of norm.[2]

In the alcaic stanza, where he does not have to take Roman examples into account, Horace sporadically permits a short in the first syllable;[3] metrically, this is the least stable position of the hendeca- and enneasyllable, as is usual in most metres at the beginning of a line. The resolution of a long syllable into a double short or the contraction of a double short to a long syllable – phenomena that are generally alien to Aeolic versification – is (probably)[4] not found in Horace, although he possibly paves the way for it by standardising the long syllables.

1.1.2 Synapheia

Horace's use of synapheia is inconsistent. Synapheia, understood as prosodic continuity across line break, manifests itself in (1) the lack of a word boundary at the end of a line, (2) prepositions separated by line-end from their immediate-

---

[1] I chose these three because of their frequency in the *Odes* and their significance for Seneca.
[2] With one exception in Carm. 1.15.36 *ignis Iliacas domos*, 'the fire [will burn down] the houses of Troy,' a reading which is, however, textually disputed.
[3] E.g. Hor. Carm. 1.9.1 *Vides ut alta stet nive candidum*, 'Do you see how [Soracte] stands there shining with its blanket of deep snow'; Carm. 1.16.19 *stetere causae, cur perirent*, '[anger too] is the [chief] reason why [cities] have been... levelled.'
[4] For *consilium*, 'advice,' (Carm. 3.4.41) and *principium*, 'beginning,' (Carm. 3.6.6), possibly to be understood as choriambs, see below.

ly following object, and (3) synaloepha[5] across line breaks. The lack of hiatus between lines is also a form of synapheia.

Synapheia is strongly developed in Horace's sapphic stanza, which has the lowest number of hiatuses of the three metres examined (1.1% of lines compared to 2.2% of lines in the alcaic stanza and 2.5% in the lesser asclepiads). But in general hiatuses are found in all types of Horatian verse.[6]

More striking forms of synapheia (which are already anticipated in Catullus[7]) are found in Hor. Carm. 1.2.19–20 (*Iove non probante u|xorius amnis*, 'the river... without Jove's permission, [flowed far and wide over the left bank], like a fond husband'[8]), Carm. 1.25.11–12 (*magis sub inter|lunia vento*, '[while the Thracian] wind [riots] ever more [boisterously] as the moonless nights [draw near]') and Carm. 2.16.7–8 (*purpura ve|nale neque auro*, 'cannot be bought by jewels or purple').

1.1.3 Caesurae

The line segmentation in the sapphic stanza (except the adonic in every fourth line), in the alcaic stanza, and in the (stichic) lesser asclepiad is treated more strictly by Horace than by Alcaeus, Sappho, and Catullus. However, he uses line segmentation differently in the various metres. In lines of eleven or twelve syllables, Horace always sets a central caesura shortly before the middle of the line, in a way not unlike that found in the most common Roman metres, the hexameter and the iambic senarius. In the alcaic and the sapphic hendecasyllable,[9] the caesura lies after the fifth syllable; in the twelve-syllable lesser asclepiad it is located after the sixth,[10] with the first half of the line still having fewer *morae*[11] than the second:

- sapphic hendecasyllable: – ᴗ – – – | ᴗ ᴗ – ᴗ – –
- alcaic hendecasyllable: – – ᴗ – – | – ᴗ ᴗ – ᴗ –
- lesser asclepiad: – – – ᴗ ᴗ – | – ᴗ ᴗ – ᴗ –

---

[5] Or elision, the coalescing or the elimination of the last vowel or diphthong of a word before a word starting with a vowel.
[6] While Alcaeus is particularly strict between the third and fourth line of the alcaic stanza: see Page 1955, 323.
[7] Catul. 11.11–12 *ulti|mosque Britannos*, 'the Britons, remotest of men.'
[8] Translations are taken from the relevant Loeb editions unless stated otherwise.
[9] In Catullus this caesura is found in 60% of the sapphic hendecasyllables.
[10] This is frequently found in Alcaeus's poems, where, however, word boundary often occurs after the seventh syllable.
[11] One *mora* is the time unit equivalent to a short syllable, a *longum* is two *morae* long.

Only in the sapphic hendecasyllable is there an alternative caesura after the sixth syllable. Two observations can be made: One concerns the number and sequence of the secondary caesura and will be dealt with later, the other concerns the 'purity' of the caesura.[12] While in his alcaic hendecasyllable and the lesser asclepiad the caesura is obscured from time to time by *caesura latens* or a preceding monosyllable, Horace waives this licence almost entirely in the sapphic hendecasyllable,[13] which suggests that for Horace, at least, a position more restricted in its mandatory segmentation leaves more freedom in its realisation.

In the ennea- and hendecasyllable of the alcaic stanza, on the other hand, tripartition is the rule – indeed, in the enneasyllable, word boundary is most rare between the three consecutive long syllables. There is a bridge inherited from Alcaeus[14] between the fourth and fifth syllable, since the only way for a word boundary to be located at this position is when there is a monosyllable before it, and the end of a monosyllable does not count as a full word boundary. Thus we find lines such as Hor. Carm. 1.31.15 *impune.* | *me͡ pascunt* | *olivae*, '... in safety. As for me, I eat olives,' which does not violate the bridge; in fact, there is only one line that has word boundary after the fourth syllable, thus violating the bridge:[15] Hor. Carm. 1.26.11 *hunc Lesbio*[16] *sacrare plectro*, 'to sanctify [Lamia] with... the quill of Lesbos.'

It is also exceedingly rare to find a word boundary after the fifth syllable which is not followed by a monosyllable. Most frequent are word boundaries after the third syllable and the antepenultimate; this, however, is little more than a strong tendency:

⏓ – ⏑ ⦂ – ͡ – – ⦂ ⏑ – –

The hendecasyllable is also divided into three parts, albeit in a less fixed way. Here, too, I would posit a bridge between the sixth and seventh syllable (which also means that there is never word-end after the two opening dactyls),

---

12 This will also play a role in Seneca's verses.
13 There are (potentially) four instances of *caesura latens*, two of which are, however, followed by a monosyllable, so we can assume that the secondary caesura is in effect instead. In the other two cases, an adjective is connected to its noun via synaloepha.
14 Although synaloepha is allowed: see Page 1955, 323.
15 Nisbet / Hubbard 1970, xli, point out the one line with word boundary after the fourth syllable (implying that the position is a bridge but not explicitly calling it such), without mentioning the instances where the fourth syllable is a monosyllable.
16 It is probably no accident that the word that stops at the bridge is a Greek word. Greek words in Roman verse are associated with licences and can be found particularly often in irregular hexameter endings, e.g. Stat. Theb. 6.563 *nota parens cursu; quis Maenaliae Atalantes*, 'His mother is famous for her running. Who [would not know of] Maenalian Atalanta's...'

as the only permissible word boundary at this position is after a monosyllable. Although word boundaries form several different patterns in this metre, there is a clear preference for word boundaries after the third or fourth syllable (or, put differently, after four or six *morae*), and after the seventh or eighth syllable (after ten or eleven *morae*):[17]

$$- \cup \cup \mid - \mid \cup \cup \overset{\frown}{} - \mid \cup \mid - -$$

The beginning of the line resembles a hexameter, and there is clear evidence that the classical hexameter shares some characteristics with the hendecasyllable as it is used by Horace. After all, a hexameter whose first two metra are dactyls is just the same up to the penthemimeral caesura.[18]

In a regular hexameter we have either word boundary at the penthemimeres, i.e. after the tenth *mora*, or, if there is word boundary after the eleventh *mora*, i.e. the *kata triton trochaion*, we find word-end after the sixth *mora* (at the trithemimeres position) or sometimes after the fourth *mora* (only when the first metrum is a dactyl, the position is called *kata proton daktylon*).[19]

It is also striking that in less than 5% of the hendecasyllables there is neither word boundary after the tenth *mora* (which is exactly the position of the penthemimeres in the hexameter) nor the combination of word boundary after the forth or sixth *mora* and word boundary after the eleventh *mora*. Thus in more than 95% of cases we find a word boundary pattern that is a regular one in the hexameter.

The combination of word boundary after the sixth and eleventh mora (6+11) is here more frequent than 6+10, whereas 4+10 is more frequent than 4+11.[20] This may be due to the fact that 4+11 is rarer in the hexameter; but it is also possible

---

17 Horace probably regarded the position after the fourth syllable as an equivalent to an established caesura. It can be seen in Carm. 2.13.16 *caeca timet aliunde fata*, ' ...expect unseen death from any other quarter,' where a *brevis in longo*, which normally is restricted to pre-caesura positions, occurs.
18 And in the hexameter, too, word boundary right before the penthemimeres is avoided.
19 Although this type of verse is not frequent, it appears often enough not to be regarded as exceptional; in the *Aeneid* it is found more than fifty times, (e.g. Verg. A. 1.366 *moenia surgentemque novae Karthaginis arcem*, 'the huge walls and rising citadel of new Carthage'). In this case, the first metrum has to be a dactyl in the hexameter; in the hendecasyllable there is, of course, no alternative. Likewise, there has to be the *kata triton trochaion* in the hexameter; in the hendecasyllable it occurs automatically. In fact, Horace himself uses this pattern in one of his hexameters in the *Odes*, Carm. 1.28.29 *ab Iove Neptunoque sacri custode Tarenti*, 'from kindly Jove and Neptune, the protector of holy Tarentum.'
20 Statius has in Silv. 4.5 the same tendency and avoids 4+11 altogether; only Silv. 4.40 does not belong in any of the categories 6+11, 6+10, and 4+10.

that it is done this way to avoid the congruence of *arsis* and word accent throughout the verse since word boundary at 6 or 10 prohibits the congruence in the preceding words, while boundaries at 4 or 11 enforce it.

1.2 Repetition

1.2.1 Word Boundary Series

When one examines the technical composition of Horace's *Odes*, every now and then one comes across concordances and harmonies that appear to be intended and meaningful but are also difficult to quantify. If, for example, we look at the word boundaries in the alcaic ennea- and hendecasyllables, we cannot fail to note striking reduplications and series. I will give two examples:

(1) Carm. 2.19.7 shows an extremely rare combination of word boundaries after the third and fifth syllable (− − ⏑ | − − | − ⏑ − −) in the alcaic enneasyllable, which is followed by the (popular) word boundary combination after the second, fourth, and eighth syllable (− ⏑| ⏑ − | ⏑ ⏑ − ⏑ | − −) in the hendecasyllable. In the subsequent stanza, exactly the same pattern appears in the ennea- and hendecasyllable; the probability of this occurrence at a given point[21] is almost 0.0003 %; the probability of an occurrence at any point is 0.096 %. The observed word boundary pattern in Carm. 2.19.7 can therefore hardly be assigned to chance, although it does not necessarily mean that it was meant to have a particular effect. It is doubtful that the pattern was perceptible to a listener, especially since there are intervening lines.

(2) The case is similar in Carm. 2.19, where each enneasyllable of the first four stanzas (out of eight total) contains a word boundary after the fifth syllable, while the next four stanzas has a word boundary after the fourth (making a series of 55554444). This, too, is hardly coincidental. The likelihood of this happening in a given eight consecutive stanzas stands at 0.078 %. This extremely low probability strongly suggests that the repetition is intentional, even if a listener had little chance of discerning this detail, as it occurs only every fourth line.

We might term this phenomenon 'responsion': a technical detail (such as word boundaries or synaloepha) is repeated (possibly in a modified manner) to form a visible pattern. This responsion is hard to quantify – it is easy to

---

[21] If estimating on the basis of the pattern frequency in Horace's alcaic stanzas: 3 / 321 for the word boundaries in the enneasyllable, 52 / 321 in the hendecasyllable.

find examples of subtle responses of one kind or another – and there is no obvious way to compare it to a baseline expectation.

At any rate, examples like the ones given above illustrate an unobtrusive feature of Horace's lyrical works that just might be part of the symmetry felt by readers.[22]

1.2.2 Peculiarities

Two cases in which Horace creates a technical link in the text by deviating from his usual versification technique are worth mentioning:

(1) There are two curious lines where we have to assume either a prosodic or a metrical licence:

> *vos lene consilium et datis et dato*
> You... give him gentle advice, and [are glad to] have given it
> (Carm. 3.4.41)

> *hinc omne principium, huc refer exitum*
> For every beginning seek their approval; to them attribute its outcome
> (Carm. 3.6.6)

Strikingly, the expressions are centred around the otherwise usual caesura positions (synaloepha with a monosyllable usually generates a word boundary after said monosyllable, but in the alcaic hendecasyllable the caesura would come just before *et* and *huc*). There are further similarities: in both instances, there seems to be a double short at the position where the long syllable before the caesura is expected. In each case it is realised by two <i>, situated within a choriambic word, and slurred with a following monosyllable. Common extenuating circumstances for this unusual construction are inapplicable: after all, there is no metrically bulky proper name involved, let alone a Greek one. Even if it were Horace's concern to use exactly the word-forms *principium* and *consilium*, there would have been a cosy spot available for them just after the caesura.

Whether we interpret these exceptions as a metrical licence, in that a long syllable is substituted by a double short, or a prosodic one, in that the second <i> is consonantal, is not crucial to the question of duplication; in my view,[23] however, the latter explanation is the likelier one.[24]

---

22 E.g. Nisbet / Hubbard 1970, xxiii, speak of a 'symmetry that has seldom been aimed at in English lyric since the seventeenth century.'
23 Likewise Nisbet / Rudd 2004, 70 without discussion.

Leaving aside the question of how to interpret these exceptional cases, it is of course highly improbable that Horace happened to use these similar structures independently; yet neither the placement within the ode / stanza nor the syntactic arrangement suggests a connection between them. As both instances are found in the Roman Odes, there is a potential link on the level of content, if not an obvious one. It seems more probable to me that Horace in this case did not so much try to connect the two *loci* than repeat the peculiarity in order to avoid the impression of a unique experiment. It also seems to me that Horace attempts to avoid such an impression on other occasions as well: for example, the peculiar synapheia generated by ignoring the line-end between the third sapphic hendecasyllable and the adonic is also not unique,[25] nor is the choice of a six syllable end-word in the lesser asclepiad.[26]

(2) The following case is slightly different: a technical detail that is only visible at a microscopic level occurs at two *loci* and thus connects them. Only twice does Horace use a single word boundary in an entire alcaic hendecasyllable, and in both cases it occurs after the fourth syllable: Carm. 3.1.48 and Carm. 3.6.48, the final lines of the first and the final Roman Ode. Both verses have the same syntactic arrangement (noun in the accusative followed by a comparative form), which means that the parallelism is clear and suggests that it was intended.

This means that Horace often uses twice what could have been unique aberrations.[27] He thus avoids the impression that the deviations were purely experi-

---

24 Horace allows other prosodic liberties when, for example, in three cases he scans the end syllable -*et* in verbs as long despite a following initial vowel (Hor. Carm. 2.13.16 *caeca timet aliunde*, '[does not] expect unseen [death] from any other quarter'; Carm. 2.6.14 *angulus ridet, ubi*, 'that corner [of the world] smiles.... There'; Carm. 3.5.17 *si non periret immiserabilis*, 'if [the young captives] were not left to die without pity') or when he seems to cram a caesura behind a verbal prefix (Hor. Carm. 1.37.5 *antehac nefas de|promere Caecubum*, 'Before this it was sacrilege to bring the Caecuban out'). He also permits hypermetrical lines and *caesurae latentes*, which I would count among the prosodic licences. It would also be a considerable coincidence if Horace just happened to use words that permit such an interpretation in exactly those two instances where he also discards the Aeolic versification principle. Additionally, as double shorts are generally substitutes for a long syllable, this position is not the most straightforward one since it is only Horace that fixes this position as a *longum* (the situation will be different for Seneca, who inherits a fixed metrical scheme).
25 Hor. Carm. 1.2.19–20, 1.25.11–12, 2.16.7–8; somewhat less convincing, since it is scattered across books 3 and 4: 3.8.3–4 and 4.6.11–12.
26 Hor. Carm. 1.1.12, 3.30.4.
27 In line with this, two further singularities should be pointed out, although these are a matter of textual criticism. Usually, one aims at normalisation in restoring the (allegedly) correct wording of a text: readings that are or seem to be atypical of Horace are more likely to be rejected in favour of more regular readings. If the 'principle' of doubled peculiarities also extends to Aeolic

ments. But more significantly, he also uses this technique as a subtle way to forge connections between poems, thus weaving the texture of his lyric poetry even more densely together.

1.2.3 Agglomeration of Impurities

A generally difficult issue in examining versification is the question of the extent to which lines within a text are independent from one another. What effect does a certain verse have on the one that follows it (or comes even later), what phenomena affect the subsequent lines? There is clear evidence for interlineal dependency in Horace's *Odes* in at least two respects: in the case of synaloepha and the use of the secondary caesura after the sixth syllable (which only applies to the sapphic stanza).

If one pays attention to the lines that contain synaloepha in Horace's *Odes*, one easily comes to suspect that their occurrence is 'agglomerated' (i.e. unequally distributed across the *Odes*). For example, in Carm. 3.21 lines 3, 18, 19, 20, and 21 (out of a total of twenty-four lines) contain synaloepha; in Carm. 3.29 (sixty-four lines in total), it is lines 3, 5, 7, 9, 12, 15, 16, 17, 25, 26, 46, 49, 50, 55, and 59. A basic way to quantify this impression would look something like this: one would calculate first the likelihood of a line containing synaloepha (assuming this to be independent of whether the preceding or following line contains one) and then the (conditional) probability of a line containing synaloepha if the preceding line contains it. This way, only pairs of lines and no larger units are examined; upon performing this calculation, the result is indeed that the probability of a verse containing synaloepha rises by more than 40% if the preceding line contains it.[28]

The picture is similar for the secondary caesura in the sapphic hendecasyllable, although this only concerns a small number of the odes; it only occurs in

---

bases and hiatus, the following instances would need to have a different reading or another instance with the same phenomenon: Carm. 1.15.36 *ignis Iliacas domos*, 'the fire [will burn down] the houses of Troy,' the one trochaic base currently to be found in editions, and Carm.1.28.24 *capiti inhumato*, 'to my unburied skull,' the only hiatus in Horace's odes.

28 I counted 772 lines in sapphic stanzas, 73 of which contained one or more synaloephas, and 11 cases of consecutive verses containing synaloepha, which is actually too conservative because there is no synaloepha in the adonius; this results in $p(vi) = 73 / 772 = 0.095$, $p(vi|vi-1) = 0.151$, a rise by 58.9%; in the alcaic stanzas 1204 lines, 170 with synaloepha, 34 line pairs with synaloepha, resulting in $p(vi) = 170 / 1204 = 0.141$, $p(vi|vi-1) = 0.2$, a rise by 41.8%; in the lesser asclepiads 80 lines, 14 with synaloepha, 5 line pairs with synaloepha: $p(vi) = 14 / 80 = 0.175$, $p(vi|vi-1) = 0.357$, a rise by 104%.

the *Carmen Saeculare* and in the fourth book with any considerable frequency. In the first three books, there is only one ode with more than one secondary caesura (Carm. 1.10); in the four other odes that contain this secondary caesura, it occurs – in another odd instance of reduplication – twice in the first line (each time in an invocation of a god or a muse, as in the first line of the *Carmen Saeculare*), and twice in the eleventh line. If we take the *Carmen Saeculare* as a starting point and observe those lines that contain the secondary caesura (note that doubly even line numbers are *Adonei*, where it cannot occur), our result is the following: lines 1, 14, 18, 19, 35, 39, 43, 51, 53, 54, 55, 58, 59, 61, 62, 70, 73, 74.[29]

It is evident at first sight that the secondary caesura comes in chunks, which prompts us to check by means of a simple calculation if the observation can be captured statistically. If we only consider *Odes* 4 and the *Carmen Saeculare*, calculate the probabilities of any line containing the secondary caesura, and then compare the outcome with the probability of a line with secondary caesura being followed by another such line, we get the following results:[30]

	$p(sc_i)$	$p(sc_i|sc_{i-1})$
Saec.	0.33	0.5
Carm. 4.2	0.22	0.33
Carm. 4.6	0.15	0.0
Carm. 4.11	0.11	0.5

Except for Carm. 4.6, where no consecutive verses with secondary caesura are found, the conditional probability is much higher in all cases; if the secondary caesurae were randomised, one would expect the same probability in both columns. In the face of these statistics, one must draw the conclusion that Horace agglomerates the secondary caesurae across his later lyric output.

It is not obvious how we are to interpret this: the statistical evidence might be taken to mean that certain stanzas seemed to the author more apt for impur-

---

[29] Or, cleansed of the adonics: 1, 11, 12, 14, 15, 27, 30, 33, 39, 40, 41, 42, 44, 45, 46, 47, 53, 55, 56.
[30] The table is to be read as follows: the middle column lists the probabilities of a line containing the secondary caesura (estimated by relative frequency). The *Carmen Saeculare*, for example, contains the secondary caesura 19 times in 57 sapphic hendecasyllables, thus resulting in a relative frequency estimate of 19 / 57 = 0.33. The right column lists the conditional probabilities of a line containing the secondary caesura if its preceding line also contains the secondary caesura. In the *Carmen Saeculare*, 9 of the lines with a secondary caesura follow such a line, too. As the first line cannot have a preceding line, it has been discarded from the calculation, thus giving an estimate of 9 / 18 = 0.5.

ities, or that Horace found the phenomenon more harmonious when situated in adjacent lines, or that he judged that a single impurity would stand out in an undesirable way. At the very least, however, the results indicate that, for example, synaloepha is not something that just 'happens' but can be part of the stylistic make-up of a text. We would need to perform more work on other authors to put the results into perspective. A small experiment on Ovid's *Metamorphoses* suggests that the agglomeration of synaloepha does not occur there. 22.9% of hexameters contain synaloepha, and 23.2% of these hexameters are preceded by a line containing synaloepha. The two numbers are very close to each other, suggesting little correlation.

2 Seneca

2.1 Stricter Usage of the Trimeter and the Hexameter

2.1.1 Trimeter

While in earlier Latin drama the iambic senarius was the main metre, Seneca used the stricter iambic trimeter in his dramas, which are thus the earliest extant Roman dramas in this metre. The most striking point in his versification is the final iambic word found in the vast majority of lines that stems from avoiding an iambic fifth foot *and* observing Porson's Law.[31]

It is highly likely that earlier Roman poets wrote plays in trimeters,[32] first and foremost Ovid in his *Medea*; but it is less clear that Seneca's predecessors were equally strict in their treatment of Porson's law. A notable contemporary of Seneca who has left us a good number of trimeters, Petronius, observes the contemporary rules that apply for the hexameter, pentameter, and hendecasyllables; in his *Troiae Halosis*, a poem in trimeters, he does admittedly prefer the line ending with an iambic word but also writes many verses that are built differently. If the final iambic word had already been firmly established, we can presume that Petronius would have observed that custom.[33]

Horace only uses trimeters in his *Epodes*, and is not bound by Porson's Law, except, strikingly, in the one poem in which he uses stichic trimeters, Epod. 17. He does allow the fifth foot to be iambic, however, and therefore allows line-

---

[31] I.e. a word boundary is not allowed in a spondaic fifth foot; Porson's Law is commonly observed in Greek trimeters, except comedies, but not in Latin iambic verse: see Raven 1965, 54.
[32] To that effect Strzelecki 1963.
[33] Even Trimalchio keeps his pentameter endings two-syllabled.

ends that are not permissible in Senecan technique (like Epod. 17.3 *non loquenda numina*, '[by] the divinity [of Diana] that must not be provoked').

2.1.2 Hexameter

Seneca's hexameter versification is extremely pure as well. There is not a single synaloepha, whether in the plays' hexameters (which only occur in the *Medea* and the *Oedipus*) or in the *Apocolocyntosis*. In the hexameters within the plays, he also has a very strong preference for the penthemimeres (only two of the twenty-six hexameters have the combination of trith- and hephthemimeres instead) and a very balanced style, showing a penchant for lines of the 'golden' type (e.g. Oed. 233 *mitia Cadmeis remeabunt sidera Thebis*, 'kindly stars will return to Thebes, the city of Cadmus,' a genuine golden line[34]). Eleven of the twenty-six lines in the plays conform to this pattern (sometimes with an additional subjunction or pronoun); many more are at least comparable. This style also leads to coincidence of line-end and sense pause in most lines.

This feature is not as strongly developed in the *Apocolocyntosis*, where one unique longer series of stichic hexameters demands a more flowing character. Still, the caesurae are observed impeccably: There is no *caesura latens*, no synaloepha, and no monosyllables before a caesura. Seneca uses both side caesurae only in conjunction with the *kata triton trochaion*, and every final word is either a di- or trisyllable.

One line that stands out among Seneca's hexameters is the *spondiacus* in Med. 113, which, however, has the classic dispondaic final word with preceding dactyl, and even forms a golden line. In a way, this hexameter is in line with Seneca's usage of Horatian metres: instead of allowing himself fewer technical licences, he simply adopts a different kind of hexameter when he does decide to vary.

Horace's hexameters in his *Odes*[35] are formed in alignment with the standard of contemporary epic, which allows some variation: he does allow synaloepha, including in the last third of the line (but in the most common form where a short syllable is elided before a trisyllabic final word), including *caesura latens*; he does allow a four-syllabled final (Greek) word[36] as well as lines with *kata tri-*

---

[34] A genuine golden line has the form a b V A B (where a and b are adjectives, V a verb, and A and B are the nouns the adjectives refer to).
[35] The hexameter of satire is, for reasons of genre, much looser and is not comparable to hexameters in a lyric context.
[36] Hor. Carm. 1.7.1.

ton trochaion without both side caesurae,[37] and he also uses a *spondiacus* once. The pattern mentioned above, which consists of a line containing a verb and two adjective-noun pairs is not found in Horace; sense-pause is rare at line-end, which is to be expected as the hexameters take up the first and third line of stanzas consisting of four lines.

We will observe this pattern again in what follows: Seneca prefers a stricter approach to versification, while Horace goes for more variety at the cost of the odd impurity.

2.2 Reception of Horatian Metres

Seneca's choral passages consist in part of anapaests,[38] in part of several different Aeolic metres in various configurations (listed in order of increasing 'imbalance,' as one might call it):
1. A choral passage is written in one single metre.
2. A choral passage consists of blocks of metres.
3. A choral passage contains several single lines in changing metres.
4. A choral passage contains longer polymetrical passages.

The configurations, of course, vary from play to play: In the *Phoenissae* there are no choral songs. In the *Troades* and in the *Thyestes* we see the simplest configuration, i.e. one metre per choral passage; in the *Hercules Furens* (and in the spurious *Hercules Oetaeus* as well), one of the choral songs is divided into two blocks; the same phenomenon occurs in the *Medea*, where, however, passages not written in trimeters are also found outside the choral songs. In the *Phaedra*, the non-anapaestic choral songs consist of many smaller units; in the *Agamemnon*, we have only one choral song made up of several metres, which, however – in addition to anapaests – consists of a longer polymetrical passage. The *Oedipus*, finally, features two polymetrical sections and choral songs consisting of several metres.

If we hazard a ranking of the plays by metrical 'imbalance,' we would arrive at something like the following list:
 1. *Phoenissae*
 2./3. *Troades, Thyestes*

---

[37] Hor. Carm. 1.28.15 and 29 (the latter is the aforementioned type with *kata proton daktylon* and *hephthemimeres*).
[38] Interesting as they are in themselves, they are beyond the scope of this chapter, where the focus is on the metres that Horace uses as well.

4. *Hercules Furens*
5. *Medea*
6./7. *Agamemnon*, *Phaedra*
8. *Oedipus*

Whether this ranking can be transferred to the plays' chronology is unclear. Fitch draws a parallel to other linguistic and stylistic peculiarities and considers the metrically more complex plays to be the earlier works.[39] That the spurious and later tragedies *Hercules Oetaeus* and *Octavia* would have to be ranked in the top half of the above list might add support to his view.

Since we are especially considering Seneca's adaptation of Horatian metres, it should be noted that the treatment of the sapphic hendecasyllable in connection with the adonic also varies from play to play and does not, unfortunately, fit so well with the ranking described above. We can distinguish:

- simple sapphic hendecasyllables without adonics (in the *Hercules Furens*, in one of two longer series in the *Phaedra*)
- a series of hendecasyllables concluded by an adonic (in the *Thyestes* and in one of the two longer series in the *Oedipus*, also once in the *Hercules Oetaeus*)
- periodic series of hendecasyllables coupled with an adonic (in the *Medea*, where in two cases a series of seven and three hendecasyllables respectively are followed by one adonic)
- hendecasyllables interspersed with adonics without recognisable pattern (in both longer series in the *Troades*, once in the *Phaedra*, where the passage also concludes with an adonic, once in the *Oedipus*)

Within these smaller structures, the metrical regularity deviates slightly from those of the larger structures (as described above): for example, in the *Troades*, whose composition might be described as 'simple' in that every choral passage consists of a single metre, the adonics are inserted randomly into the sapphic hendecasyllables. It serves as a reminder that macro- and micro-structures do not necessarily go hand in hand. It is possible, albeit speculative, that Seneca traded off regularity in the one against the other.

Beyond the choral passages as well, Seneca occasionally integrates other metres without exhibiting much regularity: the three parts of catalectic trochaic tetrameters, for example, are of different, albeit comparable length (ten to twelve

---

39 Fitch 1981.

lines). The arbitrary[40] change of metres in some plays without any visible patterns in numerical structures or in the order of different metres is legitimated by genre, but still forms a stark contrast with Horace, for the Augustan poet adheres to doubly even line counts and often, as seen above, crafts patterns spanning over several stanzas. If Fitch is correct in the relative dating of Seneca's tragedies, it is quite possible that Seneca himself discarded his own arbitrary arrangements to some degree.

2.2.1 Technical Purity

As happens in other areas of Roman poetry over time,[41] we can detect an increasing technical purity in the treatment of Aeolic versification from Horace to Seneca. Whereas, as discussed above, Horace used the secondary caesura after the sixth syllable in the sapphic hendecasyllable sparingly at first, but later more often, Seneca refrains from using it in his hendecasyllables at all. He does not use the *caesura latens* either, which occurs frequently in Horace; his central caesurae in the lesser asclepiads are not weakened by monosyllabic words (not even adjacent monosyllables that are metrically almost identical to a disyllable), nor are they absent altogether.

The boundary at line-end is further strengthened by the fact that monosyllabic words are completely absent in this position, as are hypermetrical verses and even missing word boundaries.[42]

Just as Horace turned Catullus's tendency to use a spondee as the Aeolic base into a norm, Seneca additionally refrains from varying syllable quantities – a phenomenon that still exists in some Horatian lines. Instead, Seneca establishes the long syllable as a norm in these positions. Hiatus does not occur at all in Seneca (it is also very rare in Horace). Synaloepha, on the other hand, does occur in Seneca but also less frequently than in Horace. In addition to these items, there are few exceptions in the polymetra, where, however, colometry and classification of metre may be uncertain.

---

[40] Not necessarily unmotivated, though – just think of Medea's magical song with the trochaic tetrameters Med. 740–751 and the iambic epode Med. 771–786.
[41] As seen in the development of the hexameter, especially regarding caesura and allowed final words, in the development of the pentameter with the disyllable ending, and also the iambic senarius from Plautus to, say, Phaedrus.
[42] For each of these phenomena we find examples in Horace.

2.2.2 Breaking the Rules

Irrespective of technical purity, Seneca does allow himself an un-Aeolic liberty: he resolves a long syllable into a double short or contracts a double short into a long syllable.[43] One might say that he does not bend a rule through prosodic licence but – in for a penny, in for a pound – breaks one in the following ways:
- sapphic hendecasyllable:
  $- \cup - \cup \cup - | \cup \cup - \cup - -$
  $- \cup - - - | - - \cup - -$
- lesser asclepiad:
  $- \cup \cup - \cup \cup - | - \cup \cup - \cup -$
  $- - - - - | - \cup \cup - \cup -$

Thus, there is not much left from the Aeolic versification principle (that is, the Aeolic base and a fixed number of syllables). Rather, these verses are distinctly Roman as they follow the way Romans usually adapt Greek verses: a very fixed caesura after a long syllable and the possibility of mutual substitution of double short and *longum*. Even if these substitutions occur only in a modest number of instances, they seem to work as in the hexameter. If we thought of a series of arsis and thesis even in metres that are not based on a fixed metrum, we would probably arrive at (a) $\pm \cup \pm - \pm | \cup \cup \pm \cup \pm -$ for the hendecasyllable and at (b) $\pm - \pm \cup \cup \pm | \pm \cup \cup \pm \cup \pm$ for the lesser asclepiad.

Only the unmarked syllables meet with substitutions – just as in the hexameter. It is also striking that at those positions where a long syllable is resolved into a double short (that is, in the fourth syllable of the sapphic hendecasyllable and in the second syllable of the Asclepiad), there was originally only an optional *longum*. Therefore, it is possible that only the Roman (Horatian) fixing of the long syllable created the licence for this substitution.[44] Prudentius, incidentally, follows Seneca in this practice, Statius in Silv. 4.7 does not; both reject the secondary caesura in the sapphic hendecasyllable. Thus, they provide an example for the fact that in Roman poetry, individual authors may establish licences for their successors but may also revoke them.

---

[43] He is not the first Roman to do so, see Catul. 55; but here in the phalaecian hendecasyllables, the choriamb is replaced by a molossus in a steady alternating series; additionally, there are Hor. Carm. 3.4.37 and Carm. 3.6.6 (as discussed above), where it remains unclear whether the metrical scheme is changed or whether this is due to a prosodic phenomenon.

[44] I am not sure whether this 'Romanisation,' so to say, reveals poetological tendencies. It does seem to be the case, though, that Seneca (unlike Horace) turns much more towards his Roman predecessors than towards Greek ones.

2.3 Experimentation

2.3.1 The Alcmanicus

The Alcmanicus, i.e. the acatalectic dactylic tetrameter, is a rare guest in Roman (and Greek) poetry; when it does appear, it is only for a few lines. Its stichic usage prior to Seneca is found in short passages in Ennius,[45] Accius,[46] and Pomponius Secundus.[47] In Seneca, as in his predecessors, there is one comparably short passage where three consecutive Alcmanici occur: Phaed. 761–763.[48]

What is exceptional about this verse is the fact that the last metrum is invariably realised as a dactyl and, since the last syllable needs to be short, it cannot be treated as an anceps. Thus, we find only syllables with a short vowel. But since even syllables with a short vowel are long if the syllable does not end on an open vowel, the issue of synapheia comes to the fore:[49] indeed, at least

---

[45] Enn., *Alexander*, 43–46 Jocelyn
iamque mari magno classis cita
texitur. exitium examen rapit.
adveniet. fera velivolantibus
navibus complevit manus litora.
'And now upon the mighty main a fast fleet is built; it carries a swarm of deaths; a wild horde will come and cover the shores with sail-fluttering ships.'

[46] Acc. *Antigona*, 4.140–141 Ribbeck
Heus, vigiles, properate, expergite
Pectora tarda sopore, exsurgite!
'Ho! Men of the watch, hurry there! Wake up your senses slow from sleep. Get up!'

[47] Pomponius Secundus, *ex incertis fabulis* 2.9–12 Ribbeck
Pendeat ex umeris dulcis chelys
Et numeros edat varios, quibus
Adsonet omne virens late nemus,
Et tortis errans qui flexibus.
'From the shoulders should hang the sweet lyre and generate manifold rhythms to which all the widely flourishing grove responds, and which, wandering in whirling turns' (my own translation).

[48] Anceps forma bonum mortalibus,
exigui donum breve temporis,
ut velox celeri pede laberis!
'Beauty—a doubtful boon for mortals, a brief and short lived gift, how fleeting, how swiftly passing!'

[49] As a syllable ending on a consonant is only open if the following word begins with a vowel when the consonant can be attributed to the next syllable; so e.g. *clamat avis* is segmented *cla-ma-ta-vis*. In verses without synapheia this phenomenon cannot occur across a line-end.

within these verse groups, synapheia is observed. If a line ends with a consonant, the next one begins with a vowel and vice versa.[50]

If we consider the first longer segment of these tetrameters, Sen. Oed. 449–466, we find a different scenario:

Te Tyrrhena, puer, rapuit manus,	
et tumidum Nereus posuit mare,	450
caerula cum pratis mutat freta:	
hinc verno platanus folio viret	
et Phoebo laurus carum nemus;	
garrula per ramos avis obstrepit;	
vivaces hederas remus tenet,	455
summa ligat vitis carchesia.	
Idaeus prora fremuit leo,	
tigris puppe sedet Gangetica.	
Tum pirata freto pavidus natat,	
et nova demersos facies habet:	460
bracchia prima cadunt praedonibus	
inlisumque utero pectus coit,	
parvula dependet lateri manus,	
et dorso fluctum curvo subit,	
lunata scindit cauda mare:	465
et sequitur curvus fugientia	
carbasa delphin.	

Nereus calmed the swollen seas, and changed the deep-blue waters to meadows; so there were plane trees verdant with spring foliage, and laurels whose groves are dear to Phoebus; birds vied in chattering among the branches, the oars were covered with vigorous ivy, grapevines twined at the mastheads; a lion from Ida roared at the prow, a tiger from Ganges sat in the stern. Then the frightened pirates swim in the sea, and as they sink take on new forms: first the robbers' arms fall away, their chests are squashed to join their bellies, little hands hang down at their sides, they dive in the waves with curving backs, cut through the sea with crescent tails: and the sails of the fleeing ship are chased by humpbacked dolphins.
(Oed. 449–466)

First, it is noteworthy that in every line the penthemimeral caesura is observed (as was already the case in Pomponius Secundus), which makes the verses reminiscent of hexameters with punctuation at the bucolic diaeresis;[51] second, there is no enjambement at all. Synapheia, however, seems to be observed only spor-

---

50 Note that the final -s in Ennius's lines does not count as consonantal.
51 Bucolic punctuation is – after Lucretius – always preceded by a dactylic metrum in Roman hexameters, which divides a line into a tetrameter and an adonic, just like in Oed. 465–466 – a terrific idea of Seneca's.

adically. A closer look reveals that it can be found in those line transitions where two main clauses are coordinated by a copula (*et* or *-que*), whereas it is not strictly observed at two unconnected main clauses. In fact, we see hiatuses even where one would assume there is heavy punctuation (451 to 452, 456 to 457, 465 to 466). It is not at every point of stronger division that synapheia is neglected, but it is hardly coincidental that there is synapheia between lines that are linked more closely.

Because of the few extant lines in this metre, it cannot be said with certainty whether Seneca only played around with this partial breach of synapheia; it is, however, remarkable that in the *Hercules Oetaeus* there is also a longer passage of these tetrameters[52] in which indeed – except for one hiatus at a stronger syntactic division – synapheia is observed throughout.

2.3.2 Oed. 882–914

There is another passage in the *Oedipus* that could be called an experiment as it seems to be a metre made up by Seneca and is used only once: the variation of glyconics in lines 882–914.

The metrical scheme is as follows:

$$- \cup \vdots - \overline{\smile\smile} - | \cup -$$

In contrast to regular glyconics there is no Aeolic base, which Seneca would have treated as a mandatory spondee anyway,[53] but always a trochee. Instead of the glyconic choriamb there is frequently (even in the majority of lines) a molossus. And finally, all lines end with an iambic word unlike in Seneca's other glyconics, in which only roughly half the lines end this way.

If this is not a regular glyconic verse, then – as Steinmetz ingeniously concluded – it must be a kind of glyconic correlating with the second half of a trimeter: there, too, the second syllable is necessarily short, the fourth element is realised more frequently as a *longum* (at times as a double short) and the line usually ends with an iambic word. This way, according to Steinmetz, Seneca 'macht den metrischen Kenner darauf aufmerksam, dass man diesen Vers [the glyconic] auch vom iambischen Trimeter ableiten und als akephalen *dimetrus fi-*

---

[52] Her. O. 1944–1976.
[53] There is one exception in the polymetra, Oed. 711, where the verse could be a variation of a known colon.

nalis verstehen kann.'⁵⁴ Yet the most striking aspect in this realisation of the glyconics, as Töchterle rightly points out, is that this way a 'vollkommen symmetrisches Gebilde'⁵⁵ is created that is nicely connected to the main theme of the song.

Although I would not generally put mere metrical *lusus* past Seneca and although I do not see why the usage of the molossus instead of the choriamb would emphasise the symmetry,⁵⁶ the link between metre and content appears to be plausible here. For not only is the metrical scheme palindromic with regard to the quantities, but there is also a word boundary after the second syllable in more than 75% of lines (twenty-five of thirty-three), which is a substantially higher number than expected in a regular trimeter after the penthemimeres. All this furthers the symmetry of the metre, a symmetry appropriate in a passage about the *aurea mediocritas*.⁵⁷

It is also striking that after three initial lines that contain the choriamb, the fourth line – after preceding *temperem Zephyro levi* ('I would trim [my sails] to the light westerly wind') – contains the molossus for the first time in the contrastive *vela, ne pressae gravi* ('...the sails..., lest [the sailyards shake] in a heavy [gale]'). Thus it seems the choriamb was used intentionally at the beginning of the passage, where the reader should be especially sensitive because of the novelty of the metre; the upshot is that the choriamb is used whenever the metaphorical ship goes along without difficulty, the molossus whenever it experiences trouble. While it does not occur consistently through the entire passage, a connection between metrical configuration and content is very plausible here, too.

2.4 Mimetic Metrics?

At times, metrical peculiarities can be clearly connected to the content; this is often intuitively plausible but must almost always remain speculative, simply because there are hardly any formal methods to make use of in order to prove a connection. However, a rather intuitive or associative approach may have also been decisive for the ancient poets themselves. It can be said with some certainty

---

54 Steinmetz 1970, 103.
55 Töchterle 1990, 567.
56 As Töchterle 1990, 567, argues. In fact, this position, as it is in the thesis of the verse, is the only one available for the substitution if we assume here the same technique Seneca used in the sapphic hendecasyllables and lesser asclepiads (see above).
57 On this ode cf. also Tarrant in this volume, 108–111.

that the more peculiar a metrical feature appears, the more confidently we can suppose it lends itself to interpretation.[58]

Although we have seen at least one such example in the previous section, I would like to present three further instances where one might speak of 'mimetic metrics.'

- *Thyestes* 100 *sequor*, 'I follow!'
  Half-lines are presumably a Senecan innovation, at least if we assume the half-lines of the *Aeneid* to be unintentional (which I do) even if they facilitated the introduction of half-lines in other works. In any case, it is an amusing idea of Seneca's to have the half-line *sequor* 'follow' a longer utterance by Tantalus right before the Fury becomes the speaker; it is as if it were the line itself that spoke. Of the three other incomplete trimeters perhaps Tro. 1103 *in media Priami regna* ('into the midst of Priam's kingdom') has a similar punch line; at this point the verse, too, ends right 'in the middle'.
- *Medea* 636 *sumere innumeras solitum figuras*, 'given to adopting countless shapes'
  As discussed above, Seneca at times replaces long syllables with double shorts in verses that should have a fixed number of syllables. In this choral song written in sapphic stanzas (first of four, then of nine lines[59] each) the word *innumeras* has been set. It not only increases the number of syllables by emphasising the multitude itself but also puns on *numeri*. Indeed, the other instance of a resolved *longum* not containing a Greek proper name[60] is of a similar kind, as the words *varii* (Tro. 836 *An ferax varii lapidis Carystos*, 'Or Carystos, rich in many-hued marble') and *celeres* (Ag. 817 *tardius celeres agitare currus*, 'to drive his speeding chariot more slowly') take up corresponding positions.
- *Medea* 744 *rota resistat membra torquens...*, 'the wheel that tortures limbs may stop'
  Two[61] of the eleven catalectic trochaic tetrameters in this passage exhibit a somewhat striking rhythm, in that the first half of the line is itself divided

---

58 We always have to consider the possibility that metrical peculiarities also occur for their own sake or for variation. Moreover, a peculiarity may often stress a specific part of the text but without an inherent connection of the feature to the content. Instead it is the exceptional quality itself that prompts an interpretation.
59 I.e. the adonic occurs after eight sapphic hendecasyllables, unlike in the regular sapphic stanza where it is every fourth line.
60 At least if Zwierlein 1977, 158 is correct in athetising Tro. 1051 – to which end he makes use of this metrical feature.
61 If, with Zwierlein, we expunge line 746.

into two parts of equal length: there is word boundary after the fourth element, which violates Havet's Law.[62] In the first of the two lines in particular (744) a link with the content appears plausible: At the spot where the usual flow of the verse ceases, the bone-crushing wheel also grinds to a halt.

The other verse in which the bridge is ignored (Med. 748 *vos quoque, urnis quas foratis inritus ludit labor*, 'and you who are mocked by fruitless toil with pitchers pierced by holes') does not offer such a clear a punch line, although we find at least allusions to the broken (*foratis*, 'pierced') and the sluggish (*labor*, 'toil').

3 Conclusion

What unites Horace and Seneca in their metrical compositions is the tendency to standardise the versification of their predecessors; they are in good company, as this applies, generally speaking, to Roman poetry as a whole. But Horace and Seneca did till what had until then been a fairly fallow field. In some respects Horace sowed the first seeds when it came to the naturalisation of the alcaic and sapphic verses within Latin verse (in particular by standardisation of caesurae), in other aspects he strengthened existing tendencies, for example the spondaically realised Aeolic base that Catullus had already used.

Seneca adopts the norms established by Horace and develops further restrictions. He discards individual variable positions, such as the placement of a *syllaba anceps* at the beginning of the line or the secondary caesura in the sapphic hendecasyllable, features that Horace only used with frequency in his later verse; he also dismisses stronger forms of synapheia (hypermetry, words across line break, prepositions before line boundaries). He does not continue to employ *brevis in longo*, nor monosyllabic words before caesurae, and instances of synaloepha are far fewer than in Horace. Impurities or prosodic licences are discarded.

In his avoidance of anomaly, Seneca forgoes what seems to be a context-dependent stylistic feature in Horace, who exhibits a tendency to agglomerate peculiarities (as seen in synaloepha and the secondary caesura in the sapphic hendecasyllable) across his lyric corpus. In addition, Horace seems to reduplicate certain peculiarities in a way that cannot be viewed as random. The statistical

---

[62] This law, generally ignored by Latin poets, is an equivalent to Porson's law and prohibits word-end after the fourth syllable if it is a longum ($\smile\smile - - \frown - \smile \smile \times |...$).

evidence suggests that Horace did not want the relevant feature to be considered an experiment.

Horace is to a large extent the first (or at least the most prominent) poet to create metrical schemes in a Roman mould; as far as I can see, however, he leaves them untouched once they are created. His compositions show a certain regularity; but as he has the freedom to choose which metres he uses (and indeed some of them he uses only once), this point should not be overemphasised.

Seneca, however, shows more freedom in his use and arrangement of metre – undoubtedly also for generic reasons – and makes an (apparently) unsystematic use of several metres; he suspends the Aeolic versification principle (and Romanises it) and, besides his own form of polymetry, invents a fresh metre of his own; beyond this, he also permits himself half-lines. Seneca's approach to metrical variation is situated at a higher level than that of Horace. Whereas his usage of caesurae and the syllaba anceps is strict, uniform, and prosodically sound, his metrical schemes and the arrangement of individual verses are a matter of metrical creativity.

Both authors offer certain passages in which a connection between metrical configuration and poetic content is plausible; some phenomena, however, seem to me to occur *metri gratia*.

III Themes and Concepts

Gregor Vogt-Spira
Time in Horace and Seneca

Time is a pervasive and conspicuous issue in both Horace and Seneca. The memorable phrase '*carpe diem*' has almost become a chiffre, at times emancipated from the context that gave it its original meaning. Horace's treatment of time is, however, nuanced and comprehensive: it spans the *Epodes*, *Odes*, and the late *Epistles*, and extends to the poet's self-conception and idea of literary history.[1] A similarly deep engagement can be seen in Seneca's philosophical works. It is no coincidence that the first letter to Lucilius begins with the topic of time being stolen and lost. Everything, Seneca argues, is in someone else's possession – only time is in one's own control; making correct use of one's time means to possess oneself (Sen. Ep. 1). Time is thus marked as a key topic, one that will be treated in the following letters – as it had been in earlier philosophical writings – from ever new angles.

This common interest in time may serve as the basis for examining Seneca's engagement with Horace more closely. It should be noted at the outset that both Seneca's and Horace's treatment of time is part of a shared wider discourse, one independent of questions of genre. This discourse is significantly informed by the Stoics and Epicureans, who made time a central topic and developed patterns of argumentation that were to recur in varied forms. Moreover, this intense interest in time as a phenomenon occurs within a still wider historical context: since the end of the fourth century BC, the question of what is and is not obtainable had become prevalent, a question that explored the scope of what is available, i.e. of those things that are within the control of each and every individual's way of life. Self-possession, to possess oneself, thus became a key concept; and possession of one's time, as Seneca's first letter to Lucilius makes clear, provides a path towards self-possession. This particular emphasis in the debate is evidenced not least in the rapid growth of interest in *tychē* / *fortuna*, i.e. the opposite of that which is in our control.[2] In fact, reflections on time and *fortuna* are also often linked in both Horace and Seneca.

That Horace and Seneca make use of similar phrases and, beyond that, similarly attribute importance to the topic of time is thus due to their shared partic-

---

I am most grateful to Tobias Allendorf for translating my text into English.

[1] On the complexity of the engagement with this topic, see Schwindt 2005, esp. 15–18 on Horace.
[2] Cf. Nilsson 1974, esp. 200–210; Vogt-Spira 1992, esp. 1–10.

DOI 10.1515/9783110528893-009

ipation in a common overarching discourse. One detail in this discourse is worthy of note: it is characterised by a tendency towards paradox – probably less a mannerism than a necessity that arises from the subject matter. While time is, on the one hand, an uncircumventable condition of life, it is also very difficult to pin down. Pointedness and paradox can already be found in the popular ethics of, for instance, symposiastic songs on the topic and likewise in early philosophical mappings of the concepts of time and change – such as Heraclitus's river aphorism, which is picked up by Seneca.[3] A further level of analysis is reached in Aristotle's theory of time in the fourth book of the *Physics*. His theory subsequently provides a platform for Hellenistic reflections on time, especially the question of the existence of time and of its different degrees – whether the present is a point in time and merely an arithmetic quantity or whether it has its own extension.[4] These problems are fundamental in nature and evade simple solutions.[5] It comes as no surprise, then, that the relevant discourse is wide, full of different foci, and not without contradictions. This is already true for the description of the physical phenomenon, let alone its ethical consequences.

This widespread and diverse discourse provides the necessary backdrop against which Seneca's engagement with Horace in his treatment of time is to be assessed. Given that Horace was the most prominent contributor to the discourse of time in Latin literature prior to Seneca (exceeding even Lucretius in importance), such engagement is to be expected on Seneca's part. It is thus all the more remarkable that, in contrast to the situation in Seneca's choral lyrics, only a rather small Horatian presence has been noted in his prose writings. In fact, one can only find four verbal quotations, in addition to a number of allusions, which – owing to the notorious fuzziness of what does and does not count as an allusion – cannot be quantified with certainty.[6] Insufficient knowledge of Horace on Seneca's part, however, cannot be the reason, as the numerous references to Horace in the tragedies make clear. On the contrary, Seneca's knowledge of Horace often seems obfuscated and direct quotation almost deliberately avoid-

---

[3] See below, section 2 and esp. p. 194.
[4] On the fundamental importance of Aristotle's treatment for Hellenistic theories of time, see Levi 1951, Barigazzi 1959, Neck 1964, Goldschmidt 2006. On the much-debated Aristotelian concept of time, see Wieland 1970, esp. 316–334.
[5] Discussion on the topic of time is one of the constants in the history of philosophy. An overview of the more recent debate is provided in Oaklander 2008. Frank 1989, esp. 449–450, shows how persistent the questions that Aristotle raised are.
[6] See the foundational treatment by Mazzoli 1970, 233–238, esp. 234–235, with n. 52; cf. also Berthet 1979, esp. 940–943. Three out of the four direct quotations are in the letters to Lucilius.

ed.⁷ The authors' adherence to differing philosophical schools – however we define Horace's 'Epicureanism' – does not constitute sufficient reason,⁸ nor does the difference in genre.⁹ As yet, there does not seem to be a satisfactory explanation for Seneca's reluctance to openly refer to his predecessor.¹⁰

The reason for this lies partly in the fact that the question cannot be satisfactorily answered by searching for semantic parallels between Seneca and Horace. For if one considers both authors within the discourse mentioned above as a whole, it becomes evident that, despite occasional similarities in the phrasing, they rely on completely incompatible concepts of time. It is thus necessary to sketch the basics of the Horatian and Senecan concepts of time in what follows. For reasons of space, I will restrict myself to Horace's *Odes* and Seneca's *Epistulae Morales*, works in which the topic is treated in great abundance.

1 Horace Carm. 3.29 and Seneca Ep. 12

Let us begin with a case that has long been considered a clear link between Seneca and Horace: the twelfth letter to Lucilius and Carm. 3.29. At the core of this great invitation ode to Maecenas, whose argument unfolds in a wide arc, we find a maxim common to both Kepos and Stoa as the quintessence of the piece. According to this maxim, independence and self-possession can be achieved by regarding every moment of one's life as fulfilled. Horace puts this thought into the following form, whereby the final point, i.e. of not being subject to any external power, receives particular emphasis via an elaborate tricolon:¹¹

>   Ille potens sui
> laetusque deget, cui licet in diem
>   dixisse 'vixi.' Cras vel atra
>   nube polum, Pater, occupato

---

7 Cf. Mazzoli 1970, 235–236, and Berthet 1979, esp. 944–954.
8 Cf. Tarrant 2006, esp. 2.
9 Berthet 1979, 941, n. 8 argues that the difference in genre is a reason for the few quotations; but this view is implausible, considering the numerous quotations from Virgil in Seneca's prose writings.
10 It is worth considering that Seneca may have avoided citing Horace, who never attained the status of a school author in antiquity, because his readers would not have readily recognised the quotations: see Tarrant 2006, 2; cf. also Mazzoli 1998. See further below, section 5.
11 The text of Horace is that of Shackleton Bailey's Teubner, the text of Seneca's *Epistulae Morales* is from Reynold's OCT. Translations are taken from Rudd's Loeb for the *Odes* and Gummere's Loeb for the *Epistles*.

>   vel sole puro: non tamen irritum   45
> quodcumque retro est efficiet, neque
>   diffinget infectumque reddet
>   quod fugiens semel hora vexit.

> That man will be master of himself and live a happy life who as each day ends can say 'I have lived.' Tomorrow let our Father cover the sky in dark cloud or bright sunshine, he will not cancel whatever is past, nor will he render null and void what the flying hour has once carried away.
> (Hor. Carm. 3.29.41–48)

The commentaries on Horace's *Odes* since Mitscherlich and Orelli-Baiter have routinely cited the following passage from Seneca by way of explication; Kiessling / Heinze makes the relationship explicit, stating that Seneca is here paraphrasing Horace:[12]

> Crastinum si adiecerit deus, laeti recipiamus. Ille beatissimus est et securus sui possessor, qui crastinum sine sollicitudine expectat; quisquis dixit 'vixi,' cotidie ad lucrum surgit.

> And if God is pleased to add another day, we should welcome it with glad hearts. That man is happiest, and is secure in his own possession of himself, who can await the morrow without apprehension. When a man has said: 'have lived!', every morning he arises he receives a bonus.
> (Sen. Ep. 12.9)

If one looks at the passage more closely, however, the differences are hard to overlook. First, there is the key term *vixi*, which Seneca had introduced in several earlier steps. The discussion begins with the cautionary example of a certain Pacuvius, who is said to have become wealthy in Syria – this is probably the legate Sextus Pacuvius Taurus, briefly mentioned, without further comment, in Tacitus.[13] Seneca tells us that this individual, having feasted on an opulent meal (which is sarcastically described by Seneca as a funeral offering featuring wine that Pacuvius offers to himself: *sibi parentare*), would be carried to his bedroom every night. On the way, he would be accompanied by applauding slave-boys and the refrain 'βεβίωται, βεβίωται.'[14] This is a perversion of both the tradi-

---

[12] Cf. Mitscherlich 1800, II 289 *ad* 41; Orelli / Baiter 1850–1852, 510 *ad* 41; Kiessling / Heinze 1930, 379 *ad* 41; Nisbet / Rudd 2004, 358 *ad* 41–43. Kiessling / Heinze and Nisbet / Rudd both refer to the Epicurean background. Scarpat 1975, 300 refers to 'Orazio qui echeggiato.'
[13] Tac. Ann. 2.79.2. The identification is speculative, but the scholarly consensus: cf. Koestermann 1963, vol. I 400 ad loc. and Scarpat 1975, 298.
[14] Sen. Ep. 12.8–9 *Pacuvius, qui Syriam usu suam fecit, cum vino et illis funebribus epulis sibi parentaverat, sic in cubiculum ferebatur a cena ut inter plausus exoletorum hoc ad symphoniam caneretur:* βεβίωται βεβίωται. *Nullo non se die extulit. Hoc quod ille ex mala conscientia faciebat*

tional Roman funeral procession and the key thought in *vixi*, a perversion that receives its most outstanding expression in Petronius's *Cena Trimalchionis*.[15]

The term βεβίωται is in fact attested in one of Cicero's letters to Atticus as a catchphrase circulating among the Roman elite; Cicero's urbane remark, however, commenting on L. Cornelius Balbus's building activity, is a subtle sneer at the ethical value of such an intense lifestyle as Balbus's: *verum si quaeris, homini non recta, sed voluptaria quaerenti nonne* βεβίωται?, 'but if he is asked, can't he say, as a man seeking pleasure, not virtue, *bebiōtai*?' (Cic. Att. 12.2.2.). This shows that the expression was used not least as a way of legitimising a lifestyle focused on pleasure; Seneca's satirical and critical remarks, using the example of Pacuvius, belong to this same line of discourse.[16] The βεβίωται, whose connotation is not fixed,[17] derives from an Epicurean context: Metrodorus of Lampsacus, one of Epicurus's closest disciples, is said to have called himself happy because, at any moment, he would have been able to depart this life saying 'ὡς εὖ ἡμῖν βεβίωται,' 'how well have we lived' (Metr. fr. 49 K).[18]

In Seneca's classification, Metrodorus's point would be an example of *bona* as opposed to Pacuvius's *mala conscientia*. But Seneca ignores Metrodorus at this point in the letter – even though he refers to him at other points in the *Epistulae Morales* – and instead chooses Dido's last words as his positive example, the only line that is quoted three times in Seneca's works: Verg. A. 4.653 *vixi et quem dederat cursum fortuna peregi*, 'I have lived; the course which Fortune

---

nos ex bona faciamus, et in somnum ituri laeti hilaresque dicamus: '*vixi et quem dederat cursum fortuna peregi.*', 'Pacuvius, who by long occupancy made Syria his own, used to hold a regular burial sacrifice in his own honour, with wine and the usual funeral feasting, and then would have himself carried from the dining-room to his chamber, while eunuchs applauded and sang in Greek to a musical accompaniment: "He has lived his life, he has lived his life!" Thus Pacuvius had himself carried out to burial every day. Let us, however, do from a good motive what he used to do from a debased motive; let us go to our sleep with joy and gladness; let us say: "I have lived; the course which Fortune set for me is finished".' Cf. Berno 2014, esp. 132. Mann 2006, 121 shows how Pacuvius functions as an example of acting *ex mala conscientia*.
15 Cf. Smith 1975, 211, in his commentary on c. 78. See also Schmeling 2011, 326–329.
16 Smith 1975, 211 notes that the case of Pacuvius had happened long ago (Pacuvius, if identical with the one mentioned in Tacitus, would have been legate in Syria in 19 CE), but 'Seneca's use of *illis* implies that his readers could be expected to remember.'
17 Cf. Cic. Att. 14.21.3: *Sed mihi quidem* βεβίωται; *viderint iuvenes*, 'but I have lived my life; let the young men worry,' which refers to the opposition between the old, whose life is behind them, and the young, who are now in the position of responsibility.
18 See Cicero's criticism at Tusc. 5.27.

set for me is finished.'¹⁹ Seneca introduces the line with the injunction to speak it every night before going to bed *laeti hilaresque* – despite the fact that *laetus* is hardly the state of mind Dido was in shortly before her suicide (even though in looking back she describes herself as *felix* because of her past achievements).²⁰ The decisive fact is that Seneca's choice of the example of Dido shows a subtle shift of focus: the presence of death is much more real in Seneca's rendering than it is in Horace's entanglement of temporal levels, where the future remains open. Seneca makes the theme of death concrete – albeit in satirical form – with the example of Pacuvius. Even though Kiessling / Heinze concede that Seneca 'got it right,'²¹ Seneca's paraphrase of Horace, which concludes his train of thought, is in fact completely displaced.

The Senecan shift of focus can be corroborated further if one considers the frameworks in which the respective arguments unfold. In Horace, we have an ode to Maecenas, inviting him to travel from sweltering Rome to the cool, refreshing Sabine country. The gesture of invitation links the concrete, physical pleasantness of the place – which is evoked in an elaborate manner, for example in the opposition of the cool of the country estate to the stuffiness of the city – with the injunction to retire from everyday sorrows. These sorrows, which Horace puts in perspective (why should Maecenas care what the Chinese are doing or what is happening at the Don?), are contrasted with an orientation towards the present: Carm. 3.29.32–33 *Quod adest memento | componere aequus*, 'Make sure to settle immediate problems calmly.'²² This detachment and orientation towards the present is clearly linked to a place, the physical presence at the villa. The situational parameter provides the starting point and condition for being elevated to the level of the general.

This is very different in Seneca, who disguises his argumentation with the humorous nature of his own learning process.²³ The letter begins in a graphic manner,

---

19 We are coming full circle here: for this passage, the commentaries refer to the Horatian *vixi* in Carm. 3.29: cf. Austin 1982, 189 ad loc. Berno 2014 provides a detailed discussion of all the three passages where Seneca cites the Virgilian line.
20 Cf. Mazzoli 1970, 236 on the Virgilian line: 'parole che, essendo pronunciate da Didone immediatamente prima del suicidio, sono senz'altro incongrue con la tesi morale difesa da Seneca.' Berno identifies an increasingly decontextualising method of citation: Berno 2014, 124 and 125. Literary theory has to date not sufficiently addressed the question of how far specific contexts are transported in citations and, more generally, in the practice of *imitatio*.
21 Kiessling / Heinze 1930, 380: 'Seneca hat das richtig aufgefaßt.'
22 On *curae*, see Orelli / Baiter 1850–1852 ad loc.: 'Inest in his innocens neque amicum laesura ironia; etenim et ille et omnes Romani optime noverant nihil periculi iam impendere Romano imperio ab Orientis atque Septentrionis nationibus.'
23 In the following, I paraphrase Sen. Ep. 12.1–4.

with the observation of decay: the villa is run-down – the administrator of the property explains that this is not his fault, but rather due to the age of the house. The house, however, had been extended by Seneca, who is somewhat irritated at the fact that stones not older than himself are already beginning to crumble. A further cause for irritation are the dry and knotty plane trees, which he himself had planted. The last shock is staged by Seneca as an elaborate climax: the physical decay of the son of his administrator, a boy whom he had carried in his own arms. Decaying buildings and decaying bodies – the villa gives expression to the course of time. Seneca sums up with the statement that the *suburbanum* has demonstrated to him how advanced in years he is himself.

Thus, Seneca's villa, unlike Horace's, is not viewed as a space that provides a joyful 'here and now.' It does not rescue owner and guest from *rapax tempus* – rather, it stands for the rapid river of time itself. Seneca's *paraenesis* – that one should make oneself independent of the flow of time – is, on the one hand, very close to the attitude promoted by Horace, even down to the phraseology. But the function of the physical space is actually the opposite of the Horatian model: in Seneca, there is no link between the villa as such – in its physical materiality – and a mental state.[24] One of the reasons for this is the fact that Seneca's villa is depicted as a farm estate. The owner arrives not as one enjoying *otium* but in order to survey the state of the property and to make decisions about it. That is the norm in Roman everyday life, but it is at odds with the contemporary discourse of *villeggiatura*,[25] a discourse that Seneca opposes. In this context, it becomes clear why Seneca emphasises so strongly the villa's character as a farm estate.

Owing to this Senecan construction, there is no contrast between a fulfilled present and the flow of time, the quintessence of the Horatian statement in Carm. 3.29. Rather, having made us aware of the flow of time, which is exemplified by the estate's decay, the text moves on to develop a concept of time based on the *gradus vitae*: life consists of parts as well as circles, and each smaller circle is enclosed by a bigger one (Sen. Ep. 12.6). This construction proceeds from the biggest circle, which encompasses the whole of life (from our birth to death), via *adulescentia*, *pueritia*, and *annus* (from the multiplication of which an individual *vita* is constituted), to *dies*, the smallest circle, which, however, also experiences a rising and setting. In any case, it is clear that the day is usu-

---

24 What Seneca is interested in is a more abstract, symbolic link: according to the widespread pattern 'the villa as a portrait,' the villa is used as the speaker's *speculum vitae*; cf. the subtle interpretation of Henderson 2004, 24–27.
25 On the Roman conceptualisation of rural life see Zanker 1987, 35–41.

ally the smallest unit, decisive for any reflection on time. From this, Seneca deduces that every day must be treated as if it were the last.

This exhortation, however, remains somewhat abstract: it is the result of stringent deduction, and so any positive connection with a specific locality is necessarily avoided. Thus, there is no concretisation of the present – whether we term it *dies*, *praesens tempus*, or anything else. This lack of concreteness points to a central difference in Horace's and Seneca's interventions in the discourse of time.

Horace's exhortation, *Quod adest memento | componere aequus*, has been cited above. This exhortation is emphasised as the key message by its position precisely in the middle of the poem (even down to the *morae*). At the same time, however, we can now add that the maxim functions as the first part of a central Horatian antithesis: it is followed by the image of a river.

> quod adest memento
>
> componere aequus: cetera fluminis
> ritu feruntur, nunc medio alveo
>   cum pace delabentis Etruscum   35
>   in mare, nunc lapides adesos
>
> stirpisque raptas et pecus et domos
> volventis una, non sine montium
>   clamore vicinaeque silvae,
>   cum fera diluvies quietos   40
> inritat amnis.

Make sure to settle immediate problems calmly. Everything else flows away like a river that now glides peacefully in the middle of its channel down to the Etruscan Sea, now rolls along eroded boulders, uprooted trees, livestock, and houses all mixed together amid the roar of the mountains and neighbouring woods, when a wild flood enrages its quiet streams.
(Carm. 3.29.32–41)

We can see that the antithesis does not refer to the stages of time – i.e. 'here' the present, 'there' the past and future. Rather, it is more fundamental: 'here' the present (*quod adest*), 'there' the river of time, which flows now gently, now rapidly. This is a powerful and well-developed tableau, imitating the power of the river; the enjambements between the stanzas, for instance, are significant: it is as if the borders of the stanzas are flooded by the powerful river, which only comes to rest at the very end.²⁶ The type of present at issue here is not part of this river (time), but is imagined to be something of a different quality, something that can lead an individual out of it.

2 Seneca's Use of River Imagery and Its Philosophical Background

The image of the river is one of the most common tropes for the course of life. Seneca also employs it several times. In Ep. 23, the formulation of Horace's great Maecenas Ode must have served as a model:

> Pauci sunt qui consilio se suaque disponant: ceteri, eorum more quae fluminibus innatant, non eunt sed feruntur; ex quibus alia lenior unda detinuit ac mollius vexit, alia vehementior rapuit, alia proxima ripae cursu languescente deposuit, alia torrens impetus in mare eiecit. Ideo constituendum est quid velimus et in eo perseverandum.

> There are only a few who control themselves and their affairs by a guiding purpose; the rest do not proceed; they are merely swept along, like objects afloat in a river. And of these objects, some are held back by sluggish waters and are transported gently; others are torn along by a more violent current; some, which are nearest the bank, are left there as the current slackens; and others are carried out to sea by the onrush of the stream. Therefore, we should decide what we wish, and abide by the decision.
> (Ep. 23.8)

As in Horace, this is followed by the topic of *vixi*, but the thought is developed by beginning from its failure: *male vivunt qui semper vivere incipiunt*. Those who have only just begun to live cannot be prepared for death, and their lives will always remain unfinished. Thus, as we learn from a variant of the *vixi* topos that follows soon after, one must strive to have lived enough: Sen. Ep. 23.10 *Id agendum est, ut satis vixerimus*, 'We must make it our aim already to have lived long enough.'

The points of contact are obvious; we are not dealing with different ideas of time, but with the contrast between those who act according to a long-standing and constant plan and those who are driven hither and thither by chance: the former are self-determined, the latter are dominated by external forces. The river simile thus serves as an illustration of a particular lack of autonomy: one that originates from a lack of self-possession.

---

26 The mimetic word order of the lines is discussed by Pöschl 1970, esp. 240.

The river simile is used in a different way in Ep. 58. Our experience of constant change in the world around us provides the motivation here. Nobody, Seneca says, is the same person in old age as he was when young; nobody wakes up as the same person he was the day before: Ep. 58.22–23 *Corpora nostra rapiuntur fluminum more. Quidquid vides currit cum tempore; nihil ex iis quae videmus manet*, 'Our bodies are hurried along like flowing waters; every visible object accompanies time in its flight; of the things which we see, nothing is fixed.' The general rule according to which nothing we see will remain is exemplified by reference to the present moment: *Ego ipse, dum loquor mutari ista, mutatus sum*, 'Even I myself, as I comment on this change, am changed myself.' This phrasing is an unmistakable reference to Horace's Carm. 1.11, where the host explains to his Leuconoe how the course of time is not within our control: Carm. 1.11.7–8 *Dum loquimur fugerit invida | aetas*, 'As we talk, grudging time will have run on.'[27] But in Seneca, there is no *carpe diem*: rather, the idea that nobody is the same the following morning as he was the day before leads to a famous quotation from Heraclitus: one steps into the same river twice yet, at the same time, does not step into the same river (Heraclitus B 49a D-K).[28]

The framework of this letter is provided by its engagement with Platonic metaphysics. Seneca distinguishes between six ways in which Plato understands 'being.' He counts time as the sixth and final type of being, which, together with the void, is one of those things that are invariable and always the same (Ep. 58.16–22). The question, however, of the existence of time – in technical terms, whether time should be counted among the things that exist or those that do not exist – is a central problem in the context of theories of time, which are later treated with a predominant interest in ethics rather than metaphysics. The core argument is this: while the future only exists in one's imagination, the formation of one's imagination is subject to each and every individual's control, and can thus be influenced by philosophical knowledge.

The most subtle analysis of whether time exists is given in Aristotle's *Physics*. He starts from the observation that one portion of time has existed and no longer exists, while the other has yet to arrive and does not yet exist; yet time – whether infinite time or a given period of time – is made up of one or both of these portions. But that which is made up of things which do not exist can

---

27 Cf. further below, p. 198.
28 Sen. Ep. 58.23. On the meaning of this phrase, the exact wording of which is not transmitted, see Marcovich 1967, 194–215 ('the implication of Heraclitus' river-simile is obscure,' 212); see also Kahn 1979, 168–169.

have no existence (Arist. Phys. 4.10.217b33–218a3).²⁹ Further, if an object made of parts is to exist, either all or at least some of its parts must exist for the period of its existence. Otherwise, the thing cannot exist at all. The parts of time, however, either have existed or are going to exist, and none of them *is*. More importantly, according to Aristotle, the 'now' is not a part of time: a part is a measure of the whole, and the whole must be made up of parts; but it seems as if time is not made up of 'nows' (Arist. Phys. 4.10.218a3–8). Thus, there emerges the problem of whether the 'now,' which appears to separate past from future, always remains the same or whether new 'nows' continuously appear. Both options lead to *aporia*. For, as Aristotle points out, the 'nows' would not be able to coexist simultaneously if ever-new ones arise. Nor, however, is it possible that the 'now' always remains the same, since, as soon as one picks a random period of time, there clearly emerge two different 'nows.' Otherwise, nothing would be 'before' or 'after' anything else (Arist. Phys. 4.10.218a8–30).

Aristotle's solution to this problem is to make a distinction between two aspects of *nun* (νῦν): insofar as it divides time in the sense of a succession of phases – Aristotle calls this its 'respective determination' – the *nun* is always different, but as a substratum it is always the same.³⁰ As the 'now' that is always the same, it creates a continuity of time by connecting past and present. In its other sense, it functions as the principle that delimits time: by dividing time, the 'now' is the very condition that enables one to talk about time in the first place, because, Aristotle says, that which is bounded by the 'now' is thought to be time (Arist. Phys. 4.11.219a29–30).

This distinction is also used by Seneca for his interpretation of the quotation from Heraclitus: the name of the river remains the same, whereas the water itself has flowed through it (Ep. 58.23). The simile, which at first, following on from the concrete level of the tableau, concerns the rapid flow of the river (which is also true for the flow of human life), subsequently refers in a more abstract way to

---

29 For Aristotle's *Physics*, I quote Ross's edition (Oxford University Press), translations are by Barnes (Princeton UP); the English phrasing of Aristotle follows this translation as well.
30 Arist. Phys. 4.11.219b 9–15: καὶ ὥσπερ ἡ κίνησις αἰεὶ ἄλλη καὶ ἄλλη, καὶ ὁ χρόνος (ὁ δ' ἅμα πᾶς χρόνος ὁ αὐτός· τὸ γὰρ νῦν τὸ αὐτὸ ὅ ποτ' ἦν – τὸ δ' εἶναι αὐτῷ ἕτερον – τὸ δὲ νῦν τὸν χρόνον ὁρίζει, ᾗ πρότερον καὶ ὕστερον). τὸ δὲ νῦν ἔστι μὲν ὡς τὸ αὐτό, ἔστι δ' ὡς οὐ αὐτό· ᾗ μὲν γὰρ ἐν ἄλλῳ καὶ ἄλλῳ, ἕτερον (τοῦτο δ' ἦν αὐτῷ τὸ νῦν ⟨εἶναι⟩), ὃ δέ ποτε ὄν ἐστι τὸ νῦν, τὸ αὐτό. 'Just as motion is a perpetual succession, so also is time. But every simultaneous time is the same; for the 'now' is the same in substratum – though its being is different – and the 'now' determines time, in so far as time involves the before and after. The 'now' in one sense is the same, in another it is not the same. In so far as it is in succession, it is different (which is just what its being was now supposed to mean), but its substratum is the same.' On this passage, cf. also Wieland 1970, 323–327.

time and is reformulated accordingly: every 'now' is the death of the preceding one. But given that drops of water still exist after they have flowed past, Seneca is stretching the limits of the simile's applicability here: his image in fact fails to encapsulate the core form in which time exists – a difficulty involved in all attempts at explaining time by appeal to spatial phenomena.[31]

What are we to make of the present, then, the topic in which we are most interested in this passage? For Aristotle, the present is a point in time. Stoic theory of time also deals with this problem, and discussion of it is included in Seneca's Ep. 49. Seneca reflects on what *modo* means – Ep. 49.2 *Modo amisisse te videor; quid enim non 'modo' est, si recorderis?*, 'I seem to have lost you but a moment ago. For what is not "but a moment ago" when one begins to use the memory?' – and makes the observation that memory makes even long periods of time seem small: this, he explains, is because time exists in the form of points. Stoic theory indeed treats the concept of time as made up of points, and oscillates between (1) a strictly arithmetic construction according to which a period of time is defined by two endpoints which, in turn, do not have any extension (this is Aristotle's view in the *Physics*) and (2) the assumption of a 'present moment,' which is thought to create some sort of atomic interval which cannot be divided further and thus must be the basis of perception and experience.[32]

Seneca then transforms this definition of the problem in a bold argument: for him, the problem is not about the present moment itself, but about the experience of time in general, with an excessive emphasis on the *brevitas* of our lifetime. To start with, the past – not the present – exists in the form of points for Seneca: in our *memoria*, which makes our past life present, the past is located in one location at a time, as a single unit to be perceived with one 'glance.' This means that the past no longer stretches over a period of time, an idea that Seneca expresses in the phrase, *omnia in idem profundum cadunt*, 'everything slips into the same abyss' (Ep. 49.3). All of this, however, only serves as a point of departure for Seneca in his discussion of our lifetime as existing in the form of a

---

[31] While the interpretation of the Heraclitus fragment – and with it, the opposition identified above – is debated (see above, n. 28), Seneca's use seems to be clear. It is noteworthy that Seneca's interpretation of the two meanings of 'river' parallels Aristotle explaining 'now' with two meanings; this is especially remarkable since this interpretation does not seem to appear anywhere else. It will not be possible to ascertain how far this is due to Seneca's source, which, Marcovich 1967, 211 suggests, could be Scepticism. But it is also possible to trace the idea of the stability of the river being linked to its name to Seneca himself: see Inwood 2007, 129–130. Since Seneca explicitly places his interpretation within the context of the topic of 'time,' the possibility of a connection with the famous Aristotelian theory of time (also known to Seneca) should be entertained.

[32] See the detailed discussion by Goldschmidt 2006.

point. He arrives at this idea by skillfully exploiting the fact that the measurement of time is relative, and argues that a thing which is only short in its entirety cannot contain any long period of time: thus, Seneca seems to suggest, reducing all of our past life to a single point is no great loss in terms of time. But reducing our lifetime to a single point – *punctum est quod vivimus* – is not enough for Seneca: time is even smaller than a point – *adhuc puncto minus* (Ep. 49.3), a suggestion that pointedly gets rid of the physical and arithmetical definition of time!

What Seneca wants to emphasise here is not the physically measurable passage of time, but our subjective perception of its flow and the fact that estimating a period of time depends on our standpoint: *modo* – the 'just now' he is talking about – as the *condicio humana*.[33] This is corroborated by looking at his own life: whereas time did not seem rapid to him before, the course of time seems very fast to him now that he is nearing the end of life (Ep. 49.4). The natural consequence of this is reached at the end of the letter, where Seneca points out that life – in its true sense – is independent of its duration: Ep. 49.10 *non esse positum bonum vitae in spatio eius*, 'the good in life does not depend upon life's length.' It is a topos for both Stoics and Epicureans that *eudaimonia* cannot be quantified in terms of time.[34] But one characteristic of the Senecan conception becomes very clear in Ep. 49: while *eudamonia* may not be quantifiable in terms of time, it is nevertheless positioned within the flow of time and not viewed as something of an entirely different quality, as is the case in Horace; on the contrary, an awareness of the flow of time is never absent in Seneca.

3 Horace's Use of the Discourse of Time

The above discussion will now allow us, via a third step, to contrast Seneca's and Horace's use of the discourse of time in a few brief theses. In Horace, there seems to be some kind of double-dimensionality – in the sense that a 'fulfilled' present can qualitatively lead a human subject out of the *rapax tempus*. Many situations are capable of effecting this; as an example, let us briefly consider the phenomenon in the most famous poem on the topic:[35]

---

[33] This is directed against a view that considers periods of time within physics: cf. Arist. Phys. 4.13.222b7–16.
[34] Chrysippus SVF 3.54 von Arnim; Cic. Fin. 2.87 and 3.46; Phld. De Morte col. 38.14.
[35] The complex mix of different traditions in this poem cannot be discussed here: on this, cf. Nisbet / Hubbard 1970, esp. 134–136.

> Tu ne quaesieris, scire nefas, quem mihi, quem tibi
> finem di dederint, Leuconoe, nec Babylonios
> temptaris numeros. ut melius, quidquid erit, pati,
> seu pluris hiemes seu tribuit Iuppiter ultimam,
> quae nunc oppositis debilitat pumicibus mare   5
> Tyrrhenum! sapias, vina liques et spatio brevi
> spem longam reseces. dum loquimur fugerit invida
> aetas: carpe diem quam minimum credula postero.
>
> Do not inquire (we are not allowed to know) what end the gods have assigned to you and what to me, Leuconoe, and do not meddle with Babylonian horoscopes. How much better to endure whatever it proves to be, whether Jupiter has granted us more winters, or this is the last that now wears out the Etruscan Sea against cliffs of pumice. Take my advice, strain the wine and cut back far-reaching hopes to within a small space. As we talk, grudging time will have run on. Pluck the day, trusting as little as possible in tomorrow.
> (Carm. 1.11)

Even the tone of this poem, addressed to the poet's apparent girlfriend Leuconoe, who is preoccupied with thoughts about the future and thus neglects the present, is brief to the point of curtness. The swift movement suggests that one must not waste any time. The train of thought itself is antithetical in manner: at its opening, the poem is concerned with the addressee's attitude towards the future – Leuconoe, immersed in astrology, seems to be uninterested in devoting herself to Horace at the symposium; only subsequently does the poem turn to the attitude that she ought to adopt towards the present. At first, the desire to know the future is answered with a plea for endurance (*pati*), but in line 6 there is a break and a fresh beginning with the strong injunction to make use of one's own reason. Now the antithesis is the following: on the one hand, there is the relentless flight of jealous time, on the other, the option of limiting oneself to a fulfilled present.

One might wonder whether the exhortation in line 3, to endure whatever happens, is not at odds with the injunction *carpe diem* in the final line. But this contradiction is resolved if one pays attention to the tenses: the things one is supposed to bear with endurance are put in the future tense. What is in the future cannot be enjoyed; one can only bear with patience the fact that something will happen of which one is as yet unaware. The central image that follows, however, the only one in the poem, still seems to express something beyond this: human life is compared to the sea, whereby the storms that both are subject to serve as the *tertium comparationis*. It is difficult to imagine that Leuconoe, once the future expressed here has become reality, will have any option other than to endure the weather that Jupiter has intended for her. Thus, there seems to be a double exhortation in the *pati* of the beginning and the *carpere* of the close of the poem. This seeming discrepancy can also be found by considering the exact relationship between jealous, ever-fleeing time and the day that Leuconoe is supposed to 'pluck.' Is this day itself not somehow part of 'jealous time'? Leuconoe 'plucking' it will certainly not stop time's flight.

Clearly, there are two different aspects of time at work here – and they do not neatly map onto each other. That which the usual discourse of time, such as we find it in Epicurus's *paraeneses* and in the Stoa, would formulate as a paradox appears in a concrete situation in Horace: this provides a way out of the cognitive dissonance inherent in the paradoxical structure. In the first instance, this is a matter of perception. On closer inspection, one can see that calculation – *numerus* – is a key word when it comes to the flow of time which is opposed with a different dimension of time: Leuconoe in Carm. 1.11 is not to try Babylonian *numeri*, i.e. attempt to calculate what will happen in the future based on calculations of the stars.

The Horatian ode shares several points of contact with Catullus's first *basia* poem, which also features counting as a mode of external control that is at odds with the idea of *carpe diem:* at the end of the Catullan poem, the lovers are to confuse their numbers, so that neither they themselves nor any evil-wishing third party can be sure about – or be envious of – the number of their kisses.[36] Scholars have detected attempts at incantation in the repetitiveness of the series of numbers, which, in turn, is based on a fundamental human fear.[37] But such an account does not sufficiently explain the dissolution of numbers: how could the lack of knowledge about the number of kisses – not only on the part of jealous people (the *curiosi*) but especially when it comes to the lovers themselves – protect love? It is more likely that what we are dealing with here is a subversion and transgression of one dimension of time: its flowing nature, which was evoked at the beginning of the poem in the contrast between sunrise, which is new every day, and the passage of human life, which can only ever be traversed once. In the second part of the poem, this is answered by a different way of perceiving time, the *carpe diem* of love: if this series of numbers, which is intentionally loose and undermines the mode of counting and reckoning, opens up the infinite series of countable natural numbers, the kisses must seem infinite and illimitable. Confusing the numbers, then, prevents the kisses from being ordered within the

---

36 Catul. 5.11–13. *conturbare*, which also means 'to go bankrupt,' also implies a subtle play with an economic metaphor. But this does not mean that they [sc. the lovers] 'begin all over again' (as Kroll 1960, ad loc. would have it); rather, it expresses a more general thought of 'removing from the access of others.' In this context, I refer to Schwindt 2013, a nuanced discussion of the role of counting in Catullus's *basia* poems and Hor. Carm. 1.11.
37 See Rankin 1972, 747.

flow of time from a retrospective perspective, an order that is only imposed by the individual counting them. It is precisely this confusion of numbers that guarantees that the happy 'now' of love cannot be quantified. One can therefore understand that this must apply to lovers as well as to jealous third parties: for the lovers, the choice of the temporal aspect is guided by their mental attitude.

Counting and reckoning are considered so important in this context because of a central characteristic of time itself: Aristotle defines time as ἀριθμὸς κινήσεως κατὰ τὸ πρότερον καὶ ὕστερον, 'number of motion in respect of "before" and "after"' (Arist. Phys. 4.11.219b2). The flow of time, the *fugax tempus*, comes into being through the very act of counting a series of 'befores' and 'afters.' As an alternative, we are given a situation in which such counting is renounced – Horace illustrates this in his letter to Torquatus by using the example of wine, an understandable example for physiological reasons (Ep. 1.5.16–20). This does not mean that time is not flowing past in the meantime; rather, the main thing is to adopt an attitude whereby one renounces counting and reckoning from time to time.

Horace, however, does not turn this view into an absolute truth. He keeps his distance from radically eudaimonistic positions, and this is part of the poet's characteristic quality. If anything, such radical positions only emerge as a distant ideal, mentioned merely for orientation and direction. In the ode to Grosphus the landowner, Horace explicitly says that a perfectly happy life is not possible (Carm. 2.16.25–28). The key ethical term is *aurea mediocritas:* given that the fundamental law of things is constant change, a situation that is bad for the moment will not remain that way forever (Carm. 2.10.17–18). It is worthy of note that here the 'now' is considered of little relevance: this is similar to Archilochus, who used the metaphor of the flowing river to conclude that one should not attribute too much significance to the 'now' (Archilochus fr. 67 a D 7). The fact that the unavoidable flow of time can cause anxieties is not being denied: the state of being carefree and the fulfilled 'now' of the symposium is not the norm, but an extraordinary exception. This is in accordance with the notion of the feast in the tradition of symposiastic poetry, where transitoriness is the backdrop against which the injunction to be aware of the 'now' gains its force.[38]

It is key that one grasps the opportunity of the moment. A good example of incorrect behaviour in the face of the flowing of time is provided by image of the simple peasant who patiently stands by, watching and waiting until the last drop of water in the river has drained off – but, of course, the river keeps flowing, and will do so for all eternity (Ep. 1.2.41–43). To extend the image, one could say that

---

38 On this tradition, see Nisbet / Hubbard 1970, 58–61 on Horace's first spring poem, Carm. 1.4.

enjoying the 'now' is based on the flow of time, as is emphasised again and again by Horace. On the one hand, *carpe diem* is directed towards the short space of time that is the 'now,' somehow removed from the rigours of time; on the other hand, *carpe diem* is also embedded in the greater context of flowing time, and thus thought of as subject to time's vicissitudes. Despite common misinterpretations,[39] Horace's is *not* a plea for turning the focus on the 'now' into an absolute dogma.

This becomes even more evident if one considers Horace's individual recommendations with regard to their respective addressees. Often, the Horatian plea for a turn towards the here and now is part of a corrective attempt counterbalancing certain misconceptions. A case in point is the invitation to the merchant Vergilius to a spring symposium: here, the witty injunction to bring a shell of spikenard in return for the valuable wine that he is going to drink is meant to expose the unsuitability of Vergilius's mercantile ways of thinking when it comes to *Eudaimonia* (Carm. 4.12).[40]

In general, preoccupation with material goods often serves as the occasion for developing images of time as measurable and countable. This is a tradition that had by Horace's time developed manifold modes of expression. Especially common is the topos of fleeing time: Carm. 2.5.13–14 *Currit enim ferox | aetas*, 'for time runs implacably on'; on another occasion, the time of life, especially youth, is said to *fugit retro*, 'disappear quickly into the past' (Carm. 2.11.5). The inevitability of the flow of time finds impressive expression in Horace's Postumus Ode; the message is especially forceful because the addressee, who is extremely wealthy but stingy, is too stubborn to listen to reason:

> Eheu fugaces. Postume, Postume,
> labuntur anni, nec pietas moram
>   rugis et instanti senectae
>   afferet indomitaeque morti
>
> Ah Postumus, Postumus, the fleeting years slip by, nor will piety check the onset of wrinkles, old age, and invincible death.
> (Carm. 2.14.1–4)

The remaining verses of this ode also deal with transitoriness and the inevitability of death; not until the last stanza do we get the account of the laughing heir,

---

[39] For some examples of this, see Houghton / Wyke 2009, 15, and passim. Even Nisbet / Hubbard 1970, 142 believe that it is necessary to defend the Horatian thought against allegations of hedonism.
[40] Cf. the interpretation by Zintzen 1985 / 86.

who knows better how to use up the valuable wine that had been saved and locked up by its former owner. Already Mitscherlich in his commentary picks up on the original manner in which Horace tackles the topoi, and is especially appreciative of the Horatian phrasing in *anni fugaces labuntur*[41] – a phrase that is also used by Seneca in his first letter to Lucilius.[42]

The way in which the opposition of different aspects of time is determined by different addressees can be seen most clearly in the example of Horace's complex relationship to Maecenas. Here, the antitheses, which derive from symposiastic topoi, become a vehicle for a distinction of the different spheres of life, a discussion far more fundamental than could be motivated just by a desire to induce the addressee to accept an invitation. For time plays no unimportant role in Horace's self-conception either. The detachment from time that he associates with his Sabinum not only refers to the *otium* of *villeggiatura* – it is also more generally true for his personal life: what Horace puts in the form of a paradox at the close of the great Maecenas Ode (Carm. 3.29) – security in a boat amidst the dangers of the storm – is transformed into the poet's detachment from the laws of time in the final ode (Carm. 3.30).[43]

4 Seneca's Use of the Discourse of Time

This is very different in Seneca. One of the most remarkable features of the reflections on time in the letters to Lucilius is the lack of any other dimension of time apart from its flow. The situation of 'being in time' is the specific and unavoidable *condicio humana*, which is why it is not judged negatively per se. Rather,

---

[41] Mitscherlich 1800, 480–481: 'docte et copia poetica pro, fugiunt, labuntur, praetereunt; aucta tamen hac cumulatione celeritatis notione. Nam et *labi* de veloci cursu dicitur.' Mitscherlich, who provides a quintessence of the eighteenth-century interpretation of Horace, has unfortunately been mostly forgotten in international Horatian scholarship; in Houghton / Wyke 2009, for instance, his name is not even mentioned, despite his relevance to the topic under discussion. Cf. also Vogt-Spira 2008.
[42] The phrase is well-noted as a point of contact between Seneca and Horace; Nisbet / Hubbard 1978, 226, for instance, lists Sen. Ep. 1.3 as the first parallel passage s.v. *fugaces*. Cf. also Berthet 1979, 940 and esp. 953, where the various phrasings in Sen. Ep. 1.3 are argued to be echoes of several previous texts – apart from Horace also Virgil and Ovid.
[43] On the ending of Carm. 3.29 see Zinn 1961. Graziosi 2009, 147–156 discusses Horace's statement about his being under divine protection. I cannot go into any detail here about Carm. 3.30, but cf. n. 1 above for the way in which Horace's various statements about time need to be put into relation to each other.

'being in time' is seen as a challenge, and Seneca searches in his letters for the right mode of dealing with it.

A lot can be learned from the motif of time's fleetingness: we have already seen that Seneca, in his very first letter to Lucilius, makes use of a Horatian phrase from Carm. 2.14.[44]

Both texts consider time's fleetingness as a natural condition of life, and the attitude that they promote also seems similar at first glance: Horace's conclusion, that one must not let the present flow away but rather make use of it seems close to the Senecan argument according to which life flows by if one always postpones things; thus, one ought to use today in order to be less dependent on the future (Ep. 1.2).[45] But this argument is in fact aimed at something entirely different:

> Omnia, Lucili, aliena sunt, tempus tantum nostrum est; in huius rei unius fugacis ac lubricae possessionem natura nos misit, ex qua expellit quicumque vult.
>
> Nothing, Lucilius, is ours, except time. We were entrusted by nature with the ownership of this single thing, so fleeting and slippery that anyone who will can oust us from possession. (Ep. 1.3)

Despite its fleetingness, Seneca views time as a possession. Characterising it as *res fugax ac lubrica* is only intended as a relative and not an absolute qualification: it emphasises the difficulty in adopting the right relationship towards time.[46] What comes into view here is the journey of life as a whole: this concerns Ep. 1.2 'holding every hour in one's grasp.' The 'now' is thus a function and part of the whole: *hodiernum* is not something of a different quality – rather, correct behaviour in the here and now will accumulate as the sum total of the correct life.

Thus, merely fixating on the here and now is not enough. Rarely is this expressed more explicitly than in Ep. 99, which is fashioned as a consolatory letter addressed to the father of a recently deceased son. One of the notable features of

---

44 See n. 42 above.
45 On *dum differtur vita transcurrit*, Scarpat 1975, 38 writes, 'Non può non venire in mente l'oraziano *dum loquimur fugerit invida | aetas*,' but also notes the difference in Seneca's treatment. Cf. also Berthet 1979, 953.
46 This is why it is not necessary to see the two coexisting concepts – that of fleeting time and that of valuable time – as a gesture towards a 'façon ambiguë et contradictoire dont le temps se présente à la conscience humaine,' as Armisen-Marchetti 1995, 553 does.

the letter is that this is once again done by employing a Horatian turn of phrase. The different stages of time are defined in the following way:[47]

> Anguste fructus rerum determinat qui tantum praesentibus laetus est: et futura et praeterita delectant, haec expectatione, illa memoria.
>
> People set a narrow limit to their enjoyments if they take pleasure only in the present; both the future and the past serve for our delight—the one with anticipation, and the other with memories.
> (Ep. 99.5)

For us, the key thing here is the clear statement that limiting oneself to the present is too narrow. The phrase *qui tantum praesentibus laetus est* looks like a protest against the final maxim in Hor. Carm. 3.8.27–28 *dona praesentis cape laetus horae, | linque severa,* 'gladly accept the gifts of the present hour, and let serious things go hang.' How sharply Seneca disagrees with this Horatian idea of the present becomes clear in his satirical punchline at the end, when he describes the act of limiting oneself to the 'now' as an act of 'drawing water' (*haurire*) with a 'perforated soul.'[48] In this witty transformation of the Danaids' pointless drawing of water, here applied to the concept of time, we can see that Seneca does not allow any double-dimensionality of time; he rather searches for answers in the one dimension of time's progression, in which the presence of the past via *memoria* plays a key role.

Seneca employs two fields of imagery to illustrate attitudes towards time: (1) metaphors derived from economics and (2) the imagery of fighting, war, and death. In the opening letter, he develops his 'economy of time' in an example that draws upon his own experience, thus emphasising its programmatic character:

> Fatebor ingenue: quod apud luxuriosum sed diligentem evenit, ratio mihi constat inpensae. Non possum dicere nihil perdere, sed quid perdam et quare et quemadmodum dicam; causas paupertatis meae reddam.

---

[47] The openness towards the future here is unusual: it has to do with the choice of a situation in which the addressee has to be pulled out of his excessive pain. The statement is, however, immediately qualified by a remark about the uncertainty of things to come.

[48] Sen. Ep. 99.5: *Adquiescamus iis quae iam hausimus, si modo non perforato animo hauriebamus et transmittente quidquid acceperat,* 'Let us rest content with the pleasures we have quaffed in past days, if only, while we quaffed them, the soul was not pierced like a sieve, only to lose again whatever it had received.' The image of the 'perforated soul,' used in speaking about memory, is common even in modern-day research on Alzheimer's.

I confess frankly: my expense account balances, as you would expect from one who is free-handed but careful. I cannot boast that I waste nothing, but I can at least tell you what I am wasting, and the cause and manner of the loss; I can give you the reasons why I am a poor man.
(Ep. 1.4)

The basic attitude towards time, it becomes clear, is that of calculation – a striking contrast with what we noted in Horace. The motif of time's fleetingness is here developed in order to express an antithesis: while time is the only thing that nature has given us for our possession, we are at the same time constantly in danger of losing it. Thus, Seneca's reflections are from a perspective of shortage, which is then expanded to 'poverty.' What counts is the thrifty use and constant control of one's time; this is all the more necessary given that even time used well will never be enough for all that is necessary. This logic of thrift also demands that one must start early in taking care of one's possessions, rather than starting to save when it is already too late (Ep. 1.3–5).

This model – which places emphasis on the shortage of time – is a variation of the standard moral critique of wealth: its opposite is namely wastefulness of one's time. For Seneca, one of the most serious errors is to waste one's time and let it elapse without making any use of it, whether this is because one's focus is wrong or – even worse – because of neglect. Whereas uncontrolled to-ing and fro-ing is considered the pinnacle of erroneous behaviour, focused action is stressed by Seneca as the ultimate goal – even prior to any detailed consideration of what this ought to consist of.[49] All the same, given that Seneca talks about 'gain' (someone who can say *vixi*, Ep. 12.9 points out, at the same time rises each morning to new profit),[50] a question remains: what are the goods that one ought to gain? The key term here is 'self-possession,' and it is the argumentative goal of Ep. 1 to demonstrate the way in which self-possession and the possession of time are interwoven.

'Self-possession,' however, is not a good that is secure once and for all – rather, it is a continual process. Seneca provides enlightening reflection on the specific character of time as a 'good': time, Seneca points out, cannot be refunded – not even by the most benevolent of people – and thus is not subject to the law of gift exchange, so fundamental for the ancient economy. Once time has elapsed, it is irreversibly past (Ep. 1.3). This line of argument is one of the many that point towards the systematic precedence of the past over the future, and thus also helps to explain Seneca's conception of self-possession.

---

[49] Sen. Ep. 1.1 (note the telling climactic series *male – nihil – aliud agentibus*) and elsewhere.
[50] Cf. p. 188 above.

The economic metaphors, moreover, are primarily employed in an exhortative sense, serving the argument about how to deal with shortage. This can sometimes take on humorous tones: what we call human lifetime is so tiny, Seneca says, and indeed wasted on many useless things (such as sleeping half of our life) that even in the longest of human lives the time actually spent living can only ever be a *minimum* (Ep. 99.11). This also explains why it is crucial – and this is an important point for the purpose of this paper – that the course of life always needs to be considered in its entirety.

It is worthy of note that Seneca, when dealing with the topic of time, takes pains to convey a sense of constant danger and threat. This becomes apparent in the second major cluster of imagery mentioned above, which includes metaphors of fighting, war, and death. Seneca's injunction not to fragment time or to let life elapse without using it is illustrated through the image of someone quickening speed with an enemy at his back or the cavalry on his heels. The basic situation is emphatically depicted: one is constantly hard-pressed – hence one has to escape in a swift run (Ep. 32.3).

Relying on a characteristic interpretation of a famous line from the *Georgics*, Seneca cites Virgil as his principal witness: *fugit inreparabile tempus*, 'Time flies away, and cannot be restored' (Sen. Ep. 108.24 = Verg. Georg. 3.284). One always has to be wide awake; if one does not make haste, one is lost. The swift day, Seneca continues, drives us ever forward and is itself driven forward; we are swept away without even noticing it. Staking all we have on the future, we are lazy and slow to act in the midst of impending catastrophe. This Senecan reading of the fleetness of time in Virgil is very different from the Augustan poet's original argument: on the contrary, Virgil used the phrase in order to mark a new beginning, calling himself back to his topic in an urbane way while evoking 'den Anschein einer vorausgehenden Abschweifung.'[51] Strictly speaking, Seneca's criticism would also be directed at him. From a systematic perspective, Seneca's letter is particularly interesting since it serves as the foundation for a hermeneutics of decontextualisation. This way of reading goes against established philological *interpretatio*, especially the way in which Virgil was taught in school, where the sole interest would have been directed at grammatical questions.[52]

In general, Seneca uses the existential relevance of the theme of time for intellectual polemics. A case in point is the image of the conquered city, especially popular as an image of chaotic and dangerous situations (Ep. 49.7–8).[53] The sit-

---

[51] Thus Richter 1952, 295 ad loc.
[52] Cf. Glei 1990.
[53] Quintilian uses the image of the conquered city to demonstrate how *enargeia* works (Inst. 8.3.68–69).

uation is one in which war is raging all around: old men and women are carrying stones to reinforce the walls of the city, the young warriors are waiting for their signal for a sortie, the enemy's weapons are flashing in front of the gates, and even the earth, undermined by the enemy, is shaking. The enormous labours involved in this situation are given in the context of the thought that, in such an emergency, it would be irresponsible to waste one's time with anything useless. The ludicrous syllogisms of the dialecticians are then provided as examples of those *supervacua*.

Moreover, it remains to note the conspicuous omnipresence of death in Seneca; we have observed it at the beginning of Ep. 12, in the examples of Pacuvius and Dido.[54] Regarding time as a destructive force is a topos; it is summarised, for instance, in a memorable passage of Aristotle's *Physics* (Arist. Phys. 4.12.221a30–221b3). Seneca's use of the theme, however, goes far beyond its standard application, and displays a focus that is very different from Horace's: just as his tragedies at times delight in death,[55] death is also evoked as often as possible in the *Epistulae Morales* and represents a constant, subliminal feature.

We have noted that Seneca considers 'being in time' the unavoidable *condicio humana* and does not open up a second dimension of time in the face of time's flow (as Horace had done). But the relationship between the different stages of time is complex: this creates a space for reflection that, in turn, goes beyond the immanence of the mere flow of time. One feature is particularly worthy of note in the way the present is treated here: in Seneca's definition of the present, it is not linked to any specific situations or actions, but to 'being active' itself – this contrasts with the concrete images that are at Horace's disposal in this context, and the reasons for this lie not in the difference in genre alone. The central thought concerns how one behaves with respect to the present time in a self-determined manner. This is then specifically linked to the past, the stage of time that is discussed in greatest detail. The past, Seneca points out, as the only thing to guarantee the desired security and independence, can achieve its full protreptic impact only through a particular type of presence. This presence is achieved in *conscientia:* the consciousness, in the present, of past actions and events. From this insight, Seneca develops several thoughts that are completely foreign to Horace: via memory (*memoria*), Seneca links the different stages of time and – in pointed opposition to the understanding of time as a physical phenomenon – grants the past a status of being

---

[54] See above, pp. 188–190.
[55] Cf. Winter 2014, who discusses this phenomenon within its wider intellectual context.

(Ep. 99.4).⁵⁶ This argument aims to create independence from the flow of time. The co-presence of several successful 'past presents' in our *conscientia* allows us to consider the succession of time *cum multo risu*, and thus to relativise the flow of time from that point of view – in Seneca's words: there is no difference between 'day' and 'year' (Ep. 101.9).

5 Conclusion

The Hellenistic and Roman discourse of time relies on a stable and easily manageable repertoire of argumentative patterns, but the various foci are very different. In general, there are two concepts of time: one that is concerned with the span of externally measurable and 'lived' time, and one that emphasises the flow of time, nevertheless allowing a reflective distance towards the immanence of time's flow by means of *memoria*, where our past lives and actions are internally present. Horace's concept of time, which is rather of the former category, is present in Seneca, but it is not Seneca's model: rather, its reception is subjected to a re-orientation.

This is why we need to return to our initial question: why does Seneca cite Horace so rarely or at times obscure his references? If we consider the wider context of Seneca's addressees, it might seem plausible that, unlike Virgil, Horace does not have the status of an authority because of his less widespread circulation.⁵⁷ However, we should probably assume deep knowledge of the Horatian oeuvre among the upper classes during the Neronian age. This can be inferred, for instance, from the remarkable presence of Horace in Petronius's *Satyrica*, where Horace is associated with the field of ethics as well as literary aesthetics.⁵⁸ One only needs to think of the brilliant trivialisation of the motif of *carpe diem* in the words of Trimalchio and its subtle inversion in the ship episode, when Encolpius asks Giton for a last embrace (Petr. Sat. 55.3 and 100.3).⁵⁹ Here, Horace functions as a reference point for the Roman discourse of time and *fortuna*.

It is thus possible that evoking Horace by means of allusion or citation would have had a certain signalling force. Petronius, who had quite a bit of leeway with Nero,⁶⁰ functionalises Horace in a masterly way as the measure by means of which he can parody his protagonists or, rather, contemporary attitudes through

---

56 Cf. also Montiglio 2008.
57 Cf. above, n. 10.
58 Cf. Conte 1997, esp. 47, 62–63, and 72–73 (on Eumolpus) and Stucchi 2002.
59 On these passages, see further Vogt-Spira 2002, 200–206.
60 Plut. Mor. 60 E, with Sullivan 1985b, 1669.

their actions. In the field of classical aesthetics, this is evident: the obvious example is Eumolpus, modelled on the *poeta vesanus* of Horace's *Epistle to the Pisos*. This clearly points towards Horace being considered – and used – as a representative of classicising norms.[61] It is plausible to assume that he was also considered a classic in that area of ancient ethics that concerned proper measure.

Seneca's engagement with Horace must thus also be viewed within a literary-historical context: he is dealing with a classic, a forerunner who treated the same subject matter. Whereas Seneca could acknowledge Virgil without compromising his own literary and philosophical ambitions, Horace would have been his direct competitor with respect to the discourse of time. We have seen that, despite semantic points of contact, Seneca's and Horace's concepts of time are incompatible; we have indeed noted how in one case Seneca even openly criticised Horace. While such divergence when it comes to subject matter does not encourage frequent appeal to a predecessor, it would be even less attractive for an author of the early principate – an era characterised by its predilection for novel innovation.[62]

Apart from this, one may wonder in closing whether there are specific, contemporary connotations that are associated with the citation of certain authors, a consideration that would allow a more precise historical contextualisation of authors' appeals to certain predecessors. In the eighteenth century, for instance, allusions to Epicurus – of which Frederick the Great was so fond – were interpreted as signals of atheism. In line with this, one could investigate whether there are any causes in the subject matter that made Seneca avoid the label 'Horace.'

---

[61] This does not mean that Petronius himself advocates a classicising position: see Conte 1997.
[62] Cf. Döpp 1989. This issue extends far beyond questions of personal likes and dislikes.

Barak Blum
Studiorum instrumenta: Loaded Libraries in Seneca and Horace

This paper investigates images of libraries and book collections from a selection of Seneca's and Horace's writings. It looks into parallels in the ways they evoke such imagery to convey literary, philosophical, social, and political comment, while at the same time asserting their professional identity as authors.

Book collections were part and parcel of Roman literary culture, serving as facilitators of writers' work and as its ultimate destination. They also came to be regarded as symbols of privileged class and wealth – so much so that even some with no genuine interest in books amassed and displayed them. A passage from Seneca's *De Tranquillitate Animi* (Dial. 9.9.4–7) is a *locus classicus* for this phenomenon of ostentatious collection. However, this aspect of the passage has tended to eclipse Seneca's more complex and nuanced views on libraries and their functions both here and in additional parts of his oeuvre. The paper begins with a closer analysis of this and two related passages from Ep. 2 and 45 (section 1). The themes and concepts discussed provide a springboard for further examination (sections 2–4) of book collection imagery in Ep. 108 and 39, *De Brevitate Vitae* (Dial. 10) and *De Consolatione ad Marciam* (Dial. 6), and Ep. 84. The second part of the paper (sections 5–8) turns to the exploration of pertinent images in Horace's Epod. 8, S. 2.3, 1.1, and 1.10, Ep. 1.3 and 2.1, and Ep. 1.18. The substantial conceptual and thematic overlaps identified between the two authors suggest that Seneca's particular use of library and book collection imagery constitutes a salient element in his reception of Horace.

I would like to thank the Dean Ireland Fund of the Faculty of Classics at the University of Oxford, and the Lorne Thyssen Research Fund for Ancient World Topics at Wolfson College, for supporting my travel to the conference at the University of Heidelberg. Thanks are due to the organisers and to the participants for the stimulating discussion. I am also grateful for the suggestions of the editors Martin Stöckinger, Kathrin Winter, Tom Zanker, and the copy editor Eugenia Lao, as well as for the comments of Stephen Harrison and Andrea Rotstein, in revising this paper for publication.

1 Due Measure, Meritorious Volumes, and a *horreum*

We begin with what is arguably Seneca's most famous piece on the subject of libraries:

> Studiorum quoque quae liberalissima inpensa est tam diu rationem habet quam diu modum. Quo innumerabiles libros et bybliothecas, quarum dominus vix tota vita indices perlegit? onerat discentem turba, non instruit, multoque satius est paucis te auctoribus tradere quam errare per multos. Quadraginta milia librorum Alexandriae arserunt; pulcherrimum regiae opulentiae monumentum alius laudaverit, sicut T. Livius, qui elegantiae regum curaeque egregium id opus ait fuisse: non fuit elegantia illud aut cura, sed studiosa luxuria, immo ne studiosa quidem, quoniam non in studium sed in spectaculum comparaverant, sicut plerisque ignaris etiam puerilium litterarum libri non studiorum instrumenta sed cenationum ornamenta sunt. Paretur itaque librorum quantum satis sit, nihil in apparatum.... Vitiosum est ubique quod nimium est. Quid habes cur ignoscas homini armaria ⟨e⟩ citro atque ebore captanti, corpora conquirenti aut ignotorum auctorum aut inprobatorum et inter tot milia librorum oscitanti, cui voluminum suorum frontes maxime placent titulique? Apud desidiosissimos ergo videbis quidquid orationum historiarumque est, tecto tenus exstructa loculamenta; iam enim inter balnearia et thermas bybliotheca quoque ut necessarium domus ornamentum expolitur. Ignoscerem plane, si studiorum nimia cupidine erraretur: nunc ista conquisita... sacrorum opera ingeniorum in speciem... comparantur.[1]

> For studies, too, where expenditure is most honourable, it is justifiable only so long as it is kept within bounds. What is the use of having countless books and libraries whose titles their owner can scarcely read through in a whole lifetime? The learner is not instructed but burdened by the mass, and it is much better to consign yourself to a few authors than to wander through many. Forty thousand books were burned at Alexandria; let someone else praise this library as the noblest monument to the wealth of kings, as did Titus Livius, who says it was the most distinguished achievement of the good taste and solicitude of kings. There was no 'good taste' or 'solicitude' about it, but only learned luxury, nay, not even 'learned,' since they made collections not for the sake of learning, but for show, just like many who lack even a child's knowledge of literature use books, not as tools of learning, but as decorations for the dining room. Therefore, let as many books be acquired as are enough, but none for show.... Excess in anything becomes a fault. What excuse have you to offer for one who seeks to have bookcases of citrus-wood and ivory, who collects the works of unknown or discredited authors and yawns amid so many thousands of books, who is most pleased by the outsides of volumes and their titles? Consequently it is in the houses of the laziest that you will see a full collection of orations and history with the boxes piled up to the ceiling; for by now among cold baths and hot baths a library also is built as a necessary house ornament. I would readily excuse such wandering if it were caused by ex-

---

[1] *Dialogi* passages are from Reynolds's OCT.

cessive zeal for learning. But as it is, these collections of the works of sacred genius... are bought for show.[2]
(Dial. 9.9.4–7)

Seneca here denigrates collectors of enormous libraries, arguing that too many books in a library obstruct rather than aid in learning. Worse still, overloaded libraries serve as mere decoration for the idle and the ill-educated. These negative images express criticism both at the individual and at society in general. It comes, then, as no surprise that scholarship on ancient libraries often refers to this text[3] as evidence for libraries having become yet another status symbol, vainly exhibited by some collectors with but shallow regard for their contents.[4]

This is indubitably true. However, the attention this aspect has received have left the nuances in Seneca's approach to the subject somewhat underemphasised: in this passage he maintains that spending money on a book collection is a worthy expense, provided it is done in due measure. This statement is consistent with Seneca's more general argument in preceding passages of the *De Tranquillitate Animi*, which show Seneca not to be categorically against material possessions.[5] He preaches moderation rather than complete destitution.[6]

Furthermore, libraries can and should serve as tools for study (*studiorum instrumenta*), and if kept as such even well-stocked ones may be permissible. This is the corollary of a comparison Seneca makes with the Alexandrian library, targeted probably because of the extent to which it approached the library ideal as it was usually conceived. Seneca claims that the impetus for founding that heavily laden library was misguided: it was not meant to enhance knowledge and scholarship, but rather conceived as a colossal trinket furthering the ostentatious grandeur of the rulers. It seems that this questionable motivation troubles him even more than that library's huge number of books.

A similarly complex attitude to libraries' size can be found in the sentence *onerat discentem turba, non instruit, multoque satius est paucis te auctoribus tradere quam errare per multos*. The stress can be more on *errare* than on *multos*, and *turba* conveys chaos no less than number: it is a burden if it is not read properly,

---

2 Translations of Seneca's *Dialogi* are adapted with minor changes from Basore's Loeb.
3 Frequently along with Petr. 48; Lucian. Ind. passim.
4 See e.g. Dziatzko 1897, 417; Thompson 1940, 35; Dix 1986, 152 n. 46, 266; Fedeli 1988, 47; Blanck 1992, 157; Nicholls 2005, 254; Too 2010, 104 n. 38, 109. More generally for libraries as a recommended architectural component in distinguished houses, see Vitr. 6.5.2.
5 E.g. 8.9 and 9.1.
6 For a similar approach see Sen. Ep. 5.5–6 (*Epistulae* passages are cited from Reynolds's OCT); *Exhortationes*, fr. 20 (ed. Haase 1852). Also cf. Griffin 1992, 298, noting that although Seneca's attitude to wealth varies, he mostly does not regard it as problematic in itself.

and under these circumstances it may be better to possess a smaller collection. The same holds in the case of an inventory containing books of *ignotorum auctorum aut inprobatorum*. In other words, a large book collection is not necessarily an evil in itself.

This brings us to another passage frequently mentioned together with this one,[7] usually as an example of Seneca's critique of large book collections:

> Illud autem vide, ne ista lectio auctorum multorum et omnis generis voluminum habeat aliquid vagum et instabile. Certis ingeniis inmorari et innutriri oportet, si velis aliquid trahere quod in animo fideliter sedeat.... Vitam in peregrinatione exigentibus hoc evenit, ut multa hospitia habeant, nullas amicitias; idem accidat necesse est iis qui nullius se ingenio familiariter applicant sed omnia cursim et properantes transmittunt. Non prodest cibus nec corpori accedit qui statim sumptus emittitur... Distringit librorum multitudo; itaque cum legere non possis quantum habueris, satis est habere quantum legas.... Fastidientis stomachi est multa degustare; quae ubi varia sunt et diversa, inquinant non alunt. Probatos itaque semper lege... Aliquid cotidie adversus paupertatem, aliquid adversus mortem auxili compara, nec minus adversus ceteras pestes; et cum multa percurreris, unum excerpe quod illo die concoquas. Hoc ipse quoque facio; ex pluribus quae legi aliquid adprehendo.

> Be careful, however, lest this reading of many authors and books of every sort may tend to make you discursive and unsteady. You must linger among reliable master-thinkers, and digest their works, if you would derive ideas which shall stay firmly in the mind.... Those who spend all their time in foreign travel end by having many acquaintances, but no friends. The same thing must hold true of those who devote themselves to no author, but cursorily pass over all in a hasty manner. Food does no good and is not assimilated into the body if it is ejected as soon as it is eaten... Reading many books distracts; accordingly, since you cannot read all the books which you possess, it is enough to possess as many books as you can read.... It is the sign of a squeamish appetite to toy with many dishes; for when they are manifold and varied, they cloy but do not nourish. So you should always read meritorious authors... Daily acquire something to fortify you against poverty, against death, indeed also against all other misfortunes; and after you have run over many thoughts, select one to be thoroughly digested that day. I do so myself, too; from the many things which I have read, I claim something for myself.[8]
> (Ep. 2.2–5)

This text, too, stresses due measure and moderation.[9] It recalls not just the former passage about reading, but also the leitmotif of the dialogue it forms part of, where the desired *tranquillitas* is the opposite of fickleness and inconstancy, and moderation is advised as one way to attain it.[10]

---

[7] Cf. Mazzoli 1970, 13; Scarpat 1975, 44–45; Schiroli 1981, 97; Costa 1994, 193; Setaioli 2014, 254.
[8] Translations of Seneca's *Epistulae* are adapted with minor changes from Gummere's Loeb.
[9] Also cf. Cancik 1967, 143.
[10] Cf. Scarpat 1975, 43–44.

But does this mean that large book collections are construed by Seneca as invariably illegitimate? He seems to consider as problematic not the possession of a large book collection per se, but reading it in a manner which is *vagum, instabile*, and *cursim*, i.e. disorderly and superficial. The phrase *distringit librorum multitudo* should be interpreted accordingly: the problem may be not so much an ample book collection but rather the temptation that it may pose to approach those many books cursorily and unsystematically.

That the quantity is not the major point here is also brought out by Seneca's setting himself as an example to be followed:[11] he states that he reads *plura* and, in his immediately preceding advice, says that Lucilius may read *multa* as long as he distills something substantial out of it daily. Second, discretion is advised regarding the particular books involved. Not every author would do: only *certa ingenia*[12] and the *probati*[13] will adequately nourish the reader. This reservation involves the particular content of the books and the identity of their authors.[14] The right manner of reading, applied to the right kind of books, is required to achieve the purpose of arriving at useful principles according to which one ought to live one's life: especially how to deal with the fears of hardship, death, etc., which are presented as banes (*pestes*) to be overcome by the therapeutic effect of books. In other words, these requirements from a book collection and its use are especially relevant for those interested in moral edification, particularly through philosophy.[15]

A third passage on the issue of a book collection's proportions is often mentioned in conjunction with the former two:[16]

---

11 For this tactic here also cf. e.g. Maurach 1970, 31. More generally, the philosopher is forever also a student of philosophy, as Seneca says elsewhere (e.g. Ep. 45.4). Seneca's not uncommon self-depiction in the *Epistulae* as studying is meant to encourage the addressee Lucilius to do likewise (also cf. Cancik 1967, 77), as well as, of course, the wider readership. I would add that this protreptic aim can be identified in many of the passages where reading or books are mentioned.
12 The adjective *certus* can bear the meaning of being reliable and established (see OLD s.v. certus 8).
13 Also cf. Dial. 9.9 above, with its critique of books written by *auctores inprobati*.
14 Note that the acceptable authors are not necessarily limited to 'die Klassiker' (*pace* Maurach 1970, 31), unless a very broad definition thereof is intended (such that would include, e.g. the philosopher Sextius whose writings are ardently recommended by Seneca in Ep. 64.2–5; or mime writers like Publilius, similarly praised for his relevance to philosophy in Ep. 8.8).
15 It is no coincidence that Seneca furnishes an example of reading philosophical writings later in Ep. 2.5. For his advice here applying specifically to reading philosophy books, also cf. Griffin 1992, 352.
16 E.g. Préchac-Noblot 1947, 9 n. 2; Mazzoli 1970, 12; Schiroli 1981, 97; Costa 1994, 193.

Librorum istic inopiam esse quereris. Non refert quam multos sed quam bonos habeas: lectio certa prodest, varia delectat. Qui quo destinavit pervenire vult unam sequatur viam, non per multas vagetur: non ire istuc sed errare est. 'Vellem' inquis '⟨non⟩ magis consilium mihi quam libros dares.' Ego vero quoscumque habeo mittere paratus sum et totum horreum excutere.

You complain that where you are there is a scant supply of books. It does not matter how many, but how good they are; a fixed reading benefits; a varied one delights. One who wishes to arrive at the appointed end must follow a single road and not wander through many. What you suggest is not travelling, it is wandering. 'I would rather,' you say, 'have you give me advice and books in equal measure.' Indeed, I am ready to send you all the books I have, to ransack the entire granary.
(Ep. 45.1–2)

The quality of the books one has, Seneca says, is more important than their quantity. This does not amount to a wholesale attack on book collections. With the crucial factor being the nature of the books, Seneca would presumably approve a large collection if it comprised only proper books (*boni*). Moreover, the criteria for legitimacy once more include the manner of reading: the *lectio* needs to be *certa*, and *errare* and *vagari* are discouraged.[17] This criterion seems to be linked with that of utility versus enjoyment: *non refert quam multos sed quam bonos habeas: lectio certa prodest, varia delectat*. However, though the phrase probably means that useful reading is considered superior to pleasurable reading,[18] it does not follow that they are mutually exclusive. In fact, Seneca elsewhere implies that reading philosophy books can also be pleasurable.[19]

Notably, this passage also makes it evident that Seneca himself possesses a library, referred to by the metaphor of a granary (*horreum*).[20] The phrasing is not incidental, but rather conforms to the image of a book collection as a source of sustenance, which he already established,[21] and will later re-employ.[22] Seneca at-

---

[17] Cf. *certis ingeniis* and *vagum et instabile*, in Ep. 2 above.
[18] Cf. Mazzoli 1970, 12.
[19] See e.g. Ep. 39.2.
[20] Also cf. Marino 2011, 209, taking *quoscumque habeo mittere paratus sum et totum horreum excutere* here to mean 'pronto a mandarti tutti i volumi che ho e a vuotare la mia biblioteca.' Similarly, Préchac-Noblot 1947, 10 clearly take *horreum* as a figurative apposition to a library: 'prêt à expédier ma bibliothèque, à fouiller tout mon grenier.' Also see TLL 6.3.2987.74–76 s.v. *horreum* I.A.1.b.β.
[21] In Ep. 2 above (*innutriri, cibus, alunt*).
[22] The noun can also have the sense of a storehouse for other kinds of food and equipment (see OLD s.v. *horreum* 2), and can figuratively denote a beehive (see TLL 6.3.2988.29–31 s.v. I.B.1). This is noteworthy since in Ep. 84 (discussed below) Seneca likens readers of varied books to bees foraging for food.

tests that he is willing to send Lucilius as many books from his library-granary as Lucilius would wish. This statement, too, suggests that under the right conditions Seneca does not object to one's possession or reading of numerous books, even in the context of philosophical study, the overarching theme of Ep. 45.

2 Reading the Philosophers: a Path to the *vita beata*

The value of studying philosophy books as a means for moral progression plays a part in two further passages. First, in Ep. 108:

> Illud admoneo, auditionem philosophorum lectionemque ad propositum beatae vitae trahendam... ut... captemus... profutura praecepta et magnificas voces et animosas quae mox in rem transferantur.
>
> My advice is that the study and reading of the philosophers should be applied to the idea of living the happy life... so that... we would seek... precepts which will help us, utterances of courage and spirit which may soon be used to our advantage.
> (Ep. 108.35)

Seneca advises Lucilius to read the books of philosophers with an eye to moral improvement. He does not, however, give here general advice to read only philosophical works. Nor does he say that whatever one reads is to be read with the object of such improvement. What he says in this passage pertains specifically to reading philosophy treatises,[23] and even in this case Lucilius is not asked to limit the number of books he is reading, but only to apply whatever he reads to moral development.[24]

We learn more on how a book collection can contribute to such progression in Ep. 39:

> Commentarios quos desideras, diligenter ordinatos et in angustum coactos, ego vero componam; sed vide ne plus profutura sit ratio ordinaria quam haec quae nunc vulgo breviarium dicitur... Illa res discenti magis necessaria est, haec scienti; illa enim docet, haec admonet. Sed utriusque rei tibi copiam faciam.... interim multos habes quorum scripta nescio an satis ordinentur. Sume in manus indicem philosophorum: haec ipsa res expergisci te coget, si videris quam multi tibi laboraverint. Concupisces et ipse ex illis unus esse;

---

23 Also cf. Préchac-Noblot 1962, 182.
24 Seneca makes a similar argument in Ep. 89.18.

habet enim hoc optimum in se generosus animus, quod concitatur ad honesta. Neminem excelsi ingenii virum humilia delectant et sordida: magnarum rerum species ad se vocat et extollit... felix qui ad meliora hunc impetum dedit: ponet se extra ius dicionemque fortunae; secunda temperabit, adversa comminuet et aliis admiranda despiciet. Magni animi est magna contemnere ac mediocria malle quam nimia; illa enim utilia vitaliaque sunt, et haec eo quod superfluunt nocent.

I shall indeed arrange for you, in careful order and narrow compass, the annotations which you request; but consider whether you may not get more help from the customary method than from that which is now commonly called a 'breviary'... The former is more necessary to the learner, the latter to the knower. For the one teaches, the other stirs the memory. But I shall give you an abundance of both.... meanwhile, you have many authors whose works are presumably kept sufficiently in order. Pick up the *index* of the philosophers: that very act will compel you to wake up, when you see how many have been working for your benefit. You will desire eagerly to be one of them yourself. For this is the most excellent quality that the noble soul has within itself, that it can be roused to honourable things. No man of exalted gifts is pleased with that which is low and mean; the vision of great achievements summons him and uplifts him.... happy is the man who has given it this impulse towards better things! He will place himself beyond the jurisdiction of chance; he will wisely control prosperity; he will lessen adversity, and will despise what others hold in admiration. It is the quality of a great soul to scorn great things and to prefer that which is moderate rather than that which is excessive. For the one condition is useful and life-giving; but the other does harm because it is overly abundant.
(Ep. 39.1–4)

Seneca prepares to send Lucilius a great deal (*copia*) of philosophy books as well as of notes and abridgements thereof.[25] He advises him that studying philosophy requires reading the books themselves, not just their summaries.[26] Urging Lucilius to make use of his own (i.e. Lucilius's) library, he explains how it would contribute to his moral improvement: the philosophers' teachings would inspire him to better himself (*concitatur ad honesta*), allow him to resist the disruptive influence of random positive and negative circumstances (*extra ius dicionemque fortunae*), develop a sounder perception of the value of things instead of blindly seeking what is commonly thought to be desirable (*aliis admiranda*), and realise the advantages of moderation (*quod superfluunt nocent*).

As a preliminary step, Seneca recommends taking in hand the *index philosophorum*. In this context, the noun probably means either book labels attached to

---

[25] Seneca also promises to send books together with reading aids in Ep. 6.5.
[26] For similar advice see Ep. 33.4–5 and cf. Setaioli 2014, 253 n. 108. Moreover, Ep. 33 also echoes Ep. 2: just like in the latter cursory reading is not useful in attaining significant moral progress, so in the former abridged and annotated reading. The philosophers' books are better read in their entirety.

their rolls, or a book inventory list.[27] Looking at the philosophers' names and titles on the *index* would make Lucilius understand how essential reading their works is for him, and prompt him to do so.[28]

3 Alternative Patrons, Superior Leisure, and *publica monumenta*

Keeping close company with one's book collection is conducive to moral progress, since it also provides an alternative to subjecting oneself to the hazards involved in conventional social obligations. This is shown in a passage from *De Brevitate Vitae*:

> Soli omnium otiosi sunt qui sapientiae vacant, soli vivunt; nec enim suam tantum aetatem bene tuentur: omne aevum suo adiciunt.... Disputare cum Socrate licet, dubitare cum Carneade, cum Epicuro quiescere, hominis naturam cum Stoicis vincere, cum Cynicis excedere.... quidni ab hoc exiguo et caduco temporis transitu in illa toto nos demus animo quae inmensa, quae aeterna sunt, quae cum melioribus communia? ... Hos in veris officiis morari puta [licet dicamus] qui Zenonem, qui Pythagoran cotidie et Democritum... qui Aristotelen et Theophrastum volent habere quam familiarissimos. Nemo horum non vacabit, nemo non venientem ad se beatiorem, amantiorem sui dimittet... Horum te mori nemo coget, omnes docebunt; horum nemo annos tuos conteret, suos sibi contribuet; nullius ex his sermo periculosus erit, nullius amicitia capitalis, nullius sumptuosa observatio.... Quae illum felicitas, quam pulchra senectus manet, qui se in horum clientelam contulit! Habebit... quos de se cotidie consulat, a quibus audiat verum sine contumelia, laudetur sine adulatione, ad quorum se similitudinem effingat.
>
> Of all men they alone are at leisure who take time for philosophy, they alone live; for they do not only attend to their own lifetime: they join every period to their own... We may argue with Socrates, doubt with Carneades, find peace with Epicurus, overcome human nature with the Stoics, exceed it with the Cynics... why should not we turn from this paltry and

---

27 For the former see OLD s.v. *index* 3a; TLL 7.1.1143 s.v. II.C.1.a. For the latter see OLD 5; TLL 7.1. 1143–1144 II.C.3. Note that both lexica specify the current Seneca passage as an instance of the latter sense. Also cf. Préchac-Noblot 1945, 159 who translate 'une table des philosophes,' and Marino 2011, 187 'il catalogo dei filosofi.' The same noun appears in Dial. 9.9.4 above, similarly in the context of libraries, and is there taken to mean book labels by Costa 1994, 193, and by Waltz 1950, 89 ('étiquettes'), but 'cataloghi' by Schiroli 1981, 97, and likewise in the TLL entry.
28 And thereby become one of them (see here: *et ipse ex illis unus esse*), or at least shape himself according to their model (see Dial. 10.15.2: *ad quorum se similitudinem effingat*, quoted below). The *index* could also concretely support library use by offering some help in locating relevant books: labels save time that would otherwise be spent in unrolling books to check their identity. An inventory might also be helpful, especially if a library is well organized (as seems to be the case here: *scripta... satis ordinentur*).

fleeting time and devote all our soul to what is boundless, eternal, and shared with our betters?... Consider that they alone are engaged in the true duties of life, who wish to have every day as their most intimate friends Zeno, Pythagoras, Democritus, Aristotle, Theophrastus... No one of these will be unavailable, no one will fail to have his visitor leave happier, more devoted to himself... No one of these will force you to die, but all will teach you how to; no one will wear out your years, but give you his own; no conversation with these will be perilous, no friendship will endanger your life, the courting of none will be extravagant... What happiness, what fair old age awaits one who dedicated himself as a client to these! He will have friends... whom he may consult every day about himself, hear truth without insult, praise without flattery, and after whose likeness he may fashion himself. (Dial. 10.14.1–15.2)

This account of the benefits gained by reading the philosophers[29] explains how it furnishes the combined guidance of ages past in searching for the truly blissful way of life.[30] The right use of time, a concept intrinsic to the *De Brevitate Vitae*, thereby finds particular expression.

Furthermore, time spent with one's philosophy book collection is not only a superior *otium*, but also a superior *officium*, with correspondingly better *beneficia* than those conferred in return for the fulfillment of other duties. In fact, embedded in this account is a passage where Seneca amusingly shows how chasing after the favour of flesh-and-blood patrons is troublesome, humiliating, and futile.[31] It is evidently contrasted with what precedes and follows, where philosophy books are presented as accessible and helpful, and as offering patronage capable of bringing their client-readers to a state of existential happiness.[32]

The advice to associate with one's books and abstain from regular patron-client relationships goes against social convention, and may also have political undertones. The emperors, after all, were at the head of the patronage hierarchy. The dialogue *De Brevitate Vitae* was published sometime between 48 and 55 CE, probably when its addressee Paulinus, whom Seneca tries to convince to withdraw to *otium*, served as *praefectus annonae*,[33] i.e. most likely in the latter

---

[29] That the references to philosophers are to their books is also maintained by, e.g. Duff 1915, 148; Grimal 1966, 63; Edwards 2014, 341. It is noteworthy that, despite Seneca's Stoicism, the recommended reading options represent a wide variety of philosophical schools.

[30] This trans-temporal aspect is also extra-temporal, allowing one to tap into eternity (similarly cf. Edwards 2014, 341), including the future (see later in Dial. 10.15.5 and cf. Grimal 1966, 66; Williams 2003, 21).

[31] Dial. 10.14.3–4 (not quoted).

[32] For this contrast also cf. Williams 2003, 23.

[33] See, e.g. Williams 2003, 20; Marshall 2014, 36.

half of Claudius's reign,[34] though the first year of Nero's cannot be excluded.[35] Seneca was involved in politics at this time, but scars from his long exile (41–48 CE) decreed by Claudius may well have lingered, as may have the memories of what comforted Seneca during that troubled time.[36] This description of the advantages of seeking philosophical books' company over that of conventional patrons, can express some degree of frustration and disillusionment with Roman society and its regime. At this stage, however, Seneca's wish for retirement was more an ideal than a reality.[37]

Yet book collections in Seneca's works can serve not only as an escape from society, but also as a way to change it: public libraries immortalise authors in the collective memory, and thereby aid in the formation of values, morals, and national identity. That is how they are presented in what is probably Seneca's most pointed use of library imagery for political comment, in *De Consolatione ad Marciam*:

> Ut vero aliquam occasionem mutatio temporum dedit, ingenium patris tui, de quo sumptum erat supplicium, in usum hominum reduxisti et a vera illum vindicasti morte ac restituisti in publica monumenta libros quos vir ille fortissimus sanguine suo scripserat. Optime meruisti de Romanis studiis: magna illorum pars arserat; optime de posteris, ad quos veniet incorrupta rerum fides, auctori suo magno inputata; optime de ipso, cuius viget vigebitque memoria quam diu in pretio fuerit Romana cognosci, quam diu quisquam erit qui reverti velit ad acta maiorum, quam diu quisquam qui velit scire quid sit vir Romanus, quid subactis iam cervicibus omnium et ad Seianianum iugum adactis indomitus, quid sit homo ingenio animo manu liber. Magnum mehercules detrimentum res publica ceperat, si illum... non eruisses.

> When, however, changed times gave an opportunity, you recovered for the benefit of men the talent of your father which had brought him ultimate punishment, and you saved him from true death and returned the books which that bravest man had written with his own blood to their place in the commemorative public buildings. You have done the greatest service to Roman scholarship: a large part of it had been burned; the greatest service to

---

34 Also cf. Duff 1915, xiv, proposing the range 48–50 CE; Grimal 1966, 4, arguing for 49 CE, shortly after Seneca was recalled from exile, and at the same time as he married Paulinus's daughter.
35 Cautiously suggested by Griffin 1992, 406–407.
36 Also cf. Dial. 10.15.4: *Hi... te in illum locum, ex quo nemo deicitur, sublevabunt* ('These... will raise you to a place from which no one is cast away'); and again the above quoted 10.15.1: *horum te mori nemo coget*, keeping in mind that exile was often conceptualised by Romans as death.
37 Later, when political circumstances became overbearing (from 62 CE on), Seneca made several attempts to retire from Nero's service. Though these were not very successful (see Tac. Ann. 14.53–56, 15.45; Suet. Nero 35.5), he did spend much of his time away, immersed in studies, reading philosophy and poetry, and composing philosophical treatises, including the *Epistulae* (see especially Ep. 8.1–3, 7–9; 67.2).

posterity: to them will come an uncorrupted historical account whose fidelity had cost its author dear; the greatest service to the man himself, whose memory thrives and will thrive as long as it will be worthwhile to learn Roman history, as long as there will be anyone who wishes to review the deeds of our ancestors, as long as there will be someone who wishes to know what a Roman man is, unconquered when all necks were bowed and forced under the yoke of Sejanus, what it is to be free in talent, mind, and hand. A great loss indeed the state would have suffered had you not rescued... him.
(Dial. 6.1.3–4)

In an attempt to comfort Marcia following the death of her son, Seneca praises her virtue. Among the first expressions of this praise in the dialogue is the description of her dutiful conduct towards the literary legacy of her father, the historian Cremutius Cordus.[38] She has restored his books to the public libraries (*publica monumenta*),[39] years after their burning in 25 CE following a *maiestas* accusation brought on by one of Sejanus's lackeys.[40]

The image of the public libraries in this context may have political undertones directed at specific personages. The *De Consolatione ad Marciam* is usually dated to Caligula's reign (37–41 CE). It is not implausible that the attack on Sejanus (executed in 31 CE) in this passage also implicitly reproves the former emperor Tiberius, to whom the praetorian prefect owed his power. Tiberius – so Seneca may insinuate – allowed things to deteriorate to such a degree that the writings of innocent and patriotic men such as Marcia's father were banned. Though Seneca seems to use Tiberius as a positive example of enduring grief later on in the dialogue,[41] distinguishing him from Sejanus in this particular,[42] they are nevertheless mentioned together in a way that emphasises their close ties.[43] Another possibility is that Seneca here vicariously applauds Caligula, trying to win favour by demonstrating how different the new regime is from the former.[44] This would cohere with the evidence that the rehabilitation of Cremutius's books, among those of other writers, was accomplished by Caligula's permission.[45]

---

[38] Also cf. Costa 2013, 7.
[39] For this sense here also cf. OLD s.v. *monumentum* 2b; Viansino 1990, 464.
[40] See Tac. Ann. 4.34.1–2, 4.35.4; Suet. Tib. 61.3; D.C. 57.24.2–4. Cf. e.g. Manning 1981, 29.
[41] 15.3. Cf. Abel 1967, 20; Griffin 1992, 397.
[42] Cf. Manning 1981, 85.
[43] They are described as standing side by side at the funeral of Tiberius's son, while the rest of the Roman people watch some distance away.
[44] Also cf. Costa 2013, 20–21.
[45] See Suet. Cal. 16.1. Also cf. Manning 1981, 30; Costa 2013, 20 and 21 n. 56. Indeed, it would also make a case in favour of those who date the dialogue to the beginning of Caligula's rule (see e.g. Abel 1967, 15, 159; Viansino 1990, 15–16; Costa 2013, 20. For a later dating see e.g. Manning

There is also a more general political implication: the power of the ruler over literature. A change of regime (*mutatio temporum*) can bring about changes in circulation policies. This, in turn, affects the citizenry and the state. In his enthusiastic encomium of the redemption of Cremutius's oeuvre, Seneca thus conveys a message about the wider importance of keeping meritorious books in the public libraries, about how they can benefit the many (*in usum hominum*).[46] Through their preservation of books, libraries consolidate not just personal but also collective memory and morality: they provide opportunities for the next generations (*posteri*) to engage in self-improvement by access to exempla of Roman *virtus* (*Romana cognoscere*; *scire quid sit vir Romanus*).[47] In other words, they not only enhance scholarship (*studia*) in the narrow sense, but also function as a didactic tool helping readers become better citizens, and thus promoting the well-being of the Roman state (preventing the *res publica* from *detrimentum capere*).

To the authors, the libraries give an immortality of sorts, allowing them to transcend time.[48] The preservation and restoration of Cremutius's books to the libraries is presented as saving him from death (*a vera illum vindicasti morte*). Those books are equated with his life,[49] indeed also with his body, as they are figuratively said to have been written with his very blood (*sanguine suo scripserat*).

4 An Author's Collection

The figure of a writer's oeuvre as a body appears not only in public connotations, but also in the private sphere. Seneca discusses the boons of reading books for an author's *corpus* in Ep. 84:

> Sunt autem, ut existimo, necessariae, primum ne sim me uno contentus, deinde ut, cum ab aliis quaesita cognovero, tum et de inventis iudicem et cogitem de inveniendis. Alit lectio ingenium et studio fatigatum, non sine studio tamen, reficit. Nec scribere tantum nec tan-

---

1981, 4; Griffin 1992, 397; Marshall 2014, 34), since after the 'honeymoon' period of his reign that emperor is said to have seriously considered banning the works of Homer, Virgil, and Livy from the libraries (Suet. Cal. 34.2).

46 For the significance of the quality of books' authors as a criterion in determining the legitimacy of a book collection, cf. Ep. 2 and 45.

47 On private libraries as offering inspiration to moral self-edification by setting examples, cf. Ep. 39 and Dial. 10.15.

48 Cf. the parallel transcendence for readers in Dial. 10.14.

49 For this passage's depiction of the close ties between the author's life and books, also cf. Langlands 2004, 117.

tum legere debemus: altera res contristabit vires et exhauriet (de stilo dico), altera solvet ac diluet. Invicem hoc et illo commeandum est et alterum altero temperandum, ut quidquid lectione collectum est stilus redigat in corpus.

> Yet [reading] is, I hold, indispensible – first, to keep me from being satisfied with myself alone, second, after I have learned what others had found out by their studies, to enable me to judge their discoveries and reflect upon discoveries yet to be made. Reading nourishes a mind wearied with study, yet study also refreshes. We ought not only write or only read: the former will cast a gloom over our power and exhaust it; the latter will make it flabby and watery. One should have recourse to them alternately, blending one with the other, so that whatever has been gathered by reading may be reduced to a body by the pen. (Ep. 84.1–2)

Seneca here discusses the proper balance between reading and writing. In spite of some prior reservation, he asserts that reading is essential for philosophical study and writing. It raises intellectual acuity and moral self-awareness by advancing one's knowledge and reminding how much one does not know. It develops one's judgement of the merit of what one reads, and encourages pondering matters that have not yet been satisfactorily settled by others. Reading books stimulates, nourishes, and prepares the mind, thereby helping in composition.[50] Thus, three notions from earlier passages reappear here: moderation as a virtue in reading,[51] books as nourishment,[52] and books as tools for study,[53] a prerequisite for the philosopher-writer.

In Ep. 84.3 Seneca elaborates on the process by which reading nourishes the *ingenium* and helps in composition: *Apes... debemus imitari, quae vagantur et flores ad mel faciendum idoneos carpunt:*[54] one should read in a manner resembling that by which the bees gather and prepare their food. That also means to read widely. This advice stands only in apparent contrast to Ep. 2, which warns against excessive 'wandering' in reading: while varied reading is recommended in Ep. 84.3, the recommendation is nonetheless qualified by the rest of the

---

50 Also cf. Cancik 1967, 85; Graver 2014, 284.
51 Which does not necessarily amount to reading a small number of books (see the above discussion of Dial. 9.9, Ep. 2, and Ep. 45).
52 Ep. 2 (for this echo also cf. e.g. Summers 1910, 284; Maurach 1970, 31; Scarpat 1975, 50; Setaioli 2014, 254 n. 119); Ep. 45.
53 Dial. 9.9, Ep. 39.
54 'We should imitate... the bees, who flit about and cull the flowers that are suitable for producing honey.'

phrase, i.e. one is encouraged to read many books, but they should only be adequate ones.⁵⁵

The elaboration is carried on later in the epistle:

> Nos quoque has apes debemus imitari et quaecumque ex diversa lectione congessimus separare... deinde adhibita ingenii nostri cura et facultate in unum saporem varia illa libamenta confundere, ut etiam si apparuerit unde sumptum sit, aliud tamen esse quam unde sumptum est appareat. Quod in corpore nostro videmus... idem in his quibus aluntur ingenia praestemus, ut quaecumque hausimus non patiamur integra esse, ne aliena sint.
>
> We, too, ought to imitate those bees, and sift whatever we have gathered from a varied course of reading... then, by applying the skill and care of our talent, we should blend those varied flavours into one compound, so that even if it reveals where it was taken from, it nevertheless is clearly a thing different from it. This is what we see nature doing in our bodies... So it is with the food that nourishes our talents – we should see to it that whatever we have drawn would not be allowed to remain unchanged, otherwise it will not be ours.
> (Ep. 84.5–6)

From this multifarious reading something should be distilled, which, though it shows the influence of the books read, is nonetheless new, or newly reconfigured.⁵⁶ This creation, the result of reading followed by writing, is a book, eventually several books, forming an entity which in itself is likened to a *corpus*,⁵⁷ so that the author-philosopher also has, as it were, an alternate body.⁵⁸

To recapitulate, in the passages examined in the four sections above we have identified Seneca's criteria for determining the legitimacy of libraries: proper measure, moderation, and avoidance of excess; the quality of the books (and their writers) comprising the collection; the manner of approaching it; and the purpose for which it is collected. Moreover, we saw the interaction of these criteria, and the concepts which lie behind them, with book collection images in numerous themes: as luxurious ornaments; as tools for study; as nourishment and guides for moral edification and the attainment of a blessed existence; as superior alternatives to the vicissitudes of patron-client relationships; as expressions of rulers' power and involvement with literature; as reflections of authors'

---

55 For another solution, cf. Graver 2014, 274, putting the emphasis in both epistles on the reader's assimilation of the material.
56 Cf. Cancik 1967, 86. On this Senecan admixture of imitation and originality in the process of reading-literary composition also cf. Mazzoli 1970, 95; Setaioli 2014, 254.
57 As in Ep. 84.2 above.
58 Also cf. Graver 2014, 287.

bodies and lives; and as vital nutrients during the imitative-creative process of literary composition.

Horace provides an instructive parallel with Seneca in his deployment of library and book collection imagery. The next four sections explore pertinent Horatian passages, and show the conceptual and thematic relationships between Seneca and the Augustan poet.

5 Dubiously Learned Luxury

We begin our exploration of Horace with Epod. 8:[59]

> esto beata, funus atque imagines
> ducant triumphales tuum,
> nec sit marita quae rotundioribus
> onusta bacis ambulet;
> quid quod libelli Stoici inter Sericos   15
> iacere pulvillos amant?
> illitterati num magis nervi rigent...?
>
> Be as rich as you like. Suppose that the masks of triumphal ancestors escort your cortege! Suppose that no wife be weighed down with fatter pearls as she walks proudly by! What of the fact that little Stoic volumes tend to nestle on your cushions of Chinese silk? Does that make my organ (which can't read) any stiffer...?[60]
> (Epod. 8.11–17)

In this poem Horace is asked by a woman for the reason of his lack of sexual prowess. He reacts with a harsh invective. Starting with a graphic description of the woman's old age and ugliness, he moves on in lines 11–17 to what would seem to be her more positive assets, yet he does so with mordant irony. Her distinguished lineage is mentioned in the context of her prospective death, recalling his attack on her elderliness earlier in the epode,[61] and suggesting a difference between the respectable ancestors and their shameful descendant.[62] Her riches are referred to by mentioning the opulent jewellery which she haughtily flaunts. The poet's concession that no married woman parades with larger gems hints that her conduct is unbecoming of a virtuous Roman woman.

---

59 Horace passages are from Shackleton Bailey's Teubner edition.
60 The translation is adapted with minor changes from Rudd's Loeb.
61 Cf. Kiessling / Heinze 1930, 520; Mankin 1995, 155–156; Watson 2003, 303.
62 Also cf. Watson 2003, 302.

This ironic description of her allegedly redeeming qualities is heightened by the rhetorical questions introducing her Stoic philosophy book collection and the presumptions involved in it (15–17). The poet scoffs at its presence, prominently displayed on the precious and exotic silken cushions in the woman's bedroom during their rendezvous. He mocks her erroneous assumption that such a display would impress potential suitors and would override any deleterious effects on their virility caused by her bad looks. The scene thus implies that she ostentatiously exhibits the book collection with no great interest in actually reading it.[63] To her, it and its trappings serve the same function as the portraits of her renowned ancestors and her pompous pearls. In other words, she is like the *ignari* later derided in Seneca's *Dial.* 9.9, whose libraries are nothing more than expressions of *luxuria*, being mere *ornamenta* with no other assigned purpose.

Even if the scene as Horace presents it is taken to mean that the woman has been consulting her book collection, it appears that her manner of study was shallow or amateurish. This is again brought out by the particular circumstances, as well as by the nature of the inventory:[64] the books are of Stoic philosophy, and they lie on luxurious cushions from the Far East, in the bedroom of a woman whose morals Horace seems to question. The Stoics' severe views on virtue were famous,[65] as was their fierce objection to luxury. Therefore, the portrayal of the book collection conveys the impression that the woman has failed to comprehend the lessons that ought to have been learned from it,[66] or to realise them in her way of life. Thus she has fallen prey to a danger similar to one of those Seneca warns of in Ep. 2, i.e. the one inherent in a superficial manner of reading, which deters proper assimilation. Therefore, instead of progressing towards a morally happy life, the *vita beata* that reading the philosophers is said to promote in Seneca's Ep. 108 and *Dial.* 10.14–15, the woman in this epode is *beata* (line 11) only in the inferior, material sense of being wealthy.

---

63 Cf. e.g. Pseudo-Acro (ed. Keller 1904) ad loc.; Giri 1951, 351; Romano 1991, 977; Watson 2003, 305.
64 Also cf. Giri 1951, 351; Romano 1991, 977; Mankin 1995, 156; Watson 2003, 305.
65 Indeed, *rigent* in line 17 is also a pun on the renowned moral rigidity of Stoic tenets (also cf. Mankin 1995, 156).
66 It is possible that there is a secondary, implicit, failure here – that of the books themselves. They are described as 'loving' their plush perch and complicity in conceivably illicit amours (on *amant* in line 16 similarly cf. Mankin 1995, 157). The description of the collection's self-indulgence and licentiousness may join that of its possessor's in representing a criticism of the discrepancy between the teachings of Stoicism and the actual 14 conduct of some strains of Stoics more generally (for the latter, also cf. Kiessling / Heinze 1930, 520; Watson 2003, 306).

6 Rewoven Texts vs. Bloated *corpora*

Another confrontation concerning the purpose of a book collection and the manner of its perusal is presented in S. 2.3:

> 'Sic raro scribis, ut toto non quater anno
> membranam poscas, scriptorum quaeque retexens,
> iratus tibi quod vini somnique benignus
> nil dignum sermone canas. quid fiet? at ipsis
> Saturnalibus huc fugisti sobrius. ergo   5
> dic aliquid dignum promissis: incipe. nil est.
> culpantur frustra calami immeritusque laborat
> iratis natus paries dis atque poetis.
> atqui vultus erat multa et praeclara minantis,
> si vacuum tepido cepisset villula tecto.   10
> quorsum pertinuit stipare Platona Menandro,
> Eupolin Archilocho, comites educere tantos?
> invidiam placare paras virtute relicta?
> contemnere miser. vitanda est improba Siren
> Desidia, aut quidquid vita meliore parasti   15
> ponendum aequo animo.'

'So seldom do you write, that not four times in all the year do you call for parchment, unweaving all the writings, and are angry with yourself because, generous with wine and sleep, you turn out no poetry worth talking about. What will be the end? You have fled here even in the Saturnalia, yet sober. Well, tell something worthy of your promises: begin. Nothing comes. In vain you blame the pen, and the innocent wall, born when gods and poets were angry, suffers. Yet your look portended great and glorious things, if your country cottage welcomed you, free, under its warm roof. What was the use of packing Plato with Menander, Eupolis with Archilochus, taking such weighty comrades? You plan to appease envy by deserting virtue? You wretch will earn contempt. You must shun the wicked siren Sloth, or be content to drop whatever you have gained in better times.'[67]
(S. 2.3.1–16)

The poem begins with a quotation of Damasippus' moralising speech to Horace, accusing him of meagre literary output. He derides the poet for self-indulgence and for escaping from the city to the country even during public festivities, yet still struggling with writer's block. Not even a book collection brought to his little estate appears to boost his writing. At first glance, then, Horace seems to be merely a drowsy idler with a library, not unlike the *oscitantes desidiosissimi* Seneca later denigrates in Dial. 9.9. However, a closer look reveals a balance be-

---

[67] Translations of Horace's *Satires* and *Epistles* are adapted with minor changes from Fairclough's Loeb.

tween reading, writing, imitation, and innovation in a writer's work, which somewhat resembles what Seneca advises in Ep. 84.

Horace is undoubtedly also laughing at himself, but his main target in this satire is Damasippus,[68] who confuses the poet's *otium* and writing tribulations, part of the work and polishing process, with simple *desidia*.[69] He erroneously assumes that poetic output is measured merely by speed and quantity. He is also mocked for his over-simplistic view of the function and manner of use of book collections, i.e. failing to realise that while a book collection is necessary for literary composition, it is not sufficient. It also has to be properly perused, supporting a careful *labor limae*. Horace here is not blindly copying the books of other authors, nor senselessly unravelling his own, as Damasippus perhaps takes *retexens* to mean, but persistently unwinding and reweaving both the texts of others and his own drafts into something new. Simple copying would not have caused writer's block.

Horace, then, has the last laugh, and all the more so since this attack on his conduct, working methods, and alleged inability to bring poems to their completion, is described in this satire: a completed piece, contained in a book the reader now reads, and, moreover, with its three hundred and twenty-six lines, the longest poem by far of all the eighteen satires. This irony is enhanced by the fact that most of the poem quotes Damasippus's long tirade.[70] Horace manages both to repeal the charge of not writing enough and to avoid the pitfall of inconsistency with his own literary standards: he dissociates his poetic persona from excessive writing by making Damasippus responsible for the excess.

Another reason why readers of this satire would realise the irony in Horace's presentation of Damasippus's accusations is that they are already familiar with the author's poetics from the first book of the *Satires*. Horace there often reveals his conception of literary composition by attacking those who do not conform to it. On certain occasions this criticism is articulated by depictions of poets who are so voluminous that their bloated corpora end up filling whole libraries (their own). The first is at the end of S. 1.1:

> Iam satis est. ne me Crispini scrinia lippi
> compilasse putes, verbum non amplius addam.

> It's already enough. Not a word more will I add, or you'll think I have pillaged the bookboxes of bleary-eyed Crispinus.
> (S. 1.1.120–121)

---

[68] A recent and zealous convert to Stoicism (S. 2.3.16–45).
[69] Also cf. Kiessling / Heinze 1921, 218; Commager 1962, 41; Muecke 1993, 131–132.
[70] Also cf. e.g. Oliensis 1998, 55–56; Cucchiarelli 2001, 158.

Crispinus seems to have been an over-prolific Stoic writer and poetaster.[71] Though excessive reading might also be involved,[72] Horace implies that Crispinus's own excessive and indiscriminate writings are the major component of his library,[73] whose nature is also indicated by its contrast with *satis* and *ne amplius*.[74] Throughout S. 1.1 Horace makes fun of those who desire something else or more than what they have, rather than being satisfied with their lot and means.[75] Thus, lines 120–121, with which the poem ends, fit in with the general theme: the finale of Crispinus's book collection and Horace's mock fear of the reader suspecting that he pilfered from it, convey the importance of moderation and due measure in literary composition.[76] Simultaneously, this image emphasises the importance of originality in composition.

An additional instance of an unrestrained literary corpus is found in S. 1.10:

> quid vetat et nosmet Lucili scripta legentis
> quaerere, num illius, num rerum dura negarit
> versiculos natura magis factos et euntis
> mollius ac si quis pedibus quid claudere senis,
> hoc tantum, contentus amet scripsisse ducentos   60
> ante cibum versus, totidem cenatus, Etrusci
> quale fuit Cassi rapido ferventius amne
> ingenium, capsis quem fama est esse librisque
> ambustum propriis?

What forbids us, too, when reading Lucilius's writings, to ask whether it was his harsh nature or that of his themes that denied him verses more finished and more soft of gait than if one were merely content with enclosing words in six feet, and proud of having written two hundred lines before and after supper, as was the talent of Etruscan Cassius, more headstrong than a rushing river, whose books and book boxes, so 'tis told, were burned along with him?
(S. 1.10.56–64)

---

[71] Cf. Porphyry (ed. Holder 1894) and Pseudo-Acro ad loc.; Kiessling / Heinze 1921, 21; Brown 1995, 100.
[72] His designation as *lippus* can account for more than one kind of literary activity (cf. Cucchiarelli 2001, 70 n. 46).
[73] Also cf. Cucchiarelli 2001, 79.
[74] Furthermore, in S. 1.4.8–21, following a critique of Lucilius's verbosity and neglect of *labor scribendi recte*, Horace refers to Crispinus as an even worse instance of those failings. Crispinus there challenges Horace to a poetry contest in which the winner would be the one who writes more. Such a criterion, together with his style's portrayal as imitating bellows, may also play a part in accounting for his library in S. 1.1.
[75] Neatly summarised in S. 1.1.106–107.
[76] Also derived from Callimachean poetics, for the presence of which in this passage cf. e.g. Freudenburg 1993, 192; Gowers 2012, 60–61.

Earlier in the poem, Horace recognised Lucilius as his predecessor in Latin satire, and acknowledged his literary merits, yet in this passage he states his faults: rapid, negligent composition, and an unwillingness to remove the unnecessary. The inevitable result is roughness in his poetic writings. The critique of Lucilius is elaborated by a comparison with an even worse poet,[77] the wordy Cassius.[78] His unbridled writing is said to have resulted in his poetry books filling up several book boxes, amounting to a veritable library. This corpus is clearly presented as not having been of a quality which justified its keeping and perusal: it was burned together with its author's corpse.

In this portrayal of Cassius's inferior corpus there are two elements which also appear in Seneca: the analogy between a writer's body and his works, as in Ep. 84 and Dial. 6.1, and a concern with the quality of a book collection as a criterion for its legitimacy, as in Ep. 2 and 45. A combination of both can be found in the castigation of those who keep in their libraries the corpora of bad authors (*corpora auctorum inprobatorum*) in Dial 9.9.

In the passages from S. 1.1 and 1.10 Horace's Callimachean poetics, sprinkled with his habitual allegiance to *aurea mediocritas* and moderation, is specifically applied to poetry through the images of monochrome book collections, quasi-libraries containing the copious oeuvre of their owners. Horace employs these images as vivid markers of the literary redundancy and ineptitude of certain contemporary poets, thus building negative models with which he contrasts himself. In S. 1.10 they also play a role in Horace's more complex critique of Lucilius, who is both his model and his anti-model. Horace operates in a similar generic sphere and recognises his debt to his predecessor, yet naturally wishes to differentiate himself and assert his originality as a poet. Book collection images constitute one of the ways in which he accomplishes these aims.

7 Palatine Policies

The problematic issues of literary standards and originality resurface in two passages that mention the Palatine public library. The first is in Ep. 1.3:

> quid mihi Celsus agit, monitus multumque monendus   15
> privatas ut quaerat opes et tangere vitet

---

[77] For the same tactic cf. S. 1.4.8–21 (cf. n. 74 above), whose attack on Lucilius is explicitly paraphrased in S. 1.10.50–51, 57–62.
[78] For the influence of Callimachus on this passage cf. e.g. Commager 1962, 40; Gowers 2012, 330, 331.

> scripta Palatinus quaecumque recepit Apollo,
> ne, si forte suas repetitum venerit olim
> grex avium plumas, moveat cornicula risum
> furtivis nudata coloribus? ipse quid audes?   20
> quae circumvolitas agilis thyma? non tibi parvum
> ingenium, non incultum est et turpiter hirtum.

What, pray, is Celsus doing? He was warned and must often be warned to search for home treasures and avoid touching whatever writings Palatine Apollo has admitted, lest, if some day perhaps the flock of birds would come to reclaim their feathers, the poor crow, stripped of stolen colours, would arouse laughter. And yourself – what do you venture on? Around what beds of thyme are you busily flitting? Your talent is not small, nor is it rough and bristly.
(Ep. 1.3.15 – 22)

Horace here inquires after the literary pursuits of two authors. Celsus's meddling with the library shows him to be a second-rate poet or worse. Likened to a naughty little bird stealing the feathers of others, he is bluntly and unimaginatively imitating poetry,[79] paying no heed to Horace's repeated warnings to restrain his use of the Palatine library's holdings.

Florus, on the other hand, appears to provide a positive example of engaging with a book collection as part of the process of literary composition. He is described as flying around the thyme flowers like a bee. Florus's energetic (*agilis*) hovering may also imply a more robust and controlled mode of reading, drawing something substantial from many, without drawing excessively from any one flowering plant.[80]

The implied statement on the proper versus improper manner in which authors use book collections may be recalled in the advice that Seneca later gives the reader-writer in Ep. 84. Reading of various models is there encouraged, but while it is allowed for traces of their influence to be discerned in the writing, the writer must nevertheless produce something uniquely his own. Another image the two authors share in this context is that of the bee as a positive literary figure for the wide-reading writer.[81]

---

[79] For this passage as a comment on the difference between illegitimate and legitimate *imitatio*, also cf. e.g. Kiessling / Heinze 1914, 40; Mayer 1994, 128, 129.
[80] That line 21 refers to what Florus is reading as well as to what he is writing is already asserted by Pseudo-Acro ad loc.
[81] In addition, cf. Horace Carm. 4.2.27 – 32, where he likens, in similar terms, the process of his own poetic composition to a bee's work. The echoes of that passage in Seneca's Ep. 84 have also been noted by e.g. Summers 1910, 285; Graver 2014, 287.

Returning to Horace, it is also noteworthy that in lines 16–17 *privatae opes* form an evident contrast with the public library.[82] The phrase may be construed in more than one sense, referring figuratively to drawing on one's own mental resources, and also more concretely to using one's own book resources.[83] Both senses join in conveying the idea of the need for at least an element of originality in composition.

It is perhaps not just malpractice by library visitors that troubles Horace. His attitude to the Palatine library itself is ambivalent. Not only does it furnish the conditions for increased unoriginality, but its policies and criteria for the admission of books may also be called into question. The phrase *quaecumque recepit Apollo* can have ironic undertones, with a possible implication of heterogeneous quality. This brings us to the second appearance of this library:

> verum age, et his qui se lectori credere malunt
> quam spectatoris fastidia ferre superbi   215
> curam redde brevem, si munus Apolline dignum
> vis complere libris et vatibus addere calcar,
> ut studio maiore petant Helicona virentem.

But do bestow, upon those, too, who prefer to entrust themselves to a reader rather than suffer the disdain of a scornful spectator, a moment's attention, if you wish to fill with volumes that gift worthy of Apollo, and to goad bards to seek verdant Helicon with greater zeal.
(Ep. 2.1.214–218)

Here is a call by Horace for Augustus to encourage non-dramatic poets, so as to fill the Palatine library.[84] Yet reservations emerge soon thereafter (lines 229–244):[85] Horace criticises some poets' books as unworthy to enter the library, and suggests that judgement ought to be exercised to prevent this.

Hor. Ep. 2.1 in its entirety is a manifesto alerting Augustus to the defects of Roman literary taste. The reference to the library in the temple of Palatine Apollo needs to be seen in this light. One of Augustus's pet projects, it appears to suffer

---

82 Also cf. Mayer 1994, 128.
83 Notably, *opes* later appears as an apposition to a private book collection in Hor. Ep. 1.18 (discussed below). For an indication of the importance of a private book collection to the poet's work also cf. Ep. 2.1.111–113, and S. 2.3 (discussed above).
84 It acknowledges Augustus's power as supreme arbiter of library admission (for which also see Ep. 1.3.17 above, and cf. e.g. Horsfall 1993, 62), yet at the same time shows him to be in need of instruction and advice by Horace (on this interplay of dependence and independence cf. Oliensis 1998, 193; Feeney 2002, 173, 184).
85 See especially lines 229–231, 241–244.

from this general problem, with the solution requiring more active involvement on the ruler's part.[86]

However, this is further complicated by Horace's possible insinuation of excessive pressure by Augustus,[87] even if Horace does soften this hint by stating that poets are to blame for this. There are also intimations of certain expectations of Augustus regarding the form and content of current poems, which do not always accord with poets' inclinations. Indeed, Horace himself vicariously makes a case for more tolerance towards alternative genres of poetry in his *recusatio* later on in the epistle.[88]

So it appears that, here too, moderation is preached. On the one hand, firmer intervention in literary culture, so that old-fashioned and inferior contemporary poetry would not overwhelm other poetic efforts. This should also find expression in greater discretion in libraries' book admission policy. And, on the other hand, Augustus should allow greater freedom for poets, by also encouraging composition in new genres and styles which are currently underrepresented. This should be the way to fulfill Augustus's wish to fill the Palatine library.

Two general points of resemblance with this passage can be detected in Seneca's writings. First, there is an insistence that some authors' inferior quality renders them ineligible to be included in a book collection: the *inprobati auctores* in the inexcusable libraries of Dial. 9.9, in contrast with the *idonei*, *boni*, and *certa ingenia* recommended for reading in Ep. 2, 45, and 84. Second, there is a concern with admission into and exclusion from the public libraries, and the (implied) involvement of the regime in these policies: the case of Cremutius Cordus's books and the *publica monumenta* in Dial. 6.1.

8 *Tranquillitas animi* with a Good Stockpile of Books

Horace's attitude towards the public libraries may also be tinged with the individualism and reluctance to be part of the crowd that are so typical of his persona. The big city, with its mundane duties and social obligations, does not

---

[86] Also cf. Brink 1982, 239.
[87] Lines 226–228. Also cf. Rudd 1989, 113, who, despite thinking that Horace here partly exaggerates, identifies a kernel of truth. In addition, there are indications that Augustus put pressure on Horace to compose more poetry, resulting in the fourth book of the *Odes* and in Ep. 2.1 itself (See Suet. *Vita Horatii* 38–52, ed. Rostagni 1944).
[88] Lines 250–259.

often agree with him.⁸⁹ His preference of the country over urban life is at times conveyed by images of the book collection in his own rural home.⁹⁰ The most striking instance is in Ep. 1.18:

> Inter cuncta leges et percontabere doctos
> qua ratione queas traducere leniter aevum,
> ne te semper inops agitet vexetque cupido,
> neu pavor et rerum mediocriter utilium spes;
> virtutem doctrina paret naturane donet;   100
> quid minuat curas, quid te tibi reddat amicum;
> quid pure tranquillet, honos an dulce lucellum
> an secretum iter et fallentis semita vitae.
> Me quotiens reficit gelidus Digentia rivus,
> quem Mandela bibit, rugosus frigore pagus,   105
> quid sentire putas? quid credis, amice, precari?
> sit mihi quod nunc est, etiam minus, et mihi vivam
> quod superest aevi, si quid superesse volunt di;
> sit bona librorum et provisae frugis in annum
> copia, neu fluitem dubiae spe pendulus horae.   110
> Sed satis est orare Iovem quae ponit et aufert:
> det vitam, det opes. aequum mi animum ipse parabo.

> Amid all this, read and question the learned how you can pass your days in tranquillity. So that ever-needy greed, or fear and hope for things of little use wouldn't drive and harass you; does wisdom beget virtue or does nature bestow it? What lessens care? What will make you a friend to yourself? What gives unadulterated calm? Office, sweet small gain, or a secluded journey and a path of life unnoticed? What do you think I feel, whenever the cold river Digentia, which the frost-wrinkled village Mandela drinks, refreshes me? What, friend, do you suppose I pray for? May I have what I have now or even less, may I live what remains of my life, if the gods wish for any remainder. May I have a goodly supply of books and food to last the year, and may I not waver to and fro with the hope of an uncertain hour. But 'tis enough to pray Jupiter for what he gives and removes: to grant life, to grant resources. A balanced mind I will provide myself.
> (Ep. 1.18.96–112)

The epistle contains Horace's advice to Lollius, a guidebook, as it were, for the perplexed *cliens*. In this passage, however, the poet turns to question the wisdom of becoming an active client to begin with. This questioning process is bound up

---

89 For an account of the tensions between the country and the city in Horace's poetry, cf. Harrison 2007b.
90 See, e.g. S. 2.3.1–16 (discussed above). Also cf. S. 2.6.60–62, where, following an account of the hassles of Rome, Horace yearns for his peaceful country retreat, with its private book collection and leisure.

with reading:[91] a philosophical investigation of the value of material gain, of virtue, and of the nature of the truly desirable life. Eventually, Horace supplies his own (ideal) recipe: the peace and quiet of the country, a significant element of which is the presence of a large book collection. This collection is presented as essential to the poet, to the degree that it is equated with the physical sustenance supplied by the farm. Its quality is probably a mediating factor.[92]

Notably, the last item on Horace's list (*neu fluitem dubiae spe pendulus horae*) is swiftly withdrawn from his prayer: he would achieve this *aequus animus* himself, by means of the preceding two items. The rural villa and its library are a place where outer and inner tranquillity converge. It is also a place embodying a life of *aurea mediocritas:* no excessive prestige or wealth, yet no deprived ascetic existence, but *copia* for body and soul. Ultimately, nothing is wished for beyond what is *satis*.

Later depictions of book collections and their contexts in Seneca contain many correspondences with this passage: there is an interplay between a sense of proper measure, as in the *modus* and *satis* propounded in the warnings of Dial. 9.9 and Ep. 2; a welcome abundance, such as that indicated by the willingness to send Lucilius a *copia* of books in Ep. 39 and a storehouse of them in Ep. 45; and the importance of an inventory's quality, as in the advice to read the *probati, certa ingenia, boni,* and *idonei* in Ep. 2, 45, and 84, vs. the spurned *improbati* in Dial. 9.9.[93]

Also present in Seneca is the value of a book collection as nourishment and supplies, designated in Ep. 2, 45, and 84 by *cibus, libamenta,* and *horreum,* and their capacity to *innutriri* and *alere*. The refuge a book collection offers from societal demands and burdensome patrons, as alternative *clientela* relationships for those who *sapientiae vacant* and thus spend their *aevum* in concomitant superior *otium* and *officium,* can be found in Dial. 10.14–15. Libraries' ability, as *studiorum instrumenta* and *discenti necessaria,* to facilitate self-edification, is referred to in Dial. 9.9 and Ep. 39. Their related assistance by setting an example and guidance for realising one's moral potential appears in Dial. 10.15 and

---

91 Chiefly, it seems, philosophers' works, yet implicitly also Horace's own (similarly cf. Oliensis 1998, 172; Moles 2002, 156).
92 *Librorum copia* is modified by the adjective *bona* which, besides imparting an added sense of its dimensions, may also relate the nature of the books comprising the collection. *Doctos* can similarly connote a statement on the kind of authors Lollius is exhorted to read. It is not, however, restricted to Epicurean writings (for allusions to several philosophical schools in lines 96–103, cf. e.g. Wilkins 1926, 224; Moles 2002, 156).
93 In Seneca, too, said quality does not depend on the books' adherence to any particular philosophical sect, as Dial. 10.14–15 demonstrate (also cf. n. 14 above).

Ep. 39: the opportunity they provide for genuine *consulere*, for *se effingere ad eorum similitudinem*, for inspiring the wish to become *ex illis unus*, and so to be *concitari ad honesta*. Their aid in recognising the folly of fears and imprudent expectations, as the *auxilium adversus paupertatem*, *mortem*, and *ceteras pestes*, and as a means to putting oneself beyond the *ius dicionemque fortunae*, comes up in Ep. 2 and 39. They are thus conducive to a quieter life of tranquil contentment, self-possession, and true happiness, the boon of becoming *amantior sui* and achieving *felicitas* and *beata vita* in Ep. 108 and Dial. 10.14–15.

9 Conclusion

From the investigation carried out in this paper it emerges that libraries in the writings of Seneca and Horace are loaded with multiple functions, operating as *studiorum instrumenta* on several levels. Book collection imagery is instrumental in articulating the views of both authors on literature and its interactions with morals, society, and politics. It thereby also contributes to the construction and presentation of their professional identities as writers. Moreover, their particular portrayals of libraries and book collections demonstrate considerable correspondence in themes as well as concepts. To be sure, there is also some variation. A conspicuous instance is Horace's secondary use of some book collection images to poke fun at certain Stoics. Yet a degree of difference is only to be expected from two authors working in different periods, genres, and with differing philosophical affiliations. Nevertheless, the numerous affinities in their employment of book collection imagery suggest that Horace provides a significant backdrop for Seneca in this regard.

Elena Giusti
The Metapoetics of Liber-ty. Horace's Bacchic Ship in Seneca's *De Tranquillitate Animi*

While Bacchus is unsurprisingly well represented in Seneca's tragic corpus,[1] the same god of wine, tragedy, and the irrational makes a poor fit with the rationalising Stoicism of his philosophical prose work. Indeed, to examine Bacchus in the *De Tranquillitate Animi* (Dial. 9) is to examine Bacchus in philosophical Seneca *tout court*, since the last chapter of the dialogue (9.17) is the only prose passage in which Seneca mentions Bacchus explicitly. But this is not the only reason why Dial. 9.17 is a *unicum*. This highly debated chapter has often appeared inconsistent with Seneca's precepts, not least those preached in the very same dialogue, because it invites Seneca's interlocutor Serenus to enter into an elated state of mind, that of Platonic-Democritean *enthousiasmos*[2] and frenzied poetic sublimity, which scarcely seems to sit with the previously proposed notion of *tranquillitas*. These inconsistencies can be unravelled from a philosophical perspective once we analyse them in light of the dialogue's context and sources; similarly, two later passages in the epistles to Lucilius (Ep. 28 and 108), which feature Bacchus by association and have been at the heart of the same controversy over whether or not Seneca admits the poetic sublime, help shed light on the importance of contextualising these passages before interpreting Seneca's views.[3] Yet this necessary emphasis on contextualisation ends up relativising

---

[1] Bacchus appears in relation to Thebes (Her. F. 134, 1286; Phoen. 602), revelry (Ag. 724, Phaed. 445, Thy. 467, Her. O. 701), as a point of comparison (Her. F. 16–17, 66, 472–5; Her. O. 94), and mostly as wine (Her. F. 697, Ag. 886, Thy. 65, 687, 701, 900, 915, 973, 983, 987). He is present throughout the *Oedipus*, where he is the subject of an Ode (Oed. 403–508) that has been closely compared to Horace's Carm. 2.19 by Stevens 1999. On Bacchus in Roman drama see now Schiesaro 2016, although it does not cover Seneca's tragedies.
[2] Mazzoli 1970, 47–48; see Democr. D-K B18 and B21; Pl. Ap. 22b-c, Phdr. 245a, Ion 534b, Lg. 682a, 719c; cf. the pair in Cic. Div. 1.80 and de Orat. 2.194. On *enthousiasmos* in the Presocratics see Delatte 1934; on the hypothesis that the whole concept of poetic *enthousiasmos* is Plato's legacy, Tigerstedt 1970; on the relationship between Democritus's fragments and Plato, Mansfeld 2004.
[3] On the *querelle* between Mazzoli and Setaioli see Del Giovane 2015a, 11 with bibliography. Michel 1969 suggests that the sublimity of *magnitudo animi* expressed in Ep. 41, 94, and 120 and depicted in the tragedies is also indebted to Longinus's definition of the *hupsos* as μεγαλοφροσύνης ἀπήχημα, 'the echo of a noble mind' (Longin. 9.2); on the Senecan sublime and Stoic *meg-*

DOI 10.1515/9783110528893-011

Seneca's injunctions, and it seems to indicate that Seneca plays a double game with the sublime, which unrolls around a set of oppositions (listed in the Appendix to this chapter) and allows him to avoid taking a firm stance when it comes to accepting it.

This double game is more easily understood if we acknowledge that a strict philosophical perspective does not exhaust the complex message of the *De Tranquillitate:* a strong poetic and specifically metapoetic vein runs through the dialogue alongside its more explicit philosophical content. If we may read the addressee as a double for the speaker, Serenus's restlessness is mirrored by Seneca's inconstant attitude towards literary sublimity and by his inability – or rather conscious refusal – to reconcile the contradictory aspects of poetry and philosophy in a coherent whole. This is perhaps not only a feature of intellectually honest philosophers, but more specifically of the inherent 'negative capability' of literary geniuses.[4] The same fickleness and inconsistency displayed by Serenus and Seneca are shared by Horace, whose erased presence throughout the dialogue, and particularly at Dial. 9.17, brings out the literary character of the *De Tranquillitate* and its metapoetic vein.[5] When considered under this Horatian lens, even the main metaphor of the dialogue, the sea voyage of Serenus's distressed mind, ends up entangled in implications of the poetic sublime, and Dial. 9.17, with Bacchus as its patron deity and Horace as its main model, turns into a metapoetic reflection on both Serenus's and Seneca's literary and poetic ambitions.

1 A Foreword on Ep. 28 and 108

Seneca's Ep. 28 and 108 show explicitly how inappropriate *enthousiasmos* is to the development of the *proficiens*, but just as clearly these negative connotations are bound within the specific context of the letters, and as such are liable to disappear once rid of their framework. Ep. 28 starts by discouraging Lucilius from using travel as a means to get rid of 'his sadness and heaviness of mind' (Ep. 28.1

---

alopsuchia see also Mazzoli 1970, 46–59 and 1991, 180–183; on Seneca's *De Tranquillitate* and Longinus see Armisen-Marchetti 1989, 53–59 and Staley 2010, 42–47.
4 Negative capability describes the artistic ability to contemplate the world without feeling the need to reconcile its contradictions in a coherent system; the concept was coined by John Keats (in a letter dated 22 December 1817) with reference to Shakespeare: '*Negative Capability*, that is when man is capable of being in uncertainties, mysteries, doubts, without any irritable reaching after fact and reason.'
5 On Horace's absent presence see n. 68.

tristitiam gravitatemque mentis).⁶ To do that, Lucilius 'must lay aside the burden of his soul' (Ep. 28.2 *onus animi deponendum est*), an *insidens pondus* similar to the one that Virgil's Sibyl tries to shake from her heart:

> talem nunc esse habitum tuum cogita qualem Vergilius noster vatis inducit iam concitatae et instigatae multumque habentis in se spiritus non sui:
>   bacchatur vates, magnum si pectore possit
>   excussisse deum.
> vadis huc illuc, ut excutias insidens pondus…
>
> Think that your behaviour is like that of the seer – as our Virgil described her – excited and spurred, having in herself much inspiration that is not her own:
>   The seer raves like a Bacchante, if perchance she may shake
>   the great god from her heart.
> You wander here and there, to rid yourself of the burden that lies within you…
> (Sen. Ep. 28.3 [Verg. A. 6.78–79])

The verb *bacchari* here is the only reference to Bacchus in the *Epistulae Morales*, and it is indirect at that, since the *magnus deus* who occupied the Sibyl's heart was actually Apollo, as specified in the line that preceded Seneca's quotation (Verg. A. 6.77) and which Seneca has here omitted. It could be argued that the erasure of Apollo helps to present *enthousiasmos* in negative terms as a direct consequence of Bacchus's influence,⁷ as much as the parallel involvement of Bacchus and Apollo in *enthousiasmos* is unsurprising.⁸ Such alteration and de-contextualisation of Virgil's text also seems to highlight our need to interpret the Sibyl's *enthousiasmos* in the light of the letter's prescriptions. The passage provides no direct refutation of Bacchic *enthousiasmos*, just as the context does not advise against travel *a priori*, but uses the image of the raving Sibyl

---

6 Seneca's text is from Reynolds's OCT unless otherwise indicated. Translations are freely adapted from Gummere's Loeb for the *Epistulae Morales* and Basore's Loeb for the *Dialogi*.

7 Already Heraclitus apparently accepted the Apolline *enthousiasmos* of the Sibyl (D-K B92 *apud* Plu. Moralia 397 A) and condemned frenzy inspired by Dionysus, a god comparable to Hades (D-K B15 *apud* Clem.Al. Protr. 22); on the interaction between the two passages see Delatte 1934, 6– 21. In contrast to Apolline *enthousiasmos*, Dionysiac frenzy was not initially poetic, see Tigerstedt 1970, 176–177.

8 In the first line of the *Oedipus*'s so-called 'Bacchus Ode,' Bacchus, appearing in a positive light, is introduced with the phrase *lucidum caeli decus*, 'bright ornament of heaven' (Oed. 405), a phrase that Horace famously uses for Apollo and Diana in the second line of the *Carmen Saeculare*. The description echoes a similar phrase applied to Apollo by Oedipus (Oed. 250 *o sereni maximum mundi decus*, 'greatest ornament of the clear world,' also used at Her. F. 592), see Boyle 2011, 210–211. Cf. also the famous line from Ovid's *Medea*, fr. 2 Ribbeck *feror huc illuc, vae, plena deo*, 'I am carried hither and thither, alas, full of the god,' with Gowers 2016, 567 asking: 'Bacchus, or Apollo?'.

as a necessary step to shake off the restlessness of one's soul before starting to travel. 'Any change of place,' as Seneca himself claims later in the same epistle, 'will become pleasurable once that evil is removed' (Ep. 28.4 *at cum istuc exemeris malum, omnis mutatio loci iucunda fiet*).[9]

Something similar happens in Ep. 108, which equates pupils enchanted by the phrases of the philosophers with the ecstatic worshippers of Cybele:

> quidam veniunt ut audiant, non ut discant, sicut in theatrum voluptatis causa ad delectandas aures oratione vel voce vel fabulis ducimur. magnam hanc auditorum partem videbis cui philosophi schola deversorium otii sit. non id agunt ut aliqua illo vitia deponant, ut aliquam legem vitae accipiant qua mores suos exigant, sed ut oblectamento aurium perfruantur. aliqui tamen et cum pugillaribus veniunt, non ut res excipiant, sed ut verba, quae tam sine profectu alieno dicant quam sine suo audiunt. quidam ad magnificas voces excitantur et transeunt in adfectum dicentium alacres vultu et animo, nec aliter concitantur quam solent Phrygii tibicinis sono semiviri et ex imperio furentes. rapit illos instigatque rerum pulchritudo, non verborum inanium sonitus.
>
> Some come to hear and not to learn, just as we are led to the theatre for the pleasure of delighting our ears, whether by speech, or by song, or by the plays. You will see that a large part of the listeners regard the philosopher's lecture room as a lounging-place for their leisure. They do not set about to lay aside any faults there, or to receive a life's rule by which they may test their habits; they merely wish to have full enjoyment of the delights of the ears. And yet some even arrive with notebooks, to note down not the subject matter, but only the words, so that they may repeat them to someone else with as little profit to the others as they themselves received when they heard them. Some are stirred at the magnificent phrases, and they adapt themselves, with enthusiasm in their face and in their soul, to the emotion expressed by the speakers, just like the emasculated Phrygian priests are used to being roused by the sound of the flute and go mad by command. They are enchanted and excited by the beauty of the subject matter, not by the jingle of empty words.
> (Sen. Ep. 108.6–7)

I agree with Setaioli that the comparison with the 'emasculated Phrygian priests' appears far from dignifying,[10] not because the Corybantes also have contemptible connotations elsewhere in Seneca,[11] but because these pupils are described immediately after another group which is here equally condemned: those who note down the teacher's empty words (*verba*), without grasping the meaning

---

9 The motif is already in Democr. D-K 247.
10 See Setaioli 1985, 804–805; 2000, 145–146 and Gunderson 2015, 20; Mazzoli 1970, 130 reads the simile, and the whole last group of pupils, as unambiguously positive, and in opposition to the previous ones, even though Seneca inserts no adversative conjunction to highlight this change; similarly Mazzoli 1991, 192–194; Schiesaro 1997, 100 and 2003, 23–24; and, more cautiously, Del Giovane 2015a, 11–12.
11 Sen. Dial. 7.26.8; cf. Quint. Inst. 5.15.22 with Setaioli 2000c, 145–146.

of the teaching (*res*). However, the sentence directly following the comparison sheds doubt on these negative connotations: it specifies that if there is a problem with this last group of pupils, then it is not *enthousiasmos* in itself, but the fact that they do not understand that this is aroused not by the 'jingle of empty words' (*verborum inanium sonitus*) but rather by 'the beauty of the subject matter' (*rerum pulchritudo*).[12] Similarly, the problem with the previous group of pupils was not that they took notes (arguably a commendable activity), but the fact that their aim was to note down the *verba* rather than the *res*. As in Ep. 28, *enthousiasmos* is neither negative nor positive – its connotation depends on the context. When Seneca tells us that it is the *rerum pulchritudo* of the philosophical doctrines and its high moral *telos* that has stirred the pupils, even the apparently negative comparison with the Corybantes may be reinterpreted in a positive light.[13] As confirmation of this, the *magnificae voces* of the philosophers reappear positively as long as they can quickly be translated into the *res* itself (Ep. 108.35 *magnificas voces et animosas, quae mox in rem transferantur*, 'magnificent utterances, full of spirit, which may at once be turned into facts'). Still in the same letter, Seneca claims that in order to follow Attalus's teachings, and to demonstrate that he is capable of abstinence, he keeps his 'stomach unacquainted with wine' (Ep. 108.16 *vino carens stomachus*); and yet, shortly afterwards, he corrects himself by recommending moderate abstinence, which is even more difficult to practice (Ep. 108.16 *modum servem et quidem abstinentiae proximiorem, nescio an difficiliorem*, 'I have observed a limit which is indeed close to abstinence, and possibly even more difficult'). Both total abstinence and moderate abstinence are to be interpreted as different exercises in wisdom. Only the context and the grade of one's learning will determine which of the two is recommended for one's practice at a specific point in time.

The same connections of Bacchus with travel, *enthousiasmos*, and wine that we have seen in the *Epistulae Morales* reappear in the *De Tranquillitate* with similar inconsistencies. In addition, Bacchus here also figures as an image for literary or poetic aspirations and as a possible metaphor for freedom of speech in Neronian political discourse. More than anything, the *Epistulae Morales* show

---

[12] To put it with Mazzoli 1991, 195, the good pupil should be able to read 'oltre la superficie dei *verba*, la filigrana delle *res*.' Cf. Gunderson 2015, 21: 'they have things half-right, these half-men (*semiviri*).' On Seneca's condemnation of aesthetic hedonism see Mazzoli 1970, 26–28, 74–76.
[13] On the positive connotations of both *enthousiasmos* and the simile, see Mazzoli 1991, 192–194 and Del Giovane 2015a, 11–12. Comparison with Plato (Del Giovane 2015a, 10, 12–14) is instructive, since Plato's Corybantes have been subject to a similar debate: see Wasmuth 2015 for the argument that they are used as an image of Socratic philosophical activity, a 'remedy for unhealthy souls,' and a preparatory stage for philosophical learning.

us the importance of interpreting these aspects of the god as grounded within the precise context of Seneca's prescriptions. The Phrygian priests are presented in negative terms if we think that the pupils are stirred by the *verba* and not by the *res*, but they also become an image of the irrational, sublime excitement aroused by philosophy if the same *enthousiasmos* is stirred by the philosophical themes rather than the philosopher's words. A similar double tension is present in the *De Tranquillitate*, and it underscores the difference between Seneca's preaching of philosophical practice and the literary aspirations of both Seneca and his interlocutor Serenus.

2 The Contradictions of the *De Tranquillitate*

The *De Tranquillitate* opens with a far-from-serene Serenus[14] presenting his mysterious distress to Seneca as if he were speaking to a physician of the soul and asking for a diagnosis.[15] Serenus is not sick, but he is not in good health either;[16] he is certain that his malady, whatever it is, cannot be cured by the mere passing of time, which in his case may implant the sickness even more.[17] Serenus divides his symptoms into three spheres: style of life, public life, and 'studies' (*studia*),[18] and in all three cases he starts by demonstrating to Seneca that he has been following Stoic precepts, but has not managed to stick to them.

He starts by defending himself preemptively, giving a long account of his frugal ways of life (Dial. 9.1.5–7), only to admit that the sight of luxury and opulence 'dazzles his mind' (Dial. 9.1.8 *praestringit animum*):[19] after his frugality, this splendour surrounds him and entices him almost like a magic spell (Dial. 9.1.9 *circumfudit me ex longo frugalitatis situ venientem multo splendore luxuria et undique circumsonuit*, 'coming from a long abandonment to thrift, luxury has poured around me the wealth of its splendour, and echoed around me on

---

[14] Motto / Clark 1993a, 141: 'a rather ironic and disquieting cognomen.'
[15] Dial. 9.1.2 *quare enim non verum ut medico fatear?*, 'why should I not confess the truth to you as to a physician?'; 9.1.4 *dicam quae accidant mihi, tu morbo nomen invenies*, 'I shall tell you what befalls me – you will find a name for my malady.'
[16] Dial. 9.1.2 *nec aegroto nec valeo*, 'I am neither sick nor well.'
[17] Dial. 9.1.3 *vereor ne consuetudo... hoc vitium mihi altius figat*, 'I fear that habit... may cause this fault of mine to become more deeply implanted.'
[18] Lotito 2001, 29 recognises these spheres as 'the world of objects / material life,' of 'community and society,' and 'of words and writing, of the communication and objectification of ideas.'
[19] Cf. Dial. 9.1.9 *paulum titubat acies, facilius adversus illam animum quam oculos attollo*, 'my sight falters a little, for I can lift up my heart towards it more easily than my eyes.'

every side').²⁰ This sight does not make him morally worse (*peior*), but it does make him *tristior* (Dial. 9.1.9 *recedo itaque non peior, sed tristior*, 'and so I come back, not worse, but sadder'), pointing to the vocabulary of melancholic depression (*tristitia*) that the physician Seneca will recognise more explicitly in his diagnosis.²¹ A similar structure applies to Serenus's description of his symptoms as regards to public life (Dial. 9.1.10–12): he claims that he has been following Stoic precepts when he repeats to himself that he should 'let no one rob him of one single day' and 'enjoy the tranquillity that is remote from public and private concerns' (Dial. 9.1.11 *nemo ullum auferat diem... ametur expers publicae privataeque curae tranquillitas*).²² And yet, he is easily persuaded to 'rush back' into public life by the earthly ambition to follow and surpass noble *exempla* found in the literature (Dial. 9.1.12 *sed ubi lectio fortior erexit animum et aculeos subdiderunt exempla nobilia, prosilire libet in forum*, 'but when my mind has been aroused by reading of great bravery, and noble examples have applied the spur, I want to rush into the forum'). Mention of Serenus's readings takes him to describe the third category of symptoms, *studia*. Unlike the Corybantic pupils, Serenus knows that he must prefer *res* to *verba*, subject matter to words:

> in studiis puto mehercules melius esse res ipsas intueri et harum causa loqui, ceterum verba rebus permittere, ut qua duxerint hac inelaborata sequatur oratio: 'quid opus est saeculis duratura componere? vis tu non id agere ne te posteri taceant? morti natus es, minus molestiarum habet funus tacitum. itaque occupandi temporis causa in usum tuum, non in praeconium aliquid simplici stilo scribe: minore labore opus est studentibus in diem.'
>
> And in my studies I think that it is – by Hercules! – better to fix my eyes on the theme itself and to speak for it, entrusting the words to the theme so that unstudied language may follow wherever the theme may lead. I say: 'What need is there to compose something that will last for centuries? Will you not give up striving to keep posterity from being silent about you? You were born for death; a silent funeral is less troublesome! And so, to pass the time, write something in simple style, for your own use, not for publication; those who study for the day have less need for labour.'
> (Sen. Dial. 9.1.13)

As in the previous cases, there are already a number of elements here that point to the implicit subversion of the Stoically inflected precepts that Serenus seems to know all too well: the interjection *mehercules*, the swift and abrupt reduplication of Serenus as the actor and addressee in his own *prosopopeia*, the hurried direct

---

20 As Lotito 2001, 31 notes, since he aspired to become senator (Dial. 9.1.10), luxury must have been difficult to avoid for the well-to-do historical Serenus.
21 See Kazantzidis 2011, 160–180, and below.
22 Serenus seems to have read the *De Brevitate Vitae*, see Cavalca Schiroli 1981, 56.

questions, the dramatic oxymoron *morti natus es*, which turns the sentence into an exclamation, and even a likely allusion to Horace's *carpe diem*.²³ All these elements end up transforming what should be an *inelaborata oratio* into precisely the opposite, the *oratio sollicita*, 'agitated style,' that, according to Seneca, 'does not suit the philosopher' (Ep. 100.5 *oratio sollicita philosophum non decet*).²⁴ They emphasise the restlessness of Serenus's soul – a restlessness that keeps him from being the sober-minded writer, philosopher, or orator that he wishes to be. Indeed, in the next paragraph, the soul is uplifted to *megalophrosune* (*cogitationum magnitudine*) and the *oratio*, no longer *inelaborata* – and, like that of Virgil's Sibyl,²⁵ no longer Serenus's own – takes him to the sublime:

> rursus ubi se animus cogitationum magnitudine levavit, ambitiosus in verba est altiusque ut spirare ita eloqui gestit et ad dignitatem rerum exit oratio; oblitus tum legis pressiorisque iudicii sublimius feror et ore iam non meo.

> Then again, when my mind has been uplifted by the greatness of its thoughts, it becomes ambitious of words, and with higher aspirations it desires higher expression, and language issues forth to match the dignity of the theme; forgetful then of my rule and of my more restrained judgement, I am swept to loftier heights by an utterance that is no longer my own. (Sen. Dial. 9.1.14)

Serenus finally explains that his malady is grounded in 'a frailty of good intention' (Dial. 9.1.15 *bonae mentis infirmitas*) which does not allow him to stick to the Stoic precepts in the three aforementioned cases. Introducing us to the sea-journey metaphor that will permeate the dialogue, he claims to be 'distressed not by a tempest, but by seasickness,' ναῦς-ea (Dial. 9.1.17 *non tempestate vexor sed nausea*); therefore, he asks Seneca to provide him with 'a remedy that may put this fluctuation to rest' (Dial. 9.1.17 *remedium quo hanc fluctuationem meam sistas*), and to 'deem him worthy of being indebted to Seneca for tranquillity' (Dial. 9.1.17 *dignum me putes qui tibi tranquillitatem debeam*).

If we were looking for consistency in Seneca's work, we would expect Seneca's reply to Serenus to be in line with the precepts of Ep. 108, a recommendation to prefer the *res* to the *verba*, philosophical subject-matter to (literary) style. However, that line of thought is here championed by Serenus rather than by Seneca, whose response to the third category of Serenus's symptoms is quite sur-

---

23 Cavalca Schiroli 1981, 58.
24 See Cavalca Schiroli 1981, 57; cf. Ep. 75 with Mazzoli 1991, 183–187 on the opposition between *oratio inelaborata* and *sollicita*, of which the latter is here accepted as far as it is useful, but perhaps with slightly more indulgence than expected.
25 Cf. *ore iam non meo* and Verg. A. 6.49–50 *maiorque videri | nec mortale sonans*, 'she seemed bigger, and did not sound mortal,' with Cavalca Schiroli 1981, 58.

prising. Seneca does not provide an actual diagnosis for Serenus's malady: at Dial. 9.2.10 he refers to the symptoms as *taedium* ('boredom'), *displicentia sui* ('dissatisfaction with one's self'), and *otii sui tristis atque aegra patientia* ('sad and languid endurance of one's leisure'). He speaks of the malady as *maeror marcorque* ('mourning and melancholy'), a choice of words that seems to imply an identification of Serenus's illness with Aristotelian melancholy, *tristitia*.[26] However, Seneca lingers instead on the opposite state of mind, and on how to achieve it. Just as Serenus had equated his malady with seasickness, Seneca establishes a firm parallel between *tranquillitas*, which the Greeks called *euthumia*, like Democritus in his treatise *peri euthumiēs* (Dial. 9.2.3), and *galēnē*, *tranquillitas maris* (Dial. 9.2.1 *tranquilli maris*, 'tranquil sea').[27] This state of mind consists of a sort of *ataraxia* (Dial. 9.2.3 *non concuti*, 'to be unshaken')[28] and a 'peaceful state,' a sort of golden mean, 'never uplifted nor ever cast down' (Dial. 9.2.4 *placido statu... nec attollens se umquam nec deprimens*).

Seneca's answer to Serenus with regard to the *studia* at the end of the dialogue also starts by reiterating this rhetoric of the *modus*, and then states that in order to achieve *tranquillitas* 'the mind must be diverted to amusements' (Dial. 9.17.4 *mens est... ad iocos devocanda*). As authoritative examples, he mentions Cato's drinking and Scipio's dancing, and in both cases he reiterates the practice of moderation, all of which is in line with the previous precepts (Dial. 9.17.4 – 7). The real inconsistencies start between Dial. 9.17.8 and the end of the work: Dial. 9.17.8 already strikes the reader because of its inconsistency with Dial. 9.2.13 – 15, where Seneca, as in Ep. 28, had rejected *mutatio loci* as a remedy to cure Serenus's distress. Now, however, he recommends it:

> et in ambulationibus apertis vagandum, ut caelo libero et multo spiritu augeat attollatque se animus; aliquando vectatio iterque et mutata regio vigorem dabunt convictusque et liberalior potio. non numquam et usque ad ebrietatem veniendum, non ut mergat nos, sed ut deprimat; eluit enim curas et ab imo animum movet et ut morbis quibusdam ita tristitiae medetur; Liberque non ob licentiam linguae dictus est inventor vini, sed quia liberat servitio curarum animum et adserit vegetatque et audaciorem in omnis conatus facit.

---

[26] On the term see Cael.Aur. de Morb. Chron. 1.180 *melancholici semper tristes ac nulla paene hilaritate laxati esse videantur*, 'those suffering from melancholy are always sad and are practically never cheerful and relaxed.' On Seneca's diagnosis of Serenus's malady as *dusthumia* and *tristitia*, see the whole discussion in Kazantzidis 2011, 161 – 179.

[27] On the not entirely accurate translation of *euthumia* as *tranquillitas*, see Setaioli 1988, 105 – 106; Lotito 2001, 11 – 12; Cic. Fin. 5.23 translates it as *securitas*. On the sea metaphor, which is shared by Plutarch's *On Tranquillity of Mind* and probably betrays a diatribic substratum, see Donini / Gianotti 1979, 107 – 109; Cavalca Schiroli 1981, 60 – 61; Lotito 2001, 15 – 20.

[28] On *tranquillitas* and *ataraxia* see Striker 1996, 183 – 195.

> And, too, we ought to take walks out-of-doors in order that the mind may be enlarged and uplifted by the open air and much breathing; sometimes it will get new vigour from a journey by carriage and a change of place and festive company and generous drinking. At times we ought to reach the point even of intoxication, not drowning ourselves in drink, yet succumbing to it; for it washes away troubles, and stirs the mind from its very depths and heals its sorrow just as it does certain ills of the body; and the inventor of wine is not called the Releaser on account of the licence it gives to the tongue, but because it frees the mind from bondage to cares and emancipates it and gives it new life and makes it bolder in all that it attempts.
> (Sen. Dial. 9.17.8)

In addition to the abrupt about-face on the subject of *mutatio loci*, inconsistency with the beginning of the dialogue is also shown by an acceptance of lofty excesses which seems to run contrary to the moderation required by *tranquillitas*, in particular the notion that an 'augmentation' and uplifting of the soul (*augeat attollatque se animus*) could be useful in achieving tranquillity. The emphasis on the adjective *liber* in the first two lines (*caelo libero* and *liberalior potio*) anticipates the praise for *Liber* / Bacchus, the god of wine who 'liberates from worries'. This is the climax of the paragraph, where Seneca accepts the use of wine not just in moderation, but actually to the point of intoxication (*ebrietas*),[29] so that it may even 'draw us down,' *ut deprimat* – precisely the same verb used, at Dial. 9.2.4, to describe what *euthumia* should *not* do.[30] At Dial. 9.17.9, the acceptance of Bacchus / wine, and of the liberation (*libertatem*) it provides, is highlighted again, to the point where sobriety is even defined as *tristis*, precisely the adjective that seems to point to the diagnosis of Serenus's malady:[31]

> sed ut libertatis ita vini salubris moderatio est... sed nec saepe faciendum est, ne animus malam consuetudinem ducat, et aliquando tamen in exultationem libertatemque extrahendus tristisque sobrietas removenda paulisper.
>
> But, as in freedom, so in wine there is a wholesome moderation... Yet we ought not to do this often, for fear that the mind may contract an evil habit, but there are times when it must be drawn into rejoicing and freedom, and gloomy sobriety must be banished for a while.
> (Sen. Dial. 9.17.9)

---

[29] Cavalca Schiroli 1981, 137–138 thinks instead that this is not the unrestrained *ebrietas* that Seneca condemns elsewhere (on which see Motto / Clark 1993a, 155–161), but *methē* regulated by *metriotēs*.
[30] Berger 1960, 351 notes that we would expect here a verb with precisely the opposite sense (*attollat* vel sim.); Cavalca Schiroli 1981, 138 explains the verb away by noting that it is a milder corrective of *mergere*, but the inconsistency with Dial. 9.2.4 remains.
[31] Cf. Sen. Dial. 3.1.13 with Mazzoli 1970, 56.

Finally, Seneca moves from equating intoxication from wine and poetic inspiration to accepting precisely that frenzy that Serenus had identified as one of the symptoms of his distress. Dial. 9.17.10 contains three quotations – from 'a Greek poet,'[32] Plato,[33] and Aristotle[34] – that accept the excesses of a frenzied *melancholia* in the case of poets and artistic geniuses. Subsequently, Seneca re-proposes Serenus's description of poetic *enthousiasmos*, making its connection to Virgil's Sibyl even more explicit:[35]

> nam sive Graeco poetae credimus 'aliquando et insanire iucundum est,' sive Platoni 'frustra poeticas fores compos sui pepulit,' sive Aristoteli 'nullum magnum ingenium sine mixtura dementiae fuit': non potest grande aliquid et super ceteros loqui nisi mota mens. [11] cum vulgaria et solita contempsit instinctuque sacro surrexit excelsior, tunc demum aliquid cecinit grandius ore mortali. non potest sublime quicquam et in arduo positum contingere, quam diu apud se est; desciscat oportet a solito et efferatur et mordeat frenos et rectorem rapiat suum eoque ferat, quo per se timuisset escendere.
>
> For whether we believe with the Greek poet that 'sometimes it is a pleasure also to rave,' or with Plato that 'the sane mind knocks in vain at the door of poetry,' or with Aristotle that 'no great genius has ever existed without some touch of madness' – be that as it may, the lofty utterance that rises above the attempts of others is impossible unless the mind is excited. When it has scorned the vulgar and the commonplace, and has soared far aloft fired by divine inspiration, then alone it chants a strain too lofty for mortal lips. So long as it is left to itself, it is impossible for it to reach any sublime and difficult height; it must forsake the common track and be driven to frenzy and champ the bit and run away with its rider and rush to a height that it would have feared to climb by itself.
> (Sen. Dial. 9.17.10 – 11)

It is hard to resist the temptation to interpret this passage as an endorsement of the poetic sublime, so much so that Seneca's words almost invite us to revisit our view of the Corybantes in Ep. 108. However, as in the *Epistulae Morales*, this endorsement can also be explained away through contextualisation. I find it difficult to endorse Setaioli's opinion that the passage is not a direct response to Se-

---

32 Anacreon (D'Agostino 1929, 65); Menander (Mazzoli 1970, 178–179); or perhaps Alcaeus (see Cavalca Schiroli 1981, 139). Setaioli 1988, 61–63, 108 n. 427 suggests that Seneca's gnomology listed it as anonymous, but anonymity may also serve to emphasise the Horatian paternity of the Latin version, see below.
33 Cf. Pl. Phdr. 245a.
34 Cf. the pseudo-Aristotelian Pr. XXXi (on which more below), with Kazantzidis 2011, 176–179.
35 Cf. Verg. A. 6.49–50 *maiorque videri* | *nec mortale sonans*, 'she seems bigger, and does not sound mortal' and Dial. 9.17.11 *grandius ore mortali*, with Mazzoli 1970 n. 94; see also Dial. 10.2.2 *more oraculi*, 'like an oracle,' with Schiesaro 1997, 100; 2003, 24. The passage is reminiscent of Pl. Ion 534b, while the imagery of the horse is taken again from the *Phaedrus*; see Cavalca Schiroli 1981, 140.

renus,³⁶ but it is true that Seneca here is ambiguously shifting the genre of this sublime flight. Here Seneca clearly refers to poetry, as the Platonic quotation testifies, and we are going to see shortly how specifically the poetry of Horace is present *sous rature* in this passage, in which Seneca possibly finds it more authoritative to attribute the first quotation (*aliquando et insanire iucundum est*, 'sometimes it is a pleasure also to rave') to an anonymous Greek poet rather than his probable Latin source (the phrase is very close to Hor. Carm. 3.19.18 *insanire iuvat*, 'it is a pleasure to rave,' or Carm. 4.12.28 *dulce est desipere in loco*, 'it is delightful to play the fool occasionally').³⁷ Conversely, it is not at all clear what category of *studia* Serenus was referring to in the description of his symptoms at the beginning of the dialogue. While the term *oratio* ('style,' Dial. 9.1.13 and 1.14) is applicable to both prose and poetry,³⁸ and is used by Serenus simply to refer to the choice and order of the *verba*, the comparison with Ep. 108 may suggest that we were dealing there with philosophical prose.³⁹ However, since Serenus is a public figure with certain political aspirations for his *cursus honorum* (Dial. 9.1.10) and has previously expressed concern about his behaviour in public life, the emphasis on speech and the repetition of *oratio* may indicate his involvement in public speeches, and his possible tendency to adorn them with poetic licence.

The idea that Serenus is indeed referring to his use of poetry in public speeches may gain credence by comparison with two passages from Quintilian's *Institutio* 10 regarding the use and abuse of poetic licence. At Inst. 10.1.27–8, Quintilian specifies that the orator, by reading poetry, may well receive 'inspiration in thought' (*in rebus spiritus*) and 'sublimity in language' (*in verbis sublimitas*), but he should be careful 'not to follow the poets in everything' (*non per omnia poetas esse oratori sequendos*), especially not in their 'freedom of vocabulary' (*libertas verborum*) or 'licence in developing tropes' (*licentia figurarum*). Similarly, at Inst. 10.5.4 he claims that 'the lofty spirit of poetry can help in raising the tone of oratory' (*sublimis spiritus attollere orationem potest*) and yet 'the bolder use of words permitted by poetic licence' (*verba poetica libertate audaciora*) 'does not exhaust beforehand the more desirable possibility of saying

---

36 Setaioli 2000c, 149–155, where he also considers Dial. 9.17 as an isolated episode, 'incidental and accessory... almost a footnote.'
37 Cf. also Hor. Ep. 1.19.2–3 *nulla placere diu nec vivere carmina possunt,* | *quae scribuntur aquae potoribus*, 'no poems can please long, nor live, which are written by water-drinkers.'
38 See TLL s.v. *oratio* 2a. Technically prose is referred to as *oratio soluta* and poetry as *oratio numerosa*, but prose is often referred to simply as *oratio* (OLD s.v. *oratio* 3b; TLL s.v. *oratio* 2c); on *oratio* for poetry see the example from Quint. Inst. 10.5.4, quoted below.
39 Lotito 2001, 33–34; Setaioli 2000c, 150.

the same things in ordinary terms' (*non praesumunt*⁴⁰ *eadem proprie dicendi facultatem*). It is interesting to note that these passages equate poetry with *libertas* and *licentia*, and specify that this freedom can only be granted to the orator in moderation. This is paralleled by Seneca's reply to Serenus, in which he also tries to put a limit to Bacchus's *licentia*, but he does so rather in passing. According to Dial. 9.17.8, we can abandon ourselves to 'Liber, who is said to be the inventor of wine not because he can give us *licentia linguae*, but because he helps us in *liber*ating our soul from bondage to cares' (Dial. 9.17.8 *Liber non ob licentiam linguae dictus est inventor vini, sed quia liberat servitio curarum animum*). And yet Seneca's denial of *licentia linguae* is puzzling, since Liber 'emancipates our soul and makes it stronger' (17.8 *adserit vegetatque*) and 'bolder in *all its attempts*' (17.8 *audaciorem in omnes conatus*). It is possible that such attempts also pertain to the writing of philosophy or oratory, in which *poetica libertas*, according to Quintilian, makes words *audaciora*.

Bearing in mind that the specification that Liber makes the soul bolder 'in all its attempts' complicates the matter, we can conclude that on the face of it Seneca's praise of Bacchus does not invite Serenus to feel free to say whatever he likes in whatever genres he likes; rather, it allows him to indulge in poetry to cure his soul from worries, as long as the *studia* refer to poetry, and not to oratory or philosophical prose, as it seemed instead from Serenus's request. This limitation of the precepts to the poetic sphere may also explain the surprising acceptance of *mutatio loci* at Dial. 9.17.8. Indeed, while Quintilian, at Inst. 10.3.22–23, denies the utility of 'the freedom of the open air' (*caeli libertas*) and the 'charm of the landscape' (*amoenitas locorum*) for inducing 'sublime thoughts and richer inspiration' in the orator (*sublime animum et beatiorem spiritum*), searching for solitude is what poets do, according to Tacitus (Dial. 9), or the incipit poem of Horace's Odes (Carm. 1.1.30–32).⁴¹ This kind of freedom / *libertas*, which is allowed to poets, mirrors the licence / *licentia* that is allowed to poetry, and poetry only. And yet in the imperial age it would seem that poetic licence has turned into something slightly more dangerous: in her subtle reading of Horace's *Ars Poetica* 9–13, Lowrie has recently argued that from the Augustan age onwards it is no longer the case that poets are allowed to dare whatever they please; rather, they must ask and be granted permission and indulgence (Ars 11 *hanc veniam petimusque damusque vicissim*, 'we have asked and granted this licence in turn [i.e. to dare what one wishes in poetry]'). As Lowrie puts it, 'this

---

40 I follow Peterson 1891, 155 and do not accept Watt's conjecture *praecludunt*.
41 Also note, with Montiglio 2006, 568, that Seneca's bee simile for the poets in Ep. 84 conveys the importance of poetic wandering, albeit at the metaliterary level of reading.

correction regards... the social authorization of the limitation itself'; it is 'a movement... from republican *potestas* to imperial *venia*.'[42] Already by the time of Horace, and more so in the Neronian period, liberty, even in the realm of poetry, has been transformed into indulgence.

3 From the Philosophical to the Poetical Sublime

If we omit Liber's role in making the soul bolder 'in all its attempts,' we have seen how Seneca's acceptance of the sublime becomes less troublesome if we limit it to poetry and avoid applying it to philosophical prose or oratory. However, indulgence in poetic *enthousiasmos*, and in intoxication from wine, still appears somewhat surprising at the end of a Stoic treatise on *tranquillitas animi*. If poetry was not part of Serenus's *studia* from the start, it is far from clear why Seneca would bring it up in the dialogue, especially in the last section, which should respond structurally to Serenus's requests. On the other hand, even if we allow poetry to be part of Serenus's *studia*, it still remains to explain why Seneca would allow Serenus's melancholic affliction to expand into the poetic realm.

To start with, since it is clear that Serenus's melancholy can only be accepted if it pertains to poetic inspiration, one may wonder whether Seneca draws, from ps.-Aristotle's *Problemata* XXXi, a distinction between depressive melancholy, caused by an excess of cold black bile in the body, and the frenzied, creative melancholy of the genius / artist, which is instead caused by an excess of hot black bile.[43] A melancholic type, as someone who possesses black bile in excess, is naturally prone to both types. Interestingly, however, already in Aristotle's text, the excess of hot black bile is said to produce precisely *euthumia*, in the sense of 'cheerfulness' or 'euphoria,' rather than 'tranquillity':

> καὶ ἡ χολὴ δὲ ἡ μέλαινα φύσει ψυχρὰ καὶ οὐκ ἐπιπολαίως οὖσα, ὅταν μὲν οὕτως ἔχῃ ὡς εἴρηται, ἐὰν ὑπερβάλλῃ ἐν τῷ σώματι, ἀποπληξίας ἢ νάρκας ἢ ἀθυμίας ποιεῖ ἢ φόβους, ἐὰν δὲ ὑπερθερμανθῇ, τὰς μετ' ᾠδῆς εὐθυμίας καὶ ἐκστάσεις καὶ ἐκζέσεις ἑλκῶν καὶ ἄλλα τοιαῦτα.

---

[42] Lowrie 2014, 130.
[43] On the interactions between melancholic depression, madness, and poetic inspiration from Aristotle into Greek and Latin literature I have learnt a great deal from Kazantzidis 2011, which I hope will soon appear as a monograph. See Kazantzidis 2011, 176–179 for a fuller account on the connections between ps.-Aristotle's melancholy and the *De Tranquillitate*.

Now black bile, which is naturally cold and does not reside on the surface when it is in the condition described, if it is in excessive quantity in the body, produces apoplexy or numbness, or despondency or fear; but if it becomes overheated, it produces cheerfulness with song, and madness, and the breaking out of sores and so forth.
(Ps.-Arist. Pr. XXXi 954a 21–27)

The problem therefore resides in a correct understanding and translation of Greek *euthumia*: surely *tranquillitas*, but also euphoria, like the *euthumia* used again by Aristotle to describe the state of cheerfulness induced by wine (Ps.-Arist. Pr. XXXi 955a 1–2 ποιεῖ εὐθύμους, 'it makes them euphoric').[44] Hence, the two different types of melancholy – cold and hot, or depression and frenzy (the second of which can actually have positive effects) – correspond to two different types of *euthumia*: *tranquillitas* and cheerfulness / euphoria, the second of which is actually compatible with the hot melancholic type.[45] From a medical point of view, the drinking and dancing described by Seneca with regard to Cato and Scipio undoubtedly heat the soul, the body, and the black bile – a necessary condition for a state of *enthousiasmos* or *mania*.[46] When *tranquillitas* is analysed under a Peripatetic lens, it accepts an enthusiastic and sublime state and transforms itself into Aristotelian *euthumia* / *euphoria*, but also divine inspiration[47] and philosophical *libertas*.[48]

A second way to solve the problem from a medical perspective would be to turn to Celsus's remarks on melancholy.[49] In the *De Medicina*, Celsus claims that the melancholic should abstain from wine (Cels. 3.18.17), but he also recommends as therapy the type of entertainment to which the patient was attracted when sane (Cels. 3.18.18). Therefore, if Serenus is a poet, indulgence in poetry, even in compliance with his melancholic frenzy, is part of the cure for achieving

---

44 See Mazzoli 1970, 55–56. Diogenes Laertius (D.L. 9.45) testifies to the existence of a tradition that interpreted Democritus's *euthumia* in hedonistic terms; see Lotito 2001, 12 n. 1.
45 See the Appendix.
46 Cf. Nat. 4.b.13.5. On the importance of heat in Democritus's physiology of *enthousiasmos*, see Delatte 1934, 28–79.
47 On which see Berger 1960, especially on the connections with Posidonius.
48 As in Ep. 75.18 *expectant nos, si ex hac aliquando faece in illud evadimus sublime et excelsum, tranquillitas animi et expulsis erroribus absoluta libertas*, 'there await us, if we escape from these low dregs to that sublime and lofty height, peace of mind and, when all error has been driven out, absolute liberty.' Also note that the 'Bacchic frenzy of philosophy' is Platonic (Smp. 218b3–4), see Casadesús Bordoy 2013. See Mazzoli 1970, 59 and Lotito 2001, 38 on the equivalence between euphoria, absolute liberty, and *autarkeia*. Schiesaro 1997, 99 and 101 suggests that 'the same state of enthusiastic lack of control' is shared by both philosophical excitement and artistic creation.
49 On Celsus and the *De Tranquillitate*, see Kazantzidis 2011, 169–171.

euthumia in opposition to the *dusthumia* that he falls into when he is prey to an excess of cold black bile.⁵⁰ Seneca's treatment of Serenus in Dial. 9.17 is neatly 'homeopathic,'⁵¹ and poetry figures in the cure, to use Mazzoli's formulation, as a 'euthumic pharmakon,' a 'balsam for the passions.'⁵²

However, neither of these solutions explains the compatibility between the acceptance of frenzied poetical composition and Seneca's Stoic precepts.⁵³ In an influential but controversial study, Martha Nussbaum argues that what she calls the Stoic 'cognitive view of poetry' (championed by Chrysippus, probably Zeno, Seneca, and Epictetus) considers passions as modifications and judgements of the rational faculty of the soul.⁵⁴ Poetry, with its ability to stir passions, is accepted as long as the Stoic philosopher drives his listeners, readers, or spectators through it by means of a constant 'critical detachment' towards the passions, characters, and actions therein presented.⁵⁵ From this point of view, a passage of Plutarch's *How the Young Man Should Study Poetry* is especially relevant, and it expresses this view with the same ship metaphor found in the *De Tranquillitate:* here, Plutarch claims that philosophers should not avoid poetry and steer clear of it, but rather should 'stand their pupils up against some upright standard of reason, and bind them there securely, straighten and watch over their judgement, so that they will not carried away by pleasure towards that which will harm them.'⁵⁶ If we consider the *De Tranquillitate* to be Serenus's sea voyage with Seneca as moral and philosophical guide, then we may distinguish between what Seneca suggests to Serenus at the beginning of the dialogue and his prescriptions at the end of it. In other words, if Serenus has learnt something

---

50 Cf. Dial. 9.6.4–6 on the apparently Democritean idea that *ars* must adapt to the *vis ingenii*, with Mazzoli 1970, 61–62.
51 Berger 1960.
52 Mazzoli 1970, 73.
53 On Stoicism and poetry, see especially DeLacy 1948; on Seneca and poetry, Mazzoli 1970.
54 Nussbaum 1993, 100; in contrast, the 'non-cognitive view' (held by Posidonius and probably Diogenes of Babylon) accepted the Platonic tripartition of the soul and considered passions as movements of the irrational part of the soul, which cannot be modified by a modification of judgements. On the Stoics' rejection of the existence of the irrational part of the soul and their view of affections of the soul as affections, motions, and judgements of reason, see Frede 1986. On passions and the Stoics, see also Inwood 1985, 127–181 and Graver 2007.
55 The observation leads Nussbaum 1993, 148 to argue that Senecan drama 'actively impedes sympathetic identification, promoting critical spectatorship and critical reflection about the passions'; this specific point is challenged by Schiesaro 1997 and 2003, but see in response Staley 2010, 32–34 and 43–45.
56 Plu. Moralia 15D, see Nussbaum 1993, 131. This sounds specifically like Odysseus and the Sirens, the topic which opens Seneca's Ep. 31: it is notable that it is Seneca's letter itself that helps Lucilius to be deaf to the allurement.

throughout the dialogue, and thus has managed to overcome the depressive side of his melancholy, then at that point, and at that point only, he could be encouraged to achieve, under the guidance of his Stoic helmsman, the poetic aspirations that he dreaded at the end of his request.

This is one way of solving the matter through a Stoic acceptance of poetic inspiration, but the best solution is to turn to Democritus, who wrote the lost treatise on *euthumia*.[57] We know that for Democritus, as for Seneca, *euthumia* is a product of *metriotēs*, moderation.[58] A perhaps perverse way to interpret this is to suppose that towards the end of the dialogue Seneca follows the precept of moderation so closely that he comes to imply that not only the teaching of *tranquillitas*, but also his instruction for moderation, requires itself a moderate application.[59] Therefore one is allowed, contrary to Celsus's judgement, to indulge in wine, or to avoid following too strictly Seneca's previous suggestions concerning *mutatio loci*. The injunction to indulge in entertainment as a relaxation of the soul would be in line with Seneca's portrait of Democritus as the laughing philosopher both in the *De Tranquillitate* (Dial. 9.15.2) and the *De Ira* (Dial. 4.10.5).[60] Moreover, Seneca also provides us with a description of Democritus as apparently mad, or frenzied (Ep. 79.14 *quamdiu videbatur furere Democritus!*, 'how long did men believe Democritus to be mad!'). All this ties in well with the recognition that Democritus apparently denied the possibility of being a good poet without being mad.[61] This view is found, among other places, in Cicero[62] and in Horace's *Ars Poetica*, in which the poets, according to Democritus, are not just insane (*vesani*), but should also be fled by the philosopher (*qui sapit*):[63]

---

57 See especially Berger 1960, 361–366. Panaetius and Athenodorus of Tarsus also wrote treatises on *euthumia*; see D'Agostino 1929, 66–67; Cavalca Schiroli 1981, 15–16; [J.-M.] André 1989, 1742–1744, 1768; Mutschler 2014, 158. On Panaetius as an almost certain intermediary see Barigazzi 1962; Mazzoli 1970, 51; Setaioli 1988, 98–107 (certain that Seneca did not read Democritus directly); Gill 1994, 4609–4624; Lotito 2001, 12–13; on the possible influence of Posidonius, see Berger 1960 and Mazzoli 1970, 54–55.
58 Democr. D-K B191, see Laurenti 1980, 547–548 and Lotito 2001, 58–59.
59 Conversely, *metriotēs* may contain *megalopsuchia*, see Mazzoli 1970, 54–55.
60 See D'Agostino 1929, 69.
61 Democr. D-K B18. See Delatte 1934, 28–79.
62 Cic. Div. 1.80 and de Orat. 2.194.
63 Horace's text is from Klingner's Teubner unless otherwise indicated. Translations are taken or adapted from Fairclough's Loeb for the *Ars*, *Satires*, and *Epistles*, and Bennet's Loeb for the *Odes* and *Epodes*.

> ingenium misera quia fortunatius arte
> credit et excludit sanos Helicone poetas
> Democritus

Because Democritus believes that native talent is a greater boon than wretched art, and shuts out from Helicon poets in their sober senses.
(Hor. Ars 295–297)

> ut mala quem scabies aut morbus regius urget
> aut fanaticus error et iracunda Diana,
> vesanum tetigisse timent fugiuntque poetam
> qui sapiunt...

As when the accursed itch plagues a man, or the disease of kings, or a fit of frenzy and Diana's wrath, so men of sense fear to touch a crazy poet and run away...
(Hor. Ars 453–456)

This contradiction between philosophy and poetry, *tranquillitas* and poetic madness, will have been at the very heart of Democritus's philosophical teachings, whatever his lost treatise on *euthumia* may have preached. Serenus can cure his cold melancholy in his private and public life, but there is no way that he can be a good poet without keeping that excess of black bile in his body. What is interesting, however, is that Serenus himself sees a way out that Seneca does not allow: to give up his poetic ambitions as *supervacua* and start writing for himself, without the aspiration to achieve immortality through poetry and writing. This option, according to the philosopher and tragedian Seneca, can only be utopian, and the end of the dialogue metapoetically turns the same question onto Seneca himself: is the *De Tranquillitate*, like all the rest of Seneca's philosophical and poetic production, really written *in usum sui*, or *in usum Sereni*?[64] Or does it rather envisage, and eventually also desire, the literary immortality that Seneca will no doubt achieve?[65]

4 Horace's Bacchic Ship

Poetry, especially Horace's poetry, provides a clue to understanding how the inconsistency of the *De Tranquillitate*, when analysed through both a Democritean and a poetic lens, ends up turning the end of the dialogue into a metapoetic

---

[64] On the hypothesis that Seneca writes Dial. 9.17 away from public life, see D'Agostino 1929, 77; Lefèvre 2003, 165.
[65] See Lefèvre 2003, 157–158.

commentary on Seneca's own aspirations. The paradox of the dialogue closely recalls a similar paradox in Horace's *Ars Poetica*, apparently a treatise on how to write poetry, which ends up reminding us of Democritus's mad poet and subtly implies that, no matter what, good poetry cannot be taught.[66] Furthermore, the *Ars Poetica* also contains, in Kazantzidis's words, a clear friction between Horace's need to ridicule the mad poet, and appear as 'a sober-minded critic,' and his confession of 'a strong attraction to it, almost to the point of identification.'[67] Horace himself has been fluctuating throughout all his career between the more sensible, technical side of his poetry and its Bacchic, sublime afflatus: in the *Ars Poetica*, on the one hand, he tries to purge himself of his bile (Ars 301–302 *o ego laevus, | qui purgor bilem*, 'fool that I am, purging myself of my bile!'), but on the other he implicitly equates himself with Democritus's mad poet, the exceptional genius, when he claims that if he had not purged himself, he would have been superior to any other poet (Ars 303 *non alius faceret meliora poemata*, 'no one else would compose better poems'). A reading of the *De Tranquillitate* through the lens of Horatian allusions brings out precisely this trajectory from sensible, philosophical doctrine to the sublime heights of lyric inspiration, a trajectory which is an integral part both of Horace's literary career and of Seneca's dialogue.

In the first part of the dialogue, Seneca makes ample, though not explicit, use of Horace's hexametric poems in order to bolster his philosophical points. And yet these models already contain the inconsistencies between philosophical and poetic life. A prime example of this is Seneca's use of the topos of *mutatio loci* at Dial. 9.2.13 in relation to Horace's S. 2.7 and Ep. 1.11 and 1.14:

> inde peregrinationes suscipiuntur vagae et invia litora pererrantur et modo mari se modo terra experitur semper praesentibus infesta levitas...
>
> Hence men undertake wide-ranging travel, and wander over remote shores, and their fickleness, always discontented with the present, gives proof of itself on land and now on sea...
> (Sen. Dial. 9.2.13)

In S. 2.7, in which Horace's slave Davus criticises his master on the basis of his 'fickleness,' the figure of Horace comes close to Serenus, in terms of knowing the correct precepts but being unable to follow them. Among such precepts, we also find the notion that a constant wish to change place is the sign of a fickle soul (cf. *levis*, 'fickle,' at S. 2.7.29 and the *infesta levitas* of Dial. 9.2.13), and of one that

---

66 See especially Oliensis 2009, 452.
67 Kazantzidis 2011, 191; see the whole treatment of Horace as a melancholic genius at 190–222.

cannot bear to be with itself (S. 2.7.111–113; cf. Dial. 9.2.15). Davus's precepts are presented as desirable, but Horace the poet, in his bad temper, is in Davus's words 'either mad or verse-making' (S. 2.7.117 *aut insanit... aut versus facit*). Ep. 1.11, closing with the recommendation to keep an *aequus animus* (Ep. 1.11.29–30) that seems to correspond with Seneca's *tranquillitas*, shows Horace preaching again against *mutatio loci* (Ep. 1.11.27 *caelum, non animum mutant, qui trans mare currunt*, 'those who rush across the sea change their clime, not their mind');[68] and yet lines 8–10 still betray Horace's inner desire to seclude himself from the world and be forgotten (Ep. 1.11.9 *oblitusque meorum, obliviscendus et illis*, 'forgetting my friends, and by them forgotten'). Similarly, in Ep. 1.14 Horace reverses S. 2.7, in so far as he now speaks to a slave and seems to have learned from Davus's teachings: he lives a life of frugality in the countryside, in contrast to the leisure that he used to enjoy in the city, and now knows that not the place, but rather 'the mind is at fault, since it never escapes from itself' (Ep. 1.14.13 *in culpa est animus, qui se non effugit umquam*). And yet inconsistencies taint the epistle from the beginning, when Horace first claims that he considers happy the man who dwells in the countryside (Ep. 1.14.10 *rure ego viventem, tu dicis in urbe beatum*, 'I call him happy who lives in the country; you him who dwells in the city') and then goes on to argue that the *locus* actually makes no difference in terms of happiness. Shortly after, although he claims that he is finally 'consistent with himself' (Ep. 1.14.16 *me constare mihi*), he continues to be 'dragged to Rome by hateful business' (Ep. 1.14.17 *trahunt invisa negotia Romam*); and when this happens, he is again as *tristis* as Serenus (Ep. 1.14.16 *discedere tristem*, 'I depart in gloom').

If we read the inconsistency on the topos of *mutatio loci* in Dial. 9.2 and 9.17 under the lens of Horatian intertextuality, we see a clear continuity between Horace's fickleness in the *Satire* and the two *Epistles* and the inconsistencies expressed by Seneca once he brings the philosophical teachings of his dialogue to encompass poetic creativity and literary ambition. As Montiglio has argued with regard to Seneca's stigmatisation of and yet fascination for travel in Ep. 104, in Dial. 9.17.8 the philosopher is also 'himself transported by the distracting activity

---

[68] Clearly alluded to by Seneca at Ep. 28.1 *animum debes mutare, non caelum*, 'you must change your mind, not the clime,' but passed over in silence in favour of an explicit quotation from Virgil; similarly, at Dial. 9.2.14, Seneca explicitly quotes Lucretius, hiding his Horatian debt: see Mazzoli 1970, 236; Cavalca Schiroli 1981, 67; and the present volume, especially the Introduction, and the contributions by Berno (with further bibliography at n. 1), Tischer (cf. esp. n. 72), Vogt-Spira at n. 6 (also with further bibliography), and Edwards at n. 16. Mindt's chapter is also relevant for its discussion of a similarly allusive approach in Martial to both Horace and Seneca.

he censures':[69] travel, to start with, and poetry to follow. This acceptance of *mutatio loci* signals a diversion in the journey of Serenus's ship, and the entrance into the realm of Horatian poetry: this is divinely inspired poetry, *mania* caused by an excess of hot black bile, in which one cannot apply the same teachings preached in the case of Serenus's excess of cold black bile in the spheres of both personal and public life. *Mutatio loci* takes us directly to Bacchus / Liber, not just in his guise as god of wine, as Seneca would have us believe, but as Horace's sublime metapoetic metaphor *par excellence*, the primary symbol of the flight of the inspired poetic mind; and it also takes us further to the Sibylline *enthousiasmos* driven by Apollo. Indeed, the metapoetic coupling of Bacchus and Apollo as an image of divine, and sublime, poetic inspiration, reminds us closely of the famous pair of *Odes* on Horace's Bacchic / Apolline flight, Carm. 2.19 and 2.20.[70] If we consider them together, Bacchus's inspiration in Carm. 2.19, which produces a cheerfulness (Carm. 2.19.1–7 *mens... laetatur*, 'my mind... rejoices') comparable to *euthumia / euphoria*, causes Horace in Carm. 2.20 to be uplifted like Serenus (cf. Carm. 2.20.1 *ferar*, 'I shall be uplifted,' and Dial. 9.1.14 *sublimius feror*, 'I am swept to loftier heights') to the status of 'two-formed poet' (Carm. 2.20.2–3 *biformis... vates*) and transformed into Apollo's bird, the swan. The two poems also retain Horace's poetic need for *mutatio loci* in distancing himself from the world (cf. Carm. 2.19.1 *in remotis rupibus*, 'on distant crags' and Carm. 2.20.3 *neque in terris morabor*, 'nor will I linger on earth' with Dial. 9.17.11 *desciscat oportet a solito*, 'it must forsake the common track').

Moreover, the Bacchic image also reminds us of another, earlier, poem which I have argued elsewhere must be considered the first instance of Horace's Dionysiac poetics of inebriation: Horace's Epod. 9.[71] The reference is strengthened by Seneca's pun, at Dial. 9.17.8, on Liber who 'liberates the mind from bondage to cares' (*Liber... quia liberat*), which may echo the last line of the *Epode*, where the fear for the battle of Actium is similarly 'loosened by Lyaeus' (Epod. 9.38 *Lyaeo solvere*).[72] The connection between Dionysiac inebriation and the musical / poetic frenzy that allows Horace to compose a Bacchic song fits well with Horace's use of Bacchus as a metapoetic figure later in the *Odes*, and with Seneca's

---

69 Montiglio 2006, 566. See Montiglio 2006, 568–569 for her analysis of the links between travel and poetic composition in Ep. 79. Cf. also Seneca's practical behaviour at the end of Ep. 56 (Ep. 56.15), where he chooses to leave his noisy quarters, even though the *locus* does not matter.
70 On Seneca's reception of Carm. 2.19 in the *Oedipus* see Stevens 1999. On Horace's 'Bacchic poetics' in these poems, see Silk 1969, Batinsky 1990–1991, and Schiesaro 2009.
71 See Giusti 2016.
72 A clear bilingual pun on the etymology of Lyaeus from λύειν = *solvere*.

similar mixture of Bacchus, frenzy, and poetic aspirations. Moreover, the dialogue and the *Epode* are also brought together by the metaphor of the ship, and of wine / Bacchus as the *remedium* sought by Horace to placate his 'seasickness,' *nausea* (Epod. 9.34–35 *vel quod fluentem nauseam coerceat | metire nobis Caecubum*, 'pour for us Caecuban, so that it may dam our flowing nausea'). Serenus, at Dial. 9.1.17, had asked Seneca to offer him precisely a *remedium* that would placate his *nausea* or *fluctuatio*; it is an interesting coincidence that Seneca ends up suggesting precisely the *remedium* that Horace asks for himself in Epod. 9: Bacchic inebriation, and poetic inspiration. *Nausea* of course means 'seasickness,' and is used as a powerful metaphor for describing Serenus's melancholic distress, but it is also the term used to describe the nausea caused by excessive drinking.[73] Therefore, *nausea* is as two-faced as melancholy and *euthumia*:[74] on the one hand, in private and public life, we find cold black bile, depressive melancholy, *nausea* as seasickness, which have their opposite in *euthumia / tranquillitas*; on the other, when melancholy refers to the poetic realm, we find hot black bile, frenzied / mad melancholy, *nausea* as *ebrietas* and *euthumia* as euphoria, or even poetic inspiration.

Just like melancholy and *euthumia*, and like the whole of the *De Tranquillitate*, Seneca's metaphor of the ship is also *biformis*, or two-faced: on the one hand, this is the ship of philosophy, found in Plutarch's *How The Young Man Should Study Poetry*, and the sea of *tranquillitas* may appear similar to the 'life without waves' (βίος ἀκύμων) of Plutarch's *Tranquillity of Mind*.[75] Moreover, until the very last chapter, this is also the ship of Horace's ode on the 'golden mean' (Carm. 2.10), which advises Licinius to think about storms before setting out for a sea voyage (Carm. 2.10.2–3 *dum procellas | cautus horrescis*, 'while cautiously fearing the storms') and to shorten his sails when encountering a favourable wind (Carm. 2.10.22–24 *sapienter... contrahes vento nimium secundo | turgida vela*, 'wisely reef your sails when they are swollen by too fair a breeze!'), passages comparable to Dial. 9.11.7, with its injunction to start a voyage with the possibility of a storm in mind (*magna pars hominum est, quae navigatura de tempestate non cogitat*, 'a great number of men will plan a voyage without thinking of storms') or Dial. 9.4.7, where virtue 'is forced to draw in her sails' (*cogitur in vela contrahere*).[76] However, when it is time for literary aspirations to be

---

[73] See Giusti 2016, 135 n. 27, with bibliography.
[74] See Appendix.
[75] Moralia 465 A8–9, although this refers to *alupia* rather than *euthumia*.
[76] Cf. also Dial. 9.5.5 *in periculosa navigatione subinde portum petas*, 'just as if you were making a perilous voyage, put into harbour from time to time' with Horace's injunction to his 'state ship' at Carm. 1.14.2–3 *fortiter occupa | portum!*, 'one final effort now, make port!'.

under the spotlight, the ship turns itself into the Bacchic ship of Horace's sea-symposium in Epod. 9, and into the Dionysiac ship of the Tyrrhenian pirates as described by Philostratus: 'embowered with vine ivy, with clusters of grapes swinging above it, indeed a *thauma*' (Im. 1.19.4). In this context, the laughter of Dionysus from the prow of the ship (Im. 1.19.6) superimposes itself on the laughter of Democritus, the frenzied philosopher.

For both Horace and Seneca it holds true that, as in Dial. 9.5.4, *non est... servare se obruere*, 'saving oneself does not mean burying oneself' – at least in water. But the final movement of the *De Tranquillitate*, as in Horace's Bacchic lyrics, allows the ship to be weighed down, if not submerged, by wine (Dial. 9.17.8 *non ut mergat nos, sed ut deprimas*, 'not drowning ourselves in drink, yet succumbing to it'), which 'washes away troubles' (Dial. 9.17.8 *eluit enim curas*). This also allows the acceptance of insanity / frenzied melancholy, through a quotation which, as we have noted, Seneca presents as deriving from a Greek poet, but which in fact alludes quite openly to Horatian lyric (Dial. 9.17.10 *aliquando et insanire iucundum est*, 'sometimes it is a pleasure also to rave,' cf. Carm. 3.19.18 and 4.12.27–28).[77] When it comes to literary ambition, Serenus's ship takes a direct turn and points *in altum*,[78] mirroring the ship of Horace's Bacchic flight in Epod. 9 and anticipating the inspired drive of Carm. 2.19 and 2.20. Within these images, a bond is established between the two philosophers, Seneca and Serenus, and the poet Horace. We have a Roman group that matches the three Greek authorities presented at Dial. 9.17.10: Plato, Aristotle, and the anonymous Greek poet. This bond ties Horace, Serenus, and Seneca together in their euphoric acceptance of the frenzied melancholy of geniuses, and in their ambition to achieve sublime literary heights and immortality through fame.

5 Conclusion

Both in Epod. 9 and in the *De Tranquillitate* Liber's / Lyaeus's role is to liberate the mind from worries, possibly in both cases political worries: it liberates Horace from the 'fear and worry for / of Caesar's situation' (Epod. 9.37 *curam metumque Caesaris rerum*),[79] and it lets Serenus, prefect of the watch under Nero and a front man for Nero's amorous intrigues (Tac. Ann. 13.12–13), take a break from his public duties and indulge in relaxing and pleasurable activities, such as po-

---

[77] See above and n. 32. It is precisely the similarity to Horace's passages that have made some scholars incline towards Alcaeus: see Setaioli 1988, 62–63.
[78] On the 'elative' aspect of the Senecan sublime, see Mazzoli 1991, 179.
[79] Mankin 1995, 181: 'a vague and perhaps deliberately ambiguous phrase.'

etry induced by wine.[80] In imperial times, as Lowrie notes, Liber cannot permit complete *licentia* to either Horace's or Serenus's tongue, especially in oratory or in philosophical / political writing, but he can transfer that licence to the realm of *carmina* and their allegorical language.

And yet the same allegorical language also ends up encompassing the mysteries of this treatise. On the one hand, to contextualise Seneca's endorsement of intoxication from poetry and wine within this Democritean and possibly Peripatetic treatise means to exonerate the philosopher from taking responsibility for the applicability of his own words to any situation (Dial. 9.17.8 *in omnis conatus*). On the other, the freedom provided by Liber also allows us to use the *De Tranquillitate* as Seneca used *Aeneid* 6 in Ep. 28: to excise Apollo and keep Bacchus, to shake off the rest of the dialogue and apply Dial. 9.17 to Seneca's aspiration in his literary prose or to the sublime flight of his own *carmina*, the tragedies. But to treat the world of poetry, as the *De Tranquillitate* itself teaches us, would be an altogether different story.[81]

---

80 On the historical Serenus see Cavalca Schiroli 1981, 9–11; Motto / Clark 1993a, 133–134; Lotito 2001, 20–24. On Serenus as Seneca's *alter ego* and on the dialogue's possible reflection of Seneca's situation at around 61 CE, see Motto / Clark 1993a, 148–149; Lefèvre 2003, 156–159; 164–165: 'se... Sereno, su richiesta di Seneca, fa da prestanome a Nerone, a maggior ragione sarà disposto in futuro a prestare il proprio nome per l'amico.' On the dating of the dialogue see D'Agostino 1929, 76–77; Cavalca Schiroli 1981, 16–18.
81 For that, see the work of Alessandro Schiesaro 1997 and 2003. I dedicate this chapter to him, in gratitude for always prioritising *rerum pulchritudo* in his lectures without dismissing the jingle of my empty words. I am especially grateful to the editors, Martin Stöckinger, Kathrin Winter, and Tom Zanker, for their patience and valuable criticism; to Emily Gowers, Philip Hardie, John Henderson, and Fiachra Mac Góráin for their comments; to Barbara Del Giovane and Francesca Romana Berno for their Senecan advice, and to George Kazantzidis for showing me his DPhil dissertation.

Appendix:
The Oppositions of the *De Tranquillitate*

spheres of symptoms	private and public life	*studia*
Seneca's response	Dial. 9.2–16	Dial. 9.17
genre	philosophy; oratory	poetry
bile	cold black bile	hot black bile
melancholy	depressive melancholy	frenzied melancholy
opposite state	*euthumia / tranquillitas*	*euthumia / euphoria*
symptom	*nausea* as seasickness	*nausea* as intoxication from wine
metaphor	the ship of philosophy	Horace's Bacchic ship
mutatio loci	rejected	accepted
sublime *enthousiasmos*	rejected	accepted

Alexander Kirichenko
Constructing Oneself in Horace and Seneca

While many of the papers in this volume deal with intertextual connections between Horace and Seneca, the aim of this contribution is to highlight some of the most conspicuous differences between the two authors, which to my mind are significantly more revealing than the similarities. To underline this contrast, I will discuss Horace and Seneca in two separate sections. I will demonstrate that, on the one hand, both draw structural analogies between personal ethics, imperial politics, and literary aesthetics, so that these three conceptual domains can be perceived to form a tight nexus, within which each element is notionally inseparable from the other two. But on the other hand, I will argue that Horace and Seneca rely on radically different principles in constructing their respective images of ethics, politics, and poetics and that this difference not only reflects the two authors' respective philosophical leanings but is also indicative of the transformation undergone by Roman culture from Augustus to Nero.

1 Horace

Horace begins to establish an analogy between his poetic persona, his poetry, and Octavian's Rome in *Satires* 1, his earliest published collection. The first three poems of *Satires* 1 not only formulate but also enact the ethical ideal of being at one with oneself. In S. 1.1, the notion of restraining one's appetite in order to become content with what is enough (*satis*)[1] is imitated by the text itself, as the poem, whose erratic conversational tone can easily be interpreted as excessive loquacity, concludes with an emphatic *iam satis est* – I won't add another word (121 *verbum non amplius addam*)![2] In S. 1.2, Horace similarly imitates the moral injunction to find one's inner centre (cf. 1.2.28 *nil medium est*, 'there is no middle'). He wonders why, in order to satisfy their sexual appetite, men either go to a stinking brothel or risk their reputations, fortunes, and lives by pursuing

---

[1] Hor. S. 1.1 passim, esp. 1–12 and 68–70. See Fraenkel 1957, 90–97; Knorr 2004, 15–30; Schlegel 2005, 21–25; Hooley 2007, 32–38.
[2] Freudenburg 1993, 110–114 and 2001, 27–44; Dufallo 2000; Gowers 2012, 60. On the 'chatty style' of S. 1.1 and on the scholarly reception of the ensuing inconsistencies, see Sharland 2010, 75–98. On Horace's speaker in the diatribe satires as a *doctor ineptus* 'prone to long-winded digressions, false logic and pat endings' (Gowers 2012, 58), see Freudenburg 1993, 3–51; Turpin 1998.

DOI 10.1515/9783110528893-012

aristocratic matrons or manipulative actresses, although the middle way – sex with a slave boy or with a freedwoman – is so easily accessible (1.2.28–119).[3] This notion of the golden mean he enacts by putting an imaginary dialogue between a misguided adulterer and his penis (69–70 *numquid a te | magno prognatum deposco consule cunnum*, 'do you really think I need a cunt born of a great consul?') exactly in the middle of the poem.[4] And likewise, the form of S. 1.3 effectively imitates the most salient aspect of its content: the ideal of equanimity in dealing with one's friends. The first eighteen and a half lines (1–19) are taken up by a portrayal of the singer Tigellius Hermogenes, whose inconsistencies make him appear like an incongruous hodge-podge of quotations that fail to amount to a coherent identity: 18–19 *nil fuit umquam | sic impar sibi*, 'there has never been anything so unequal to itself.'[5] In perfect symmetry, the last eighteen and a half lines (124–142 *si dives, qui sapiens est... vivam te rege beatus*, 'if he who is wise is rich... I'll live happily with you as king') portray a Stoic whose unrealistically high standard of inner unity turns him into a laughingstock of the whole town. Between these two extremes, both spatially and conceptually, is a defence of Horatian pragmatism, whose practitioner is conscious of his own *vitia minora* (20), tolerates similar minor blunders in his friends, and reasonably hopes that they will treat him the same way.[6]

In the first three poems, poetic language emphatically does what it preaches: form iconically merges with content,[7] demonstrating what it means to be at one

---

[3] Fraenkel 1957, 76–86; Lefèvre 1975; Gigante 1999; Henderson 1999, 173–201; Knorr 2004, 41–70; Schlegel 2005, 25–30; Gibson 2007, 19–42; Hooley 2007, 38–42; Sharland 2010, 115–122.
[4] The dialogue is introduced at S. 1.2.68, i.e. the first line of the second half of the 134-line-long poem – the middle of the poem putting on display 'the middle' of the male body. Cf. Gowers 2012, 86: 'H.'s satirical vision homes in directly on the *medium corpus*.' On Horace's talking penis, see also Plaza 2006, 83–90; Sharland 2010, 110–115.
[5] After this gnomic pronouncement, there is a notable break introducing a dialogue with an imaginary interlocutor, in which the speaker presents his ethical stance: 19 *nunc aliquis dicat mihi, quid tu?* 'Now, someone may say, and what about you?' etc. On the figure of Tigellius Hermogenes in Horace's *Satires* 1, see Gowers 2012, 92. On Tigellius's inconsistencies, see Sharland 2010, 37–40.
[6] Cf. esp. Hor. S. 1.3.68–72. Note that this passage is also located right in the middle of the poem. On Stoicism and Epicureanism in S. 1.3, see Kemp 2009, with further references. Cf. Hooley 2007, 42–45; Sharland 2010, 151–156. On Lucretius behind Horace's Epicurean voice, see Ferri 1993, 33–57; Plaza 2006, 273–279; Gowers 2012, 120–121. For a summary of earlier scholarly debates on the structure of S. 1.3, see Knorr 2004, 71–90 (esp. 71: 'Bis heute ist jedoch nicht ausreichend geklärt, wie die einzelnen Teile miteinander verbunden sind'). See also Schlegel 2005, 30–37.
[7] The concept of iconicity (the analogy between form and content, characteristic of representational images rather than of arbitrary linguistic signs) goes back to the semiotic theory of Charles

with oneself. But while enacting this philosophical ideal, Horace presents himself as a moralist largely devoid of any personal characteristics and, apart from the pun linking *satis, satur,* and *satura,* makes no explicit statements about the genre identity of his poetic diatribes.[8] It is only in S. 1.4 that he endows both his speaker and his text with specific personal and cultural memories. Quite tellingly, both are portrayed as gaining their distinct identities by means of imitation – the speaker imitating moral exempla pointed out by his father and the text imitating its literary models. According to Horace's father, it is only by imitating or avoiding specific *auctores* (122 *habes auctorem quo facias hoc,* 'you have a role model for doing this') that one can become a unique – morally sound – individual, whose *mediocria vitia* allow for a harmonious existence within society.[9] By presenting his poetry as one of such innocuous flaws Horace effectively establishes an analogy between his eclectic self and his intertextual poem. To underscore this analogy, he begins his poem by evoking a few literary *auctores* who have contributed to the unique literary identity of his satires. Lucilius's directness, itself inspired by Old Comedy, is presented as the main inspiration for the content and tone of his *Satires,* while his verbosity and lack of formal elaboration make him the opposite of Horace's own preoccupation with self-sufficiency and formal perfection (1–13). By comparing Lucilius's unpolished style to the famously muddy waters of Callimachus's programmatic *Hymn to Apollo,*[10] Horace stresses that he applies to the Lucilian satiric material the Callimachean ideal of aesthetic purity.[11] And finally, Horace's disingenuous statement that his poems cannot count as poetry at all, because they fail to use Ennius's epic dic-

---

Sanders Peirce. On Peirce's categorisation of different kinds of signs (symbol, index, icon), as well as on the complicated fate of the concept of iconicity in the modern humanities, see De Cuypere 2008. Cf. Kirichenko 2016. Quite importantly, this concept seems to be partly anticipated in Philodemus's poetics, which postulates the fundamental inseparability of *res* and *verba* in poetry: [D.] Armstrong 1995, Porter 1995, Fuhrer 2003. On the relevance on this Epicurean background to Horace's *Satires,* see Oberhelman / Armstrong 1995.
8 Cf. Freudenburg 2001, 18–19 and 23–44.
9 Cf. Oliensis 1998, 24–26. Note, too, that Horace's father, imparting to his son the crucial lesson on the mechanics of ethical imitation, is likely to be himself a product of literary imitation, modelled on an easily recognisable character type of New Attic (and Roman) comedy: Leach 1971; Freudenburg 1993, 33–39.
10 Hor. S. 1.4.11–13. Cf. Call. Ap. 108–109 Ἀσσυρίου ποταμοῖο μέγας ῥόος, ἀλλὰ τὰ πολλὰ | λύματα γῆς καὶ πολλὸν ἐφ' ὕδατι συρφετὸν ἕλκει ('The stream of the Assyrian river is massive, but what it sweeps along in water is silt and a lot of garbage').
11 Scodel 1987; Freudenburg 1993, 158–160 and 2001, 45–46; Oliensis 1998, 22; Zetzel 2002, 40–45; Gowers 2012, 157.

tion,¹² indirectly draws attention to his text's dense conceptual unity, which can remind one of the organic unity ascribed by Aristotle to the plots of the Homeric poems:¹³ in contrast to Ennius, Horace's poem indeed appears to be a stable construction that can by no means be reduced to *disiecti membra poetae* (62 'disjointed limbs of the poet').¹⁴ As a result, poetic intertextuality and moral exemplarity merge into a comprehensive conceptual unity.

The construction of Horace's poetic persona continues in the subsequent poems of *Satires* 1. The emphasis shifts, however, from the generalised moral and aesthetic ideal to the speaker's situation in space and time. In S. 1.5, Horace portrays himself as a humble client accompanying his patron-friend on an important political mission to Brundisium – and enacts his inferior social position by focusing exclusively on meaningless trifles: he obviously knows his place within the social hierarchy and is keen to overstep no boundaries.¹⁵ In S. 1.6, he presents the place he has found for himself among Maecenas's friends as a realisation of the ethical programme formulated in the first three satires: his status as a freedman's son enjoying aristocratic leisure without having to fulfill any aristocratic duties emerges as an embodiment of the golden mean.¹⁶ The anecdotal trivialisation of Brutus's 'regicide' in S. 1.7 implicitly links this newly gained balance to Horace's putting behind him his own involvement in the meaningless chaos of the civil wars,¹⁷ while in S. 1.8 the expulsion of the ominous witch Canidia from the Esquiline – the site of Maecenas's house – by Priapus's fart creates a similarly trivialised image of the seemingly effortless purification of Rome from

---

12 Hor. S. 1.4.39–41 and 57–62. The verses quoted here by Horace (60–61 *postquam Discordia taetra | Belli ferratos postis portasque refregit*, 'when dreadful Discord broke the iron-clad posts and gates of War') are from Ennius's *Annals* (225–226 Skutsch): Gowers 2012 ad loc.
13 Arist. Po. 1450b31–1451a35 (cf. 1459a30–34). Cf. Freudenburg 1993, 149–150; Gowers 2012, 169.
14 Cf. Oberhelman / Armstrong 1995; Oliensis 1998, 23; Gowers 2012, 167.
15 Cf. Fraenkel 1957, 105–112; Ehlers 1985; Gowers 1993b and 2012, 182–186; Freudenburg 1993, 201–205; Oliensis 1998, 26–30; Reckford 1999; Cucchiarelli 2001; Plaza 2006, 262–268; Hooley 2007, 52–55; Schmitzer 2009. On Horace in S. 1.5 practising the theory of satire advocated by him in S. 1.4, see Cucchiarelli 2001, 17–21; Freudenburg 2001, 51–58; Schlegel 2005, 59–76.
16 Horace's insistent emphasis on his servile pedigree (S. 1.6.6, 45–46; probably, a construct derived from the Greek diatribe tradition: Williams 1995) is contrasted with his leisurely existence of philosophical solitude and self-contentment (111–131), which, in the poem's fiction, he has been enabled to enjoy by Maecenas. Cf. Fraenkel 1957, 101–105; Rudd 1966, 36–53; Du Quesnay 1984, 43–52; Oliensis 1998, 34–36; Freudenburg 2001, 58–71; Gowers 2012, 212–219.
17 The litigation between Persius and Rupilius Rex, presided over by M. Brutus – Julius Caesar's tyrannicide, under whose command Horace himself had fought at Philippi (cf. Carm. 2.7) –, ends with a pun on Brutus's 'regicide': S. 1.7.33–35. See Du Quesnay 1984, 36–39; Henderson 1994; Gowers 2002 and 2012, 250–252.

the pollution caused by that chaos.¹⁸ Likewise, the way in which in S. 1.9 Horace jokingly presents himself as rescued by Apollo from an annoying poetaster, who is ready to go to any lengths to infiltrate Maecenas's household, casts the meritocratic circle of Maecenas's friends almost as a divinely protected space of moral and aesthetic purity.¹⁹ Finally, S. 1.10 superimposes onto the literary-critical discourse initiated in S. 1.4 the notion of a close correlation between poetics and history. By stating that, if Lucilius had been transposed to 'our age,' he would purify his poetry of all its imperfections (which essentially amounts to saying that he would write Horatian satire),²⁰ Horace in effect reveals his own poetry as an iconic representation of Octavian's Rome (or rather of Maecenas's circle as the best that contemporary Rome has to offer), which turns out to embody the same principles of self-sufficiency and purity as Horace's persona and Horace's Callimachean poetics.²¹

The tight nexus of ethics, politics, and poetics determines the production of meaning in Horace's later poetry as well. It is most emphatically in *Epistles* 1 that Horace again foregrounds the structural analogies among all three components of this nexus. The poems of *Epistles* 1 pick up many themes rehearsed in *Satires* 1,²² but they are characterised by a radically different structure of authority: unlike in the *Satires*, where Horace stages the process of defining his place within the new Roman establishment, here he has clearly found that place – both literally, at his own country estate, and conceptually, as a successful author of several books of poetry.²³ For that reason, he can afford to communicate with his friends, even with Maecenas himself, from a distance, refusing to write any more lyric poetry, purporting instead to concentrate on what he claims would

---

18 On Canidia as a symbol of the civil wars, see Oliensis 1998, 64–101.
19 Hor. S. 1.9.78 *sic me servavit Apollo*, 'This is how Apollo saved me.' Cf. Fraenkel 1957, 112–118; Rudd 1966, 74–85; Du Quesnay 1984, 52–53; Henderson 1993; Schmitzer 1994, 25–30; Oliensis 1998, 24; Schlegel 2005, 118; Gowers 2012, 303–304. There is a highly suggestive analogy between Apollo protecting the purity of Maecenas's house in S. 1.9 and Apollo advocating the ideal of aesthetic purity in Callimachus's *Hymn to Apollo*, to which Horace alludes at S. 1.4.11–13: cf. Hor. S. 1.9.49 *domus hac nec purior ulla est* ('No house is purer than this one') and Call. Ap. 110–111 Δηοῖ δ' οὐκ ἀπὸ παντὸς ὕδωρ φορέουσι μέλισσαι, | ἀλλ' ἥτις καθαρή ('The bees bring water to Deo not from every source, but only from one that is pure'). Cf. [J. F.] Miller 2009, 39–44.
20 Hor. S. 1.10.67–71. Cf. Du Quesnay 1984, 27–32; Keane 2006, 111–113; Hooley 2007, 64–67; Gowers 2012, 304–309.
21 Cf. Oliensis 1998, 39–41.
22 Cucchiarelli 2010. Cf. Kilpatrick 1986, Johnson 1993.
23 Cf. Oliensis 1998, 155–157, for a comparison between Horace's stance in *Epistles* 1 and three earlier collections dedicated to Maecenas – *Satires* 1, the *Epodes*, and *Odes* 1–3.

better suit his advanced age – the philosophical task of ordering his inner self[24] – and authoritatively imparting to others the ethical lessons that he has learnt in *Satires* 1.[25]

As Horace now portrays himself as an intellectually, poetically, and politically mature individual inhabiting a private space of his own, the system of analogies that he establishes between philosophy, literature, and society undergoes a notable change too. While in *Satires* 1 Horace portrays himself as dependent on his father for constructing his persona out of moral exempla casually observed on the street, in *Epistles* 1 he consciously selects a variety of authoritative philosophical teachings – not only Epicurean, but also Stoic, Aristippean, and Cynic – to create the generalised image of a philosophical life that suits a unique personality.[26] And while in *Satires* 1 the construction of the poet's ethically refined persona serves to underscore the adulatory image of the 'purified' society of Maecenas's circle, in *Epistles* 1 the poet's eclectic self mirrors the composite space of the empire as a whole: on the one hand, Horace's country estate fuses features of seemingly incompatible landscapes into an integrated unity and emerges as a metaphorical projection of the geographically vast empire;[27] on the other, Rome's control over various domains at the empire's borders is presented as responsible for establishing a golden-age-like peace in Italy itself,[28]

---

24 Hor. Ep. 1.1.1–11. Kilpatrick 1986, 1–7; Freudenburg 2002a. On the political significance of a similar *recusatio* in Ep. 2.2, see Freudenburg 2002b. Cf. Johnson 1993, 1–3; Reckford 2002, 2–7; Günther 2010, 1–46.
25 See e.g. Ep. 1.17 and 1.18, where Horace authoritatively explicates to his addressees the mechanics of social advancement, which clearly evokes the process of looking for a niche within the aristocratic establishment staged in *Satires* 1.
26 Moles 2002, esp. 157: '[I]ndividuals must make their own philosophical choices. They must balance one philosophical position against another. They must read and re-read the text, much of whose complexity derives from the poems' kaleidoscopic shifts of viewpoint, which create an interactive dynamic which itself constitutes a kind of Socratic dialectic. And they must constantly interface this complex text with the complexities of life.' On the influence of Philodemus's eclectic Epicureanism on Horace's philosophical outlook in *Epistles* 1, see [D.] Armstrong 2004. Cf. Mayer 1986. On the significance of the epistolary form as a vehicle of philosophical didacticism, see Morrison 2007.
27 Horace describes his estate as combining features of both Tarentum and Thrace (Ep. 1.16.11–14). Cf. Ep. 1.3.3, where the Hebrus is part of a catalogue of imperial landscapes controlled by Rome.
28 Hor. Ep. 1.12.25–29 *ne tamen ignores quo sit Romana loco res, | Cantaber Agrippae, Claudi virtute Neronis | Armenius cecidit; ius imperiumque Phraates | Caesaris accepit genibus minor, aurea fruges | Italiae pleno defudit Copia cornu* ('So that you know how things are in Rome: Cantabria has been crashed by Claudius's valour, Armenia by Tiberius's; Phraates has humbly ac-

which in turn guarantees that Horace can fully dedicate himself to ordering his inner self in the serene isolation of his villa.

Concomitantly, *Epistles* 1 is paradoxically cast as both an aesthetically elitist manifesto of philosophical inwardness and as a potential bestseller whose readership is notionally coextensive with the geographical expanses of the empire – from Rome to North Africa and Spain (Hor. Ep. 1.20.1 and 13 *Uticam... Ilerdam*). In the final poem (Ep. 1.20), Horace pictures a surprising transformation of his philosophically eclectic self into a freshly polished bookroll (2 *Sosiorum pumice mundus*),[29] as desperate for public attention as a young slave prostitute (2 *ut prostes*) – a bookroll destined to be soiled by the dirty fingers of the reading folk (11 *manibus sordescere vulgi*), to be fed on by bookworms (12 *tineas pasces*), to be used by rustic schoolchildren in writing exercises (17–18 *ut pueros elementa docentem | occupet extremis in vicis balba senectus*), and ultimately to preserve forever the fame of the author's transient life wherever the book is read (19–28).[30]

And finally, even more emphatically than *Satires* 1, *Epistles* 1 likens the process of philosophical self-fashioning to the construction of intertextual poetry. Horace describes his moral progress in Ep. 1.1 as similar to literary composition and, at the same time, as a prerequisite for any future writing of poetry.[31] His warning to Celsus in Ep. 1.3 to abstain from plagiarising the classical texts stored in Augustus's library at the temple of Palatine Apollo (there would be nothing left of his poetry if one were to remove all the borrowings)[32] echoes his assertion that his own moral self-fashioning consists in creatively amalgamating, rather than in copying, identifiable philosophical teachings (1.1.13–15). And in a similar vein, in Ep. 1.19 he contrasts the servile crowd of plagiarists (1.19.19 *o imitatores, servum pecus*) with his own transformation of the Greek iambic tradition in the *Epodes*,[33] which in turn forms an analogy to his creative absorption of Greek philosophy in Ep. 1.1. As in *Satires* 1, poetic intertextuality emerges in *Epistles* 1

---

cepted on his knees Caesar's rule; the golden Plenty has poured fruits over Italy from her full horn').
29 For the booksellers Sosii, cf. Hor. Ars 345.
30 Harrison 1988; Ferri 1993, 131–133; Oliensis 1998, 175–181; Trinacty 2012b, 72–74. See also Ferri 1993, 134–137, on connections between Horace's *sphragis* in Ep. 1.20 and the mode of communication characteristic of private funerary inscriptions. Cf. Feeney 2002, 175.
31 Hor. Ep. 1.1.12 *condo et compono* ('I lay foundation and arrange'). For the ambiguity in this phrase, see Moles 2002, 145; Trinacty 2012b, 57 58.
32 Hor. Ep. 1.3.15–20. Cf. Trinacty 2012b, 63–64.
33 Hor. Ep. 1.19.21–24. Cf. Carm. 3.30. Oliensis 1998, 173–174; Freudenburg 2002a, 134–140; Porter 2002, 26–27; Glinatsis 2012; Trinacty 2012b, 68–70. On the importance of the iambic tradition for the overall conception of *Epistles* 1, see Morrison 2006.

as a metaphor for both ethics and politics, staging a notional fusion between the most intimate and the most open of spaces – one's inner self and the empire.

In *Epistles* 1, Horace foregrounds the inextricable interdependence between his poetry and the empire: poetry is cast as both indispensable for conceptualising the imperial world and crucially dependent for its spread and survival on the empire's Latin-speaking readership. In Ep. 2.1, Horace enacts a similar merger between his own persona and the poetic image of Augustus. The *Epistle to Augustus* begins by establishing a contrast between the *princeps*, worshipped as a god during his lifetime, and Horace, who disingenuously wonders why one cannot be considered a canonical poet before one dies (Ep. 2.1.1–27).[34] On a closer look, however, it becomes apparent that the divine status of Augustus is a poetic construct rooted exclusively in Horace's own oeuvre. The divine honours paid Augustus during his lifetime are contrasted with those accorded *post mortem* to Romulus, Bacchus, the Dioscuri, and Hercules (Ep. 2.1.5–17), all of whom are presented in Carm. 4.8 as owing their deification to poetry alone (Carm. 4.8.22–34).[35] Similarly, the altars, at which 'we' worship Augustus, echo Horace's depictions of private sacrifices to Augustus throughout the *Odes*,[36] while the universally shared opinion that 'there will never be, nor has there ever been, anything like Augustus' (Hor. Ep. 2.1.17 *nil oriturum alias, nil ortum tale fatentes*) evokes the passage of Carm. 4.2 in which Horace stresses that 'the fate and the good gods have never given, nor will they ever give, the world anything better' than the *princeps* (4.2.37–39 *quo nihil maius meliusve terris | fata donavere bonique divi | nec dabunt*). Horace then continues to highlight his own contribution to the consolidation of the regime by indirectly alluding to the *Carmen Saeculare* at the very centre of the poem.[37] And finally, towards the end of the epistle Horace lists Augustus's glorious deeds, which, as he disingenuously claims, he would certainly praise in song if only he had the talent; on a closer look, however, this list does not contain a single item that would not find a correspondence in *Odes* 4.[38] Thus, by strategically placing – at the beginning, the middle,

---

[34] Brink 1982, 464–466; Kilpatrick 1990, 5–6.
[35] Cf. Hor. Carm. 3.3.9–18, where the divinity Augustus is similarly assimilated to that of Hercules, the Dioscuri, Bacchus, and Romulus.
[36] Cf. Hor. Ep. 2.1.16 *iurandasque tuum per numen ponimus aras* ('We build altars at which we swear by your divinity') and Carm. 3.14; 4.2.53–60, 4.5.29–40, 4.15.25–32.
[37] Hor. Ep. 2.1.132–138. Fraenkel 1957, 391; Oliensis 1998, 192; Feeney 2002, 181.
[38] Hor. Ep. 2.1.250–257 *nec sermones ego mallem | repentis per humum quam res componere gestas | terrarumque situs et flumina dicere et arces | montibus impositas et barbara regna tuisque | auspiciis totum confecta duella per orbem | claustraque custodem pacis cohibentia Ianum | et formidatum Parthis te principe Romam, | si quantum cuperem possem quoque* ('Rather than these earth-crawling talks | I'd prefer to compose accounts of great deeds, | describe the locations

and the end of the epistle – allusions to his earlier works that have strengthened Augustus's claims to eternity, Horace presents the image of Augustus's immortality as a poetic construction.

But Horace's faux-naïve complaint about not having yet been accorded the status of a classic indirectly acknowledges that his own poetic immortality is intimately linked to his immortalisation of Augustus. By reducing classical Roman poets – the likes of Ennius (Ep. 2.1.50–52) – to a pile of *disiecta membra*,[39] and by presenting contemporary theatrical productions as ephemeral combinations of spectacular effects – with exotic animals, soldiers, and spoils of war inundating the stage with no regard for the meaning or the coherence of the whole (Ep. 2.1.182–201) –[40] he casts his own poetry as the only contemporary art form worthy of being admitted as a new canonical classic into Augustus's library in the temple of Apollo on the Palatine.[41] The contrast between the venal playwright's dependence on the fickle whims of the theatregoing populace and the poet's dependence on Augustus's approval alone serves to corroborate this claim.[42] That Horace's praise of Augustus is an equally important criterion for the canonisation of his work as the work's quality is emphasised by the comparison between poetry and visual art: while Alexander the Great allowed only the best artists – the painter Apelles and the sculptor Lysippus – to portray him the way he wanted to be remembered by posterity (Ep. 2.1.237–241), Augustus has

---

of lands and rivers, forts built | on the peaks of mountains, and barbarous kingdoms, of the end | of all war, throughout the world, by your command, | of the iron bars that enclose Janus, guardian of peace, | of Rome, the terror of the Parthians, ruled by you, | if only I could do as much as I long to'). Cf. Carm. 4.4.17–18; 4.14, esp. 11–12 *arces | Alpibus impositas tremendis* ('Forts built on the peaks of the awe-inspiring Alps'); 4.5, esp. 25 *quis Parthum paveat...?* ('Who would be afraid of the Parthians...?'); 4.15, esp. 4–9 *tua, Caesar, aetas | fruges et agris rettulit uberes | et signa nostro restituit Iovi | derepta Parthorum superbis | postibus et vacuum duellis | Ianum Quirini clausit* ('Caesar, your age has restored rich crops to the fields, at last brought back to our Jupiter the standards snatched from the haughty Parthian pillars, and closed the temple of Janus Quirinus now freed from wars'). On the *recusatio* of Ep. 2.1, see Barchiesi 2001, 83–85; Lowrie 2002; Freudenburg 2014.

39 Horace's criticism here is quite similar to his criticism of Lucilius (and implicitly, Ennius) in S. 1.4: he emphatically stresses that a few successful lines, which one can occasionally find in archaic Roman poetry, are not enough to endow the whole with the sense of comprehensive unity: Hor. Ep. 2.1.73–75. On Horace's critique of canonical Roman poetry in Ep. 2.1, see Brink 1982, 466–475; Kilpatrick 1990, 6–9; Citroni 2013.
40 Goldberg 1996, esp. 271–272. Cf. Feeney 2002, 183 184.
41 Hor. Ep. 2.1.216–218. For Augustus's library on the Palatine as a collection of works that have attained the classical status, see Ep. 1.3.17. Cf. Horsfall 1993, 61–62; Oliensis 1998, 193–194.
42 Hor. Ep. 2.1.213–215. Cf. Brink 1982, 476–482; Kilpatrick 1990, 8–9; Santirocco 1995, 238–242.

been lucky enough to have good poets immortalising his idealised image even more efficiently than visual artists (Ep. 2.1.248–250). Since Virgil and Varius – the only poets he explicitly singles out (Ep. 2.1.247) – are already dead, Horace emerges as the only surviving member of Maecenas's circle who can still carry on the collective effort of immortalising Augustus.[43] His unique status is finally highlighted by the concluding comparison of an inept poetic encomium to an unflattering portrait – the eventual consignment of such an inferior poem to the wastebasket (Ep. 2.1.264–267) once again stressing the crucial dependence of the survival of Augustus's *post mortem* image on the classical status of Horace's poetry. Viewed *sub specie aeternitatis*, Horace and Augustus virtually merge with each other:[44] Augustus's immortality is as crucially dependent on Horace's poetry as the immortality of his poetry is dependent on Augustus's political power and influence.

Thus, throughout his *sermones* (both the *Satires* and the *Epistles*),[45] Horace consistently enacts the analogy between ethics, politics, and poetics. Conspicuously enough, the authenticity of each of these three domains is not predicated upon a unique ontological essence, but originates solely from a creative mixture of multiple preexisting elements. Despite Horace's emphasis on the eclecticism of his philosophical preferences, there is something distinctly Epicurean about the way he uses his intertextual poetics as a metaphor for both nonessentialist ethics and imperial politics. To begin with, Horace's conception of the authenticity of his poetry as an outcome of creative appropriation of multiple literary prototypes is reminiscent of the materialistic poetics of Lucretius, who consistently stresses the analogy between the emergence of the endless diversity of the material world from atoms and the construction of meaning from preexisting elements of language.[46] Furthermore, the emphatic fusion of form and subject matter in Horace's poetry also finds a parallel in Epicurean poetics – in Philodemus's *De Poematis*, where poetic form is conceived of as essentially coextensive (or even identical) with meaning.[47] This conspicuous trait of Horace's poetry is largely in keeping with the strong Epicurean undercurrent that character-

---

[43] Feeney 2002, 174–177.
[44] On the suggestive conflation between Horace and Augustus in the conclusion of Ep. 2.1, see Feeney 2002, 185–187.
[45] On both the *Satires* and the *Epistles* as different kinds of *sermones* (cf. Ep. 2.1.250), see Cucchiarelli 2010.
[46] Cf. Lucr. 2.1018–1021: Beer 2008, 118–165; Noller 2015.
[47] Cf. Phld. Po. 5 Col. 13. [D.] Armstrong 1995; Porter 1995; Beer 2008, 88–106. On connections between Philodemus's Epicurean poetics and Horace, see Oberhelman / Armstrong 1995, Fuhrer 2003, [D.] Armstrong 2004.

ises the poetics of Augustan literature in general, Virgil's indebtedness to Philodemus being perhaps the most notable case in point.[48] Finally, it captures the pervasive stress on artistic creativity not only in Augustan poetry but also, more generally, in Augustan culture and ideology, where the creation of something genuinely new is usually conceived of as synonymous with the projection onto the present of an amalgam of multiple cultural models inherited from the past.[49]

2 Seneca

In the *Satires*, Horace repeatedly contrasts his own – essentially Epicurean – outlook on both ethics and aesthetics with attitudes displayed by the Stoics. Most conspicuously, he opposes his own aesthetic ideal of elaborate precision and harmony between form and meaning with the formless verbosity of Stoic philosophers.[50] In addition, he highlights the advantages of his own ethical pragmatism by juxtaposing it in S. 1.3 with the Stoics' unattainable moral ideal. As I mentioned above, the poem ends by depicting a failed attempt to implement the unrealistic standard of inner cohesion exemplified by the Stoic sage: when confronted with reality, this ideal is effectively shattered to pieces by laughter, leading to the misguided philosopher's metaphorical bursting (136 *rumperis*) and thus making him barely distinguishable from the singer Tigellius Hermogenes, who at the beginning of the poem is cast as the embodiment of inner fragmentation (18–19 *nil fuit umquam | sic impar sibi:* 'there has never been anything so unequal to itself').[51]

Ironically enough, Seneca's writings can be perceived as illustrating the predicament of a Stoic philosopher ridiculed by Horace. Seneca, too, advocates a holistic view of ethics and employs highly verbose protreptic rhetoric in order to inculcate this view in his recipients. Furthermore, Seneca's texts are also thoroughly informed by the anxiety of the imminent disintegration of a seemingly

---

48 See. e.g. the contributions to [D.] Armstrong et al. 2004.
49 The theme comes under extensive investigation in Zanker 1987 and Galinsky 1996.
50 The two (otherwise unknown) Stoics named in Horace's *Satires* by name are Crispinus (1.1.120, 1.3.139, 1.4.14) and Stertinius (2.3), both portrayed as incarnations of senseless longwindedness: Gowers 2012, 84–85; Sharland 2009.
51 Cf. Kemp 2009. Quite tellingly, the singer Hermogenes makes another appearance in the Stoic's – characteristically paradoxical – speech, which completely blurs the distinction between this caricature image of inner disruption and the improbably monolithic self of the Stoic sage (Hor. S. 1.3.129–133). Cf. Freudenburg 1993, 114–117; Gowers 2012, 144.

monolithic worldview, and thus inadvertently reveal the inherent fragility of the Stoic philosophical project in general. But rather than inviting Horace's self-congratulatory satiric laughter,[52] some of Seneca's texts allow one to experience the gap between the schematic constructions of philosophy and the unruliness of the world as a tragic fact of human existence. More specifically, both Seneca's own writings and the later literary tradition of his life invite one to construe the gap between ideal and reality characteristic of Nero's imperial politics as one of the most palpable manifestations of this fundamental non-coincidence. As a result, Seneca's inherently frustrating quest for the forever-receding philosophical ideal turns out to be much better suited for representing the conceptual disintegration of the Neronian empire than Horace's artefact-like construction of Augustan Rome, in which the maker, the medium, and the object of representation forever merge into an indivisible unity.

Seneca's philosophical writings contain occasional passages that seem to echo Horace's analogy between intertextuality and moral exemplarity, in that they stress the formative role that any philosophical or literary text can play in the construction of an integrated self (e.g. Sen. Ep. 8.8). One of the most memorable among these passages can be found in Ep. 84, whose main theme is the role of reading and writing in the process of moral self-improvement. For best results, one should do both, transforming what one has read in books written by others into one's own original texts, the way the bees turn nectar into honey.[53] This Horatian image[54] introduces what reads like a veritable manifesto of 'moral intertextuality,' which evokes the conjunction between nonessentialist ethics and intertextual poetics enacted by Horace most notably in the *Satires* and the *Epistles*.

But this seemingly 'atomistic' view of moral self-fashioning, which goes hand in hand with Seneca's frequent sympathetic references to Epicurean philosophy,[55] emerges in fact as nothing but a concession to the limitations of human

---

[52] Ironically, however, the discrepancy between the unattainable philosophical ideal preached by Seneca and the significantly more lax circumstances of his own life has traditionally – from Tacitus (cf. Ann. 13.42) to modern scholarship – led to vitriolic accusations of hypocrisy, which not only reflect many readers' classicising bias but also accidentally resemble Horace's ridicule of the inherent fragility of the Stoics' idealism. On Seneca's hypocrisy, see Jones 2014, with further references.
[53] Sen. Ep. 84.5–8. See Schönegg 1999, 69–72; Graver 2014, with further references.
[54] Hor. Carm. 4.2.27–32, Ep. 1.3.21. Cf. Pi. P. 10.53–54. To complicate matters, Seneca introduces the apian imagery by quoting at Ep. 84.4 a Virgilian passage (A. 1.432–433): Trinacty 2014, 13–16.
[55] On Epicurus in Seneca's *Epistulae Morales*, see Wildberger 2014, Schiesaro 2015 with further references.

cognition incapable of perceiving the truth all at once.[56] Unlike Horace, Seneca is far from conceiving of literary models and moral exempla as building blocks from which one can construct a cohesive self. Rather, they serve to sharpen one's view on the arduous task of Stoic moral progress understood as a gradual approximation (*oikeiōsis*) of the 'occurrent,'[57] disorderly, self of a *proficiens* to the normative, fully integrated, self of the Stoic *sapiens*.[58] In Seneca, it is this normative ideal that functions as the only true model of imitation.[59] The awareness of the bewildering multiplicity of alternative cultural models is thus only a preliminary step towards empowering one's *hēgemonikon* – the rational self that constitutes the innate core of human personality.[60] In contrast to Horace's construction of the self on the basis of multiple cultural prototypes, the process of therapeutic self-fashioning enacted by Seneca is based on the notion of concentrated self-inspection, which should ideally result in a holistic perception of the truth and in a

---

56 Cf. Sen. Ep. 89.2 *nobis autem, quibus perrumpenda caligo est et quorum visus in proximo deficit, singula quaeque ostendi facilius possunt, universi nondum capacibus* ('We, however, who must break through the mist and whose vision fails even for what is near at hand, can be shown with greater ease each separate object as we are not yet capable of comprehending the totality'). See Kirichenko 2013, 221–222.
57 I.e. empirically observable: see Long 2009.
58 For the concept of *oikeiōsis* in Stoicism, see e.g. Bees 2004; Brennan 2005, 154–168. For *oikeiōsis* in Seneca, see e.g. Sen. Ep. 4–6 and esp. 121. Cf. Wessels 2014, 34–41. For the *sapiens* in Seneca, see Sen. Ep. 9.8–17, 59.14–17, 71.26–28. Cf. Long 2009, 32–33; Bartsch 2006, 192–208; Gill 2006, 249–266 and 2009, 70–76; Jones 2014, 412–413; Bartsch 2015, 188–192; Williams 2015b, 187–190.
59 Cf. Long 2009, 32.
60 Cf. Graver 2007, 21–24. Quite importantly, Seneca repeatedly draws a contrast between the multiplicity of cultural models (conceived of in literary or theatrical terms) and the concentrated process of Stoic self-fashioning. E.g. in Ep. 88 Seneca stresses that the multifaceted erudition that one builds up by studying the *artes liberales* does no harm only as long as it does not distract one from the task of philosophical self-integration, while in Ep. 120 (esp. 22) he points out that one has to recognise that humans are fundamentally *multiformes* – playing throughout their lives a multiplicity of different roles – in order to begin to practise the philosophical ideal consisting in playing only the role of oneself. Cf. Star 2012, 65–69; Bartsch 2015, 193–198. Most crucially, the fact that Seneca corroborates this view by quoting verbatim the Tigellius Hermogenes passage from Horace's S. 1.3 (11–17 = Sen. Ep. 120.20 and Hor. S. 1.3.19 *impar sibi* = Sen. Ep. 120.22) draws attention to the fundamental difference between Horace's and Seneca's conceptions of self-fashioning: while the Horatian self is a well-balanced 'intertextual' mixture of multiple prototypes (contrasted with a slavish copy), the Senecan normative self (the state of being *par sibi*: Sen. Ep. 120.10) is a projection of the unified ideal of Stoic virtue (cf. 120.8 *imaginem... virtutis*).

self-transformation conceived of as a liberation of the self from external accretions.[61]

A similar ideal of normative self-fashioning is presupposed in Seneca's tragedies.[62] But in contrast to the philosophical writings, the tragedies emphatically draw attention to the inherent fragility of that ideal. Most of their characters are aware of being caught in a radically metatheatrical world, in which they have no other choice but to reenact a variety of prefabricated literary models, until that world is – sometimes quite literally – blown to smithereens.[63]

The *Phaedra* is a case in point. Phaedra herself is a split personality who does not seem to possess an identity of her own: not only does she long for what she knows has to be avoided (699 *fugienda petimus*; cf. Horace, S. 1.2.75, 1.3.114 *fugienda petendis*), but she also displays no integrated perception of her experiences, conceptualising them as a mosaic of quotations from her family's mythological past.[64] For instance, she interprets her love for Hippolytus in terms both of Pasiphae's love for the bull and Ariadne's love for Theseus; she wants Hippolytus to be forever banned to the underworld, the way the Minotaur was hidden in the labyrinth; or she compares his dismembered body to one of the Minotaur's victims.[65] In a similar vein, Phaedra's nurse fragments reality by projecting onto it a self-contradictory series of philosophical platitudes: for instance, when she attempts to persuade Phaedra to put an end to her fatal attraction to Hippolytus, she calls the divinisation of love an excuse invented by humans to justify their lack of self-restraint,[66] but when she assesses the odds of talking Hippolytus into an affair with his stepmother, she equates having

---

[61] On self-inspection in Seneca, see Edwards 1997; Bartsch 2006, 191–208; Ker 2009b; Dietsche 2014. On the holistic perception of the truth in Seneca, cf. Sen. Ep. 89.1–2. In Ep. 90 (esp. 90.28–29), Seneca compares the perception of the philosophical truth with an initiation rite. On the importance of such holistic vision for philosophical cognition in Seneca, see Solimano 1991, esp. the chapter 'Visione e conoscenza' (92–103). On self-transformation, see esp. Sen. Ep. 6.1 *intellego, Lucili, non emendari me tantum sed tranfigurari* ('I feel, Lucilius, that I'm being not only reformed but also transformed'). See Edwards 1997, 31–32; Jones 2014, 405–413.
[62] On the fundamental (rhetorical and conceptual) compatibility between *Seneca tragicus* and *Seneca philosophus*, see Kirichenko 2013, esp. 207–279, with further references.
[63] Cf. Boyle 1997, 112–137; Littlewood 2003, 172–258; Fitch / McElduff 2008; Kirichenko 2013, 18–165.
[64] Kirichenko 2013, 35–59. In addition, Phaedra's character is constituted by allusions to earlier Roman poetry. On the intertextual construction of Seneca's Phaedra (with a strong emphasis on Ovidian intertexts), see Trinacty 2014, 67–93.
[65] See Sen. Phaed. 113–119 (Pasiphae and the bull, cf. 142–143 and 687–689: Boyle 1985, 1316–1320); 645–666 (Ariadne and Theseus: [R.] Armstrong 2006, 290–292); 119–123 (Hippolytus as the Minotaur, cf. 174–177); 1170–1173 (Hippolytus as the Minotaur's victim).
[66] Sen. Phaed. 195–203. Wiener 2006, 60–68; [S.] Fischer 2008, 107–115.

(from the legal viewpoint, incestuous) sex with living in accordance with nature.[67]

Hippolytus, on the other hand, appears at first to be fully at one both with himself and with a unified philosophical ideal, as in his self-righteously ascetic life he attempts to put into practice a private version of the mythological golden age.[68] It is thus highly significant that Hippolytus's confrontation with Phaedra's fragmenting view of reality results in a figurative dissolution of his utopian self-perception into a primordial chaos,[69] in a reduction of his seemingly monolithic worldview to the status of a mere fiction,[70] and ultimately in a literal dismemberment of his body, which in the last act of the tragedy is displayed on stage as a formless mass of *disiecta membra*.[71] Theseus, too, is a victim of fragmentation. Reduced to the raw heroism of killing monsters and challenging the powers of the underworld, his character seems at first to be quite monolithic. His determination to have Hippolytus killed also falls into this paradigm, as he perceives his son, too, as the worst imaginable monster.[72] But this seemingly solid identity also falls apart with the dismemberment of Hippolytus's body, whose shocking appearance forces Theseus to recognise his heroic ethos as the ultimate source of his abominable crime (Phaed. 1249 *Hippolytus hic est? crimen agnosco meum*, 'Is this Hippolytus? I recognise my crime').

Thus, the spectacle of Hippolytus's disintegrated body is figured in the play as a dismantlement of a worldview that consists exclusively of borrowed literary discourses. The conspicuous contrast between Phaedra's and Theseus's reactions to this spectacle further underscores the philosophical momentum of the play. To Phaedra, the void that emerges from the instantaneous realisation of

---

[67] Sen. Phaed. 481 *proinde sequere naturam ducem* ('Then follow nature as your guide'). Cf. Ep. 5.4.
[68] Sen. Phaed. 525–539. Cf. Ov. Met. 1.89–112. See Segal 1986, 77–105; Critelli 1998; Bellandi 2007, 66–70.
[69] Sen. Phaed. 674–676 *omnis impulsus ruat | aether et atris nubibus condat diem, | ac versa retro sidera obliquos agant | retorta cursus* ('Let the entire sky collapse and hide the light of day with black clouds, let the stars veer from their courses and move in the opposite direction').
[70] Sen. Phaed. 915–919 *ubi vultus ille et ficta maiestas viri | atque habitus horrens, prisca et antiqua appetens, | morumque senium triste et affectus graves? | o vita fallax, abditos sensus geris | animisque pulcram turpibus faciem induis* ('Where is this man's feigned earnestness of expression, that rugged look of his imitating the olden ways, his moral severity rivalling that of an elder, his serious behaviour? O dishonest life, you conceal your true thoughts deep inside and put a pretty mask on a base spirit'): Trinacty 2014, 45–46.
[71] Sen. Phaed. 1256–1258 *disiecta genitor membra laceri corporis | in ordinem dispone et errantes loco | restitue partes* ('Arrange in order, father, the torn limbs of this mangled body and put together in one place the scattered fragments'). Cf. Most 1992; Kirichenko 2013, 41–42.
[72] Cf. Boyle 1985, 1318–1319; Kirichenko 2013, 48–49.

the fictitiousness – falseness – of such a 'literary' life is synonymous with her life's end.[73] To Theseus, on the contrary, it marks a new beginning. The last scene of the tragedy, in which Theseus attempts to put together his son's fragmented body, is a strikingly vivid image that highlights the arduousness of constructing even a semblance of unity in the midst of discursive confusion. Quite significantly, this attempt is presented as a potentially never-ending and painfully frustrating process, since there are simply too many disfigured pieces that have to be put together and since its goal consists in making Hippolytus's dead body fit for burial.[74] But what the futility of this process forces one to recognise is, most importantly, the fundamental pointlessness of any attempt to construct one's self from borrowed discourses – a realisation that in the world of Seneca's philosophical writings would function as an indispensable precondition for the beginning of a Stoic self-transformation.

Thus, while Horace draws an analogy between moral self-fashioning and poetic intertextuality, Seneca emphatically contrasts the amalgamation of preexisting cultural discourses with the process of attaining the ideal of integrated selfhood. A similar difference can be observed in the images that Horace and Seneca draw of imperial politics. As we have seen, in the *Epistle to Augustus* Horace foregrounds the function of his poetry as forever preserving the literary construction of Augustus's immortality. To underscore the immortalising nature of such a poetic image, Horace implicitly contrasts it in *Odes* 4 with the image of the transient human body that one sees reflected in the mirror: the image of one's physical decay displayed by the mirror is presented as effectively ruptured by time – the mirror symbolising both the subject's anxiety about the future and his / her longing for the past;[75] by contrast, a poetic memorial creates an autonomous reality, which consists in an ingeniously crafted arrangement of literary reminiscences,

---

[73] On Phaedra's suicide, see Palmieri 1999, 47–82.
[74] Note that Theseus's re-fashioning of his son's dead body is referred to as *corpus fingere* (1265), which further emphasiszes the illusory status of the entire enterprise (cf. 195–196 *deum esse amorem turpis et vitio favens | finxit libido*; 915 *ficta maiestas*; 1194 *mentita finxi*), and that the reconstruction is emphatically provisional and almost arbitrary: Sen. Phaed. 1265–1268 *hoc quid est forma carens | et turpe, multo vulnere abruptum undique? | quae pars tui sit dubito; sed pars est tui: | hic, hic repone, non suo, at vacuo loco* ('What's this ugly, shapeless thing, torn with wounds on all sides? I don't know which part it is; but it's a part of you. Put it here, here – not in its own place but an empty place').
[75] The image of the mirror explicitly appears only in Carm. 4.10, where Horace predicts that Ligurinus will regret his current unresponsiveness to the poet's erotic advances when he grows old and sees his changed appearance in the mirror: Hor. Carm. 4.10.6–8. Cf. Putnam 1986, 177–183. But the remaining 'non-political' poems of *Odes* 4 also function like notional mirrors reminding their beholders of the relentless passage of time. Cf. Hor. Carm. 4.1, 11, 12, 13.

and is therefore largely insusceptible to the vicissitudes of temporal reality.[76] In a striking contrast to Horace, Seneca constructs his idealised image of Nero in *De Clementia* as a metaphorical mirror. Unlike Horace's mirror, however, the Senecan one does not reflect physical transience but postulates the normative notion of the ideal ruler in which Nero is encouraged to recognise himself.[77] Significantly enough, although in *De Clementia* Augustus constitutes the main model for the new emperor,[78] Nero is declared to be by far superior to his predecessor. The main reason for his superiority is that, unlike the historically and culturally complex image of Augustus, the image of young Nero is in effect a *tabula rasa* untainted by any painful memories of the past.[79] Concurrently, this pristine image cannot be presented as an intertextual construct of the kind that Horace creates in order to immortalise Augustus but is understood as a natural given, which Nero is now expected to bring to fruition.[80] In a sense, Nero's self-recognition in this normative image is analogous to the process of *oikeiōsis*, the approximation of the 'occurrent' self of a *proficiens* to the fully integrated self of a Stoic *sapiens*, which Seneca sometimes conceptualises in his philosophical writings in terms of specular self-inspection.[81] In this case, however, Nero's task does not consist in self-improvement but in preserving the purity of the innate perfection attributed to him by Seneca.[82] Moreover, Seneca projects the same conceptual schema onto imperial society at large. While Horace's textualised Augustus is akin to an artefact placed in a cultic context, which turns Rome

---

[76] As in Ep. 2.1, in Carm. 4.8 Horace draws an analogy between poetry and visual art (giving preference to the former: 1–12) and emphasises that it is not the praiseworthy deeds per se but the fact that they have been mentioned in poetry that serves to immortalise the *laudandus* (22–27): Thomas 2011, 185–186. Similarly, the fact that in Carm. 4.9 Horace praises the Augustan general Lollius, who had only recently suffered a devastating defeat from the Gauls (the so-called *clades Lolliana*: Tac. Ann. 1.10.3, Suet. Aug. 23; cf. Ambrose 1965, Sage 1994), as the embodiment of an entire catalogue of standard philosophical virtues shows that the poet's power consists precisely in granting immortality to anyone he chooses and on any grounds he sees fit.
[77] Sen. Cl. 1.1.1 *scribere de clementia, Nero Caesar, institui, ut quodam modo speculi vice fungerer et te tibi ostenderem perventurum ad voluptatem maximam omnium* ('I have decided to write about clemency, Nero Caesar, so that I can act as some kind of mirror and show you to yourself as one who will reach the greatest pleasure of all'). Armisen-Marchetti 2006; Bartsch 2006, 183–229; Rimell 2015b, 124–126.
[78] Sen. Cl. 1.9.1–12 and 1.15.3–16.1
[79] Cf. Sen. Cl. 1.11.1–3. On the image of Augustus in *De Clementia*, see Braund 2009, 61–64.
[80] Bartsch 2006, 184.
[81] Cf. Sen. Dial. 4.36.1: Bartsch 2006, 187–188; Ker 2009b, 180–181.
[82] Note, too, that the ideal self displayed by Nero is not a casually donned mask but the emperor's true essence: Sen. Cl. 1.1.6. Like the Stoic sage of Ep. 120.22 (see note 60 above), Seneca's Nero only plays the role of himself. Cf. Bartsch 2006, 227–228.

into a community of grateful worshippers powerfully drawn to that image and yet adoring it from a respectful distance,[83] Seneca's image of Nero is deeply essentialist. Just as the ideal ruler reflected in Seneca's mirror functions in a manner analogous to the Stoic *hēgemonikon*,[84] so Nero himself is portrayed as a kind of normative mirror for his subjects: he is supposed to rule them by offering himself for imitation and to infuse the state with life the way the mind animates the body (cf. Sen. Cl. 1.4.1).[85]

Inevitably, the image displayed in Seneca's normative mirror is much more unstable than the one produced by Horace's immortalising memorial. While Horace's intertextual construct is emphatically immune to the passage of time, the functioning of Seneca's mirror is very much dependent on the future actions of the object it purports to reflect. This realisation suffuses Seneca's text with profound anxiety: as he explicitly points out, any deviation from the postulated norm would plunge the utopia he constructs into a state of primordial chaos.[86] Needless to say, the subsequent historical development of Nero's 'occurrent self' will justify Seneca's anxiety with a vengeance. Thus, Seneca's idealised image of Nero in *De Clementia*, ironically enough, proves to be as prone to disintegration as the utopian self-perception of Seneca's Hippolytus, which similarly results in a notional cosmic catastrophe.

It is highly revealing that the inherent vulnerability of Seneca's political utopia constitutes one of the main themes of the pseudo-Senecan *Octavia* – one of the earliest instances of Senecan reception in Latin literature.[87] Like Hippolytus in the *Phaedra*, Seneca in this play is a character whose seemingly coherent ethics is shattered to pieces by a confrontation with recalcitrant reality. Unsurprisingly, his musings on the advantages of philosophical seclusion over the prominent position at the top of imperial politics include a cliché-ridden – as in the *Phaedra*, essentially Ovidian – description of the golden age, which he contrasts with the veritable cosmic dissolution that is the reign of Nero.[88] The reasons for

---

[83] Cf. e.g. Hor. Carm. 1.2, 3.3, 3.14, 4.5, 4.15; Ep. 2.1.16–17.
[84] On the Stoic background of *De Clementia*, see Braund 2009, 64–73, with further references.
[85] Cf. Scipio's Stoicising view at Cicero, *De Re Publica* 2.69 that one of the functions of the ideal ruler is *ut sese... sicut speculum praebeat civibus* ('to show himself... as a mirror to the citizens').
[86] Sen. Cl. 1.4.2 *tam diu ab isto periculo aberit hic populus quam diu sciet ferre frenos, quos si quando abruperit vel aliquo casu discussos reponi sibi passus non erit, haec unitas et hic maximi imperii contextus in partes multas dissiliet* ('This people will stay away from that danger as long as it knows how to endure the reins; for if it ever breaks them or does not allow them to be restored after they have been shaken off by some chance, this unity and this cohesion of the great empire will disintegrate into many parts').
[87] Boyle 2008, xiii–xvi. Cf. Taylor 2010.
[88] Oct. 391–434. Cf. Ov. Met. 1.89–150. For further parallels, see Boyle 2008, 174–181.

Seneca's disillusionment become apparent in his dialogue with Nero, where countless near-quotations from *De Clementia* are revealed as meaningless hot air by the emperor, who stubbornly refuses to recognise himself in Seneca's utopian mirror.[89] As a result, this mirror effectively breaks into pieces, leaving Seneca himself almost as fragmented and as unequal to himself as the characters (which, as I mentioned above, include Stoic philosophers) that Horace sketches in the *Satires* to highlight the stable construction of his own Epicurean persona.

Thus, both Seneca's literary works (philosophical and dramatic alike) and the later literary tradition of his life reveal the gap between the urgency of implementing the philosophical ideal of integrated selfhood and the arduousness, or even the impossibility, of reaching that ideal:[90] while the images that Horace constructs both of himself and of his world are conceived of as ingeniously crafted artefacts designed to preserve forever their reassuringly idealised view of the reign of Augustus, the images created by Seneca both in the tragedies and in the *Epistulae Morales* are thoroughly infused with desire for what may in fact be utterly unattainable. This drastic difference manifests itself at the level of literary expression as well. As I argued above, Horace's Epicurean poetics foregrounds the fundamental constructedness of his poetry, whose goal consists in preserving forever an artefact-like image of Augustan Rome and whose meaning emerges from an intricate interplay between obliquely evoked intertextual memories and subtly drawn analogies between form and subject matter. Seneca, on the other hand, is preeminently concerned with immediately affecting his recipients, both emotionally and cognitively, in order to make them change the way they perceive reality and ultimately to change the way they are.[91] The protreptic nature of much of Seneca's literary production is largely responsible for some of the most conspicuous characteristics of his poetics.

It is a commonplace of ancient rhetorical theory that one of the most efficient ways of cajoling the recipient into acting in the manner intended by the speaker consists in *enargeia* – a rhetorical technique designed to make the recipient experience the illusion of seeing with her own eyes the images, or *phantasiai*, of what is being described by the speaker.[92] Significantly enough, there is a terminological overlap between this aspect of rhetorical theory and Stoic episte-

---

[89] Oct. 435–592. Cf. Manuwald 2002; Braund 2009, 80–82. For parallels, see Boyle 2008, 181–217.
[90] Cf. Long 1996, 150–151; Jones 2014, 402–403.
[91] On the protreptic nature of Seneca's tragedies, see Kirichenko 2013, 207–279.
[92] Webb 2009. See e.g. Plu. Mor. 347a; Quint. Inst. 6.2.29–30. Pseudo-Longinus sees the effect of 'rhetorical *phantasia*' as the virtual enslavement of the listener: Ps.-Longin. Subl. 15.9. Goldhill 2007, 4.

mology,⁹³ which postulates sense impressions – also called *phantasiai* – as the sole basis not only of human cognition⁹⁴ but also of human action: the so-called cognitive impression (*phantasia katalēptikē*) is understood as being so vivid (*enargēs*) as to effect in the beholder a kind of inner transformation (*alloiōsis*: D.L. 7.50), to force her to accept the truthfulness of the impression,⁹⁵ and ultimately to act on the basis of that acceptance.⁹⁶ While Horace, as Philip Hardie appositely points out, is 'one of the least pictorial of Latin poets,'⁹⁷ Seneca demonstrates an inordinate propensity for emotionally charged, emphatically pictorial, visualisations – both in the tragedies and in the philosophical writings.⁹⁸ By resorting to visualising rhetoric, Seneca effectively turns techniques taught by rhetorical theory into an instrument of Stoic cognition, creating vivid secondary sense impressions designed to enable the recipient to undergo an instantaneous inner transformation.⁹⁹ In order to enhance the protreptic / therapeutic effect of this rhetoric, Seneca employs different forms of affective *amplificatio* (constructing individual sentences, larger passages, or even entire dramatic plots as crescendos that gradually heighten the emotional pitch from the relatively harmless to the virtually unbearable)¹⁰⁰ in order to make the recipients more receptive to

---

93 *Pace* Bartsch 2007, who postulates a radical distinction between the 'philosophical *ekphrasis* or *phantasia*' and the 'rhetorical / poetic *ekphrasis* or *phantasia*.' For the terminological continuity, see e.g. Ps.-Longin. Subl. 15.11; Kirichenko 2013, 225–233.
94 See e.g. D.L. 7.49, LS 39 A, *SVF* 2.52.
95 Cf. S.E. M. 7.255, LS 40K. Gerson 2009, 100–111.
96 Stob. 2.88.2–6. On the Stoic notion of *phantasia*, see Long / Sedley 1987, 238–243; Watson 1988, 38–58; Brennan 2005, 51–61; Wildberger 2006, 338–340; Wessels 2014, 141–160.
97 Hardie 1993, 120.
98 Cf. Solimano 1991; Schönegg 1999, 179–194; Aygon 2004. Needless to say, the visuality of Seneca's rhetoric is by far not the only conspicuous characteristic of his style. On further aspects of literary form in Seneca's writings, see Traina 1987, Armisen-Marchetti 1989, Setaioli 2000, Williams 2015a.
99 Seneca repeatedly highlights the transformative effect of emotionally charged 'impressions' both in the tragedies and in the prose works (cf. Sen. Ep. 57.6 *sensi ergo, ut dicebam, quandam non quidem perturbationem, sed mutationem*: 'So, as I said, what I felt was not some kind of inner commotion, but a transformation') and constructs his own texts as such potentially transformative 'impressions.' Kirichenko 2013, esp. 207–248.
100 Again, Seneca not only repeatedly describes the process of rising affective intensity (e.g. Sen. Ep. 7, esp. 7.3; Thy. 744–745; Med. 904–905) but also enacts it in his writings – particularly in the tragedies, whose last scenes, featuring raw spectacles of bodily dismemberment or mutilation, are routinely presented as surpassing in horror the increasingly harrowing literary images with which the recipient has been bombarded in the course of each play: Seidensticker 2007 (on the *comparativus Senecanus*); Kirichenko 2013, 17–165 (and 225–230, on similar strategies in prose writings).

the philosophical cure.[101] It is precisely the predominance of this crescendo pattern that seems to be partly responsible for the notorious disregard for the internal consistency of plot and character in Seneca's tragedies[102] – a feature that stands in stark contrast not only to Horace's classicist precepts in the *Ars Poetica* but also to his practice of constructing well-balanced poetic artefacts.

And finally, the contrast between the memorialising function of Horace's poetic constructs and the protreptic immediacy of Seneca's visuality is symptomatic of the transformation of Roman culture from Augustus to Nero. While Augustan culture constantly foregrounds innovation achieved through creative appropriation of multiple cultural models, Neronian (and, more generally, imperial) culture is preeminently concerned with an emulative theatricality that aims to create the illusion that observable reality greatly surpasses its cultural prototypes in myth, literature, and history (including Augustus as a model for Nero).[103] Seneca's rhetorical crescendos certainly reflect this overall emulative tendency. But as in other Neronian authors (Persius, Lucan, and Petronius),[104] Seneca's motivation for laying bare the hopelessly imitative character of contemporary culture seems to consist primarily in the desire to highlight the desperate urgency of striving for the forever-unattainable ideal of – aesthetic and ethical – authenticity.

---

101 In order to heal, Seneca's Stoic therapy must hurt. Cf. Epict. 3.23.30 ἰατρεῖόν ἐστιν, ἄνδρες, τὸ τοῦ φιλοσόφου σχολεῖον· οὐ δεῖ ἡσθέντες ἐξελθεῖν, ἀλλ' ἀλγήσαντας ('The philosopher's school is a surgery room: one must leave it after enduring pain, not pleasure'). Perhaps this explains Seneca's propensity for graphic representations of suffering and violence both in the prose works and in the tragedies: Edwards 1999, Wessels 2014.
102 Cf. Kirichenko 2013, 230–248, with further references.
103 Cf. Bartsch 1994, 1–62; Schiesaro 2003, 13–16; Ker 2009a, 113–146; Kirichenko 2013, 169–205; Littlewood 2015, Rimell 2015b. For the age of Nero as a superior version of the age of Augustus, cf. Sen. Apoc. 4.1.3–9 and Calp. Ecl. 1.77–88: Kirichenko 2013, 173–180, with further references. Note also that Seneca conceived of himself as emulating Maecenas: Mayer 1982, 315; Ker 2015, 120.
104 On a similar tension between derivativeness and authenticity in Persius, Lucan, and Petronius, see Kirichenko 2014, with further references.

IV **Modes of Quotation and Issues of Reception**

Ute Tischer
Nostra faciamus. Quoting in Horace and Seneca

A quotation, in the literary sense, is a marked reference of one text to another realised via a partial repetition of the other text. According to this basic definition, the quoting author makes explicit in some way that he is referring to the quoted text, and, consequently, puts himself in a relation to this text. By including parts of a previous utterance, he allows someone else's *Weltanschauung* to enter his own speech, and may also indicate the kind of discourse in which he is taking part.

In this contribution, I would like to describe and compare the ways in which Seneca in his *Epistulae Morales* and Horace in his *Satires* and *Epistles* use quotation. Both authors are clearly in favour of literary quotation and both use it in all its variety: as an allusive echo, as a covert reminiscence, as an anonymous statement, as a reference, or as a word-for-word rendition that includes an identification of the source. Both are similar in their critical standpoint when it comes to moral issues but differ in their choice of genre. This relationship of similarity and difference renders a comparison between them useful and interesting, and allows us to ask about the conditions that serve as a basis for quotation, as well as the form and the function of quoting. In what follows, I therefore will focus on two aspects: first, the conditions under which similar citational forms occur in each of the two corpora and second, why formally similar quotations may nevertheless serve different communicative purposes. The main focus in this study will be on distinctly marked references.

A comparison will establish a relationship between Horace and Seneca and uncover several lines of connection in style and subject matter; at the same time, it will also highlight several differences between the two poets' corpora. The outline of my study suggests that we look for explanations for these similarities and differences first of all in contexts and attitudes both authors either share or do not share. Consequently, the main aim of my argument will not be to either establish or refute a relationship of literary reception between the two authors. At the end, however, I shall briefly touch on the vexing question as to why Seneca cites Horace's works as rarely as he does, proposing as a possible answer the differences between the two poets' attitudes towards quoting.

My study will be conducted in five steps: (1) in a short theoretical section I would first like to define the most important criteria of comparison that serve to describe both quotations and the process of quoting. (2) After that I will provide an overview of the formal characteristics of the quotations found in both authors, before (3) exemplarily analysing two pairs of quotations from Seneca and Horace in order to demonstrate the connection of form and function in quotation by means of concrete examples. I will then (4) identify several contextual features that serve as the authors' guidelines for quoting. In a final step (5) I will discuss the extent to which the similarities and differences found between the authors may either be explained through contextual factors or as concrete decisions of literary reception.

1 Descriptive Categories of Quotation and a Model of Quoting

A quotation can be described as a sequence of signs that is part of a text and has a special semantic status within it. This status is due to an act of reference, i.e. due to the sequence in question being a noticeable repetition of another text. It is this manifest act of either word-for-word or analogous repetition that I designate by the term 'quoting'; the result of this act is a quotation.[1]

In contrast to the actual process of quoting, the quotation itself can be observed in the text and therefore also described. Following the definition that I have just provided, quotations may essentially be distinguished and defined by four integral features: every quotation (1) is part of a quoting text, (2) stems from a certain pre-text, (3) is embedded and reproduced in a certain way, and (4) is marked in some way or other by the quoting text as a quotation.[2] Every quotation is realised according to these four categories – quoting text, pre-text, quotation segment, and marking – but each category may manifest itself differently at different times.

The effect and function of a quotation within the quoting text, however, cannot be fully ascertained by this method; full comprehension may only be achieved by a shift in focus from the actual quotation to the act of quoting as a communicative process. Besides the quoting text itself, the parties involved in this form of communication are (1) the citing author and (2) the reader as an interpreter. Furthermore, this is an intertextual form of communication, in that both of these communicative partners need to turn to the cited pre-text for it to work. A precondition for this is that both quoting author and his reader are willing to work together: the author reads and interprets the pre-text, selects

---

[1] Compagnon 1979, 50–55; cf. Böhn 2007, 843.
[2] On the categories of the characteristics of quotations see Plett 1988; Holthuis 1993, 89–113.

the sequence to be quoted, inserts it in his own text, and marks it as a repetition. The reader, in turn, recognises the passage as a quotation and activates his knowledge of the quotation's origin to make sense of it.

In order for this indirect form of communication to be successful, a cultural bond between author and recipient is a further prerequisite. For one thing, this implies the need for a 'grammar of quoting,' i.e. for a system of signs that author and reader share and that regulates what may be considered a quotation, what it can mean, what can be cited in the first place, etc. For another thing, the act of quoting involves the communicative partners' shared contexts and shared cultural knowledge: for example, knowledge of the pre-text as the quotation's point of reference, knowledge of the current communicative situation (which in this case would, *inter alia*, be partly defined by the genre of the quoting text),[3] and finally knowledge of the rules and norms of quoting that apply in the particular situation. As a consequence, if we wish to interpret a quotation and grasp its specific, intertextual meaning, we need to ask (1) how the act of quoting as a communicative process between author and reader is shaped by certain framing conditions and (2) what the intended communicative goals might be.[4]

A comparison of the citational styles of Horace and Seneca thus needs to proceed from a description of the quotations found in their texts, this description being based on the four integral characteristics of all quotations mentioned above, i.e. the features of quoting text and the quoted text, faithfulness to the original text, and the way the quotation is marked. On the basis of these textual observations, individual quotations ought to be compared, with especial attention paid to the way in which the intertextual communication between citing author and reader proceeds. A prerequisite for this, in turn, is the identification of the framing conditions, i.e. of the concepts and notions that influence quoting.

---

[3] On the prescription of norms conditioned by the genre of the quoting text see Plett 1988, 89.
[4] Cf. Tischer 2010, 99–103. The extension of the communicative model by an intertextual dimension is described by Stocker 1998, esp. 99; cf. also Compagnon 1979, 55–57. On intertextual reading see Holthuis 1993, esp. 29–39.

2 The Practice of Quotation in Horace's Hexametric Poetry and Seneca's *Epistulae Morales ad Lucilium*

2.1 Quotation in Horace

Horace's *Satires* and *Epistles* are hexametric poems, although their titles suggest that they are prose works. They therefore belong to an area of literary production to which ancient critics have assigned a set of functions and aesthetic norms different from those ascribed to prose. When it comes to intertextuality, the use of allusive dialogue is especially characteristic of Latin poetry. The term 'allusive dialogue' here denotes a technique of 'competition' (*aemulatio*) between authors and their literary precursors carried out via allusive reminiscences. Typically, the sources are not explicitly mentioned, and the passages taken from the pre-text are modified and recombined. Apart from distant echoes, in the case of such reminiscences the text offers no assistance to the reader; instead it asks for his cooperation and challenges his literary competence.[5] Horace, too, stands in this tradition, not just in his *Odes* but also in his hexametric poems: a kind of intertextual dialogue may be observed in his texts, which mainly manifests itself in implicit markings of citations and paraphrases, and typically refers back to other poetic texts, e.g. to Lucilius, his precursor in satire, or to Lucretius as a philosophical point of reference.[6]

Next to these typically poetic allusions, however, there are also a considerable number of references in which Horace either names the pre-text explicitly, or gives a virtually literal rendition of the text, or sometimes even both. To this end, Horace draws on poetic texts as well as on prose, mentions Latin as well as Greek names, and in some cases sticks surprisingly close to the wording of even rather long source passages.[7]

All in all, about forty such quotations can be discerned in Horace's *Satires* and *Epistles*, i.e. a frequency of roughly one such quotation in 3.5 pages or in

---

[5] Important studies are Pasquali 1942, Conte 1974, Farrell 1991, Clausen 2002.
[6] Regarding Horace's reception of Lucilius cf. *inter alia* Fiske 1966; Tarrant 2007, 67–69; Schlegel 2010; regarding Lucretius cf. Giesecke 2000, 95–131.
[7] Examples would be e.g. S. 1.2.37–38 (Enn. Ann. 494–495 Skutsch); 1.2.92 (Philodem. AP 5.132.1); S. 1.4.60–61 (Enn. Ann. 225–226 Skutsch; cf. Porph. Hor. S. 1.4.56–57); S. 2.3.61–62 (Pac. Iliona v. 197 Ribbeck) and S. 2.3.259–271 (Ter. Eu. 46–63); see below section 3.1.

ninety lines of verse.⁸ Their distribution, however, is irregular: five of the eighteen satires and thirteen of the twenty-two epistles do not use this kind of quotation, and the second book of the *Epistles* is almost free of such reminiscences.⁹ Precise citations such as those just described would not be conspicuous in a prose text. In comparison with other examples of Roman poetry, especially epic poetry and drama, however, such forms of citation and their accumulation are indeed very unusual. One possible interpretation of these findings is that when it comes to these quotations Horace is modelling his technique of citation on that of prose.

2.2 Quotation in Seneca

Seneca, with his mixture of diatribe and epistolary forms (discussed by Del Giovane in this volume), stands in the tradition of philosophical prose shaped by Cicero. Many features of Cicero's quoting style in his philosophical oeuvre, to which Seneca explicitly refers,[10] can be recognised in the *Epistulae Morales*.[11] A striking feature is the frequency of citations marked in such a way that they can easily be recognised as quotations.[12] Very often, they are embedded as direct or indirect speech, and so marked as part of a former speech context.[13] On top of

---

[8] Measured by the Teubner edition of Shackleton Bailey 2008, 165–309, in which the *Satires* and *Epistles* (spanning 3612 lines of verse) take up 144 pages.

[9] The pieces richest in quotations are S. 1.2 (six quotations), 2.3 (four quotations), and Ep. 1.19 (five quotations); there are only two proper quotations in the second book of *Epistles* (485 lines of verse).

[10] Sen. Ep. 107.10–11. However, Seneca shows only superficial similarities to the very allusive quoting style used in Cicero's letters, which is very different in nature and often witty; cf. Coleman 1974, 279–280; 287.

[11] On Cicero's quotations in his philosophical writings see Spahlinger 2005 as well as Salamon 2004 and 2006. A comparison of poetic quotations in Cicero's and Seneca's philosophical works is provided by Dueck 2009.

[12] Two hundred and sixty citations and references can be found in Seneca's 124 surviving epistles; in Reynolds's Oxford edition from 1965, in which the *Epistulae Morales* take up about 540 pages, this yields a frequency of roughly one quotation in two pages, cf. the overview of Gambla 1981, 125–130. In the *Tusculanae Disputationes*, Cicero's richest work when it comes to quotations, the frequency is about 1.5 quotations per page (ca. 185 quotations in 277 pages in the edition by Fohlen / Humbert 1931).

[13] One might offer Ep. 5.7, with its quotation from Hecato, as one example of this rendering of quotation as 'speech': *Sed ut huius quoque diei lucellum tecum communicem, apud Hecatonem nostrum inveni cupiditatum finem etiam ad timoris remedia proficere. 'Desines' inquit 'timere, si sperare desieris.' Dices, 'quomodo ista tam diversa pariter sunt?' Ita est, mi Lucili: cum videantur*

that, further explicit or implicit forms of marking may be added, such as identification of the source by name, citational formulae, or clear contrast with the surrounding co-text. The texts and genres from which Seneca quotes are diverse; specific types of pretext tend to be coupled with specific forms of presentation and marking. Seneca cites prose texts in particular, mainly the precursors of his own genre, by explicitly naming his source and often also by using indirect speech, although rarely in a word-for-word rendition. This, too, conforms to Ciceronian practice since, as was already the case for Cicero, the majority of Seneca's prose quotations are taken from Greek philosophical works; just like Cicero, Seneca translates his Greek quotations into Latin and by doing so adapts them to the language of the quoting text.[14]

Almost half of the quotations found in the *Epistulae Morales*, however, do not derive from prose but rather from Latin (and sometimes also from Greek) poetry.[15] Unlike prose citations, these quotations very often occur without any indication of source and frequently even without any verbal marker indicating the presence of a quotation.[16] Their presentation, however, almost always sticks so closely to the actual wording that the metre of the cited passage remains discernible.[17] This preservation of metrical form is of such apparent importance that Seneca even translates Greek lines of verse metrically into Latin in certain instances.[18] The implicit nature of the marking and the high degree of faithfulness

---

dissidere, coniuncta sunt. 'But I wish to share with you today's profit also. I find in the writings of our Hecato that the limiting of desires helps also to cure fears: "Cease to hope," he says, "and you will cease to fear." "But how," you will reply, "can things so different go side by side?" In this way, my dear Lucilius: though they do seem at variance, yet they are really united.' (All translations of Seneca's letters here and in what follows are from the Loeb edition of Gummere). See also below n. 46.

14 Unlike in Cicero's published works, Greek quotations are not completely ruled out here; a literal rendition in the original language (Metrodorus) can be found in Ep. 99.25, and another one in *De Ira*, Dial. 3.1.20.8 (Homer); on the treatment of Greek quotes see Setaioli 1988, esp. 23–24; 47–91.

15 One hundred and sixteen of about 260 quotations, i.e. ca. 47%, are poetic quotations. A very large proportion of these are quotations from Virgil (65 of 116, i.e. 56%).

16 Out of all of the 116 poetic quotations, 66 are cited without indication of source.

17 One hundred and three of the 116 references to poetry are rendered in metre; this does not automatically imply that they are faithful renderings as well, but as far as it can be verified through surviving pre-texts Seneca mostly renders these quotes word-for-word.

18 Ep. 107.11 (a hymn by Cleanthes, SVF fr. 527 von Arnim), 115.14 (apparently a compilation of verses by Euripides, cf. fr. adesp. 181.1, 461, 326 Nauck²). Another verse by Euripides in Ep. 49.12 (Ph. 469) is merely rhythmised, in Ep. 63.2 two passages by Homer are paraphrased (Hom. Il. 19.228–229, 24.602–617), another two in Ep. 40.2 (Hom. Il. 3.221–222, 1.247–249).

to the original text are obviously connected here:[19] by inserting a metrical passage into a prose text, a formal contrast is produced between the surrounding text and the citation, a dislocation that may be further heightened by stylistically and textually conspicuous features. This contrast leads to the prominence of such passages on account of their very form, so that further marking becomes unnecessary.[20] This, in turn, creates opportunities for other types of covert quoting, in which the citation may remain discernible as 'guest' speech, to adapt the terminology of Stephen Harrison,[21] or may be virtually 'incorporated' into the author's own 'host' speech. Even though Seneca makes creative use of these possibilities, he generally follows the practice established at least since Cicero in his use of poetic quotations, which enables him to draw on the aesthetic potential of poetic speech. Hence, allusive references, common in Horace and in poetry in general, are a possible but not particularly prominent stylistic device in the *Epistulae Morales*. The distribution of quotations is similar in its irregularity to that found in Horace: 28 of 124 epistles do not quote at all while quotations pile up in others.[22]

All in all, Seneca's technique of quotation in the *Epistulae Morales* can be described as mostly in line with the genre. Although he quotes intensively and in a varied fashion, he nonetheless remains within a set of conventions that is also observable in other pieces of expository prose. If Seneca and Horace share certain features, as I intend to demonstrate, this will be due less to Seneca than to Horace, who goes against the conventions of his genre in following the citational forms of prose.

---

19 Of the sixty-six passages cited without any indication of source, sixty-three are rendered in metre; a faithful rendition here is not a consequence of implicit quoting, however, since explicitly identified quotations, too, are often rendered in metre (forty of fifty).
20 In modern theorising on the act of quoting and on the marking of quotations, contrasts in rhythm hardly play a part; cf. Spahlinger 2005, 209–210. For contemporary readers of Horace and Seneca, however, who received literature mainly through hearing or reading aloud, the beginning of a metrical quote must have been considerably more marked, cf. Johnson 2010, 3–16 on ancient reading practice.
21 Cf. Harrison 2011, 16.
22 Especially rich in quotations are, *inter alia*, Ep. 88 (seven quotes), 94 (fourteen), and 108 (fifteen quotes), in which Seneca partly discusses problems of the rendition of texts and of the processing of sources.

3 A Comparison of Quotations in Seneca and Horace

By way of example, in this section I will present a comparison of two pairs of quotations from Horace and Seneca that are as formally similar as possible. The comparison is designed to illustrate both the extent of the congruities and the points of difference between the authors. In both examples the same pre-text author is cited. To further elucidate the intertextual connections, the passage of the pre-text from which the quotation is taken and the passage of the quoting text are both presented (I have underlined quotations, setting paraphrases in italics).

3.1 Two Quotations Taken from Terence: Hor. S. 2.3.259–271 (Ter. Eu. 46–63) and Sen. Ep. 95.53 (Ter. Hau. 77)

In my first pairing, the Horatian example is a quotation taken from S. 2.3, the diatribe of the bankrupt Damasippus, who has converted to the Stoic doctrine (S. 2.3.259–271). This character renders in direct speech the *praecepta* of a certain Stertinius on general madness; in the passage at hand, the specific form of madness is that of love:

amator | exclusus qui distat, agit ubi secum eat an non, | quo rediturus erat non <u>arcessitus</u>, et haeret | invisis foribus? '<u>nec nunc, cum me vocet</u> ultro, | accedam? <u>an potius mediter finire dolores? | exclusit; revocat; redeam? non, si obsecret</u>.' ecce | servus non paulo sapientior 'o <u>ere, quae res | nec modum habet neque consilium, *ratione modoque* | *tractari non vult.* in amore haec sunt *mala,* bellum, | pax rursum: haec si</u> quis tempestatis prope ritu | mobilia et caeca fluitantia sorte <u>laboret | reddere certa</u> sibi, <u>nihilo plus *explicet ac* si | insanire *paret* certa ratione</u> modoque.'

Ph.] Quid igitur faciam? <u>non eam ne nunc</u> quidem | <u>quom *accersor* ultro? an potius</u> ita me comparem | <u>non perpeti meretricum contumelias? | exclusit; revocat; redeam? non si me obsecret</u>.

Pa.] ... | proin tu, dum est tempus, etiam atque etiam cogita, | <u>ere; quae res</u> in se <u>neque consilium neque modum | habet</u> ullum, eam <u>*consilio regere non potes.* | in amore haec</u> omnia insunt *vitia*: iniuriae, | suspiciones, inimicitiae, indutiae, | <u>bellum, pax rursum</u>: incerta <u>haec si tu *postules*</u> | ratione <u>certa *facere*, nihilo plus *agas* | *quam* si *des operam* ut cum ratione insanias</u>.

How differs the lover who, when shut out, debates with himself _whether to go or not to_ where, though not _invited_, he meant to return, and hangs about the hated doors? 'Shall I not go even now, when she _invites_ me of her own accord? Or rather, _shall I think of putting an end to my affliction?_ She shut me out. She calls me back. Shall I return? No – not if she implores [me].'
Now listen to the slave, wiser by far of the two: 'My master, a thing that admits of neither method nor sense _cannot be handled by rule and method._ In love inhere these _evils_ – first war, then peace: things almost as fickle as the weather, shifting about by blind chance, and _if one were to try to reduce_ them to fixed rule for himself, he would no more set them right than if he _aimed_ at going mad by fixed rule and method.'[23]
(Hor. S. 2.3.259–271)

Ph.] What am I to do then? Not go even when she _invites_ me herself? Or would it be better to set myself _not to put up with the insults of such women?_ She shut me out, now she recalls me; am I to go back? No, not if she implored me.

Pa.] ... So while there's time think it over, Sir, pretty closely. When a thing lacks method and measure, _no method of advice can direct it._ Love has in it all these _evils:_ wrongs, jealousies, quarrels, reconcilements, war, then peace again. If you _tried_ to _turn_ these uncertainties into certainties by a system of reasoning, you'd _do_ no more good _than if you set yourself_ to be mad on a system.

(Ter. Eu. 46–63)

This quotation may be contrasted with an excerpt from Seneca's ninety-fifth epistle, in which the philosopher asks whether _praecepta_ are an apt or even necessary means to philosophical instruction. Seneca answers in the affirmative: as long as the precept does not apply to concrete actions but to attitudes;[24] from Ep. 95.51 onwards, the focus shifts to the attitude that is to be inculcated toward human coexistence:

Ecce altera quaestio, quomodo hominibus sit utendum. Quid agimus? quae damus praecepta? Natura nos cognatos edidit, cum ex isdem et in eadem gigneret; haec nobis amorem indidit mutuum et sociabiles fecit. Illa aequum iustumque composuit; ex illius constitutione miserius est nocere quam laedi; ex illius imperio paratae sint iuvandis manus. Ille versus et in pectore et in ore sit:

Me.] Chreme, tantumne ab re tuast oti tibi aliena ut cures ea quae nil ad te attinent?

---

[23] All translations of Horace's hexametric poetry here and in what follows are from the Loeb edition of Fairclough. Translations of Terence are from the Loeb edition of Sargeaunt.
[24] Sen. Ep. 95.44. On the role of quotations as _praecepta_ in Seneca see Mazzoli 1970, 97–99.

'homo sum, humani nihil a me alienum puto.'
Habeamus in commune: ⟨in commune⟩ nati sumus. Societas nostra lapidum fornicationi simillima est, quae, casura nisi in vicem obstarent, hoc ipso sustinetur.

Then comes the second problem, – how to deal with men. What is our purpose? What precepts do we offer?... Nature produced us related to one another, since she created us from the same source and to the same end. She engendered in us mutal affection, and made us prone to friendships. She established fairness and justice; according to her ruling, it is more wretched to commit than to suffer injury. Through her orders, let our hands be ready for all that needs to be helped. Let this verse be in your heart and on your lips:
'I am a man; and nothing in man's lot do I deem foreign to me.'
Let us possess things in common; for birth is ours in common. Our relations with one another are like a stone arch, which would collapse if the stones did not mutually support each other, and which is upheld in this very way.

(Sen. Ep. 95.51–53)

Ch.] homo sum: humani nil a me alienum puto.
vel me monere hoc vel percontari puta: rectumst ego ut faciam; non est te ut deterream.
Me.] mihi sic est usu'; tibi ut opu' factost face.

Me.] Chremes, have you so much time to spare from your own affairs that you can attend to another man's with which you have no concern?
Ch.] I am a man, I hold that what affects another man affects me. You may take it that I am offering advice or asking a question, which you like, so that if you are right I may do as you, if you are wrong I may scare you out of this.
Me.] *I* have got to do this; *you* may do what you find necessary for your own case.

(Ter. Hau. 75–80)

Both authors are citing from Terence's comedies, Horace from the *Eunuchus* (Eu. 46–63), Seneca from the *Heautontimorumenos* (Hau. 77), and in both cases the quoted sequence is taken from the catchy first scene of each play: Horace's quotation recalls the exposition of the *Eunuchus*, a scene in which the two main protagonists, Phaedria, a young man unhappily in love with a hetaera, and his *servus callidus*, appear for the first time in the play. The line quoted by Seneca involves the self-characterisation of the prying old man Chremes in the first scene of the *Heautontimorumenos*.[25] Terence was known from the stage and, as early as the first century BCE, read in schools.[26] It can be assumed, therefore, in both cases that the text and the passage from which Seneca and Horace cited were familiar to their intended readership. Furthermore, when Horace and

---

[25] Concerning quotes from Terence in Seneca cf. Mazzoli 1970, 198–201.
[26] Cf. Hor. Ep. 2.1.59–61 as well as Lefèvre 2002, 250–251.

Seneca integrated these two passages into their texts, both quotations had already long been used as moral aphorisms. Cicero stands as a witness for this in both cases: the passage taken from the *Eunuchus* had been quoted by Cicero in Tusc. 4.76 to illustrate the flaw of *inconstantia animi*, just as in Horace S. 2.3; in Off. 1.30 Cicero had referred back to the same lines from *Heautontimorumenos* that Seneca later used in order to discuss the problems of human coexistence.[27]

Neither Seneca nor Horace identifies the cited text by the author's name. Horace, however, while he does not explicitly mark the quotation as such, at least makes it stand out by not presenting it as pronounced by the speaker's 'I,' but in a dialogue between two characters introduced abruptly into the text: an *amator exclusus* and his slave. Seneca marks the cited segment by means of a syntactic pause and rhythmic contrast to the surrounding text, as well as through the explicit hint *ille versus*, which not only implies 'guest' speech but also indicates that the words are taken from a poetic text. Thus, despite its anonymity, Seneca highlights his quotation from Terence more clearly than Horace does.

Both authors strive for a word-for-word rendition: Seneca renders Terence's lines faithfully and consequently also preserves its original metre (iambic senarius). In Horace's case, a comparison with the pre-text shows an elaborate mosaic of literal repetitions, rearrangements, slightly modified expressions, and paraphrases, which culminates in a line almost entirely adopted in verse 262. By making only minimal alterations, he manages to integrate the comedy's iambic senarii into his hexametric poem without having to sacrifice the wording of the pre-text. Therefore, this passage can be read as an attempt to reconcile literal quotation with the need, common to all poetic texts, to assimilate the quoted lines to the rhythm of the quoting text – a need that does not pertain to prose as Seneca's quotations in verse show.

In spite of these formal similarities, the way in which the quotations refer to their pre-texts and the intensity of the intertextual link differ greatly in each case: Horace not only orients himself by the wording of Terence's text; he also adopts both the distribution of speech and the roles of the young man and his slave from the comedy. By doing so, he creates the impression of two comedic figures suddenly entering the satire to perform their given parts in direct speech as if on stage. That is not all, because the quotation from *Eunuchus* seems to have a double reference: it is also an intertextual allusion to Lucilius, who had incor-

---

[27] Both passages are among Cicero's favourites; further quotes and allusions to Eu. 46–63 in N.D. 3.72; to Hau. 77 in Leg. 1.33, Fin. 3.63.

porated the very same passage into a satire as well (Lucil. 730–737 Marx).[28] Seneca, in contrast, neither offers any hints as to the original context from which the lines are quoted, nor tells us which character spoke them. Moreover, one look at the pre-text shows that he not only deliberately decontextualised the quoted segment but has also reinterpreted the passage. Within the context of the comedy the line is certainly not an expression of the human spirit but an excuse for curiosity and *polypragmosynē*.[29] Thus, whereas Horace relies on the reader's knowledge of the Terentian context for his quotation, Seneca's use of the quotation forces the reader to renounce the original context. Both authors, however, use the quotation to serve their moral argumentation: in Horace, the comedic figure of the young man is turned into a negative *exemplum* for the inconstancy of human desires; on a more positive note, Seneca derives the quintessence of his *praeceptum* for social behaviour from the sophistic self-justification of a prying old man.[30]

3.2 Two Quotations Taken from Cato: Hor. S. 1.2.31–35 (Cato Dict. fr. 75 Jordan) and Sen. Ep. 94.27 (Cato Agr. fr. 10 Jordan)

My second pair of examples consists of two quotations taken from Cato. In S. 1.2.23–46 Horace thematises extreme behaviour that, according to him, misses the target of the golden mean, e. g. in amorous affairs. He illustrates the character type of those who only pursue prostitutes by means of a 'divine phrase by Cato' (*sententia dia Catonis*):

nil medium est. sunt qui nolint tetigisse nisi illas quarum subsuta talos tegat instita veste; contra alius nullam nisi olenti in fornice stantem. quidam notus homo cum exiret fornice, 'macte virtute esto' inquit sententia dia Catonis. 'nam simul ac venas inflavit taetra libido, huc iuvenes aequom est descendere, non alienas permolere uxores.'[31]

(a) Cato, cum vidisset ex lupanari adulescentem exeuntem, laudavit eum et ait: Macte nova virtute, puer. (b) Catone transeunte quidam exiit de fornice; quem, cum fugeret, revocavit et laudavit. Postea cum frequentius eum exeuntem de eodem lupanari vidisset, dixisse fertur: adulescens, ego te laudavi, tamquam huc intervenires, non tamquam hic habitares.

---

28 As shown by Fiske 1966, 393–397.
29 Cf. also Jocelyn 1973, esp. 23–25, and 42–44 to the line's reception in Seneca.
30 On the topic of Latin poetic citations in the *Epistulae Morales* in general see Gambla 1981; on their moral functionalisation see Berno 2011b, esp. 245 and Berno 2006, esp. 56–57.
31 In punctuation I differ from Shackleton Bailey's text, who prints S. 1.2.33–35 (*nam simul – uxores*) without quotation marks; for the punctuation adopted here cf., among others, Borzsák

There is no middle course. Some men would deal only with women whose ankles are hidden by a robe with low-hanging flounce; another is found only with such as live in a foul brothel. When from such a place a man he knew was coming forth, 'A blessing on thy well-doing!' runs Cato's revered utterance; 'for when shameful passion has swelled the veins, 'tis well that young men come down hither, rather than tamper with other men's wives.'
(Hor. S. 1.2.28–35)

(a) When Cato saw a young men coming out of a brothel, he praised him and said: 'A blessing on your fresh bravery, my son!' (b) A certain individual came out of a brothel, when Cato was passing by. He tried to run away, but Cato called him back and praised him. Later, after having seen him frequently coming out of the same brothel, Cato is reported to have said: 'Young man, I praised you as someone who visits this place, not as someone who lives here.'[32]
(Cato Dict. fr. 75 Jordan in Ps.-Acr. Hor. S. 1.2.31–32)

Seneca uses an aphorism by Cato in Ep. 94.27 to prove that *praecepta* may have a moral impact through their authority alone (i.e. without any argumentation).

> 'Si dubia sunt' inquit 'quae praecipis, probationes adicere debebis; ergo illae, non praecepta proficient.' Quid quod etiam sine probationibus ipsa monentis auctoritas prodest? sic quomodo iurisconsultorum valent responsa, etiam si ratio non redditur. Praeterea ipsa quae praecipiuntur per se multum habent ponderis, utique si aut carmini intexta sunt aut prosa oratione in sententiam coartata, sicut illa Catoniana: '<u>emas non quod opus est, sed quod necesse est; quod non opus est asse carum est</u>,' qualia sunt illa aut reddita oraculo aut similia: 'tempori parce,' 'te nosce.'

> 'But if,' comes the answer, 'your precepts are not obvious, you will be bound to add proofs; hence the proofs, and not the precepts, will be helpful.' But cannot the influence of the monitor avail even without proofs? It is like the opinions of a legal expert, which hold good even though the reasons for them are not delivered. Moreover, the precepts which are given are of great weight in themselves, whether they be woven into the fabric of song, or condensed into prose proverbs, like the famous Wisdom of Cato: '<u>Buy not what you need, but what you must have. That which you do not need, is dear even at a farthing,</u>' Or those oracular or oracular-like replies, such as 'Be thrifty with time!' 'Know thyself!'
> (Sen. Ep. 94.27–28, cit. Cato Agr. fr. 10 Jordan)

The works by Cato that Horace and Seneca are drawing on here are both inaccessible to us today. The aphorism cited by Horace displays the characteristics of an anecdote and is classed with the *dicta memorabilia* (Dict. fr. 75, p. 110 Jordan), a collection of aphorisms Cicero describes as witticisms.[33] The quotation Seneca

---

1984. That these verses belong to Cato's speech (and not to the narrator) is not least suggested by the scholium cited above. In verse 33 I prefer Borzsák's *taetra* to Shackleton Bailey's *tecta*.
32 Translation by U.T.
33 Cic. Off. 1.104: ...*iocandi genus... elegans, urbanum, ingeniosum, facetum... ut ea, quae a sene Catone collecta sunt, quae vocantur* ἀποφθέγματα. '...a sort of jest... refined, polite, clever, witty...

takes from Cato, the effect of which he compares to that of a poetic expression, seems to originate from the context of *De Agricultura* (Agr. fr. 10, p. 79 Jordan).

Both quotations are explicitly marked by name and both emphasise the prominence of the passages quoted. Horace additionally stresses the quotation's authoritative status (*sententia dia*) whereas Seneca is particularly interested in the prose character of the *sententia* and its message, which is condensed to the extreme. In both cases the quotation is presented in direct speech and consequently creates the impression of a word-for-word rendition. In Horace, however, Cato's aphorism itself paradoxically 'speaks' in the manner of an oracle and Seneca, too, presents the quotation not as rendition of speech but as a maxim, which he links with oracles in what follows. In both cases one can reasonably doubt the faithfulness to the passage in which the quotation was originally lodged. In the satire, for example, the way the *sententia* is framed as an anecdote in itself suggests that Horace at the very least did not quote directly from one of Cato's works; that he versified Cato's words is in any case likely.[34]

Furthermore, the scholium cited above, which explains Horace's reference to Cato, shows that the anecdote must have been longer in its original form, and that its close presented the impact of Cato's authority in a negative light. Moreover, suspicions have also been voiced with regard to Seneca's quote from Cato: it has been argued that Cato's *praeceptum* was not just short but also shortened – it is possible that it acquired the concise form we now find in the text only through Seneca.[35]

As in the previous example, one should note that the citations in Seneca and Horace are formally very similar. The kind of connection they help to establish between the quoting and quoted texts, however, differs and so, consequently, does the role they play and the function they have within the argumentation. In Horace, Cato's aphorism, introduced as an authority, supports a certain form of behaviour (i.e. having affairs with prostitutes rather than *matronae*) that Horace himself does not approve of;[36] and the reader who paid attention to the intertextual reference to Cato's anecdote would have been in a position

---

like those collected by old Cato under the title of 'Bons Mots' (or Apophthegms)' (translation from the Loeb of Miller).

[34] Cf. Gowers 2012, 98: in the protreptic tradition, the sentence was ascribed to several different individuals.

[35] The first part of the sentence opens up a contrast between what is merely useful (*quod opus est*) and what is absolutely necessary (*quod necesse est*); the second part, in contrast, refers to what is *not* useful. Cf. possible emendations suggested by Boeckh and Ritschl in Jordan's app. crit. ad loc. p. 79.

[36] Cf. Hor. S. 1.2.73–76.

to understand that the *vitium*, which Cato praised as the lesser evil, was not neutralised by this praise but indeed reinforced. As a result, Cato's *praeceptum* is ironised and his authority challenged within the Horatian satire.[37] Seneca proceeds very differently: in his text, the quotation is taken out of its original context and extended metaphorically from the economic sphere of country estate administration to become a general precept of life. Only thus is it turned into a self-evident *praeceptum* apt for illustrating Seneca's argumentation. The content of the cited text has as little consequence as its context; what is of paramount importance to Seneca is the universal maxim, the authority of which is unchallenged and asserted by Cato's authorship alone.

4 The Contextual Framework of Quotation in Seneca and Horace

As is to be expected in view of the large number of quotations involved, the observations that I have made with respect to the preceding examples are of no general validity.[38] The main criterion for selecting the above examples was that the pairs of quotations resemble each other as closely as possible with respect to their pre-text, marking, and faithfulness to the original. Nevertheless, both of these cases display great differences when it comes to the quotation's intensity and our interpretation of the reference. Although Horace and Seneca quote in a similar way, they differ in the degree to which they take the original context into account, in the specific aspects of the pre-text that they activate, and in the way they evaluate the pre-text.

A comparable tension between affinity and distance becomes apparent when we consider the authors' respective attitudes towards quoting, as revealed in their texts.

---

[37] Cf. Freudenburg 1993, 25–26, 42; Hooley 1999, unnumbered; Gowers 2012, 98–99. Here, too, Horace additionally seems to allude to Lucilius and perhaps to Ennius, who uses the phrases *dia sententia* (Lucil. fr. 1316 Marx = Porph. Hor. S. 1.6.12, with commentary ad loc.) and *macte virtute* (Lucil. fr. 225 Marx) as well.

[38] Thus there are, for instance, also intertextually active quotes in Seneca; examples, especially from Virgil, are e.g. discussed in Krauss 1957; Setaioli 1965, Coleman 1974, 280–282; De Vivo 1992; and Berno 2011b.

4.1 Attitudes towards the Pre-Text: A Moral Reading of Poetry

A first tension would seem to lie in the two authors' citational references to poetry and the motivation behind them. As the quotations from Terence discussed earlier have shown, quotations taken from a poetic text very often serve to augment moral points in both Seneca and Horace. The basis for this tendency is a manner of reading poetry in which poetic texts are not considered from an aesthetic point of view but from a moral one.[39] This issue is explicitly addressed by both authors.

Horace demonstrates such a reading in detail in Ep. 1.2.1–31, using the example of Homer.[40] He explains that the 'author of the Trojan War' presents 'what is beautiful, what is reprehensible, what is useful and what is not useful' via his characters, and indeed does so 'more accurately and better' than Chrysippus and Crantor, two eminent philosophers (1–4). According to Horace, Homer reveals human errors and their consequences, as well as their opposites, i.e. virtue and wisdom, by means of his examples (17–31).[41] The morally attentive reader relates these depictions to himself, learns from them, and draws consequences for his own way of life (27–31).

Seneca deals with the 'philosophical' reading of poetry in particular detail in Ep. 108. Using a line from Virgil (G. 3.284) as an example, he defines his 'philosophical' reading in sharp contrast not only to an aesthetic reception (Sen. Ep. 108.6), but also to the approach of a *grammaticus* (24–29). According to Seneca, when studying Virgil's line the *grammaticus* is mainly interested in the words and their syntactic-semantic connection (24), whereas the philosopher is more interested in the words' message for the individual reader and the consequences to be drawn from it (25).[42] Seneca openly admits that, as a consequence, the poetic work of art has to be assigned its function with regard to the recipient's intentions and needs (28).

A frequent side effect of the moral reading of poetry is a striking recklessness towards the pre-text. Seneca, for example, endows the line taken from the *Georgics* discussed in Ep. 108 with a sententious quality that it did not have in its

---

39 Cf. Quint. Inst. 1.8.4–12.
40 On the problems regarding this example of reading poetry in Hor. Ep. 1.2 and their implications cf. Keane 2011, Hunter 2014.
41 Cf. Hor. Ep. 1.2.17–18: *quid virtus et quid sapientia possit, | utile proposuit nobis exemplar Ulixen.* 'Of the power of worth and wisdom he has set before us an instructive pattern in Ulysses.'
42 The same goes for reading prose, e.g. Cicero, cf. Ep. 108.30–34.

original context;⁴³ Horace reads his Homer in Ep. 1.2 so anachronistically that Homer's Phaeacians, who lead a paradisiacal life, are turned into dawdlers without plan or ambition and thus serve to anticipate the worthlessness of Horace's contemporaries.

Hence, when Horace and Seneca in these and other passages cite poetry or refer to it, both assume that the poetic text has an *auctoritas* that can be put to fruitful use for moral improvement.⁴⁴ They differ, however, in how this should be realised: Horace mainly obtains the desired instruction by using the characters of, for instance, Terence and Homer as *exempla* for certain modes of behaviour. Seneca, by contrast, brings out the potential of poetry for concise and catchy phrases, from which *praecepta* may be gained for a moral way of life.⁴⁵

4.2 Text Type: Dialogue and Diatribe

In both authors the text is sprinkled with quotations stylised as 'guest' speech. Seneca generally prefers to make this guest speech audible as the 'voice' of the quoted authors; they 'speak' the quotes taken from their texts and thus often partake in the argumentation, as it were.⁴⁶ In other cases, as the quotation taken from Cato in Ep. 94.27 discussed earlier illustrates, the guest speech bursts into the 'host' speech of the quoting text as a maxim or dictum. Sometimes the speaker's 'I' internalises this 'other voice,' as, for example, in the quotation from Terence in Ep. 95.53: here, the 'I' in the quoted line could be both the persona of the anonymously invoked author or that of the likewise anonymous fig-

---

43 In Virgil this line merely serves as a link used to announce the transition from one topic (rutting season of horses) to the next one (sheep husbandry) by hinting at the time lost to love affairs, cf. Virgil G. 3.280–288. For striking reinterpretations of quotations from Virgil in Seneca cf. also Krauss 1957, 1–2.
44 Cf. Sen. Ep. 8.8.
45 Cf. Ep. 108.8 on poetry's 'potential for truth': *Non vides quemadmodum theatra consonent quotiens aliqua dicta sunt quae publice adgnoscimus et consensu vera esse testamur?* 'Have you not noticed how the theatre re-echoes whenever any words are spoken whose truth we appreciate generally and confirm unanimously?'. On the part poetry plays in Seneca, e.g. as a source of *praecepta* cf. Dingel 1974, 28–38 and Mazzoli 1970, esp. 103–108.
46 Apart from common phrases for introducing quotes, such as *ut ait Epicurus*, 'as Epicurus says' (Ep. 25.4) and *Epicurus... inquit*, 'Epicurus says' (Ep. 7.11), we repeatedly encounter formulations in which the quoted authors appear to be present, cf. e.g. *negat Cicero*, 'Cicero denies' (Ep. 49.5); *Vergilio licet credas*, 'you may believe on the authority of Virgil'; *Vergilius probabit tibi*, 'Virgil will prove it' (Ep. 58.2–3); *errare mihi visus est, qui dixit*, 'mistaken, in my opinion, is the one who said' (Ep. 66.2); *Posidonius iudicat*, 'Posidonius holds' (Ep. 90.5).

ure of comedy; at the same time, however, it could also be the persona of the Senecan letter-writer or that of the addressee.

In Horace, too, it may be the quoted author himself who utters the quotation and is thereby responsible for it.[47] More frequently, however, Horace shifts the quoted speech onto a third party, be it a figure from drama, as in the quotation from Terence in S. 2.3.259–271 (discussed above), or a *fictus interlocutor* who presents the quotation as his own speech and opinion.[48]

Quotations presented in such a way bring the invoked pre-text to life and give it a dialogic character. By doing so they conform to a narrative style that by no means only applies to quotation, but which belongs to diatribe: even without falling back on a pre-text, in both Horace and Seneca other voices and figures repeatedly appear or are addressed, contradict, agree or ask questions. Horace explicitly names this conversational style, which is linked to the notion of plain and informal everyday speech, as characteristic of his satirical poetry;[49] Seneca, too, describes his letter-writing as *sermo*.[50] Such a 'conversation,' he adds, brings didactic advantages because, in contrast to a lecture, it sinks into the soul 'bit by bit' (*minutatim*) with its effect lasting longer due to personal engagement.[51] This same effect, for Seneca, is the aim of quotations. Just like the quotation from Cato in Ep. 95.27 mentioned above, they add the authority of the speaking author of the pre-text, and in the case of poetic quotations they promote the moral message by their aesthetic impact.[52] Horace does not give any explicit statement on these points. However, his summoning of dramatic and epic figures as moral *exempla* via quotations (illustrated e.g. in S. 2.3 or Ep. 1.2) has a similar effect; nevertheless, it is only on rare occasions and then mostly in his *Epistles* that this speech of poets and fictional characters has an immediate moral impact.[53] By contrast, especially in the *Satires* the suggestions

---

[47] This phenomenon is only found in the *Satires*, e.g. in *Philodemus ait sibi*, 'says Philodemus to himself' (S. 1.2.121); *Chrysippus dicat*, 'Chrysippus would say' (S. 1.3.127); *Chrysippus ponit*, 'Chrysippus estimates as' (S. 2.3.287).
[48] Quotations as character speech are also found in Ep. 1.7.40 (Telemachus); Ep. 1.16.73 (an anonymous figure of Euripides); as speech by *interlocutores* particularly frequent in S. 1.2, cf. S. 1.2.20 (*ut pater ille Terenti*); 92 (an anonymous quote by Philodemus) and 105 (an anonymous quote by Callimachus); in S. 2.3.62 a passage from Pacuvius is chanted by the theatre audience.
[49] Hor. S. 1.4.41–42. Cf. the discussion in Freudenburg 1993, 120–150; Oberhelman / Armstrong 1995; Kemp 2010, 68–76; Gowers 2012, 164.
[50] Sen. Ep. 38.1; cf. also Ep. 75.1.
[51] On the characteristic diatribe style as a contextual feature shared by Horace and Seneca see Mazzoli 1970, 238; Coleman 1974, 288–289.
[52] Cf. Sen. Ep. 94.27 and 108.11.
[53] Next to Ep. 1.2.1–31 mainly Ep. 1.7.40–43 and 1.16.69–79.

pronounced by cited authors or discussed by the speaker's 'I' are in most cases not positive but dubious and negative.[54] Thus, in contrast to most of the poets' speeches found in Seneca, the didactic quality of quotation in Horace is achieved indirectly and *ex negativo*.[55]

4.3 Adoption of the Pre-Text: Acquisition and Digestion

A third aspect of quoting reflected in the writing of Seneca and Horace concerns the correct handling of pre-texts. Horace thematises them with a view towards imitation (*imitatio*). Again, we generally hear what imitation is not supposed to be: both the 'herd of slaves' of *imitatores* in Ep. 1.19.1–20, who take the poet at his word and drink wine because he praises the god of wine, and the 'aping' imitator (*simius iste*) in S. 1.10.25–29, who takes the imitation of Greek models literally by mixing Greek words into his Latin speech, adopt the wrong approach. The philosophical convert Damasippus, who in S. 2.3.34 'dutifully copies' (cf. *descripsi docilis*) the *praecepta* prescribed by his newly discovered guru Stertinius in over 250 lines of verse in direct and allegedly literal speech, belongs to this category.[56] Correct imitation, in contrast, does not care about what everyone wants to see time and again (S. 1.10.45–47) and while it respects the model, it nevertheless preserves a critical distance to it and tries to surpass it (S. 1.10.56–61). This freedom, as far as the model is concerned, leads to new creations that are due not to the model's content but to its form and spirit (Ep. 1.19.21–34).[57] The same freedom is assumed by the poet in turning to philosophical engagement in Ep. 1.1; instead of favouring an individual master's words, the poet goes his own way in an eclectic fashion, and does not bow to any exclusive scheme of philosophy (Ep. 1.1.10–19).

In part, Seneca deals with the topic of handling sources under quite similar headings, but his focus is on acquisition rather than imitation (as Horace has

---

[54] Cf., *inter alia*, quotes and paraphrases in S. 1.2.20–22 (Terence); 92 (Philodemus); 107–108 (Callimachus); 1.3.126–128 (Chrysippus); 2.3.43–45 and 286–287 (the Stoa is ironised in each case by a dubious speaker).
[55] According to his presentation in S. 1.4.105–120, Horace received his own moral education from his father in the same way. For further discussion of persona in Horace and Seneca, see the contribution of Kirichenko in this volume.
[56] Hor. S. 2.3.33–34: *Stertinius... unde ego mira descripsi docilis praecepta haec*, 'Stertinius, from whom I took down these wondrous lessons that I learned'; cf. S. 2.3.39 and 2.3.296–297.
[57] Cf. Hor. Ars 131–134.

it).⁵⁸ What Seneca means by this is described most clearly in Ep. 84: philosophical studies, he argues, are a balanced mixture of *lectio* and *stilus*, i.e. of reception and production. In his view, the act of reading involves one in collecting bits and pieces, whereas the act of writing involves blending the bits into a whole, a *corpus* (Ep. 84.2). In the following, Seneca compares this process of intellectual incorporation of pre-texts to the bees' production of honey from nectar (Ep. 84.3–5), to the digestion of food (Ep. 84.6–7), and to the polyphonic harmony of a choir or orchestra (Ep. 84. 9–10). The result of this process is a new, distinct element, even if its origin remains detectable (Ep. 84.5), and only in this new, digested form does it nurture the mind. Intellectual digestion, however, implies an agreement with the quoted source to the point that the two become identified, to such a degree that the sources that helped to shape the new philosophical / literary product become irrelevant.⁵⁹

The consequence of this attitude is that if reception is done correctly and involves the right pieces of text, there is no guest-like quality left – even if someone else's words are rendered literally. In opposition to those who 'favour the exact wording' and ask for the source of the quotation, Seneca only deems relevant the content of what is quoted; if that content is acceptable, its origin becomes irrelevant: *quod verum est, meum est* ('Any truth is my own property' Ep. 12.11).⁶⁰ Acquisition, however, costs effort (Ep. 84.11) and whoever shuns the effort performs it inadequately, an idea that is illustrated by the example of the rich freedman in Ep. 27.5–8, who keeps educated slaves and believes himself to own whatever knowledge they possess. As in the case of the Horatian *imitatores*, this kind of engagement with texts orients itself towards an outer effect (pretense of educa-

---

58 On the processing of sources in Seneca, particularly with regard to quotations, see Krauss 1957, esp. 116–117.
59 Sen. Ep. 84.7: *Concoquamus illa; alioqui in memoriam ibunt, non in ingenium. Adsentiamur illis fideliter et nostra faciamus, ut unum quiddam fiat ex multis, sicut unus numerus fit ex singulis cum minores summas et dissidentes conputatio una conprendit. Hoc faciat animus noster: omnia quibus est adiutus abscondat, ipsum tantum ostendat quod effecit.* 'We must digest it; otherwise it will merely enter the memory and not the reasoning power. Let us loyally welcome such foods and make them our own, so that something that is one may be formed out of many elements, just as one number is formed of several elements whenever, by our reckoning, lesser sums, each different from the others, are brought together. This is what our mind should do: it should hide away all the materials by which it has been aided, and bring to light only what it has made of them.' On the metaphor of digestion as part of a cognitive framework for speaking about communicative procedures see Short 2013; for the connection between digestion, quotation, and construction of identity cf. Graver 2014, esp. 285.
60 Cf. Sen. Ep. 8.8.10, 9.20–21, 16.7, 19.9, 21.9, and others.

tion in front of guests), focuses on the traditional (Homer, Hesiod), and is shameful and fruitless.

Both Horace and Seneca emphasise that in dealing with sources and models the result should be a creation of one's own. For Horace this involves autonomy and critical distance, for Seneca it rather means a kind of 'dispossession' of the pre-text. Hence, for Horace, quoting all too frequently bears the charge of *furtum*, whereas for Seneca plagiarism exists only from the viewpoint of a *grammaticus*, not from that of a philosopher.[61]

4.4 Didactic Purpose: Quoting as Part of the Curriculum

From the preceding remarks it is evident that Horace and Seneca often are not only similar in how they use quotations, but also in their ideas about how and why another text should be incorporated into one's own, and about how the source-texts are to be processed. In the use of quotation for didactic purposes, however, Seneca far outdoes Horace. In Ep. 33 he argues that quoting (i.e. the more or less literal and marked presentation of a pre-text's fragments) is entitled to its own place only at the beginning of the philosophy student's curriculum.[62] He therefore asks the addressee of the thirty-third epistle, who still demands further quotations for *praecepta* (Ep. 33.1; 3), to study Stoic doctrine not in small portions but as a whole and as a system (Ep. 33.5). According to Seneca, it is now time to shift the focus from repeating mnemonics to expressing the masters' words as one's own (Ep. 33.7). The step has to be taken from being an *interpres* of others' opinions to being an *auctor* who is productive in his own right, a step from remembering to knowing, from studying to teaching, because this, he points out, is the only way new insights may be gained (Ep. 33.8–10).

According to Seneca's view, learning by means of quotations is only one of the steps towards completely acquiring the philosophical doctrine embodied in the quoted pre-texts – a process described as 'digestion' in Ep. 84.[63] Progress in this process of acquisition also involves an emancipation from pre-texts as teach-

---

[61] Compare the concerns regarding the poet and friend Celsus in Hor. Ep. 1.3.15–20 with Sen. Ep. 108.34 (grammatical study of source material) and 38 (every philosopher could have said what one philosopher said).
[62] On the didactic use of quotations in Ep. 1–29 see Setaioli 1988, 182–222; Freise 1989, esp. 546–554; Hachmann 1996.
[63] On the connection between Sen. Ep. 33 and the digestion imagery used in Ep. 84 see Graver 2014, esp. 282.

ers: the truth belongs to everyone and those who have voiced it do not have an exclusive right to it, but have merely helped pave the way for others (Ep. 33.11).

The student's process of learning and acquiring knowledge finds its practical reflex in the teacher's didactic methods. At the end of almost each of the first twenty-nine epistles, Seneca presents his addressee with a quotation in direct speech, usually taken from Epicurus, which he describes as 'daily wages' or a 'gift'.[64] As the reading proceeds, he repeatedly refers to the irrelevance of the source compared to the content;[65] he forestalls the student who inquires after the origin of the *praecepta*,[66] and from Ep. 22 onwards he starts to stress that the presentation of other people's property is to end soon.[67] Finally, in Ep. 29.10 he announces the end of 'debt-creation,' and none of the following letters receives a closing quotation. They are supplanted by a postulation, expressed ever more impatiently, for the reader to finally gain independence.[68]

5 Parallel or Reception?

If, at this point, we look back at Seneca and Horace as quoting authors, a number of surprising overlaps are to be found in their techniques of quoting. These are surprising because poetry and prose are generally perceived, not only in classical reflections on literature but also in modern scholarship, as two separate areas of communication comprising their own strategies and rules – and this goes for quotation as well. In effect, this study has shown that Horace as a poet and Seneca as a prose writer were confronted with different demands and possibilities when integrating literal repetitions of another text into their own. What has become even more obvious, however, is that the differences caused by these factors are levelled by congruities in other aspects. These include similar thematic interests (moral philosophy), the choice of a similar style of argumentation (diatribe), and shared attitudes in dealing with earlier texts and in processing them within one's own literary production.

This finding could be explained in two different ways: on the one hand, Horace in many places uses quotations not in a typically poetic way, i.e. allusively, but rather quotes in prose style, i.e. in direct speech, explicitly marked and, in the case of poetic quotations, oriented closely around the wording of the pre-text

---

[64] Cf. e.g. Ep. 5.7 *diei lucellum*, 6.7 *diurna mercedula*, Ep. 10.5 *munusculum*, 12.10 *peculium*.
[65] For instance Ep. 8.8–10, 9.20–21, 16.7, 21.9.
[66] Cf. Ep. 14.17–18, 15.9, 16.7.
[67] Cf. Ep. 22.13, 26.8.
[68] Cf. Ep. 39.1–2, 71.6, 75.7, 84.7.

(compare the paper of Trinacty in this volume). While in doing so he takes up the generic forms of satire and (prose) letters, he also explicitly distances himself from higher poetic genres and writes (allegedly at least) *sermones*, i.e. 'speech in prose.' The similarity of the quoting procedure of his moralistic poetry to Seneca's philosophical prose letters could thus be explained through Horace's transgression of genre boundaries.

On the other hand, we need to pose the obvious question of whether these similarities could be a phenomenon of reception, i.e. whether they might be the result of Seneca's acquaintance with Horace's works, and thus of Seneca processing and possibly even referring to Horace's poetry in his own text – either by what he quotes or how he quotes.

With regard to the general character of Seneca's quoting practice, one has to answer in the negative. As illustrated above, Seneca's method of citation is oriented towards a set of norms that can also be observed in other prose texts and especially in philosophical prose; thus, it is rather Cicero who should be put forward as a role model here. Besides, in the greater part of his work, Seneca does not use Horace as a source or authority either, despite many thematic parallels, and despite the conviction expressed in his letters that poetry is an excellent medium for conveying moral doctrines.[69] Apart from a single reminiscence in the *Apocolocyntosis*, which principally concerns an unusual word,[70] he quotes from Horace only at the end of his corpus of *Epistulae*.[71] Although each of these three references, uniformly taken from the first book of *Satires*, are cited in verse, they depict Horace less as a satirist or poet than as a moralist in the tradition of the diatribe.[72] In each of these three cases, Seneca takes over a Horatian *exemplum* and shows his clear approval. Twice he utters the verses from his own persona without any introduction, only later to identify them as quotations taken from Horace; this reinforces the impression that Seneca has internalised the other author's point of view.[73]

---

[69] Ep. 108.10.
[70] Apoc. 13.3 (Hor. Carm. 2.13.34): *Itaque quamvis podagricus esset, momento temporis pervenit ad ianuam Ditis, ubi iacebat Cerberus vel, ut ait Horatius, 'belua centiceps.'* 'So, although he was gouty, he came in an instant to the gateway of Dis where lay Cerberus or, as Horace says, "the hundred-headed beast".' (Translation from the Cambridge edition of Eden). What apparently triggers the quotation here is the Horatian hapax *centiceps* used in reference to Cerberus, not the content of the ode.
[71] Ep. 86.13 (Hor. S. 1.2.27); Ep. 119.13 (Hor. S. 1.2.114–116); Ep. 120.20 (Hor. S. 1.3.11–17).
[72] Cf. Berthet 1979, 943–945; Del Giovane 2014, as well as Del Giovane's essay in the present volume.
[73] On Horatian quotations in Seneca see Mazzoli 1970, 233–238; Berthet 1979; Gambla 1981, 63–77.

It seems that, in his moralising impetus, Horace was indeed close to Seneca. Nevertheless, Seneca's work, apart from those three late hints of appreciation mentioned in the last paragraph, raises the suspicion that the philosopher intentionally rendered the poet invisible. There are some correlations when it comes to quotations and quoted texts, which could be explained if Seneca's quotation were encouraged by reading Horace. A reading of S. 1.2, where Horace paraphrases Hau. 121–150, might have inspired Seneca to choose the aforementioned Terentian quotation from Hau. 77 in Ep. 95.53, which belongs to the same scene in this comedy.[74] The same satire (S. 1.2) might even have encouraged Seneca to use a Catonian quotation in Ep. 122.2, which seems to stem from the same context as Horace's Catonian anecdote mentioned above (S. 1.2.31–35).[75] Thus in a number of cases, at least, it is possible that Horace's works and his usage of quotations induced Seneca to quote the same authors and texts. However, Seneca's text does not betray any desire for the reader to notice these source connections. They clearly differ from quotations with 'double reference' like the example in S. 2.3.259–271 discussed above, where Horace is quoting Terence and at the same time alluding to Lucilius's usage of the same Terentian quote. The same goes for a number of congruities in motive, where, disconcertingly, Horatian quotations are missing.[76] To sum up, we can say with confidence that Seneca knew Horace's work, but he makes little effort to put his reading into effect by means of allusion or quotation.

A possible reason for this may be found in the subtle but nevertheless noticeable differences in the passages that I have discussed: Horace's quotations often convey their moral message by means of a negative example; Horace himself assumes a critical attitude towards his pre-texts and maintains the distance between the pre-text and his own writing even while imitating it. Seneca, on the contrary, frequently prefers quotations that can immediately be adopted by the

---

74 Cf. Hor. S. 1.2.20–22. Both are taken from the entry scene: Horace renders a paraphrase of the self-description of the self-tormenting character Menedemus in Ter. Hau., esp. 121–150; Seneca cites with Hau. 77 the self-description of the prying Chremes. Another possible echo of Hor. S. 1.2 in the same letter (Sen. Ep. 95.67) is discussed in Berno 2011b, 239–240.

75 The quotation in Ep. 122.2 (Cato Dict. fr. 76 Jordan) is the second of only two quotes from Cato in Seneca's works (the other is the passage in Ep. 94.27 illustrated above). Similarly to the Catonian anecdote cited by Horace in S. 1.2.31–35, its counterpart in Sen. Ep. 122.2 is concerned with people who tend to exaggerate (here: by turning the night into day); cf. Cic. Fin. 2.23, which apparently paraphrases the same passage from Cato. Both Catonian fragments could thus stem from the same context; Jordan puts them directly behind one another in his edition as Dict. fr. 75 Jordan (= Hor. S. 1.2.31–35) and frg. 76 Jordan (= Sen. Ep. 122.2).

76 For a collection of Senecan passages that possibly go back to a reading of Horace cf. Mazzoli 1970, 235 and n. 52, as well as Berthet 1979.

philosophical student-addressee as moral *praecepta* even without referring back to the context of the pre-text; he supports a reception of acquisition and digestion, in which the reader's distance to the pre-text is to be neutralised as much as possible.

Quotation, as I have defined it, is the repetition of speech, whose effectiveness is based on the difference between guest and host speech. Horace's method of citation, which maintains a distance from the pre-text, makes the 'other speech' active on the level of meaning, and thereby enables quotation in its proper sense. Seneca also quotes, but in his case the repetition of the pre-text is a step towards a complete disengagement from the source material. Once the destination is reached and the pre-text has been entirely internalised, quotation comes to an end.

Nina Mindt
Horace, Seneca, and Martial: 'Sententious Style' across Genres

In this paper, I intend to extend the triple 'inter-' in 'interactions, intertexts, and interpretations' between Horace and Seneca to a third author: Martial. I shall inquire into the cross-generic similarities in writing strategies that bind the three authors and their genres together. In doing so, I shall touch on certain theoretical questions concerning intertextuality, genre, and persona.

My starting point is Martial himself and his explicit and implicit engagement with Horace and Seneca. My paper outlines some features shared by Horace and Seneca that led them to be inscribed into Martial's epigrams. Which characteristics made Horace and Seneca attractive to Martial? In addressing this question, I shall not point out every allusion, reuse, or transformation of Horace and Seneca in Martial (there are many of them, from mere poetic reminiscences to clear intertextual operations),[1] but rather analyse their technique and writing strategy as a whole (*Schreibweise / écriture*), as well as certain topics related to that specific technique. The term 'writing strategy' is apt for analysing characteristics of content, diction, and style in different genres. Of course, neither Horace nor Seneca wrote epigrams in the strict generic sense, and Martial did not write tragedy, lyric, satire, or epistles (aside from the prose prefaces to some of his *libelli*), but the genres in which they wrote do interact in clear ways.

In my first section, 'Horace and Seneca through Martial's Eyes,' I open with some general observations concerning the similarities between these three authors, especially regarding their *sermo*-style, and I point to the payoffs as well as to the problems of such a comparative analysis.[2] After outlining where and how Martial mentions Horace and Seneca by name in my second section, 'Explicit References to Horace and Seneca in Martial's Epigrams,' I concentrate on the

---

[1] For the influence of Horace on Martial in general see Wagner 1880, 17–25 and, briefly, Sullivan 1991, 103–104. For the presence of Seneca in Martial see Borgo 2009. Further literature is given throughout the chapter. No systematic survey of the triangular relationship between the three has as yet been undertaken.
[2] Since there are too many points of contact between the three authors to be discussed in a paper of this length, I have selected the most important characteristics in Horace and Seneca when viewed through the lens of epigram.

DOI 10.1515/9783110528893-014

hidden impact of both authors on Martial:[3] these authors appear more often, and in different ways, in Martial's poetry than the epigrammatist's open references to them would suggest. Though Martial names Horace and Seneca explicitly, he does not emphasise the real impact that these two authors had on his epigrams. For my third section, 'Sententious Writing,' I choose one central feature shared by all three authors, analysing the use and purposes of *sententiae* in their works. The fourth section, 'Horace, Seneca, and Martial as "Philosophers",' concentrates on the more or less 'philosophical' points at which Martial interacts with Horace and Seneca. The closing remarks in the final section, 'Epigrammatic Writing in Horace and Seneca?', stress that literary genres can help as heuristic tools to bring into focus the similarities and affinities, and sometimes even interactions, between classical authors.

1 Horace and Seneca through Martial's Eyes

Martial, a 'meta-poet par excellence,'[4] is highly aware of the role played by literary history and poets within his epigrams.[5] On a number of occasions he composes a kind of intra-poetic literary history, referring especially to Greek and Latin 'classics' and their literary genres. He makes implicit references by means of allusions or intertextual techniques,[6] and explicit references by mentioning names, but always of course with a purpose applicable to epigram and its status within the hierarchy of literary genres. This is what I mean by the term 'epigrammatic' canon, a canon designed for epigrammatic purposes.[7]

Rimell describes Martial's engagement with the literary tradition as follows:

---

[3] See Mindt 2013a, 175–196 ('Martial's "hidden canon"'), a chapter that discusses Horace and the *Senecae* in Martial. This was the starting point for the current inquiry concerning the relationship between all three authors.
[4] Janka 2006, 279.
[5] Cf. Neger 2012.
[6] 'Intertextuality' is defined as an irreducible system of linguistic relations between texts (associated with poststructuralist theory) and 'allusion' as a conscious authorial practice of quotation or reference to another text (associated with traditional philological methods). While I am aware of this distinction in scholarship, I use both terms, since I assign a certain agency to the author of a text managing the intertextual references to other authors and their texts.
[7] Cf. Mindt 2013a; Mindt 2013b; Mindt 2014.

In many ways, Martial does his best to ruin Latin literature as we know it, dumbing down, graffiti-ing over, in short *epigrammatising* everything from Vergil's *Aeneid* to Ovid's *Metamorphoses* and Horace's *Odes*.[8]

The expression 'epigrammatising everything' is fitting, 'ruin' and 'dumbing down' are not entirely fair, since their connotations and implications seem highly negative. Furthermore, the direction is not only 'down,' but also 'up': the end result may be the elevation of the epigrammatic genre by means of engagement with 'higher' genres. There is a complex interaction at work involving various directions of exchange and reciprocal effects. Moreover, Martial not only epigrammatises high literary genres, but also 'smartens up' genres lower than epic and lyric for the purposes of his own poetics. Thus, it is better to speak of 'transformation' with regard to Martial's methods.[9] In considering this transformation, brought about by Martial's epigrammatic lens, I pose the question of what we can deduce about all three authors from Martial's perspective on Horace and Seneca. What cross-generic similarities are there in their writing (in terms of diction and content)? Do they share certain features or are the similarities a result of Martial's reception? I will argue that these three authors wrote in a chain of reception and transformation, within which each subsequent author adapts a specific persona (or several specific personae) of his predecessor for the purposes of his own poetry, and exploits it / them for his own ends.

It is striking to note that Martial (in a manner perhaps reminiscent of Bloom's 'anxiety of influence') conceals authors who have in fact influenced him to a significant degree, such as the contemporary Greek epigrammatists – and indeed Horace and Seneca.[10] Martial does not mention the importance of ei-

---

8 Rimell 2009, 209.
9 I use the term 'transformation' in a precise way. A concept of 'transformation' has been developed by the Collaborative Research Centre 'Transformations of Antiquity' at Berlin (SFB 644 'Transformationen der Antike'). Compared with 'reception,' the concept of 'transformation' interprets the process not as a merely retroactive one and does not concentrate only on the perspective of the recipient. The central theoretical concept of transformation enables us to conceive of references to the source material not as the unilateral 'reception' of a static object. Instead, we analyse them as the interrelations of mutually dependent constructions of self and other. The object of reference is not something stable and fixed; rather, the act of transformation generates the object itself, creates something new. For these interrelations, the SFB project has created the term *allelopoiesis*, from Greek *allelon* ('mutual' / 'reciprocal') and *poiesis* ('production'). The categories 'transformation mode' and 'transformation type' permit the development of a detailed analysis and description of the process. See Böhme et al. 2011.
10 Bloom treats the relationship of a text not only to its predecessors, but also to its readers; see Bloom 1975, 97: 'The reader is to the poem what the poem is to his precursor – every reader is therefore an Ephebe, every poem a forerunner, and every retracing an act of "influencing," that

ther Horace's *sermo* or Seneca's prose style for his own poetry, although he makes use of some of their techniques.[11] In Epigram 7.46, it is likely that Martial alludes to the Horatian oxymoron *Musa pedestris* (S. 2.6.17).

> Commendare tuum dum vis mihi carmine munus
>   Maeonioque cupis doctius ore loqui,
> excrucias multis pariter me teque diebus,
>   et tua de nostro, Prisce, Thalia tacet.
> Divitibus poteris musas elegosque sonantes   5
>   mittere: pauperibus munera πεζά dato.

While you are wishing to recommend your present to me by a poem and to speak more skilfully than Homeric lips, you rack both me and yourself alike for many days, and your Thalia, Priscus, at my expense, remains silent. You can send to rich men verses and sounding elegies: to poor men send prosaic gifts.[12]
(Mart. 7.46)

This epigram enters the *pauper dives* discourse and dramatises its consequences for the poet-persona cast as a *pauper-poeta* ('the poor client needs the generosity of his patrons,' a commonplace in Martial). Martial uses the Greek technical term 'in prose' in the final line of the epigram to facilitate a play on words (with the Latin *tunica pexa*):[13] Priscus should not wait for poetic inspiration to accompany gifts with dedicatory poems; instead Martial asks for *munera* πεζά – a new woollen toga or prose. If we read this in relation to poetics, which transfers the point of view from 'Martial' as recipient to 'Martial' as producer of poetry, Martial prefers epigram to epic or elegy, as it belongs to the 'pedestrian muse.' Martial's poetics stand in marked contrast to loud-voiced and bombastic poetry. He activates the metaphors of the Horatian *saturae Musaque pedestris*[14] and *sermones humi repentes* (Ep. 2.1.250 – 251; cf. S. 1.4.39 – 42).

The 'pedestrian muse,' represented in Martial's epigram by the Muse Thalia, produces prose or a special kind of down-to-earth poetry that resembles ordina-

---

is of being influenced by the poem and of influencing any other reader to whom your reading is communicated.'
[11] For example, elements that can be traced back to the genre of mime (such as dialogism or dialogisation, dramatisation, and colloquialism) that characterise the oral dimension in Martial's epigrams are present also in Horace and Seneca.
[12] Translations, if not indicated otherwise, are my own. The editions for Martial and Horace are Shackleton Bailey's; the text of Seneca is taken from Rosenbach's edition of the complete philosophical works.
[13] See Galán Vioque 2002 ad loc.
[14] Hor. S. 2.6.17: *quid prius illustrem saturis Musaque pedestri?* ('to whom should I sooner give renown with my satires and my prosaic Muse?').

ry conversation (in Greek, ἡ πεζὴ λέξις). ἡ πεζὴ λέξις brings us to *sermo*, 'conversation' or 'dialogue.'

Seneca's ideal conception of his *Epistulae Morales* is in fact that they should be conversational. The familiar quotidian diction and imagery of Seneca evokes at a textual level the informality of spoken *sermo*.[15]

> Qualis sermo meus esset si una desideremus aut ambularemus, inlaboratus et facilis, tales esse epistulas meas volo, quae nihil habent accersitum nec fictum. [2] Si fieri posset, quid sentiam ostendere quam loqui mallem.
>
> I want that my letters should be just what my conversation would be if you and I were sitting together or taking walks together, spontaneous and easy; for my letters have nothing strained or artificial about them. [2] If it were possible, I would prefer to show, rather than to say what I am feeling.[16]
>
> (Sen. Ep. 75.1–2)

Seneca's style (I refer here especially to his epistolary style) tends towards 'a more lapidary – perhaps more truly Latin – style, which is based on parataxis and the juxtaposition of pointed phrases.'[17] These remarks are appropriate for Martial as well.

On the concealed relationship between Martial and Horace, Merli rightly states: 'While the intertextual relationship to Catullus is manifest, rich in *motti* and quotes and thus serves in a sense as a trademark for the genre of epigram, Martial's relationship to Horace is less apparent.'[18] Martial's relationship to Horace is certainly less apparent but it does exist: scholars have proposed reading certain epigrams of Martial as 'satires in miniature'[19] and it is highly likely, although impossible to prove, that Martial wrote them with Horace in mind. Regarding Martial's relationship to Seneca, it has been observed that the *brevitas* of Seneca's diction and point occasionally even surpasses that of Martial.[20] Therefore, Seneca's writing can at times be characterised as essentially 'epigrammatic.' Horace, too, displays features of Hellenistic epigram in his lyric: as schol-

---

15 Cf. von Albrecht 2014, 710 ('colloquialisms are in harmony with the personal tone of his prose works, their closeness to dialogue and epistolary style'); cf. also Williams 2015a, 136. On the *sermo cotidianus* in Seneca's language see Setaioli 2000b.
16 The final statement – *quid sentiam ostendere quam loqui mallem* – could be a further explanation of Seneca's sententious style since Quintilian provides the following etymology of *sententia* (Quint. Inst. 8.5.1): *Sententiam veteres quod animo sensissent vocaverant* ('The ancients used the word *sententia* to mean what they felt in their minds').
17 Coleman 1974, 286.
18 Merli 2006, 270.
19 Sullivan 1991, 104.
20 See Sullivan 1991, 101.

ars have noted, there is a certain generic hybridity in the *Odes*, and at times Horace appears to 'epigrammatise' lyric.[21] Hence we may apply the adjective 'epigrammatic' to some of the characteristics of Seneca and Horace, even though they were not epigrammatists in a strict generic sense as Martial was. We should not forget that it is Martial himself who has to a certain extent defined what we understand under the term 'epigram.' Yet there is also a generic hybridity in his epigrams, due in part to the way he attempts to integrate ancient literary history into them.

2 Explicit References to Horace and Seneca in Martial's Epigrams

Martial refers several times explicitly to Horace and to Seneca. These explicit characterisations need not correspond with Martial's actual use of their works,[22] and indeed, as we will see, they do not. In two epigrams, Martial name-drops Horace as a canonical author, a famous member of the circle of Maecenas (together with Virgil and Varius): 1.107.3–4 (*otia da nobis, sed qualia fecerat olim | Maecenas Flacco Vergilioque suo*: 'give me leisure, but leisure such as once Maecenas provided for his Flaccus and his Virgil') and 12.3.1–2 (*quod Flacco Varioque fuit summoque Maroni | Maecenas*: 'what Maecenas was to Flaccus and Varius and illustrious Maro'). In 8.18.5–6 (once again in combination with Virgil), Horace is described as a lyric poet following in the footsteps of Pindar: *sic Maro nec Calabri temptavit carmina Flacci, | Pindaricos nosset cum superare modos* ('so Maro did not even attempt the lyrics of Calabrian Flaccus although

---

21 See Höschele 2009, 79: 'In this context it appears by all means striking that Horace both inscribes epigram into lyric and bids farewell to the lyric genre by "epigrammatizing" its very emblem [*scil.* the lyre, N. M.]. Maybe it goes too far to speak of a two-way appropriation here (epigram-into-lyric-into-epigram), but I dare say that Horace offers us a poetic experiment that quite deliberately confronts one genre with the other.' See also Acosta-Hughes / Barbantani 2007 on the interactions between lyric and epigram. On Horace's reception of the epigrammatic genre see Buchmann 1974. Cf. Harrison 2011 on 'generic enrichment,' by which he means the incorporation of elements of one generic system into another 'for the purposes of perceived expansion and variation of the "host" genre' (ibid. 21).
22 On the presence of Horace's work in Martial's epigrams see Wagner 1880, 17–25, and, briefly, Sullivan 1991, 103–104; see Neger 2012, 240–252, on the impact of Horace's *Satires* and *Epodes*; see Mendell 1922 and Szelest 1963 on Martial's satiric epigrams; see Donini 1964 on Epod. 2 and other *carmina* in Mart. 1.49; see Duret 1977 in detail on Epod. 12 and Martial. Roman 2001, 123–127, notes themes and motifs that Martial shares with Horace. For the (relatively) current state of research see Beltrán et al. 2005, 84–87 (further literature ibid., 110–111).

he might have surpassed the measures of Pindar'). In 5.30.2 (*Calabra lyra:* 'the Calabrian lyre') and 12.94.5 (*fila lyrae movi Calabris exculta Camenis:* 'I struck the strings of a lyre practised by the Calabrian Muses') Horace represents lyric poetry in general. Interestingly, all the epigrams that refer to Horace designate him as lyric poet, never as author of the *Epistles*, *Epodes*, or *Satires*. A distinction by genre when discussing literary history is a standard approach throughout ancient literary criticism (cf. e. g. Quintilian Inst. 10), and Martial assigns to Horace the label 'lyric poet';[23] the role of 'the Roman satirist' is assigned to Lucilius (Mart. 12.94.7), not at least because of his explicit naming as such by Horace himself in the *Satires* (e. g. S. 1.10.48).[24] It is therefore interesting to note that for Martial (in his explicit references to Horace) Horace is always a lyric poet, whereas Seneca in his *Epistulae Morales* only quotes from the *Satires*; still, the way in which Martial and Seneca use Horace does not differ as much as this may suggest, as I will explain below.

Seneca the Younger is also explicitly present in Martial's epigrammatic production consistently over the years CE 85 / 86 – 101. The first reference to Seneca in Martial's oeuvre is 1.61.7 (*duosque Senecas*), where Martial mentions him together with his father. The epigram is about a hometown's pride in its famous sons, in Seneca's case Corduba (1.61.8). Martial names Seneca five times in all, but in these explicit references he treats him not so much as a philosopher or poet with personal intellectual characteristics,[25] but rather as a member of the *Senecae*, a family of patrons, idealising him as a man of the good old days. This becomes clear in two of the five epigrams:

> Pisones Senecasque Memmiosque
> et Crispos mihi redde, sed priores
>
> Give me back the Pisos, and the Senecas, and the Memmiuses, and the Crispuses – but those of former days.
> (Mart. 12.36 – 37)

> Atria Pisonum stabant cum stemmate toto
>   et docti Senecae ter numeranda domus,
> praetulimus tantis solum te, Postume, regnis.

---

23 On *Horatius lyricus* in Martial see Mindt 2013a, 175 – 182.
24 See Mindt 2013a, 182 – 184. On Lucilius in Martial see Neger 2012, 236 – 239 ('Martial und der *primus inventor* der römischen Satire').
25 See Borgo 2009.

> When the Pisos' hall stood with all its ancestry, and learned Seneca's house illustrious for its triple names, I put you alone, Postumus, before so great patronage.
> (Mart. 4.40.1–3)

The only explicit characterisation of Seneca (or better, the *Senecae:* Seneca the Elder, the Younger, and Lucan) remains somewhat unspecific: *doctus*. Thus far, Martial has used explicit references to the *Senecae* in describing his own place within the social system of literature, that is to say, within the patron-client relationship, but he does not go into specifics about their style and content, or even his own relationship with them.

The other two epigrams of Martial that name Seneca the Younger (7.44 and 7.45) will lead us to Seneca as author and reveal his closeness to Martial and his genre. They also build a bridge to my analysis (in section four) of the influence of Seneca (and Horace) on Martial and the way the epigrammatist received and transformed him in his epigrams.

> Maximus ille tuus, Ovidi, Caesonius hic est,
>   cuius adhuc vultum vivida cera tenet.
> Hunc Nero damnavit; sed tu damnare Neronem
>   ausus es et profugi, non tua, fata sequi:
> aequora per Scyllae magni comes exulis isti,   5
>   qui modo nolueras consulis ire comes.
> Si victura meis mandantur nomina chartis
>   et fas est cineri me superesse meo,
> audiet hoc praesens venturaque turba fuisse
>   ille te, Senecae quod fuit ille suo.   10

Here, Ovidius, is your Maximus Caesonius, whose lineaments the living wax still preserves. He it was Nero condemned; but you dared to condemn Nero, and to follow the fortunes of a banished man, not your own: over Scylla's seas you went as the great exile's companion, you who had lately refused to be companion of a consul. If those names shall live which are entrusted to my pages, and if it may be that I survive my own ashes, this shall the men of today and of tomorrow hear that you were to him all that he was to his Seneca.
(Mart. 7.44)

> Facundi Senecae potens amicus,
> caro proximus aut prior Sereno,
> hic est Maximus ille, quem frequenti
> felix littera pagina salutat.
> Hunc tu per Siculas secutus undas,   5
> o nullis, Ovidi, tacende linguis,
> sprevisti domini furentis iras.
> Miretur Pyladen suum vetustas,
> haesit qui comes exuli parentis.

Quis discrimina comparet duorum?   10
Haesisti comes exuli Neronis.²⁶

The powerful friend of the eloquent Seneca, next to his dear Serenus, or dearer still, that Maximus is here, whom in many a page the happy letter greets. This is he whom you – no tongue, Ovidius, should withhold your name! – followed over Sicilian waters and spurned the wrath of an infuriate despot. Let old time admire its Pylades, who as companion clung to one banished by his parent. Who could compare the perils of the two? You, as companion, clung to one banished by Nero!
(Mart. 7.45)

These two epigrams recall an important fact in Seneca's biography: the exile. The exile is not only important as a biographical fact *extra opus* but also plays a significant role in Seneca's oeuvre, most obviously in the *consolationes*. Further, two epigrams of a *Seneca impersonatus*,²⁷ the pseudo-Seneca of the *Anthologia Vossiana*, also concern this important piece of Seneca's biography,²⁸ and another six epigrams assume the scenario of exile.²⁹ I consider the epigrams of pseudo-Seneca to be later than Martial,³⁰ so I do not postulate that they had an impact on him. It is significant, however, that Seneca himself could be imagined to be an author of epigrams, since he used a new form of prose with a tendency towards *sententiae*.

3 'Sententious' Writing

3.1 The Term *'sententia'*

The *sententia* was a rhetorical device of great importance in Roman rhetoric, literature, and public life during the early Principate. In a literary context the Latin term can refer to a generalising maxim or something like a prose epigram.³¹ Both of these are present in Horace, Seneca, and Martial. Bluntly put, these authors

---

26 For these epigrams see Galán Vioque 2002, 278–288.
27 Holzberg 2004, 423–444.
28 Epigr. 2 and 3 Prato / Dingel = AL 228 and 229 Shackleton Bailey.
29 Epigr. 6, 14, 18, 19, 21, and 25 Prato / Dingel.
30 See Holzberg 2004, 436, and Breitenbach 2009 and 2010 with further literature on the chronological priority.
31 For the theory behind the use of maxims and epigrams as developed by the ancient rhetoricians see Sinclair 1995 and Kirchner 2007, but also Holloway 1998, 43–45. For the history of the term *sententia* see Sinclair 1995, 120–122. On *sententiae* in Seneca see Dinter 2014; see also Casamento 2011 (on proverbs and maxims more generally).

have in common a 'sententious' writing technique. Seneca the Elder and Quintilian often mention the growing tendency in the early Principate to use *sententiae* – intended as striking generalisations – in lieu of arguments, and in particular to end each short narrative passage with such a *sententia*. The general and broader definition of *sententia* is given in the *Rhetorica ad Herennium* and in Quintilian:

> Sententia est oratio sumpta de vita, quae aut quid sit aut quid esse oporteat in vita, breviter ostendit, hoc pacto.
>
> A *sententia* is a declaration derived from social behaviour, which succinctly presents either what is or what ought to be a fact of life.
> (Rhet. Her. 4.17.24)

> Antiquissimae sunt quae proprie, quamvis omnibus idem nomen sit, sententiae vocantur, quas Graeci gnomas appellant.
>
> Oldest of all – and properly called *sententiae*, though the same name serves for all types – are what are called in Greek *gnōmai*.
> (Quint. Inst. 8.5.3)

The examples of *sententiae* collected by the elder Seneca from contemporary declaimers illustrate the prevailing interest of this epoch in *sententiae*.

As well as bearing the sense 'proverb' or 'gnomic generalisation,' the term *sententia* in Seneca the Elder already also designates a form of penetrating epigram.[32] The rhetoricians' elaborate classification of *sententiae* and *ridicula dicta* would also seem to include the various types of striking conclusion found in Martial's epigrams.[33] Many of the excerpts from declamations cited by the elder Seneca consist of a series of short expository passages that conclude with a *sententia*, each of which would provide material for the kind of epigram in which Martial excelled.[34] Some *sententiae* composed in other genres prior to the time of Martial can still be called 'epigrammatic.'[35] While it certainly did not originate with him, Martial did much to reinforce this technique of using a

---

[32] See Dinter 2014, 320. On the use of *sententiae* in epigrammatic form in Seneca the Elder see Balbo 2011, 29 (on Con. 7.3.8).
[33] On 'epigram and rhetoric' and the use of *sententiae* see Mindt forthcoming.
[34] Barwick 1959 and Salemme 1976, 93–97, on the influence of rhetoric on Martial.
[35] See Kirchner 2007, 190: 'Furthermore, the term *sententia* is also employed in a broader sense to denote a pointed phrase or a short paradoxical epigram.' Winterbottom in his Loeb edition of Seneca the Elder translates *sententia* as 'epigram.'

pointe, the rhetorical structure that introduces a witticism at the very end of the poem.[36]

But point and wit are not the same, and pointedness is not in itself witty or humorous. Martial paid much attention to the closure of his epigrams in general and formulated the end of his poems in various ways.[37] The witty surprise, the witty *pointe*, is only one possibility. Martial's epigrams also often end with a *sententia* in the broader sense or with a quotation;[38] and the close of the poem may also resolve a paradox or a supposed contradiction. It often presents two stark alternatives or opposing statements. Martial uses a large range of different types of closure that can be categorised as *sententiae*. Yet the *argumentum e contrario* does not always work: that the style of Seneca can be described by the adjective 'sententious' is beyond doubt and, as I will show, sometimes even 'epigrammatic' applies; but Seneca's *sententiae* mainly use antithesis and paradox, sometimes in an unexpected way, but with no real 'jokes.'

To label Horace 'epigrammatic' would seem, in some ways, even more problematic. But simple, universalising judgements (such as Ep. 1.2.56 *semper avarus eget*: 'the greedy are never satisfied') recur across the poet's works,[39] most frequently as *epiphenomena* in order to illustrate or sum up the narrative to which they are attached,[40] but also as *promythia* which open a passage or often even an entire poem.[41] Therefore, a certain 'sententiousness' has been attributed to Horace as well.[42] A list of *sententiae* in Horace, sometimes even with a *pointe*, would be unwieldy in an essay such as this, and therefore I limit myself to but a few examples:[43]

---

36 In the Latin literature before Martial certain poems of Catullus (e.g. Catul. 32, 42, 55, and 56) end with a *pointe*, but rarely in the so-called 'epigrammatic' part of his *Carmina* (Catul. 69–116), see Fain 2008, 47–48. Therefore, Lessing disregards Catullus for his theory of *pointe*. From other Latin epigrammatists before Martial too little has survived to make a clear statement about poetic structure.
37 See Sullivan 1991, 217–227.
38 On the closeness of proverb, *sententia*, and quotation see several contributions in Lelli (ed.) 2009, 2010, 2011.
39 On proverbs, *gnōmai*, and philosophical / didactic / moralistic *sententiae* in Horace, see Guglielmo 2010.
40 See Dinter 2009, 101 and 103, on *sententiae* in Horace at the endpoint of a passage or even a poem (with a list of the most striking examples). Compare Rosenthal 1897, 16.
41 Cf. Dinter 2009, 104, and Rosenthal 1897, 17.
42 Dinter 2009, 97.
43 Rosenthal 1897 offers a detailed study of Horace's *sententiae* and aims to collect them all.

> Dum vitant stulti vitia, in contraria currunt.
>
> In avoiding a vice, fools run to its opposite.
> (Hor. S. 1.2.24)

> Virtus est vitium fugere et sapientia prima | stultitia caruisse.
>
> To flee vice is the beginning of virtue, and to have got rid of folly is the beginning of wisdom.
> (Hor. Ep. 1.1.41–42)

Even in Horace we sometimes find aphoristic diction and a style rich in point. His first epistle ends with a concluding *sententia* (*ad summam*) including an *aprosdoketon:*

> ad summam: sapiens uno minor est Iove, dives,
> liber, honoratus, pulcher, rex denique regum,
> praecipue sanus, nisi cum pituita molesta est.
>
> In sum: the wise man is second only to Jupiter, rich, free, honoured, handsome, truly a king of kings, healthy, above all, unless he has a cold in the head!
> (Hor. Ep. 1.1.106–108)

Save for the metre, these lines could certainly be from an epigram by Martial.

As indicated above, rhetorical *sententiae* are typical elements of the so-called 'modern style,' and the younger Seneca was greatly influenced by this style in general and by this rhetorical device in particular.[44] The influence of Seneca the Elder on his works also results in similar turns of phrase involving *sententiae*.[45] There are parallels with both *Senecae* in Martial[46] – for example, one can note similarities in theme, phraseology, and attitude between Martial's epigram on Cicero and Antony (Mart. 5.69), Seneca the Elder (Suas. 6 and 7 and Controv. 7.2), and Seneca the Younger.[47] Seneca the Younger writes about Cicero and Antony twice, in *De Ira* (Dial. 4.2.3) and *De Tranquillitate Animi* (Dial. 9.16.1).

---

[44] See e.g. Traina 1987, 25–27 on the importance of the *sententia* ('La cellula stilistica di Seneca e della sua età è la frase, la *sententia*'). For the tradition of Seneca's rhetorical style with 'a diction rich in short, rhythmical sentences, with an epigrammatic turn in both content and form,' see von Albrecht 2014, 701.

[45] For examples, see Trinacty 2009, 261 and Rolland 1906, 63–65.

[46] Sullivan 1991, 102 (n. 39): 'Martial reworks in verse form so many themes dear to contemporary rhetorical declamation that it is unlikely that he was unacquainted with the famous Handbooks of Seneca's father.'

[47] See Mindt 2013a, 37–42.

In the latter passage, Seneca gives a good example of his new rhetorical (and potentially epigrammatic) style:

> Ubi bonorum exitus mali sunt, ubi Socrates cogitur in carcere mori, Rutilius in exilio vivere, Pompeius et Cicero clientibus suis praebere cervicem, ...necesse est torqueri tam iniqua praemia fortunam persolvere.
>
> When the ends of good men are bad, when Socrates is forced to die in prison, Rutilius to live in exile, Pompey and Cicero to offer their necks to their own clients..., we must be distressed that Fortune pays her rewards so unjustly.
> (Sen. Dial. 9.16.1)

The expression *ubi bonorum exitus mali sunt* ('when good men come to bad ends') is an example of Seneca's *brevitas* and represents one of his *sententiae*. Seneca is full of them, in every genre: in the philosophical dialogues, his epistles, and his tragedies. One can imagine that Martial read Seneca with pleasure and admiration.

In Seneca's tragedies, *sententiae* are even more frequent than in his Greek models.[48] Seneca uses them often in the *peroratio* of a monologue (and avoids them, in contrast, in the chorus).[49] In Sen. Thy. 470 – a good example of an epigrammatic paradoxical *sententia* from Seneca's tragedies – Thyestes finishes his speech as follows: *immane regnum est posse sine regno pati* ('It is a vast kingdom to be able to endure without kingdom'). This phrase has been accurately described as 'a paradoxical Stoic epigram.'[50] And Atreus ends one of his speeches with *quod nolunt, velint* (Thy. 212: 'They must want what they do not want').

In Seneca's *Epistulae Morales* we sometimes find an epigrammatic *sententia* at the beginning of the letter, e.g. Ep. 61: *desinamus, quod voluimus, velle* ('let us cease to want what we wanted'). Often a *sententia* comes up at the end: Ep. 106, for example, ends epigrammatically with the following famous *sententia* (Ep. 106.12): *non vitae, sed scholae discimus* ('we do not learn for life, but for school'). This would fit well with Martial's epigrams on school themes, e.g. Mart. 12.68 and 10.62. But *sententiae* appear not just at the beginning or end

---

48 On *sententiae* in *Seneca tragicus* see e.g. Dinter 2014, 322. On the function of the *sententiae* in speeches see Boyle 2014, xlviii: '*Sententiae* in such speeches are not only used for rhetorical punctuation and closure (see Med. 55) but serve also a larger dramatic purpose, namely to display – even in a sense create – a mind, as it grapples with itself and its moral and existential context.'
49 Cf. Tarrant in this volume, 97–99. See Billerbeck 1988, 126: 'abschließende Sentenzen sind ein Hauptmerkmal von Senecas Stil.' Cf. Sen. Ag. 144, 610; Her. F. 201, 328, 462, 874; Med. 55, 109, 150–167; Oed. 86, 909–910; Phaedr. 430, 735; Tro. 162–163, 291, 425, 954.
50 Meltzer 1988, 320.

of a work – one might compare the *sententia* with a *fulmen in clausula* found at Ep. 93.3:

> Non vixit iste sed in vita moratus est, nec sero mortuus est, sed diu.
>
> A person like him has not lived, he has merely tarried awhile in life. Nor he died late in life; he has simply been a long time dying.

Sometimes a whole passage of Seneca can be analysed using Lessing's *Inhalt* ('set-up') and *Aufschluß* ('resolution'), terms that Lessing created for his theory of epigrams in his work *Zerstreute Anmerkungen über das Epigram und einige der vornehmsten Epigrammatisten* from 1771 (which was largely based on Martial). Like Martial, Seneca also uses *sententiae* as one possible technique for the 'resolution' of a poem.

3.2 *Sententiae* and *personae*

So far I have focused on the rhetorical and technical aspects of composition in *sententiae*. We have seen that all three authors possess a sententious writing technique. In what follows I shall concentrate on the function of *sententiae* with respect to the authors' personae and on the content itself.

One feature that is without doubt shared by all three authors is their self-fashioning within the context of 'first-person literature' (to adapt the term 'first-person poetry' to include prose literature as well).[51] There are cross-generic similarities in the representation of the author's persona and the importance accorded to it.[52] In the case of Horace and Martial, a 'functional affinity'[53] has been

---

[51] For Horace, self-fashioning and the roles the poet adopted in his poetry have been well explored, e.g. Oliensis 1998; see also Feeney 2009. For Seneca's self-fashioning see Bartsch / Wray 2009, Trinacty 2014 passim, and Littlewood 2015.

[52] For Martial, see Puelma 1995, 453 n. 35: 'Neu bei Martial gegenüber den üblichen Themenzyklen der griechischen Epigrammdichtung ist die stark persönliche, autobiographische Aufmachung seiner epigrammatischen Situationsbilder, besonders der des ‚römischen Dichters.' Diese Eigentümlichkeit teilen Martials Epigrammata im Verhältnis zu den griechischen Vorbildern mit den anderen Gattungsformen biotischer Dichtung, wo der Autor als Berichterstatter bunter eigener Lebenserfahrungen von betont exemplarischer Bedeutung für die Allgemeinheit der Leser auftritt.' Puelma refers especially to the *Satires* of Lucilius and Horace.

[53] Roman 2001, 123: 'functional affinity, in the general conception of his [i.e. Martial's] role as writer, with Horace and other imperial poets: he depicts various moments of a private citizen's life of *otium*; integrates motifs of imperial propaganda within the fabric of his small, first-person genre; avoids satirising named contemporaries; ...and pursues Horace's identification of writing

observed in their conception of their role as writer.⁵⁴ Horace and Martial create several personae, some of which overlap. Aside from their poet-persona, this becomes most obvious in the cases of personae such as *philosophus, praeceptor,* and *amicus*. Seneca in his writings also takes on several roles, most prominently the role of philosopher, friend, and teacher. There are, therefore, functional affinities and similar strategies in using the author's voice – despite all the differences.⁵⁵ The *sententia* is one rhetorical device they share: *sententiae* help the persona to underline the text's message.

Sententious writing is a technique that helps to convey the message of the text and to attribute authority to one's persona.⁵⁶ *Sententiae* play an important role in defining the 'author's' voice.⁵⁷ Seneca not only makes full use of *sententiae*, maxims, and verse or prose proverbs, but also reflects on their function in three *Epistulae* (Ep. 33, 94, and 95). They have great weight, as he himself declares:⁵⁸

> Praeterea ipsa quae praecipiuntur per se multum habent ponderis, utique si aut carmini intexta sunt aut prosa oratione in sententiam coartata.
>
> Moreover, the precepts which are given are of great weight in themselves, whether they be woven into the fabric of song, or condensed into prose epigrams.
> (Sen. Ep. 94.27)

In the same epistle, Seneca defends the use of *praecepta* in the form of *sententiae*:

---

with rustic autarky in poems describing villas and the country.' On Horace's impact on the description of *villae* in Martial see Fabbrini 2007.
54 In her study of the relation between Martial's tenth book and the *Satires* and *Epistles* of Horace, Merli 2006 has convincingly shown that Horace is Martial's model for the *secessus rusticus*, and that Martial pursues Horace's identification of writing with rustic autarky in poems describing villas and the country.
55 See Kirichenko on the differences in the act of 'constructing oneself' in Horace and Seneca in this volume.
56 On *auctoritas* through *sententiae* see Sinclair 1995.
57 Cf. Dinter 2014, 324: 'For according to ancient views *sententiae*, when pieced together, serve to convey a sense of an author, a figure behind the aphorisms with his own distinctive personal agenda.' For the ancient concept of persona and author see Mayer 2003.
58 However, in commenting to Lucilius on the style of his teacher Fabianus he seems to be sceptical about style that sets form over content: *sensus honestos et magnificos habes, non coactos in sententiam, sed latius dictos* ('you have noble and splendid ideas, not gathered together into a *sententia* but spoken more freely,' Sen. Ep. 100.5). On the rejection of a *brevitas* that obscures the sense, see Merchant 1905.

Quis autem negabit feriri quibusdam praeceptis efficaciter etiam imperitissimos? Velut his brevissimis vocibus, sed multum habentibus ponderis: 'Nil nimis.' 'Avarus animus nullo satiatur lucro.' 'Ab alio exspectes, alteri quod feceris.' Haec cum ictu quodam audimus, nec ulli licet dubitare aut interrogare 'quare?'; adeo etiam sine ratione ipsa veritas lucet.

Moreover, who can deny that even the most inexperienced are effectively struck by the force of certain precepts? For example, by such brief but weighty saws as: 'Nothing in excess.' 'The greedy mind is satisfied by no gains.' 'You must expect to be treated by others as you yourself have treated them.' We receive a sort of shock when we hear such sayings; no one ever thinks of doubting them or of asking 'Why?'. So much, indeed, does mere truth, unaccompanied by reason, shine forth.
(Sen. Ep. 94.43)

Seneca inserts existing *sententiae* and creates new ones to convey his practical ethics. Note that the second *vox* is reminiscent of the *sententia* from Horace, Ep. 1.2.56: *semper avarus eget*. *Sententiae* are especially useful for didactic purposes, as Seneca declares in Ep. 33.7: *ideo pueris et sententias ediscendas damus* ('that is why we give boys *sententiae* to memorise'). But later, one should not only reproduce them, but create one's own: *Dicat ista, non teneat... impera et dic quod memoriae tradatur, aliquid et de tuo profer* (Ep. 33.7: 'Let him say such things, not hold on to them... Take command and say something that could be committed to memory, say something of your own creation'). These passages reveal the practice of reception and production of *sententiae* in Seneca the Younger.

3.3 *Sententia:* the Practice of Reception and Production

Ancient readers used to excerpt, collate, and recycle *sententiae*. The famous anthology of *sententiae* from the mimes of Publilius Syrus is only one outstanding example of this practice. Horace and Seneca knew about this form of reception, would have expected their own works to be excerpted, and perhaps even promoted their own 'excerptability' by their sententious writing technique. The layers of reception and production get mixed when authors use *sententiae* (anonymous and identifiable ones, as well as their own). It has recently been argued that Horace and Seneca created their own anthology, a 'best of' collection, through their *sententiae*.[59]

---

[59] Dinter 2009, 97 ('I propose to read Horace's *sententiae* as a readers' digest of the poet's self-projection, the "best of Horace" or "essential Horace" – and, most particularly, as Horace's legacy to his text') and, almost in the same words, Dinter 2014, 321 ('I propose reading Seneca's

Later readers did exactly that with Horace: they distilled from his *sententiae* a *Horatius ethicus*.⁶⁰ The even more overtly sententious style of Seneca eased his excerptability into *florilegia*. I would argue that Martial was an early precursor of the medieval and Renaissance excerptions from Horace and Seneca on another level as well: Martial inserts his predecessors into his epigrammatic poetry. As for Martial himself, the *brevitas* of his epigrams means that cuts are seldom needed prior to inclusion in collections of phrases, proverbs, and mottoes.

To give a late example of this tendency, one that documents well the problems of contamination and mixing of levels that accompanied the use of *sententiae*, we may turn briefly to the early modern period. Otto Vaenius in the seventeenth century wrote in his preface to the *Horatii Emblemata* that he had drawn philosophical *sententiae* from Horace and illustrated them.⁶¹

> Otto Vaenius, Q. Horatii Flacci Emblemata 1607, LECTORI SEV SPECTATORI.
> Damvs hic vobis, Lector seu Spectator benevole, Sententias, quas Emblemata vulgo vocant, ex Q. Horatio Flacco, Lyricorum principe, desumptas, tabulisque in æs incisis illustratas... itaque in hoc libello non pauca Ethicæ, sive Moralis, ac Stoicæ Philosophiæ dogmata, imaginibus expressa.

> Otto Vaenius, The Emblemata of Q. Horatius Flaccus 1607, TO THE READER OR VIEWER.
> Here I give Sententiae to you, benevolent Reader or Viewer, commonly called Emblemata, taken from Q. Horatius Flaccus, the leader under the lyric poets, illustrated by plates chased in bronze... Therefore, in this book there are many aphorisms of Ethics or Moral Philosophy and Stoic Philosophy, expressed with images.

Further on in the work, Vaenius seems to have taken the phrase *volat irrevocabile tempus* from Horace. Vaenius's first two examples for this *sententia* and its emblem (i.e. its corresponding image), run as follows:

> Lib. 4. Od. 7
> Inmortalia ne speres, monet annus et almum
>   quae rapit hora diem.
> Frigora mitescunt Zephyris, ver proterit aestas,
>   interitura simul
> pomifer autumnus fruges effuderit, et mox
>   bruma recurrit iners.

---

sententiae as the readers' digest, the best of, essential Seneca – and, most particularly, as Seneca's legacy to his text').
60 On the reception of Horace's *sententiae* see Dinter 2009, 106–108; on Horace in the medieval *Flores Sententiarum* and Erasmus's *Adagia* see Guglielmo 2010, 191–192, with further literature.
61 On Vaenius and Horace see Mayer 2009.

> Sen. lib. 9 Epist.: Diem nox premit, dies noctem, Aestas in Autumnum desinit, Autumno Hiems instat, quae Vere compescitur; omnia sic transeunt ut revertantur. Tibi autem nemo restituet annos, nemo iterum te tibi reddet. Ibit qua coepit aetas nec cursum suum aut revocabit aut supprimet. Non illa se Regis imperio, non favore populi longius proferet.

Vaenius combines Hor. Carm. 4.7.7–12 (his first quotation)[62] with two passages from the philosophical writings of Seneca; although he only mentions Seneca's *Epistulae*, the source of the second part of the quotation from Seneca is in actual fact *De Brevitate Vitae*:

> diem nox premit, dies noctem, aestas in autumnum desinit, autumno hiemps instat, quae vere conpescitur; omnia sic transeunt ut revertantur.
>
> Night is close at the heels of day, day at the heels of night; summer ends in autumn, winter rushes after autumn, and winter softens into spring; all nature in this way passes, only to return. (trans. Gummere)
> (Sen. Ep. 24.26)

> ...Nemo restituet annos, nemo iterum te tibi reddet. Ibit qua coepit aetas nec cursum suum aut revocabit aut supprimet... Non illa se regis imperio, non favore populi longius proferet.
>
> No one will bring back the years, no one will bestow you once more on yourself. Life will go where it started, and will neither reverse nor check its course... It will not prolong itself at the command of a king, or at the applause of the people.
> (Sen. Dial. 10.8.5)

Vaenius is thus something of a forerunner when it comes to investigating the interaction of Horace and Seneca.

The issue becomes more complex when we note that Vaenius also cites Virgil's *Georgics* (his third quotation):

> Optima quaeque dies miseris mortalibus aevi
> prima fugit; subeunt morbi tristisque senectus
> et labor, et durae rapit inclementia mortis.[63]
> (Virg. G. 3.66–68)

This passage is quoted by Seneca in Ep. 108. In this letter, Seneca also quotes Verg. G. 3.324: *fugit inreparabile tempus*, not quoted by Vaenius as a Virgilian in-

---

[62] 'Not to hope for things to last forever is what the year teaches, and the hour that speeds the pleasant day. Cold is ameliorated by West Winds, spring treads on summer. They will perish at the same time crops poured out by fruit-bearing autumn, and soon lifeless winter returns.'
[63] 'The best days are the first to fly by for the wretched mortals. Then sickness and sorry old age and toil come, and the mercilessness of a cruel death carries us off.'

tertext. With a small change from *fugit* to *volat* (perhaps from Cicero, Tusc. 1.31.76: *volat enim aetas*) we come to the *sententia* '*Volat inreparabile tempus*' that serves as the heading of Vaenius's page – even though this is a *sententia* that Horace never actually wrote. Perhaps this example illustrates how difficult it is to trace influences in multilayered intertexts with any degree of certainty, to define the pattern of influence, and to determine the amount of contextual information that remains.

On account of this, some preliminary points concerning the role of *sententiae* (especially gnomic ones) in analyses of intertextuality are in order: had certain formulations already become so proverbial that it no longer mattered whether they were from Horace or Seneca? Had certain concepts formulated by Horace (and other Augustan writers) become commonplaces already for Seneca (and / or Martial)? What was the role of (rhetorical) education in the transmission of *sententiae*? Did handbooks of wise sayings excerpted from Horace already exist in Seneca's time, and from Horace and / or Seneca in Martial's? Did these authors use such collections or did they draw directly from the works, or both? If an author uses these handbooks, he would presumably tend not to take into account the generic aspect of what Genette has called 'architextuality.'[64] But even without the use of collections, *sententiae* have a cross-generic quality. There was without doubt a pool of proverbial maxims and wise sayings that our authors shared, but since Seneca's engagement with Horace, and Martial's with both Horace and Seneca, are not limited to their use of *sententiae*, I am convinced that Seneca and Martial mostly drew directly from Horace's oeuvre – and that Horace and Seneca were used to 'smarten up' the *auctoritas* of Martial's epigrams.

4 Horace, Seneca, and Martial as Philosophers, and their Philosophy of Real Life

In the following section I shall concentrate on the one hand on Horace and Seneca's shared persona as philosophers writing in a sententious style, and on the other on Martial as a philosophical epigrammatist. Although Seneca is the only true philosopher among these authors when taken from a strictly generic point of view, all three give advice about life. That even Martial enjoys the role – or better, pose – of philosopher is obvious from the relatively high number

---

[64] See Genette 1997, 1: 'the entire set of general or transcendent categories – types of discourse, modes of enunciation, literary genres – from which emerges each singular text.'

of moralising epigrams in his collection, and especially those that contain what might be called a philosophy of life, even if this is simply popular philosophy endowed with existential messages.[65]

A further interesting aspect of Martial's two epigrams about Seneca's exile quoted above (Ep. 7.44 and 7.45) is that they are about friendship, specifically friendship that had survived blows of fate. Martial deploys the figures of Seneca and his friends Annaeus Serenus and Caesonius Maximus as *exempla* to illustrate true friendship. Clearly, there is a light philosophical message in these epigrams. Moreover, it is perhaps not only the historical Seneca who is present in these epigrams but also Seneca's philosophy, in that Martial highlights friendship, a topic quite central to Seneca's writing.[66] In choosing Seneca's friends as prominent *exempla*, Martial points also to the content of Seneca's philosophy: in Ep. 63, Seneca deals with the death of close friends, and also talks about his grief when Annaeus Serenus died.[67] It may not be an accident that the letter itself is full of epigrammatic diction. As Ker notes, 'Seneca's philosophy of friendship is encapsulated in the following epigrammatic statement':[68]

> Quem amabas extulisti: quaere quem ames. Satius est amicum reparare quam flere.
>
> You have buried someone you loved. Look for someone you may love. It is better to replace a friend than to weep for him.
> (Sen. Ep. 63.11)

Seneca the philosopher can also be an epigrammatist, as Martial the epigrammatist can also be a philosopher. This can be seen especially in several epigrams in which Martial combines philosophical advice from Horace and Seneca regarding one's way of life, e.g. in 5.20 and 5.58:[69]

---

[65] On Martial as a philosopher with moral views see Schäfer 1983, Heilmann 1984 and 1998, and Frings 1985. Holzberg 2002, 81–85, esp. 85, adds that we have to be cautious about taking Martial's philosophical claims too seriously since they are often self-deprecating. Canobbio 2011 passim sets the term 'philosophical' in quotation marks to relativise the characterisation of Martial as 'philosopher' in a strict sense. For Horace and satire as popular philosophy see Mendell 1920.

[66] On philosophy and friendship in Seneca's *Epistulae* see Ker 2009, 109 and Edwards 2015.

[67] Sen. Ep. 63.14: *Haec tibi scribe, is qui Annaeum Serenum carissimum mihi tam inmodice flevi ut, quod minime velim, inter exempla sim eorum, quos dolor vicit* ('I write these words to you, I who wept so excessively for my dear friend Annaeus Serenus, that, despite of my wishes, I am among the examples of those who have been overcome by grief').

[68] Ker 2009, 109.

[69] Cf. Canobbio 2011, 18: 'Il tema della *vera vita* è affrontato in tre epigrammi (20; 58; 64) [in Martial's fifth book of epigrams, N. M.] che combinano l'invito oraziano a *vivere hodie* con quello

Horace, Seneca, and Martial: 'Sententious Style' across Genres — 335

> Si tecum mihi, care Martialis,
> securis liceat frui diebus,
> si <u>disponere tempus otiosum</u>
> et <u>verae</u> pariter <u>vacare vitae</u>,
> ...
> Nunc <u>vivit</u> neuter <u>sibi</u>, bonosque
> soles effugere atque abire sentit,
> qui <u>nobis pereunt et inputantur.</u>
> <u>Quisquam vivere cum sciat, moratur?</u>

> If you and I, dear Martialis, were permitted to enjoy careless days, if permitted to dispose an idle time, and both alike to have leisure for genuine life... Today neither man lives for himself, and he feels the good days are flitting and passing away, that perish for us and are scored to our account. Does any man, when he knows how to live, delay?
> (Mart. 5.20.1–4, 11–14)

Verbal expressions regarding life and time are drawn from Seneca (lines 3, 4, 11, 13, 14), and *vita vera* recurs already in Horace (Ep. 2.2.144: *sed verae numerosque modosque ediscere vitae*, 'but rather to learn the notes and tunes of life itself').[70]

> Cras te victurum, cras dicis, Postume, semper.
>   Dic mihi, cras istud, Postume, quando venit?
> ...
> Cras vives? Hodie iam vivere, Postume, serum est:
>   ille sapit quisquis, Postume, vixit heri.

> 'Tomorrow you will live, tomorrow,' you are always saying, Postumus. Tell me, when does that 'tomorrow' arrive, Postumus?... Tomorrow will you live? To live today, Postumus, is already too late. He is wise, whoever he be, Postumus, who lived yesterday.
> (Mart. 5.58.1–2, 7–8)

This epigram makes obvious allusions to several poems of Horace – Carm. 2.14 to Postumus, Carm. 1.9.13 (*quid sit futurum cras, fuge quaerere*: 'cease to ask what tomorrow will bring forth'), and the famous *carpe diem* poem Carm. 1.11 – but also to Seneca's doctrine that time should be used in the right way.[71]

Another good example is Mart. 10.47, which contains parallels not only to Seneca's *De Vita Beata*, but also to the ideals put forward by Horace (e.g. in S. 2.6.59–76, with its relaxed dining in a rustic, quasi-Epicurean setting, or in Hor. S. 2.4.95 *vitae praecepta beatae*, 'instructions for a happy life'):

---

senecano a *vivere sibi* e dai quali si evince un messaggio esistenziale, vagamente filosofico, relativo al buon uso del tempo.'
70 Cf. Canobbio 2011 ad loc.
71 Cf. Canobbio 2011 ad loc.

> Vitam quae faciant beatiorem,
> Iucundissime Martialis, haec sunt:
> Res non parta labore, sed relicta;
> Non ingratus ager, focus perennis;
> Lis numquam, toga rara, mens quieta; 5
> Vires ingenuae, salubre corpus;
> Prudens simplicitas, pares amici;
> Convictus facilis, sine arte mensa;
> Nox non ebria, sed soluta curis;
> Non tristis torus, et tamen pudicus; 10
> Somnus, qui faciat breves tenebras:
> Quod sis, esse velis nihilque malis;
> Summum nec metuas diem nec optes.

The things that make life happier, most genial Martialis, are these: means not acquired by labour, but bequeathed; fields not unkindly, an ever blazing hearth; no lawsuit, the toga seldom worn, a quiet mind; a free man's strength, a healthy body; frankness with tact, congenial friends, pleasant companionship, a dining without art; nights not drunken, but freed from cares; a bed not gloomy and yet chaste; sleep such as makes the darkness brief; that you wish to be what you are, and prefer nothing; nor dread your last day, nor long for it. (Mart. 10.47)

On the one hand, this poem could be taken as evidence that the philosophies of Horace and Seneca should not be assigned too strictly to philosophical schools (Epicurean versus Stoic) – at any rate, they coexist harmoniously in Martial's epigram. Perhaps this is an effect of the banalisation (the so-called 'dumbing down') of the philosophical language and ideals of Horace and Seneca.[72] On the other hand, it is also evidence of the rhetorical and didactic strategies in the sententious writing of the philosophical personae of Horace, Seneca, and Martial: Martial ends his epigram with a philosophical *sententia*, just as Horace might have done to close the argumentation in his philosophical epistles, or Seneca in his treatises. Indeed, there are strong parallels between the close of Martial's poem and Seneca's *De Vita Beata* (Dial. 7.5.1): *potest beatus dici, qui nec cupit nec timet beneficio rationis* ('one may describe the happy man as someone who neither desires nor fears thanks to the gift of reason'). For this Stoic concept Seneca in Ep. 5 refers to Hecato of Rhodes:[73]

---

[72] See Piazzi 2004, esp. 75.
[73] Hecato was a pupil of Panaetius. Among his works mentioned by Diogenes Laertius are the *Chreiai* ('Maxims'), perhaps the source for Seneca. For Seneca's quoting of *sententiae* see Tischer in this volume.

Sed ut huius quoque diei lucellum tecum communicem, apud Hecatonem nostrum inveni cupiditatum finem etiam ad timoris remedia proficere. 'Desines' inquit 'timere, si sperare desieris.'

But I wish to share with you today's profit, too. I find in the writings of our Hecato that the limiting of desires helps also to cure fears: 'Cease to hope,' he says, 'and you will cease to fear.'
(Sen. Ep. 5.7)

Using *sententiae* that concern the right way to live (Seneca cites Hecato, Martial alludes to Seneca) is to take part in the didactic strategies of philosophical writing. Rhetorical, philosophical, and literary claims overlap.

The interactions among different traditions and genres become complex and circular at this point: the *dicta* and *sententiae* come not only from the Roman rhetorical schools, but from the Greek philosophical tradition. It is revealing that in some of the cases in which Martial seems to borrow from Seneca the *sententia* is not from Seneca himself, but is a quotation from other Stoic philosophers of the Roman era – for example, Hecato (Sen. Ep. 9.6: *si vis amari, ama*, 'if you want to be loved, love' – Mart. 6.11.10: *ut ameris, ama* 'to be loved, love') or Athenodorus (Sen. Ep. 10.5: *tunc scito esse te omnibus cupiditatibus solutum, cum eo perveneris, ut nihil deum roges nisi quod rogare possis palam*, 'Know that you are free from all desires when you have reached such a point that you pray to the deity for nothing except what you can pray for openly'; and Mart. 1.39.6: *et nihil arcano qui roget ore deos*, 'and who asks nothing from the gods secretly'). The Stoics set a high value on literature as a medium for philosophical expression.[74] They made extensive use of rhetorical forms such as *sententiae* or diatribe. Seneca's general willingness to employ all the literary and rhetorical arts in expounding his ethical doctrine enables us to see a connection between the Hellenistic diatribes and the *Epistulae Morales*.[75] The Hellenistic diatribes had influenced Cicero's *Paradoxa Stoicorum* and the *Satires* of Horace as well. And the *Satires* and *Epistles* of Horace on moral themes are in many respects our closest precedent for what Seneca was doing in prose.[76]

Martial and the genre of epigram add something to these considerations. This body of work shows how authors of first-person literature engage with each other cross-generically to construct their respective personae and define their poetics, the poetics of life, for their philosophy of life. Diatribe, moral sermon, satire, moral epistle, moral and satiric epigram (both Greek and Latin),

---

[74] See e.g. Colish 1985, 58–60 with further literature.
[75] For the diatribic character of the *Epistulae Morales* see e.g. Hamacher 2006, 37–41.
[76] See Coleman 1974, 289.

pointed and / or philosophical *sententia* all mingle, and it becomes problematic to distinguish the generic source (whether Greek or Latin) from which the authors have drawn, since the traditions often overlap.[77]

Sometimes Martial puts inherited content into epigrammatic form without any notable differences arising from the change of genre; but sometimes he seems to transform the philosophy of Horace or Seneca rather significantly. Two examples will make this evident.

First, the philosophical problem of the *commutatio loci* ('change of place') is formulated several times both in Horace and in Seneca.[78] They use almost identical wording:

> <u>caelum, non animum mutant</u>, qui <u>trans mare</u> currunt.[79]
>
> Those who rush across the sea change their clime, not their mind / soul.
> (Hor. Ep. 1.11.27)
>
> Hoc tibi soli putas accidisse et admiraris quasi rem novam quod peregrinatione tam longa et tot locorum varietatibus non discussisti tristitiam gravitatemque mentis? <u>Animum debes mutare, non caelum</u>. Licet vastum <u>traieceris mare</u>, licet, ut ait Vergilius noster,
>   'terraeque urbesque recedant,'
> sequentur te quocumque perveneris vitia.
>
> Do you suppose that it has happened to you alone and are you surprised as if it were a novelty that after such long travel and so many changes of places you have not shaken off the gloom and the heaviness of your mind? You need to change your mind / soul, not the clime. Though you may cross vast spaces of sea, and though, as our Virgil remarks, 'lands and cities are left,' your faults will follow you wherever you travel.
> (Sen. Ep. 28.1)

The underlined *sententia* found in these excerpts of Horace and Seneca could have been written by Martial. Indeed, Martial makes use of a *sententia* from Seneca on the same topic: he ends Epigram 7.73 on Maximus, a man who constantly changes residence, with these words: *quisquis ubique habitat, Maxime, nusquam habitat* ('he who stays everywhere, stays nowhere'). Seneca in Ep. 2.2 wrote a very similar aphorism: *nusquam est qui ubique est* ('he is nowhere, who is everywhere'). Seneca is referring to a practice of reading that does not

---

[77] See Sullivan 1991, 104, n. 46: 'The problem is to distinguish, if at all possible and worthwhile, the topics Martial takes from Roman satire proper, the primary Greek source or satiric Greek epigram, since these often overlap' (with further literature).
[78] See Introduction, 5–6.
[79] On this *sententia* in Horace and its concluding function in Sen. Ep. 1.11.27 see Guglielmo 2010, 202.

focus on the important authors but which is unstable. The epigrammatist in turn refers to a more practical 'wisdom' when talking about changing residences: 'unstable' becomes 'unsettled.' In a maxim of worldly wisdom, a *sententia*, Seneca offered rich material that could be adapted to the genre of epigram with little change.

For the so-called dumbing down or deflation of a philosophical maxim within the epigrammatic genre, I would like to add one example of Martial's epigrammatic transformation of Horace:

> Qualem, Flacce, velim quaeris nolimve puellam?
>   nolo nimis facilem difficilemque nimis.
> Illud quod medium est atque inter utrumque probamus:
>   nec volo quod cruciat nec volo quod satiat.[80]
>
> Do you ask, Flaccus, what sort of girl I like or dislike? I dislike one too yielding, and one too coy. That middle type between the two I approve: I like not that which racks me, nor like I that which satiates.
> (Mart. 1.57)

The question in the first line recalls the first lines of Horace, Carm. 1.11.1–2 (*tu ne quaesieris... quem mihi quem tibi..., Leuconoe...*). This poem features the famous maxim *carpe diem* (1.11.8). Martial does not pick up this concept, but that of the golden mean instead. Certainly, this is found in authors besides Horace and is, like the topos of choosing the right partner, part of the tradition of Greek epigram,[81] but for a Roman reader Horace would doubtless have been the most important precursor: he formulates the same maxim in Carm. 2.10.5–6 very explicitly (*auream quisquis mediocritatem | diligit* 'whoever chooses the golden mean').[82] After the first line of Martial's epigram, which clearly recalls Horace, the following two lines also seem to point to Horace in particular as a model. Martial in the final line transforms the concept of the golden mean into a criterion for the choice of female sex-partners. This fits with the poetics of real life and the sexualised genre of epigram.

---

[80] On this epigram see Citroni 1975, 191–192, and Howell 1980, 241–243.
[81] Citroni 1975, 191–192, lists parallels from the *Anthologia Palatina*. See already Prinz 1911, who points especially to Straton, AP 12.200. See also Höschele 2006, 58–61, who finds more coincidences with Rufinus. She hides in note 168 the important hint that it will be no surprise, 'dass der Adressat des Martial-Epigramms ebenso heißt wie der berühmteste römische Vertreter der *aurea-mediocritas*-Philosophie, Q. Horatius Flaccus' (ibid. 60).
[82] Degl'Innocenti Pierini 1992 shows that the Horatian *aurea mediocritas* occurs in Seneca's tragedies.

But Horace himself, already in S. 1.2, had explained the problem of extremes (S. 1.2.28 nil medium est) when choosing between *matronae* and *meretrices* as sexual partners. The satiric 'I' defines his attitude to sex in line 119: *namque parabilem amo Venerem facilemque* ('for I desire an easily acquired and simple type of love'). Martial corrects the definition of the golden mean where the satiric 'I' of Horace's S. 1.2 fails: nolo nimis facilem *difficilemque nimis.* | illud quod medium est.... Martial's reading of the golden mean in Horace's later works may have been influenced by Horace the satirist, a Horace who in many respects may be closer to his own genre.[83]

Reminiscences of the Horatian *Satires* in Martial have been observed several times.[84] The *Satires* influenced Martial not only in terms of content,[85] but also in the strategies he took to defend certain characteristics of his poetry. Like Horace, Martial avoids naming contemporaries in his satiric epigrams in favour of satirising types, a technique that can also be found in Seneca. In 10.33 Martial professes *parcere personis, dicere de vitiis* (10.33.10 'to spare individuals, to speak of vices') and that his verses are free from *aerugo* (line 5). These are central ideas in Horace's S. 1.4.[86] Compare:

> Simplicior priscis, Munati Galle, Sabinis,
>   Cecropium superas qui bonitate senem,
> Sic tibi consoceri claros retinere penates
>   Perpetua natae det face casta Venus:
> Ut tu, si viridi tinctos aerugine versus   5
>   Forte malus livor dixerit esse meos,
> Ut facis, a nobis abigas, nec scribere quemquam

---

[83] The poetics of real life, also in diction, are expressed clearly in the preface of Martial's first book of epigrams (cf. Mart. 1 praef. 3): *iocorum nostrorum simplicitate* ('the simplicity / straightforwardness of my jokes')... *lascivam verborum veritatem, id est epigrammaton linguam* ('the frank and lewd language, that is the language of epigram'); and in Epigram 11.20.10: *Romana simplicitate loqui* ('to speak with Roman plainness'). S. 1.2 of Horace clearly uses the *lascivam verborum veritatem* as well.
[84] Cf. Szelest 1963, 27–37; Salemme 1976, 86–92; Sullivan 1991, 104.
[85] Like Horace, Martial prefers to satirise types, e.g. the legacy hunter (see Mart. 2.40, esp. 4.56, 5.39, 6.62 and 63, 8.27, 9.8 and 48, 11.44, 12.90). This is a popular topic in satire in general, but perhaps Martial also had Horace's famous S. 2.5 in mind (esp. 4.56). The dedication of chains by a former slave in Mart. 3.29 (*Has cum gemina compede dedicat catenas,* | *Saturne, tibi Zoilus, anulos priores*) may allude to Hor. S. 1.5.65–66 (...*donasset iamne catenam* | *ex voto Laribus, quaerebat*...), the only direct parallel, cf. Fusi 2006, 258–263. Martial's sceptic epigrams on *vetulae* (Mart. 3.93, 9.37, and 11.29) seem more motivated by the eighth and twelfth *Epode* than similar epigrams in the *Anthologia Palatina*, cf. Grassmann 1966, 23–28.
[86] See Neger 2012, 244, and in general her chapter 6.2, 'Horaz: Satire und Iambik,' with further literature.

> Talia contendas carmina, qui legitur.
> Hunc servare modum nostri novere libelli,
> <u>Parcere personis, dicere de vitiis.</u>
>
> Munatius Gallus, more simple in manners than the Sabines of old, more virtuous than the Athenian old man (Socrates), so may the chaste Venus bless your union, and give you to inherit the noble mansion of your father-in-law, as you exculpate me when perchance malicious envy shall call my verses steeped in poisonous gall, and as you insist that no poet, who is read, composes such verses. In all my books my rule has ever been to spare the person, to denounce the vice.
> (Mart. 10.33)
>
> hic nigrae sucus lolliginis, haec est
> <u>aerugo</u> mera; quod vitium procul afore chartis
> atque animo prius;...
> ...exemplis vitiorum quaeque notando.
>
> Here is the very ink of the cuttlefish; here is venom unadulterated. That such malice shall be far from my pages, and first of all from my heart; ...by using examples to brand each of the vices.
> (Hor. S. 1.4.100–102, 106)

Several contributions to this volume discuss the interaction between Horace and Seneca regarding the connection between philosophy and literature. Martial's persona as poet-philosopher corroborates these interactions. Sullivan categorises Martial as a 'social poet and an acute... critic of contemporary society.'[87] This statement is in fact true of all three authors: they are *castigatores morum*. They share certain views when it comes to practical ethics, and they share techniques for presenting them. The following passage from Seneca illustrates this chain of Horace – Seneca – Martial:

> Callidus non difficilem aditum praebuit inmodica cupientibus spesque inprobas nihil re adiuturus verbis fovit; at peior <u>Opimio</u>, si lingua asper, voltu gravis cum invidia fortunam suam explicuit. Colunt enim detestanturque felicem et, si potuerint, eadem facturi odere facientem. [3] Coniugibus alienis ne clam quidem sed aperte ludibrio habitis suas aliis permisere. Rusticus, inhumanus ac mali moris et inter matronas abominanda condicio est, si quis coniugem suam in sella prostare vetuit et vulgo admissis inspectoribus vehi perspicuam undique. [4] Si quis nulla se amica fecit insignem nec alienae uxori annuum praestat, hunc <u>matronae</u> humilem et sordidae libidinis et <u>ancillariolum vocant</u>. Inde decentissimum sponsaliorum genus est adulterium et in consensu viduitas caelibatusque: <u>nemo uxorem duxit, nisi qui abduxit.</u>
>
> A man is shrewd if he does not make himself difficult of access to those who come with immoderate desires, and encourages their wild expectations by his words although in real-

---

87 Sullivan 1987, 260; see also Sullivan 1991, 104–105.

ity he intends to give them no help; but he is worse than Opimius, if he, sharp of tongue, stern in countenance, flaunts his own good fortune with jealousy. For they admire and imprecate the prosperous man, and they hate him for doing the same things that they would do if they could. [3] They make a laughing-stock of other men's wives, not even secretly, but openly, and then surrender their own wives to others. The man is boorish, ignorant and guilty of bad manners and a detestable condition under the married women, if he forbids his wife to appear in public in a litter and to ride exposed on every side to the view of observers who everywhere approach her. [4] If someone makes himself conspicuous by not having a mistress and does not supply an allowance to another man's wife, the married women say that he is a poor sort and is addicted to low pleasures and affairs with maid-servants. The result of this is that adultery has become the most seemly sort of betrothal and celibacy: no man has taken a wife unless he has taken away a wife.
(Sen. Ben. 1.9.2–4)

Seneca in this philosophical text uses types, just like Horace's *Satires* and Martial's satiric epigrams: he begins with the *callidus* and the 'poor rich man.' This paradox of the 'poor rich man' is a commonplace in ancient moral sermonising and is used several times both by Horace and Seneca.[88] The name 'Opimius,' however, occurs in Horace S. 2.3.142: *pauper Opimius argenti positi intus et auri* ('Opimius, a poor man for all his stored up silver and gold'). Seneca, by choosing the same name for the type 'rich poor man,' is probably hinting directly at Horace. Martial puts the same topos into his Epigram 8.19, which consists only of a monostich: *Pauper videri Cinna vult; et est pauper* ('Cinna wishes to appear poor, and he is poor'). Barwick 1959 has rightly pointed out the parallels between sections 3 and 4 of the Senecan paragraph and Martial's Epigram 12.58:

Ancillariolum tua te vocat uxor, et ipsa
    Lecticariola est: estis, Alauda, pares.

Your wife calls you an admirer of servant maids, and she herself is an admirer of litter-bearers. You are a pair, Alauda.
(Mart. 12.58)

Horace, Seneca, and Martial share the same commonplaces in moral writing and, as the allusions among them have shown, they are aware that they share

---

[88] Hor. S. 2.3.142: *pauper Opimius argenti positi intus et auri* ('Opimius, a poor man for all his gold and silver hoarded up within'); Hor. Carm. 3.16.28: *magnas inter opes inops* ('a poor man in the midst of wealth'); Sen. Her. F. 168: *congesto pauper in auro* ('poor in cumulated gold'); Sen. Ep. 74.4: *in divitiis inopes* ('in wealth needy'). See also Publilius Syrus, T 3: *tam deest avaro quod habet quam quod non habet* ('The miser wants as much that which he has as that which he has not'); Cic. Parad. 3.52: *avari... non modo non copiosi ac divites, sed etiam inopes ac pauperes existimandi sunt* ('misers... are not only to be deemed not well-off and rich, but actually needy and poor.').

them – that they stand in a tradition that crosses genres. We can characterise Martial as moral satirist, Horace as philosophical satirist, or Seneca as epigrammatic philosopher: to provide one final example, Seneca ends his criticisms of *adulterium* in the above excerpt with an epigrammatic *dictum*, with *pointe* and wordplay between *ducere* and *abducere*.

5 Epigrammatic Horace and Seneca?

When we read Horace and Seneca through Martial's eyes, these authors appear to have certain epigrammatic characteristics. Perhaps this is only due to the allelopoetic effect of transformation, that is, the way in which the act of reception or transformation effects a change in the source-material.[89] After we, as observers of the transformation process, have noted that Martial rewrote topics already treated by Horace and / or Seneca, these authors themselves and their texts seem to possess certain epigrammatic features. Martial's selectivity and our own perspective create a new Horace and a new Seneca, both more epigrammatic than they had 'objectively' been. Furthermore, the relationship between Horace, Seneca, and Martial is certainly no exclusive one, and we could proceed from other authors or genres as well.[90] But nevertheless: If we use genre as a heuristic element, it can help us to bring into focus the similarities, affinities, and sometimes even interactions between these three authors.

---

[89] See n. 9.
[90] We might briefly consider an analogous case: some of the *Epistulae* of Pliny the Younger, nearly contemporaneous with Martial, have epigrammatic characteristics and fall into the category of moral epistles. Pliny's *Epistulae* have been compared to the *Epistles* of Horace and the 'quasi-epistolary' writing of Martial. Neger 2015, 144 defines the relationship Martial – Pliny and Pliny – Martial and their genres as 'reciprocal intertextuality between the *Epistulae* and the *Epigrams*.' There is without doubt a cross-generic interaction between Pliny's *Epistulae* and Martial's epigrams (on epigrammatic features in Pliny see Mindt forthcoming). It is striking that we find certain functional affinities between Martial and Horace in Martial's prose prefaces (which take the form of letters). Apart from the prose prefaces, Martial's epigrams from Book 10 play with the conventions of the epistolary genre, a genre used by Horace and Seneca. We can define the affinities between these three authors as epistolographic as well as epigrammatic, and it is therefore better to avoid thinking too strongly in terms of genres.

Victoria Moul
Seneca, Horace, and the Anglo-Latin 'Moralising Lyric' in Early Modern England

The modern perception of Horace is of a lyric poet of evanescent pleasure, of 'wine, women, and song,' and of a distinctively dispassionate and sometimes ironic tone.[1] Although there are occasional traces of this Horace in early modern English poetry, Horatian imitation in this period is dominated by a quite different version of the Roman poet – a perception of Horace as above all a great moralist, both in lyric and hexameter poetry, and a moralist rooted strongly in the everyday realities of courtly life, the demands of patronage, and the pleasures and compromises of panegyric.[2] Richard Tottel's popular *Songes and Sonnettes* (often referred to as 'Tottel's miscellany') of 1557, for instance, includes no fewer than three versions of Carm. 2.10, titled not with reference to Horace, but in terms of their moralising force: 'Praise of mean and constant estate' (no. 32), 'Of the golden mean' (no. 253), and 'The mean estate is to be accounted the best' (no. 163).[3] The volume includes a fourth poem with an almost identical title – 'Of the meane and sure estate' (no. 128) – although this is not in fact a version of Carm. 2.10 but rather Thomas Wyatt's rendering of the final part of the second chorus from Seneca's *Thyestes*, 391–403:

> Stond who so list upon the slipper wheele,
> Of hye astate and let me here rejoyce.
> And use my life in quietnesse eche dele,
> Unknowen in court that hath the wanton toyes,
> In hidden place my time shal slowly passe
> And when my yeres be past withouten noyce

---

1 See for example Harrison 2007c.
2 Burrow 1993; Moul 2010, especially 9–12. The *Epistles* and *Odes* Book 2, with its moral and philosophical themes, and Book 4, with an emphasis upon panegyric, are accordingly particularly popular in early modern translations and imitations; whereas modern criticism has tended to find those collections less rewarding than Books 1 and 3.
3 Each of these poems is presented anonymously, although the first (no. 32) is known to be by Henry Howard, Earl of Surrey. For a fuller discussion of these poems, see Moul 2016. Tottel's work was revised and reprinted eight times between 1557 and 1587, and was the first in a series of popular verse anthologies of this kind. Other poets translated or imitated in the collection (though without explicit acknowledgement) include Lucretius, Seneca, Martial, Boethius, Ausonius, Petrarch, Bonifacio, Serafino, Sannazaro, Collinutio, Beza, Haddon, Scaliger, and Muret. On the role of translation in these collections, see Greene 1999. Wyatt's Horatian epistles are also printed in Tottel's miscellany.

DOI 10.1515/9783110528893-015

Let me dye olde after the common trace
For gripes of death doth he to hardly passe
That knowen is to all: but to him selfe alas
He dyeth unknowen, dased with dreadfull face.[4]

Stet quicumque volet potens
aulae culmine lubrico:
me dulcis saturet quies.
obscuro positus loco
leni perfruar otio,
nullis nota Quiritibus
aetas per tacitum fluat.
sic cum transierint mei
nullo cum strepitu dies,
plebeius moriar senex.
illi mors gravis incubat
qui, notus nimis omnibus,
ignotus moritur sibi.

The editors of the excellent recent edition of the miscellany, in their notes on this poem, stress that such titles encompass two distinct meanings of the word 'mean': 'the "mean" (i.e. lowly) estate is not to be confused with the "mean" (i.e. middle) estate praised in poems on the golden mean, such as poems 32, 163, and 253 [that is, the translations of Horace, Carm. 2.10].'[5] But the overlap of these terms in the titles of the miscellany reflects a 'blurring' of the source texts too. Several of the imitations of Carm. 2.10 make more explicit than the Latin original the connection between the tall pine tree, towers, and mountain-tops of the third stanza and high office, the realm of courts and palaces.[6] Similarly, several of the poems on the advantages of virtuous obscurity over wealth and high office – the theme of Seneca's chorus – introduce imagery of sailing

---

[4] Text quoted from Holton / MacFaul 2011. Gillespie 2015 places Wyatt's version at the head of a tradition of English translations of this chorus. An alternative and more often quoted version of the same poem, beginning 'Stond who so list upon the Slipper toppe | Of courtes estates, and lett me heare reioyce | and use my quyet without lett or stoppe | unknowe in courte, that hath suche brackishe ioyes' is found in the Arundel Harington MS (311), see Hughey 1960.

[5] Holton / MacFaul 2011, 449. Other examples of poems describing poverty or simplicity of life (a 'mean estate') as the most virtuous include Wyatt's long verse epistle to John Poyns, 'Of the meane and sure estate written to John Poins', (no. 134), 'They of the meane estate are happiest' (no. 140), and 'The meane estate is best' (no. 160).

[6] An expansion probably suggested by Horace's phrase *invidenda... aula* (Carm. 2.10.7–8). On echoes of Horace's 'golden mean' in Seneca, see Degl'Innocenti Pierini 1992.

influenced by Horace.⁷ Seneca's moralising choruses are themselves of course dependent upon and reminiscent of Horace – compare for instance the combination of 'golden mean' and sailing imagery (indebted especially to Horace, Carm. 2.10) in Oed. 882–914 and Med. 599–606, and the substantial borrowings from Horace, including Carm. 1.1 and Epod. 2, in Her. F. 125–204.

In Tottel's collection, similar generalising titles are given for a version of Horace, Carm. 4.4 ('All worldly pleasures vade,' no. 166), Surrey's translation of Martial 10.47 (no. 31, 'The meanes to attain happy life'), and a further poem, which does not appear to be a translation of any particular classical poem ('The pore estate to be holden for best,' no. 169), but which incorporates an acrostic on the name of Edward Somerset, who had fallen from power in 1549 and was executed in 1552:

> Experience now doth shew what God us taught before,
> Desired pompe is vaine, and seldome doth it last:
> Who climbes to raigne with kinges, may rue his fate full sore.
>
> ...
>
> Such as with oten cakes in poore estate abides,
> Of care have they no cure, the crab with mirth they rost,
> More ease fele they then those, that from their height down slides
> Excesse doth brede their wo, they saile in Scillas cost,
> Remainying in the stormes tyll shyp and al be lost.
> Serve God therefore thou pore, for lo, thou lives in rest,
> Eschue the golden hall, thy thatched house is besT.⁸

The last line of this poem alludes to Carm. 2.10, and the address to a named individual also recalls Horace, but the sustained and explicit moralising is closer in tone to Seneca. Poems of this sort were an enduringly popular kind of early modern lyric, representing some of the most widely circulated types of poem in manuscript miscellanies; they are closely related to the classical tradition, as the overlap between translation and looser imitation in Tottel's volume demonstrates, but they have barely been considered in terms of classical reception because they do not fit well into the models of classical imitation which have been most influential upon studies of English literature in recent years.⁹

---

7 As in no. 169 quoted below: 'they saile in Scillas cost, | Remainying in the stormes tyll shyp and al be lost'; see also no. 160, 'The meane estate is best': 'The wofull ship of carefull sprite...' (lines 13–18).
8 The last letter of the poem is capitalised to indicate the final letter of the acrostic-telestic, spelling out 'Edward Somerset.'
9 Greene 1982, for instance, focuses upon the tension and dissonance of what he calls 'dialectical' imitation; this concept is linked to Pigman's 'eristic' imitation (Pigman 1980). These read-

In this chapter I want to explore the overlap between imitation of Horace and Seneca in sixteenth- and seventeenth-century moralising lyrics of this kind, and in both English and Latin, since these lyrics – in common with most fashions in early modern English literature – are found in both languages, and indeed often (especially in manuscripts) in bilingual presentation. Analyses of allusion and intertextuality usually work by breaking a poem down into constituent and contributing elements, often emphasising, at least in the more interesting readings, the sophisticated 'conversation' or even competition created between competing allusions.[10] This is not a satisfactory model for poetry of this sort. What is effective and memorable about these generalising lyrics is not usually their allusive structure: there is no real sense of 'dialogue' between Horatian and Senecan elements in most of these poems.[11] Their power derives rather from the force of their authority, an impression created partly by a sense of multiple overlapping precedents, each in themselves morally as well as aesthetically authoritative, augmented, in some instances, by the counterpoint between general sentiments and the specific personal or contemporary contexts in which such poems were placed not only (or even mostly) by their authors, but also by those who read, transcribed, and circulated them.[12]

This congruence of Horatian and Senecan translation and imitation has attracted no critical attention partly because it is found most obviously in the kind of widely circulated lyrics which, though appearing in multiple print and manu-

---

ings, in which an individual poet grapples with and even outdoes authoritative earlier texts, naturally also tend to stress authorial personality and individual 'self-fashioning.' (Pigman's discussion of his other categories of imitation, 'transformative' and 'dissimulative,' still tends to stress the author's unique response to one specific – even if concealed – model.) This kind of theoretical approach works well for many early modern poets, including Jonson (discussed at length by Greene 1999, 264–293; see also Moul 2010) but is less useful for the kind of poem analysed here, which is much less concerned with the individual identity either of the author or of a specific source text. The authorship of these poems is frequently obscure or confused, and in a sense irrelevant, and yet the literary authority and popularity of these pieces is real.

10 This is for instance key to the analysis of Jonson's intertextuality in my own earlier work, Moul 2010.

11 Although I certainly do not mean to be dogmatic on this point, and where there did seem to me to be a real sense of intertextual 'conversation' between source-texts, I have commented to that effect.

12 A fuller study would incorporate imitations and translations of the metrical portions of Boethius as well, since they often appear alongside Horatian and Senecan material in this period, or are translated by the same authors. See e. g. Thomas Wyatt, 'He ruleth not though he raigne over realmes that is subject to his own lustes,' no. 122 in Tottel's *Songes and Sonnettes*, as well as the manuscript poems of John Polwhele, Richard Fanshawe, and the author of BL [British Library] Harley MS 3910.

script miscellanies, have not often been included in modern anthologies; but also because our modern patterns of education and scholarship, both in classics and English literature, make the existence of a substantial zone of 'Horatio-Senecan' lyric – a point which must have been obvious to the point of banality to educated early modern readers – hard to discern. There are three main reasons for this. First, the elements of Horatian lyric least popular today, both in teaching and scholarship – hymns, moralising, and panegyric lyric – map almost precisely onto the most widely appropriated poems in sixteenth- and seventeenth-century England.[13] Second, Seneca's drama is no longer a centrepiece of early classical education, as it was in the early modern period; and although Seneca has attracted attention in the context of early modern classical reception, such work has focused largely upon the development of Renaissance drama, and paid relatively little attention to the lyric qualities of the Senecan chorus, or the frequency with which such passages were excerpted and translated.[14] Finally, studies of English poetry in the sixteenth and seventeenth centuries have largely ignored neo-Latin verse, despite the great quantity of Latin material found in both print and manuscript sources of the period.[15] This refusal to engage with what we actually find in early modern literary sources has occluded the bilingualism of literary culture: time and again, a resonant English lyric which does not look or sound markedly 'Horatian' or 'Senecan,' especially to the scholar who associates Seneca with drama (not lyric) and Horace with erotic or sympotic (not moralising or political) verse, is found in contemporary manuscripts accompanied by a Latin version, or Latin companion poem, which makes the Horatio-Senecan associations of the piece quite plain.[16]

---

[13] As a representative starting point, see for instance the selection chosen for inclusion by Ashmore for his 1621 volume, discussed further below. In each section of the volume (Horatian translations, epigrams, 'country life' and 'blessed life' poems) Ashmore reproduces just the kind of loosely thematic subsections that one tends to find in manuscript verse collections of the period.
[14] Particularly important here is the influence of popular contemporary anthologies of extracts: see for instance Mirandula 1507, Maior 1534, Dornavius 1619, Langius 1625. The major forthcoming anthology by Gillespie (Gillespie forthcoming) will include a section on both Seneca and Horace. On Seneca's lyric appropriation of Horace, see e.g. Stevens 1999, Degl'Innocenti Pierini 1992, Spika 1890.
[15] The only overview remains Bradner 1940, though see also Davidson 2007, 25–93 and my own forthcoming monograph (Moul forthcoming). The only English poet whose Latin work has attracted sustained attention is John Milton; his literary bilingualism is frequently presented as an unusual or unique phenomenon, whereas it is in most respects typical.
[16] In the title of this chapter, I have used the phrase 'Anglo-Latin' to refer to this phenomenon, which is intended to encompass pieces of neo-Latin poetry by English authors, English poems

The enthusiasm for literary translation – and, standing closely behind it, the educational practice of 'double translation,' first from Latin into the vernacular and then of the (corrected) vernacular translation 'back' into Latin – is of central importance to this phenomenon.[17] Tottel makes no distinction between translations, freer imitations, and 'original' poems (not in any case a category he would probably have recognised): none of the titles in the volume indicate that the poem is a translation.[18] Both print and manuscript sources of the sixteenth and seventeenth century reflect this: translations, or sequences of translations, frequently appear in volumes which demonstrate the taste for, and production of, the sort of moralising lyrics with which this chapter is concerned.

British Library Harley MS 3910 is a typical example; a small paper book of 147 leaves, it contains a large variety of English and Latin poetry in various hands, with many examples of bilingual presentation: that is, copies of the Latin and English versions of a poem recorded alongside one another.[19] None of the entries are dated, although the poems included, and events referred to, suggest that it dates from the 1620s.[20] The most relevant sequence for the purposes of this study begins on fol. 76^v, with an eight-line extract from the opening of Horace, Carm. 3.3 (*Iustum et tenacem propositi virum...*) accompanied on the facing page (fol. 77^r) by an English translation:

> A Just and setled man, resolued aright;
> Not Ciuicke rage forcing to things vnfitt,
> Not cruellest Tyrants terrifying sight
> Nor feircest stormes wch the swolne ocean splitt;

---

which are either translations or close imitations of specific Latin pieces, and also the characteristic juxtaposition of Latin and English versions of poems in the manuscript record.
17 [W. E.] Miller 1963.
18 Though occasionally the text itself suggests it: e.g. the first line of poem 31 (a translation of Martial), 'Martial, the things that do attain | The happy life, be these, I finde.'
19 For instance, Latin poems by William Alabaster accompanied by English translations by Hugh Holland on fols. 51^v–53^r; Latin epigrams with English translations on fols. 56^r, 56^v; a Latin song from John Barclay's *Euphormio* with an English translation on the facing page, fols. 75^v–76^r.
20 See the online *Catalogue of English Literary Manuscripts* http://www.celm-ms.org.uk/repositories/british-library-harley-3000.html#british-library-harley-3000_id667535. The final section of the volume contains many poems in Latin and English commemorating the death of Thomas Murray, Secretary to Charles, Prince of Wales, who died in 1623. In a recent article Gillespie dates two of the translations in this MS to the early eighteenth century (Gillespie 2015), but correspondence with him has confirmed that this was based on a mistranscription, and he now concurs with a dating from around 1620. This revised dating will be reflected in Gillespie (forthcoming).

> Nor Thundring Joues high hand can e're affright
> Or shake his solid mind from her fix't plight
> Yea, though the shatter'd world in peeces fall,
> The ruines strike him, not appall'd at all./[21]

The following double-page spread (fols. 77ᵛ–78ʳ) contains the Latin text, with facing translation, of the same section from the second chorus of Seneca's *Thyestes* already given above: in fact, the opening eight lines of Carm. 3.3 is one of the identifiable sources for Seneca's chorus, as the sequence of entries here suggests.[22] This notebook, though, records not one but two distinct versions of the poem, the first considerably longer than the second (thirty-two compared to twelve lines), though both apparently indebted to Wyatt's version.[23]

> Let him that listeth liue at court
> In all the pomp and princely port
> That place affords of Princes grac't
> And on the top of greatness plac't
> So slippery and so prone to fall
> And so precipitate with all:
> Let him that list, with vast desire
> Not reason-bounded swell to' aspire;
> Let quietness and sweete content
> Still satisfy my soule, not bent
> To high designes, but being retyred
> Vnto some place, of none admired,
> Or enuy'd, nor in the obvious eye
> Of prying critiques, or the dye
> Of their rash doomes: so plac't I shall
> Enioy my peace & rest with all
> Free to my selfe, not vnder checke
> Of haughty seigniors at their becke,

---

21 fol. 77ʳ. This is a very commonly excerpted and translated passage in miscellanies of the period; compare for instance Cambridge University Library MS Dd. 14. 8, fol. 25ᵛ (a translation of the same passage).
22 Compare Hor. Carm. 3.3.1–8 and Sen. Thy. 348–364. For discussion of the Horatianism of this chorus, see Tarrant 1985, 137.
23 BL Harley MS 3910, fols. 77ᵛ–79ʳ. Both of these versions are printed in Gillespie's recent short anthology of translations just of this passage (Gillespie 2015). I have not been able to identify the author of these poems. Translations of this passage survive by many English poets; Gillespie also prints examples by Jasper Heywood, Robert Sidney, Abraham Cowley, Matthew Hale, Andrew Marvell, John Wright, John Norris of Bemerton, Robert Dobbins, John Rawlet, Richard Bulstrode, Daniel Baker, George Granville, Thomas Morrell, John Cotton, Richard Polwhele, and Goldwin Smyth, as well as several anonymous versions.

> Not crouching, nor in cringing posture,
> Playing, for gains, the slye imposture,
> But plac't in quiet in mine owne,
> Of Great ones neither markt, nor knowne
> My life shall slyly steale away,
> Like brookes which, trilling, never stay;
> So when my daies are ouerpast
> Not noysd, or noted; at the last
> A poore old man, and ripe for death
> I shall surrender this my breath:
> A heauy death on that man lyes
> Who to much knowne to all men, dyes
> So farre estranged from his [ei]one,
> That he is to himself vnknowne.
> (fols. 78ʳ–79ᵛ)

> Let him that list, vpon the slippery hill
> Of courtly fauor build his lofty tower,
> in humble valley I securely will
> and safely rest within my lowly bower;
>   while, in obscurity to states vnknowne,
>   like a still riuollet my yeares slyde on –
> So, without noyse when I haue runne my race,
> from worldly care & perturbation free,
> then, to the graue a gods name let me passe
> a plaine ould fellow: better yet then he,
>   whom all men know too well, and yet alone
>   alas, he dies vnto himself vnknowne.
> Another transl: of yᵉ same.
> (fol. 78ᵛ)

These three translations are in fact only the beginning of a sequence of classical translation, all with facing Latin text, which assembles passages of Seneca, Horace, Martial, and Boethius, namely: the second chorus of Seneca's *Medea*; the first chorus of the *Agamemnon*; *Phaedra* 483–558; Horace, Carm. 2.3, 2.14, 2.15, 3.23, 4.7, 4.9; Martial 9.17, 10.47, and 11.40; Boethius, *De Consolatione Philosophiae* 1, metrum 4; 3, metrum 6.[24] There is an obvious thematic coherence to this selection; compare for instance the translation of the first chorus of the *Agamemmnon* (translating lines 57–74), which begins:

---

[24] BL Harley MS 3910, fols. 76ᵛ–99ʳ. Some further translations (e. g. of Catul. 63; Hor. Carm. 4.7; Mart. 9.47, 10.47, 11.40) appear in the more varied material (including a large amount of contemporary Latin verse) in the rest of the volume, but without the same thematic coherence.

> O deceitfull kingdomes Fate,
> In their greatest, and best estate
> Placing their high-crested state
> Doubtfully, precipitate.
> Scepters n'ere in quiet sway
> Nor e're kept their certaine day
> Care on care doth them perplex
> And new stormes their minds still vexe:
> Not the Lybicke sea so raues
> Rowling roaring waues on waues;
> Nor the Euxine so turmoiles
> Or from his huge dpeth so boiles
> When the frosty neighbour-Pole
> Doth his freer course countroul
> As the state & port of kings
> Fortune wheeling, headlong flings
> To be feared they feare, desire,
> Night to them no safe retyre...
> (fol. 84^r)

with the version of Boethius, Cons. 1.4:

> He that is still, in setled state
> And vnderfoote hath trode proud Fate,
> And either Fortune can behold
> with an undaunted looke & bold,
> Him, no seas rage, nor threatning surge
> W^{ch} from the bottome stirr'd doth vrge
> Nor mountaines casting smoake & fire,
> from horrid riftes, wch all admire,
> Nor feircest lightnings from aboue,
> vsd to strike highest towres, shall moue
> why doe fond men so much admire,
> Madd Tyrants rage, & strengthlesse ire?
> Lay by vaine Hope, & Feare, & then
> Thou shalt disarme the rage of men.
> But he that feares, or wishes; hee
> Being vnsetled, and not free,
> Hath Lost his sheild, & place; and knitt
> A Chaine, to be drag'd-on by itt./
> (fol. 93^r)

and that of Horace, Carm. 2.3, beginning:

> Still keepe an euen mind in thy distresse,
> And temper'd from loose mirth in good successe;

> Thou art to Dye, whether in discontent
> And wasting sadnes all thy tyme be spent...
> (fol. 94ʳ)

The selected texts have significant overlaps in theme and tone, but these are emphasised and augmented by the translations, which reuse certain words ('And so precipitate with all,' translating Thy. 341–342; 'Doubtfully, precipitate,' translating Ag. 58) and phrases ('He that is still, in setled state,' Boe. Cons. 1.4.1; 'Still keepe an even mind,' Carm. 2.3.1; 'Meane estat's doe longer last,' translating Ag. 102; 'In their greatest and best estate,' translating Ag. 57). The Latin that stands behind these examples is often quite different: towards the end of the version of the *Agamemnon* chorus, for instance, the English line 'Meane estat's doe longer last' (fol. 86ʳ) translates the Latin line *modicis rebus longius aevum est* (fol. 85ᵛ, Ag. 102), where English 'estates' translates Latin *rebus* ('things,' 'matters,' 'situation'). At the beginning of the same poem, the line 'In their greatest, and best estate' (fol. 84ʳ) uses the same English word to translate the Latin phrase *magnis... bonis* (Ag. 57). The sense of ethical coherence is intensified by the close relationship between the English words 'estate' and 'state,' both of which had a different and wider range of meanings in early modern English than they do today.[25] 'State' recurs very frequently in the sequence: the phrase 'setled state,' for instance, appears both in the translation of Boethius, Cons. 1.4.1 – 'He that is still, in setled state' translating *Quisquis composito serenus aevo* (fols. 92ᵛ–93ʳ) – and in the translation of Horace, Carm. 4.9 ('From her right and setled state,' fol. 98ʳ), associating via the translation two ostensibly rather different poems.[26]

These repeated words and phrases have a cumulative force, partly simply by virtue of their recurrence in the sequence itself, and partly by their ethical and literary resonance, reaching back, via Jonson, to Elizabethan and Tudor lyric, and indeed (as in 'Meane estat's doe longer last') to Tottel's miscellany itself. The translations are also quite substantial expansions, as the *mise-en-page* of the manuscript makes immediately clear: some pages have as few as eight lines on the left (Latin) side against twenty-three on the right, and the expansions focus upon the moralising passages most closely related to the 'theme'

---

[25] See for instance OED s.v. 'state,' obsolete usages related to wealth, status, and the natural or proper condition of something, often with an overlap with 'estate': I.1.b. (b), 2.a., 5.a., 5.b., 6.a., 6.b., 7.a, and II.15, 18, 19, 22, 23. The word could even mean the royal throne itself (II.17.a.).
[26] The author of this sequence may have been influenced by Ben Jonson in particular, in whose work 'state' recurs particularly frequently and with a markedly resonant and ethically significant range of meaning, see Moul 2010, 190 and n. 42.

of the collection: in the translation of the *Agamemnon* chorus, for instance, the memorable phrase 'as the state & port of kings' (line 15) translates the much less striking *regnum casus* (Ag. 71). The line from the translation of Carm. 4.9, 'From her right and setled state' (fol. 98ʳ), already noted above as an example of the repetition of key words and phrases across the sequence, is also a significant expansion: the only Latin word to which the phrase corresponds directly is the single adjective *rectus* ('upright,' Carm. 4.9.36).

Many of these translations contain effective passages, and several are successful English poems in their own right, though the parallel text format (which is maintained throughout) and the presence of some lines, such as 'Doubtfully, precipitate,' which are hard to follow without reference to the Latin, suggest that they were intended to be appreciated in close conversation with the Latin texts. But even where the translations are undistinguished, such sequences, found commonly in late sixteenth- and seventeenth-century manuscript miscellanies, offer a clear demonstration of the standard literary associations which linked the lyrics of Horace, Seneca, Boethius, and a selection of other individual pieces (such as Martial 10.47, Claudian's 'Old Man of Verona,' and even versions of the first Psalm).[27] Whereas modern readers and scholars might tend to stress the *individuality* of authors – emphasising for instance the differences in style, tone, and political context of Horace and Seneca, and the role of Seneca's lyrics as dramatic choruses – the typical early modern reader valued the sense of a common purpose and a moral consensus.[28]

---

[27] Compare for instance the earliest surviving manuscript of Richard Fanshawe's well-known translations of Horace (BL Add MS 15228). This manuscript, dating from the 1630s, includes in addition to translations from the *Odes* (1.1, 1.2, 1.4, 1.5, 1.8, 1.13, 1.18; 2.3, 2.8, 2.10, 2.14; 3.7, 3.11, 3.20, 3.24; 4.2, 4.3, 4.4, 4.7; Epod. 16), a long series of translations of the metrical portions of Boethius (an almost continuous sequence from 1.1–5.5), a version of Psalm 45, and thirteen of Martial's epigrams (1.63, 5.62, 8.2, 8.30, 8.56, 8.70, 10.2, 10.23, 10.26, 10.50, 10.66, 12.44, 12.48). Similar if less extensive clusters of translations, including the Seneca *Thyestes* passage, are found through to the early eighteenth century. See e. g. Bodleian Rawl. poet. 90 (early eighteenth century, including Marvell's translation of the *Thyestes* extract) and Rawl. poet. 173 (about 1705), including some of Dryden's translations of Horace alongside John Glanville's version of the Senecan chorus.

[28] Interestingly, where such sequences appear in material dating from the civil war period, the selection of translated material often reflects the political upheaval: see for instance John Polwhele's notebook, Bodleian MS Eng. poet. fol. 16, the early stages of which offer a typical 1630s blend of tributes to Ben Jonson and George Herbert with Horatian translations (Carm. 1.1, 2.14, and a fragment of the *Ars Poetica*) before, apparently in direct response to the events of 1649, breaking suddenly into an extraordinary sequence of heavily revised and explicitly politicised versions of Horace (Carm. 1.14 [twice], 1.33, 4.9; Epod. 5, 7, and 16; Ep. 1.18) and Boethius

But the 'Horatio-Senecan' phenomenon can be traced beyond the (porous) boundaries of translation, whether of individual pieces or in sequences, and into the larger realm of English lyric, both in printed collections and in manuscript sources. Certain lyrics of this sort are almost ubiquitous in manuscript miscellanies of the first part of the seventeenth century, though not usually well represented in anthologies of sixteenth- and seventeenth-century poetry today. Bodleian MS Rawl. poet. 31, dating from c. 1620–1633, is a typical example: identified authors include Sir John Harrington, Henry Wotton, Ben Jonson, John Donne, and Edward Herbert, and the material by Donne and Jonson in particular has attracted attention.[29] This manuscript collection includes, on adjacent pages, two typical examples of the tradition we are tracing here: Henry Wotton's popular poem, 'How happy is he born and taught' (fol. 5ʳ) and Thomas Campion's 'The man of life upright' (fol. 5ᵛ), the latter of which I give below:

> The man of life upright,
>   Whose guiltless hart is free
> From all dishonest deedes,
>   Or thought of vanitie,
>
> The man whose silent dayes
>   In harmless joyes are spent,
> Whome hopes cannot delude,
>   Nor sorrow discontent,
>
> That man needes neither towers
>   Nor armour for defence,
> Nor secret vautes to flie
>   From thunders violence.
>
> Hee onely can behold
>   With unafrighted eyes
> The horrours of the deepe,
>   And terrours of the Skies.

(Cons. 1, metra 2–7; 2, metra 1–8; 3, metra 1–6, twenty translations). I have not however discussed this sequence in more detail since it does not include Seneca.

29 Several of the pieces in this manuscript by Jonson or his associates (e.g. Jonson's translation of Epod. 2; his 'To Sir Robert Wroth,' a related poem; and a partial translation of Ep. 1.18, probably by Jonson's friend Sir John Roe) have a moral force and belong more broadly to this tradition, though their longer length, the sharpness of their allusive relationship, especially with the Horace of the *Epodes* and *Epistles*, and their use of prominent named addressees, represent a distinct, albeit related, kind of poem. Jonson's poems of this sort are some of the best-studied moralising verse of this period, but they are not 'moralising lyrics' of the generalising (and often anonymous) type considered here.

> Thus, scorning all the cares
>   That fate, or fortune brings,
> He makes the heav'n his booke,
>   His wisedome heev'nly things,
>
> Good thoughts his onely friendes,
>   His wealth a well-spent age,
> The earth his sober Inne,
>   And quiet Pilgrimage.[30]

Campion's poem takes its cue (and, in manuscript versions, often its title, 'Integer Vitae') from Horace, Carm. 1.22 (*Integer vitae scelerisque purus*), the first eight lines of which are loosely paraphrased in the opening four stanzas of Campion's poem (compare the relationship between Seneca, Thy. 348–364 and Horace, Carm. 3.3.1–8, noted above). But the focus and unity of Campion's lyric is quite different from the Horatian ode which (typically for Horace) moves after line 8 from the idea that the good man is safe from harm, to a related but distinct suggestion that the lover in the grip of his obsession is equally proof from harm, even in the harshest of environments. The irony is augmented by Horace imagining *himself* (not Fuscus, the addressee of the poem) as the preoccupied lover. The tone of these two poems is quite different: there is nothing arch about Campion's account of what the good man might hope to escape; whereas Horace's list (2–8) is markedly over-the-top. Lines 2–8 of Horace's ode, as well as the later description of exotic wanderings (17–24), are probably indebted to Catullus 11.1–12; and the poem is also linked metrically to Catullus 11 and 51 (the latter itself a version of Sappho), both well-known poems about Lesbia.[31] The alert reader discerns literary self-consciousness, a suggestion of erotic adventure and a degree of irony in Horace's poem well before its explicit thematic 'turn' to the erotic from line 10 onwards. Campion's popular poem, by contrast, raises no such uncertainties of tone, and in both form and content has links to hymnody.[32]

---

[30] Text cited from Davis 1967, 43. Campion's poem was first published as no. 18 in his *Booke of Ayres* (1601).
[31] Indeed, Catul. 11 and 51 are often read as the beginning and end of the 'Lesbia cycle.' See Ancona 1994, 113–121, 168, n. 33.
[32] On links between Psalm 1 and Carm. 1.22, see Hamlin 2004, 67–68; on the popularity and literary importance of neo-Latin psalm paraphrases, see Green 2014. Ashmore's 1621 volume (see further below) concludes with a version of the first psalm. Several influential neo-Latin versions of the psalms, such as those by George Buchanan and Marcantonio Flaminio, used Horatian lyric metres. There is also evidence of Campion's poem influencing translations of Horace's

The tonal stability and moral seriousness of Campion's lyric, despite the poem's obvious debt to Horace, is not ultimately particularly Horatian: but both those characteristics *are* typical of Senecan choruses and the metrical portions of Boethius. Seneca's choruses and the metrical parts of *De Consolatione Philosophiae* are of course indebted to Horace metrically, lexically, and thematically, although they have a quite different tone and 'feel' to them from anything that Horace wrote. Indeed, John Ashmore's *Certain Selected Odes of Horace, Englished* (1621), often cited as the first collection of English translations of Horace's *Odes*, demonstrates both the moral associations of Horatian lyric at this period, and the sense of the moralising subgenre of poems on how to live well, of which Horace himself is only a part. The subtitle of the book continues: *With Poems (Antient and Modern) of divers Subjects, Translated. Whereunto are added, both in Latin and English, sundry new Epigrammes, Annagramms, Epitaphes,* and the work is in fact divided into four parts: the translations and imitations of Horace (1–28); a section of mostly contemporary epigrams, presented in Latin and English (29–79); a section entitled 'The Praise of a Country Life' (81–87) including poems and extracts by Martial and Virgil as well as neo-Latin examples; and a final section 'Of a Blessed Life,' once again a mixture of ancient and modern poems.³³

That final section includes an English lyric with a Latin title, *Lipsii laus, & vota Vitae beatae*:

> Hes like the gods, and higher then
> The rest-less Race of mortall Men,
> That wisheth not, or (in despaire)
> The doubtful Day of Death doth feare.
> In whom Ambition doth not raigne,
> That is not vext with hope of Gaine,
> That trembles not at Threats of Kings,
> Nor Darts that angry *Iove* down flings;
> But, firmely seated in one Place,
> Vulgar Delights doth scorne, as base:
> That of his Life one *Tenor* keeps;
> Secure that wakes, secure that sleeps.
>   If I might live at mine owne pleasure,

---

ode: Richard Fanshawe's translation of Carm. 1.22, first printed in 1652 and probably dating from the previous decade, alludes to Campion's famous poem in its opening line ('Who lives upright, and pure of heart'), though the tone of Fanshawe's translation is much closer to that of Horace than Campion's lyric.

33 The Horatian lyrics chosen for translation in the first part are: Carm. 1.1, 1.5, 1.13, 1.22, 1.23, 1.26, 2.10, 2.14, 2.15, 2.16, 2.18, 3.9, 3.30, 4.3, 4.7, 4.8, and Epod. 2.

I would no Office seek, nor Treasure;
Nor captive Troups should me attend,
As to my Charret I ascend
Drawne by white Steeds, with Shouts and Cries;
A Spectacle to gazing Eyes.
   In Places I remote would be:
Gardens and Fields should solace me:
Ther, at the bubbling waters noyse,
I with the Muses would reioyce.
   So, when my *Lachesis* hath spun
The thread of Life, she well drewn on;
Not unto any man a Foe,
I full of Years from hence would goe,
   And Date my dayes in quiet state,
   As my good *Langius* did of late.

This is, as the title suggests, a translation of a Latin poem by Justus Lipsius:

Ille est par superis Deis,
Et mortalibus altior
Qui fati ambiguum diem
Non optat levis, aut timet.
   Quem non ambitio impotens
Non spes sollicitat lucri:
Quem non concutiunt metu
Regum praecipites minae
Non telum implacidi Iovis.
Uno sed stabilis loco
Vulgi ridet inania:
Securoque oritur dies,
Securo cadit & dies.
   Vitam si liceat mihi
Formare arbitriis meis:
Non fasces cupiam aut opes,
Non clarus niveis equis
Captiva agmina traxerim:
   In solis habitem locis,
Hortos possideam atque agros,
Illic ad strepitus aquae
Musarum studiis fruar.
   Sic cum fata mihi ultima
Pernerit Lachesis mea;
Non ulli gravis aut malus,
Qualis Langius hic meus,
Tranquillus moriar senex.

Lipsius's lyric was a popular poem, and Ben Jonson's heavily marked copy has survived.[34] Despite the Catullan allusion of the opening line, it is derived in particular from Seneca. Indeed, a contemporary work, Philip Camerarius's *Operae horarum subcisivarum* quotes Lipsius's poem (which is reproduced in full) in a chapter, 'Commendatio privatae vitae,' which begins by quoting Seneca, Phaed. 483–495 (p. 341) and then comments explicitly on the links between Lipsius's lyric and the metrical portions of Boethius (p. 342).[35] The phrase *ambitio impotens* (5), however, is borrowed from the same chorus of the *Thyestes* so often translated and imitated at this period (*quem non ambitio impotens | et numquam stabilis favor | vulgi praecipitis movet*, 350–352). Lipsius has transformed the 'never stable' popular favour of Seneca's chorus into the true stability (*uno sed stabilis loco*, 10) of the wise man, while the fickleness of the mob (*vulgi praecipitis*) is transferred to the unpredictability and violence of royal power (*regum praecipites minae*, 8).[36] There are multiple further parallels between Lipsius's poem and the final two choruses of Seneca's *Oedipus*, which are themselves indebted to Horace at many points. In particular, Oed. 882–910 is written in the same unusual palindromatic glyconic metre[37] used here by Lipsius, and the subject of that chorus is fate and the *media via*. Oed. 980–997 does not have the same metre but includes many of the same tropes.[38]

Ashmore's collection demonstrates the 'bilingualism' of the vogue for moralising lyrics of this kind: original Latin and English poems stand alongside English translations from both classical and neo-Latin. Indeed, the Latin 'feel' or associations of English lyrics in this tradition, far from obvious to the modern reader, are reflected in the contemporary habit, particularly evident in surviving

---

[34] Bryan / Evans 1996, 181–182, notes that this poem is one of the most heavily marked pages in Jonson's (well annotated) copy of Lipsius's works. The entire poem is underlined. For full details of Jonson's copy of Lipsius, see McPherson 1974, 59–60.

[35] *Operae horarum subcisivarum, sive meditationes historicae*, first published in Nuremburg in 1591, with several further editions. The page numbers I have given refer to the 1609 Frankfurt edition of this work. Translations were produced in French (1610), English (1610), and German (1625–1630).

[36] See also comparable expressions in the *Thyestes* chorus: *regnorum magnis fallax | Fortuna bonis*, 57–58; *ut praecipites regum casus | Fortuna rotat*, 71–72. For line 10, compare also Oed. 909–910: *quidquid excessit modum | pendet instabili loco* and Her. F. 200: *humilique loco sed certa sedet*.

[37] On the glyconic metre and the 'golden mean' in Oed. 882–914 see the chapters by Geiger, 177–178, and Tarrant, 108–111, in this volume.

[38] Other parallels include Lipsius 14–15 and Oed. 882–883; Lipsius 23–24 and Oed. 986; Lipsius 27 (final line) and Oed. 899 (Daedalus as *callidus senex*). I am grateful to Kathrin Winter for pointing out the links to the *Oedipus* here.

manuscript sources, of translating English poems of this type into (almost, as it were, 'back' into) Latin verse.

Henry Wotton (1568–1639), whose ubiquitous 'The Character of the Happy Life' has already been mentioned, was one of the masters of the suggestive moralising lyric in the late sixteenth and early seventeenth centuries, and many Latin translations of his poems are found in manuscript sources. His works have largely slipped out of the lyric 'canon' but copies are found very widely in manuscript collections throughout the seventeenth century – the Catalogue of English Literary Manuscripts, for instance, lists sixty-three copies of 'The Character of the Happy Life.'[39]

But perhaps the most striking example of the translation of English into Latin lyric concerns Wotton's fine poem, found in many manuscripts with varying titles, and published in Izaak Walton's *Reliquiae Wottonianae* of 1651 in the following form:

Upon the sudden Restraint of the Earle *of* Somerset, *then falling from favor*

Dazel'd thus, with height of place,
Whilst our hopes our wits beguile,
No man markes the narrow space
'Twixt a prison, and a smile.

Then, since fortunes favours fade,
You, that in her armes doe sleep,
Learne to swim, and not to wade;
For, the Heart of Kings are deepe.

But, if Greatness be so blind,
As to trust in towers of Aire,
Let it be with Goodness lin'd,
That at'least, the Fall be faire.

---

39 On the manuscript transmission of 'The Character of the Happy Life,' see Main 1955, Pebworth 1978 (plus plates) and Røstvig 1962. Røstvig's work remains an invaluable study of one particular (though quite broadly interpreted) version of the 'happy life' lyric – namely, the form which concentrates on, or at least includes an element of a rural setting for the description of human contentment. She looks only at the development of the form from 1600 (particularly the works of Ben Jonson) onwards, and does not consider sixteenth-century texts such as those included in Tottel's miscellany. She does not consider the relationship of these poems to the broader class of 'moralising' lyrics, in both English and Latin, under discussion here, though she deserves considerable credit for emphasising the importance of neo-Latin as well as classical and English authors, especially in relation to Casimir Sarbiewski, discussed further below.

> Then though darkned, you shall say,
> When Friends faile, and Princes frowne,
> *Vertue* is the roughest way,
> But proves at night a *Bed of Downe*.⁴⁰

This poem was probably written, as the title in this edition suggests, about the spectacular fall in 1616 of Robert Carr, the Earl of Somerset, a royal favourite for around a decade, who, with his wife Frances, was charged with and convicted of the murder by poison of Sir Thomas Overbury, who had opposed the marriage. Extant examples of the poem in both print and manuscript, however, often give it either a generic title ('On the sudden restraint of a favourite') or link the poem to the fall of another prominent individual, such as Walter Raleigh (imprisoned for marrying without the Queen's permission in 1591; later executed for treason against James I in 1618), Francis Bacon (found guilty of taking bribes in 1621), George Villiers, Duke of Buckingham (impeached in 1626, eventually assassinated in 1628), and William Davison (secretary to Queen Elizabeth I, who was made the scapegoat for the execution of Mary, Queen of Scots, in 1587). In some instances, the poem is in fact said to be *by* the unfortunate favourite, as in Bodleian MS Rawl. poet. 166, p. 83, where the lyric is titled 'By yᵉ most Illustrious Prince George Duke of Buckingham &c.', or a copy in the Leeds Archives WYL 156/237, fol. 56ᵛ, which ascribes the poem to Sir Walter Raleigh.⁴¹

This is a lovely and memorable poem, which is at once timelessly imprecise and politically highly suggestive – a quality it shares with many of Horace's moralising lyrics and also with Seneca's choruses, especially if they are read as stand-alone poems. It belongs recognisably to the kind of politico-moral 'generalising lyric' under discussion. Nevertheless, there is nothing very obviously Horatian or Senecan about the poem, especially from the perspective of a modern classicist: it is not a translation, or even a close imitation, and it has no marked classicising touches. The only existing article dedicated to the poem does not relate it in any way to the classical tradition.⁴² But contemporary readers *did* read the poem as part of that Horatio-Senecan tradition which is the subject of this article. 'Dazel'd thus, with height of place' is found in at least five manuscripts (to my knowledge) accompanied by multiple Latin translations, and in each case the Latin versions make the association with Horace and Sene-

---

40 Walton 1651, 522.
41 The two copies relating the poem to 'Secretary Davison' are both in the same manuscript in the Bradford Archives (32D86/17, fol. 26ᵛ and fol. 124ᵛ). For full details of the various ascriptions of the poem, see Pebworth 1977.
42 Pebworth 1977.

ca plain, both in terms of metre, lexical choices, and specific allusions.[43] I give below an edited transcription of one stanza, alongside the Latin translations which accompany it in four of the five sources.[44] The Latin on the right is in sapphic stanzas, on the left in alcaics.

> Then though darkened he may say
> While friends sinke & princes frowne
> Vertue is the hardest way
> Yet at night a bed of Downe

Tunc lapsus alto culmine gloriae	Tunc amicorum fugiat corona
Dum cauta fallit turba clientium	Et necem princeps rigido minetur
Et rex minatur; dura, cantet,	Ore, cantabit, placidum est cubile
Dulce parat pietas cubile.	Ardua virtus.[45]

The striking *mise-en-page* of these double translations, with the sapphic and alcaic versions of the poem set alongside one another in the same way in all four

---

[43] Four sources reproduce the English poem in a central column interspersed stanza by stanza with a double Latin translation in parallel columns, sapphics on the right, alcaics on the left (BL MS Harley 6038, fol. 44[r-v], BL MS Harley 1221, fol. 110[r], BL Add MS 72439, fol. 148[r] and Nottingham MS PW V 518). The two Latin translations are, bar minor differences in spelling and punctuation, the same in all four of these manuscripts. The fifth manuscript (Bodleian MS Rawlinson poet. 166, p. 82) preserves a further three (different) Latin translations, two of which include 'alternative' translations for one stanza (in one case the first stanza, in another the last). This probably suggests some kind of informal challenge or competition among friends to translate the poem into Latin. Several of Wotton's other poems are also found in Latin translations in manuscript sources of the period. Other Latin translations of Wotton noted by CELMS include a Latin version of his 'Ode to the King' (Bodleian MS Sancroft 89, pp. 57–58) and four of his widely-circulated poem on the Queen of Bohemia (Bodleian MS Douce 357, fol. 19[r]; BL Add MS 47111, fol. 7[r-v]; Folger MS V.a.103, Part I, fol. 53[r-v]; The Family Album, Glen Rock, Pennsylvania, [Wolf MS], p. 3). It is likely that others are extant but unidentified, since the Latin verse in manuscript collections of this period has barely been studied, is almost always inadequately catalogued, and is only rarely included in first-line indexes of manuscript verse. For this reason, Latin versions even of well-known poems are likely to have been missed unless they have been titled as such, or are clearly presented alongside or in close proximity to the English poem they translate.

[44] All five of these manuscripts add a fifth stanza, not reproduced here; this fifth stanza is discussed by Pebworth 1977, 161–163, who considers it a later addition.

[45] The variant readings between the four manuscripts preserving these two translations are very few, and confined largely to matters of punctuation and capitalisation. The text reproduced is based on Harley MS 6038, with minor emendations based on the other witnesses. Pebworth 1977 notes only the two Harley manuscripts and does not discuss the Latin translations. The Latin translations are anonymous, though I hope to publish further on their likely authorship in due course.

manuscripts, immediately suggests a markedly Horatian interpretation of the poem. Indeed, the Latin versions are full of echoes of Horace: in this section, the phrase *turba clientium* (line 2 of the penultimate stanza) is borrowed from Carm. 3.1.13, also a poem in Alcaic stanzas. But these lines are also forcefully Senecan: in the first line of the same stanza, the phrase *tunc lapsus alto culmine gloriae* borrows from the same much-imitated passage, the second chorus of Seneca's *Thyestes*, with which this essay began: *stet quicumque volet potens | aulae culmine lubrico* (391–392). The translator at this point has in fact conflated two separate passages of the *Thyestes*, blending an allusion to the second chorus – which implies but does not explicitly state the possibility of falling from high office (*culmine lubrico*) – with Thyestes's own speech near the end of the play, where he describes himself as *ex alto culmine lapsum* (927). The translation in this way combines Horace's generalised disdain for popular favour with a much sharper reference to the explicit and memorably horrific evocation of personal disaster in the *Thyestes*: a blend of associations which responds to the roots of these 'moralising lyrics,' as this essay has discussed, in translation of exactly these kinds of classical texts, while also suggesting the personalised and specific force of a poem widely interpreted at the time as being about (or even by) a particular victim of spectacular political misfortune.

This oscillation between specific and generalising force is a feature of many of the poems belonging to this tradition that were written and published, especially by royalist authors, under pressure of the English Civil War (1642–1651) and its immediate aftermath. Verse collections by Robert Herrick (*Hesperides*, 1648), Mildmay Fane (*Otia Sacra*, 1648), Richard Lovelace (*Lucasta*, 1649 and *Posthume Poems*, 1659), and Henry Vaughan (1650) all reflect an engagement with this tradition, sharpened by circumstance.

Robert Herrick's 'His Age: Dedicated to his Peculiar Friend, Mr John Wickes, under the name of Postumus,' first published in *Hesperides* (1648), is one example of this kind of poem which is found in contemporary manuscript miscellanies as well as in print.[46] In common with many of the longer lyric poems of the period – such as Lovelace's 'The Grasse-hopper,' 'Advice to my best Brother,' and even (though to very different political effect) Marvell's 'Horatian Ode' – Herrick's poem has a well-recognised Horatian base: as the name 'Postumus' implies, the opening of the poem follows Horace, Carm. 4.7 (the ode to Postumus), though it extends beyond it, continuing with a sequence of imitations of the moralising passages of Horace, including both lyric (Carm. 2.16 and 2.18) and hexam-

---

[46] Beal, *Catalogue of English Literary Manuscripts, 1450–1700* records ten copies.

eter (S. 2.6 and Ep. 1.10).⁴⁷ But observations of this sort are of limited help: despite the satisfaction for the scholar in 'spotting' the Horatian allusions, the overall effect of the poem is not very much *like* reading Horace at all. None of Horace's *Odes* are devoted so uniformly to moralising, and the moralising sentiments which in Herrick's poem are piled up, one after another, are found individually in Horace, often at the beginning or the end of a given poem, and almost always distanced or complicated by what follows or precedes. Moreover, the handful of Horace's *Odes* which are of anything close to the length of Herrick's poem are his grandest panegyric celebrations of public office and achievement. Formally, the closest analogues of this almost obsessive appropriation of Horatian motifs are found outside Horace: in these formal terms, Herrick's poem is indebted both to Seneca's choruses and their imitation (as for instance in the lyric by Lipsius discussed above) and, almost certainly, to the vogue for more insistently and consistently philosophical and moralising 'Horatian' poems initiated by the odes of the enormously popular Latin Jesuit poet Casimir Sarbiewski (first published in 1625; first English translations published 1646).⁴⁸

Similar observations can be made about Richard Lovelace's 'The Grass-hopper. To my Noble Friend, Mr. Charles Cotton. Ode,' first published in *Lucasta* (1649). This well-known and still frequently anthologised poem has often been described as Horatian, and does indeed have an Horatian core: the two stanzas addressed directly to Cotton (lines 21–28) are based on Horace, Carm. 1.9 and perhaps also Epod. 13.1–8, and the whole poem, as Joanna Martindale puts it, 'suggests' the Soracte ode.⁴⁹ Scholars have been quick to note that the opening twelve lines on the grasshopper are based not upon Horace but rather a poem

---

47 The most important Horatian sources are Carm. 1.4, 2.14, and 4.7, with identifiable elements drawn also from S. 2.6, Ep. 1.10, and Carm. 2.16 and 2.18. There is a fine discussion of this poem in Martindale 1993, 77–80. Lovelace, 'Advice to my best Brother' is based loosely upon Hor. Carm. 2.10, a poem which probably also stands behind Mildmay Fane's lyric 'How to ride out a Storm' (*Otia Sacra*, 161).
48 H[ils] 1646. The volume prints a selection of Sarbiewski's poetry (twenty-five odes, three epodes, six epigrams) with facing English translations. A prefatory English poem imagines Horace and Sarbiewski seated together upon the summit of the Muses' hill. On Sarbiewski, see Schäfer 2006.
49 Martindale 1993, 74. See also D. C. Allen, who, in a sensitive reading, remarks: 'The remedy for the moment is provided by the doctrine of Horace [i.e. in stanzas 6–7], although the inner conviction of an infinite present, once satisfaction is procured, is totally Christian' (Allen 1960, 80–92). Allen does not mention Sarbiewski, but this remark applies equally well to Sarbiewski's own Latin lyric poetry.

from the Greek *Anacreontea* 43.⁵⁰ Except that, as Martindale pointed out in passing, Lovelace's model is almost certainly not directly Anacreon, but rather Sarbiewski's own Anacreontic grasshopper poem, *Odes* 4.23:

> O, quae populae summa sedens coma,
> Coeli roriferis ebria lacrymis,
> Et te voce Cicada,
> Et mutum recreas nemus.
>
> Post longas hiemes, dum nimium brevis
> Aestas se levibus praecipitat rotis,
> Festinos, age, lento,
> Soles excipe jurgio.
>
> Ut se quaeque dies attulit optima,
> Sic se quaeque rapit: nulla fecit satis
> Umquam longa voluptas,
> Longus saepius est dolor.[51]

Most interesting, however, for the purposes of this essay, is the blend of elements in the final stanza of Lovelace's poem:

> Thus richer than untempted Kings are we,
>   That asking nothing, nothing need:
> Though Lord of all what Seas imbrace; yet he
>   That wants himselfe, is poore indeed.

The first couplet here, as Scodel has noted, adapts Seneca's *Thy.* 388–90: *Rex est qui metuet nihil, | rex est qui cupiet nihil: | hoc regnum sibi quisque dat.*[52] But Lovelace's conclusion combines Seneca not, as we might have expected, with Horace directly, but rather with lines drawn once again from the 'Polish Horace,' Sarbiewski:

---

[50] See McDowell 2008, 128; Allen 1960, 80–92. Abraham Cowley's poem, 'The Grasshopper,' is an imitation of the Greek lyric, on which see Mason 1990. On the vogue for the Anacreontea, see O'Brien 1995.
[51] Lovelace's image of the grasshopper drinking the tears of dew, often described as an original elaboration on his part upon the Greek poem (e.g. McDowell 2008, 128) comes directly from Sarbiewski ('Coeli roriferis ebria lacrymis,' 2).
[52] Scodel 2002, 232, also cited by McDowell 2008, 129 n. 41. But compare also Sarbiewski *Odes* 4.3, 'Regnum sapientis.' Tarrant 1985, 146 considers lines 388–389 to be possible interpolations; however, they appear to have been accepted as authentic by the poets and translators under discussion.

> Divitem nunquam, Tiberine, dices,
> Cuius Eois potiora glebis
> Rura, fortunae sine face pulcher
>   Rivus inaurat:
> Quem per insigneis geniale ceras
> Stemma claravit; vaga quem per urbes
> Quem per & gentes radiante vexit
>   Gloria curru.
> Pauper est, qui se caret; & superbè
> Ipse se librans, sua rura latam
> Addit in lancem, socioque fallent
>   Pondus in auro...
> (*Odes* 4.34.1–12)[53]

The importance of Sarbiewski's lyrics to English poets of the seventeenth and eighteenth centuries has been remarked upon several times, usually by reference primarily to existing translations of his works into English, of which there are a strikingly large number.[54] Poets of the mid-seventeenth century who engaged directly with Sarbiewski, in translation or imitation, include Mildmay Fane, Henry Vaughan, Abraham Cowley, Sir Edward Sherburne, Edward Benlowes, and Andrew Marvell as well as Lovelace and Herrick.[55] Samuel Coleridge planned

---

[53] The combination of Seneca and Sarbiewski at the end of the poem is discussed briefly by McDowell 2008, 138. Neither Scodel nor McDowell note the existence of Sarbiewski's 'grasshopper' poem, perhaps because *Ode* 4.23 is not one of those printed and translated in George Hil's 1646 English edition. McDowell (2008, 128) claims 'the first three stanzas [of Lovelace's grasshopper] are derived from *Anacreontea* 43.' He also suggests that Lovelace's poem is a response to Stanley's version of *Anacreontea* 43, published in 1647, discussed at some length by McDowell within his fine analysis of Lovelace's poem (McDowell 2008, 128–130).

[54] Seven paraphrases of Sarbiewski's odes were published in Henry Vaughan's *Olor Iscanus* (1651); seven also in the poems of Sir Edward Sherburne, also published that year. There are at least seven separate English versions of Sarbiewski, *Odes* 2.5 (a long poem of eighty-eight lines on leaving behind worldly things), including versions by Abraham Cowley and Isaac Watts. Lovelace's *Lucasta* (1649) includes a translation of Sarbiewski, *Odes* 4.13 ('To his Dear Brother Colonel F. L. immoderately mourning my Brother's untimely Death at Carmarthen'), a poem also translated, among English poets alone, by Henry Vaughan, Isaac Watts, and Thomas Yalden. John Hall's 1649 elegy for Henry, Lord Hastings, published in *Lachrymae Musarum*, is also an adaptation of Sarbiewski's *Ode* 4.13 (on which see Clarke 2005). On Sarbiewski and English poetry, see, briefly but very effectively, Davidson 2007, 31–32, and, the most accessible resource on Sarbiewski in English, Fordonski / Urbanski 2010.

[55] See in general Røstvig 1954, Fordonski / Urbanski 2010, Gömöri 2011, and Money 2006. On Edward Benlowe's *Theophila* (1652) and Sarbiewski, see Røstvig 1954–1955. On versions of Sarbiewski, *Odes* 4.13, Arens 1963. On Sarbiewski and Watts, Birrel 1956. On Sarbiewski and Johnson, see Baldwin 1995, 40.

(though never finished) a complete translation.[56] But his stylistic influence ranges well beyond individual translations or imitations: Sarbiewski's odes are forcefully and movingly Horatian in their metre and diction – they are inconceivable without Horace; but Sarbiewski himself cited Martial and Seneca as his most important influences after Horace himself,[57] and Sarbiewski's critical writings cite Seneca on several occasions.[58] Sarbiewski's odes are on average significantly longer than those of Horace, and in their meditative circling around a given ethical point resemble Seneca's moralising choruses more than any of Horace's own lyrics. They are much more consistently moralising than Horace himself, both in the proportion of poems devoted to moralising themes, and in the lack of any tendency to turn aside from or aslant to the moralising force of a poem which is so distinctive of Horace's own lyric output.[59] His explicitly Christian and often devotional lyrics repeatedly start from Horace, but also seek to augment and sometimes directly confront the pagan poet, as in his third epode, 'Palinodia. Ad secundam libri Epodoon Odam Q. Horatii Flacci. Laus otii Religiosi,' beginning: *At ille, Flacce, nunc erit beatior, | Qui mole curarum procul | Paterna liquit rura, litigantium | Solutus omni jurgio.*

Indeed, Sarbiewski's lyrics – and especially the subset of them most often translated or imitated in England – fit precisely within the blended tradition of Latin moralising lyric which is the subject of this essay, a point which no doubt partly explains their great popularity. In several instances, George Hils's choice of English titles for the poems makes this connection plain: Odes 4.3, for instance, is titled in Hils's volume 'That we ought to be of an even and upright mind against the inconstancy of fortune.' Sarbiewski offered English readers a 'Christian Horace' who accorded more closely than Horace himself with the most influential aspects of the English 'Horatian' tradition at the time.

Indeed, just as Lovelace's 'Grass-hopper' ends with a highly conventional quatrain which sounds (and indeed in a sense is) broadly 'Horatian' but which in its details is drawn most directly from Seneca and Sarbiewski (that is, a Christian Horace), so in several collections of this period we find Sarbiewski standing in for Horace in sequences of translation: Henry Vaughan's *Olor Iscanus* (1651) juxtaposes translations of Ovid's exile poetry, Boethius, and Sarbiewski; half a century later, Isaac Watts, a dissenting poet and the first of the great Eng-

---

56 Brown 1997, 173–194.
57 See e.g. Li Vigni 2005, 12.
58 Stawecka 1972, e.g. 176, 190, 280.
59 'The lyrics of the "divine Casimire" single out *beatus ille* motifs with much greater frequency than had previously been the case and also fuse them more fervently with Christian ideas,' Røstvig 1962, 14.

lish hymn writers, likewise turns to Sarbiewski, a Polish Jesuit, rather than to Horace directly.[60]

Wotton's 'Dazl'd thus' is a beautiful example of a type of poem which is immediately recognisable to any sensitive and experienced reader of English poetry, a mode of verse which has persisted relatively unchanged through successive waves of poetic fashion: this is not the poetry of Elizabethan sonneteers or love elegists; nor is it recognisably 'metaphysical' verse; and it is certainly not Augustan satire. Poetry of this kind has an enduring, if enduringly unfashionable, role in English literature: Kipling's poem 'If,' for instance, is an expansion of the theme – of consistent virtue and restraint in the face of both good and ill fortune – which is the subject of Seneca's most widely translated chorus (Thy. 336–403) as well as the opening lines of Horace Carm. 4.9, and indeed Sarbiewski's *Odes* 2.1. Kipling's poem was voted Britain's favourite poem in a 1995 BBC opinion poll; Wotton's 'How Happy is he Born and Taught' was apparently George Washington's favourite hymn;[61] and the hymns of Watts and Wesley are still sung regularly in Christian churches of many denominations around the world.

Kipling is almost as out of fashion as Wotton and Watts, but he was a fine reader of Horace, and his memorable immortalisation of a peculiarly English brand of stoicism descends directly, via Jonson, Wotton, and the English hymn book, from Horace and Seneca.[62] Recent classical criticism has shown little interest in Horace's moral and philosophical lyrics (less so than in the philosophical content of his hexameter verse), and has done almost nothing with Horace as a religious poet, although many of his odes are formally hymns, a point of great importance for his early modern readers. For a sense of that Horace, we do best to read not criticism, but poetry: the poetry of Seneca and Boethius, but also of Wyatt, Wotton, Sarbiewski, Lovelace, Vaughan, and Watts.

---

[60] It is particularly striking that Watts (1674–1748), a prominent nonconformist – that is, belonging to a Protestant congregation which was not part of the Church of England – who, barred from Oxford and Cambridge as a result, had been educated at the dissenting academy at Stoke Newington and apparently never traveled outside England should have been so strongly influenced by Sarbiewski. Watts made many translations of Sarbiewski, for which see Fordonski / Urbanski 2010, 125–150. Watts also wrote his own Latin poetry, several of which were published in *Horae Lyricae* (1706). Watts's early English poetry includes 'The Happy Man,' a clear example of the tradition traced in this essay. On Watts and Wesley as lyric poets, see Davie 1974, 3–6 and 1978, 19–54.

[61] Spann / Williams 2008, 5–8.

[62] Kipling wrote several poems titled as odes from 'Book V' of Horace; on Kipling's Horace see Medcalf 1993.

Table of Correspondences

The following is an edited table of correspondences between Horace and Seneca; we hope that it will aid further investigation of the relationship between these authors. The sources are Zingerle (1873), Spika (1890), Kapnukajas (1930), Berthet (1979), and Mazzoli (1974 and 1998), as well as the correspondences made by the contributors and editors of the present volume. When taken together with the notes in the principal commentaries (e. g. Tarrant on the *Agamemnon*), this table records the bulk of previous scholarly discussion of the relationship between these two authors. Our goal has been (1) to gather as many correspondences as possible together in the one place, while (2) using a critical eye when it comes to the inclusion of parallels. We are very much aware that it is impossible to gather all the correspondences in such a format (from a brief glance at the table it will be clear that there are large gaps), while some parallels are clearly weaker than others. Scholars may find it particularly useful to use this table in conjunction with databases such as the Tesserae Project of the University of Buffalo (http://tesserae.caset.buffalo.edu) in order to establish and document fresh points of contact.

We have also sought to provide some indication as to what the connection consists in. It should be borne in mind that our categories are rough and that there is substantial overlap between them. They are also broad: for example, 'V' can denote a parallel in which the same word is found with different meanings, as well as a parallel in which different yet synonymous words are employed. As mentioned in the Introduction, authorial intention is not assumed in the compilation of these lists.

Larger sections of text (e. g. Carm. 3.1.5 – 8) are listed before smaller ones (e. g. Carm. 3.1.5 – 6). Page numbers in brackets refer to passages in the volume where the relevant correspondence is discussed. The key is as follows:

V	Verbal parallel
M	Motif, imagery
N	Name
PHI	Philosophical theme
quote	Verbatim quotation
*	Structural parallel
%	Inversion of thought

We hope that readers will take these tables as we offer them – as a possible starting point for investigating the relationship of Horace and Seneca that reveals quite clearly how much there is yet to be done.

DOI 10.1515/9783110528893-016

Correspondences Seneca – Horace

Seneca, prose works

Seneca	Horace	
Apocolocyntosis		
Apoc. 13.3	Carm. 2.13.34	quote (p. 3, 37, 311)
De Beneficiis		
Ben. 1.12.3	Ep. 1.11.18	M
Ben. 2.16.2	S. 1.1.106–107	PHI
Ben. 5.17.7	Carm. 1.9.13–18	PHI, V
	Carm. 3.29.41–48	PHI, V
	Ep. 1.4.13–14	PHI, V
Ben. 7.2.4	Carm. 2.16.25–26	M, PHI (p. 48)
	Carm. 3.16.21–22	M (p. 47–48)
	S. 2.2.110	M, PHI (p. 48–49)
Ben. 7.3.2	Carm. 3.16.21–22	M (p. 47–48)
Ben. 7.10.6	Carm. 3.16.13–15	PHI (p. 46–47)
De Clementia		
Cl. 1.1.1	Carm. 4.10	M (p. 280–281)
Cl. 1.7.2	Carm. 4.5.6–8	M
Cl. 1.8.2	S. 1.6.112	V
De Providentia		
Dial. 1.3.9–10	Carm. 3.1.17–24	N, M
	Carm. 3.5.13–56	N, M
De Ira		
Dial. 3.1.2	Ep. 1.2.62	V, PHI (p. 116)
Dial. 3.12.5	Carm. 3.2.13	PHI
Dial. 4.2.5	Ars 101–102	V
Dial. 4.36.1–3	Carm. 4.10	M (p. 280–281)
Ad Marciam de Consolatione		
Dial. 6.1.3–4	Ep. 2.1.214–218 & 229–244	M (p. 233–234)
De Vita Beata		
Dial. 7.15.4	Carm. 4.9.45–50	V, PHI
Dial. 7.26.1	Ep. 1.10.47	PHI
Dial. 7.26.7	Carm. 3.1.2–8	V, M

De Tranquillitate Animi

Dial. 9.1.13	Carm. 1.11.8	V (p. 245–246)
Dial. 9.1.14	Carm. 2.20.1	PHI, V (p. 259)
Dial. 9.1.17	Epod. 9.34–35	V (p. 260)
Dial. 9.2.13	Carm. 2.6.11–20	N, PHI
Dial. 9.2.13 & 15	Ep. 1.8.12	M
Dial. 9.2.13–15	S. 2.7.28–29	PHI (p. 257–258)
	Ep. 1.11	PHI, V (p. 257–258)
	Ep. 1.14.12–13	PHI (p. 257–258)
Dial. 9.3.7	Carm. 2.15	PHI, M
	Carm. 2.18.19–26	M, V
	Carm. 3.1.33–34	M, V
	Carm. 3.24.3–4	M, V
Dial. 9.4.7	Carm. 2.10.22–24	V (p. 260)
Dial. 9.5.5	Carm. 1.14.2–3	M (p. 260)
Dial. 9.8.5	Carm. 3.16.27–28	V, PHI (p. 50–51)
Dial. 9.9.4–7	S. 2.3.1–16	M (p. 228–229, 234)
	Ep. 1.18.96–112	M (p. 235–236)
Dial. 9.11.7	Carm. 2.10.2–3	V, M (p. 260)
Dial. 9.17.8	Epod. 9.38	V (p. 259)
Dial. 9.17.10	Carm. 3.19.18	V (p. 249–250, 261)
	Carm. 4.12.27–28	V (p. 249–250, 261)
	Ep. 1.19.2–3	M (p. 249–250)
Dial. 9.17.10–11	Ars 295–297 & 301–303 & 453–456	PHI (p. 256–258)
Dial. 9.17.11	Carm. 2.19	PHI (p. 259)
	Carm. 2.20	PHI (p. 259)

De Brevitate Vitae

Dial. 10.9.1	Carm. 1.4.15	PHI
	Carm. 1.11.6–8	M, PHI (p. 7–9)
Dial. 10.9.3	Carm. 3.30.4–5	V, PHI (p. 7–10)
Dial. 10.14–15	Ep. 1.18	M (p. 227, 235–237)

Ad Polybium de Consolatione

Dial. 11.8	Carm. 2.9.17–20	M, *
Dial. 11.18.2	Carm. 3.30.3–5	V, M (p. 16–18)

Ad Helviam Matrem de Consolatione

Dial. 12.11.4	Carm. 3.16.27–28	V, PHI (p. 50–51)

Epistulae Morales

Ep. 1.1	Carm. 1.9.13–18	PHI
	Carm. 3.29.41–48	PHI, V
	Ep. 1.4.13–14	PHI
Ep. 1.2	Carm. 1.4.15	PHI
	Carm. 1.11.6–8	PHI
Ep. 1.3	Carm. 2.14.1–2	V (p. 201–203)

Table of Correspondences

Ep. 2	Ep. 1.18.96–112	M (p. 235–237)
	Ep. 2.1.214–218 & 229–244	M (p. 233–234)
Ep. 2.5	Carm. 3.16.22–23	V, M
Ep. 2.6	Carm. 1.1.9	PHI, M
	Carm. 3.16.25–28	PHI, M
	Epod. 2.67–70	PHI, M
	S. 1.1.66–67	PHI, M
	S. 1.2.114–115	PHI, M
Ep. 12	Carm. 3.29	PHI, V (p. 187–193)
Ep. 12.1–4	Carm. 3.29.32–33	PHI (p. 190)
Ep. 12.6	S. 2.6.25–26	V
Ep. 12.9	Carm. 1.9.13–18	PHI
	Carm. 3.29.41–48	PHI, V (p. 187–188)
	Ep. 1.4.13–14	PHI, M
Ep. 12.11	Ep. 1.1.14	V
Ep. 18	S. 2.2	PHI (p. 80)
Ep. 18.3–4	Carm. 2.16.37–40	PHI (p. 77)
	S. 1.1.92–94	PHI (p. 77)
	S. 1.2.24–28	PHI (p. 77)
	S. 2.2.65–66	PHI (p. 77)
	S. 2.3.4–5	V, PHI
Ep. 19.9	Carm. 2.10.23–24	V
Ep. 23.8	Carm. 3.29.32–41	V, M (p. 192–193)
Ep. 24.26	Carm. 2.18.15–16	M
	Carm. 4.7.7–12	M, PHI (p. 332)
Ep. 25.1	Ep. 1.2.64	V
Ep. 28.1	Carm. 2.16.19–20	M, PHI
	S. 2.7.28–29	M
	Ep. 1.8.12	M
	Ep. 1.11.25–27	V, M (p. 5–6, 258, 338)
	Ep. 1.14.12–13	M
Ep. 33.5	S. 1.2.92–93	V
Ep. 34.3	Ep. 1.2.40	V, %
Ep. 38.1	S. 1.4.41–42	M (p. 306)
Ep. 39	Ep. 1.18.96–112	M (p. 234–236)
Ep. 41.7	Carm. 1.1.9–10	PHI
	Carm. 3.16.25–28	PHI
	Epod. 2.67–70	PHI
	S. 1.1.66–67	PHI
	S. 1.2.114–115	PHI
Ep. 45	Ep. 1.18.96–112	M (p. 231, 235–236)
	Ep. 2.1.214–218 & 229–244	M (p. 233–234, 236)
Ep. 47.14–16	S. 2.7	PHI, M (p. 87)
Ep. 56.5	Carm. 2.16.10–11	V, PHI
Ep. 58.5	Ep. 2.2.115–119	M, V
Ep. 58.22–23	Carm. 1.11.7–8	PHI, M (p. 194)
Ep. 60	Ep. 1.4	PHI, M (p. 53–71)

Ep. 60.4	Ep. 1.4.15–16	M, V (p. 65)
Ep. 74.4	Carm. 3.16.28	M, V (p. 342)
	S. 2.3.142	M, V (p. 342)
Ep. 74.7	Carm. 3.16.27–28	V, PHI (p. 50–51)
	Carm. 3.29.49–52	V, M
Ep. 75.1	Ep. 2.1.250–251	M (p. 75–76)
Ep. 76.13	Carm. 1.14.14–15	V, M
Ep. 76.15	Carm. 1.1.9	PHI
	Carm. 3.16.25–28	PHI
	Epod. 2.67–70	PHI
	S. 1.1.66–67	PHI
	S. 1.2.114–115	PHI
Ep. 79.14	Ars 295–297	PHI (p. 255–256)
Ep. 84	Carm. 4.2.27–32	M (p. 232, 276)
	S. 2.3.1–16	M (p. 228–229 & 234)
	Ep. 1.3.15–22	M (p. 231–232, 276)
	Ep. 2.1.214–218 & 229–244	M (p. 233–234)
Ep. 86.13	S. 1.2.27	quote (p. 3–4, 74–75, 311)
	S. 1.4.92	V (p. 76)
Ep. 89.20	Carm. 2.15	PHI
	Carm. 2.18.19–26	M, V
	Carm. 3.1.33–34	M, V
	Carm. 3.24.3–4	M, V
Ep. 93.6	Carm. 1.9.13–1	PHI
	Carm. 3.29.41–48	PHI
	Ep. 1.4.13–14	PHI
Ep. 96.4–5	S. 1.1.15–19	V, PHI (p. 34–36)
Ep. 99.5	Carm. 3.8.27–28	V, % (p. 204)
Ep. 101.4	Carm. 1.4.15	PHI, V
	Carm. 1.11.6–8	PHI
Ep. 104.8	Carm. 2.16.18–19	V, PHI
	S. 2.7.28–29	M
	Ep. 1.8.12	M
	Ep. 1.11.25–30	M, V, PHI
	Ep. 1.14.12–13	M
Ep. 108	Ep. 1.18.96–112	M (p. 227, 235–237)
Ep. 108.15–16	S. 2.3	PHI (p. 84)
Ep. 115.5	Carm. 3.23.13–20	M, V
Ep. 119.6	Ep. 1.2.46–49	V, PHI (p. 38–39)
Ep. 119.14	S. 1.2.114–116	quote (p. 38–41, 75, 81–82, 311)

Naturales Quaestiones
Nat. 1.1.7	S. 2.5.39	V
Nat. 1.2.8	Carm. 2.16.1–6	V
Nat. 3 praef. 7	Carm. 2.10.13	V, M
Nat. 6.32.4	Carm. 3.3.1–8	M

Seneca, tragedies

Seneca	Horace	
Hercules Furens		
Her. F. 33–34	Carm. 4.4.59–60	M
Her. F. 125–204	Carm. 1.1	M (p. 347)
	Carm. 3.3.9–48	M
	Epod. 2	M (p. 347)
Her. F. 139–140	Carm 1.4.4	V
Her. F. 141–145	Carm. 3.13.3–5	V
	Carm. 3.18.9	V, M
Her. F. 152–154	Carm. 1.3.10–16	M
Her. F. 152	Carm. 1.14.14	M
Her. F. 162–163	Ep. 2.2.85	V
Her. F. 164–165	Epod. 2.7–8	V, %
Her. F. 166–168	Carm. 1.29.1–2	V
	Carm. 3.16.28	M, PHI (p. 342)
	S. 1.1.70–71	PHI, M
	S. 2.3.142	M, PHI (p. 342)
	Ep. 2.2.12	M
Her. F. 174–178	Carm. 1.11.7–8	M
Her. F. 178–185	Carm. 1.7.17	PHI
	Carm. 1.9.13–18	PHI
	Carm. 1.11	PHI
	Carm. 1.18	PHI
	Carm. 2.10.6–8	PHI
	Carm. 3.1.16	PHI, M
	Carm 4.13.14–16	M, PHI
Her. F. 181–189	Carm. 1.3.26 & 38	M
	Carm. 1.4.16	PHI
	Carm. 1.28.19–20	PHI
	Carm. 2.3.25–28	PHI
	Carm. 2.18.32–34	PHI
	Carm. 2.20.8	V, M
	Carm. 3.1.14–16	PHI
	Epod. 13.15	PHI
Her. F. 181–182	Carm. 2.3.15–16	V, %
Her. F. 192–200	Carm. 2.16.35–40	M
Her. F. 192–195	Carm. 1.1.3–6	V
	Carm. 4.3.4–6	V
	S. 2.7.28–29	V
Her. F. 197	Carm. 1.1.30–31	V
	S. 2.7.28–29	V
Her. F. 198	Carm. 1.9.17	V
	Carm. 3.14.25	V
Her. F. 199–200	Carm. 2.10.5–8	V, M

(cont.)	Carm. 2.16.37	V
Her. F. 201	Carm. 2.10.9–12	V
Her. F. 533–568	Carm. 4.8.29–30	M
	Carm. 3.24.9–11	V (p. 156)
Her. F. 537	Carm. 3.24.17	V
Her. F. 548–551	Carm. 1.3.25–28	V
Her. F. 549	Carm. 2.13.21	V
Her. F. 552–553	Carm. 1.12.25–32	M
	Carm. 4.8.31	V, N
Her. F. 554–557	Carm. 1.4.13–14	M, V
	Carm. 2.14.9–18	M, V
Her. F. 559	Carm. 2.6.9	M, V
	Epod. 13.15–16	M
Her. F. 566	Carm. 1.3.36	V, %
Her. F. 572–576	Carm. 1.12.7–12	V, M
	Carm. 3.11.13–14	M
	Ars 393	M
Her. F. 573	Ars 395	M
Her. F. 578	Carm. 3.10.11	V
Her. F. 836	Carm. 1.21.7	V
Her. F. 838–839	Carm. 2.17.25–26	M
	Ep. 2.1.60–61	M
Her. F. 852–853	Carm. 1.21.1–2	M
	Carm. 3.14.10–11	M
Her. F. 864–866	Carm. 1.3.32	M
	Carm. 1.4.15–18	M, *
	Carm. 1.28.19	M
Her. F. 869	Carm. 2.14.9–12 & 18	M
Her. F. 870	Carm. 2.8.17	V
Her. F. 874	Carm. 1.11.8	V, %
Her. F. 875–894	Carm. 1.37	PHI
Her. F. 877	Carm. 2.17.30–31	V
Her. F. 880–881	Carm. 3.6.42	V, M
Her. F. 882	Carm. 2.12.6	V
Her. F. 892	Ep. 1.16.79	M
Her. F. 1059	Carm. 3.21.24	V
Her. F. 1074	Carm. 1.4.13	M
	Carm. 2.18.32–33	M
	Carm. 3.1.14–15	M
Her. F. 1115–1117	Carm. 1.10.11–12	V, M
	Carm. 1.21.11–12	V, M
	Saec. 61–62	V, M
Her. F. 1124–1125	Carm. 1.10.2–4	V
Her. F. 1128	Carm. 1.12.23–24	V
Her. F. 1129	Carm. 3.12.10–11	V
Her. F. 1316	Carm. 1.3.36	V

Troades

Tro. 69–72	Carm. 1.15.1–2	N, M
Tro. 70	Carm. 3.3.26	V
Tro. 73	Carm. 1.9.1–2	V
	Carm. 3.25.10	V
Tro. 77–78	Carm. 1.15.10–11	M
Tro. 85–87	Carm. 2.1.21–22	V
Tro. 124–127	Carm. 3.3.26–28	M
	Carm. 4.9.22–24	M
Tro. 128–129	Carm. 2.4.9–12	M
Tro. 144 & 148–149	Carm. 1.10.13–16	V
Tro. 145–155	Carm. 1.37.29–32	M
	Carm. 4.2.34–36	M
Tro. 162–164	Carm. 3.2.13	M, V
Tro. 377	Carm. 3.30.6–7	V, PHI
Tro. 385	Carm. 1.3.33–34	V, PHI
Tro. 390	Carm. 2.3.25	PHI
Tro. 403–404	Carm. 3.11.15–17	M
Tro. 441	Ars 360	V
Tro. 712	Carm. 1.1.1	V
Tro. 814–860	Carm. 1.22	N
	Carm. 2.6	N
Tro. 829	Carm. 3.4.51–52	V
Tro. 848	Carm. 1.15.22	N
Tro. 855	Carm. 1.6.8	N
Tro. 857	S. 2.5.3–4	N
Tro. 1020–1021	Carm. 2.16.33–34	M
	Carm. 3.16.25–27	M
	Epod. 4.13	M
Tro. 1022	Carm. 1.18.5	V
	Carm. 3.21.18	V

Phoenissae

Phoen. 277–278	Epod. 7.20	V (p. 134)

Medea

Med. 13	Epod. 5.53–54	V (p. 119)
Med. 43	Epod. 1.12	V
Med. 60	Carm. 4.2.59–60	V, M
Med. 62–63	Carm. 1.5.13	V
Med. 82–89	Carm. 1.12.21–27	V, M
	Carm. 3.3.13–15	V, M
Med 87	Carm. 1.12.22	V, N
Med. 97–98	Saec. 35–36	V, M
Med. 99–100	Carm. 4.10.4–5	V
Med. 111	Carm. 1.37.4	V
Med. 161	Ep. 1.2.17	V (p. 118)

Med. 174–175	Ep. 1.2.63	V (p. 117)
Med. 301–379	Carm. 1.3	M, V
Med. 301–302	Carm. 1.3.9–11 & 25	V, M
Med. 305–308	Carm. 1.3.9–11	V, M
Med. 311–312	Carm. 1.3.14	V, M
Med. 329–334	Carm. 1.1.11–14	V, M
	Carm. 2.10.2–4	V, M
	Epod. 2.1–4	V, M
Med. 331–334	Carm. 1.1.11–15	V
Med. 335–336	Carm. 1.3.21–24	V, M
Med. 346	Carm. 3.27.28	V
Med. 358	Carm. 1.24.13	V
Med. 370	Carm. 1.7.29	V
Med. 373–374	Carm. 4.15.21–24	V
Med. 537	Ep. 1.2.40–41	V, PHI (p. 114–115)
Med. 558	Ep. 1.2.62	V, PHI (p. 116)
Med. 560–567	Ep. 1.2.37–41	V, PHI (p. 114–115)
Med. 579–582	Carm. 1.25.11–15	M
Med. 588–590	Carm. 1.12.6	V, M
Med. 591–594	Carm. 1.16.5–12	V, PHI
Med. 595	Carm. 1.2.30	V
Med. 595–598	Carm. 1.2.1–20	M
	Carm. 4.5.17–20	V, M
Med. 599–606	Carm. 2.10	M (p. 346–347)
Med. 599–602	Carm. 4.11.25	N
Med. 607–609	Carm. 1.3.9–11	M
Med. 611	Ep. 1.2.20–22	M
Med. 612	Carm. 1.32.7–8	M
Med. 622–629	Carm 1.24.13–14	V, N
Med. 625–630	Carm. 1.12.7–12	N, V
Med. 632–633	Carm. 1.4.16–20	M
Med. 638	Carm. 1.3.36	M
Med. 660–661	Epod. 10.13–14	M
Med. 668	Carm. 1.2.1	V
Med. 715	Epod. 11.5–6	V
Med. 849–852	Carm. 3.15.9–10	M
Med. 858	Carm. 1.13.5–6	M
Med. 859	Epod. 7.15	V, M
Med. 861	Carm. 1.13.5–6	M
Med. 866–869	Ep. 1.2.11–13	V, PHI (p. 117)
Med. 877–878	Carm. 2.9.10–12	M
Med. 918–919	Ep. 1.2.40–41	V, PHI (p. 114–115)
Med. 970–971	Epod. 5.89–90	V, M (p. 121)

Phaedra

Phaed. 1–53	Carm. 1.9	M, * (p. 154–155)
Phaed. 274–275	Carm. 4.1.5	N, V (p. 123–124)

(cont.)	Carm. 1.19.1–4	N, V (p. 122–123)
Phaed. 281–283	Carm. 1.13.8	M
Phaed. 291–293	Carm. 1.4.19–20	M
	Carm. 4.1.8	V (p. 124)
Phaed. 303–308	Carm. 3.27.25–29	M
Phaed. 346	Epod. 6.15	V, M
Phaed. 387–388	Carm. 4.9.14	V
Phaed. 406	Carm. 3.22.1	V
Phaed. 409–411	Saec. 1–2	V
Phaed. 412	Carm. 3.22.4	V
Phaed. 488	Carm. 3.2.20	V
Phaed. 508	Epod. 2.26	V
Phaed. 516–539	Epod. 2	PHI, M
Phaed. 634–635	Carm. 4.1.29–32	V (p. 125)
Phaed. 699	S. 1.2.75	V (p. 278)
	S. 1.3.114	V (p. 278)
Phaed. 700–701	Carm. 4.1.37–40	M (p. 127–128)
Phaed. 736–834	Carm. 2.11.5–24	PHI
Phaed. 737–738	Carm. 2.16.23–24	V
Phaed. 742	Ep. 2.1.48–49	V
Phaed. 743–752	Carm. 2.9.10–12	V, M
	Carm. 3.9.21–22	V, M
Phaed. 744–752	Epod. 15.1–2	V, M
Phaed. 748	Carm.1.12.47–48	V
	Epod. 15.2	V
Phaed. 764–768	Carm. 4.7.9–12	M
	Epod. 11.6	M
Phaed. 764–765	Carm. 2.11.9–10	V
Phaed. 764	Carm. 2.11.9–10	V, M
Phaed. 768–772	Carm. 4.10.3–8	V, M (p. 125–126)
Phaed. 769–772	Carm. 4.13.17–18	PHI, M
	Epod. 17.21–22	V, M
Phaed. 773	Carm. 2.11.5–6	V, M
Phaed. 774	Carm. 2.11.16	V, *
	Carm. 4.12.26	V, *
	S. 2.6.96	V, *
Phaed. 795–800	Carm. 1.19.5–8	V (p. 126–127)
Phaed. 801	Carm. 1.12.41	V, M
Phaed. 961–965	Carm. 1.12.13–16	V, M
Phaed. 966–971	Carm. 4.7.9–12	V, M
Phaed. 972–974	Carm. 2.10.15–17	V, M
Phaed. 975–977	Carm. 1.34.12–13	M
Phaed. 978–980	Carm. 1.34.14–16	M
	Carm. 3.29.49–52	M
Phaed. 983	Carm. 1.1.7–8	M
Phaed. 1123–1153	Carm. 2.10	PHI, M
Phaed. 1124–1127	Carm. 3.29.9–12	V, M

Phaed. 1128–1136	Carm. 2.10.9–12	V, M
Phaed. 1138–1139	Carm. 2.10.6–7	V, M
Phaed. 1141–1143	Carm. 1.34.14–16	V, M
	Carm. 3.29.49–53	V, M
Phaed. 1179–1180	Carm. 4.1.37–40	M (p. 128)
Phaed. 1183–1184	Saec. 27–28	V (p. 132)

Oedipus

Oed. 47	Epod. 3.15	V
Oed. 114	Ep. 1.1.45	V
	Ep. 1.6.6	V
Oed. 115	Carm. 2.9.24	V
Oed. 117	Carm. 1.29.1	V
	Carm. 2.12.24	V
	Carm. 3.24.2	V
	Ep. 1.7.36	V, M
Oed. 118–119	Carm. 1.19.11–12	V, M
	Carm. 2.13.17–18	V, M
Oed. 121–122	Saec. 9–11	V
Oed. 124–125	Carm. 1.3.32–33	PHI, V
Oed. 126–128	Carm. 1.24.16–18	PHI
	Carm. 1.28.15–16	PHI
Oed. 127	Carm. 1.4.16	V
Oed. 131–132	Carm. 1.28.19	V, M
Oed. 133–148	Carm. 3.23.5–8	V, M
Oed. 138–139	Carm. 3.23.12–13	V, M
Oed. 145–148	Epod 16.61–62	V, M
Oed. 149	Carm. 1.17.8–9	V
	Epod. 16.20	V
Oed. 151	Epod. 16.51	V
Oed. 156–158	Carm. 3.23.5–8	M, *
Oed. 156	Epod. 16.55	V
Oed. 166–166b	Carm. 2.3.25–27	V, M
	Carm. 3.1.16	V
Oed. 167	Carm. 2.18.34–36	M
Oed. 176–176b	Carm. 1.9.2–3	M
Oed. 177	Carm. 3.13.6–7	M
Oed. 250	Saec. 2	V (p. 241)
Oed. 403–508	Carm. 2.19	N, M, *
Oed. 403–405	Saec. 1–5	V (p. 129, 241)
Oed. 405–407b	Carm. 1.7.3	N
Oed. 424–425	Carm. 3.3.13–15	V, M
Oed. 430	Carm. 3.25.20	V
Oed. 432–438	Carm. 3.25.8–12	V, M
Oed. 442	Carm. 2.19.14–15	N, M
Oed. 467–468	Epod. 15.19–20	N, V
Oed. 469	Carm. 3.8.23	V

Oed. 470	Carm. 3.4.34	V, M
Oed. 471	Carm. 2.19.16	N, M
Oed. 473–474	Carm. 3.24.11–16	V, M
Oed. 473	Carm. 3.24.38	V
Oed. 478	Carm. 2.9.23	N, %
Oed. 491–492	Carm. 2.19.10–12	V, M
Oed. 498–500	Carm. 3.20.14	V
Oed. 506	Carm. 2.9.10–12	M
Oed. 709–712	Carm. 3.6.1–2	V, M
Oed. 712	Carm. 3.4.61–62	N
Oed. 724–725	Epod. 16.10	M
Oed. 726–727	Carm. 4.4.63–64	V, M
Oed. 731–734	Carm. 2.1.17–22	V, M (p. 149–150)
Oed. 748	Carm. 3.6.1–4	M
Oed. 882–914	Carm. 2.10	PHI, M (p. 177–178)
Oed. 882–891	Carm. 2.10.5–8	PHI, V (p. 108–111)
Oed. 886	Carm. 1.14.6	V
Oed. 887–914	Carm. 2.10	M (p. 347, 360)
Oed. 887–889	Carm. 2.10.23–25	V, M
	Carm. 3.29.62–64	V
Oed. 890–891	Carm. 2.10.5–6	V, M
Oed. 892–898	Carm. 4.2.2–4	N, M
Oed. 896–897	Carm. 2.2.7	M
Oed. 898	Carm. 4.2.2–4	V, %
Oed. 899–905	Carm. 1.3.34–35	N, M
Oed. 980–997	Carm. 2.10	PHI (p. 360)
Oed. 981–983	Epod. 13.15–16	M
Oed. 983–986	Saec. 25–28	V, M
Oed. 989	Carm. 3.29.45–48	V, M
Oed. 991–991b	Carm. 2.6.9	M
	Carm. 2.16.39	M
Oed. 992–994	Carm. 2.13.13–14	V, PHI
	Carm. 2.13.19–20	V, PHI
	Carm. 2.14.2–4	V, PHI
	Carm. 2.14.15–16	V, PHI
	Carm. 2.16.17–20	V, PHI

Agamemnon

Ag. 57–107	Carm. 2.10	PHI, *
Ag. 64–70	Carm. 1.22.5	V
	Carm. 2.6.3–4	V
	Carm. 2.20.13–16	V
Ag. 71–76	Carm. 2.16.9–22	V, PHI
	Carm. 3.1.37–40	V
Ag. 75–89	Carm. 1.34.12–13	V
Ag. 77–82	Carm. 1.2	V, M, PHI
Ag. 83–102	Carm. 1.34	V, M

Ag. 90–97	Carm. 2.10	V, *
Ag. 96	Carm. 2.10.11–12	V
Ag. 98–102	Carm. 1.34.12–16	V, M
Ag. 102–107	Carm. 2.10.1–4	V (p. 110–111)
	Carm. 3.29.62–64	V (p. 110–111)
Ag. 103–105	Carm. 2.10.13–14	V
	Carm. 3.16.22–24	V
	Carm. 3.16.29–32	PHI, M
Ag. 310–387	Carm. 4.6.31–40	M
Ag. 310	Carm. 1.21.2	V
	Carm. 4.6.37	V
Ag. 312–314	Carm. 2.5.21–24	M
Ag. 322–339	Carm. 1.21	N, M
	Carm. 1.22	M, V
Ag. 322–332b	Carm. 2.10.18–20	M, V
Ag. 322–323	Carm. 3.8.23–24	V
Ag. 324–326b	Carm. 1.21.11–12	V
Ag. 324–325	Carm. 1.22.3–4	V
	Carm. 3.4.60	V
Ag. 327–331b	Carm. 2.1.37–40	V, M
	Carm. 3.3.69–72	V, M
Ag. 334–334b	Carm. 3.4.42–44	V
Ag. 335–339	Carm. 3.4.49–52	V, *
Ag. 340–344	Carm. 1.7.8–9	V, N
Ag. 356–358b	Carm. 4.6.7–8	V
Ag. 367–369b	Carm. 3.22.1–4	V
	Saec. 13–16	N
Ag. 376–379	Carm. 4.6.1	N
Ag. 384–384b	Carm. 3.1.8	M
Ag. 385–387	Carm. 1.2.35–36	V
Ag. 598–610	Carm. 3.3.1–18	V, * (p. 11–15, 105–107, 147–149)
Ag. 602–604	Carm. 3.3.7–8	V, M, %
Ag. 605–610	Carm. 4.9.46–52	V, PHI
Ag. 670–677	Carm. 4.12.5–8	N, M
Ag. 677–680	Carm. 4.3.19–20	V, M
Ag. 686–690	Carm. 1.16.5–8	M
Ag. 769–771	S. 1.1.68–69	V, M
Ag. 808–809	Carm. 1.7.8–9	V, M
Ag. 820–821	Carm. 2.9.10–12	V, %
Ag. 828	Carm. 3.3.9–10	M
Ag. 835–836	Carm. 4.4.61–62	M
Ag. 840–841	Carm. 2.14.7–8	N
Ag. 859–860b	Carm. 2.19.29–32	M, V
	Carm. 3.11.17–20	M, V
Ag. 861	Carm. 2.2.1	V
Ag. 862–866	Carm. 1.2.52	V

Ag. 862–864	Carm. 3.3.26–27	V, M
Ag. 867	Ars. 179	V

Thyestes

Thy. 26–27	Carm. 1.24.1–2	V
Thy. 44	Epod. 7.19–20	V (p. 134)
Thy. 67	Epod. 7.1	V (p. 134)
Thy. 122–175	Carm. 1.6.8–9	V, metre
	Carm. 2.13	PHI, *
	Carm. 2.14	PHI, *
Thy. 123	Carm. 1.1.3–4	M
	Carm. 4.2.17–19	M
	Carm. 4.3.4–6	M
Thy. 134–135	Carm. 3.6.46–48	V, M
Thy. 137	Carm. 2.18.36–38	V
Thy. 140 & 142–143	Carm. 1.1.14	N, M
Thy. 147–148	Carm. 1.28.7	M
Thy. 152	Epod. 17.66	N, M
Thy. 205–207	Carm. 3.14.13–16	M, % (p. 101–103)
	Carm. 4.5.25–28	M (p. 102–103)
	Carm. 4.15.17–20	M (p. 101–103)
	Carm. 4.15.25–32	M (p. 102–103)
Thy. 212	Carm. 3.14.13–16	M (p. 101–103)
	Carm. 4.5.25–28	M (p. 102–103)
	Carm. 4.15.17–20	M (p. 101–103)
	Carm. 4.15.25–32	M (p. 102–103)
Thy. 336–403	Carm. 4.9.1–4	PHI (p. 369)
Thy. 338	Carm. 3.16.21–22	M (p. 47–48)
Thy. 339–340	Epod. 7.1–2	V, M
Thy. 344–403	Carm. 3.3	PHI, M
Thy. 348–349	Carm. 2.16.13–16	V, PHI
Thy. 348–368	Carm. 3.3.1–8	V, M (p. 351)
Thy. 350	Carm. 3.2.17	PHI
Thy. 351–352	Carm. 3.2.19–20	M
Thy. 356–357	Carm. 1.1.10	V
Thy. 358–362	Carm. 3.1.25–28	V, M
	Carm. 3.3.2–6	V, M
Thy. 363–364	Carm. 3.1.17–18	V, M
Thy. 365	Carm. 2.10.5–8	PHI
Thy. 366–368	Carm. 4.9.47–52	PHI
Thy. 376–377	Carm. 4.15.21	V
Thy. 381–384	Carm. 1.22.1–4	PHI
Thy. 391–395	Carm. 3.16.18–20	V, M
Thy. 393–403	Carm. 2.10.6–8	V, M
	Carm. 2.16.37	V, M
Thy. 394–395	Carm. 2.3.5–12	M, PHI
	Carm. 3.1.21–22	M, PHI

(cont.)	Carm. 3.1.45–48	M, PHI
Thy. 394	Carm. 2.16.37	M, PHI
	Carm. 2.17.32	V, PHI
Thy. 459–460	Carm. 3.1.33	V
Thy. 546–622	Carm. 1.25	M, PHI
	Carm. 1.34	M, PHI
Thy. 557	Carm. 2.14.13	V
Thy. 573–576	Carm. 2.1.17–19	V (p. 151–152)
Thy. 574–575	Epod. 2.5	V
Thy. 583	Epod. 17.32–33	V
Thy. 588–589	Carm. 1.12.29–32	V, M
Thy. 598	Carm. 1.34.12	V
Thy. 604–606	Carm. 2.13.13–14	M, PHI
Thy. 607	Carm. 1.12.15–16	V, M
Thy. 609	Carm. 1.16.22	M, PHI
	Carm. 3.6.5	M, PHI
Thy. 610–611	Carm. 3.4.67–68	M, PHI
Thy. 612	Carm. 3.1.5–8	M
	Carm. 3.4.47–48	M
Thy. 615–616	Carm. 2.10.13–15	M, PHI
	Carm. 2.10.21–24	PHI
Thy. 619–620	Carm. 1.11.9	V, PHI
	Carm. 4.7.17–18	V, PHI
Thy. 791	Saec. 2	V
Thy. 795–797	Carm. 2.9.10–12	V, N
Thy. 801	Carm. 3.6.43	V
	Carm. 3.13.11	V
Thy. 805–812b	Carm. 3.4	M
Thy. 805–806	Carm. 2.19.21–22	M
	Carm. 3.1.7–8	M
Thy. 805–806	Carm. 3.4.49–58	M
Thy. 807–808	Carm. 3.4.77–78	N, M
	Carm. 3.11.21–22	N
Thy. 807–808	Carm. 4.6.1–3	M
Thy. 809–810	Carm. 3.4.53–54	N, M
	Carm. 3.4.75–76	V
Thy. 810–812b	Carm. 3.4.51–52	V, M
Thy. 848–849	Carm. 1.4.1–2	V
	Carm. 4.7.9	V
	Ep. 1.10.15–16	V, N
Thy. 850–874	Carm. 2.17.13–20	M
Thy. 855–856	Ep. 1.10.15–16	V, N
Thy. 858–859	Carm. 2.17.17–18	N, V
Thy. 863–864	Carm. 2.17.19–20	N, V
Thy. 885–895	Carm. 1.12.51–52	M (p. 104–105)
	Carm. 1.12.57–58	M (p. 104–105)
	Carm. 3.1.5–6	M (p. 104–105)

(cont.)
Thy. 886   Carm. 3.6.5–8   M (p. 104–105)
Thy. 933   Carm. 1.1.36   V (p. 105)
                  Carm. 3.3.8   V

Correspondences Horace – Seneca

Horace, *Odes* and *Epodes*

Horace	Seneca	
Odes 1		
Carm. 1.1	Her. F. 125–204	M (p. 347)
Carm. 1.1.1	Tro. 712	V
Carm. 1.1.3–6	Her. F. 192–195	V
Carm. 1.1.3–4	Thy. 123	M
Carm. 1.1.7–8	Phaed. 983	M
Carm. 1.1.9–10	Ep. 41.7	PHI
Carm. 1.1.9	Ep. 2.6	PHI, M
	Ep. 76.15	PHI
Carm. 1.1.10	Thy. 356–357	V
Carm. 1.1.11–15	Med. 329–334	V, M
Carm. 1.1.14	Thy. 140 & 142–143	N, M
Carm. 1.1.30–31	Her. F. 197	V
Carm. 1.1.36	Thy. 886	V (p. 105)
Carm. 1.2	Ag. 77–82	V, M, PHI
Carm. 1.2.1–20	Med. 595–598	M
Carm. 1.2.1	Med. 668	V
Carm. 1.2.30	Med. 595	V
Carm. 1.2.35–36	Ag. 385–387	V
Carm. 1.2.52	Ag. 862–866	V
Carm. 1.3	Med. 301–379	M, V
Carm. 1.3.9–11	Med. 301–302	V, M
	Med. 305–308	V, M
	Med. 607–609	M
Carm. 1.3.10–16	Her. F. 152–154	M
Carm. 1.3.14	Med. 311–312	V, M
Carm. 1.3.21–24	Med. 335–336	V, M
Carm. 1.3.25–28	Her. F. 548–551	V
Carm. 1.3.25	Med. 301–302	V, M
Carm. 1.3.26 & 38	Her. F. 181–189	M
Carm. 1.3.32–33	Oed. 124–125	PHI, V
Carm. 1.3.32	Her. F. 865–866	M
Carm. 1.3.33–34	Tro. 385	V, PHI
Carm. 1.3.34–35	Oed. 899–905	N, M
Carm. 1.3.36	Her. F. 566 & 1316	V, %

(cont.)	Med. 638	M
Carm. 1.4.1–2	Thy. 848–849	V
Carm. 1.4.4	Her. F. 139–140	V
Carm. 1.4.13–14	Her. F. 554–557	M, V
Carm. 1.4.13	Her. F. 1074	M
Carm. 1.4.15–18	Her. F. 865–866	M, *
Carm. 1.4.15	Dial. 10.9.1	PHI
	Ep. 1.2	PHI
	Ep. 101.4	PHI, V
Carm. 1.4.16–20	Med. 632–633	M
Carm. 1.4.16	Her. F. 181–189	PHI
Carm. 1.4.16	Oed. 127	V
Carm. 1.4.19–20	Phaed. 291–293	M
Carm. 1.5.13	Med. 62–63	V
Carm. 1.6.8–9	Thy. 122–175	V
Carm. 1.6.8	Tro. 855	N
Carm. 1.7.3	Oed. 405–407b	N
Carm. 1.7.8–9	Ag. 340–344	V, N
	Ag. 808–809	V, M
Carm. 1.7.17	Her. F. 178–185	PHI
Carm. 1.7.29	Med. 370	V
Carm. 1.9	Phaed. 1–53	M, * (p. 154–155)
Carm. 1.9.1–2	Tro. 73	V
Carm. 1.9.2–3	Oed. 176–176b	M
Carm. 1.9.13–18	Ben. 5.17.7	PHI, V
	Ep. 1.1	PHI
	Ep. 12.9	PHI
	Ep. 93.6	PHI
	Her. F. 178–185	PHI
Carm. 1.9.17	Her. F. 198	V
Carm. 1.10.2–4	Her. F. 1124–1125	V
Carm. 1.10.11–12	Her. F. 1115–1117	V, M
Carm. 1.10.13–16	Tro. 144 & 148–149	V
Carm. 1.11	Her. F. 178–185	PHI
Carm. 1.11.6–8	Dial. 10.9.1	M, PHI (p. 7–9)
	Ep. 1.2	PHI
	Ep. 101.4	PHI
Carm. 1.11.7–8	Ep. 58.22–23	PHI, M (p. 194)
	Her. F. 174–178	M
Carm. 1.11.8	Dial. 9.1.13	V (p. 245–246)
	Her. F. 874	V, %
Carm. 1.11.9	Thy. 619–620	V, PHI
Carm. 1.12.6	Med. 588–590	V, M
Carm. 1.12.7–12	Her. F. 572–576	V, M
	Med. 625–630	N, V
Carm. 1.12.13–16	Phaed. 961–965	V, M
Carm. 1.12.15–16	Thy. 607	V, M

Carm. 1.12.21–27	Med. 82–89	V, M
Carm. 1.12.22	Med 87	V, N
Carm. 1.12.23–24	Her. F. 1128	V
Carm. 1.12.25–32	Her. F. 552–553	M
Carm. 1.12.29–32	Thy. 588–589	V, M
Carm. 1.12.41	Phaed. 801	V, M
Carm. 1.12.47–48	Phaed. 748	V
Carm. 1.12.51–52	Thy. 885–895	M (p. 104–105)
Carm. 1.12.57–58	Thy. 885–895	M (p. 104–105)
Carm. 1.13.5–6	Med. 858 & 861	M
Carm. 1.13.8	Phaed. 281–283	M
Carm. 1.14.2–3	Dial. 9.5.5	M (p. 260)
Carm. 1.14.6	Oed. 886	V
Carm. 1.14.14–15	Ep. 76.13	V, M
Carm. 1.14.14	Her. F. 152	M
Carm. 1.15.1–2	Tro. 69–72	N, M
Carm. 1.15.10–11	Tro. 77–78	M
Carm. 1.15.22	Tro. 848	N
Carm. 1.16.5–12	Med. 591–594	V, PHI
Carm. 1.16.5–8	Ag. 686–690	M
Carm. 1.16.22	Thy. 609	M, PHI
Carm. 1.17.8–9	Oed. 149	V
Carm. 1.18	Her. F. 178–185	PHI
Carm. 1.18.5	Tro. 1022	V
Carm. 1.19.1–4	Phaed. 274–278	N, V (p. 122–123)
Carm. 1.19.5–8	Phaed. 795–800	V (p. 126–127)
Carm. 1.19.11–12	Oed. 118–119	V, M
Carm. 1.21	Ag. 322–339	N, M
Carm. 1.21.1–2	Her. F. 852–853	M
Carm. 1.21.2	Ag. 310	V
Carm. 1.21.7	Her. F. 836	V
Carm. 1.21.11–12	Her F. 1115–1117	V, M
	Ag. 324–326b	V
Carm. 1.22	Tro. 814–860	N
	Ag. 322–339	M, V
Carm. 1.22.1–4	Thy. 381–384	PHI
Carm. 1.22.3–4	Ag. 324–325	V
Carm. 1.22.5	Ag. 64–70	V
Carm. 1.24.1–2	Thy. 26–27	V
Carm. 1.24.13–14	Med. 622–629	V, N
Carm. 1.24.13	Med. 358	V
Carm. 1.24.16–18	Oed. 126–128	PHI
Carm. 1.25	Thy 546–622	M, PHI
Carm. 1.25.11–15	Med. 579–582	M
Carm. 1.28.7	Thy. 147–148	M
Carm. 1.28.15–16	Oed. 126–128	PHI
Carm. 1.28.19–20	Her. F. 181–189	PHI

Carm. 1.28.19	Her. F. 864–866	M
	Oed. 131–132	V, M
Carm. 1.29.1–2	Her. F. 166–168	V
Carm. 1.29.1	Oed. 117	V
Carm. 1.32.7–8	Med. 612	M
Carm. 1.34	Ag. 83–102	V, M
	Thy. 546–622	M, PHI
Carm. 1.34.12–16	Ag. 98–102	V, M
Carm. 1.34.12–13	Phaed. 975–977	M
	Ag. 75–89	V
Carm. 1.34.12	Thy. 598	V
Carm. 1.34.14–16	Phaed. 978–980	M
	Phaed. 1141–1143	V, M
Carm. 1.37	Her. F. 875–894	PHI
Carm. 1.37.4	Med. 111	V
Carm. 1.37.29–32	Tro. 145–155	M

Odes 2
Carm. 2.1.17–22	Oed. 731–734	V, M (p. 149–150)
Carm. 2.1.17–19	Thy. 573–576	V (p. 151–152)
Carm. 2.1.21–22	Tro. 85–87	V
Carm. 2.1.37–40	Ag. 327–331b	V, M
Carm. 2.2.1	Ag. 861	V
Carm. 2.2.7	Oed. 896–897	M
Carm. 2.3.5–12	Thy. 394–395	M, PHI
Carm. 2.3.15–16	Her. F. 181–182	V, %
Carm. 2.3.25–27	Oed. 166–166b	V, M
	Her. F. 181–189	PHI
Carm. 2.3.25	Tro. 390	PHI
Carm. 2.4.9–12	Tro. 128–129	M
Carm. 2.5.21–24	Ag. 312–314	M
Carm. 2.6	Tro. 814–860	N
Carm. 2.6.3–4	Ag. 64–70	V
Carm. 2.6.9	Her. F. 559	M, V
	Oed. 991–991b	M
Carm. 2.6.11–20	Dial. 9.2.13	N, PHI
Carm. 2.8.17	Her. F. 870	V
Carm. 2.9.10–12	Med. 877–878	M
	Phaed. 743–752	V, M
	Oed. 506	M
	Ag. 820–821	V, %
	Thy. 795–797	V, N
Carm. 2.9.17–20	Dial. 11.8	M, *
Carm. 2.9.23	Oed. 478	N, %
Carm. 2.9.24	Oed. 115	V
Carm. 2.10	Med. 599–606	M (p. 346–347)
	Phaed. 1123–1153	PHI, M

(cont.)	Oed. 882–914	PHI, M (p. 177–178)
	Oed. 887–914	M (p. 347, 360)
	Oed. 980–997	PHI (p. 360)
	Ag. 57–107	PHI, *
	Ag. 90–97	V, *
Carm. 2.10.1–4	Ag. 102–107	V (p. 110–111)
Carm. 2.10.2–4	Med. 329–334	V, M
Carm. 2.10.2–3	Dial. 9.11.7	V, M (p. 260)
Carm. 2.10.5–8	Her. F. 199–200	V, M
	Oed. 882–891	PHI, V (p. 108–111)
	Thy. 365	PHI
Carm. 2.10.5–6	Oed. 890–891	V, M
Carm. 2.10.6–8	Her. F. 178–185	PHI
	Thy. 393–403	V, M
Carm. 2.10.6–7	Phaed. 1138–1139	V, M
Carm. 2.10.9–11	Phaed. 1128–1131	V, M
	Her. F. 201	V
Carm. 2.10.11–12	Phaed. 1132–1136	V
	Ag. 96	V
Carm. 2.10.13	Nat. 3 praef. 7	V, M
Carm. 2.10.13–15	Thy. 615–616	M, PHI
Carm. 2.10.13–14	Ag. 103–105	V
Carm. 2.10.15–17	Phaed. 972–974	V, M
Carm. 2.10.18–20	Ag. 322–332b	M, V
Carm. 2.10.21–24	Thy. 615–616	PHI
Carm. 2.10.22–24	Dial. 9.4.7	V (p. 260)
	Ep. 19.9	V
Carm. 2.10.23–25	Oed. 887–889	V, M
Carm. 2.11.5–24	Phaed. 736–834	PHI
Carm. 2.11.5–6	Phaed. 773	V, M
Carm. 2.11.9–10	Phaed. 764–765	V, M
Carm. 2.11.16	Phaed. 774	V, *
Carm. 2.12.24	Oed. 117	V
Carm. 2.12.6	Her. F. 882	V
Carm. 2.13	Thy. 122–175	PHI, *
Carm. 2.13.13–14	Oed. 992–994	V, PHI
	Thy. 604–606	M, PHI
Carm. 2.13.17–18	Oed. 118–119	V, M
Carm. 2.13.19–20	Oed. 992–994	V, PHI
Carm. 2.13.21	Her. F. 549	V
Carm. 2.13.34	Apoc. 13.3	quote (p. 3, 37, 311)
Carm. 2.14	Thy. 122–175	PHI, *
Carm. 2.14.1–2	Ep. 1.3	V (p. 201–203)
Carm. 2.14.2–4	Oed. 992–994	V, PHI
Carm. 2.14.7–8	Ag. 840–841	N
Carm. 2.14.9–18	Her. F. 554–557	M, V
Carm. 2.14.9–12 & 18	Her. F. 869	M

Carm. 2.14.13	Thy. 557	V
Carm. 2.14.15–16	Oed. 992–994	V, PHI
Carm. 2.15	Ep. 89.20	PHI
Carm. 2.15	Dial. 9.3.7	PHI, M
Carm. 2.16.1–6	Nat. 1.2.8	V
Carm. 2.16.9–22	Ag. 71–76	V, PHI
Carm. 2.16.10–11	Ep. 56.5	V, PHI
Carm. 2.16.13–16	Thy. 348–349	V, PHI
Carm. 2.16.17–20	Oed. 992–994	V, PHI
Carm. 2.16.18–19	Ep. 104.8	V, PHI
Carm. 2.16.19–20	Ep. 28.1	M, PHI
Carm. 2.16.23–24	Phaed. 737–738	V
Carm. 2.16.25–26	Ben. 7.2.4	M, PHI (p. 48)
Carm. 2.16.33–34	Tro. 1020–1021	M
Carm. 2.16.35–40	Her. F. 192–200	M
Carm. 2.16.37–40	Ep. 18.3–4	PHI (p. 77)
Carm. 2.16.37	Her. F. 199–200	V
	Thy. 393–403	V, M, PHI
Carm. 2.16.39	Oed. 991–991b	M
Carm. 2.17.13–20	Thy. 850–874	M
Carm. 2.17.17–18	Thy. 858–859	N, V
Carm. 2.17.19–20	Thy. 863–864	N, V
Carm. 2.17.25–26	Her. F. 838–839	M
Carm. 2.17.30–31	Her. F. 877	V
Carm. 2.17.32	Thy. 394	V, PHI
Carm. 2.18.15–16	Ep. 24.26	M
Carm. 2.18.19–26	Ep. 89.20	M, V
	Dial. 9.3.7	M, V
Carm. 2.18.32–34	Her. F. 181–189	PHI
	Her. F. 1074	M
Carm. 2.18.34–36	Oed. 167	M
Carm. 2.18.36–38	Thy. 137	V
Carm. 2.19	Oed. 403–508	*, N, M
	Dial. 9.17.11	PHI (p. 259)
Carm. 2.19.10–12	Oed. 491–492	V, M
Carm. 2.19.14–15	Oed. 442	N, M
Carm. 2.19.16	Oed. 471	N, M
Carm. 2.19.21–22	Thy. 805–806	M
Carm. 2.19.29–32	Ag. 859–860b	M, V
Carm. 2.20	Dial. 9.17.11	PHI (p. 259)
Carm. 2.20.1	Dial. 9.1.14	PHI, V (p. 259)
Carm. 2.20.8	Her. F. 181–189	V, M
Carm. 2.20.13–16	Ag. 64–70	V

Odes 3

Carm. 3.1.2–8	Dial. 7.26.7	V, M
Carm. 3.1.5–8	Thy. 612	M

Carm. 3.1.5–6	Thy. 885–895	M (p. 104–105)
Carm. 3.1.7–8	Thy. 805–806	M
Carm. 3.1.8	Ag. 384–384b	M
Carm. 3.1.14–16	Her. F. 181–189	PHI
Carm. 3.1.14–15	Her. F. 1074	M
Carm. 3.1.16	Her. F. 178–185	PHI, M
	Oed. 166–166b	V
Carm. 3.1.17–24	Dial. 1.3.9–10	N, M
Carm. 3.1.17–18	Thy. 363–364	V, M
Carm. 3.1.21–22	Thy. 394–395	M, PHI
Carm. 3.1.25–28	Thy. 358–362	V, M
Carm. 3.1.33–34	Dial. 9.3.7	M, V
	Ep. 89.20	M, V
Carm. 3.1.33	Thy. 459–460	V
Carm. 3.1.37–40	Ag. 71–76	V
Carm. 3.1.45–46	Thy. 394–395	M, PHI
Carm. 3.2.13	Dial. 3.12.5	PHI
	Tro. 162–164	M, V
Carm. 3.2.17	Thy. 350	PHI
Carm. 3.2.19–20	Thy. 351–352	M
Carm. 3.2.20	Phaed. 488	V
Carm. 3.3	Ag. 589–658	V, M
	Thy. 344–403	PHI, M
Carm. 3.3.1–18	Ag. 593–610	V, * (p. 11–15, 105–107, 147–149)
Carm. 3.3.1–8	Nat. 6.32.4	M
	Thy. 348–368	V, M (p. 351)
Carm. 3.3.2–6	Thy. 358–362	V, M
Carm. 3.3.7–8	Ag. 602–604	V, M, %
Carm. 3.3.8	Thy. 933	V
Carm. 3.3.9–48	Her. F. 125–204	M
Carm. 3.3.9–10	Ag. 828	M
Carm. 3.3.13–15	Med. 82–89	V, M
	Oed. 424–425	V, M
Carm. 3.3.26–28	Tro. 124–127	M
Carm. 3.3.26–27	Ag. 862–864	V, M
Carm. 3.3.26	Tro. 70	V
Carm. 3.3.69–72	Ag. 327–331b	V, M
Carm. 3.4	Thy. 805–812b	M
Carm. 3.4.34	Oed. 470	V, M
Carm. 3.4.42–44	Ag. 334–334b	V
Carm. 3.4.47–48	Thy. 612	M
Carm. 3.4.49–52	Ag. 335–339	V, *
Carm. 3.4.49–58	Thy. 805–806	M
Carm. 3.4.51–52	Tro. 829	V
	Thy. 810–812b	V, M
Carm. 3.4.53–54	Thy. 809–810	N, M
Carm. 3.4.60	Ag. 324–325	V

Carm. 3.4.61–62	Oed. 712	N
Carm. 3.4.67–68	Thy. 610–611	M, PHI
Carm. 3.4.75–76	Thy. 809–810	V
Carm. 3.4.77–78	Thy 807–808	N, M
Carm. 3.5.13–56	Dial. 1.3.9–10	N, M
Carm. 3.6.1–4	Oed. 748	M
Carm. 3.6.1–2	Oed. 709–712	V, M
Carm. 3.6.5–8	Thy. 885–895	M (p. 104–105)
Carm. 3.6.5	Thy. 609	M, PHI
Carm. 3.6.42	Her. F. 880–881	V, M
Carm. 3.6.43	Thy. 801	V
Carm. 3.6.46–48	Thy. 134–135	V, M
Carm. 3.8.23–24	Ag. 322–323	V
Carm. 3.8.23	Oed. 469	V
Carm. 3.8.27–28	Ep. 99.5	V, % (p. 204)
Carm. 3.9.21–22	Phaed. 743–752	V, M
Carm. 3.10.11	Her. F. 578	V
Carm. 3.11.13–14	Her. F. 572–576	M
Carm. 3.11.15–17	Tro. 403–404	M
Carm. 3.11.17–20	Ag. 859–860b	M, V
Carm. 3.11.21–22	Thy 807–808	N
Carm. 3.12.10–11	Her. F. 1129	V
Carm. 3.13.3–5	Her. F. 141–145	V
Carm. 3.13.6–7	Oed. 177	M
Carm. 3.13.11	Thy. 801	V
Carm. 3.14.10–11	Her. F. 852–853	M
Carm. 3.14.13–16	Thy. 205–207	M, % (p. 101–103)
	Thy. 212	M (p. 101–103)
Carm. 3.14.25	Her. F. 198	V
Carm. 3.15.9–10	Med. 849–852	M
Carm. 3.16.13–15	Ben. 7.10.6	PHI (p. 46–47)
Carm. 3.16.18–20	Thy. 391–395	V, M
Carm. 3.16.21–22	Ben. 7.2.4	M (p. 47–48)
Carm. 3.16.21–22	Ben. 7.3.2	M (p. 47–48)
	Thy. 338	M (p. 47–48)
Carm. 3.16.22–24	Ag. 103–105	V
Carm. 3.16.22–23	Ep. 2.5	V, M
Carm. 3.16.25–28	Ep. 2.6	PHI, M
	Ep. 41.7	PHI
	Ep. 76.15	PHI
Carm. 3.16.25–27	Tro. 1020–1021	M
Carm. 3.16.27–28	Ep. 74.7	V, PHI (p. 50–51)
	Dial. 9.8.5	V, PHI (p. 50–51)
	Dial 12.11.4	V, PHI (p. 50–51)
Carm. 3.16.28	Ep. 74.4	M, V (p. 342)
	Her. F. 166–168	M, PHI (p. 342)
Carm. 3.16.29–32	Ag. 103–105	PHI, M

Carm. 3.18.9	Her. F. 141–145	V, M
Carm. 3.19.18	Dial. 9.17.10	V (p. 249–250, 261)
Carm. 3.20.14	Oed. 498–500	V
Carm. 3.21.18	Tro. 1022	V
Carm. 3.21.24	Her. F. 1059	V
Carm. 3.22.1–4	Ag. 367–369b	V
Carm. 3.22.1	Phaed. 406	V
Carm. 3.22.4	Phaed. 412	V
Carm. 3.23.5–8	Oed. 133–148	V, M
	Oed. 156–158	M, *
Carm. 3.23.12–13	Oed. 138–139	V, M
Carm. 3.23.13–20	Ep. 115.5	M, V
Carm. 3.24.2	Oed. 117	V
Carm. 3.24.3–4	Dial. 9.3.7	M, V
Carm. 3.24.3–4	Ep. 89.20	M, V
Carm. 3.24.9–11	Her. F. 533–568	V (p. 156)
Carm. 3.24.11–16	Oed. 473–474	V, M
Carm. 3.24.17	Her. F. 537	V
Carm. 3.24.38	Oed. 473	V
Carm. 3.25.8–12	Oed. 432–438	V, M
Carm. 3.25.10	Tro. 73	V
Carm. 3.25.20	Oed. 430	V
Carm. 3.27.25–29	Phaed. 303–308	M
Carm. 3.27.28	Med. 346	V
Carm. 3.29	Ep. 12	PHI, V (p. 187–193)
Carm. 3.29.9–12	Phaed. 1124–1127	V, M
Carm. 3.29.32–41	Ep. 23.8	V, M (p. 192–193)
Carm. 3.29.32–33	Ep. 12.1–4	PHI (p. 190)
Carm. 3.29.41–48	Ben. 5.17.7	PHI, V
	Ep. 1.1	PHI, V
	Ep. 12.9	PHI, V (p. 187–188)
	Ep. 93.6	PHI
Carm. 3.29.45–48	Oed. 989	V, M
Carm. 3.29.49–53	Phaed. 1141–1143	V, M
Carm. 3.29.49–52	Ep. 74.7	V, M
	Phaed. 978–980	M
Carm. 3.29.62–64	Oed. 887–889	V
	Ag. 102–107	V (p. 110–111)
Carm. 3.30.3–5	Dial. 11.18.2	V, M (p. 16–18)
Carm. 3.30.4–5	Dial. 10.9.3	V, PHI (p. 7–10)
Carm. 3.30.6–7	Tro. 377	V, PHI

Odes 4

Carm. 4.1.5	Phaed. 274–275	N, V (p. 123–124)
Carm. 4.1.8	Phaed. 291–293	V (p. 124)
Carm. 4.1.29–32	Phaed. 634–635	V (p. 125)
Carm. 4.1.37–40	Phaed. 700–701	M (p. 127–128)

(cont.)	Phaed. 1179–1180	M (p. 128)
Carm. 4.2.2–4	Oed. 892–898	N, M
	Oed. 898	V, %
Carm. 4.2.17–19	Thy. 123	M
Carm. 4.2.27–32	Ep. 84	M (p. 232, 276)
Carm. 4.2.34–36	Tro. 145–155	M
Carm. 4.2.59–60	Med. 60	V, M
Carm. 4.3.4–6	Her. F. 192–195	V
	Thy. 123	M
Carm. 4.3.19–20	Ag. 677–680	V, M
Carm. 4.4.59–60	Her. F. 33–34	M
Carm. 4.4.61–62	Ag. 835–836	M
Carm. 4.4.63–64	Oed. 726–727	V, M
Carm. 4.5.6–8	Cl. 1.7.2	M
Carm. 4.5.17–20	Med. 595–598	V, M
Carm. 4.5.25–28	Thy. 205–207	M (p. 102–103)
	Thy. 212	M (p. 102–103)
Carm. 4.6.1–3	Thy 807–808	M
Carm. 4.6.1	Ag. 376–379	N
Carm. 4.6.7–8	Ag. 356–358b	V
Carm. 4.6.31–40	Ag. 310–387	M
Carm. 4.6.37	Ag. 310	V
Carm. 4.7.7–12	Ep. 24.26	M, PHI (p. 332)
Carm. 4.7.9	Thy. 848–849	V
Carm. 4.7.9–12	Phaed. 764–768	M
	Phaed. 966–971	V, M
Carm. 4.7.17–18	Thy. 619–620	V, PHI
Carm. 4.8.29–30	Her. F. 533–568	M
Carm. 4.8.31	Her. F. 552–553	V, N
Carm. 4.9.1–4	Thy. 336–403	PHI (p. 369)
Carm. 4.9.14	Phaed. 387–388	V
Carm. 4.9.22–24	Tro. 124–127	M
Carm. 4.9.45–50	Dial. 7.15.4	V, PHI
Carm. 4.9.46–52	Ag. 605–610	V, PHI
Carm. 4.9.47–52	Thy. 366–368	PHI
Carm. 4.10	Cl. 1.1.1	M (p. 280–281)
	Dial. 4.36.1–3	M (p. 280–281)
Carm. 4.10.3–8	Phaed. 768–772	V, M (p. 125–126)
Carm. 4.10.4–5	Med. 99–100	V
Carm. 4.11.25	Med. 599–602	N
Carm. 4.12.5–8	Ag. 670–677	N, M
Carm. 4.12.26	Phaed. 774	V, *
Carm. 4.12.27–28	Dial. 9.17.10	V (p. 249–250, 261)
Carm. 4.13.14–16	Her. F. 178–185	M, PHI
Carm. 4.13.17–18	Phaed. 769–772	PHI, M
Carm. 4.15.17–20	Thy. 205–207	M (p. 102–103)
	Thy. 212	M (p. 102–103)

Carm. 4.15.21–24	Med. 373–374	V
Carm. 4.15.21	Thy. 376–377	V
Carm. 4.15.25–32	Thy. 205–207	M (p. 101–103)
	Thy. 212	M (p. 101–103)

Carmen saeculare

Saec. 1–5	Oed. 403–405	V (p. 129, 241)
Saec. 1–2	Phaed. 409–411	V
Saec. 2	Oed. 250	V (p. 241)
	Thy. 791	V
Saec. 9–11	Oed. 121–122	V
Saec. 13–16	Ag. 367–369b	N
Saec. 25–28	Oed. 983–986	V, M
Saec. 27–28	Phaed. 1183–1184	V (p. 132)
Saec. 35–36	Med. 97–98	V, M
Saec. 61–62	Her F. 1115–1117	V, M

Epodes

Epod. 1.12	Med. 43	V
Epod. 2	Her. F. 125–204	M (p. 347)
	Phaed. 516–539	PHI, M
Epod. 2.1–4	Med. 329–334	V, M
Epod. 2.5	Thy. 574–575	V
Epod. 2.7–8	Her F. 164–165	V, %
Epod. 2.26	Phaed. 508	V
Epod. 2.67–70	Ep. 2.6	PHI, M
	Ep. 41.7	PHI
	Ep. 76.15	PHI
Epod. 3.15	Oed. 47	V
Epod. 4.13	Tro. 1020–1021	M
Epod. 5.53–54	Med. 13	V (p. 119)
Epod. 5.89–90	Med. 970–971	V, M (p. 121)
Epod. 6.15	Phaed. 346	V, M
Epod. 7.1–2	Thy. 339–340	V, M
Epod. 7.1	Thy. 67	V (p. 134)
Epod. 7.15	Med. 859	V, M
Epod. 7.19–20	Thy. 44	V (p. 134)
Epod. 7.20	Phoen. 277–278	V (p. 134)
Epod. 9.34–35	Dial. 9.1.17	V (p. 260)
Epod. 9.38	Dial. 9.17.8	V (p. 259)
Epod. 10.13–14	Med. 660–661	M
Epod. 11.5–6	Med. 715	V
Epod. 11.6	Phaed. 764–768	M
Epod. 13.15–16	Her. F. 559	M
	Oed. 981–983	M
Epod. 13.15	Her. F. 181–189	PHI
Epod. 15.1–2	Phaed. 744–752	V, M

Epod. 15.2	Phaed. 748	V
Epod. 15.19–20	Oed. 467–468	N, V
Epod. 16.10	Oed. 724–725	M
Epod. 16.20	Oed. 149	V
Epod. 16.51	Oed. 151	V
Epod. 16.55	Oed. 156	V
Epod. 16.61–62	Oed. 145–148	V, M
Epod. 17.21–22	Phaed. 769–772	V, M
Epod. 17.32–33	Thy. 583	V
Epod. 17.66	Thy. 152	N, M

Horace, hexameter poetry

Horace	Seneca	
Satires 1		
S. 1.1.15–19	Ep. 96.4–5	V, PHI (p. 34–36)
S. 1.1.66–67	Ep. 2.6	PHI, M
	Ep. 41.7	PHI
	Ep. 76.15	PHI
S. 1.1.68–69	Ag. 769–771	V, M
S. 1.1.70–71	Her. F. 166–168	PHI, M
S. 1.1.92–94	Ep. 18.3–4	PHI (p. 77)
S. 1.1.106–107	Ben. 2.16.2	PHI
S. 1.2.24–28	Ep. 18.3–4	PHI (p. 77)
S. 1.2.27	Ep. 86.13	quote (p. 3–4, 74–75, 311)
S. 1.2.75	Phaed. 699	V (p. 278)
S. 1.2.92–93	Ep. 33.5	V
S. 1.2.114–115	Ep. 2.6	PHI, M
	Ep. 41.7	PHI
	Ep. 76.15	PHI
	Ep. 119.14	quote (p. 38–41, 75, 81–82, 311)
S. 1.3.11–17	Ep. 120.20–21	quote (p. 3, 9, 75, 277, 311)
S. 1.3.19	Ep. 120.22	V (p. 277)
S. 1.3.114	Phaed. 699	V (p. 278)
S. 1.4.41–42	Ep. 38.1	M (p. 306)
S. 1.4.92	Ep. 86.13	V (p. 76)
S. 1.6.112	Cl. 1.8.2	V
Satires 2		
S. 2.2	Ep. 18	PHI (p. 80)
S. 2.2.65–66	Ep. 18.3–4	PIII (p. 77)
S. 2.2.110	Ben. 7.2.4	M, PHI (p. 48–49)
S. 2.3	Ep. 108.15–16	PHI (p. 84)
S. 2.3.1–16	Ep. 84	M (p. 228–229, 234)

(cont.)	Dial. 9.9.4–7	M (p. 228–229, 234)
S. 2.3.4–5	Ep. 18.3–4	V, PHI
S. 2.3.142	Ep. 74.4	M, V (p. 342)
	Her. F. 166–168	M, PHI (p. 342)
S. 2.5.3–4	Tro. 857	N
S. 2.5.39	Nat. 1.1.7	V
S. 2.6.25–26	Ep. 12.6	V
S. 2.6.96	Phaed. 774	V, *
S. 2.7	Ep. 47.14–16	PHI, M (p. 87)
S. 2.7.28–29	Ep. 28.1	M
	Ep. 104.8	M
	Dial. 9.2.13–15	PHI (p. 257–258)
	Her. F. 192–195	V
	Her. F. 197	V

Epistles 1

Ep. 1.1.14	Ep. 12.11	V
Ep. 1.1.45	Oed. 114	V
Ep. 1.2.11–13	Med. 866–869	V, PHI (p. 117)
Ep. 1.2.17	Med. 161	V (p. 118)
Ep. 1.2.20–22	Med. 611	M
Ep. 1.2.37–41	Med. 560–567	V, PHI (p. 114–115)
Ep. 1.2.40	Ep. 34.3	V, %
Ep. 1.2.40–41	Med. 537	V, PHI (p. 114–115)
	Med. 918–919	V, PHI (p. 114–115)
Ep. 1.2.46–49	Ep. 119.6	V, PHI (p. 38–39)
Ep. 1.2.62	Dial. 3.1.2	V, PHI (p. 116)
	Med. 558	V, PHI (p. 116)
Ep. 1.2.63	Med. 174–175	V (p. 117)
Ep. 1.2.64	Ep. 25.1	V
Ep. 1.3.15–22	Ep. 84	M (p. 231–232, 276)
Ep. 1.4	Ep. 60	PHI, M (p. 53–71)
Ep. 1.4.13–14	Ben. 5.17.7	PHI, V
	Ep. 1.1	PHI
	Ep. 12.9	PHI, M
	Ep. 93.6	PHI
Ep. 1.4.15–16	Ep. 60.4	M, V (p. 65)
Ep. 1.6.6	Oed. 114	V
Ep. 1.7.36	Oed. 117	V, M
Ep. 1.8.12	Dial. 9.2.13 & 15	M
	Ep. 28.1	M
	Ep. 104.8	M
Ep. 1.10.15–16	Thy. 848–849	V, N
	Thy. 855–856	V, N
Ep. 1.10.47	Dial. 7.26.1	PHI
Ep. 1.11	Dial. 9.2.13–15	PHI, V (p. 257–258)
Ep. 1.11.18	Ben. 1.12.3	M

Ep. 1.11.25–27	Ep. 28.1	V, M (p. 5–6, 338, 258)
Ep. 1.11.25–30	Ep. 104.8	M, V, PHI
Ep. 1.14.12–13	Ep. 28.1	M
	Ep. 104.8	M
	Dial. 9.2.13–15	PHI (p. 257–258)
Ep. 1.16.79	Her. F. 892	M
Ep. 1.18	Dial. 10.14–15	M (p. 227, 235–237)
Ep. 1.18.96–112	Dial. 9.9.4–7	M (p. 235–236)
	Ep. 2	M (p. 235–237)
	Ep. 39	M (p. 234–236)
	Ep. 45	M (p. 231, 235–236)
	Ep. 108	M (p. 227, 235–237)
Ep. 1.19.2–3	Dial. 9.17.10	M (p. 249–250)

Epistles 2

Ep. 2.1.48–49	Phaed. 742	V
Ep. 2.1.60–61	Her. F. 838–839	M
Ep. 2.1.214–218 & 229–244	Dial. 6.1.3–4	M (p. 233–234)
	Ep. 2	M (p. 233–234)
	Ep. 45	M (p. 233–234, 236)
	Ep. 84	M (p. 233–234)
Ep. 2.1.250–251	Ep. 75.1	M (p. 75–76)
Ep. 2.2.12	Her. F. 166–168	M
Ep. 2.2.85	Her. F. 162–163	V
Ep. 2.2.115–119	Ep. 58.5	M, V

Ars Poetica

Ars 101–102	Dial. 4.2.5	V
Ars 179	Ag. 867	V
Ars 295–297	Ep. 79.14	PHI (p. 255–256)
Ars 295–297	Dial. 9.17.10–11	PHI (p. 256–258)
Ars 301–303	Dial. 9.17.10–11	PHI (p. 256–258)
Ars 360	Tro. 441	V
Ars 393–395	Her. F. 572–576	M
Ars 453–456	Dial. 9.17.10–11	PHI (p. 256–258)

Works cited

Abel, K. (1967) *Bauformen in Senecas Dialogen*, Heidelberg.
Acosta-Hughes, B. / Barbantani, S. (2007) 'Inscribing Lyric,' in: Bing, P. / Bruss, J. S. (eds.) *Brill's Companion to Hellenistic Epigram*, Leiden, 429–457.
Ahl, F. (2008) *The Two Faces of Oedipus: Sophocles' Oedipus Tyrannus and Seneca's Oedipus*, Ithaca (NY).
Allen, D. C. (1960) *Image and Meaning: Metaphoric Traditions in Renaissance Poetry*, Baltimore (MD).
Allendorf, T. S. (2013) 'The Poetics of Uncertainty in Senecan Drama,' *Materiali e discussioni per l'analisi dei testi classici* 71, 103–144.
Ambrose, J. W. (1965) 'The Ironic Meaning of the Lollius Ode,' *Transactions of the American Philological Association* 96, 1–10.
Ancona, R. (1994) *Time and the Erotic in Horace's Odes*, Durham (NC) / London.
Anderson, W. B. (ed. and trans.) (1965) *Sidonius: Poems and Letters*, 2 vols., Cambridge (MA).
André, J. (ed.) (1981) *Anonyme latin, Traité de Physiognomie*, Paris.
André, J.-M. (1989) 'Sénèque: "De brevitate vitae," "De constantia sapientis," "De tranquillitate animi," "De otio.",' in: *Aufstieg und Niedergang der römischen Welt* II.36.3, 1724–1778.
Arens, J. C. (1963) 'Sarbiewski's Ode Against Tears Imitated by Lovelace, Yalden and Watts,' *Neophilologus* 47, 236–239.
Armisen-Marchetti, M. (1989) *Sapientiae facies: étude sur les images de Sénèque*, Paris.
Armisen-Marchetti, M. (1995) 'Sénèque et l'appropriation du temps,' *Latomus* 54, 545–567.
Armisen-Marchetti, M. (2006) '*Speculum Neronis*: un mode spécifique de direction de conscience dans *De Clementia* de Sénèque,' *Revue des Études Latines* 84, 185–201.
Armstrong, D. (1995) 'The Impossibility of Metathesis: Philodemus and Lucretius on Form and Content in Poetry,' in: Obbink (1995), 210–233.
Armstrong, D. (2004) 'Horace's *Epistles* 1 and Philodemus,' in: Armstrong, D. / Fish, J. / Johnston, P. A. / Skinner, M. B. (eds.) *Vergil, Philodemus, and the Augustans*, Austin (TX), 267–298.
Armstrong, R. (2006) *Cretan Women: Pasiphae, Ariadne, and Phaedra in Latin Poetry*, Oxford.
Ashmore, J. (1621) *Certain Selected Odes of Horace, Englished*, London.
Austin, R. G. (ed.) (1982) *Vergil. Aeneidos liber quartus*, Oxford.
Axelson, B. (1967) *Korruptelenkult. Studien zur Textkritik des unechten Seneca-Tragödie Hercules Oetaeus*, Lund.
Aygon, J.-P. (2004) *Pictor in fabula: l'ecphrasis – descriptio dans les tragédies de Sénèque*, Brussels.
Balbo, A. (2011) 'Tra sententia e proverbio. Problemi di paremiografia in Seneca il Vecchio,' in: Lelli, E. (ed.) *ΠΑΡΟΙΜΙΑΚΩΣ. Il proverbio in Grecia e Roma*, Pisa / Rome, 11–34.
Baldwin, B. (1995) *The Latin and Greek Poems of Samuel Johnson*, London.
Baratte, F. (1986) *Le trésor d'orfèvrerie Romaine de Boscoreale*, Paris.
Baraz, Y. / Van den Berg, C. (2013) 'Intertextuality. Introduction,' *American Journal of Philology* 134, 1–8.

Barchiesi, A. (2001) *Speaking Volumes: Narrative and Intertext in Ovid and Other Latin Poets*, London.
Barigazzi, A. (1959) 'Il concetto del tempo nella fisica atomistica,' in: Untersteiner, M. (ed.), *Epicurea in memoriam Hectoris Bignone. Miscellanea philologica*, Genoa, 29–59.
Barigazzi, A. (1962) 'Democrito e il proemio del De Tranquillitate animi di Plutarco,' *Rivista di Filologia e Istruzione Classica* 90, 113–129.
Barnes, J. (1984) *The Complete Works of Aristotle. The Revised Oxford Translation*, Princeton (NJ).
Bartsch, S. (1994) *Actors in the Audience. Theatricality and Doublespeak from Nero to Hadrian*, Cambridge (MA).
Bartsch, S. (2006) *The Mirror of the Self: Sexuality, Self-Knowledge, and the Gaze in the Early Roman Empire*, Chicago.
Bartsch, S. (2007) '"Wait a Moment, *Phantasia*": Ekphrastic Interference in Seneca and Epictetus,' *Classical Philology* 102, 83–95.
Bartsch, S. (2015) 'Senecan Selves,' in: Bartsch / Schiesaro (2015), 187–198.
Bartsch, S. / Freudenburg, K. / Littlewood, C. (eds.) (2017) (forthcoming) *The Cambridge Companion to the Age of Nero*, Cambridge.
Bartsch, S. / Schiesaro, A. (eds.) (2015) *The Cambridge Companion to Seneca*, Cambridge.
Bartsch, S. / Wray, D. (eds.) (2009) *Seneca and the Self*, Cambridge.
Barwick, K. (1959) *Martial und die zeitgenössische Rhetorik*, Berlin.
Basore, J. W. (ed.) (1963–1965) *Seneca, Moral Essays*, 3 vols., 3rd edition, Cambridge (MA).
Batinsky, E. E. (1990–1991) 'Horace's Rehabilitation of Bacchus,' *Classical World* 84, 361–378.
Beal, P. (s. a.) *Catalogue of English Literary Manuscripts 1450–1700*, http://www.celm-ms.org.uk.
Beer, B. (2008) *Lukrez und Philodem: Poetische Argumentation und poetologischer Diskurs*, Basel.
Bees, R. (2004) *Die Oikeiosis Lehre der Stoa. I. Rekonstruktion des Inhalts*, Würzburg.
Bellandi, F. (2007) 'Il sangue e l'altare: Ippolito cacciatore e il sacrificio cruento (a proposito di Seneca, Phaedra 498–500),' *Materiali e discussioni per l'analisi dei testi classici* 58, 43–72.
Beltrán, J. A. / Encuentra, A. P. / Fontana, G. C. / Iso, J. J. / Magallón A. I. / Marina, R. (2005) *Marco Valerio Marcial: Actualización científica y bibliográfica. Tres décades de estudios sobre Marcial (1971–2000)*, Zaragoza.
Benlowes, E. (1652) *Theophila*, London.
Beretta, M. (2014) 'Immaginare Lucrezio. Note storiche sull'iconografia lucreziana,' in: Beretta, M. / Citti, F. / Iannucci, A. (eds.) *Il culto di Epicuro. Testi, iconografia, paesaggi*, Florence, 193–225.
Berger, M.-P. (1960) '"Tristis sobrietas removenda" (Sen., De tranq. an., XVII, 9),' *L'antiquité classique* 29, 248–268.
Berlincourt, V. / Galli Milić, L. / Nelis, D. (2016), 'Introduction,' in: Berlincourt, V. / Galli Milić, L. / Nelis, D. (eds.) *Lucan and Claudian: Context and Intertext*, Heidelberg, 1–9.
Berno, F. R. (2006) 'Il cavallo saggio e lo stolto Enea. Due citazioni virgiliane in Seneca (epist. 95.67–71; 56.12–14),' *Acta classica* 49, 55–77.
Berno, F. R. (2008) 'Seneca e la semantica della pienezza,' *Bollettino di Studi Latini* 38, 549–566.

Berno, F. R. (2011a) 'Epistulae morales ad Lucilium' The literary encyclopedia, accessed 18/01/2016: http://wwwlitencyc.com/php/sworks.php?rec=true&UID=32192.
Berno, F. R. (2011b) 'Seneca, Catone e due citazioni virgiliane (Sen. epist. 95, 67–71 e 104, 31–32),' Studi Italiani di Filologia Classica 9 (4th series), 233–253.
Berno, F. R. (2014) 'Il saggio destino di Didone. Aen. IV 653 in Seneca (vit. b. 19, 1; benef. 5, 17, 5; ep. 12, 9),' Maia 66, 123–136.
Berthet, J.-F. (1979) 'Sénèque lecteur d'Horace d'après les Lettres à Lucilius,' Latomus 38, 940–954.
Berti, E. (2004) 'Aspetti del moralismo nell'epica di Lucano,' in: Auriemma, E. / Esposito, P. (eds.) Lucano e la tradizione dell'epica latina. Atti del Convegno Internazionale di Studi, Fisciano-Salerno, 19–20 ottobre 2001, Naples, 109–135.
Billerbeck, M. (1988) Senecas Tragödien. Sprachliche und stilistische Untersuchungen, Leiden.
Biondi, G. G. (1984) Il nefas argonautico. Mythos e Logos nella Medea di Seneca, Bologna.
Birrel, T. A. (1956) 'Sarbiewski, Watts and the Later Metaphysical Tradition,' English Studies 37, 125–132.
Bishop, J. D. (1968) 'The Meaning of the Choral Meters in Senecan Tragedy,' Rheinisches Museum 111, 197–219.
Blanck, H. (1992) Das Buch in der Antike, Munich.
Blänsdorf, J. (1998) 'Senecas Kritik am Menschenbild des Horaz,' in: Radke, A. E. (ed.) CANDIDE IUDEX, Beiträge zur augusteischen Dichtung. Festschrift für Walter Wimmel zum 75. Geburtstag, Stuttgart, 35–46.
Bloom, H. (1975) Kabbalah and Criticism, New York.
Bloom, H. (1997) The Anxiety of Influence, 2nd edition, Oxford.
Böhme, H. (2011) 'Einladung zur Transformation,' in: Böhme / Bergemann / Dönike / Schirrmeister / Töpfer / Walter / Weitbrecht (eds.), 7–37.
Böhme, H. / Bergemann, L. / Dönike, M. / Schirrmeister, A. / Töpfer, G. / Walter, M. / Weitbrecht, J. (eds.) (2011) Transformation. Ein Konzept zur Erforschung kulturellen Wandels, Munich.
Böhn, A. (2007) 'Zitat,' in: Burdorf, D. / Fasbender, C. / Moennighoff, B. (eds.) Metzler Lexikon Literatur. Begriffe und Definitionen, 3rd edition, Stuttgart / Weimar, 843.
Bonandini, A. (2010) Il contrasto menippeo: prosimetro, citazioni e commutazione di codice nell'Apocolocyntosis di Seneca. Con un commento alle parti poetiche, Trento.
Bonsangue, V. (2004) 'Il cipiglio del console. Allusioni e riscritture comiche nella In Pisonem di Cicerone,' Pan 22, 201–223.
Borgo, A. (2009) 'Quanti e quali Seneca nella letteratura latina? Il Seneca di Marziale,' Vichiana 11, 34–44.
Borzsák, S. (ed.) (1984) Q. Horatius Flaccus: Opera, Leipzig.
Bottiglieri, A. (2002) La legislazione sul lusso nella Roma repubblicana, Naples.
Boyle, A. J. (ed.) (1987) Seneca's Phaedra, Leeds.
Boyle A. J. (1985) 'In Nature's Bonds: A Study of Seneca's Phaedra,' in: Aufstieg und Niedergang der römischen Welt II.32.2, 1284–1347.
Boyle A. J. (2008) Octavia (attributed to Seneca). Edited with Introduction, Translation, and Commentary, Oxford.
Boyle, A. J. (1997) Tragic Seneca: An Essay in the Theatrical Tradition, New York.

Boyle, A. J. (ed.) (2011) *Seneca: Oedipus. Edited with Introduction, Translation, and Commentary*, Oxford.
Boyle, A. J. (ed.) (2014) *Seneca: Medea. Edited with Introduction, Translation, and Commentary*, Oxford.
Bradley, K. (1994) *Slavery and Society at Rome*, Cambridge.
Bradner, L. (1940) *Musae Anglicanae: A History of Anglo-Latin Poetry 1500–1925*, London.
Braund, S. (2009) *Seneca:* De Clementia, Oxford.
Breitenbach, A. (2009) *Kommentar zu den Pseudo-Seneca-Epigrammen der* Anthologia Vossiana, Hildesheim.
Breitenbach, A. (2010) *Die Pseudo-Seneca-Epigramme der* Anthologia Vossiana. *Ein Gedichtbuch aus der mittleren Kaiserzeit*, Hildesheim.
Brennan. T. (2005) *The Stoic Life: Emotions, Duties, and Fate*, Oxford.
Brink, C. O. (1982) *Horace on Poetry.* Epistles, Book II. *The Letters to Augustus and Florus*, Cambridge.
Brown, M. (1997) 'Towards an Archaeology of English Romanticism: Coleridge and Sarbiewski,' in: Brown, M. (ed.) *Turning Points: Essays in the History of Cultural Expressions*, Stanford (CA), 173–194.
Brown, P. M. (ed. and transl.) (1995) *Horace* Satires *I: with an Introduction, Text, Translation and Commentary*, Warminster.
Bruno, G. (1993) 'La *strenua inertia* oraziana e un'interpretazione della *iunctura* in Seneca filosofo,' in: Bruno, G. (ed.) *Letture oraziane*, Venosa, 43–54.
Brunschwig, J. (1986) 'The Cradle Argument in Epicureanism and Stoicism,' in: Schofield / Striker (1986), 113–144.
Bryan, L. / Evans, R. C. (1996) 'Jonson's Response to Lipsius on The Happy Life,' *Notes and Queries* 43, 181–182.
Buchmann, J. (1974) *Untersuchungen zur Rezeption hellenistischer Epigrammatik in der Lyrik des Horaz*, diss. Constance.
Burnyeat, M. F. 1997. 'Postscript on Silent Reading,' *Classical Quarterly* 47, 74–76.
Burrow, C. (1993) 'Horace at Home and Abroad: Wyatt and Sixteenth Century Horatianism,' in: Martindale / Hopkins (1993), 27–49.
Busch, S. (2002) 'Lautes und leises Lesen in der Antike,' *Rheinisches Museum* 145, 1–45.
Bußfeld, B. (1935) *Die polymetrischen Chorlieder in Senecas Oedipus und Agamemnon*, Bochum (diss. Münster).
Camerarius, P. (1591) *Operae horarum subcisivarum, sive meditationes historicae*, Nuremberg.
Camerarius, P. (1609) *Operae horarum subcisivarum, seu meditationes historicae*, Frankfurt.
Camerotto A. (2009) *Luciano di Samosata. Icaromenippo o L'uomo sopra le nuvole*, Alessandria.
Cancik, H. (1967) *Untersuchungen zu Senecas Epistulae morales*, Hildesheim.
Canobbio, A. (2011) *M. Valerii Martialis Epigrammaton liber quintus*, Naples.
Canter, H. V. (1925) *Rhetorical Elements in the Tragedies of Seneca*, Urbana (IL).
Casadesús Bordoy, F. (2013) 'Dionysian Enthusiasm in Plato,' in: Berbabé, A. / Herrero de Jáuregui, M. / Jiménez San Cristóbal, A. I. / Martín Hernández, R. (eds.) *Redefining Dionysos*, Berlin / Boston (MA), 386–400.
Casamento, A. (2011) 'Benifici proverbiali (tra Pubilio e Seneca),' in: Lelli, E. (ed.), *ΠΑΡΟΙΜΙΑΚΩΣ. Il proverbio in Grecia e Roma*, Pisa / Rome, 47–54.

Castagna, L. / Vogt-Spira, G. (eds.) (2002) *Pervertere: Ästhetik der Verkehrung. Literatur und Kultur neronischer Zeit und ihre Rezeption*, München / Leipzig
Catrein, C. (2003) *Vertauschte Sinne. Untersuchungen zur Synästhesie in der römischen Dichtung*, Munich.
Cavalca Schiroli, M. G. (ed.) (1981) *Lucio Anneo Seneca:* De Tranquillitate Animi, Bologna.
Cèbe, J.-P. (ed.) (1996) *Varron*, Satires Ménippées, vol. XI: Prometheus liber – Sesqueulixes, Paris.
Champlin, E. (2003) *Nero*, Cambridge (MA).
Citroni Marchetti, S. (1991) *Plinio il Vecchio e la tradizione del moralismo romano*, Pisa.
Citroni Marchetti, S. (1997) 'Lusso,' in: *Enciclopedia Oraziana* II, Rome, 561–564.
Citroni Marchetti, S. (2012) *Plinio il Vecchio e la tradizione del moralismo romano*, Pisa.
Citroni, M. (1975) *M. Valerii Martialis epigrammaton liber primus*, Florence.
Citti, F. (2000) *Studi oraziani: tematica e intertestualità*, Bologna.
Citti, F. (2012) '*Spes dulce malum*. Seneca e la speranza,' in: Citti, F. Cura sui. *Studi sul lessico filosofico di Seneca*, Amsterdam, 25–51.
Clarke, S. A. (2005) 'Royalists Write the Death of Lord Hastings: Post-Regicide Funerary Propaganda,' *Parergon* 22, 113–130.
Clausen, W. (2002) *Vergil's Aeneid. Decorum, Allusion and Ideology*, Munich / Leipzig.
Coffey, M. / Mayer, R. (eds.) (1990) *Seneca:* Phaedra, Cambridge.
Coleman, R. (1974) 'The Artful Moralist: A Study of Seneca's Epistolary Style,' *Classical Quarterly* 24, 276–289.
Colish, M. L. (1985) *The Stoic Tradition from Antiquity to the Early Middle Ages, I. Stoicism in Classical Latin Literature*, Leiden.
Commager, S. (1962) *The Odes of Horace: A Critical Study*, New Haven (CT).
Compagnon, A. (1979) *La seconde main ou le travail de la citation*, Paris.
Conte, G. B. (1974) *Memoria dei poeti e sistema letterario. Catullo, Virgilio, Ovidio, Lucano*, Turin.
Conte, G. B. (1986) *The Rhetoric of Imitation*, Ithaca (NY).
Conte, G. B. (1997) *L'autore nascosto. Un'interpretazione del 'Satyricon,'* Bologna.
Costa, C. D. N. (1994) *Four Dialogues:* De vita beata, De Tranquillitate animi, De Constantia sapientis, Ad Helviam Matrem de consolatione, Warminster.
Costa, S. (2013) *Quod olim fuerat: La rappresentazione del passato in Seneca prosatore*, Hildesheim.
Critelli, M. G. (1998) 'L'Arcadia impossibile: elementi di un'età dell'oro nella *Phaedra* di Seneca,' *Rivista di cultura classica e medioevale* 40, 71–76.
Cucchiarelli, A. (2001) *La satira e il poeta: Orazio tra Epodi e Sermones*, Pisa.
Cucchiarelli, A. (2010) 'Return to Sender: Horace's *sermo* from the *Epistles* to the *Satires*,' in: Davis (2010), 291–318.
Cucchiarelli, A. (ed.) (2015) *Orazio: L'esperienza delle cose* (Epistole, Libro I), Venice.
Cugusi, P. (1983) *Evoluzione e formedell'epistolografia latina nella tarda repubblica e nei primi due secoli dell'impero*, Rome.
Curley, T. F. (1986) *The Nature of Senecan Drama*, Rome.
Curtius, E. R. (1993) *Europäische Literatur und lateinisches Mittelalter*, 11th edition, Tübingen / Basel.
D'Agostino, V. (1929) 'Seneca e il *De Tranquillitate Animi*,' *Athenaeum* 7, 51–84.
Damon, C. (trans.) (2012) *Tacitus:* Annals, London.

Damschen, G. / Heil, A. (eds.) (2014) *Brill's Companion to Seneca. Philosopher and Dramatist*, Leiden.
Danielewicz, J. (1997) 'Natura,' in: *Enciclopedia Oraziana* II, Rome, 586–589.
Davidson, P. (2007) 'British Baroque,' in: Davidson, P. *The Universal Baroque*, Manchester, 25–93.
Davie, D. (1974) *Augustan Lyric*, London.
Davie, D. (1978) *A Gathered Church: The Literature of the English Dissenting Interest, 1700–1930*, Oxford.
Davis, G. (ed.) (2010) *A Companion to Horace*, Malden (MA).
Davis, P. J. (1993) *Shifting Song. The Chorus in Seneca's Tragedies*, Hildesheim.
Davis, W. R. (1967) *The Works of Thomas Campion*, New York.
De Cuypere, L. (2008) *Limiting the Iconic*, Amsterdam.
De Pretis, A. (2004) *Epistolarity in the First Book of Horace's Epistles*, Piscataway (NY).
De Vivo, A. (1992) 'Seneca, la citazione virgiliana, la paura del terremoto (nat. 6,2,2),' in: de Vivo, A. / Spina, L. (eds.) *'Come dice il poeta...' Percorsi greci e latini di parole poetiche*, Naples, 119–130.
De Vos, A. (2014) 'Intertextuelle Bezüge zwischen Horaz, carmen 3,30 und Seneca, ad Polybium de consolatione (dialogus 11),' unpublished seminar paper (12 pages), Heidelberg.
Degl'Innocenti Pierini, R. (1992) '*Aurea mediocritas:* la morale oraziana nei cori delle tragedie di Seneca,' *Quaderni di Cultura e di Tradizione Classica* 10, 155–171. Reprinted in: Degl'Innocenti Pierini, R. (1999) *Tra filosofia e poesia. Studi su Seneca e dintorni*, Bologna, 39–57.
Degl'Innocenti Pierini, R. (2013) 'Medea e Canidia, Canidia e Medea: percorsi intertestuali tra Orazio giambico e Seneca tragico,' *Studi italiani di filologia classica* 11, 257–266.
Del Giovane, B. (2012) 'Seneca, Scipione e l'ombra di Cicerone: a proposito dell'epistola 86,' *Prometheus* 38, 155–174.
Del Giovane, B. (2014) 'Tra moralismo diatribico e *sal niger* oraziano: per l'esegesi dell'epistola 119 di Seneca,' *La biblioteca di classicocontemporaneo* 1, 32–47.
Del Giovane, B. (2015a) 'Attalus and the Others: Diatribic Morality, Cynicism and Rhetoric in Seneca's Teachers,' *Maia* 67, 3–24.
Del Giovane, B. (2015b) *Seneca, la diatriba e la ricerca di una morale austera. Caratteristiche, influenze, mediazioni di un rapporto complesso*, Florence.
DeLacy, P. (1948) 'Stoic Views of Poetry,' *American Journal of Philology* 69, 241–271.
Delatte, A. (1934) 'Les conceptions de l'enthousiasme chez les philosophes présocratique,' *L'Antiquité Classique* 1, 5–79.
Di Marco, M. (1981) 'Riflessi della polemica antiepicurea nei *Silli* di Timone. 2. Epicuro, il porco e l'insaziabile ventre,' *Elenchos* 4, 59–91.
Di Virgilio, R. (1998) 'Romanità dell'effimero in Seneca,' *Paideia* 53, 149–171.
Dickison, S. (1977) 'Claudius: *Saturnalicius princeps*,' *Latomus* 36, 634–47.
Dietsche, U. (2014) *Strategie und Philosophie bei Seneca: Untersuchungen zur therapeutischen Technik in den Epistulae morales*, Berlin / Boston (MA).
Dilke, O. A. W. (ed.) (1966) *Horace: Epistles, Book 1*, 3rd edition, London.
Dingel, J. (1974) *Seneca und die Dichtung*, Heidelberg.
Dinter, M. (2009) 'Laying down the Law: Horace's Reflection in his *Sententiae*,' in: Houghton / Wyke (2009), 96–108.

Dinter, M. (2014) 'Sententiae in Seneca,' in: Wildberger / Colish (2014), 319–342.
Dionigi, I. (1980) 'L'epistola 1.1 di Orazio e il proemio del *De otio* di Seneca (tradizione filosofica e riflessione autobiografica),' *Bollettino di Studi Latini* 10, 38–49.
Dix, T. K. (1986) *Private and Public Libraries at Rome in the First Century B.C.: A Preliminary Study in the History of Roman Libraries*, diss. University of Michigan, Ann Arbor (MI).
Dodson-Robinson, E. (ed.) *Brill's Companion to the Reception of Senecan Tragedy*, Leiden.
Döpp, S. (1989) '*Nec omnia apud priores meliora*. Autoren des frühen Principats über die eigene Zeit,' *Rheinisches Museum* 132, 73–101.
Donini, G. (1964) 'Marziale I 49: Horatius in Martiale,' *American Journal of Philology* 85, 56–60.
Donini, P. L. / Gianotti, G. F. (1979) *Modelli filosofici e letterari. Lucrezio, Orazio, Seneca*, Bologna.
Dornavius, C. (1619) *Amphitheatrum sapientiae socraticae joco-seriae*, Hanau.
Du Quesnay, I. M. Le M. (1984) 'Horace and Maecenas: The Propaganda Value of *Sermones* I,' in: Woodman, A. J. / West, D. (eds.) *Poetry and Politics in the Age of Augustus*, Cambridge, 19–58.
Dubrueil, P. (2013) *Le marché aux injures à Rome. Injures et insultes dans la littérature latine*, Paris.
Dueck, D. (2009) 'Poetic Quotations in Latin Prose Works of Philosophy,' *Hermes* 137, 314–334.
Dufallo, B. (2000) '*Satis / satura*: Reconsidering the 'Programmatic Intent' of Horace's *Satires* 1.1,' *Classical World* 93, 579–590.
Duff, J. D. (ed.) (1915) *L. Annaei Senecae Dialogorum Libri X, XI, XII: Three Dialogues of Seneca*, Cambridge.
Dunbabin, K. M. D. '*Sic erimus cuncti*... The Skeleton in Graeco-Roman art,' *Jahrbuch des Deutschen Archäologischen Instituts* 101, 185–255.
Duret, L. (1977) 'Martial et la deuxième Epode d'Horace: quelche réflexions sur l'imitation,' *Revue des Études Latines* 55, 173–192.
Dziatzko, K. (1897) 'Bibliotheken,' in: *Realencyclopädie der classischen Altertumswissenschaft* III.1, 405–424.
Eden, P. T. (1984) *Seneca: Apocolocyntosis*, Cambridge.
Edmunds, L. (1992) *From a Sabine Jar. Reading Horace, Odes 1.9*, Chapel Hill (NC).
Edwards, C. (1997) 'Self-scrutiny and self-transformation in Seneca's Letters,' *Greece & Rome* 44, 23–38
Edwards, C. (1999) 'The Suffering Body: Philosophy and Pain in Seneca's *Letters*,' in: Porter, J. (ed.) *Constructions of the Classical Body*, Ann Arbor (MI), 252–268.
Edwards, C. (2009) 'Free yourself! Slavery, freedom and the self in Seneca's *Letters*,' in: Bartsch, S. / Wray, D. (2009) 139–59.
Edwards, C. (2014) 'Ethics V: Death and Time,' in: Damschen / Heil (2014), 323–341.
Edwards, C. (2015) 'Absent Presence in Seneca's Epistles: Philosophy and Friendship,' in: Bartsch / Schiesaro (2015), 41–53.
Edwards, C. (2017) (forthcoming) 'Seneca and the Quest for Distinction in Nero's Golden Age,' in: Bartsch / Freudenburg / Littlewood (2017) (forthcoming).
Ehlers, W.-W. (1985) 'Das 'Iter Brundisium' des Horaz *Serm.* 1.5,' *Hermes* 113, 69–83.
Fabbrini, D. (2007) *Il migliore dei mondi possibili. Gli epigrammi ecfrastici di Marziale per amici e protettori*, Florence.

Fairclough, H. R. (ed. and trans.) (1929) *Horace:* Satires, Epistles *and* Ars Poetica, Cambridge (MA).
Fairclough, H. R. (ed. and trans.) (1999), *Virgil:* Eclogues, Georgics, Aeneid *I–VI*, revised edition by G. P. Goold, Cambridge (MA).
Fantham, E. (1982) *Seneca's* Troades. *A Literary Introduction with Text, Translation, and Commentary*, Princeton (NJ).
Fantham, E. (2013) 'The First Book of *Letters*,' in: Günther, H.-C. (ed.) *Brill's Companion to Horace*, Leiden, 407–430.
Farrell, J. (1991) *Vergil's Georgics and the Traditions of Ancient Epic. The Art of Allusion in Literary History*, Oxford.
Fedeli, P. (1988) 'Biblioteche private e pubbliche a Roma e nel mondo romano,' in: Cavallo, G. (ed.) *Le biblioteche nel mondo antico e medievale*, Rome, 29–64.
Fedeli, P. (1996) 'Personaggi letterari,' in: *Enciclopedia Oraziana* I, Rome, 601–610.
Fedeli, P. (ed.) (1997) *Q. Orazio Flacco, Le Opere, II.4. Le Epistole e l'arte poetica*, Rome.
Feeney, D. (1998) *Literature and Religion at Rome: Cultures, Contexts, and Beliefs*, Cambridge.
Feeney, D. (2002) '*Una cum scriptore meo.* Poetry, Principate and the Traditions of Literary History in the *Epistle to Augustus*,' in: Woodman / Feeney (2002), 172–187.
Feeney, D. (2009) 'Becoming an Authority: Horace on his own Reception,' in: Houghton / Wyke (2009), 16–38.
Ferri, R. (1993) *I dispiaceri di uno epicureo: uno studio sulla poetica delle epistole oraziane*, Pisa.
Ferri, R. (ed.) (2003) Octavia: *A Play Attributed to Seneca*, Cambridge.
Finzi, R. (2014) *L'onesto porco. Storia di una diffamazione*, Milan.
Fischer, B. (2007) *The Sculpted Word. Epicureanism and Philosophical Recruitment in Ancient Greece*, Berkeley (CA) / Los Angeles (CA) / London.
Fischer, B. (2014) 'Ripensando *The sculpted Word*. Come ricostruire e interpretare la statua di Epicuro oggi,' in: Beretta, M. / Citti, F. / Iannucci, A. (eds.) *Il culto di Epicuro. Testi, iconografia, paesaggi*, Florence, 177–192.
Fischer, S. (2008) *Seneca als Theologe*, Berlin / New York.
Fischer, S. (2014) 'Systematic Connections Between Seneca's Philosophical Works and Tragedies,' in: Damschen / Heil (2014), 745–768.
Fish, J. (1998) 'Is Death Nothing to Horace? A Brief Comparison with Philodemus and Lucretius,' *Cronache ercolanesi: bollettino del Centro internazionale per lo studio dei papiri ercolanesi* 28, 99–104.
Fiske, G. C. (1966) *Lucilius and Horace. A Study in the Classical Theory of Imitation*, Hildesheim (reprint of the 1920 edition).
Fitch, J. G. (1981) 'Sense-Pause and Relative Dating in Seneca, Sophocles and Shakespeare,' *American Journal of Philology* 102, 289–307.
Fitch, J. G. (1987a) *Seneca's Hercules Furens*, Ithaca (NY) / London.
Fitch, J. G. (1987b) *Seneca's Anapaests. Metre, Colometry, Text, and Artistry in the Anapaests of Seneca's Tragedies*, Atlanta (GA).
Fitch, J. G. (ed. and trans.) (2002) *Seneca. Hercules, Trojan Women, Phoenician Women, Medea, Phaedra*, Cambridge (MA).
Fitch, J. G. (ed. and trans.) (2004) *Seneca: Oedipus, Agamemnon, Thyestes, [Seneca]: Hercules on Oeta, Octavia*, Cambridge (MA).

Fitch, J. G. / McElduff, S. (2008) 'Construction of the Self in Senecan Drama,' in: Fitch, J. G. (2008) (ed.) *Seneca*, Oxford, 157–181.
Fitzgerald, W. (1978) 'Lucretius' Cure for Love in the *De Rerum Natura*,' *Classical World* 78, 73–86.
Fitzgerald, W. (2000) *Slavery and the Roman Literary Imagination*, Cambridge.
Fohlen, G. (ed.) / Humbert, J. (trans.) (1931) *Cicéron, Tusculanes*, 2 vols., Paris.
Fordonski, K. / Urbanski, P. (2010) *Casimir Britannicus: English Translations, Paraphrases and Emulations of the Poetry of Maciej Cazimierz Sarbiewski*, revised edition, London.
Formicola, C. (1995) 'Orazio e Albio (*Carm.* I 33 e *Ep.* I 4),' in: Gigante, M. / Cerasuolo, S. (eds.) *Letture oraziane*, Naples, 233–265.
Fowler, D. P. (2000) 'On the Shoulders of Giants. Intertextuality and Classical Studies,' in: Fowler, D. P. (2000) *Roman Constructions. Readings in Postmodern Latin*, Oxford, 115–137 (= [1997] *Materiali e discussioni per l'analisi dei testi classici* 39, 13–34).
Fraenkel, E. (1957) *Horace*, Oxford.
Frangoulidis, S. / Harrison, S. J. / Manuwald, G. (eds.) (2016) *Roman Drama and its Contexts*, Berlin / Boston (MA).
Frank, G. (1989) 'Das Paradox der Zeit und die Dimensionszahl der Temporalität,' *Zeitschrift für philosophische Forschung* 43, 449–471.
Frank, T. (1925) 'On Augustus' References to Horace,' *Classical Philology* 20, 26–30.
Frede, M. (1986) 'The Stoic Doctrine of the Affections of the Soul,' in: Schofield / Striker (1986), 93–110.
Freise, H. (1989) 'Die Bedeutung der Epikur-Zitate in den Schriften Senecas,' *Gymnasium* 96, 532–556.
Freudenburg, K. (1993) *The Walking Muse: Horace on the Theory of Satire*, Princeton (NJ).
Freudenburg, K. (2001) *Satires of Rome: Threatening Poses from Lucilius to Juvenal*, Cambridge.
Freudenburg, K. (2002a) '*Solus sapiens liber est*: Recommissioning Lyric in *Epistles* I,' in: Woodman / Feeney (2002), 124–140.
Freudenburg, K. (2002b) 'Writing to/through Florus: Sampling the Addressee in Horace, *Epistles* 2.2,' *Memoirs of the American Academy in Rome* 47, 35–55.
Freudenburg, K. (ed.) (2005) *The Cambridge Companion to Roman Satire*, Cambridge.
Freudenburg, K. (ed.) (2009) *Horace: Satires and Epistles*, Oxford
Freudenburg, K. (2014) '*Recusatio* as Political Theatre: Horace's Letter to Augustus,' *Journal of Roman Studies* 104, 105–132.
Freudenburg, K. (2015) 'Seneca's *Apocolocyntosis*,' in: Bartsch / Schiesaro (2015), 93–105.
Friedrich, O. (ed.) (1994) *Publilii Syri Mimi Sententiae*, Hildesheim (reprint of the 1880 edition).
Frings, U. (1985) '"Glückseliges Leben", literarisch, theologisch,' *Der Altsprachliche Unterricht* 28, 76–85.
Fuentes González, P. P. (1997) *Les diatribes de Télès: Introduction, texte revu, traduction et commentaire des fragments (avec en appendice une traduction espagnole)*, Paris.
Fuentes, M. C. G. (1999) 'Presencia horaciana en los coros de Séneca,' *Cuadernos de Filología Clásica. Estudios Latinos* 16, 89–106.
Fuhrer, T. (2003) 'Was ist gute Dichtung? Horaz und der poetologische Diskurs seiner Zeit,' *Rheinisches Museum* 146, 346–364.
Funaioli, G. (1914) 'Recitationes,' *RE*, 435–446.

Fusi, A. (2006) *M. Valerii Martialis Epigrammaton liber tertius*, Hildesheim.
Fussell, P. (1979) *Poetic Meter and Poetic Form*, 2nd edition, New York.
Gagliardi, D. (1988) *Un'arte di vivere. Saggio sul primo libro delle epistole oraziane*, Rome.
Gaheis, A. (1895) *De troporum in L. Annaei Senecae tragoediis generibus potioribus*, Vienna.
Galán Vioque, G. (2002) *Martial, Book VII. A Commentary*, Leiden.
Galimberti, A. (2001) 'Seneca e la guerra,' in: Sordi, M. (ed.) *Il pensiero sulla guerra nel mondo antico*, Milan, 195–207.
Galinsky, K. (1996) *Augustan Culture: An Interpretive Introduction*, Princeton (NJ).
Gambla, R. J. (1981) *Verse Quotation in the Epistulae Morales of Seneca*, diss. Northwestern University, Evanston (IL).
Genette, G. (1997), *Palimpsests: Literature in the Second Degree*, trans. C. Newman / C. Doubinsky, Lincoln (NE).
Gerber, E. (1883) *De versibus Senecae tragici ex Horatio derivatis*, Mährisch-Schönberg.
Gerson, L. P. (2009) *Ancient Epistemology*, Cambridge.
Gianotti, G. (1979) 'Dinamica dei motivi comuni,' in: Donini, P. / Gianotti, G. (eds.) *Modelli filosofici e letterari. Lucrezio, Orazio, Seneca*, Bologna, 5–148.
Gibson, R. (2002) '"Cf. E. g.": A Typology of "Parallels" and the Function of Commentaries on Latin Poetry' in: Kraus, C. / Gibson, R. (eds.) *The Classical Commentary: Histories, Practices, Theory*, Leiden, 331–358.
Giesecke, A. (2000) *Atoms, Ataraxy, and Allusion. Cross-generic Imitation of the De rerum natura in Early Augustan Poetry*, Hildesheim.
Gigante, M. (1993) *Orazio: una misura per l'amore: lettura della satira seconda del primo libro*, Venosa.
Gill, C. (1983) 'Did Chrysippus Understand Medea?' *Phronesis* 28, 136–49.
Gill, C. (1994) 'Peace of Mind and Being Yourself: Panaetius to Plutarch,' in: *Aufstieg und Niedergang der römischen Welt* II.36.7: 4599–4640.
Gill, C. (2006) *The Structured Self in Hellenistic and Roman Thought*, Oxford.
Gill, C. (2009) 'Seneca and Selfhood: Integration and Disintegration,' in: Bartsch / Wray (2009), 65–83.
Gillespie, S. (2015) 'Seneca ex Thyestes: A Collection of English Translations 1557–1800,' *Translation and Literature* 24, 203–218.
Gillespie, G. (forthcoming) *Newly Recovered English Classical Translations, 1600–1800*, Oxford.
Giri, G. (1951) *Orazio: Odi ed Epodi commentati*, Rome.
Giusti, E. (2016) 'Dithyrambic Iambics: Epode 9 and its General(s') Confusion,' in: Bather, P. / Stocks, C. (eds.) *Horace Epodes: Contexts, Intertexts, and Reception*, Oxford, 131–151.
Glei, R. (1990) 'Von Probus zu Pöschl: Vergilinterpretation im Wandel,' *Gymnasium* 97, 321–340.
Glinatsis, R. (2012) 'Horace et la question de l'*imitatio*,' *Dictynna* 9, 2–14.
Goldberg, S. M. (1996) 'The Fall and Rise of Roman Tragedy,' *Transactions of the American Philological Association* 126, 265–286.
Goldberg, S. M. (2014) 'Greek and Roman Elements in Senecan Tragedy,' in: Damschen / Heil (2014), 639–652.
Goldhill, S. (2007) 'What is Ekphrasis for?' *Classical Philology* 102, 1–19.
Goldschmidt, V. (2006) *Le système stoïcien et l'idée de temps*, Paris.

Gömöri, G. (2011) '"The Polish Swan Triumphant": The English Reception of Maciej Kazimierz Sarbiewski in the Seventeenth Century,' *The Modern Language Review* 106, 814–833.
Goodyear, F. R. D. (1972) *The Annals of Tacitus, Books 1–6*, vol. 1, Cambridge.
Goold, G. P. (ed. and trans.) (1995), *Catullus, Tibullus, Pervigilium Veneris*, translation of Catullus by F. W. Cornish, 2nd edition, Cambridge (MA).
Gowers, E. (1993a) *The Loaded Table: Representations of Food in Roman Literature*, Oxford.
Gowers, E. (1993b) 'Horace, Satire 1.5: An Inconsequential Journey,' *Proceedings of the Cambridge Philological Society* 39, 48–66.
Gowers, E. (2005) 'The Restless Companion: Horace, *Satires* 1 and 2,' in: Freudenburg (2005), 48–61.
Gowers, E. (2012) *Horace. Satires. Book I*, Cambridge.
Gowers, E. (2016) 'Noises Off: The *Thyestes* Theme in Tacitus' Dialogus,' in: Frangoulidis / Harrison / Manuwald (2016), 555–571.
Grassmann, V. (1966) *Die erotischen Epoden des Horaz: literarischer Hintergrund und sprachliche Tradition*, Munich.
Graver, M. R. (2007) *Stoicism and Emotion*, Chicago (IL) / London.
Graver, M. R. (2014) 'Honeybee Reading and Self-Scripting: *Epistulae Morales* 84,' in: Wildberger / Colish (2014), 269–293.
Graziosi, B. (2009) 'Horace, Suetonius, and the *Lives* of the Greek poets,' in: Houghton / Wyke (2009), 140–160.
Green, R. P. H. (2014) 'Poetic Psalm Paraphrases,' in: Ford, P. / Bloemendal, J. / Fantazzi, C. (eds.) *Brill's Encyclopaedia of the Neo-Latin World*, Leiden, 461–469.
Greene, R. (1999) 'The Lyric,' in: Norton, G. P. (ed.) *The Cambridge History of Literary Criticism. Volume III: The Renaissance*, Cambridge, 216–228.
Greene, T. M. (1982) *The Light in Troy: Imitation and Discovery in Renaissance Poetry*, New Haven (CT).
Griffin, M. T. (1992) *Seneca: A Philosopher in Politics*, 2nd edition, Oxford.
Griffin, M. T. (2013) *Seneca on Society. A Guide to* De Beneficiis, Oxford.
Griffin, M. T. / Inwood, B. (eds.) (2011) *Seneca, On Benefits*, Chicago (IL) / London.
Grilli, A. (1983) 'Orazio e l'epicureismo (ovvero *serm.* 1,3 ed *ep.* 1,2),' *Helmantica* 34, 267–292.
Grimal, P. (1966) *L. Annaei Senecae De Brevitate Vitae: Sénèque Sur la Brièveté de la Vie: Édition, introduction et commentaire*, 2nd edition, Paris.
Grimal, P. (1978) *Sénèque ou la conscience de l'Empire*, Paris.
Guglielmo, M. (1997) 'L'educazione dei giovani secondo Seneca,' in: Lana, I. (ed.) *Seneca e i giovani*, Venosa, 55–90.
Guglielmo, M. (2010) 'I proverbi nel primo libro delle *Epistole* di Orazio,' in: Lelli, E. (ed.) *ΠΑΡΟΙΜΙΑΚΩΣ. Il proverbio in Grecia e Roma*, Pisa / Rome, 191–206.
Gummere, R. M. (ed. and trans.) (1917–1925) *Seneca: Ad Lucilium Epistulae Morales*, Cambridge (MA).
Gunderson, E. (2015) *The Sublime Seneca: Ethics, Literature, Metaphysics*, Cambridge.
Günther, H.-C. (2010) *Die Ästhetik der augusteischen Dichtung: Eine Ästhetik des Verzichts. Überlegungen zum Spätwerk des Horaz*, Leiden.
Günther, H.-C. (2013) 'The *Carmen Saeculare*,' in: Günther, H.-C. (ed.) *Brill's Companion to Horace*, Leiden, 431–443.
Guzzo, G. P. (2006) *Argenti a Pompei*, Milan.

H[ils], G. (1646) *The Odes of Casimire. Translated by G.H.*, London.
Haase, F. (1852) *L. Annaei Senecae Operum Quae Supersunt Supplementum*, Leipzig.
Hachmann, E. (1996) 'Die Spruchepiloge in Senecas *Epistulae morales*,' *Gymnasium* 103, 385–410.
Halbauer, O. (1911) *De diatribis Epicteti*, diss. Leipzig.
Hamacher, U. G. (2006) *Senecas 82. Brief an Lucilius: Dialektikkritik illustriert am Beispiel der Bekämpfung des metus mortis. Ein Kommentar*, Munich.
Hamlin, H. (2004) *Psalm Culture and Early Modern English Literature*, Cambridge.
Hardie, P. (1990) 'Ovid's Theban History: The First 'Anti-Aeneid'?' *Classical Quarterly* 40, 224–235.
Hardie, P. (1993) '*Ut pictura poesis?* Horace and the Visual Arts,' in: Rudd, N. (ed.) *Horace 2000: A Celebration. Essays for the Bimillennium*, London, 120–139.
Hardie, P. (ed.) (2013) *Ovidio Metamorfosi, vol. VI: libri XIII–XV*, Milan.
Hardie, P. (2016) 'Introduction: Augustan Poetry and the Irrational,' in: Hardie, P. (ed.) *Augustan Poetry and the Irrational*, Oxford, 1–33.
Harrison, G. W. M. (ed.) (2000) *Seneca in Performance*, London.
Harrison, G. W. M. / Liapis, V. (eds.) (2013) *Performance in Greek and Roman Theatre*, Leiden.
Harrison, S. J. (1988) 'Deflating the *Odes*: Horace, *Epistles* 1.20,' *Classical Quarterly* 38, 473–476.
Harrison, S. J. (ed.) (2007a) *The Cambridge Companion to Horace*, Cambridge.
Harrison, S. J. (2007b) 'Town and Country,' in: Harrison (2007a), 235–247.
Harrison, S. J. (2007c) 'The Reception of Horace in the Nineteenth and Twentieth Centuries,' in: Harrison (2007a), 334–346.
Harrison, S. J. (2011) *Generic Enrichment in Vergil and Horace*, 2nd ed., Oxford.
Harrison, S. J. (2017) (forthcoming) *Horace: Odes, Book II*, Cambridge.
Harvey, R. H. (1981) *A Commentary on Persius*, Leiden.
Heilmann, W. (1984), '"Wenn ich frei sein könnt für ein wirkliches Leben…" Epikureisches bei Martial,' *Antike und Abendland* 30, 47–61.
Heilmann, W. (1998) 'Epigramme Martials über Leben und Tod,' in: Grewing, F. (ed.) *Toto notus in Orbe. Perspektiven der Martial-Interpretation*, Stuttgart, 205–219.
Heinze, R. (1889) *De Horatio Bionis imitatore*, diss. Bonn.
Heinze, R. (1890) 'Ariston von Chios bei Plutarch und Horaz,' *Rheinisches Museum* 45, 497–523.
Heinze, R. (1960) 'Die lyrischen Verse des Horaz,' in: Heinze, R. *Vom Geist des Römertums*, Stuttgart, 227–294.
Henderson, J. G. W. (1983) 'Poetic Technique and Rhetorical Amplification: Seneca *Medea* 579–669,' in: Boyle, A. J. (ed.) (1983) *Seneca Tragicus. Ramus Essays on Senecan Drama*, Berwick (Victoria), 94–113.
Henderson, J. G. W. (1993) 'Be Alert Your Country Needs Lerts: Horace, *Satires* 1.9,' *Proceedings of the Cambridge Philological Society* 39, 67–93.
Henderson, J. G. W. (1994) 'On Getting Rid of Kings: Horace, *Satire* 1.7,' *Classical Quarterly* 44, 146–170.
Henderson, J. G. W. (1998) 'Polishing off the politics: Horace's Ode to Pollio (Odes 2.1),' in: Henderson, J. G. W. *Fighting for Rome. Poets and Caesars, History and Civil War*, Cambridge, 108–162.

Henderson, J. G. W. (1999) *Writing Down Rome: Satire, Comedy, and other Offences in Latin Poetry*, Oxford.
Henderson, J. G. W. (2004) *Morals and villas in Seneca's Letters: Places to Dwell*, Cambridge.
Hense, O. (1893) *Seneca und Athenodorus*, Freiburg.
Hense, O. (1909) *Teletis reliquiae. Recognovit prolegomena scripsit*, 2nd edition, Tübingen.
Hett, W. S. (ed. and trans.) (1955) *Aristotle, 14. Minor Works:* On Colours, On Things Heard, Phyisiognomics, On Plants, On Marvellous Things Heard, Mechanical Problems, On Indivisible Lines, Situations and Names of Winds, On Melissus, Xenophanes, and Gorgias, Cambridge (MA).
Heyworth, S. J. (1995) 'Dividing Poems', in: Pecere, O. / Reeve, M. D. (eds.) *Formative Stages of Classical Traditions: Latin Texts from Antiquity to the Renaissance*, Spoleto, 117–148.
Hicks, R. D. (ed. and trans.) (1972), *Diogenes Laertius*, Lives of Eminent Philosophers, Cambridge (MA).
H[ils], G. (1646) *The Odes of Casimire*, London.
Hinds, S. (1998) *Allusion and Intertext: Dynamics of Appropriation in Latin Poetry*, Cambridge.
Hinds, S. (2011) 'Seneca's Ovidian *Loci*,' *Studi italiani di filologia classica* 9, 5–63.
Hine, H. M. (ed. and trans.) (2000) *Seneca:* Medea, Warminster.
Hine, H. M. (2004) '*Interpretatio Stoica* of Senecan Tragedy,' in: Billerbeck, M. / Schmidt, E. A. (eds.) *Sénèque le tragique*, Vandoeuvres (Geneva), 173–220.
Hine, H. M. (ed.) (2010) *Seneca:* Natural Questions, Chicago (IL).
Hirzel, R. (1895) *Der Dialog. Ein literarhistorischer Versuch*, 2 vols., Leipzig.
Holder, A. (1894) *Pomponi Porfyrionis Commentum in Horatium Flaccum*, Innsbruck.
Holloway, P. A. (1998) 'Paul's Pointed Prose: The *Sententia* in Roman Rhetoric and Paul,' *Novum Testamentum* 40, 32–53.
Holthuis, S. (1993) *Intertextualität. Aspekte einer rezeptionsorientierten Konzeption*, Tübingen.
Holton, A. / MacFaul, T. (eds.) (2011) *Tottel's Miscellany: Songs and Sonnets of Henry Howard, Earl of Surrey, Sir Thomas Wyatt and Others*, London.
Holzberg, N. (2002) *Martial und das antike Epigramm*, Darmstadt.
Holzberg, N. (2004) 'Impersonating the Banished Philosopher. Pseudo-Seneca's *Liber Epigrammaton*,' *Harvard Studies in Classical Philology* 102, 423–444.
Hooley, D. M. (1997) *The Knotted Thong. Structure and Mimesis in Persius*, Ann Arbor (MI).
Hooley, D. M. (1999) 'Horace's Rud(e)-imentary Muse: Sat. 1.2,' *Electronic Antiquity* 5, unpaginated.
Hooley, D. M. (2007) *Roman Satire*, Oxford.
Hornby, N. (1995) *High Fidelity*, New York.
Horsfall, N. (1993) 'Empty Shelves on the Palatine,' *Greece & Rome* 40, 58–67.
Höschele, R. (2006) *Verrückt nach Frauen. Der Epigrammatiker Rufin*, Tübingen.
Höschele, R. (2009) 'Epigrammatizing Lyric: Generic Hybridity in Horace's Odes,' in: Da Rocha Pereira, M. H. / Ribeiro Ferreira, J. / De Oliveira, F. (eds.) *Horácio e a sua perenidade*, Coimbra, 71–88.
Houghton, L. B. T. / Wyke, M. (eds.) (2009), *Perceptions of Horace. A Roman Poet and His Readers*, Cambridge.
Howell, P. (1980) *A Commentary on Book One of the Epigrams of Martial*, London.
Hughey, R. W. (ed.) (1960) *The Arundel Harington Manuscript of Tudor Poetry*, 2 vols., Columbus (OH).

Hunter, R. (2014) 'Horace's other Ars poetica: Epistles 1.2 and ancient Homeric criticism,' in: A. Ferenczi (ed.) *New approaches to Horace's* Ars poetica, *Materiali e discussioni per l'analisi dei testi classici*, Special Issue 72, 19–41.

Husner, F. (1924) *Leib und Seele in der Sprache Senecas. Ein Beitrag zur sprachlichen Formulierung der moralischen* adhortatio, Leipzig.

Hutchinson, G. O. (2013) *Greek to Latin: Frameworks and Contexts for Intertextuality*, Oxford.

Inwood, B. (1985) *Ethics and Human Action in Early Stoicism*, Oxford.

Inwood, B. (2005) *Reading Seneca: Stoic Philosophy in Rome*, Oxford.

Inwood, B. (transl.) (2007) *Seneca. Selected Philosophical Letters, translated with an Introduction and Commentary*, Oxford.

Jakobi, R. (1988) *Der Einfluß Ovids auf den Tragiker Seneca*, Berlin / New York.

Janka, M. (2006) 'Paelignus, puto, dixerat poeta (Mart. 2.41.2): Martial's Intertextual Dialogue with Ovid's Erotodidactic Poems,' in: Gibson, R. / Green, S. / Sharrock, A. (eds.) *The Art of Love. Bimillennial Essays on Ovid's Ars Amatoria and Remedia Amoris*, Oxford / New York, 279–297.

Jocelyn, H. D. (1973) 'Homo sum: humani nil a me alienum puto (Terence, Heauton timorumenos 77),' *Antichthon* 7, 14–46.

Jocelyn, H. D. (1979) 'Horace, Epistles 1,' *Liverpool Classical Monthly* 4, 145–147.

Jocelyn, H. D. (1982) 'Diatribes and Sermons,' *Liverpool Classical Monthly* 7, 3–7.

Jocelyn, H. D. (1983) '*Diatribes* and the Greek book-title Διατριβαί,' *Liverpool Classical Monthly* 8, 89–91.

Johnson W. R. (2010) 'The Epistles,' in: Davis (2010), 319–333.

Johnson, W. A. (2010) *Readers and Reading Culture in the High Roman Empire. A Study of Elite Communities*, Oxford / New York.

Johnson, W. R. (1993) *Horace and the Dialectic of Freedom: Readings in Epistles 1*, Ithaca (NY).

Jones, M. (2014) 'Seneca's Letters to Lucilius: Hypocrisy as a Way of Life,' in: Wildberger / Colish (2014), 393–429.

Kahn, C. H. (ed. and transl.) (1979) *The Art and Thought of Heraclitus. An Edition of the Fragments with Translation and Commentary*, Cambridge.

Kapnukajas, C. K. (1930) *Die Nachahmungstechnik Senecas in der Chorliedern des* Hercules furens *und der* Medea, diss. Leipzig.

Kaster, R. A. (ed. and trans.) (2011) *Macrobius:* Saturnalia, Cambridge (MA).

Kazantzidis, G. (2011) *Melancholy in Hellenistic and Latin Poetry: Medical Readings in Menander, Apollonius Rhodius, Lucretius and Horace*, diss. Oxford.

Keane, C. (2006) *Figuring Genre in Roman Satire*, Oxford.

Keane, C. (2011) 'Lessons in Reading: Horace on Homer at Epistles 1.2.1–31,' *Classical World* 104, 427–450.

Keller, O. (ed.) (1904) *Pseudacronis Scholia in Horatium Vetustiora, vol. II: Scholia in Sermones Epistulas Artemque Poeticam*, Leipzig / Stuttgart.

Kemp, J. (2009) 'Irony and aequabilitas: Horace, Satires 1.3,' *Dictynna* 6, 84–107.

Kemp, J. (2010) 'A Moral Purpose, A Literary Game: Horace, Satires 1.4,' *Classical World* 104, 59–76.

Kennedy, D. F. (1993) *The Arts of Love*, Cambridge.

Kenney, E. J. (1982) 'Books and Readers in the Roman World,' in: Kenney, E. J. / Clausen, W. V. (eds.) *The Cambridge History of Classical Literature*, Cambridge, 1–32.

Ker, J. (2009a) *The Deaths of Seneca*, Oxford.
Ker, J. (2009b) 'Seneca on Self-Examination: Rereading *On Anger* 3.36,' in: Bartsch / Wray (2009), 160–187.
Ker, J. (2015) 'Seneca and Augustan Culture,' in: Bartsch / Schiesaro (2015), 109–121.
Keseling, P. (1941) 'Horaz in den Tragödien des Seneca,' *Philologische Wochenschrift*, 190–192.
Kiessling, A. / Heinze, R. (eds.) (1930) *Q. Horatius Flaccus: Oden und Epoden*, 7th edition, Berlin.
Kiessling, A. / Heinze, R. (eds.) (1921) *Q. Horatius Flaccus: Satiren*, 5th edition, Berlin.
Kiessling, A. / Heinze, R. (eds.) (1914) *Q. Horatius Flaccus: Briefe*, 4th edition, Berlin.
Kilpatrick, R. S. (1986) *The Poetry of Friendship: Horace, Epistles I*, Edmonton (Alberta).
Kilpatrick, R. S. (1990) *The Poetry of Criticism: Horace, Epistles II and Ars Poetica*, Edmonton (Alberta).
Kilpatrick, R. S. (1996) 'Epistole,' in: *Enciclopedia Oraziana* I, Rome, 304–309.
Kindstrand, J. F. (1976) *Bion of Borysthenes: A Collection of the Fragments with Introduction and Commentary*, Uppsala.
Kindstrand, J. F. (1986) 'Diogenes Laertius and the *Chreia* tradition,' *Elenchos* 7, 217–243.
Kirchner, R. (2007) '*Elocutio*: Latin Prose Style,' in: Dominik, W. (ed.) *Companion to Roman Rhetoric*, Malden (MA), 181–194.
Kirichenko, A. (2013) *Lehrreiche Trugbilder: Senecas Tragödien und die Rhetorik des Sehens*, Heidelberg.
Kirichenko, A. (2014) '*Satura* und Pikareske: Der unendliche Spaß der *Satyrica* Petrons,' *Zeitschrift für Literaturwissenschaft und Linguistik* 175, 24–48.
Kirichenko, A. (2016) 'The Art of Transference: Metaphor and Iconicity in Pindar's *Olympian 6* and *Nemean 5*,' *Mnemosyne* 69, 1–28.
Klingner, F. (ed.) (2008), *Q. Horatius Flaccus: Opera*, 3rd edition, Berlin / New York.
Kloss, G. (2009) 'Von Zeiten und Rhythmen. Zu Tac. ann. 3, 55,' *Wiener Studien* 122, 123–143.
Knauer, G. N. (1964) *Die Aeneis und Homer. Studien zur poetischen Technik Vergils, mit Listen der Homerzitate in der Aeneis*, Göttingen.
Knorr, O. (2004) *Verborgene Kunst: Argumentationsstruktur und Buchaufbau in den Satiren des Horaz*, Hildesheim.
Knox, B. M. W. (1968) 'Silent reading in antiquity,' *Greek, Roman and Byzantine Studies* 9, 421–435.
Koestermann, E. (1963–1968) *Cornelius Tacitus: Annalen*, 4 vols., Heidelberg.
Kohn, T. (2013) *The Dramaturgy of Senecan Tragedy*, Ann Arbor (MI).
Koster, S. (1983) 'Horatius princeps,' in: Koster, S. *Tessera. Sechs Beiträge zur Poesie und poetischen Theorien der Antike*, Erlangen, 31–46.
Krauss, H. (1957) *Die Vergil-Zitate in Senecas Briefen an Lucilius*, diss. Hamburg.
Krenkel, W. A. (ed. and transl.) (2002) *M. Terentius Varro Saturae Menippeae*, 3 vols., Sankt Katharinen.
Kristeva, J. (1967) 'Bakhtine. Le mot, le dialogue et le roman,' *Critique* 239, 438–461.
Kroll, W. (ed.) (1960) *C. Valerius Catullus*, 4th edition, Stuttgart.
Kugelmeier, C. (2007) *Die innere Vergegenwärtigung des Bühnenspiels in Senecas Tragödien*, Munich.

Kurth, T. (1994) *Senecas Trostschrift an Polybius. Dialog 11. Ein Kommentar*, Stuttgart / Leipzig.
La Penna, A. (1993) 'Autarkeia e saggezza mondana nelle *Epistole*,' in: La Penna, A. *Saggi e studi su Orazio*, Florence, 187–195.
Lana, I. (1992) 'La Scuola dei Sestii,' in: s. n. (ed.) *La langue latine, langue de la philosophie. Actes du colloque organisé par l'École française de Rome avec le concours de l'Université de Rome 'La sapienza' (Rome, 17–19 mai 1990)*, Rome, 197–211.
Langius, J. (1625) *Anthologia sive Florilegium rerum et materarium selectarum*, Strasbourg.
Langlands, R. (2004) 'A Woman's Influence on a Roman Text: Marcia and Seneca,' in: McHardy, F. / Marshall, E. (eds.) *Women's Influence on Classical Civilization*, London, 115–126.
Laurenti, R. (1980) 'L'εὐθυμία di Democrito in Seneca,' in: Romano, F. (ed.) *Democrito e l'atomismo antico, Atti del Convegno Internazionale Catania 18–21 aprile 1979*, Catania, 533–552.
Laurenti, R. (1997) 'Morale,' in: *Enciclopedia Oraziana* II, Rome, 571–581.
Lavan, M. (2011) 'Slavishness in Britain and Rome in Tacitus' *Agricola*,' *Classical Quarterly* 61, 294–305.
Lavery, G. (1980) 'Metaphors of War and Travel in Seneca's Prose Works,' *Greece & Rome* 27, 147–157.
Leach, E. W. (1971) 'Horace's *pater optimus* and Terence's Demea: Autobiographical Fiction and Comedy in *Sermo* 1.4,' *American Journal of Philology* 92, 616–632.
Lee, M. O. (1969) *Word, Sound, and Image in the Odes of Horace*, Ann Arbor (MI).
Lefèvre, E. (1975) '*Nil medium est*. Die früheste Satire des Horaz 1.2,' in: Lefèvre, E. (ed.) *Monumentum Chiloniense: Studien zur augusteischen Zeit: Kieler Festschrift für Erich Burck zum 70. Geburtstag*, Amsterdam, 311–346.
Lefèvre, E. (2002) 'P. Terentius Afer,' in: Herzog, R. / Schmidt, P. L. (eds.) *Handbuch der lateinischen Literatur der Antike*, vol. I: W. Suerbaum (ed.) *Die archaische Literatur von den Anfängen bis Sullas Tod. Die vorliterarische Periode und die Zeit von 240 bis 78 v. Chr.*, Munich, 232–254.
Lefèvre, E. (2003) 'Anneo Sereno e il dialogo *de tranquillitate animi* di Seneca,' in: Gualandri, I. / Mazzoli, G. (eds.) *Gli Annei: Una famiglia nella storia e nella cultura di Roma imperiale. Atti del Convegno internazionale, Milano-Pavia, 2–6 maggio 2000*, Como, 153–165.
Lelli, E. (2009–2011) (ed.) *ΠΑΡΟΙΜΙΑΚΩΣ. Il proverbio in Grecia e Roma*, Pisa / Rome.
Leo, F. (1878) *De Senecae Tragoediis observationes criticae*, vol. I, Berlin.
Leo, F. (1889) 'Die beiden metrischen Systeme des Alterthums,' *Hermes* 21, 280–301.
Leonhardt, J. (1989) 'Die beiden metrischen Systeme des Altertums,' *Hermes* 117, 43–61.
Levi, A. (1951) 'Il concetto del tempo nelle filosofie dell'età ellenistica,' *Rivista critica di storia della filosofia* 6, 209–216.
Li Vigni, A. (2005) *Poeta quasi creator: Estetica e poesia in mathias Casimir Sarbiewski*, Palermo.
Littlewood, C. A. J. (2004) *Self-Representation and Illusion in Senecan Tragedy*, Oxford.
Littlewood, C. A. J. (2015) 'Theater and Theatricality in Seneca's World,' in: Bartsch / Schiesaro (2015), 161–173.
Littlewood, C. A. J. (2016) 'Seneca, Horace and the Poetics of Transgression,' in: Frangoulidis / Harrison / Manuwald (2016), 363–378.

Long, A. A. (1996) *Stoic Studies*, Cambridge.
Long, A. A. (2009) 'Seneca and the Self: Why Now?' in: Bartsch / Wray (2009), 20–36.
Long. A. A. / Sedley, D. N. (eds.) (1987) *The Hellenistic Philosophers*, 2 vols., Cambridge.
Lotito, G. (2001) *Suum esse: forme dell'interiorità senecana*, Bologna.
Lovelace, R. (1649) *Lucasta*, London.
Lowrie, M. (1997) *Horace's Narrative Odes*, Oxford.
Lowrie, M. (2002) 'Horace, Cicero and Augustus, or the Poet Statesman at *Epistles* 2.1.256,' in: Woodman / Feeney (2002), 158–171.
Lowrie, M. (2009) *Writing, Performance and Authority in Augustan Rome*, Oxford.
Lowrie, M. (2014) 'Politics by Other Means in Horace's *Ars Poetica*,' *Materiali e discussioni per l'analisi dei testi classici* 72, 121–142.
Lowrie, M. (2015) '*Rege incolumi*: Orientalism, Civil War, and Security at *Georgics* 4.212,' in: Günther, H.-C. (ed.) *Virgilian Studies. A Miscellany dedicated to the Memory of Mario Geymonat*, Nordhausen, 322–342.
McCarter, S. (2015) *Horace between Freedom and Slavery: The First Book of the* Epistles, Madison (WI).
McDowell, N. (2008) *Poetry and Allegiance in the English Civil Wars: Marvell and the Cause of Wit*, Oxford.
McGann, M. J. (1969) *Studies in Horace's First Book of* Epistles, Brussels.
McPherson, D. (1974) *Ben Jonson's Library: An Annotated Catalogue*, special issue, *Studies in Philology* 71.
Main, C. F. (1955) 'Wotton's "The Character of a Happy life",' *The Library* 10 (5th series), 270–274.
Maior, G. (1534) *Sententiae veterum poetarum*, Magdeburg.
Mankin, D. (ed.) (1995) *Horace: Epodes*, Cambridge.
Mann, W.-R. (2006) 'Learning how to die: Seneca's use of *Aeneid* 4.653 at *Epistulae morales* 12.9,' in: Volk / Williams (2006), 103–122.
Manning, C. E (1981) *On Seneca's "Ad Marciam"*, Leiden.
Mansfeld, J. (2004) 'Democritus, Fragments 68B18 and B21 DK,' *Mnemosyne* 57, 484–488.
Manuwald, G. (2002) 'Der 'Fürstenspiegel' in Senecas *De clementia* und in der *Octavia*,' *Museum Helveticum* 59, 107–126.
Manuwald, G. (2011) *Roman Republican Theatre*, Cambridge.
Marcovich, M. (ed.) (1967) *Heraclitus. Greek Text with a Short Commentary*, Merida.
Marino, R. (2011) *Seneca: Lettere a Lucilio*, Siena.
Mariotti, I. (ed.) (2007) *G. Sallustio Crispo, Coniuratio Catilinae*, Bologna.
Marshall, C. W. (2014) 'The Works of Seneca the Younger and Their Dates,' in: Damschen / Heil (2014), 33–44.
Martin, J. (1960) 'Zwei Interpretationsversuche zu Horaz,' in: s. n. (ed.) *Studi in onore di L. Castiglioni*, Florence, vol. II, 595–611.
Martindale, C. / Hopkins, D. (eds.) (1993) *Horace Made New: Horatian influences upon British writing from the Renaissance to the twentieth century*, Cambridge
Martindale, J. (1993) 'The best master of virtue and wisdom: the Horace of Ben Jonson and his heirs,' in: Martindale / Hopkins (1993), 50–85.
Marx, F. (ed.) (1993) *Incerti auctoris de ratione dicendi ad C. Herennium lib. IV*, Stuttgart (reprint of the 1923 edition).

Marx, W. (1932) *Funktion und Form der Chorlieder in den Seneca-Tragödien*, Köln (diss. Heidelberg).
Mason, T. (1990) 'Abraham Cowley and the Wisdom of Anacreon,' *Cambridge Quarterly* 19, 103–137.
Mastrorosa, I. G. (2000) 'Similitudini, metafore e lessico militari nella trattatistica retorica latina. Cicerone e Quintiliano,' in: Sconocchia, S. / Toneatto, L. (eds.) *Lingue tecniche del greco e del latino. Atti del III Seminario internazionale sulla letteratura scientifica e tecnica greca e latina*, Bologna, 277–310.
Maurach, G. (1970) *Der Bau von Senecas Epistulae Morales*, Heidelberg.
Maurach, G. (2001) *Horaz. Werk und Leben*, Heidelberg.
Mayer, R. (1982) 'Neronian Classicism,' *American Journal of Philology* 103, 305–318.
Mayer, R. (1986) 'Horace *Epistles* I and Philosophy,' *American Journal of Philology* 107, 55–73.
Mayer, R. (ed.) (1994) *Horace, Epistles, Book I*, Cambridge.
Mayer, R. (2003) 'Persona<l> Problems,' *Materiali e discussioni per l'analisi dei testi classici* 50, 1–26.
Mayer, R. (2009) '*Vivere secundum Horatium*: Otto Vaenius' *Emblemata Horatiana*,' in: Houghton / Wyke (2009), 200–218.
Mazzoli, G. (1970) *Seneca e la poesia*, Milan.
Mazzoli, G. (1989) 'Le *Epistulae morales* di Seneca. Valore letterario e filosofico,' in: *Aufstieg und Niedergang der Römischen Welt* II.36.3, 1823–1877.
Mazzoli, G. (1991) 'Seneca e la poesia,' in: Grimal, P. (ed.) *Sénèque et la prose latine*, Vandœuvres (Geneva), 177–217.
Mazzoli, G. (1998) 'Seneca,' in: *Enciclopedia Oraziana* III, Rome, 62–64.
Medcalf, S. (1993) 'Horace's Kipling,' in: Martindale / Hopkins (1997), 217–235.
Meltzer, G. (1988) 'Dark Wit and Black Humor in Seneca's *Thyestes*,' *Transactions of the American Philological Association* 118, 309–330.
Ménage, J. (1692) *In Diogenem Laertium Aegidii Menagii. Observationes et emendationes, hac editione plurimum auctae*, Amsterdam.
Mendell, C. W. (1920) 'Satire as Popular Philosophy,' *Classical Philology* 15, 138–157.
Mendell, C. W. (1922) 'Martial and the Satiric Epigram,' *Classical Philology* 17, 1–20.
Merchant, F. I. (1905) 'Seneca the Philosopher and His Theory of Style,' *The American Journal of Philology*, 26, 44–59.
Merli, E. (2006) 'Identity and Irony: Martial's Tenth Book, Horace, and the Tradition of Roman Satire,' in: Nauta, R. / van Dam, H.-J. / Smolenaars, J. J. L. (eds.) (2006) *Flavian Poetry*, Leiden, 257–270.
Michel, A. (1969) 'Rhétorique, tragédie, philosophie: Sénèque et le sublime,' *Giornale italiano di filologia* 21, 245–257.
Miller, F. J. (ed. and trans.) (1999) *Ovid: Metamorphoses*, 2 vols., revised edition by G. P. Goold, Cambridge (MA).
Miller, J. F. (2009) *Apollo, Augustus, and the Poets*, Cambridge.
Miller, P. A. (2012) 'Imperial satire as Saturnalia,' in: Braund, S. / Osgood, J. (eds.) *Companion to Persius and Juvenal*, Oxford, 312–334.
Miller, W. (ed. and trans.) (1990) *M. Tullius Cicero: De officiis*, Cambridge (MA).
Miller, W. E. (1963) 'Double Translation in English Humanistic Education,' *Studies in the Renaissance* 10, 163–174.

Minarini, A. (1977) *Q. Orazio Flacco. La satira 1,1*, Bologna.
Minarini, A. (1997) 'Una epistola perduta di Seneca e una reminiscenza oraziana,' *Paideia* 52, 263–274.
Mindt, N. (2013a) *Martials 'epigrammatischer Kanon,'* Munich.
Mindt, N. (2013b) 'Griechische Autoren in den Epigrammen Martials,' *Millennium Jahrbuch* 10, 501–556.
Mindt, N. (2014) 'Cicero und Seneca d.J. in den Epigrammen Martials,' *Gymnasium* 121, 69–89.
Mindt, N. (forthcoming) 'Epigram and Rhetoric,' in: Henriksén, C. (ed.) *A Companion to Ancient Epigram*, Malden (MA).
Mirandula, O. (1507) *Illustrium Poetarum Flores*, Venice (influential revised edition [1538], Strasbourg).
Mitscherlich, C. G. (ed.) (1800) *Q. Horatius Flaccus: Opera*, 2 vols., Leipzig.
Moles, J. (2002) 'Poetry, philosophy, politics and play: *Epistles* I,' in: Woodman / Feeney (2002), 141–157. Reprinted in: Freudenburg (2009), 308–332.
Moles, J. (2007) 'Philosophy and ethics,' in: Harrison (2007a), 165–180.
Moles, J. (2012) 'Diatribe,' in: Hornblower, S. / Spawforth, A. (eds.) *The Oxford Classical Dictionary*, 4th edition, Oxford, 446–447.
Money, D. (2006) 'Aspects of the Reception of Sarbiewski in England: From Hils, Vaughan, and Watts to Coleridge, Bowring, Walker and Coxe,' in: Urbanski, P. (ed.) *Pietas humainistica: Neo-Latin Religious Poetry in Poland in European Context*, Frankfurt, 157–187.
Montiglio, S. (2006) 'Should the Aspiring Wise Man Travel? A Conflict in Seneca's Thought,' *American Journal of Philology* 127, 553–586.
Montiglio, S. (2008) *'Meminisse iuvabit:* Seneca on Controlling Memory,' *Rheinisches Museum* 151, 168–180.
Moretti, G. (1995) *Acutum dicendi genus. Brevità, oscurità, sottigliezze e paradossi nelle tradizioni retoriche degli Stoici*, Bologna.
Morgan, L. (2010) *Musa Pedestris: Metre and Meaning in Roman Verse*, Oxford.
Morgan, J. / Harrison, S. J. (2008), 'Intertextuality,' in: Whitmarsh, T. (ed.) *The Greek and Roman Novel*, Cambridge, 218–236.
Morrison, A.D. (2006) 'Advice and Abuse: Horace, *Epistles* 1 and the Iambic Tradition,' *Materiali e discussioni per l'analisi dei testi classici* 56, 29–61.
Morrison, A. D. (2007) 'Didacticism and Epistolarity in Horace's *Epistles* 1,' in: Morello, R. / Morrison, A. D. (eds.) *Classical and Late Antique Epistolography*, Oxford, 107–131.
Morton Braund, S. (ed. and trans.) (2004) *Juvenal and Persius*, Cambridge (MA).
Motto, A. L. / Clark, J. R. (1993a) *Essays on Seneca*, Frankfurt.
Motto, A. L. / Clark, J. R. (1993b) 'The Art of Paradox in Seneca's *Epistle* 60,' in: Motto / Clark (1993), 99–104.
Moul, V. (2010) *Jonson, Horace and the Classical Tradition*, Cambridge.
Moul, V. (2016) 'Horace,' in: Cheney, P. / Hardie, P. (eds.) *The Oxford History of Classical Reception in English Literature. Volume 2: 1558–1660*, Oxford, 539–556.
Moul, V. (forthcoming) *Latin and English Poetry in Britain, 1550–1770*, Cambridge.
Muecke, F. (1993) *Horace Satires II: with an Introduction, Translation and Commentary*, Warminster.

Müller, J. (2014) 'Did Seneca Understand Medea? A Contribution to the Stoic Account of *Akrasia*,' in: Wildberger / Colish (2014), 65–94.
Muñoz Martín, M. N. (1995) *Teoría epistular y conceptión de la carta en Roma*, Granada.
Mutschler, F.-H. (2014) '*De Tranquillitate Animi*,' in: Damschen / Heil (2014), 153–159.
Nauta, R. (1987) 'Seneca's *Apocolocyntosis* as Saturnalian literature,' *Mnemosyne* 40, 69–96.
Neck, G. (1964) *Das Problem der Zeit im Epikureismus*, diss. Heidelberg.
Neger, M. (2012) *Martials Dichtergedichte. Das Epigramm als Medium der poetischen Selbstreflexion*, Tübingen.
Neger, M. (2015) 'Pliny's Martial and Martial's Pliny: the Intertextual Dialogue between the *Letters* and the *Epigrams*,' in: Devillers, O. (ed.) *Autour de Pline le Jeune, en hommage à Nicole Méthy*, Bordeaux, 131–144.
Negri, A. M. (1988) 'La fortuna letteraria dell'*inertia* (Hor. *Ep.* I, 2, 28; Sen. *tranq.* 12, 3),' *Paideia* 43, 177–188.
Nelis, D. (2001) *Vergil's* Aeneid *and the* Argonautica *of Apollonius Rhodius*, Leeds.
Newman, R. J. (1989) '*Cotidie meditari*: theory and practice of the *meditatio* in imperial Stoicism,' in: *Aufstieg und Niedergang der römsichen Welt* II.36.3, 1473–1517.
Newton, T. (ed.) (1927 [1581]) *Seneca. His Tenne Tragedies Translated into English*, London.
Nicholls, M. (2005) *Roman Public Libraries*, diss. Oxford.
Nilsson, M. P. (1974) *Geschichte der Griechischen Religion*, vol. II, 3rd edition, Munich.
Nisbet, R. G. M. / Hubbard, M. (1970) *A Commentary on Horace: Odes, Book I*, Oxford.
Nisbet, R. G. M. / Hubbard, M. (1978) *A Commentary on Horace: Odes, Book II*, Oxford.
Nisbet, R. G. M. / Rudd, N. (2004) *A Commentary on Horace: Odes, Book III*, Oxford.
Noller, E. M. (2015) '*Re et sonitu distare*: Überlegungen zu Ordnung und Bedeutung in Lukrez, De Rerum Natura 1, 814–829,' in: Haß, C. D. / Noller, E. M. (eds.) *Was bedeutet Ordnung – was ordnet Bedeutung? Zur bedeutungskonstituierenden Ordnungsleistungen in Geschriebenem*, Berlin / Boston (MA), 137–172.
Nussbaum, M. C. (1993) 'Poetry and the passions: two Stoic views,' in: Brunschwig, J. / Nussbaum, M. C. (eds.) *Passions & Perceptions: Studies in Hellenistic Philosophy of Mind, Proceedings of the Fifth Symposium Hellenisticum*, Cambridge, 97–149.
O'Brien, J. (1995) *Anacreon Redivivus. A Study of Anacreontic Translation in Mid-Sixteenth-Century France*, Ann Arbor (MI).
O'Gorman, E. (2005) 'Citation and authority in Seneca's *Apocolocyntosis*,' in: Freudenburg (2005), 95–108.
Oaklander, L. N. (ed.) (2008), *The Philosophy of Time. Critical Concepts in Philosophy*, 4 vols., London.
Obbink, D. (ed.) (1995) *Philodemus on Poetry: Poetic Theory and Practice in Lucretius, Philodemus, and Horace*, Oxford.
Oberhelman, S. / Armstrong, D. (1995) 'Satire as Poetry and the Impossibility of Metathesis in Horace's *Satires*,' in: Obbink, D. (1995), 233–254.
Oliensis, E. (1998) *Horace and the Rhetoric of Authority*, Cambridge.
Oliensis, E. (2009) 'Fashioning Men: the Art of Self-Fashioning in the *Ars Poetica*,' in: Freudenburg (2009), 451–479.
Oltramare, A. (1926) *Les origines de la diatribe romaine*, Lausanne.
Op Het Veld, C. (2000) *Quem putas perisse praemissum est. Ein Kommentar zu Senecas 93.und 99. Brief*, Aachen.

Opelt, I. (1965) *Die lateinischen Schimpfwörter und verwandte sprachliche Erscheinungen*, Heidelberg.
Orellius, I. G. / Baiterius, I. G. (1850–1852) *Q. Horatius Flaccus*, 3rd edition, vol. I, Zürich.
Page, D. L. (1955) *Sappho and Alcaeus, an introduction to the study of ancient Lesbian poetry*, Oxford.
Palmieri, N. (1999) *L'eroe al bivio: modelli di 'mors voluntaria' in Seneca tragico*, Pisa.
Pantzerhielm Thomas, S. (1936) 'De quarta primi epistularum Horatii libri epistula interpretando,' *Eranos* 34, 41–46.
Parker, H. N. (2009) 'Books and Reading Latin Poetry,' in: Parker, H. N. / Johnson, W. A. (eds.), *Ancient Literacies. The Culture of Reading in Greece and Rome*, Oxford, 186–229.
Paschalis, M. (2011) 'Petronius and Virgil. Contextual and Intertextual Readings,' in: Doulamis, K. (ed.) *Echoing Narratives. Studies of Intertextuality in Greek and Roman Prose Fiction*, Groningen, 73–98.
Pasquali, G. (1942) 'Arte allusiva,' *Italia che scrive* 25, 185–187.
Pebworth, T.-L. (1977) 'Sir Henry Wotton's "Dazel'd Thus, with height of Place" and the Appropriation of Political Poetry in the Earlier Seventeenth Century,' *The Papers of the Bibliographical Society of America* 71, 151–169.
Pebworth, T.-L. (1978) 'New Light on Sir Henry Wotton's "The Character of a Happy Life",' *The Library* 10 (5th series), 223–226.
Pellegrino, M. (1982) 'Il *topos* dello *status rectus* nel contesto filosofico e biblico (a proposito di *Ad Diognetum* 10, 1–2),' in: Pellegrino, M., *Ricerche patristiche*, II, Turin, 391–399.
Pennacini, A. (1982) 'Bioneis sermonibus et sale nigro,' in: Della Corte, F. (ed.) *Prosimetrum et Spoudogeloion*, Genoa, 55–61.
Pennacini, A. (1989) 'Bione di Boristene. La retorica al servizio della filosofia,' in: s. n. (ed.). *Mnemosynum: studi in onore di Alfredo Ghiselli*, Bologna, 451–456.
Pennacini, A. (2007) 'Riso e conoscenza in testi pagani: diatriba cinica e satira romana,' in: Mazzucco, C. (ed.) *Riso e comicità nel cristianesimo antico. Atti del convegno di Torino (14–16 febbraio 2005) e altri studi*, Alessandria, 59–78.
Peterson, W. (ed.) (1891) *M. Fabi Quintiliani Institutionis Oratoriae Liber Decimus*, Oxford.
Petrochilos, N. K. (1974) *Roman Attitudes to the Greeks*, Athens.
Piazzi, L. (2004) 'Elementi diatribico-moralistici negli epigrammi di Marziale,' *Atene e Roma: rassegna trimestrale dell'Associazione Italiana di Cultura classica* 49, 73–78.
Pighi, I. B. (1965) *De Ludis Saecularibus*, Amsterdam.
Pigman, G. W. (1980) 'Versions of Imitation in the Renaissance,' *Renaissance Quarterly* 33, 1–32.
Plaza, M. (2006) *The Function of Humour in Roman Verse Satire: Laughing and Lying*, Oxford.
Plett, H. F. (1988) 'The Poetics of Quotation,' in: Petöfi, J. S. / Olivi, T. (eds.) *Von der verbalen Konstitution zur symbolischen Bedeutung – From verbal constitution to symbolic meaning*, Hamburg, 313–334.
Porter, D. H. (2002) 'Playing the Game: Horace, *Epistles* 1,' *Classical World* 96, 21–60.
Porter, J. (1995) 'Content and Form in Philodemus: The History of an Evasion,' in: Obbink (1995), 97–147.
Pöschl, V. (1970) 'Die große Maecenasode des Horaz (c. III 29),' in: Pöschl, V., *Horazische Lyrik. Interpretationen*, Heidelberg, 198–245.
Préaux, J. (ed.) (1968), *Horace, Épîtres, livre I*, Paris.
Préchac, F. (ed.) / Noblot, H. (transl.) (1945–1962) *Sénèque: Lettres a Lucilius*, Paris.

Prince, M. (2013) 'Canidia Channels Medea: Rereading Horace's Epode 5,' *Classical World* 106, 609–620.
Prinz, K. (1911), *Martial und die griechische Epigrammatik*, Vienna.
Puelma, M. (1995) 'Dichter und Gönner bei Martial,' in: Fasel, I. (ed.) *Labor et lima. Kleine Schriften und Nachträge*, Basel, 415–466.
Putnam, M. C. J. (1972) 'Horace and Tibullus,' *Classical Philology* 67, 81–88.
Putnam, M. C. J. (1986) *Artifices of Eternity: Horace's Fourth Book of Odes*, Ithaca (NY).
Putnam, M. C. J. (2000) *Horace's Carmen Saeculare*, New Haven (CT).
Rankin, H. D. (1972) 'The Progress of Pessimism in Catullus, Poems 2–11,' *Latomus* 31, 744–751.
Raven, D. S. (1965), *Latin Metre*, London.
Reckford, K. (1999) 'Only a Wet Dream? Hope and Skepticism in Horace, Satire 1.5,' *American Journal of Philology* 120, 525–554.
Reckford, K. (2002) '*Pueri ludentes*: Some Aspects of Play and Seriousness in Horace's Epistles,' *Transactions of the American Philological Association* 132, 1–19.
Relihan, J. C. (1993) *Ancient Menippean satire*, Baltimore (MD).
Reynolds, L. D. (ed.) (1965) *L. Annaei Senecae Ad Lucilium Epistulae Morales*, 2 vols., Oxford.
Reynolds, L. D. (ed.) (1977) *L. Annaei Senecae Dialogorum Libri Duodecim*, Oxford.
Ribbeck, O. (1875) *Die römische Tragödie im Zeitalter der Republik*, Leipzig.
Richter, W. (ed.) (1952) *Vergil. Georgica*, Munich.
Rimell, V. (2009) *Martial's Rome: Empire and the Ideology of Epigram*, Cambridge.
Rimell, V. (2013) 'The Best a Man Can Get: Grooming Scipio in Seneca Epistle 86,' *Classical Philology* 108, 1–20.
Rimell, V. (2015a) *The Closure of Space in Roman Poetics. Empire's Inward Turn*, Cambridge.
Rimell, V. (2015b) 'Seneca and Neronian Rome: In the Mirror of Time,' in: Bartsch / Schiesaro (2015), 122–134.
Roberts, D. (1987) 'Parting Words: Final Lines in Sophocles and Euripides,' *Classical Quarterly* 37, 51–64.
Rolfe, J. C. (ed. and trans.) (1946) *Aulus Gellius: The Attic Nights*, Cambridge (MA).
Rolfe, J. C. (ed. and trans.) (2013) *Sallust: The War with Catiline, The War with Jugurtha*, revised edition by J. T. Ramsey, Cambridge (MA).
Rolland, E. (1906) *De l'influence de Sénèque le père et des rhéteurs sur Sénèque le philosophe*, Ghent.
Roller, M. (2004) 'Exemplarity in Roman Culture: the Cases of Horatius Cocles and Cloelia,' *Classical Philology* 99, 1–56.
Roman, L. (2001) 'The Representation of Literary Materiality in Martial's Epigrams,' *Journal of Roman Studies* 91, 113–145.
Romano, E. (1991) *Q. Orazio Flacco, Le Opere; Vol. I: le Odi, il Carme Secolare, gli Epodi; Fasc. II: commento*, Rome.
Rosenbach, M. (ed.) (1995) *L. Annaeus Seneca, Philosophische Schriften. Lateinisch – deutsch*, 5th edition, Darmstadt.
Rosenthal, G. (1897) *De sententiis Horatianis*, Berlin.
Roskam, G. (2007) *Lathe Biosas – Live Unnoticed. On the Vicissitudes of an Epicurean Doctrine*, Leiden.
Ross, W. D. (1977) *Aristotle's Physics. A Revised Text with Introduction and Commentary*, Oxford.

Rostagni, A. (1944) *Suetonio De Poetis e biografi minori*, Turin.
Røstvig, M.-S. (1954–1955) 'Benlowes, Marvell, and the Divine Casimire,' *The Huntington Library Quarterly* 18, 13–35.
Røstvig, M.-S. (1954) 'Casimire Sarbiewski and the English Ode,' *Studies in Philology* 51, 443–460.
Røstvig, M.-S. (1962) *The Happy Man: Studies in the Metamorphosis of a Classical Ideal*, Volume 1: 1600–1700, 2nd edition, Oslo.
Rudd, N. (1966) *The Satires of Horace*, Cambridge.
Rudd, N. (1989) *Horace: Epistles Book II and Epistle to the Pisones ('Ars Poetica')*, Cambridge.
Rudd, N. (ed. and trans.) (2004), *Horace: Odes and Epodes*, Cambridge (MA).
Runchina, G. (1960) 'Tecnica drammatica e retorica nelle Tragedie di Seneca,' *Atti della Facoltà di Lettere, Filosofia e Magistero dell' Università di Cagliari* 28, 163–324.
Sage, P. W. (1994) 'Vatic Admonition in Horace *Odes* 4.9,' *American Journal of Philology* 115, 565–586.
Said, E. (1995) *Orientalism. Western Conceptions of the Orient*, 2nd edition, Harmondsworth.
Salamon, G. (2004) 'Les citations dans les Tusculanes: quelques remarques sur les livres 1 et 2,' in: Darbo-Peschanski, C. (ed.) *La citation dans l'Antiquité. Actes du colloque du PARSA, Lyon, ENS LSH, 6–8 novembre 2002*, Grenoble, 135–146.
Salamon, G. (2006) 'Les citations des philosophes dans le livre III des *Tusculanes:* forme et sens,' in: Nicolas, C. (ed.) *Hôs ephat', dixerit quispiam, comme disait l'autre... Mécanismes de la citation et de la mention dans les langues de l'Antiquité*, Grenoble, 69–79.
Salemme, C. (1976) *Marziale e la 'poetica' degli oggetti: Struttura dell'epigramma di Marziale*, Naples.
Sallmann, K. (1987) 'Lyrischer Krieg. Die Verschiebung der Genera in der Pollio-Ode 2, 1 des Horaz,' in: Boldrini, S. (ed.), *Filologia e forme letterarie. Studi offerti a F. Della Corte*, Urbino, 69–87.
Santirocco, M. (1984) 'The Maecenas Odes,' *Transactions of the American Philological Association* 114, 241–253.
Santorelli, B. (ed. and trans.) (2013) *Giovenale, Satira IV. Introduzione, Traduzione e Commento*, Berlin / Boston (MA).
Sargeaunt, J. (ed. and trans.) (1983–1986) *Terence, in two volumes*, Cambridge (MA).
Scarpat, G. (1975), *Lucio Anneo Seneca, Lettere a Lucilio, libro primo (epp. I–XII): testo, introduzione, versione e commento*, Brescia.
Scarpat, G. (1977) *Il Pensiero religioso di Seneca e l'ambiente ebraico e cristiano*, Brescia.
Schäfer, E. (1983) 'Martials machbares Lebensglück (Epigr. 5,20 und 10,47),' *Der Altsprachliche Unterricht* 26, 74–95.
Schäfer, E. (ed.) (2006) *Sarbiewski. Der polnische Horaz*, Tübingen.
Schauer, M. (ed.) (2012) *Tragicorum Romanorum Fragmenta. Vol. 1: Livius Andronicus, Naevius, Tragici minores, Fragmenta adespota*, Göttingen.
Schenk, P. (2016), 'Forms of Intertextuality in the *Epistles* of Pliny the Younger,' in: Gibson, R. / Whitton, C. (eds.) *The Epistles of Pliny*, Oxford, 332–354.
Schiesaro, A. (1997) 'Passion, Reason and Knowledge in Seneca's Tragedies,' in: Braund, S. M. / Gill, C. (eds.) *The Passions in Roman Thought and Literature*, Cambridge, 89–111.
Schiesaro, A. (2003) *The Passions in Play: Thyestes and the Dynamics of Senecan Drama*, Cambridge.

Schiesaro, A. (2009) 'Horace's Bacchic Poetics,' in: Houghton / Wyke (2009), 61–79.
Schiesaro, A. (2015) 'Seneca and Epicurus: The Allure of the Other,' in: Bartsch / Schiesaro (2015), 239–251.
Schiesaro, A. (2016) 'Bacchus in Roman Drama,' in: Frangoulidis / Harrison / Manuwald (2016), 25–41.
Schiroli, M. G. C. (1981) *Lucio Anneo Seneca:* De tranquillitate animi, Bologna.
Schlegel, C. (2005) *Satire and the Threat of Speech: Horace's* Satires Book 1, Madison (WI).
Schlegel, C. (2010) 'Horace and the Satirist's Mask: Shadowboxing with Lucilius,' in: Davis (2010), 253–270.
Schmeling, G. (2011) *A Commentary on the* Satyrica *of Petronius*, Oxford.
Schmidt, E. A. (2002) *Zeit und Form: Dichtungen des Horaz*, Heidelberg.
Schmidt, E. A. (2014) 'Space and Time in Senecan Drama,' in: Damschen / Heil (2014), 501–546.
Schmitzer, U. (1990) *Zeitgeschichte in Ovids Metamorphosen. Mythologische Dichtung unter politischem Anspruch*, Stuttgart.
Schmitzer, U. (1994) 'Vom Esquilin nach Trastevere: Hor. sat. 1,9 im Kontext zeitgenössischen Verstehens,' in: Koster, S. (ed.) *Horaz-Studien*, Erlangen, 9–30.
Schmitzer, U. (2009) 'Der Maecenaskreis macht einen Ausflug, oder: Wie Horaz die Politik zur Privatsache macht,' in: Felgentreu, F. / Mundt, F. / Rücker, N. (eds.) *Per attentam Caesaris aurem: Satire – die unpolitische Gattung?*, Tübingen, 99–115.
Schnegg-Köhler, B. (2002) *Die augusteischen Säkularspiele*, Leipzig.
Schofield, M. / Striker, G. (eds.) (1986) *The Norms of Nature. Studies in Hellenistic Ethics*, Cambridge.
Schönegg, B. (1999) *Senecas* epistulae morales *als philosophisches Kunstwerk*, Bern.
Schöpsdau, K. (2015) '*Caelum, non animum mutant, qui trans mare currunt.* Horaz (*epist.* 1, 11) und Seneca (*epist.* 28) über das Reisen,' in: Kugelmeier, C. (ed.) *Translatio humanitatis. Festschrift zum 60. Geburtstag von Peter Riemer*, St. Ingbert, 451–469.
Schork, T. (1971) '*Aemulos Reges.* Allusion and Theme in Horace 3.16,' *Transactions of the American Philological Association* 102, 515–539.
Schwindt, J. P. (2005) 'Zeiten und Räume in augusteischer Dichtung,' in: Schwindt, J. P. (ed.) *La représentation du temps dans la poésie augustéenne. Zur Poetik der Zeit in augusteischer Dichtung*, Heidelberg, 1–18.
Schwindt, J. P. (2013) 'Die Magie des Zählens. Zur cantatorischen Statur der Dichtung (Catull, cc. 5 u. 7; Horaz, c. 1, 11),' in: Dunsch, B. / Prokoph, F. (eds.), *Am langen Seil des Altertums. Beiträge aus Anlass des 90. Geburtstags von Walter Wimmel*, Heidelberg, 15–35.
Scodel, J. (2002) *Excess and the Mean in Early Modern English Literature*, Princeton (NJ).
Scodel, R. (1987) 'Horace, Lucilius, and Callimachean Polemic,' *Harvard Studies in Classical Philology* 91, 199–215.
Segal, C. (1977) 'Synaesthesia in Sophocles,' *Illinois Classical Studies* 2, 88–96.
Segal, C. (1986) *Language and Desire in Seneca's* Phaedra, Princeton (NJ).
Seidensticker, B. (2007) '*Plura non habui:* Senecas *Medea* und der *Comparativus Senecanus*,' *Phasis* 10, 1–14.
Setaioli, A. (1965) 'Esegesi Virgiliana in Seneca,' *Studi Italiani di Filologia Classica* 37, 133–156.

Setaioli, A. (1981) 'Gli "Epodi" di Orazio nella critica dal 1937 al 1972 (con un appendice fino al 1978),' in: *Aufstieg und Niedergang der römischen Welt* II.31.3, 1674–1788.
Setaioli, A. (1985) 'Seneca e lo stile,' in: *Aufstieg und Niedergang der römsichen Welt* II.32.2, 776–858.
Setaioli, A. (1988) *Seneca e i Greci. Citazioni e traduzioni nelle opere filosofiche*, Bologna.
Setaioli, A. (2000a) *Facundus Seneca: aspetti della lingua e dell'ideologia senecana*, Bologna.
Setaioli, A. (2000b) 'Elementi di *sermo cotidianus* nella lingua di Seneca prosatore,' in: Setaioli (2000a), 9–95.
Setaioli, A. (2000c) 'Seneca e lo stile,' in: Setaioli (2000a), 111–217.
Setaioli, A. (2014) 'Ethics I: Philosophy as Therapy, Self-transformation, and "Lebensform",' in: Damschen / Heil (2014), 239–256.
Shackleton Bailey, D. R. (ed.) (1990) *M. Valerius Martialis: Epigrammata*, Stuttgart.
Shackleton Bailey, D. R. (ed. and trans.) (2003), *Statius, vol. I: Silvae*, Cambridge (MA).
Shackleton Bailey, D. R. (ed.) (2008) *Q. Horatius Flaccus: Opera*, 4th edition, Berlin / New York.
Sharland, S. (2009) 'Soporific Satire: Horace, Damasippus and Professor Snore (Stertinius) in Satire 2.3,' *Acta Classica* 52, 113–131.
Sharland, S. (2010) *Horace in Dialogue: Bakhtinian Readings in the Satires*, Bern.
Shorey, P. (ed. and trans.) (1935) *Plato: Republic*, 2 vols., Cambridge (MA).
Short, W. M. (2013) '"Transmission" Accomplished? Latin's Alimentary Metaphors of Communication,' *American Journal of Philology* 134, 247–275.
Silk, E. T. (1969) 'Bacchus and the Horatian *Recusatio*,' *Yale Classical Studies* 21, 193–212.
Simpson, C. J. (2002) 'The Tomb, Immortality and the Pontifex: Some Realities in Horace Carm. 3.30,' *Athenaeum* 90, 89–94.
Sinclair, P. (1995) *Tacitus the Sententious Historian: A Sociology of Rhetoric in Annales 1–6*, University Park (PA).
Skalitzky, R. (1968) 'Good Wine in a New Vase (Horace, Epistles 1.2),' *Transactions of the American Philological Association* 99, 443–52.
Smith, M. S. (ed.) (1975) *Petronius: Cena Trimalchionis*, Oxford.
Soldo, J. (2015) 'Horace and Seneca: Interactions, Intertexts, Interpretations: Heidelberg, Seminar für Klassische Philologie 27th–29th July 2015,' *Bollettino di studi latini* 45, 717–721.
Solimano, G. (1991) *La prepotenza dell'occhio: riflessioni sull'opera di Seneca*, Genoa.
Sommer, A. (2001) '*Vivere militare est*. Die Funktion und philosophische Tragweite militärischer Metaphern bei Seneca und Lipsius,' *Archiv für Begriffsgeschichte* 43, 59–82.
Spahlinger, L. (2005) *Tulliana simplicitas. Zu Form und Funktion des Zitats in den philosophischen Dialogen Ciceros*, Göttingen.
Spann, C. E. / Williams, M. E., Sr. (2008) *Presidential Praise: Our Presidents and their Hymns*, Macon (GA).
Spika, J. (1890) *De imitatione Horatiana in Senecae canticis chori*, Vienna.
Staley, G. A. (2010) *Seneca and the Idea of Tragedy*, Oxford.
Star, C. (2012) *The Empire of the Self: Self-Command and Political Speech in Seneca and Petronius*, Baltimore (MD).
Star, C. (2016) 'Seneca *Tragicus* and Stoicism,' in: Dodson-Robinson (2016), 34–56.

Starr, R. J. (1991) 'Reading Aloud: *Lectores* and Roman Reading,' *The Classical Journal* 86, 337–343.
Stawecka, K. (ed.) (1972) *Maziej Kazimierz Sarbiewski*, Dii Gentium / Bogowie Pogan, Wrocław.
Steinmetz, P. (1970) 'Ein metrisches Experiment Senecas?' *Museum Helveticum* 27, 97–103.
Stevens, J. A. (1999) 'Seneca and Horace: Allegorical Technique in two Odes to Bacchus (Hor. "Carm." 2.19 and Sen. "Oed." 403–508),' *Phoenix* 53, 281–307.
Stocker, P. (1998) *Theorie der intertextuellen Lektüre. Modelle und Fallstudien*, Paderborn.
Stowers, S. K. (1988) 'The Diatribe,' in: Aune, D. E. (ed.) *Greco-Roman Literature and the New Testament: Selected Forms and Genres*, Atlanta (GA), 71–83.
Striker, G. (1996) *Essays on Hellenistic Epistemology and Ethics*, Cambridge.
Strzelecki, L. (1963) 'De rei metricae Annaeanae origine quaestiones,' *Eos* 53, 157–170.
Stucchi, S. (2002) 'Esempi di sapienza oraziana nel *Satyricon*. Tra svilimento e rovesciamento,' in: Castagna / Vogt-Spira (2002), 213–222.
Sullivan, J. P. (1985a) *Literature and politics in the age of Nero*, Ithaca (NY).
Sullivan, J. P. (1985b) 'Petronius' "Satyricon" and its Neronian Context,' in: *Aufstieg und Niedergang der römischen Welt* II 32.3, 1666–1686.
Sullivan, J. P. (1987) 'Martial's Satirical Epigrams,' in: Whitby, M. / Hardie, P. / Whitby, M. (eds.) *Homo Viator. Classical Essays for John Bramble*, Bristol, 259–265.
Sullivan, J. P. (1991) *Martial: The Unexpected Classic. A Literary and Historical Study*, Cambridge.
Summers, W. C. (1910) *Select Letters of Seneca: Edited with Introduction and Notes*, London.
Sutherland, E. H. (2002) *Horace's Well-Trained Reader: Toward a Methodology of Audience Participation in the Odes*, Frankfurt.
Syed, Y. (2005) 'Romans and Others,' in: Harrison, S. J. (ed.), *A Companion to Latin Literature*, Oxford, 360–371.
Syndikus, H. P. (2001) *Die Lyrik des Horaz. Eine Interpretation der Oden*, 2 vols., 3rd edition, Darmstadt.
Szelest, H. (1963) 'Martials satirische Epigramme und Horaz,' *Altertum* 9, 27–37.
Tarrant, R. J. (ed.) (1976) *Seneca: Agamemnon*, Cambridge.
Tarrant, R. J. (1978) 'Senecan Drama and Its Antecedents,' *Harvard Studies in Classical Philology* 82, 213–263.
Tarrant, R. J. (ed.) (1985) *Seneca's Thyestes. Edited with Introduction and Commentary*, Atlanta (GA).
Tarrant, R. J. (1995) 'Greek and Roman in Seneca's Tragedies,' *Harvard Studies in Classical Philology* 97, 171–198.
Tarrant, R. J. (2002) 'Chaos in Ovid's *Metamorphoses* and its Neronian Influence,' *Arethusa* 35, 349–360.
Tarrant, R. J. (ed.) (2004) *P. Ovidii Nasonis Metamorphoses*, Oxford.
Tarrant, R. J. (2006) 'Seeing Seneca Whole?' in: Volk / Williams (2006), 1–17.
Tarrant, R. J. (2007) 'Horace and Roman literary history,' in: Harrison (2007a), 63–76.
Tarrant, R. J. (ed.) (2012) *Virgil: Aeneid Book XII*, Cambridge.
Taylor, M. (2010) 'The Figure of Seneca in Tacitus and the *Octavia*,' in: Miller, J. F. / Woodman, A. J. (eds.) *Latin Historiography and Poetry in the Early Empire*, Leiden, 205–222.

Terranova, A. (1969) 'A proposito dell'*epistola* I 4 di Orazio,' *Syculorum Gymnasium* 22, 190–201.
Thomas, R. F. (1999) 'Virgil's *Georgics* and the Art of Reference,' in: Thomas, R. F. (ed.) *Reading Virgil and his Texts: Studies in Intertextuality*, Ann Arbor (MI), 114–141.
Thomas, R. F. (ed.) (2011) *Horace: Odes Book IV and Carmen Saeculare*, Cambridge.
Thompson, J. W. (1940) *Ancient Libraries*, Hamden / London.
Tigerstedt, E. N. (1970) '*Furor poeticus*,' *Journal of the History of Ideas* 31, 163–178.
Till, R. (1968) 'Horazens "Exegi monumentum" im Spiegel der Übersetzung,' in: Hörmann, F. (ed.) *Die alten Sprachen im Gymnasium*, Munich, 93–113.
Tischer, U. (2010) 'Aspekte des Zitats. Überlegungen zur Anwendung eines modernen Konzepts auf antike lateinische Texte,' in: Tischer, U. / Binternagel, A. (eds.) *Fremde Rede – Eigene Rede. Zitieren und verwandte Strategien in antiker Prosa*, Frankfurt, 93–109.
Töchterle, K.-H. (ed. and trans.) (1994) *Lucius Annaeus Seneca, Oedipus, Kommentar mit Einleitung, Text und Übersetzung*, Heidelberg.
Too, Y. L. (1994) 'Educating Nero,' in: Elsner, J. / Masters, J. (eds.) (1994) *Reflections of Nero*, London, 211–224.
Too, Y. L. (2010) *The Idea of the Library in the Ancient World*, Oxford.
Tosi, R. (2003) *Dizionario delle sentenze latine e greche*, Milan.
Traina, A. (1987) *Lo stile 'drammatico' del filosofo Seneca*, 4th edition, Bologna.
Traina, A. (1991) 'Orazio e Aristippo. Le *Epistole* e l'arte di convivere,' *Rivista di Filologia* 119, 285–305.
Traina, A. (2009) 'Il tempo e la saggezza. Introduzione,' in: Traina, A. (ed.) *Seneca. La brevità della vita*, Milan, 24th edition, 5–21.
Trinacty, C. (2009) 'Like Father, like Son? Selected Examples of Intertextuality in Seneca the Younger and Seneca the Elder,' *Phoenix* 63, 260–277.
Trinacty, C. (2012a) 'Seneca's *Apocolocyntosis* and Horace's *belua centiceps* (*Carm.* 2.13.34),' *Classical Philology* 107, 156–160.
Trinacty, C. (2012b) 'The Fox and the Bee: Horace's First Book of *Epistles*,' *Arethusa* 45, 57–77.
Trinacty, C. (2014) *Senecan Tragedy and the Reception of Augustan Poetry*, Oxford.
Trinacty, C. (2015) 'Senecan Tragedy,' in: Bartsch / Schiesaro (2015), 29–40.
Trinacty, C. (2016) '*Imago Res Mortua Est*: Senecan Intertextuality,' in: Dodson-Robinson (2016), 13–33.
Troxler-Keller, I. (1964) *Die Dichterlandschaft des Horaz*, Heidelberg.
Usener, H. (1887) *Epicurea*, Leipzig.
Van den Berg, C. (2014) *The World of Tacitus' Dialogus de Oratoribus. Aesthetics and Empire in Ancient Rome*, Oxford.
Van Geytenbeek, P. C. (1963) *Musonius Rufus and the Greek diatribe*, trans. B. L. Hijmans Jr., Assen.
Vatri, A. (2012) 'The physiology of Ancient Greek reading,' *Classical Quarterly* 62, 633–647.
Vaughan, H. (1651) *Olor Iscanus*, London.
Vegetti, M. (1983) 'Passioni e bagni caldi. Il problema del bambino cattivo nell'antropologia stoica,' in: Vegetti, M. *Tra Edipo ed Euclide. Forme del sapere antico*, Milan, 71–90.
Versnel, H. (1993) *Inconsistencies in Greek and Roman religion 2: transition and reversal in myth and ritual*, Leiden.

Veyne, P. (1988) *Roman Erotic Elegy: Love, Poetry, and the West*, trans. D. Pellauer, Chicago (IL).
Viansino, G. (1990) *Lucio Anneo Seneca: I dialoghi, Volume secondo*, Milan.
Vogt-Spira, G. (1992) *Dramaturgie des Zufalls. Tyche und Handeln in der Komödie Menanders*, Munich.
Vogt-Spira, G. (2001) 'Die Einschätzung der Zukunft in der Zeitreflexion der Antike,' *Mitteilungen der Villa Vigoni* V, 41–60.
Vogt-Spira, G. (2002) 'Ars pervertendi. I *Satyrica* di Petronio e i limiti del rovesciamento,' in: Castagna / Vogt-Spira (2002), 193–211.
Vogt-Spira, G. (2008) 'Christoph Wilhelm Mitscherlich: ein Horazkommentator der Spätaufklärung,' in: Santini, C. / Stok, F. (eds.), *Esegesi dimenticate di autori classici*, Pisa, 83–95.
Volk, K. / Williams, G. D. (eds.) (2006), *Seeing Seneca Whole. Perspectives in Philosophy, Poetry and Politics*, Leiden.
von Albrecht, M. (2008) 'Seneca's Language and Style II. Linguistic Differences and Connections between Seneca's Philosophical Works and his Tragedies,' *Hyperboreus* 14, 124–150.
von Albrecht, M. (2014) 'Seneca's Language and Style,' in: Damschen / Heil (2014), 699–744.
Vottero, D. (ed.) (1998) *Seneca, I frammenti*, Bologna.
Vretska, K. (ed.) (1976) *Sallust, De coniuratione Catilinae*, 2 vols., Heidelberg.
Wagner, E. (1880) *De M. Valerio Martiale poetarum augustae aetatis imitatore*, Regensburg.
Walton, I. (ed.) (1651) *Reliquiae Wottonianae*, London.
Waltz, R. (trad.) (1950) *Sénèque: Dialogues*, vol. IV, Paris.
Warmington, E. H. (ed. and transl.) (1936) *Remains of Old Latin II: Livius Andronicus, Naevius, Pacuvius, Accius*, Cambridge (MA).
Warmington, E. H. (ed. and transl.) (1956), *Remains of Old Latin I: Ennius and Caecilius*, 2nd edition, Cambridge (MA).
Wasmuth, E. (2015) 'ὥσπερ οἱ κορυβαντιῶντες: The Corybantic Rites in Plato's Dialogues,' *Classical Quarterly* 65, 69–84.
Waszink, J. H. (1972) 'Zum Anfangsstadium der römischen Literatur,' in: *Aufstieg und Niedergang der römsichen Welt* I.2, 869–927.
Watson, G. (1988) *Phantasia in Classical Thought*, Galway.
Watson, L. C. (2003) *A Commentary on Horace's Epodes*, Oxford.
Watts, I. (1706) *Horae Lyricae: Poems, Chiefly of the Lyric Kind*. London.
Webb, R. (2009) *Ekphrasis, Imagination and Persuasion in Ancient Rhetorical Theory and Practice*, Farnham / Burlington (VT).
Weber, H. (1895) *De Senecae philosophi dicendi genere Bioneo*, diss. Marburg.
Weinreich, O. (1923) *Senecas Apocolocyntosis. Die Satire auf Tod / Himmel- und Höllenfahrt des Kaisers Claudius*, Berlin.
Wessels, A. (2014) *Ästhetisierung und ästhetische Erfahrung von Gewalt: Eine Untersuchung zu Senecas Tragödien*, Heidelberg.
West, D. (trans.) (1997) *Horace: The Complete Odes and Epodes*, Oxford.
West, M. L. (1982) *Greek Metre*, Oxford.
Whitton, C. (ed.) (2013a), *Pliny the Younger. Epistles Book II*, Cambridge.

Whitton, C. (2013b) 'Seneca, *Apocolocyntosis*,' in: Buckley, E. and Dinter, M. (eds.) *A Companion to the Neronian Age*, Oxford, 151–169.
Wieland, W. (1970) *Die aristotelische Physik*, 2nd edition, Göttingen.
Wiener, C. (2006) *Stoische Doktrin in römischer Belletristik: Das Problem von Entscheidungsfreiheit und Determinismus in Senecas Tragödien und Lucans Pharsalia*, Munich.
Wiener, C. (2014) '"Stoic Tragedy": A Contradiction in Terms?' in: Garani, M. / Konstan, D. (eds.) *The Philosophizing Muse*, Newcastle, 187–217.
Wilamowitz-Moellendorff, U. von (1919) *Griechische Tragödie*, Berlin.
Wilamowitz-Moellendorff, U. von (1921) *Griechische Verskunst*, Berlin.
Wildberger, J. (2006) *Seneca und die Stoa. Der Platz des Menschen in der Welt*, 2 vols., Berlin / New York.
Wildberger, J. (2014) 'The Epicurus Trope and the Construction of a "Letter Writer" in Seneca's *Epistulae Morales*,' in: Wildberger / Colish (2014), 431–465.
Wildberger, J. / Colish, M. L. (eds.) (2014) *Seneca Philosophus*, Berlin / Boston (MA).
Wilkins, A. S. (ed.) (1926) *Horace*, Epistles, London.
Wilkinson, L. P. (1963) *Golden Latin Artistry*, Cambridge.
Williams, G. W. (1995) '*Libertino patre natus:* True or False?' in: Harrison, S. J. (ed.) *Homage to Horace: A Bimillenary Celebration*, Oxford, 296–313.
Williams, G. D. (ed.) (2003) *Seneca: De Otio, De Brevitate Vitae*, Cambridge.
Williams, G. D. (2015a) 'Style and Form in Seneca's Writing,' in: Bartsch / Schiesaro (2015), 135–149.
Williams, G. D. (2015b) 'Minding the Gap: Seneca, the Self, and the Sublime,' in: Volk, K. / Williams, G. D. (eds.) *Roman Reflections: Studies in Latin Philosophy*, Oxford, 172–191.
Wilson, E. (2014) *The greatest empire: a life of Seneca*, Oxford.
Wilson, M. (2001) 'Seneca's *Epistles* Reclassified' in: Harrison, S. J. (ed.) *Texts, Ideas and the Classics: Scholarship, Theory and Classical Literature*, Oxford, 164–87.
Winter, K. (2014) *Artificia mali. Das Böse als Kunstwerk in Senecas Rachetragödien*, Heidelberg.
Winterbottom, M. (ed.) (1970) *M. Fabi Quintiliani Institutionis Oratoriae libri duodecim*, Oxford.
Wiseman, P. (2015) *The Roman Audience. Classical Literature as Social History*, Oxford.
Woodman, A. J. (1998) *Tacitus Reviewed*, Oxford.
Woodman, A. J. (2012) *From Poetry to History: Selected Papers*. Oxford.
Woodman, A. J. / Feeney, D. (eds.) (2002) *Traditions and Contexts in the Poetry of Horace*, Cambridge.
Zangrando, V. (1998) 'L'espressione colloquiale nelle "Diatribe" di Epitteto,' *Quaderni urbinati di cultura classica* 59, 81–108.
Zanker, P. (1987) *Augustus und die Macht der Bilder*, Munich.
Zanker, P. (1995) *The Mask of Socrates. The Image of the Intellectual in Antiquity*, Berkeley. Italian translation: (2009) *La maschera di Socrate. L'immagine dell'intellettuale nell'arte antica*, Turin.
Zetzel, J. E. G. (2002) 'Dreaming about Quirinus: Horace's *Satires* and the Development of Augustan Poetry,' in: Woodman / Feeney (2002), 38–52.
Zingerle, A. (1873) *Zu späteren lateinischen Dichtern*, Innsbruck.

Zinn, E. (1961) 'ΆΠΟΡΟΣ ΣΩΤΗΡΙΑ. Horaz im Rettungsboot (c. III 29, 62),' in: Kroymann, J. (ed.) *Eranion. Festschrift H. Hommel*, Tübingen, 185–205.

Zintzen, C. (1985/86) 'Horaz' Einladung an einen Kaufmann (c. IV 2),' *Grazer Beiträge* 12/13, 131–145.

Zwierlein, O. (1966) *Die Rezitationsdramen Senecas*, Meisenheim am Glan.

Zwierlein, O. (1977) 'Weiteres zum Seneca Tragicus (I),' *Würzburger Jahrbücher für die Altertumswissenschaften* 3, 149–177.

Zwierlein, O. (1986) *Kritischer Kommentar zu den Tragödien Senecas*, Mainz.

Zwierlein, O. (ed.) (2007) *L. Annaei Senecae Tragoediae*, revised edition, Oxford.

Contributors and Editors

Tobias Allendorf is currently a lecturer in Classics at Magdalen College, Oxford. After studying in Heidelberg and Oxford, he came to Oxford to complete a doctoral thesis on the Chorus in Seneca's tragedies. His research has been focused on Republican and early imperial Latin literature.

Francesca Romana Berno is Assistant Professor of Latin Language and Literature at the Sapienza Università di Roma. Her interests are focused on Cicero and Seneca. She has written a book about the relationships between moral and scientific issues in Seneca's *Naturales Quaestiones* (2003), a commentary on *Epistulae Morales* 53–57 (2006), and several essays about rhetorical devices in philosophical prose works.

Barak Blum is a D.Phil. candidate in Classical Languages and Literature at the University of Oxford, Wolfson College. His research focuses on the presentation of book collections in Latin poetry. He is the author of several articles on Ovid and Graeco-Roman literary culture.

Barbara Del Giovane was awarded her Doctorate at the University of Florence in 2014 and is a postdoctoral researcher at the same institution. She has published a monograph on diatribe in Seneca, *Seneca, la diatriba e la recerca di una morale austere* (Florence 2015), together with articles on Cicero, Horace, Seneca, and ancient Rhetoric. She is currently working on poetry quoted in ancient biographies and is planning a commentary on Macrobius' *Saturnalia* 1.

Catharine Edwards is Professor of Classics and Ancient History at Birkbeck, University of London. Her books include *The politics of immorality in ancient Rome* (1993) and *Death in ancient Rome* (2007). She has written a number of articles on Seneca and is currently working on a commentary on a selection of his letters.

Jonathan Geiger has obtained degrees in computational linguistics and Latin at Heidelberg University and is currently a Ph.D. student at Heidelberg's Department of Classical Philology. He specialises in metrics and versification, using statistics to explore these issues.

Elena Giusti is Assistant Professor in Latin Literature and Language at the University of Warwick. Previously to this, she taught at the Universities of Glasgow and Cambridge. She has published articles and book chapters on Augustan poetry and is the author of a forthcoming monograph entitled *Carthage in Virgil's Aeneid: Staging the Enemy under Augustus* (Cambridge).

Alexander Kirichenko received his Ph.D. from Harvard and is currently a Privatdozent at the University of Trier and a Heisenberg Senior Research Fellow at the Humboldt University of Berlin. He is the author of *A Comedy of Storytelling: Theatricality and Narrative in Apuleius' Golden Ass* (Heidelberg 2010) and *Lehrreiche Trugbilder: Senecas Tragödien und die Rhetorik des Sehens* (Heidelberg 2013) as well as numerous articles on Greek and Roman literature.

Nina Mindt is a Privatdozent at the Humboldt University of Berlin and has been Acting Professor for Classical Philology / Latin at the University of Wuppertal since 2015. Her publications include *Manfred Fuhrmann als Vermittler der Antike. Ein Beitrag zu Theorie und Praxis des Übersetzens* (2008) and *Martials 'epigrammatischer Kanon'* (2013). Her current research interests include ancient epigram, the metapoetics of classical verse, and the transformation of antiquity.

Victoria Moul is Senior Lecturer In Latin Language and Literature at King's College London. She works mainly on the relationship between English and Latin poetry in the sixteenth and seventeenth century, with a particular interest in the cultural importance of neo-Latin literature throughout this period.

Martin Stöckinger is Academic Coordinator of the August Boeckh Centre at the Humboldt University of Berlin. Previously to this, he taught at the University of Heidelberg. He has authored a book entitled *Vergils Gaben. Materialität, Reziprozität und Poetik in den* Eklogen *und der* Aeneis (Heidelberg 2016) as well as articles on Augustan and early imperial literature.

Richard Tarrant is Pope Professor of the Latin Language and Literature at Harvard University. He has edited and commented on Seneca's *Agamemnon* and *Thyestes*. He is currently finishing a book on Horace's *Odes* and hopes to produce a new OCT edition of all of Horace.

Ute Tischer holds the position of Research Fellow at the University of Leipzig. She is currently preparing a monograph about quoting in Roman prose, concentrating primarily on the norms and concepts associated with the activity. Her research focuses, among other things, on ancient practices of interpretation, as well as on modern literary theory and its application to ancient literature.

Christopher Trinacty is Associate Professor of Classics at Oberlin College. He is the author of *Senecan Tragedy and the Reception of Augustan Poetry* and is currently writing a commentary on Seneca's *Naturales Quaestiones* 3.

Gregor Vogt-Spira holds the chair of Classical Philology / Latin at the Philipps-Universität Marburg (Germany). His publications mainly concern the early and classical periods of Roman literature, as well as Roman poetics and literary criticism, but he has also written on the historical epistemology of ancient culture and its transformation through to the modern age. He is co-editor of Julius Caesar Scaliger's *Poetices libri septem* (1994–2011) and of the series *Europäische Grundbegriffe im Wandel* (2014–).

Kathrin Winter is a lecturer in Latin language and literature at the University of Heidelberg. She has written a monograph on Seneca's tragedies, *Artificia Mali. Das Böse als Kunstwerk in Senecas Rachetragödien* (Heidelberg 2014), and several articles on Seneca, Ovid, and Horace's *Odes*.

Andreas T. Zanker is Assistant Professor of Classics at Amherst College. His first monograph is *Greek and Latin Expressions of Meaning: The Classical Origins of a Modern Metaphor* (Munich 2016); he has also published on Horace, Virgil, Velleius Paterculus, and the concept of the golden age.

General Index

Absyrtus, 120–121
allusion, 10, 15, 19–20, 71, 113, 138–141, 144–147, 149, 155–157, 186, 292, 295, 310, 312, 348, 363–365; definition, 316n6; distinguished from intertext, 139n13; metre and sound in ancient practice, 140–141. *See also* Hinds, Stephen; intertextuality
anxiety of influence, 1, 317
Aristotle, 186, 194–195, 200, 207, 268; ps.-Aristotle, *Problemata* XXXi 954a 21–27, 252–253
Augustus: associated with gods, 103–104, 108, 272; interest in literary culture, 233–234; merged with Horatian persona, 272–275; rule celebrated by Horace, 101–103, 132–133
aurea mediocritas. *See* golden mean

Bacchus, 123, 129–132, 133, 239–244; as Liber, 248, 251, 256–262
Berthet, Jean-François, 1–3, 5, 23, 38, 53n1, 76, 186–187, 202n42, 311n72
Bion of Borysthenes: connection with diatribe, 27–29, 30, 81n37; family origin, 30–31, 32; greed in, 44, 45; and Horace, 30–33, 38; Seneca's knowledge of, 33, 38–39, 49, 52; theatrical metaphor in, 35, 36
Boethius: *De Consolatione* 1.2–7, 355–356n28; 1.4, 352–354; 2.1–8, 355–356n28; 3.1–6, 355–356n28; 3.6, 352; translated/imitated in neo-Latin poetry alongside Horace and Seneca, 345n3, 348n12, 358, 360, 369; translated/imitated in neo-Latin poetry alongside Ovid and Sarbiewski, 368

Caesius Bassus, 141
Canidia, 119–121
Carmen Saeculare (Horace), 129–134, 135, 168–169
carpe diem, 7–10, 194, 197–201, 208, 335, 339. *See also* time

Cato the Elder, Agr. fr. 10 Jordan, 301; Dict. fr. 75 Jordan, 300–301
Catullus: *basia* poem, counting in, 199; Catullus 11, 140n15, 154, 357; Catullus 51, 140n15, 357; Catullus 68.33, 143n28; and Horace, 357; and Justus Lipsius, 360; and Martial, 319; *pointe* in, 325; and Seneca, 140n15; versification technique, 154, 159–161, 173, 180
Celsus, 253
choral odes, 11, 15, 94–95, 96–99, 105–107, 108–111, 122–134, 146–157, 171–173
chorus: relationship to tragic action, 94–100, 108–112; theatrical functions of, 93–94
Chrysippus, 62n42, 118, 254; mentioned in Horace, 114, 306n47, 307n54; SVF 3.54, 197n34; 3.768, 81n37
Cicero, 29, 36n48, 53, 189, 326–327, 337; *Academica* 2.139, 69n66; *Ad Atticum* 12.15, 57n15; *Cato Maior de Senectute* 83, 36n47; *De Legibus* 1.8.25, 69n66; *De Re Publica* 2.69, 282n85; *In Pisonem* 37, 60; 66, 67n57; *Paradoxa Stoicorum*, 46, 85n51, 342n88; *Tusculanae Disputationes* 1.31.76, 333; 3.16.3, 77n22; 4.80, 59n26; 5.116, 143; 5.118, 81n37; on the poets' insanity, 255; on philosophical elements in Menippean satire, 73; quotation in, 293–295, 299, 301–302, 311–312; quoted by Seneca, 304–305
citation. *See* quotation
Claudius, 88, 132–134; *Apocolocyntosis* and, 31, 73
commonplace. *See* topos
Cynicism, 21, 36–37, 45, 46–47, 48, 50–51, 270

De Consolatione ad Polybium (Seneca), 16–21
Degl'Innocenti Pierini, Rita, 1n2, 38n54, 119n25, 339n82, 346n6, 349n14
Demetrius, 36, 46–47, 50
Democritus, 219–220, 239, 247, 253–257, 261

diatribe, 27–52, 293, 306, 310–311; genre question, 27–29, 267; topoi in, 33–37, 41–42, 44–47
Dionysus, 131, 261. *See also* Bacchus
disiecta membra, 10, (*disiecti*) 268, 273, 279

Ennius, 137n5, 141n18, 175–176, 267–268, 273, 292n7, 303n37
Epicureanism: attitude to death, 81; attitude to pleasure, 67, 79, 82; contrasted with Stoicism, 56–62, 68, 148; poetics, 274–275; theory of time, 189, 197
epigram, generic considerations in, 317, 319–320. *See also* Martial
ethics, moral, (moral) philosophy, 32, 36–38, 40, 42–43, 48–49, 51–52, 56, 64, 75–76, 84, 88, 114–115, 118, 121, 156, 186, 194, 205, 209, 215, 217–219, 223–225, 236–237, 243, 245, 254, 265, 267–272, 274–277, 280, 282, 289, 299–301, 304–307, 310–313, 330–331, 334, 337, 341–343, 345, 347–350, 354–356, 358, 360–362, 364–365, 368–369
Euripides: chorus, 96–97, 155–156n71; *Medea*, 118, 120n30, 121n33; *Hippolytus*, 122n39, 123n40, 128
exile, 21, 98, 221, 322–323, 334, 368

genre, theoretical considerations of, 4–5, 147n40, 316–317, 343
golden mean, 51–52, 93, 178, 110, 236, 266, 268, 339–340, 346–347, 360

Heraclitus, 194–196
Heywood, Jasper, 153–154
Hinds, Stephen, 15, 17, 20, 52n104, 113n1, 128n52, 132n69, 139n13
Hippolytus, 122, 125, 126–128, 278–280
Homer, 222–223n45, 309, 318; quotation / paraphrase from, 30–32, 294n14, 294n18; reading, 114, 118, 304–305
Horace and Seneca, literary relationship: critical issues in, 3–21; general features, 2–3; studies to date, 1–2; Seneca's quotations of Horace, 3–4, 37–42, 81–82, 186–187, 208–209

Horace, hexametric works: *Ars Poetica* 453–456, 256; *Epistles* 1.1.41–42, 326; 1.1.106–108, 326; 1.2.11–13, 117; 1.2.37–41, 114; 1.3.15–22, 231–232; 1.4, 54–55; 1.11.25–27, 6; 1.11.27, 338; 1.18.96–112, 235; 2.1.214–218, 233; *Satires* 1.1.15–19, 34; 1.1.117–119, 71; 1.1.120–121, 85, 229; 1.2.24, 326; 1.2.28–35, 300–301; 1.2.114–116, 81; 1.4.100–102, 341; 1.4.106, 341; 1.10.56–64, 230; 2.2.84–85, 80; 2.3.1–16, 228; 2.3.259–271, 296–297
Horace, iambic / lyric works: *Carmen Saeculare* 1–4, 129; *Odes* 1.11, 198; 1.11.6–8, 7; 1.12.51–52, 104; 1.12.57–58, 104; 1.19.1–4, 123; 1.19.5–8, 127; 2.1.17–20, 149; 2.10.1–4, 111; 2.10.5–8, 110; 2.14.1–4, 201; 3.1.5–6, 104; 3.3.1–8, 11, 106–107; 3.4.41, 165; 3.6.5–8, 104; 3.6.6, 165; 3.14.13–16, 101; 3.16, 43–44; 3.29.32–41, 192; 3.29.41–48, 187–188; 3.29.62–64, 111; 3.30, 17–19; 3.30.1–5, 9; 3.30.3–5, 18; 3.30.6–7, 10; 4.1.37–40, 127–128; 4.5.25–28, 101; 4.10.3–8, 125; 4.15.17–20, 101–102; 4.15.25–32, 102; *Epodes* 5.49–55, 119; 8.11–17, 226; 17.3, 169–170

imitation, 225–226, 267, 277, 282, 307–308, 345–348, 350, 358, 362, 364–368
intertextuality, 3–5, 15–17, 20, 113, 134–135, 139, 271, 276, 280, 283, 291–292, 315–316, 348; definition, 316n6; in early modern English lyric, 348; multi-layered, meaning, 16, 333; seminal theoretical works, 4n9; Transformation(sketten), chains of reference, 16, 19–20, 315, 317, 343; translation and imitation, post-classical, 345–369. *See also* allusion; Hinds, Stephen; imitation; quotation; reception, early modern; reference

libraries and book collections, 211–237; and *otium*, 220, 234–236; proper use of, 213–215, 223–226, 227, 228, 232–233; public libraries, political implications, 221–223, 233–234; quality of, 215–

216, 229–231, 236; as status symbol, 212–213, 227; as tools for study, 213, 217–220
licence / *licentia*: metrical, 162, 165–166, 170–171, 174–180, 181 (see also metrics); Saturnalian, 73, 76–77, 83, 85, 88–89; in speech, 250–252
Livius Andronicus, 144–145; *Aegisthus* (fr. 2–4 Warmington = 9 Schauer), 144
Lucilius (satirist), 39, 46, 141n18, 230–231, 267, 269, 273n39, 312, 321
Lucilius (Seneca's correspondent). See citations of Epistulae Morales under Seneca, prose works
Lucretius, 36n48, 62, 71, 81, 82, 156, 176n51, 186, 258, 266n6, 274, 292, 345n3
Ludi Saeculares, 132–133
luxury, 38–40, 42, 44–46, 48, 50–51, 64, 77, 81–82, 226–227, 244
lyric (Roman), art of: sound and space, in Horace, 137–139, 154–155; sound and space, in Seneca, 138–139, 153–157. See also metrics
lyric, early modern, 345–369; Ashmore, John, *Lipsii laus, & vota Vitae beatae* in *Certain Selected Odes of Horace, Englished* (1621), 358–359; British Library Harley MS 3910 fol. 77ʳ, 351; fol. 78ᵛ, 352; fols. 78ʳ–79ᵛ, 351–352; fol. 84ʳ, 353; fol. 93ʳ, 353; fol. 94ʳ, 354; Campion, Thomas, in Bodleian MS Rawl. poet. 31, fol. 5ᵛ, 356–357; Justus Lipsius, 359–360; Lovelace, Richard, 'The Grass-hopper. To my Noble Friend, Mr. Charles Cotton. Ode' in *Lucasta* (1649), 366; Sarbiewski, Casimir, *Odes* 4.23, 366; 4.34.1–12, 367; Tottel, Richard, *Songes and Sonnettes*, no. 169, 347; Wotton, Henry, *Upon the sudden Restraint of the Earle of* Somerset, *then falling from favor*, version in Izaak Walton, *Reliquiae Wottonianae* (1651), 361–362; version in Harley MS 6038, emended, 363

Maecenas: in Carm. 3.16, 42–44, 50, 51; in Carm. 3.29 (Maecenas Ode), 190, 202; emulated by Seneca, 285n103; in Martial, 320; relationship with Horace, 84, 86, 105, 268–269
Martial: engagement with literary tradition, 316–317; as excerptor, 331; persona, 318, 328–329, 333–334, 336–337, 341; relationship to Horace and Seneca, 315–343; *sententiae* in, 324–325, 326, 327
Martial, *Epigrams* 1.57, 339; 4.40.1–3, 321–322; 5.20.1–4, 335; 5.20.11–14, 335; 5.58.1–2, 335; 5.58.7–8, 335; 7.44, 322; 7.45, 322–323; 7.46, 318; 10.33, 340–341; 10.47, 336; 12.36–37, 321; 12.58, 342
Mazzoli, Giancarlo, 1–5, 8–9, 23, 29, 33, 37, 53n1, 76n16, 186–187, 214–216, 225n56, 239–240, 242–243, 246n24, 248–249, 253–255, 258n68, 261n78, 297–298, 305–306, 311–312
Medea, 95, 114–122
Menippean satire, 31, 32, 34, 73
metapoetry, 115–122, 130–131, 239–263, 278
metrics, 137–157, 159–181: Horatian technique, 159–169, 173; mimetic, 137, 179–180; Senecan engagement with Horace, 14, 18, 138, 140, 146–153, 155–157, 171–173, 360; Senecan technique, other aspects, 141–142, 144–145, 154, 169–180
moderation / excess, 2, 76–86, 212–214, 222–225, 228–231, 234, 236, 247–252; leads to *euthumia*, 255. See also golden mean

Nero, 88–89, 281–283, 285. See also politics: freedom of speech; politics: in Senecan tragedy

Oedipus: of Seneca, 108–110, 129–134, 149–151; of Sophocles, 95
Ovid, 18–20, 108, 115n6, 120–121, 124n46, 131–132, 150n50, 157, 169, 241n8, 278n64, 282, 317, 368; *Metamorphoses* 15.871–872, 18

passions: anger, 59–60, 79, 116–117; fear, 59–60, 78, 80, 86; poetry's effect on, 254; regulation of, 39–40; sexual desire, 122–128; slavery as metaphor for, 86, 87; in Stoic philosophy, 59–60, 62, 254

Persius, 58–59, 285

persona, 115, 229, 234, 265–272, 305–307, 317–318, 328–329, 333–343

Petronius, 169, 189, 208–209, 285

Phaedra, 122, 124, 126–128, 278–280

Plato, 34n41, 53–54, 59n22, 60–61, 67n55, 194, 239, 243n13, 249–250, 253–254, 261

politics: freedom of speech, 85–89, 243, 250–252; and library imagery, 220–223, 233–234; its nexus with ethics and poetics, 265–285; in satiric discourse, 83–89; in Senecan tragedy, 93, 99–112, 132–134

Polybius. *See* De Consolatione ad Polybium

Porphyrio, 137, 146n38, 151n53, 230n71

power (political), 2–3, 18–19, 32, 44, 50, 88, 99–101, 108, 222–225, 222–225, 233, 274, 360

Quintilian, 141, 206n53, 250–251, 319n16, 321, 324; *Institutio Oratoria* 8.5.3, 324

quotation, 3, 6–7, 31–32, 66–67, 289–313, 331–333; definition, 289, 290; features of, 290–291; Senecan and Horatian practice compared, 296–313; use of pre-text, 304–310

reading, 212–219, 220, 223–227; moral reading of poetry, 114, 118, 121–122, 304–305; practices in antiquity, 140–141, 142–144

reception: contexts in antiquity, 142–144; distinguished from '(chain of) transformation,' 19, 317, 343; of *sententiae*, early modern, 331–333; problematised, 16, 19, 311

reference, 10–11, 15–16, 65, 208, 289–295, 302–304, 311–312, 315–317, 320–322; marked reference, 122, 289 (*see also* quotation); multiple reference, 53, 67–68; 'window,' 19

Rhetorica ad Herennium 4.17.24, 324

ruler / kings, 12–13, 88, 93, 99–101, 103–108, 111, 225, 234, 281–282, 326, 353, 355, 358, 361, 366

Sallust, 62–70

satire / satiric, 2, 32–33, 37–38, 46, 60, 73–77, 79–81, 83–87, 89, 141, 189, 190, 229, 306, 311, 315, 318–321, 328, 337–338, 340, 342–343, 369

satis (limit to desire), 38–40, 46–49, 78–79, 80–82, 230, 236, 265

Saturnalia, 73–74, 76–80, 83–89

self-consciousness, literary, 116, 124n43, 137, 157, 357. *See also* metapoetry

Seneca the Elder, 3n4, 324, 326

Seneca the Younger: exile, 221, 323, 334; involvement in politics, 220–221; relationship with Horace. *See* Horace and Seneca, literary relationship

Seneca, prose works: *De Beneficiis* 1.9.2–4, 341–342; 4.13.1, 68; *Dialogi* 6 (*De Consolatione ad Marciam*) 1.3–4, 221–222; 7.18.2, 57; 9 (*De Tranquillitate Animi*) 1.13, 245; 1.14, 246; 2.13, 257; 9.4–7, 212–213; 16.1, 327; 17.8, 247–248; 17.9, 248; 17.10–11, 249; 10 (*De Brevitate Vitae*) 8.5, 332; 9.1–3, 7–8; 14.1–15.2, 219–220; 11 (*De Consolatione ad Polybium*) 18.2, 16–17; *Epistulae Morales* 1.3, 203; 1.4, 204–205; 2.2–5, 214; 5.7, 337; 12.9, 188; 18.2, 77; 18.5, 78; 18.8, 84; 23.8, 193; 24.26, 332; 28.1, 5, 338; 28.3, 241; 39.1–4, 217–218; 45.1–2, 216; 60, 63; 63.11, 334; 75.1–2, 319; 84.1–2, 223–224; 84.5–6, 225; 86.13, 4; 93.3, 328; 94.27, 329; 94.27–28, 301; 94.43, 330; 95.51–53, 297–298; 99.5, 204; 108.35, 217; 108.6–7, 242; 119.12, 38

Seneca, tragedies: *Agamemnon* lines 102–107, 110; lines 421–422, 145; lines 589–595, 147; lines 589–603, 12–13; lines 589–609: 105–106; line 672: 142; [ps.-Sen.] *Hercules Oetaeus* lines 1983–

General Index — 437

1988, 98; *Medea* lines 560–567, 114–115; line 636, 179; line 744, 179; lines 849–852, 95; lines 866–869, 117; lines 1026–1027, 99; [ps.-Sen.] *Octavia* lines 978–982, 98; *Oedipus* lines 403–405, 129; lines 449–466, 176; lines 731–734, 149; lines 755–758, 142; lines 882–891, 108–109; lines 980–982, 109; lines 987–990, 109; *Phaedra* lines 274–278, 122–123; lines 768–772, 126; lines 795–800, 126; lines 966–967, 141–142; lines 973–974, 142; *Thyestes* line 100, 179; lines 336–338, 94; lines 391–403, 345–346; lines 573–576, 151; lines 641–645, 103; line 873, 141; lines 885–895, 105
sententia, 116, 302, 316, 323–333, 336–339
Serenus, 244–249, 250, 261–262
sermo: meaning conversation or dialogue, 2, 75–76, 306, 311, 318–319; translation of *diatribē*, 27–28, 30
Sextus Pacuvius Taurus, 188
Sophocles, *Ajax* lines 1418–1420, 96. *See also* chorus; Oedipus, of Sophocles
sound, 22, 137–140, 143–146, 149–150, 152–155, 157
space, 2–3, 137–139, 144–146, 153, 155, 191, 207, 268–270, 272, 338
Statius, 17n38, 163n20, 174
Stoicism: contrasted with Epicureanism, 62–71 (*see also* Epicureanism, contrasted with Stoicism); epistemology, 283–284; indifference to wealth, 58, 80; moral progress (*proficiens*), 56–57, 244–246, 276–278; moralising in, 74, 83–87; on passions, 59–60, 254; *sapiens*, state of, 82–83, 86, 87; *temperantia*, 77; theory of time, 196, 197

Tacitus, 4–5, 87–89, 100, 141n18, 188, 251, 276n52
Tarrant, Richard, 1, 12–14, 23, 93–112, 138, 140n14, 144n35, 147n41, 150n52, 152, 155–156, 187n10, 292n6, 351n22, 366n25
Teles, 28, 33, 35, 45, 46n84, 48, 49
Terence, 296–300, 304, 305, 312; *Eunuchus* lines 46–63, 296–297; *Heautontimorumenos* lines 75–80, 297–298
Theseus, 122, 278–280
Tibullus, 55–62, 64, 67, 71
time, 185–209; metaphors for, 203–207; in philosophical discourse, 61, 185–186, 194–196, 200, 207, 219–220, 280, 282, 335; river as trope, 191–194, 195–196, 200. *See also* carpe diem
topos, in literary criticism, 16–17, 20–21, 52
tragedy, Senecan 93–112, 113–136; poetics of space and sound, 138–139; ruler figures in, 103, 104–105, 108, 133; whether performed, 95–96, 142n25
travel, 5–6, 190, 240–243, 257–259, 338
Trinacty, Christopher, 2, 12–14, 23, 37n49, 111, 113–136, 147, 271, 276n54, 278–279, 326, 328n51

Virgil: frequently quoted by Seneca, 3, 187n9, 294n15; *Georgics* 3.66–68, 332; intertexts (excepting quotes) with Seneca, 10, 108, 113, 138–139, 156, 157; praised by Seneca, 8–9; quoted by Seneca, 5, 67–68, 79, 189–190, 206, 241, 303n38, 304–305, 332, 338; Sibyl as model of *enthousiasmos*, 241, 246, 249; and Varius, in Maecenas's circle, 274, 320

www.ingramcontent.com/pod-product-compliance
Lightning Source LLC
Chambersburg PA
CBHW051241300426
44114CB00011B/837